TV News Corp Prosecution: of Scott Peterson

A Viewer's View

by

roy g. raymond, J.D.

authorHOUSE™
1663 Liberty Drive, Suite 200
Bloomington, Indiana 47403
(800) 839-8640
www.AuthorHouse.com

First published by AuthorHouse 07/26/04

ISBN: 1-4184-8709-0 (e)
ISBN: 1-4184-8708-2 (sc)

Library of Congress Control Number: 2004095770

Printed in the United States of America
Bloomington, Indiana

This book is printed on acid-free paper.

"It is the People's belief that once a [gag] order is put in place, responsible journalists will understand that leaked information violates the court's order and is being spewed forth with an intent to circumvent justice. And if justice cannot protect the defendant then who will protect the media in the future?"

June 4, 2003, *People's Points and Authorities in Support of Limited Protective Order*

Deputy District Attorney, David Harris

Stanislaus County, California

Table of Contents

Preface

While watching TV, alot of inconsistencies in the accusations being made by TV news corporations in several criminal cases were apparent, so a few notes were written down on what was said, or at least what was heard. As the book title says, this is a viewer's view. No recordings or tapes were made, and no reruns of shows were viewed to make corrections or add more to what was heard the first time, nor were any digital enhancements performed to help with the gathering of material for this book. The shows were watched as usual and turned off when I wanted peace of mind.

When a person speaks to you, a lot of information is conveyed with their tone, volume, demeanor, and body movements. How well you know them, how you met them, and what you think of them, has some bearing on the message conveyed to you. Sometimes what they say in words, isn't what they mean at all; nor is it understood by anyone watching, that what they said with words was actually what they meant. Yet, when you put that person's words into letters and sentences, it will say what they didn't mean. So, why do we use transcripts of a person or of a court proceeding? Wouldn't a video convey a more accurate meaning from a person; if the video shows the context, setting, and ALL participants while the conversation is occurring; from beginning to end, without comment from any outside voice.

Opinion is kept to a minimum during the TV news corporation shows, sometimes even having to bite my lip, since the dog doesn't seem to understand when I'm fussing at the TV, but yet it's okay for him to howl at it from time to time, especially during Hannity and Colmes. The amount of information the news corporations can come up with also helped with keeping the comments to a minimum, since there wasn't time to write much of a comment.

In the 1950s, when the TV news came onto the television, it was time for silence. After all, the news was important. You could pretty much believe what was said on the TV news, cause it wasn't Hollywood. Through grade school and high school, it was habit to watch the eleven o'clock news most every night and not go to bed till the Johnnie Carson Show was over.

It wasn't until an older age, that the realization of just what TV news can do to a person became apparent. It can make ya, and it can break ya. So TV news watching became more of an exercise in seeing just what was being told to the American people, rather than believing in what was heard. Today, our TV news is being told to the world. Flip between news stations, and one station says that 'it happened', and another station says 'it didn't happen', and yet another station says 'we'll let you know if and when it does happen'. Guess this is a way of neutralizing any misinformation we may be getting.

So where do the news corporations get their confidential information? Would it really matter? When news is reported to the public, which later turns out to be false, can the news corps lay the responsibility for the damage caused onto an anonymous source, and say, well, we only report from reliable sources. TV news corps seem to go even further and say they are a voice for the people, to the people, and that it is their responsibility, their duty, to inform the public. Has anyone thought to ask the TV news corps; Of What? No doubt the answer will be; Why, of the news, of course.

Unfortunately, the nightmare for Scott Peterson continues indefinitely, regardless of the court's decision. The TV news corps are not going to let this affair rest until Scott is put to death, or behind bars forever. Just how this prosecution occurs, changes as quickly as the wind changes direction, but the TV news corps remain headstrong in only one direction.

Introduction

James Madison wrote that law must be written and interpreted from a respectable point of view. It would appear that Mr. Madison's words are a basis for justice itself. Once law is written respectably, and in turn, interpreted and executed respectably, the chance of law being judged, as having been written and executed in a respectable manner, increases exponentially. Attention can then be placed upon the true exercise of criminal law; is this person guilty of the crime charged, beyond a reasonable doubt, given the foregoing premise of respectability.

Thomas Jefferson wrote that, if given the choice of government without newspapers, or, newspapers without government, he would not hesitate to chose the latter. Some say it's because Mr. Jefferson also wrote that, news was fit to wrap fish in. We could assume that Thom liked to fish alot, and, or, he didn't care much for government, or newspapers.

Some may even think that Mr. Jefferson was contradicting himself. But, there's more to the story than meets the eye, or that was intended to meet certain eyes. Thom had difficulty in getting the newspapers in Virginia to print his letters, as written. An editor would make a little change in spelling here, a word added there and one taken out here; well, it just made the reading make a little more sense to more people. However, what happened in effect, was that the letters, as printed, said what Thom did not say, or what he wouldn't have said, and sometimes things that he never even thought, let alone would have said. Most people would give up after the self-humiliation caused by those who praised him, for what he didn't say, and by those who now avoided him for what he was said to have said.

Mr. Jefferson heard that some newspapers in Kentucky would print his letters, as written. So, Thom hopped on his favorite horse and rode to Kentucky.

Having driven to Kentucky from Virginia, it's a beautiful ride along Interstate 64, through the Cumberland Gap, alot of mountain views, and some wonderfully nice people. When Thom took his ride, Interstate 64 hadn't been built yet, and the trip probably took four to six months, considering it took 28 days for him to ride to Washington, D.C., some years later to be sworn in as President.

Kinda makes you wonder if a few written words could possibly mean so much to go through such effort. Never mind that Thom's horse didn't want to return to Virginia after munchin' on some of that Kentucky bluegrass. Today, if it were concerning a criminal trial, and Thom was the defendant's lawyer, he'd save himself a horse, cause the judge would issue a gag order before Thom could get him saddled up.

The Press today, as it was several hundred years ago, means more than just satisfying the gossip of a small community. Stories from one community are picked up by another and can be reprinted throughout the country. Our TV news corps show the news to the world, sometimes instantaneously. People tend to believe what their favorite show tells them. The ability of the TV news corps to influence is within nearly every household in America.

The United States Constitution states that an accused shall have the right to a public trial. This right, is an accused's right, not the public's right, nor the government's right, or the media's right. It's a right that cannot be deprived of an accused by government. Inherent within this right, is the right of the accused to have a non-public trial. It is the accused, who stands in the best position to determine if the circumstances of the process afforded to him in his individual ordeal should be broadcast to the world, or not.

The right of the accused to a fair trial, when publicity is involved, must be considered in the specific context of the individual who is the accused. Also, within this same context of a public trial and a fair trial, is the right to a trial by jury. This does not mean a fair public jury trial. Each is as separate and distinct as the words and letters they require to relay them.

The right of an accused to a jury trial was written into the Constitution, as before this, many were not tried at all and many were convicted by Royal judges. Inherent in the accused's right to a jury trial is the right to a non-jury, or trial by judge.

Today, this essential right to a jury trial has been negated and removed as an option of the accused, unconstitutionally, by the legislatures; by giving itself, government, a right to demand a jury trial. The right to a trial by judge was preserved for those times when public passion would be unable to hand down a fair decision.

When the stranger rides through town and the resident evil criminal takes advantage of the circumstance and commits a crime dear to the town's residents, knowing that with a little talk and rumor that the stranger will be strung up by sundown; only the Lord can help him if the crime was an affair.

A trial by judge prevents these unfortunate circumstances from convicting the innocent. But, with the prosecutor, a member of the executive branch, now having control of judicial constitutional procedure, the very process which begins the search for the truth between two adversarial opponents, then the judge can be eliminated from determining an accused's guilt or innocence. Once eliminated, then the jury can be predetermined to a verdict by publicity, or just a littlc talk and rumor.

We've come a long way baby, but by golly, we're right back where we started.

Although there is no definite date for this first written note about Scott Peterson, the TV news corp inquisition had been in full swing for six months.

When Laci Peterson was first reported missing, I too, thought, what a beautiful woman, not just in appearance, but in her eyes and smile. Surely, she would come back home. Within a few days, the TV news corps were asking the question, was the husband having an affair. The first I remember the question being asked as an insinuation, was with the TV video of Scott Peterson walking from his driveway towards the tree next to the street in front of their home, just days after the search for Laci began. There still seemed to be a chance, with many possibilities of how and why Laci would return, but the TV news corps began their 'let's give the public what we say they wanta know' smear campaign anyway.

The TV news corps began to force Scott Peterson to react to their barrage against him, and of course, it just had to be with a TV interview. I didn't watch the interview with Diane Sawyer, since, no matter who did the interview, it would be used to crucify Scott.

A week or so before the interview was to be shown on TV, a trained legal mind asked me if I was going to watch it, and I replied that the TV news corps had already tried and convicted Scott, and, as we both laughed aloud and said in unison, "Yea, and he hasn't even been tried yet", I continued that the TV news corps were already trying to decide on just how they would execute Scott, so a TV interview is only gonna be trouble.

What I remember from the TV news corp reports, before Scott was found to be having an affair, was that when Scott called Laci's Mom, the evening of December 24th, Laci's Mom kept telling Scott that it's okay and that Laci would be home shortly. This, Mrs. Rocha repeated to Scott several times, in her own words. This is the same phone conversation that Scott was to have said, Well, Laci's missing.

My impression was that Scott thought Laci's Mom did therefore know where Laci was, since she kept saying it'll be okay, Laci will be home, so if Scott expressed his concern more, Laci's Mom would tell Scott that she was with her Mom. This didn't happen. Sure enough Laci wasn't with her Mom.

Still there was a chance that Laci was at a friend's or family member's, maybe to come home, and since Scott was having an affair and Laci is pregnant, maybe Christmas is the time to place hurt upon Scott and not let him have anything to do with the birth of their child. This being a thought that Scott would have had to think, even if he knows Laci better than this.

But, after a week or so, if Laci were aware of the publicity in her search, she would have contacted someone to let us know she was alright. Without doing so, it still didn't mean she wasn't alright, but she would have had to be in seclusion and away from media reports, abducted and being held or worse, or a person that nobody really knew in the first place and had no intentions in coming home. This hope of life, doesn't end with suspicion and rumor.

No doubt, a man having an affair is possibly one of the most damning public bit of information to that man, when stated within the evaluation process by a group of women. It's only matched in the reverse setting, by the damning bit of information that a woman is having an affair, but it's effect is opposite, since the woman's affair isn't pubic fodder.

What does happen with this affair, is that it's used as a basis for every action taken, and therefore, every action taken is also to lie, deceive, and to get away with murder?

Where the real problem with the criminal actions begin, is the evidence. The U.S. Supreme Court has stated several times that it is okay for the executive branch to lie, cheat, deceive, and trick an American during the investigation of a crime. As has been proven many times before, and should be obvious to people as intelligent as our Supreme Court Justice's, is that you can't answer truthfully to a deceitful question, you can't argue with a lie, and trickery is but a game.

Combine this with trained professionals, good enough to fool professional criminals and others, and what chance would an average jury of twelve citizens have to not be fooled? If we have them already believing that Scott is guilty, and aware that they are under pressure to return a guilty verdict for having an affair and well....

Scott Peterson isn't the stranger riding through town, but the rumor and talk caused him to be taken out of town in the hopes of finding twelve people who could decide Scott's fate based upon the evidence as shown in court. This is not to imply that the help of the TV news corps in the particular area of helping to find those who have gone missing is not highly valued by everyone, since their equipment and personnel are, quite possibly, surpassed by no one. It is also this ability that can cause extensive damage.

Chapter One

TV News Corp Reports

The shows are in the sequence that they were viewed. From this point forward, the author's comments are within brackets. []

TV News: The judge has released government taped conversations between the press and Scott Peterson to the news media. [The TV news corps have declared themselves exempt from any 'no lie' law, or deception and intimidation in questioning Peterson.]

7/22/03

MSNBC Dan Abrams: Why are Scott Peterson's lawyers afraid of a televised preliminary hearing?

7/23/03

CNN Headline News:[Shows Scott Peterson entering the courtroom, still in a bright red jumpsuit, handcuffed and shackled. CNN states that Scott's lawyer doesn't want the preliminary hearing shown, so as to prejudice his client's jury pool and a fair trial. CNN is well aware, that courts have repeatedly stated that showing a defendant in the courtroom, while wearing handcuffs, places unfair guilt and suspicion on what might otherwise be an innocent person.]

7/26/03

CNN People in the News: [Shows a half-hour chronicle which was biased against Scott; with known facts left out, the sequence of events distorted, and an ending with a commentary against Scott on issues that actually show innocence.]

7/27/03

CNN Larry King Live: Media Coverage

Nancy Grace, of Court TV: The Constitution shrouds a defendant in unimaginable rights.
Jeanine Farris Pirro, prosecutor Westchester County, New York: The Constitution shrouds a defendant in tremendous rights and the prosecution can't get a fair trial with public attention.
Harvey Levin, of Celebrity Justice Show: When people like parents or a spouse begin to back off from police during questioning and suspicion of murdering their child or spouse, and refuse to take a lie detector exam or shout out loud for justice and instead hire a lawyer, they bring suspicion and doubt upon themselves.
Rikki Klieman, Defense Attorney: Suspicion and rumor will become charges and a conviction, with media coverage of pretrial events.

COURT TV Special, Laci Peterson Investigation:
Scott's house broken into? [The show didn't say, that the house was broken into when Scott went out of town. Remember when the TV news corps were condemning Scott for not looking for Laci, so he did. He went out of town and his house was broken into. It was reported that nothing of value was taken, just a few things. Later it was claimed to be the neighbor who had gone into the house, looking for Laci's wedding dress. Then the TV news corps condemned Scott for changing the locks on the doors of his house, asking, how is Laci supposed to get back in her own house with the locks changed.

Scott traded Laci's car, after police took his work truck, so that he could get a work truck, but the show forgets to mention this fact. They only condemn Scott for selling Laci's car while she's gone and wonder what will she drive when she comes back.

Shows Scott crying during a TV interview. They misstate that Scott told his girlfriend that he didn't kill Laci, but knows who did. Scott was asked by his girlfriend if he had anything to do with his wife's disappearance, and Scott replied, No, but I know who did.

The show leaves out that police called and intimidated Scott for months in attempts to get him to run from the area, and then called and said they were coming to arrest him, intending to make him run, after harassing him for months in a manner that they know causes adverse and unexpected behavior. A person is forced to run for safety, or fight. They showed nothing about the close scrutiny of Scott and what this may do to a person.

They showed nothing about the bodies found on the Bay shore, both before and after Laci. Said Scott's own words would convict him and show that he's a liar. Yet no proof was shown.]

8/6/03

CNN **Wolf Blitzer:** Stay tuned to find out why Scott Peterson turned down a plea bargain to avoid the death penalty, before he was charged.
Two segments later: Stay tuned for Scott Peterson and why he turned down offer that could have saved his life.
Later: The prosecution offered Scott Peterson a deal three months before charges were filed. His lawyers say that he turned it down because he's innocent. [Shows Scott in an orange jumpsuit and handcuffs in the courtroom.]

MSNBC **Dan Abrams:** New info in the Scott Peterson case. He was offered a plea bargain.
[Actually this was known early on in the investigation, soon after the police changed from Laci missing, to being a homicide. This was well before the bodies were found and was reported by the TV media, briefly.

8/7/03

ABC News Channel 8 Richmond, Virginia: New information out on Scott Peterson. New court documents show Scott was offered a plea in early January, if he told where Laci's body was. [The plea was told to us when it happened, only it wasn't repeated by TV news corps as much as it is now, since it may have helped to explain why Scott wasn't so cordial. In effect, he had been accused of killing his wife and unborn son; no body, she still may be alive, and yet he's threatened with death if he didn't tell them what they wanted to hear.]

8/11/03

Fox News Channel
Dr. Michael Baden, Forensic Pathologist: People make mistakes, misinterpret things.

8/13/03

Fox News Channel **Greta Van Susteren:** Pathologist say that the autopsy that the Peterson baby was at thirty-eight weeks of age and the sonogram was done a couple of days before 12/24 shows the baby at thirty-one weeks, with a plus or minus, of three weeks accuracy.

8/14/03

COURT TV: Scott Peterson hearing; the government prosecutor says that people do change their behavior and respond differently in public when being faced with a camera video taping them.
Rochelle Wilcox, of Court TV: In the Scott Peterson hearing, the public can only get accurate information of the court proceeding with live video coverage, not recounts of it.
[During the hearing, each time the judge speaks, we hear preaching about God. What's up? Is this divine intervention or has Court TV lost it's reputation of experience and knowledge in showing court hearings live on TV. Can't they edit out God?]
Nancy Grace, of Court TV, former prosecutor: The defense attorney, Geragos, gives inconsistent pleadings in court. First, he wants the preliminary hearing closed to all, but when the judge denies that request, Geragos changes his mind and says he wants live TV coverage. What's up with that? [Actually the defense attorney, Geragos, is not inconsistent. What he said was that if the preliminary hearing is open to the public, then live TV cameras are the only way for the public to get and see the truth of the events in the preliminary hearing.]

8/15/03

CNN Larry King Live
Nancy Grace, of Court TV, former prosecutor: The photo in the newspaper of Scott Peterson's defense team going over evidence is staged and I bet everything that Laci Peterson was not killed by a satanic cult.
Dr. Robi Ludwig, cult expert: It's rare for a satanic cult to kill someone, after all, if they did, we'd hear more about it. Why did it just stop with Laci Peterson?
Chris Pixley, Defense Attorney: Well, if you don't look at them, you probably won't find it either.

Nancy Grace: If Geragos even thinks Scott is guilty, he will shut it out completely and try everything he can to get this guy off. Completely inappropriate for the Peterson family to make statements of innocence to the press and in violation of the court's gag order. If the Rocha family did this, on how they believe Scott killed their daughter, they'd have their butts dragged into court in a heartbeat.

8/16/03

Fox News Channel **Rita Cosby:** Maybe the reason the defense team got Dr. Lee and Dr. Wecht is so the prosecutor couldn't get them. Is there a smoking gun? Stay tuned. [Rita says this with a picture of Scott Peterson. Uh, Rita, no gun has been mentioned in the Scott Peterson case, so a smoking gun would not mean anything. Rita comes back from commercial with Mo Rocca, from smokinggun.com. Rita shows Scott Peterson's picture, but with Mo Rocca's name underneath it on the TV screen. Mo tells Rita about the mistake Fox News Channel just made with his identity, but no one said that Scott Peterson isn't Mo or that Scott Peterson has nothing to do with a smoking gun.]

8/18/03

CNN: Judge bars cameras in the Scott Peterson's case; Will it help or hurt?

CNN Wolf Blitzer [CNN shows Scott Peterson in an orange jumpsuit and handcuffs coming into the court room; while talking about no cameras at the preliminary hearing. The U.S. Supreme Court states that seeing a defendant in handcuffs is inflammatory to the jury, to the public, and may cause a prejudice to believe the defendant is guilty, and, or dangerous.]

MSNBC: Does the judge in the Laci Peterson case really believe that the real killer is still on the loose? Stay tuned.
John Burris, former prosecutor, attorney: It's more of an intellectual exercise.
Paul Pfingst, prosecutor: The judge should open the court room if he really believes that and wants the real killer there.
Gary Casimir, former prosecutor, attorney: I agree, its a good intellectual exercise.

Fox News Channel **Greta Van Susteren:** Guess who got served with a subpoena when they showed up in court at the Scott Peterson's hearing? Stay tuned.
Greta: Stay tuned. No cause of death by the defense team and not dismembered before put in water. Prosecutor uses hypnosis on prosecution [defense!] witness. The age of the baby is many weeks older than he was on 12/23/02. Prosecutor subpoenas Scott Peterson's family when they get to court.
Bernie Grimm, Defense Attorney: This puts them under the gag order. [The prosecutor doesn't want the Peterson's saying that their son is innocent.]

8/19/03

CNN Larry King Live
Nancy Grace, of Court TV, former prosecutor: We'll hear the spin and not the facts of the courtroom.
Dr. Robi Ludwig, psychotherapist: Cameras distort the image to where is doesn't seem real.
Chris Pixley, Defense Attorney: The judge made a better case for closure, with his holding on no cameras, than what Geragos did, on closing the preliminary hearing to the public.
Dr. Robi Ludwig: The camera affect depends on the personalities involved and may influence the jury. It may affect the jury's decision on what to decide, if they feel pressured because of the cameras.
Larry King: Why are you sarcastically, about the judge saying the killer may still be loose? [to Nancy Grace.]
Nancy Grace: I have a First Amendment right. It's ridiculous, the perpetrator can't read the court papers. In the Simpson case; the jury was contrary to the public poll.
[headline]: **'NO CAMERAS IN LACI CASE'.**
Ted Rowlands, KTVU TV Reporter: The leaks began on the prosecution side. We have gotten a lot of information we received, but don't feel comfortable reporting on. [Shows Scott's Dad saying Scott is in jail and shouldn't be; someone's out there who did this and isn't in jail; and the investigation was flawed.]
[Geragos didn't want the gag order, but it was gagged. Geragos didn't want the prelim open, but it was opened. Geragos wanted cameras, but cameras aren't allowed. As police would say, I see a pattern developing here.]

Nancy Grace: Even before they found the bodies and when they picked up Scott, he wasn't wearing his wedding ring.
Dr. Robi Ludwig: His action in court was bizarre and have people asking if this guy is innocent.
Nancy Grace: He knows he wasn't crying in court and he was faking a tear. [Again Chris Pixley does an excellent job in putting the public and the panelists back on the reality track with evidence and innuendo that they always spin to prosecute a man, but Chris is never given the time to give an innocent person's view.]

8/21/03

Fox News Channel **Greta Van Susteren:** Why might a new doctor's x-ray in the Scott Peterson case get him off the hook? Stay tuned.
Greta: Scott Peterson spent alot of money, just weeks before Laci's death, and the feds are interested. Stay tuned.
Greta: Will new autopsy details set Scott free? Stay tuned.
Greta: Why a radiologist? Age of fetus. Stay tuned.
Dr. Michael Baden, Forensic Pathologist: The prosecution expert says the baby was near term [nine months]. The x-ray shows growth points and then is compared to sonogram.
Dr. Spitz: Don't know if x-ray will show much if there's no external injury.
Fox News Channel ticker: Up next, Scott's finances. **Jayne Weintraub**, Defense Attorney: The baby can't live when the Mom's oxygen is cut off.
Geoffrey Fieger, Defense Attorney: Your only slightly presumed innocent, and you have to prove your innocent.
[headline]: **SCOTT'S MONEY MYSTERY.** Stay tuned.
Greta: The feds want to know Scott's finances and may be involved in drugs.
Geoffrey Fleger, attorney: Maybe he was supplying the chemicals to meth labs from his fertilizer business.
Jayne Weintraub, Defense Attorney: The prosecutor is hypnotizing witness to remember if they took a walk or not.
Bernie Grimm, Defense Attorney: Over fifty percent of the public believes he is guilty, without any evidence. Two people saw Laci after she's supposed to be dead.

8/24/03

Fox News Channel **Rita Cosby:** Scott Peterson, caught on tape; Did he incriminate himself? In a conversation with Amber Frey, on tape, he said, yes, he had something to do with it.
Amber Frey: [on tape recording] Did you have anything to do with Laci's disappearance?
Scott Peterson: [on tape recording] Yes, uh uh, but No, But I know who did and I'll tell you later when I see you.
Former prosecutor: This is a confession.
Defense Attorney: Can't take this out of context. If this was a real confession, he'd have been arrested immediately.
Attorney: We have two trials in America; American Public and Media, then the real trial. We need the context it was said in.

[There's no news or ticker tapes yet about Scott Peterson's family receiving subpoenas from the prosecutor. Guess we know who's kissing whose butts in this case. Are the TV news corps scared? The very low tone and volume, or lack of volume, that Greta used to tell us that the Peterson family was subpoenaed by the prosecutor, is certainly evident that the TV news corps will lead us to follow the government prosecution in most any case.]

8/25/03

Fox News Channel [headline]: **SCOTT PETERSON'S OWN WORDS.** Frey met Scott on November 20, 2002. Scott tells Amber on Valentine's Day that he pledges love forever to her. This shows he's cold and indifferent to his wife's death.[headline]: **SELF-INCRIMINATION?**

8/26/03

Fox News Channel Hannity & Colmes
Alan Colmes: Did Scott Peterson tell Amber Frey that he knew who was responsible for Laci's disappearance? Stay tuned.
Sean Hannity: Did Scott Peterson tell Amber Frey that he knew who was responsible for Laci's disappearance? Stay tuned.
Hannity: Coming up, Did Scott Peterson tell his girlfriend that he knows what happened to Laci? Reports have some people wondering. Stay tuned.

Colmes: Did Scott admit to Amber he was involved in Laci's disappearance? Coming up. Stay tuned.
Colmes: New report on what Scott Peterson may have said to Amber Frey. Coming up. Stay tuned. We'll talk to Gloria Allred, Amber Frey's attorney.
Hannity: How will this impact the cult theory? [Hannity said this with a laughing voice.]
Gloria Allred, Amber Frey's lawyer: I won't confirm or deny the tape, but if it's true, it's damning.
Hannity: The tape says, I'll tell you later who did this. Why are you backing off from what Amber will say?
Colmes: Is it logical he killed her over his love for Amber?
Gloria Allred, Amber Frey's lawyer: Anything Amber said to me is attorney-client privilege and I can't comment on that.

Fox News Channel **Greta Van Susteren:** Later, Is the defense on the run in the Scott Peterson case and was he caught on tape admitting he has details of Laci's disappearance? [headline]: **DID SCOTT ADMIT GUILT?** Stay tuned. Shocking information on what Scott may have told his girlfriend and why does the age of the fetus matter. How old was Conner?
Dr. Michael Baden, Forensic Pathologist: 12/20 sonogram, and x-ray and they'll be a disagreement between the defense and prosecution on age; as there are variations. Age would help corroborate eye witness accounts of seeing Laci. The x-ray is better age determinate and shows abnormalities. The autopsy; thirty-five to thirty-seven weeks old and this is by prosecution experts.
Jayne Weintraub, Defense Attorney: Age is critical.
Geoffrey Fieger, attorney: Makes no difference.
Ted Williams, Defense Attorney: Age is critical.
[Fox News Channel uses teasers to lead us to the tapes of the phone calls, but the time on air was spent about the age of Conner.]
Greta: Rita [Cosby] reported the tapes. If tapes exist?
Jayne Weintraub, Defense Attorney: Amber's trying to put words in his mouth.
Ted Williams: He said 'Yes'.
Greta: First we heard he denied it, now we hear it's changed.
Bernie Grimm: Quote is, "Yes, uh uh but no."
Greta: If that's so, it's curtains.

Geoffrey Fieger: He said he knew who was involved. The defense attorney needs to pull a rabbit out of his hat. [Geoff's hung up on Amber and that the jury won't forgive Scott for that. Greta does pick up on the Michael Peterson trial, where the Durham, North Carolina court, allowed an eighteen year old death in Germany come into evidence at a current murder trial, to show similar circumstance and therefore lack of mistake or accident in the current death, that the defendant is charged with. No doubt Michael Peterson will be convicted. The conviction will be reversed, but, because the eighteen year old death was allowed into this trial, this trial conviction will then be used to convict him of the eighteen year old death, now murder. Once convicted of the eighteen year old death, then that conviction will be used to retry this current death, and he'll be convicted again. Will Michael Peterson be prosecuted for the rest of his life, in retribution for criticizing North Carolina government, or did he really kill two ladies?]

8/27/03

[Guess when the judge in the Scott Peterson case ask Court TV if they would be responsible for the 'live' feed to other news corps and was told 'yes', that this meant we weren't going to see much of the court proceedings anyway, so why allow any coverage.]

CNN: The Appeals Court opens the preliminary hearing in the Scott Peterson case to the public on 9/9/03. In the Scott Peterson case, no cameras allowed. Cameras are a discretionary call by each judge. [Actually, the judge already opened the preliminary hearing to the public with no camera allowed, and the Appeals Court merely agreed. News corps used 'new details' in the Scott Peterson case as a teaser to keep people watching yesterday.]

8/28/03

CNN **Bill Hemmer:** People's Magazine got ahold of Laci Peterson's file and discloses some sensitive information and photos of the crime scene. Stay tuned. [So where's the crime scene?]
Bill Hemmer: The Appeals Court opens the preliminary hearing in the Scott Peterson case.

MSNBC: What role will the condition of Laci Peterson's body play in the case against Scott Peterson? Stay tuned.

MSNBC: WAS BABY BORN ALIVE, stay tuned for new information in the Laci Peterson case.
Elizabeth Gleick, of People Magazine: Access to photos, the body of the baby was up on the shore fifteen feet and different condition than Laci. There were tire tracts and foot prints around the baby. The decomposition; thirty-one weeks at disappearance; Conner at thirty-five to thirty-eight weeks. There was debris and plastic on the bodies. Yes, there was tape on the bodies; not known type of tape which had a knot in the tape around the neck of Conner. There was a robbery in the area, which questions the prosecutor's view of the timeline. Eyewitness saw Laci at 10:30am, on 12/24/02. The prosecution's case is mainly circumstantial, with what we know of the facts. Will the article taint the jury pool;, we gave a balanced account and there is no gag on us. We don't have a conclusion; not our job; it's not an opinion piece. The article comes out tomorrow.

MSNBC [headline]: **Initially Scott Peterson blamed blond hair color on chlorine.**

MSNBC: The People's Magazine article says that the police claim that the break-in near Scott Peterson's home was a couple of days later; when it was the morning of 12/24/02. His hair was a professional dye job and not chlorine. All the defense has to do is poke holes in the prosecution's case.
Leonard Levine, defense attorney: Exactly.

8/29/03

Fox News Channel: The National Enquirer says, no tool marks on Laci's body. Probably postmortem dismemberment by/after in water.
Amber Frey: "Did you have anything to do with the disappearance?" [Again, it's shown that Scott said, yeah, then no, to Laci's disappearance.]
Greg: He said "Yes".

[The TV News Corps talking head attorneys have made such a joke out of satanic cults, that the cults could get away with most any crime and be laughed off as a suspect.]

Fox News Channel **Shepard Smith:** Laci's autopsy is said to be bad news for Scott's defense. Stay tuned.
Shep: If the tabloid report is true, Scott Peterson's defense is in a world of hurt. Stay tuned.
Shep: Satanic cult theory in trouble. Report says body not severed before going in water.

MSNBC
Kimberly Guilfole Newsom, Assistant District Attorney, San Francisco
[headline]: **NEW AUTOPSY DETAILS.**
Mickey Sherman, defense attorney: It doesn't mean Scott did it. Pokes some holes in the satanic cult theory. We'll have battling experts.
Brian Wice, attorney: Hope they dial down the theory. Doesn't mean he did it. [Wice makes a joke of the defense.]
Grillo, prosecutor: The report is pretty credible. I like the evidence. This shows it wasn't a cult. I'd love it if they used the cult theory and I was prosecutor.
Gloria Allred, Amber Frey's lawyer: I apologize to Laci's family, if they are watching. Geragos said he'd prove Scott's innocent and he'd show us who did it.
Kimberly Guilfole Newsom, Assistant District Attorney, San Francisco: Were autopsy details leaked to the press? If so, who did it and which side will this help? Stay tuned. Laci and Conner were buried today.
Grillo, prosecutor: He'll probably say someone else did it.
Brian Wice, attorney: Soddi defense; somebody else.
Mickey Sherman: Discovery, He can buy People's Magazine or the Enquirer. The gag order don't work.

Grillo, prosecutor**:** But now the defense knows not to use the cult theory.
Gloria Allred, Amber Frey's lawyer: They may still stick to it and attack everyone; the scene; the physical evidence; fluids; body fluids; burglary. When the judge issues a gag order, he should

enforce it. A member of the defense team went on cable TV and talked of this case and judge should know about it.

CNN ticker: Prosecutor and defense agreed to stop accusing each other of violating the gag order in Scott Peterson case.

8/30/03

MSNBC: Laci laid to rest, finally.
Sumi Das: In People's Magazine, new information in an article. The unborn was older than previously thought; thirty-five to thirty-eight weeks old. Both the defense and the prosecutor say they both violated the gag order and both agree to drop the allegations.

CNN **Elaine Quyano:** The amount of coverage in the Laci Peterson case is enormous. Interesting to see what the judge will do about the People's Magazine article. The article is a blow to ??? The tape on the baby raises questions as to what happened. We'll see what the judge says about People's Magazine.

8/31/03

Fox News Channel [headline]: **NEW EVIDENCE IN THE SCOTT PETERSON CASE.** Stay tuned. **NEW INFORMATION FILTERS IN ON THE PETERSON CASE.** Stay tuned. **NEW INFO FILTERS IN ON THE PETERSON CASE**; How will it play? Stay tuned.
Fox News Channel: Laci Peterson may have had the baby when it was alive; how will it affect the case? Stay tuned.
Fox News Channel Host, Anne Bremner, and Stacey: Experts believe that the baby was born alive. There's a September 9th hearing. It's a circumstantial case, with no direct evidence against Scott. This makes the timing of the murder off, with a full term baby, and no umbilical cord. It's a bombshell; only need one reasonable doubt. Scott was under surveillance after December 24th, constantly. There's an ace in the hole; Scott was fishing at the same place. There's no evidence to say he's guilty, and why would he say that he was there, if guilty? We don't know what the evidence is. Gag order? Violation?

Fox News Channel **Geraldo Rivera:** Were you involved? Well Yes, but no, I'll tell you later when I see you.

[Geraldo asks his two guests about what the tape recording between Scott and Amber, as if this is what the tape recording says.

The TV news corps are now calling Scott and Laci's unborn child, Aunborn child@, whereas before they called him Conner.]

Fox News Channel **Fox Magazine:** Scott teared up in court when details of Laci's and their unborn child's autopsy details were read in court. [This is the first time the I've heard a TV news corp say that Scott teared up. Fox shows an earlier hearing; video that goes back to when the bodies were found; shows Laci's family interview; police believe Laci was strangled; shows Laci's family interview, again; and shows the memorial service.]
Magazine: Tune in to Fox Magazine for all the latest details on the Scott Peterson case.

9/1/03

[News corps take each piece of information that comes out and turns it against the defendant. Especially Scott Peterson for adultery, and not so much Kobe Bryant, yet.

It will be interesting to see if the judge in the Scott Peterson case dismisses anyone from the preliminary hearing for violating the court ordered gag order. If you or I disrupted the process necessary to assure justice, do you think the judge would allow us into the courtroom?]

MSNBC: Scott Peterson due back in court tomorrow. We'll get a preview in a moment. Stay tuned.
Defense Attorney: [People Magazine article] This may help his case; there may be evidence the baby was born.
New Jersey prosecutor: Common sense show they washed up close to each other and this is a red herring.
Defense Attorney: The only physical evidence is a hair on the pliers in the boat.
New Jersey prosecutor: There's ten thousand on him, the affair, the blonde hair doesn't prove anything.

9/2/03

CNN Headline News: A hearing today in the Scott Peterson case; both sides say they aren't getting enough information from the other side to continue.

Fox News Channel: The discovery phase in the Scott Peterson case is coming to a head today. The defendant hasn't had enough time and both sides need more information from the other.
Scott Peterson's Father: Both were alive, four to five weeks after their abduction. [The Peterson's were told that they weren't welcome at the burial service for Laci.]

Fox News Channel [headline]: **PROSECUTION SHOWING ITS HAND.** The prosecutor is showing his hand in the Scott Peterson case today. We'll have the legal lowdown coming up. Stay tuned.
Former prosecutor: Are they winning the prehearing stage? The defense is bringing in hired guns.
Host: Suppose experts come up with evidence to hurt the defendant?
Former prosecutor: They won't be called [to testify].
Host: You better believe Fox will question them.
Former prosecutor: They'll be sanctions against whoever leaked the autopsy photos.

Fox News Channel: The Scott Peterson preliminary hearing has been delayed to October 20th.
Garcia, former prosecutor: The defense is preparing as if this is a jury trial rather than a preliminary hearing. [The defense needs a lot of information from the prosecutor, but we hear nothing about what the prosecutor is seeking from the defense, at the discovery hearing.]

Court TV **Lisa Bloom:** Big surprise, the defense is delaying the hearing. [Court TV shows a video of the discovery hearing.]
Judge: The defense's motion for discovery.

Defense Attorney: There's a mass volume of tapes on dog tracking, and therefore we're not ready to proceed. There are other items needed; the materials found near the body have not been turned over. I have another case in Los Angeles to last seven days and a murder case in Los Angeles and the judge there continued

for this case, and probably won't again. Is 10/20 okay? The tapes of the dogs arrived Friday, to the defense, and the video tape of the hypnotized lady and we want a hearing on her testimony, a 402 motion; also on the GPS tracking device. The lion's share of discovery is with other agencies that the prosecutor sends it to. There's fifteen hundred items in the property room to look at, some tested by the Justice Department, and they don't want us to view what they're testing, while they're testing it.
Prosecutor: We've complied completely with discovery, if we feel it's valid. We have no basis to object to 10/20 preliminary hearing.
Judge: What happens if the other case doesn't go?
Defense Attorney: The defendant is a deputy sheriff and both sides are ready to go. The other case is set in stone and ready to go. We estimate four weeks to try these and should not run longer.
Scott Peterson: I do agree. [To waiving the thirty day requirement for a preliminary hearing.]
Prosecutor: We haven't received discovery; thirty day before trial requirement. We need a witness list for the preliminary.
Defense Attorney: We haven't decided yet, but probably no witnesses.
Judge: Set the discovery hearing; 10/17 for discovery, as this one; if needed.
Defense Attorney: Witness list?
Prosecutor: Maybe a week or two from now.
Judge: Dog tracking?
Prosecutor: Yes.
Judge: Hypnosis?
Prosecutor: Yes.
Judge: GPS?
Prosecutor: Yes.
Judge: Okay, a 402 hearing on each. [Court TV hosts interrupt the video with their talking.]
Judge: Four, 402 hearings; DNA also. Insert >except' and >doing' should be >going', in the certified transcripts of the earlier hearing. [Commercial]

[Dr. Henry Lee, in the Michael Peterson case in North Carolina, stated that the prosecution was usually piecemeal with turning over discovery evidence to the defense counsel.]

Beth Karas, of Court TV: The judge thought the discovery issues could be handled by next week and gave continuance on Geragos' schedule of other trials.

Lisa Bloom, of Court TV: The strategy in the [Winona] Ryder case was delay, delay, delay; and we'll see more of this.
Beth Karas: May be another delay.
Lisa Bloom: There's other attorneys in Geragos' firm that can handle the prelim. Maybe he should take fewer cases.
James Curtis, of Court TV, former prosecutor: The judge has no control over an attorney taking cases, or if he's in another trial.

[Lisa Bloom does her best to discredit Geragos in this case, and others, as if Scott doesn't deserve a defense, nor a prosecution which abides by law or ethics; during their after-the-fact discovery hearing discussion on Court TV.]
Beth Karas: The hypnosis was to determine if the other pregnant woman was the one neighbors saw walking her dog, and not Laci.
Prosecutor's Press conference:
John Goold: Questions? A 402 hearing allows either side to ask for a hearing to determine if evidence is admitted. The witness hypnosis, dog handler, DNA. It will be at the same time as the preliminary hearing. 10/17 is a control to see if we're ready to go. The defense said they'd comply with our request. I can't comment on evidence, as the order prevents that. [Court TV interrupts the press conference.]
Lisa Bloom: What does the delay say to you? Are you buying Geragos' excuse?
Attorney: The schedule is skeptical.
James Curtis: Nothing wrong with other trials is it?
Attorney: No, not at all. You have to attend other trials.
Court TV: Tune in at 4:30pm for Nancy Grace on the Scott Peterson continuance.
Lisa Bloom: Scott looked good in court today.
Beth Karas: A new defense theory with Nancy Grace today at 4:30pm.

Court TV: Tonight at 10pm, Catherine Crier separates fact from fiction in the Scott Peterson murder trial, accused of murdering his beautiful wife, Laci. [No mention of Conner, baby, or unborn baby.]

MSNBC **Sumi Das:** The judge said to take note, that the preliminary hearing is highly unlikely to be continued again.
Paul Pfingst, prosecutor: Delay, delay, delay, helps the defense.

Brian Wice, attorney: They should have gone to a grand jury and indict. We'll see a O.J. scenario here with witnesses. The rules have changed to help exclude scientific evidence.

Fox News Channel Dayside with Linda Vester [headline]:
COMING UP, NEW LACI PETERSON DEVELOPMENTS.
Lis Wiehl, Fox News legal analyst, former federal prosecutor: Delay helps the prosecution.
Robert Tarver, Defense Attorney: Not hurt either.

Lee, Reporter: The prosecutor wants the hypnotized lady to be the one neighbors saw. The prosecution is desperate and may be trying to create a memory. One dog says Laci was taken away by car. The defense wants the veterinarian records and the dogs' hit and miss records.
Dr. Michael Baden, Forensic Pathologist: They [dogs] are wrong many times; sometimes no where near where the body is found.
Lis Wiehl, Fox News legal analyst, former federal prosecutor: They are mini-investigators; prosecutors.
Robert Tarver, Defense Attorney: You can't use the tools of investigation, as evidence.
Dr. Michael Baden, Forensic Pathologist: They're not as good at bodies, as drugs, and can't cross exam them.
Lee, Reporter: I believe the GPS failed.
Lis Wiehl, Fox News legal analyst, former federal prosecutor: It could be rock solid evidence.
Robert Tarver, Defense Attorney: We got dogs, GPS, hypnosis; Look at this, People.
Guest: GPS goes blank when it can't see the satellite.
Lee, Reporter: Ninety bags of evidence. We're talking mitochondria DNA and not just dogs, GPS, and hypnosis.

[TV news corps are now presenting Laci's picture appearing on screen with very solemn and suspenseful music.]

Fox News Channel: The Peterson's are lashing out at the Rocha's for not being allowed to attend the funeral. Mr. Peterson lashed out at the police investigation and that Scott is innocent. Mrs. Peterson lashed out at the Rocha family. [Fox shows a video of the Petersons.]

Mrs. Peterson: Felt like someone hit us, and I think Laci would have been appalled. She wouldn't have wanted this done to us. [Does this sound like lashing out? Mrs. Peterson's voice was somber, quiet, sympathetic, sincere, and hurt. Fox News Channel censored what Mr. Peterson said, if anything.]

COURT TV [As the Peterson's were leaving the court today, Court TV shows Mr. Peterson talking, which is the same video as Fox News shows Mrs. Peterson talking.]
Mr. Peterson: He's still alive; lost baby, lost freedom; what more could a man lose?
Court TV: You can't find a copy of People's Magazine in Modesto; it's sold out; says Conner was thirty-five to thirty-eight weeks, much older than should be. Blood and vomit were not found in the house.

[Court TV shows an ad to watch the latest on the Scott Peterson case with Crier, and shows Scott Peterson walking into the courtroom in an orange jumpsuit and handcuffs. Court TV knows this is inflammatory and unfairly prejudices a fair trial, both to a jury and to the public.]

Fox News Channel: The defense gets a preview of what prosecutors have planned in the Scott Peterson case today. What do they have planned? Stay tuned.

[Court TV shows Michael Peterson and Scott Peterson photos, side by side, sometimes talking about anal sex and husbands murdering their wives.]
Nancy Grace, of Court TV, former prosecutor: Isn't it strange, two Peterson's, both charged with murdering their wives. [More than once, Scott Peterson's photo is shown with Michael Peterson's name, and **NOVELIST ON TRIAL**, headline.]

[Court TV shows Scott walking into the courtroom with blonde shaggy hair, with an ad to stay tuned.]

COURT TV **Nancy Grace:** Wife and unborn child. Why delay, delay, delay?

Dr. Ferrell??: Emotions fade and you get a trial without so much emotion.
Fox News Channel ticker: Scott Peterson accused of killing wife and her fetus.
Norris, former prosecutor: Delay tactic is common in defense attorneys. Let the public lose interest in the case. Any strong case, they try to delay.
Magama: A delay hurts Peterson. He's better served if the preliminary hearing is next week.
Norris, former prosecutor: He may waive the preliminary, cause he doesn't want the public to know it's a very strong case.
Nancy Grace, of Court TV, former prosecutor: The defense would drag the Rocha's to court if they spoke. [Nancy shows Mr. Peterson talking about Scott. Yet, earlier, Nancy showed Mrs. Rocha talking to the press.]
Norris, former prosecutor: He'd be incompetent if he didn't stall.
Magama: The defense continues a case for good reason.
Catherine Crier, of Court TV, former judge**:** There's lots of discovery outstanding and we said we wouldn't see the preliminary hearing on the set date. [Wasn't it the prosecutor who wouldn't turn over discovery at the last hearing, and yet, now here, we have this again. The original delay was, and is, the prosecutor not complying with Court Rules of Procedure.]
Beth Karas, of Court TV**:** The prosecutor has complied with discovery and even willing to give information earlier than the law requires.

Catherine Crier, of Court TV, former judge: What about hypnosis?
Beth Karas: The prosecutor wants to show that, or whether she saw the brown van in the area.
Catherine Crier: Police officer who found Conner said it looked like he had been born alive.
Forensic hypnosis expert: We know that a person's memory can be enhanced or changed by watching TV, so it may not be accurate.
Lady: A woman ten blocks away and a man nearby saw Laci that morning. The woman hypnosis was to see if she saw the brown van.
Tom Lange, former O.J. cop: It's successful because they can relax and clear their mind of clutter.

MSNBC
Gloria Allred, Amber Frey's lawyer: What the public should focus on, is why the defense wants evidence suppressed that is against them. What do they want to hide?
Catherine Crier, of Court TV, former judge**:** Dogs decided Laci got in a car, and not that she went for a walk.
Gloria Allred, Amber Frey's lawyer: Hypnosis is questionable. The prosecution wants to show she looks like Laci and the defense wants to keep it out.
Catherine Crier, of Court TV, former judge**:** Prosecutors in the Laci Peterson case say they have DNA evidence that links Scott Peterson to the murder of Laci. Stay tuned.

Fox News Channel Greta Van Susteren
Bernie Grimm, Defense Attorney: The dog tracked Laci three miles down the road, then backed up and followed to the car.
Jayne Weintraub, Defense Attorney: The handler will say dog led him to Laci getting into the car.

9/3/03

CNN Larry King [12 midnight, shows a video.]
Mr. Peterson: Laci may have been alive two to six weeks after being abducted and police failed to follow up on leads that began coming in hours after she was missing. [headline]: **LACI, UNBORN SON, CONNER BURIED FRIDAY IN CALIFORNIA.**
Nancy Grace, of Court TV, former prosecutor: Laci had Never been on Scott's boat and yet Her hair was on the pliers in the boat. [Nancy interrupts Chris Pixley, so Larry King tells her not to interrupt. Nancy shows a pout and says that the defense is doing well so far and that she has First Amendment rights.]
Nancy Grace: The bloodhound told his handler that Laci left by car and didn't walk away. [Like, maybe, in a brown van?]
Mr. Peterson: The police focused on Scott and didn't want anything to get in the way of their scenario.
Caller: It was reported several months ago that Scott told Amber he knew who did it. Has this been explored?
Nancy Grace: Lee Peterson and his wife have violated the gag order, but the judge won't do anything. If Scott had taken a polygraph, police could have focused on someone else.

Dr. Robi Ludwig, psychotherapist: It concerns me that he's getting a public trial, and the effects on a fair trial.
Newspaper guy: Most of the information leaked, was leaked before the gag order and really isn't new. We keep our sources by protecting them and not letting it be known who they are and continue to get information. [Shows video of hearing today in court.]
Scott's Defense Attorney: The volume of discovery we just got from the prosecution prohibits us from going forward at this time.
Nancy Grace, of Court TV, former prosecutor: A plea was offered to Scott if he said where the bodies were, but they found the bodies before anything could happen on that. [Nancy knows this is wrong, since the charge bargain, plea bargain, and sentence bargain were attempted to be forced upon Scott, early on in the investigation, long before the bodies were found. The prosecutor is playing the civil lawsuit game, where documents are subpoenaed by one party, so the other party hands over a truck load of boxes and says, it's in there; sorta like spaghetti sauce. Surely, the huge amount of material, whether evidence or not, will hamper and slow down the opposition. This is not to be confused with, maybe the prosecutor shouldn't turn over everything, but rather, the prosecutor has a duty to justice, for he is us and we are him.]

COURT TV **Catherine Crier**, former judge**:** Police feared Scott Peterson may flee before the bodies were identified. [Actually, the police told Scott the identity of the bodies with hopes that he would run. He headed North to a golf course, not South to Mexico, as TV news corps keep reporting. This Crier Live show seems to be a rerun of a June show, and not really, the latest.]

<u>9/4/03</u>

COURT TV **Diane Dimond:** Laci Peterson's doctor denies he did a sonogram on Laci the day before she died. Coming up on Crier live, stay tuned. Will this hurt the defense? [Seems like the TV news corps want to come up with something new every day or so, even if they knew something months before or have already brought it up before and now they change a little something to get an audience.]

COURT TV **Catherine Crier**, of Court TV, former judge**:** Laci's obstetrician comes out and says that he did not perform a sonogram on December, 23rd.

Fox News Channel **Greta Van Susteren**: Why is Amber Frey under surveillance? Why is Amber hiding and has twenty-four/ seven security? Laci's doctor speaks up. Is he making a case for the defense? Laci's baby doctor is speaking up will he seal her husband's fate? The doctor is suggesting he didn't do a sonogram on December, 23rd.

9/5/03

COURT TV: Breaking news in the Kobe Bryant case and the Laci Peterson case, tonight 7pm.
Catherine Crier ad: Breaking News in the Scott Peterson case and women speak out on Kobe's infidelity today at 5pm.

COURT TV **Catherine Crier**, of Court TV, former judge**:** Will the tactical errors in the GPS system be allowed in court in the Scott Peterson case? In the Scott Peterson case we have a forensic columnist.
News Reporter: The GPS may say that Scott visited the Berkley marina quite often and the defense might want to exclude that. Like, why did he do that?
Catherine Crier: Coming up, voice analyst, what was in Scott's mind? Stay tuned.
Gloria Gomez, KOVR TV: There's a late January interview with Scott.
David Coury, Forensic Columnist: [A vocal autopsy?] It's far cry for help. He has a strained voice, but no water. There's no grief, nothing. No question from Scott on who did this. On January, 24th, Amber claims Scott called her. Scott won't waste this time on a relevant question. He didn't defend himself. He's robo. He's asking the public to help, but he's not. It's what he doesn't say that counts. He didn't look at the cell phone when it rang, he just turned it off. He didn't flinch when it went off. He's a pro. Now that I know he had the questions before the interview; Oh, that makes a big difference. [Court TV played only a few excerpts from a twenty-two to twenty-five minute interview.]

9/6/03

Fox News Channel: Police used a GPS system to track Scott Peterson, and couldn't this evidence be used in court, say, to show he was trying to escape to Mexico. [Scott was headed North to the golf course, and not South to Mexico, even though the Police called him that day and said that the bodies were identified, when they hadn't been, and that the police were coming to arrest Scott, all in a deception to try and get him to run away, which he didn't do. They heckled and harassed him constantly to try and get Scott to lash out or run, which, either way would give the Police evidence which they don't have and would be evidence manufactured by government action.]

9/7/03

Fox News Channel **Geraldo Rivera:** Scott Peterson's defense may try to prove that the baby was born alive, and personally I don't believe that, to show the court that they have the wrong man. Up next, the Laci Peterson murder case.
Stan Goldman, Fox News legal editor: Geragos may run beyond October with the other trial and the prosecutor in the Scott Peterson case has a lengthy trial coming up in November. The trial may be next summer; the preliminary hearing moved to January. The prosecution says maybe two years to trial.
Geraldo: More time to get more bogus people who could have done it.
Craig Silverman, former prosecutor, attorney: Geragos must be expecting a manslaughter conviction or he wouldn't leave Scott in jail all this time. The prosecutor must have a strong case.

Geraldo: Experts lean toward who ever hires them, from my experience as a lawyer. They say what the one who hires them wants. [Is this a confession, and what does it say about the people Geraldo hired when he was a lawyer.]
Dr. Michael Baden, Forensic Pathologist: Dr. Lee and Dr. Wecht are the best there are. They won't say anything that isn't true.
Mark Fuhrman, former O.J. cop: They won't misstate science, but they also can't say Scott Peterson wasn't involved. Geragos doesn't want the wiretaps admitted into evidence.

9/10/03

COURT TV Catherine Crier Live
Catherine Crier, of Court TV, former judge**:** Jail house informant talks about Scott Peterson. Globe Magazine, an interview with jailhouse mate of Scott Peterson. Scott had a magazine of Mexico in his car.
David Thompson: His cell mate is in for domestic abuse, break-ins, no rewards from the Globe offered to him. Jail not easy for Scott, loner, sad, keeps to self. Scott is cold hearted, still obsessed with Amber, forced to have sex in jail, talks more about dog than Laci, didn't want child with Laci, wanted to travel. [headline]: **Scott is cold hearted, still obsessed with Amber, forced to have sex in jail, talks more about dog than Laci, didn't want child with Laci, wanted to travel.**
Thompson: Scott had a gay relation with a male bar pick up; forced to have oral sex with an inmate and consented to give oral sex to an inmate shortly after arriving in jail.
Gloria Gomez, KOVR TV Reporter: There's no conformation of this [oral sex]. He continued to romance Amber after Laci's disappearance, he wanted mini-vacations with her. The hypnosis witness saw Scott loading his truck on 12/24 and talked to Scott that morning; he was in no hurry or rush. He was loading or unloading something. Don't know what. The lady was under hypnosis for three hours, about the brown van; Scott had began the conversation with her. [James Soares, the jail house informant, has a life sentence.]

Gloria Gomez: [According to James Soares] Scott had more than ten to fifteen thousand dollars, brother's ID, clothes, camping gear, and said he was going to Mexico and live off the land. He was going to buy a car with the money. He used the ID at the golf course that his brother belonged to, for a discount.
David Thompson: Scott talked to James Soares, he wanted James to remove the golf clubs from his house; that he could have them and don't tell anyone. [headline]: **SCOTT PETERSON IS CHARGED WITH MURDER OF WIFE AND UNBORN SON.**

Fox News Channel [headline]: **SCOTT PETERSON, NEW CLUE REVEALED!**
Host: Wait till you hear what cops found in Scott's car. Is it a new clue? Stay tuned.

[Fox is going to tell us that he is going to Mexico; but what Fox won't tell us is that he was headed North. Headline]: **SCOTT PETERSON, SMOKING GUN FOUND?** Stay tuned. **UP NEXT- CLUES IN SCOTT'S CAR?**
Greta Van Susteren: Up Next, New information found in Scott's car. Is there an innocent explanation or is this a conviction? KSN TV Reports a map found in car, may be an escape to Mexico.
Geoffrey Fieger, attorney: So many smoking guns in the case. Scott's on fire. [Uh, Geoff, there's no gun in the Scott Peterson's case; so all those smoking guns must prove something else.]
Jayne Weintraub, Defense Attorney: He was on his way back; Headed North. He'd already been to Mexico and was back. Remember?

9/12/03

COURT TV **Deborah Norville**: Another affair in the Scott Peterson case. New legal strategy; a parade of women, seven, may take the stand. Will this help Scott?
Gloria Gomez, KOVR TV Reporter: How seven women? Sources familiar with the defense strategy say he may admit to seven. Laci found Scott with a woman. Laci ignored Scott and never told her family about the women. Amber says Scott said his wife was never around. The defense says he said this to three others. No big deal. Laci did not tell her family about number one, so why say anything about Amber.

Jane Ronis, defense attorney: Nobody wants this in. They want a better spin than just killing his wife. Many of us carry on affairs and don't kill our wife.
James Hammer, San Francisco prosecutor: Being a liar goes to credibility and this may show what lead him to kill her. A circumstantial case is a good case.
Jane Ronis, defense attorney: If all come in, it's better than one. The prosecution shows a pattern, and went off, and killed her after a confrontation and fight.
Gloria Gomez, KOVR TV Reporter: The real motive maybe that he didn't want a child; responsibility as husband and father.
Deborah Norville: The leading cause of pregnancy death is murder. [headline]: **FIRST AFFAIR RIGHT AFTER BEING MARRIED.**

Jane Ronis, defense attorney**:** It'll be more successful at keeping out seven affairs, than one.
James Hammer, Assistant San Francisco prosecutor: We'll see with the wiretaps.
Deborah Norville: Almost impossible to get a neutral jury.
James Hammer: What he did after his wife disappeared.
Gloria Gomez: He said it'll change in three weeks and a child with Amber on the tapes.
[headline]: **CHARGED WITH HOMICIDE OF LACI AND CONNER.**

Fox News Channel: Why was another women hypnotized in the Laci Peterson case and what will she say. Stay tuned, coming up on Greta.

Fox News Channel **Laurie Dhue:** Coming up, new development in the Laci Peterson case; another women was hypnotized. Will this hurt the prosecution? Stay tuned. [headline]: **UP NEXT, MODESTO MURDER**. Up next, police hypnotized another women in the Scott Peterson case. Stay tuned to hear what she said and if the prosecutor can use it in court. Stay tuned. Tonight, new development in the Laci Peterson case. Two women are hypnotized.
Stan Goldman, Fox News legal editor: One pregnant lady was walking the dog on 12/24; to counter the defense that it was Laci. The second lady, claims she saw a brown van on 12/24 across from the Peterson home. The police say the van was there on 12/26, and robbing the home across from the Peterson home. Can't say what was said under hypnosis, only what was said before.

Gloria Allred, Amber Frey's lawyer: May allow hypnosis, may lead to evidence that's admissible. [headline]: **MURDER IN MODESTO.**
Bernie Grimm, Defense Attorney: The prosecution is trying to deflect what the defense says, and negate witness for the defense. Hypnosis tells you you're a dog and you bark.
Gloria Allred, Amber Frey's lawyer: Learn everything you can.
Ted Williams, Defense Attorney: Hypnosis ain't a slam dunk case. [headline]: **MURDER IN MODESTO.**
Gloria Allred, Amber Frey's lawyer: The attorney general said it was a slam dunk, not the prosecutor, and he referred to the body

identification of Laci. [Bolshevik]! Amber is not a mistress, she didn't know he was married. We'll see later if the prosecution plans to call her.

9/13/03

COURT TV **Diane Dimond:** The National Enquirer claims the fingerprint of Scott Peterson was on a washed up tarp; day after the body was found.
Kimberly Guilfole Newsom, Assistant District Attorney, San Francisco: There's circumstantial evidence that links him to the crime.
Diane Dimond: The Enquirer digs up good stuff. They do some hard work to get their stuff.
Chris Pixley, Defense Attorney: The article says it comes from the police. What harm to jury pool?
Diane Dimond: The defense will say he wouldn't kill over Amber, cause he had seven others.
Brian Wice, attorney: Geragos has to do something else, within camera range, he does more damage than good.
Diane Dimond: It's been so over blown by the media; everything shown.
Kimberly: Both sides have uncleaned hands; unfortunate for Laci.
Chris Pixley: This pollutes the jury pool; no cause of death; no time; no weapon, yet the majority thinks he's guilty.
Kimberly: Laci hadn't ever been on that boat; hair and pliers.
Diane: That's right, that's a very good point.

Fox News Channel **Rita Cosby:** Up next, we have some stunning developments in the Laci Peterson case, new evidence. Will it convict Scott? Stay tuned. Up next. [headline]: **NEW EVIDENCE? NEW LACI EVIDENCE?** Up next; is there new evidence in Laci Peterson case? Stay tuned. Up next; do prosecutors finally have the evidence that fingers Scott Peterson in the Laci Peterson case? Stay tuned. New allegations in the Laci Peterson murder case. The National Enquirer; the bomb shell in the case; the fingerprint on duct tape on a black tarp found. They say duct tape was found on Laci's body.
Judge Joe Doherty, of Texas Justice Show: I didn't read the article as a fingerprint of Scott, but, so newspapers can say he's guilty.

Lis Wiehl, Fox News legal analyst, former federal prosecutor: If it's true no one has the same fingerprints.
Mickey Sherman, former prosecutor, defense attorney: It was in the water for a long time; no creditability to the story.
Lis Wiehl: Even submerged, they can make a match. There can be eight-ten matches on a fingerprint; one-in-one million; one-in-eight million chances.
Judge Joe Doherty: If, if, if, equals speculation; if they match the tape; if they match the tarp; if they match the fingerprint. They could match the duct tape to tape in your house.
Mickey Sherman: It has to be a one hundred percent match on a fingerprint.
Lis Wiehl: If it's similar, it'll come in.

Fox News Channel **Geraldo Rivera:** The National Enquirer says Scott Peterson's fingerprint found on black tarp which washed up in San Francisco Bay shortly after Laci Peterson's body was found. The National Enquirer, are probably as right as main stream press. Bomb shell allegation, very near the bodies, a big tarp of duct tape was found and a fingerprint on the duct tape and it's Scott's.
Mickey Sherman, Defense Attorney: Very tough to believe, in the water for a long time.

Stan Goldman, Fox News legal editor: If a tarp was found, if a fingerprint on tape, if Scott purchased the tarp. Smoking gun here if correct. A fingerprint can be challenged in court.
Geraldo: If it exists, I hate to defend Scott. I'd think someone else would have leaked this story sooner, if the evidence, the tarp and tape were found a day or so after the bodies were found. How do you defend against something like this, if it exist?
Gerry Boyle: Say it's real, what's the defense? A terrible problem for the defendant. A circumstantial case and even if it's weak, this evidence will become stronger.
Geraldo: The hypnosis of a witness was to question the story; is the prosecution desperate?
Stan Goldman, Fox News legal editor: The police were involved in the hypnosis, not the prosecutor. This looks bad on the prosecutor. It's about the woman who saw the van the next morning; this is a defense witness and hypnotic testimony isn't admissible, and everything before the hypnosis becomes suspect. [The police detective who interrogated the lady said he didn't

know the lady was under hypnosis when he questioned her. The TV news corps don't show us this particular video anymore.]

9/14/03

Fox News Channel: Were going to talk to Scott Peterson when we come back. Stay tuned.
The prosecution is putting forth satanic cult theory with hypnosis. Hypnosis puts the jury to believe there's prompting by the prosecutor and not a very strong case. The U.S. Supreme Court has condemned hypnosis. The public doesn't view it well. It's not a slam dunk case as they said early on.

9/15/03

COURT TV **Catherine Crier**, former judge: We'll tell you about the fingerprint some thinks is Scott Peterson's. New hypnosis in the Scott Peterson case. National Enquirer reports Scott's fingerprint at the dumping place of Laci and Conner.
Former Judge Hatchett: The hypnosis will be challenged.
Oxman, defense attorney: Everybody wants to be a witness in this case.
Larry Pozner, defense attorney: People under hypnosis can lie and be influenced.
Catherine: Black tarp found near bodies with duct tape.

Judge Hatchett: If there is a fingerprint found on the tape, they better bargain.
Oxman, defense attorney: The fingerprint is probably elongated and hard to connect.
Larry Pozner, Defense Attorney: They found out in the last five years, fingerprinting is an invention of crime labs to get a conviction. Some countries don't allow fingerprints if there is a one point difference; others say if there's one-in-five are different, can't use.
[What they fail to tell us is that these ladies who were hypnotized are defense witnesses and the prosecution is discrediting them by hypnosis. What Larry says is very true. Fingerprints, teeth marks, tool marks, voice prints, and yes, DNA, have never been researched to find two just alike. Oops, teeth marks, tool marks, voice prints, and handwriting have been checked and more than

two people and tools were found just alike. The best way not to find something, is not to look for it.]

Fox News Channel **Shepard Smith:** The defense is still working on the cult theory in the death of Laci and her unborn son, Conner. The defense is testing the coat of a man arrested, who has been bragging he was involved in the murder of Laci and her unborn son, Conner.
Fox News Channel ad **Greta Van Susteren:** New evidence surfacing in the Laci Peterson case. Coming up tonight.

Fox News Channel **Greta Van Susteren:** The Laci Peterson murder case, will a coat get Scott off the hook? Stay tuned.
Greta: The Laci Peterson murder case, the press is reporting a coat of a cult leader with Raider emblem. Four people executed with a ball bat, nine miles from Modesto. Why is a trench coat important to defense? [headline]: **SCOTT'S DEFENSE**. Up next, the legal panel tells us what they'd do with the trench coat. Trench coat?
Geoffrey Fieger, attorney: Nothing. They're not cults and didn't kill innocent people.
Jayne Weintraub, Defense Attorney: Wait and see what evidence they find.
Bernie Grimm, Defense Attorney: It's inadmissible as evidence. No link to Laci or Scott.

Ted Williams, former D.C. police detective, attorney: Looking at the boogie man here. Was she killed in Modesto and carried ninety miles to frame Scott? No way. Come on.
Jayne Weintraub, Defense Attorney: How do you know she was killed in Modesto? The defense has an obligation to investigate it. It depends on what side your on, as to what's said in thought.

9/16/03

MSNBC **Keith Olbermann:** Today's top news stories. Scott Peterson; the National Enquirer magazine reports that police in Modesto say they believe they have found Scott Peterson's fingerprint on a piece of duct tape that washed up near where the bodies were found.

9/21/03

Fox News Channel Rita Cosby
Frank Muna, attorney for jailhouse informant, Cory Carrol: Cory claims he met with Scott Peterson on 11/2/02, in strip club in Fresno, California. Cory says Scott met with two members of a neo-nazi gang to steal Laci's car, so he could buy her a new one. Peterson then wanted them to kidnap Laci, then murder her. The police interviewed Cory in jail this week. He took a polygraph; okay. On 9/19/03, the police dive teams returned to Fresno Bay. [headline]: **PLOT GONE AWRY**. Scott made a solicitation for kidnapping and it went awry.
[headline]: **KIDNAPPING CLAIM.** [headline]: **Scott's sister says no way, Scott couldn't drive the distance required in amount of time allowed. He was with family that day.**
Muna: Cory told the story in June, cause he didn't know of Laci till then.
Rita Cosby: Laci and unborn child.
Craig Mitnick: Disbelieve, he's a California inmate, but says he walked away cause he didn't want anything to do with it.
Craig Silverman, former Colorado prosecutor, defense attorney: This is a dead story. Who has the motive to leak this. The inmate wants police protection and be in the public media.
Frank Muna: This information ties Scott to what happened. I was there during the polygraph. Many with a criminal history tell the truth. He'll be believed when he takes the stand.
Rita Cosby: The conversation with Amber and Scott; with the disappearance, "Yea, but no, I'll tell you later.
Los Angeles Police Sergeant, **Al DeBlanc:** There's no independent evidence to corroborate this; nothing; not what clothes; car; or anything Scott has. But, if true, it's devastating.

9/22/03

Court TV Catherine Crier ad: Coming up, new information on the Scott Peterson case, that he tried to hire a gang to kidnap Laci.

[Was Laci actually taken by someone in a brown van, and now the police are falling into this fact with a jailhouse snitch and a reformed story, so as to find Scott guilty with what police failed to investigate?]
Catherine Crier, of Court TV, former judge: Cory Lee Carroll says he met Scott to hire neo-nazis to kidnap Laci.

Frank Muna: Scott solicited Cory to steal Laci's car. Cory introduced Scott to the two men. Scott asked if they'd kidnap Laci.
Catherine: He passed a polygraph.
Muna: Yes, and police are trying to locate the two fellows. Cory went back to jail on a parole violation and didn't hear of Scott's case. He gets discharged very soon. The prosecutor wants him to stay in jail for his own protection, since the two fellows tried twice already to kill him.
John Q. Kelly, former prosecutor: These two fellows used a beige van; Dirty and Skeeter.
Brian Wice, attorney: This is as worthless as Enron stock.
[headline]: **TOXICOLOGY REPORT SHOWS CAFFEINE IN LACI'S SYSTEM. NOT PROOF CONNER WAS BORN BEFORE LACI'S DEATH.**
Muna: Cory's been told he'd be called as a witness.
John Kelly, former prosecutor: This ties into Scott saying he knew about Laci's disappearance, to Amber. [Oh, so now we're back to 'disappearance'.]
[headline]: **GERAGOS BEING INVESTIGATED BY SEC** [Securities and Exchange Commission]. [headline]: **GERAGOS SAYS FEDS TRYING TO DISCREDIT HIM.**
John Kelly, former prosecutor: Same happened to the O.J. lawyers, being investigated on where they got money.

Fox News Channel Bill O'Reilly [headline]: **PETERSON SNITCH.**
Bill O'Reilly: Apparently someone who met Scott in jail is telling on him. Stay tuned. New info.
Rita Cosby, of Fox News: Made for a TV movie; he's in jail and wants to tell the truth. This happened about a month before the disappearance. He didn't know about the case while in jail.
Bill O'Reilly: Did these guys know satan worshippers?
Rita: He saw the information about the case after he was out of solitary, and said he knows this guy. He met Scott and introduced him to two neo-nazi guys to steal Laci's car and when he walked away, he heard Scott ask the guys to kidnap Laci. The police are looking for the two guys and the inmate has passed a polygraph.

[The story here fits the facts that Scott and others have been telling police and what's been in the news of rumor. Remember the fellow in jail who showed news organizations how he could take a few news reports and make a few phone calls from jail, and come up with convicting testimony of someone that he had never met, but could easily make it appear that the person had confessed to him in jail.

Is it a coincidence that police produce this jailhouse snitch after hypnotizing witnesses that saw Laci and the brown van on 12/24/02, after Scott was supposed to have already killed her?]

MSNBC Dan Abrams [Shows Scott coming into court with handcuffs and in an orange jumpsuit.] [headline]: **LACI KIDNAPPING PLOT?**

Abrams: I'll tell you why I don't believe it. Why not sooner? Scott has an alibi. You mean he left cause he didn't want to be involved?

Frank Muna: He [Cory] didn't get out till June. He gave an approximate date, not clear of exact date [met with Scott]. He's trying to turn his life around. He was okay with meeting on car theft, but not kidnapping. I'd have left too. I was there, during the polygraph and interrogation. He's very level-headed and wants to turn life around. We've given more information [to police] than what's been released. There is corroborating evidence, what Scott did, clothes, etc. Cory couldn't have gotten this information from the news media. The polygraph was given by a retired police officer.

Abrams: Could there be any truth to allegations that Scott talked to neo-nazis about Laci's death? Stay tuned.

Colin Murray, former prosecutor: Very effective [polygraph], but not admissible. Good chance it's the truth. Easy to cross-check for a lie. Wonder if he had an agreement to talk with police.

Jeralyn Merritt, Defense Attorney: Depends on information he has on Scott; could get it anywhere. Assume they met and Scott wanted to get rid of car. The story has changed since it first broke; first car, now kidnap, then two guys involved. I was told two weeks ago, by Muna, something would break, at a conference, but he said he was under a gag order. Why a gag order then, and not now. He said from a jailhouse snitch and he'll get something in return.

Abrams: Far fetched?

Colin Murray, former prosecutor: Criminals do stupid things, so I wouldn't discount it. [Colin says Scott is a criminal and stupid, but

isn't it the snitch who is the criminal, since Scott has never been arrested before now?]
Abrams: Very dubious about this, unless corroborated.

Fox News Channel Greta Van Susteren [headline]:
TOXICOLOGY RESULTS; LACI PETERSON.
Greta: Up next, wait till you hear who showed up Friday at the spot where Laci was found. Stay tuned. The dive team returns, report shows caffeine in Laci but not in her unborn son, Conner.
Dr. Michael Baden, Forensic Pathologist: If she had a cup of coffee one hour or two before death, it would still show up in her and not necessarily in Conner. Can't tell when she had coffee, or chocolate or something with caffeine. [headline]: **FORENSIC CLUES. SCOTT'S DEFENSE.**
Dr. Michael Baden: A red herring on caffeine.
Greta: No GHB found [date rape drug].
Dr. Michael Baden: Hard to find GHB, almost impossible with decomposition. The dive team probably looking for weights, cinder blocks. Scott had a stack of cinder blocks at home, with some missing. [Huh?]
[headline]: **INMATE BOMBSHELL.**
Greta: Inmate's lawyer joins us for an exclusive interview. Stay tuned. [Exclusive to who? He's already been on many TV shows.] Hear about Scott's lover in jail.
Ted Williams, former D.C. police detective, attorney: Dr. Baden's explanation is very good.
Geoffrey Fieger, attorney: The defense is grasping at straws with caffeine not in Conner. The information was floated by the defense. Scott's unsavory character.
Jayne Weintraub, Defense Attorney: It's not a popularity contest. Experts will say it does pass on to the fetus. Pregnant women are told not to take caffeine. It may show separation from the Mom. We don't know how much caffeine was found.
Bernie Grimm, Defense Attorney: The suggestion is the child was born.
[headline]: **MODESTO MYSTERY. MORE CLUES IN THE BAY?**
Bernie Grimm: It's a floating junkyard in the Bay.
Ted Williams, Defense Attorney: They're desperate. Not a slam dunk case.

Jayne Weintraub, Defense Attorney: Desperately diving for evidence.
Greta: May be a new tip they received. Up next, new evidence and his attorney. Where was Scott on 11/29/02? An inmate says he introduced Scott to two neo-nazis; Cory Lee Carroll.
Frank Muna: He met Scott, and Scott asked if he could find someone to steal Laci's car. Cory set up a meeting and went to a hotel room. When the kidnapping came up, Cory left.
Greta: Why won't you tell us exactly what was said? He would be implicated in kidnapping, and murder is a more serious charge.
Muna: We don't want to impede the prosecutor's investigation. He passed a polygraph; much more information given there than I can say.
Greta: Met 11/29/02? More time?
Muna: More than one meeting; Cory, one or two days after Thanksgiving. The van, some say a camper, a small motor home with a van front. My client wrote letters to the parole board, the prosecutor, and other prosecutors, but no one called, so he contacted me two weeks ago. They said they had received the letters.
Greta: Is there cable [TV] in jail?
Muna: TV in pot area, but I don't know what they play on it.
Ted Williams, former D.C. police detective, attorney: Biggest con here. You know what happens to rats in prison.
Geoffrey Fieger, attorney: No more goofier than what Geragos has said for months.
Greta: Gag order, so Geragos hasn't said anything for months.
[headline]: **JAILBIRD TALL TALE?**
Geoffrey Fieger, attorney: Geragos better pray he's a liar.
Greta: His attorney just came on TV and told us what his client will say.
Bernie Grimm, Defense Attorney: Jury would only take fifteen minutes on this one [acquit].
Jayne Weintraub, Defense Attorney: Story won't check out.
Ted Williams, Defense Attorney: It's stupid.
Jayne Weintraub, Defense Attorney: Waits till now to come forward.
Geoffrey Fieger, attorney: If not true, prosecution won't use him.

[How could a meeting to get someone to steal Laci's car, so Scott could collect on insurance in order to buy Laci a new car, turn into a meeting to kidnap Laci? Once, Muna even said, to murder her. And what purpose would a kidnapping do in getting a new car? Would Scott do this, knowing his son would be born shortly? One news corp host says, yea, we know Laci hated her car and wanted a different one, yet the news corps have condemned Scott for trading Laci's car for a work truck, after police impounded Scott's work truck. He needed a truck to continue his employment, a fact which the news corps conveniently left out of their news stories. This would seem to imply that a car could be purchased without the help of insurance money. 'For the insurance money' would be a fabrication, or rather a reality for a poor person, making up this story.]

9/24/04

Fox News Channel: Cory's story is almost unbelievable, except that he passed a lie detector test.

Fox News Channel **Geraldo Rivera:** Rumors that Geragos will be replaced as attorney for Scott Peterson probably isn't true, at least not until after the preliminary hearing.

Fox News Channel **Greta Van Susteren:** Was it a hired hit? And did it go wrong. Stay tuned.
[headline]: **WAS IT A HIRED HIT?**
[Finally someone plays the tape recording of Scott and Amber.]
Amber Frey: Did you have anything to do with your wife's disappearance?
Scott Peterson: No, but I know who did and I'll tell you later, when I see you.
Muna: Need to establish the date that Scott met with Cory, cause Cory doesn't know. Scott struck up the conversation with Cory. They didn't know each other before. Scott asked if he knew someone to steal Laci's car. Cory was maintenance at the motel, and met Skeeter and Dirty; Tony and Anthony are their real names.
[headline]: **PETERSON KIDNAPPING PLOT?**
Muna: They met at a restaurant; Chili's, then at the motel later; a couple of days later.
Greta: You keep coming back with more information, as you get it. Coming up, Scott's sister says meeting was impossible. Sister says Scott was in San Diego area where the baby shower was

held. It's a seven hour drive to Modesto and one hour back to the meeting.
Gloria Allred, Amber Frey's lawyer: Not charged with conspiracy, but with murder.
[headline]: **SCOTT'S ALIBI.**
Bernie Grimm, Defense Attorney: If charged with conspiracy, Geragos would be delighted. Bring 'em in and let 'em testify.
Jayne Weintraub, Defense Attorney: Scott didn't solicit them. Think you'd go to a bar and solicit murder of wife? There's a slew of jailhouse witnesses.
Ted Williams, former D.C. police detective, attorney: No credibility to story. Listen to lawyer. Tonight he said before 11/29, but before it was a couple of days after 11/29. Get the transcripts and compare them. This attorney gives lawyers a bad name.
Gloria Allred, Amber Frey's lawyer: He didn't try to cut a deal.
Greta: Oh, there's one coming. I've seem it happen a million times as a lawyer.
Ted Williams, former D.C. police detective, attorney: A neo-nazi gang? He's a dead man walking. He was in a jail house day room, saw the story and said this is my way out.

9/25/03

Fox News Channel **Greta Van Susteren:** More about the polygraph test in the Scott Peterson case. Stay tuned. [headline]: **MONEY TRAIL CLUES. LACI'S FEARS.**
Greta: A shocker, was Laci afraid of Scott's plans before she disappeared? But first, the man who administered the polygraph is here.
Stay tuned.
Melvin King, retired policeman, from Expert Polygraph Services: Did he mention $10,000 for murder? No. I met Cory, he had alot of information; in mid-November, later November, he met Scott and Scott wanted to know if there's anybody to steal a car? No problem. Yes, he exchanged phone numbers with Scott. Later in November, Scott called Cory, after 11/25 or 11/29. Any deception? He wasn't hooked up yet. He continued with the story. He met Dirty and Skeeter; met at the restaurant, then to Cory's motel room. Cory was paid $300 for introducing the men to Scott. First to steal car, then kidnap and Cory left; nothing to do with it. Lie? No indication of lying. Did he lie about stealing car? Lie about introducing them? Lie about kidnapping? I believe he believes

what he said is true. We report it to the police and let them do what is needed.

Greta: Do you grade the polygraph test?

Melvin King: Yes, he passed. Three grades: lie; pass; and deception. I wanted to clarify the names, but I didn't. Cory says he, Scott, and a female took a picture, but he said the girl kept it. Doesn't make sense. I didn't clarify this either. He gave names and addresses.

Stan Goldman, Fox News legal editor: Did they have a brown van? We have the released phone numbers; twice a day, from Scott to Amber, before; and four times a day after the disappearance. The family not thrilled with Geragos; rumors.

Gloria Allred, Amber Frey's lawyer: Amber never gave or sold the right to sell photos of her. No legal right to do this.

Ted Williams, former D.C. police detective, attorney: She won't sue. Make his day. Gloria won't sue. He said he has the release.

Geoffrey Fieger, attorney: Amber thought somebody would look at them; she didn't take them so she could look at them herself.

Gloria Allred, Amber Frey's lawyer: How do you know? She didn't do it to sell or give away.

Geoffrey Fieger, attorney: Story parallels Geragos' defense, of two guys in a van.

Bernie Grimm, attorney: Geragos' defense dovetails the prosecution case, maybe. [Bernie uses 'murder' instead of 'disappearance' in Scott and Amber's phone call.]

Greta: Sixty-five phone calls between Scott and Amber. Stay tuned. Eighteen calls from Scott, nine days before Laci's disappearance. Forty-seven calls from Amber in the three weeks after Laci's disappearance.

Geoffrey Fieger, attorney: Motive, fishing, bodies, equals conviction.

Bernie Grimm, Defense Attorney: You'd want him in on it before the murder, not after.

Ted Williams, Defense Attorney: Content is missing ingredient; premise for motive. Other women he was involved with and didn't kill wife.

Gloria Allred, Amber Frey's lawyer: Up to the prosecutor to decide to call her [Amber] at the preliminary hearing.

Geoffrey Fieger, attorney: Yes, they'll call her.

Ted Williams, Defense Attorney: She's not that big of an issue.

Bernie Grimm, Defense Attorney: Don't know if Amber will testify at the prelim.
Ted Williams, former D.C. police detective, attorney: She'll testify at the prelim.
Greta: If they put her on and lock in her testimony, that's the prosecutor's problem.

9/26/03

Fox News Channel: The inmate's attorney says Laci died in childbirth after kidnapping, in retaliation for not being paid.

[Bit by bit, we get more info from Cory's attorney, so that attorney can keep himself in the media. What would Laci dying during childbirth have to do with retaliation? What happened to the woman who reported being raped by two men and a woman, in a van near the Peterson home, and she was told by the men, 'wait till Christmas and you'll see...? This rape victim reported this before 12/24/02.]

Fox News Channel **Shepard Smith:** Scott Peterson now has one less attorney on his legal team to help with his defense. Stay tuned. [headline]: **LEGAL SHAKEUP. LACI PETERSON MURDER CASE.**
Shep: Matthew Dalton quits the law firm, but no one will say why. He's off the Scott Peterson case.

MSNBC Dan Abrams
Catherine Crier, of Court TV, former judge: I talked to the retired police officer who administered the polygraph to Cory and he says that Cory may believe he's telling the truth or he may be telling the truth, but either way, he passed.

CNN: The Rocha family [Laci's family] files a civil suit against Scott Peterson for the wrongful death of Laci, to prevent Scott from making any money from writing a book. The Rocha's want the money to go to the victim's beneficiaries.

Fox News Channel Greta Van Susteren
Muna: The kidnappers could have dumped the body in the Bay to frame Scott, cause they didn't get paid. It's just a theory.
Greta: Why is Amber fearing for her life?

Ted Williams, Defense Attorney: Muna should take a polygraph himself. Maybe should check to see if this guy's really a lawyer.
Ron Sullivan, defense attorney: Sounds like these three guys killed Laci and trying to blame it on Scott.
Bernie Grimm, Defense Attorney: You can't disclose information, like Muna has about your client. You might as well go down and turn in your law license.
Greta: Did Amber ask for police protection? And why does Scott have one less lawyer on the defense team?
Gloria Allred, Amber Frey's lawyer: Never wise to comment on security. She's aware of the circumstances. I have concern for her security. Always should be careful, but not necessarily scared.
[headline]: **DALTON'S DEPARTURE.**
Greta: We don't know why he left.
Ron Sullivan, defense attorney: Must be something going on, or they'd tell us why he left.
Greta: Family unhappy with Geragos? Rumors?
Bernie Grimm, Defense Attorney: Natural to be stressful when family is facing Scott with death. Usually take it out on the attorney.
Gloria Allred, Amber Frey's lawyer: May not be giving case enough time.
Ted Williams, former D.C. police detective, attorney: They'll have to put some evidence on at the prelim. Their theory is she was killed in the house on 12/23.

[Were police getting close to Cory, Dirty, and Skeeter for burglary, kidnapping, and murder, so Cory adds to their crime with his story about Scott being involved? Where, and from who, did police get their original tip from?]

Fox News Channel ticker: Scott Peterson is charged with the murder of Laci and their unborn son.

MSNBC: Laci's Mom files suit to prevent Scott from profiting from Laci's death. Could an artist's Park bring clues to Laci's disappearance?
[headline]: **THE CULT THEORY.**
Fresno police: The defense hasn't been doing their homework, if they believe paintings are satanic cults. The currents in the Bay

vary greatly from day to day and did so a couple days before the body was discovered.

9/27/03

Fox News Channel [headline]: **INSIDE THE LACI PETERSON MURDER.** Join Rita today at 5pm to get the inside latest scoop that's come out in the Laci Peterson murder.

[If Scott Peterson is such an idiot, and yet Laci was and appears to be such a wonderful person, does this mean she had very poor judgment, that she could be fooled in not believing or knowing that Scott had an affair? Or was Laci's judgment just fine, but she was kidnapped anyway?]

Fox News Channel ticker: Department of Corrections says that no prison Cory was in was under lock-down at any time and any inmates in lock-down can still see TV news.

Fox News Channel **Rita Cosby:** California Corrections Department doesn't believe Cory's story is true. A spokesman says Cory was not under lock-down and shows the institutions, with dates he was in jail.
Muna: [Muna gives fourteen reasons why and how Cory didn't hear the Peterson case in the news. Muna also admits that he too had heard Conner could have been born alive.]
Dr. Michael Baden, Forensic Pathologist: Autopsy rules that out. Came out after in water for months; out of womb. Wasn't tested for caffeine in fetus.
Retired Modesto police officer: The low-rider gang is one of the most vicious and violent in California.
Muna: I believe others are out there with information. No information on progress from police.
Mickey Sherman, Defense Attorney: Scott was on TV for six days, 12/25-12/31, every day and hour. Amber called the police on 12/31, and yet she says she didn't know Scott was married. What? She didn't turn on the TV one time and she claims she didn't know. Scott called Amber four times on 12/25.
Lis Wiehl, Fox News legal analyst, former federal prosecutor: People don't usually plead guilty to a crime they didn't commit, a second time. [Was this an insight from Lis?]

9/28/03

Fox News Channel **Rita Cosby:** Muna, he says within twenty-four hours. [headline]: **CORY'S LAWYER HOPES TO HAVE PROOF OF MEETING SOON.**
Melvin King, polygraph tester: I didn't ask Cory if he was on lock-down while on the polygraph. Spent two and one-half hours with him; information needs to be investigated; don't know if truth or not, but he believes it. Satisfy yourself if true or not. It doesn't concern me if he was watching news or not; let's get to the truth, I'm not God, if polygraph was wrong, let's find out, recommend that another polygraph be given. The lady who saw Laci and won't take a polygraph, yet police say Laci killed on 12/23-12/24, and yet lady may well pass polygraph. [headline]: **12/31 TWO TIMES TALK. 12/25 FOUR TIMES TALK. 12/26 AMBER CALL SCOTT THIRTEEN TIMES. 12/30 AMBER CALL POLICE, TWENTY-TWO MINUTES. 2/14 AMBER CALL SCOTT SEVENTEEN TIMES. WHO TO BELIEVE?**
Paul Callan, retired prosecutor: Motive is to kill wife for Amber. In the initial interview, he said not a problem between he and wife. Police will use this. Use what King just said against Cory in court.
John Burris, former prosecutor, attorney: Can't imagine prosecutor using Cory's information, always looking for deal for self. Dangerous for prosecutor to use, cause it'll show they have other suspects.

9/29/03

MSNBC **Dan Abrams:** Is Scott Peterson trying to profit from Laci's death? According to Laci's Mom he is. They say in the suit filed against Scott that they have interviews, innuendo, and talk that suggests he is cutting a book or movie deal to tell his story and profit.

[One lawyer says that the suit can succeed, but not the way it is written, which is upon the unconstitutional son-of-sam law. Another lawyer says the suit is not about money, but for the Rocha family to punish Scott, and that it probably won't succeed, since the suit is based on 'maybe he's guilty', 'maybe a deal', and 'maybe a profit'. Too much speculation. Both lawyers say they'd have to prove he killed Laci first, or once a deal is made, then 'maybe' the court would act.]

Fox News Channel **Greta Van Susteren:** Exclusive new evidence in the Scott Peterson case. Learn what document was sent to police and... Stay tuned. [Fox shows a video of police searching a field.] Hired hit evidence? In the Scott Peterson case. Stay tuned. [headline]: **HIRED HIT EVIDENCE?** Cory has corroborating evidence of the meeting?
Muna: Yes, declaration submitted to the prosecutor that saw them together in Fresno. That person has agreed to be interviewed, a long-time friend of Cory's; can't question her character, she's right, either late November, Cory was doing work in her garage and Scott spoke to both of them, in Fresno. Cory was putting up shelves. Talked to both, small talk. This person, she liked Scott. No crime talk; small talk. Cory and Scott talked alone, probably set up a meeting. I spoke with her myself. Pretty, pretty reliable. Couldn't get her to lie, even if you pulled out her toenails. She was very clear about that. There may be other parties to say what occurred at the meeting; Scott, Cory, Dirty, and Skeeter. There were three to four meetings with Cory and Scott.
Greta: Go get more info and come back and let us know. Why didn't Cory come forward sooner? Stay tuned.
Geoffrey Fieger, attorney: Muna is interesting, if he backs it up, materials, and dovetails with the theory by Geragos.
Ted Williams, Defense Attorney: You have faith in Muna? Department of Corrections said Cory wasn't in lock-down. If she knew Scott, why didn't she come forward?
Jayne Weintraub, Defense Attorney: All she knows is Scott met Cory.
Bernie Grimm, Defense Attorney: We weren't light on Muna; he's a lunatic; said she was a she; said 11/29, then changed it. Geragos wants this to be true cause killers are Cory, Skeeter, and Dirty.
Greta: If he hired them, then murder for Scott too.
Jayne Weintraub, Defense Attorney: Why didn't she go to the police, instead of a declaration?
Greta: Phone calls.
Geoffrey Fieger, attorney: Jury pool polluted and guilty.
Bernie Grimm, Defense Attorney: Agree with Geoff, not criminal conduct, but heartlessness conduct used to convict him.

9/30/03

Court TV Deborah Norville

Muna: The person didn't hear about hit or kidnap; Cory was fixing shelves or fixing a bicycle. Scott came over and had small talk with Cory and this person. This person knows Scott from pictures. Does she, the person, know of Cory's record? She signed a statement that her name not be released. No problem with Cory's background.
Trent Copeland, Defense Attorney: Not giving the information early on, makes it unreliable. There's nothing physical to connect Scott with Fresno, and his family says he was with them; the sister.
Deborah Norville: Be interesting to see how much ends up in court as to what we see on TV.

10/1/03

[Prosecutors in the Michael Peterson case, Scott Peterson case, and the Kobe Bryant case, have, and are withholding evidence that they say proves the defendant committed the crime charged with, yet they won't share it with the defendant so he can defend himself, and sometimes even show he's not guilty.]

10/2/03

Court TV Catherine Crier Live
Ted Rowlands, KTVU TV Reporter: Bones found near where Laci Peterson was found; animal bones after testing. Diving, two weeks ago, for five days; a dive team from New York and ongoing.
Catherine Crier, former judge: Low riders; well it isn't going away. Police knowledge. They talked to Cory several times. Still being checked into.

Fox News Channel: Bones found near where Laci's body washed ashore, but investigators still don't know if human bones or not.

Fox News Channel **Greta Van Susteren:** What was just discovered where Laci's remains were found? Stay tuned. Up next, Kobe Bryant rulings and startling discovery in the Laci Peterson case. Stay tuned. [headline]: **NEW EVIDENCE FOUND?** New evidence found? Near where Laci's body found? Stay tuned. [headline]: **UP NEXT, MODESTO MYSTERY. GRUESOME NEW FIND.** Up next in the Laci Peterson case, find out what was just found and brought over to the coroner's office. Stay tuned. The Costa County coroner examines the bones

found; don't know if human or not. The woman found them weeks ago and took them home. [headline]: **GRUESOME FIND.**
Jayne Weintraub, Defense Attorney: No preservation of bones.
Geoffrey Fieger, attorney: Maybe show how separated. Doubt if they find any other evidence.
Ted Williams, former D.C. police detective, attorney: Found bones in the Levy case much later.
Greta: Feel bad for the family. [All say they feel bad for the family and for Scott.]
Geoffrey Fieger, attorney: What about Scott trying to buy a car in his Mom's name and gave her name? What if that turns out to be true?

10/3/03

Fox News Channel [headline]: **SINISTER PLOT?** [Shows Scott getting into the back of his pickup truck.]
Greta Van Susteren: In the Laci Peterson case; is there a sinister plot to profit from her death? Stay tuned and find out why some may think so. [headline]: **MODESTO MYSTERY**. Up later, Cory and what he says about Dirty and Skeeter; and are police looking for them. Stay tuned.
Muna: Cory heard Scott offer three thousand dollars to each, both Dirty and Skeeter, to kidnap and eight thousand dollars each to kill her. We have the phone records to show the calls. The story about someone buying his story for eight thousand dollars, by National Enquirer, Cory said no. No offers of seventy-five thousand. I'm obliged to convey offers to my client. [headline]: **HIRED HIT THEORY.**
Melvin King, polygraph tester: There were no questions on money asked, no discussion of money offer.
Muna: Cory told me right before talking to the police. I told him to answer their questions. If they didn't ask question, then he didn't answer one. The poly guy didn't ask for details.
Greta: Your story is getting larger.
Muna: No, we give police first shot. What can we release without hurting the prosecution. We talk to them and fully cooperate.
Greta: Where's Dirty and Skeeter?
Muna: Don't know if they exist. Met several people who knew them; locals in area; still looking.

Melvin King: Every question, Cory had a logical answer. Two and one-half hours; everything I asked. He impressed me, in all my years, he's probably the only one I couldn't trip up.

10/4/03

Fox News Channel [headline]: **NEW INFO ON PHONE CALLS BETWEEN SCOTT AND AMBER.**
Fox: We have new information on the recorded phone calls between Scott and Amber. Stay tuned for Rita and Geraldo for the details. [Fox shows Scott walking his dog and Amber at her TV announcement, the second TV announcement first, then they show her first TV announcement.] [headline]: **FREY FACTOR.**
Fox: We're learning more about the Laci Peterson murder, stay tuned for Rita and Geraldo tonight. [headline]: **LACI PETERSON MURDER.**

[It has been interesting to note that the news corps have gone from Laci and son, Conner; to Laci and Conner; to Laci and unborn son, Conner; to Laci and unborn fetus; to the Laci Peterson murder. They humanized Conner for the double murder charge, then dehumanized him for the evidence to be against Scott that Conner had not been born. These weren't different news corps, who had different opinions on life, expressing their individual view; but, were the same news corps, changing their word usage to combine with their right of using their public influence, to influence the public.]

Fox News Channel **Geraldo Rivera:** Much more lurid and complicated than we thought. The calls continued after the cops stopped taping.
Rita Cosby: We reported alot of this before the conversations took place. Amber and the polygraph; Melvin King; on 2/1/03, called him. Scott agreed to take a polygraph with Amber. King declined to comment. Law enforcement wanted to set up a sting, but Scott said the next day was not enough time.
Geraldo Rivera: King called and thanked you for the respect shown to him. King says that no one has disproved the story yet. Alleges Cory has stayed in motel where the meeting took place. Like Scott is living in an alternate reality.
Rita Cosby: Muna says corroborating evidence is the picture with the stripper and Cory just drops away.

Geraldo Rivera: Club says it doesn't allow cameras in the Club, unless a celebrity. [headline]: **EXCLUSIVE INFORMATION.**
Rita Cosby: Is there a bombshell in the Laci Peterson case. Stay tuned. Fox news has learned Scott offered to take a polygraph test. Amber kept asking if he had anything to do with Laci's disappearance and Scott said he'd take a lie detector test, but it was too early to get the police into sting the polygraph.
Wendy Murphy, former federal prosecutor: If guilty, the best thing to say is, of course, but you then just don't take it. He knows he'd fail it.
Judge Glenda Hatchett: He never expected it to go further than her, Amber, to convince her.
Geoffrey Fieger, attorney: I agree; it's further evidence of motive; to convince her and facilitate relations with her. Clouds the jury view and the defense is destroyed, without other evidence.
Wendy Murphy, former federal prosecutor: Court of public opinion knows he said no and they'll be the jury.
Judge Glenda Hatchett: Jury will see through the defense argument that he offered to take it.
Rita Cosby: What could police have gotten?
Wendy Murphy, former federal prosecutor: You can trick a polygraph, but when police do it, much more likely to get results they are lying and that's why he refused. [So, just whom is detecting whom?]
Judge Glenda Hatchett: Better police didn't do it, may have backfired.
Geoffrey Fieger, attorney: Agree, better to offer, but never did.

Fox News Channel At Large With **Geraldo Rivera:** Why did Amber contact Lieutenant King? Apparently to ask him to give Scott a polygraph. Stay tuned.

[Is it possible that the lady who was raped in a brown van before Laci was missing, told someone that the men were Dirty and Skeeter, and this info got to Cory through the jail or other means?]

10/7/03

Fox News Channel: In the Scott Peterson case, the defense also wants to exclude evidence from hidden tracking devices.

10/8/03

Court TV: Scott Peterson's defense is trying to quash some hair evidence because of the way police handled it. Also the tracking devices in his vehicles.

Court TV ticker: Scott Peterson, accused of murdering wife Laci and their unborn son, defense attorneys want to exclude strands of hair and other evidence and testimony from police hypnotized neighbor and tracking devices on vehicles.

Fox News Channel [headline]: **SHADES OF SIMPSON TRIAL IN SCOTT PETERSON CASE?**
Shepard Smith: Are there shades of the Simpson trial in the Scott Peterson case? Stay tuned. Mark Fuhrman coming up. [headline]: **PETERSON ATTORNEYS SAY POLICE TAINTED SOME EVIDENCE.**
Shep: Attorneys say police now have two hairs on pliers and that they put it there.
Mark Fuhrman, former O.J. cop: Weak case, so attack the police, instead of factually innocent like Geragos said. Not talking about gun, bowling ball, etc., it's hair. They could find another one anywhere. The patrol officer and detective find evidence, and give it to the lab and processed according to standards they're using in the case. Police don't give evidence to the lab, then open bag and put another hair in.
Jeralyn Merritt, Defense Attorney: Okay to challenge evidence, if unscientific; must collect, store, and handle correctly; and patrol officer doesn't wear gloves.
Tim: Course they take a page out of the O.J. book. I hate to be here talking about hair. It's a three ring circus and might as well pick up as much as can on the way to acquittal.
Jeralyn Merritt, Defense Attorney: File motions to question evidence and they become public.
Shepard Smith: Don't defense attorneys do this to make it public and we talk about it.
Jeralyn Merritt, Defense Attorney: Not done for that, but to check evidence to see if reliable or not.

Court TV ticker: Scott Peterson, charged with killing his pregnant wife Laci, and their unborn son.

Court TV **Diane Dimond:** Remember strand of hair on the pliers in the Scott Peterson case? Well the defense team now wants that evidence tossed. Stay tuned. [Court TV actually shows Scott coming into court in a suit and tie.]
[headline]: **THE RUNNING MAN?** [Shows Scott behind bars in cuffs and leg irons, where he undressed and put on jail clothes.]
Diane Dimond: Did Scott Peterson try to run and go on the lamb before police caught him? And what his defense team is up to with evidence. Stay tuned. [Shows Scott behind bars in cuffs and leg irons, where he undressed and put on jail clothes.] Was Scott Peterson planning to flee the United States shortly before his arrest? The National Enquirer reports he bought a used car using his mother's name.
Bruce Yale: Some deception going on, but he didn't try to register it in Mom's name. He didn't want notoriety using his own name to buy a car.
Diane Dimond: He knew police put a tracker on his truck; he found it; the GPS device.
Bruce Yale: If they can prove he knew of it and other stuff.
Abbe Rifkin, Florida state prosecutor: The defense is getting around the gag order with motions; what he wants public to hear. Is blood on hair; pulled out; get rid of evidence using argument that splits hairs. Knock out GPS cause unreliable; Come On.
Bruce Yale: Not desperation; doing what supposed to do. Hypnosis isn't reliable; all kinds of rules; it's a good motion. Everybody says one hair, lab, cops, etc., one hair. The two detectives pulled out the pliers without any company, and now there's two hairs. The original hair was five inches; and now if there's two hairs, two and a half inches, there's some explaining to do. May be in trouble.

10/11/03

Fox News Channel: Scott Peterson's lawyers are looking to push back his preliminary hearing. Stay tuned with Rita and Geraldo for the latest.
Geraldo Rivera: Police looking for Dirty, [Geraldo gives his real name and birth date], confirmed by Muna, that he belongs to neo-nazis; forty-five years old; extensive criminal record; living with a blonde prostitute, [Geraldo gives her first name].
Rita Cosby: This comes from Cory; so; remain skeptical of Cory; not in lock-down, lied about that; still they'll track it down.

Geraldo Rivera: Geragos in trial in Los Angeles; prosecutor delays; slam dunk for Geragos on delay, other trial, not my fault.
Rita Cosby: Both sides told there may be a delay; week or maybe more.
Geraldo Rivera: If neo-nazi pans out; dispels prosecution's case; hair in boat, what if never in the boat.
Greg: Playing the O.J. defense, go after the police.

Fox News Channel: Scott Peterson is charged with murdering his wife Laci and their unborn son. [headline]: **COURT DELAY?** [Shows Scott in court with Geragos, with a suit and tie.]

10/13/03

Fox News Channel [headline]: **STEAMY PHONE CALLS?** [With a picture of Scott and Laci.]
Greta Van Susteren: Something about phone calls and did police blotch some evidence in the beginning, intentionally? Or inadvertently?
Stay tuned.
Greta: You'll be surprised; exclusive new info on who spent hours on the phone with Laci's family while she was missing. Stay tuned.
[headline]: **MODESTO MYSTERY.**
Ted Rowlands, KTVU TV Reporter: New information; Amber Frey formed a relation on the telephone with the brother, father, and step-brother, of Laci. Amber Frey tried to broker a deal to send Scott to take a lie detector test; but fell through.
Greta: Hair?
Ted Rowlands, KTVU TV Reporter: Geragos will want that evidence suppressed; two hairs in the boat; initially, only one hair. Investigators went back and found another hair. Detective Brocchini; the Peterson family says he's been aggressive from the beginning. He'll be the Mark Fuhrman of this case.
Jayne Weintraub, Defense Attorney: Move to suppress at the preliminary hearing; why one, now two; probably from hair brush. Pliers didn't kill her. Scorned woman, Amber, she's more on the phone than affair.
Geoffrey Fieger, attorney: Not sloppy work. They can go back and find another hair. Okay, if prove she's been in the boat.

Bernie Grimm, Defense Attorney: Critical; no evidence he put her in the boat and dropped in the Bay; but the hair. Still won't carry the day.
Ted Williams, Defense Attorney: Hair not the lynchpin for anything; they were married. If this is all they have, then the prosecutor is in trouble.
Ted Rowlands, KTVU TV Reporter: Say dog hit at Scott's warehouse; they want that excluded. Scott in Berkley area alot; want that excluded, as GPS has inherent problems.
Geoffrey Fieger, attorney: Important is when he went south, when bodies were found, with money and fake ID. Amber is still most of his problems.
Greta: Why go to Berkley to look for wife?
Geoffrey Fieger, attorney: Maybe he was looking for Dirty and Skeeter.
Jayne Weintraub, Defense Attorney: Who said looking for wife? Maybe with family; sister.
Greta: He went to Berkley Manor the next day, when others were at the park where he said last seen.
Bernie Grimm, Defense Attorney: The criminal evidence against Scott wouldn't make it to a jury. They can't say how, when, where....
Greta: You get the last word.

[If Amber knew Scott was married, just a few days after Christmas, and she contacted police within a couple more days, then with the phone taps on Scott's phone, Amber could try to get Scott to say most anything, especially with the police coaching her on how to set Scott up with combining fact and fiction.

The word 'disappearance' in Amber's question to Scott, changed to 'murdering' very quickly with the news corps, once Rita Cosby broke the exclusive new info from the phone taps. Now it's slowly getting back to 'disappearance'.

With Amber combining police, psychology experts, Laci's family, polygraph experts, and her own powers of seduction, if she didn't get Scott to give a full and complete confession lasting twenty minutes or so, then Scott either isn't as dumb as media plays him to be, or he didn't do it, or both. Very soon after the event would seem to be the most likely time for a person to tell someone about it, but if police insisted Amber not see Scott in person, then he could have already known she was trying to set him up; since we already know that the police accusations and media condemnation had already begun.]

10/14/03

MSNBC **Sumi Das:** Two reasons why Amber reached out: Amber wanted the Rocha family to know she didn't know Scott was married, and that Laci would be found safe and alive. This comes from a source close to the Rocha family and not from Amber herself.

Fox News Channel **Greta Van Susteren:** Coming up; stunning news in the Scott Peterson case. Learn what he told Amber in those taped phone calls, just days after Amber went public. Up next, why did police stop taping Amber and Scott Peterson? [headline]: **MODESTO MYSTERY. AMBER'S AFFAIR.** Up next, you may be surprised who praised Amber, called her the next day for going public.
Ted Rowlands, KTVU TV Reporter: Rita gave details of relations days after 12/30, when Amber called the police. Amber kept the conversations going that day, 12/30, when Scott called her, and then Scott told her of the marriage.
Greta: January 24th she went public.
Ted Rowlands, KTVU TV Reporter: He called her, loved her, spend life with her; but public, saying affair a mistake. The preliminary, probably not Friday, maybe November 27th; to finish trial [Geragos] in Los Angeles.

10/15/03

Court TV **Susan McDougal**, former special prosecutor Kent Starr victim: Mark Geragos believes one hundred percent that Scott Peterson is innocent.

Fox News Channel: No mishandling of evidence in the Scott Peterson case, say prosecutors, of the second hair found on the pliers that the defense wants tossed out.

Fox News Channel The Factor **John Kasich:** The dogs went to the car.

Melinda McAllister, Defense Attorney: There are dog evidence standards in California; the defense questions this. Evidence of phone calls.
Jimmy Gurule, former prosecutor: Phone calls not consistent with the innocence of Scott Peterson. Dogs; critical evidence.

Fox News Channel **Greta Van Susteren:** Did Modesto police tamper with evidence from Scott's boat? **MODESTO MYSTERY**. Have police identified 'Dirty' and located him? **DIRTY IDENTIFIED?** [Fox shows a picture of Cory with the above headline.] **MODESTO MYSTERY.** Up next, one hair on Scott Peterson's boat could be key evidence, but did someone mess with it? Stay tuned. Have cops tampered with evidence?
Lewis Jared, former cop: Another herring by the defense. Like the satanist theory. Attack the evidence, the hair, as to a break in the chain of custody. Officers review evidence after being booked into evidence; is routine throughout the United States. One five-to-six inch hair, a single strand; next it appears as two; a one inch and a four inch, with damage on both ends and maybe damaged while in police custody.
MISHANDLED EVIDENCE?
Lewis: Two of the finest, Modesto police have on this case; top notch investigator.
Greta: Could be negligence?
Lewis: See when go to court.

[We didn't hear anything about Skeeter, nor Dirty. Remember when the news corps said that Scott did not go fishing in the Bay, cause his boat didn't have any salt water on it or the boat trailer. Scott produced a gas receipt and the news corps said you can pick those up off the ground. But, when the bodies were found, the news corps said Scott could have washed all the salt off the trailer and boat.]

10/16/03

Court TV **Nancy Grace**, former prosecutor: Speaking of spousal abuse, it'll come up in the Laci Peterson case, with the death of Laci and her son, Conner. Most of you know, most abuse happens when the woman is pregnant.

MSNBC **Dan Abrams:** New information in the Laci Peterson case. Witnesses hypnotized in the Laci Peterson case, wait till you hear as they prepare to testify in that case. The preliminary hearing is next week. The defense motions to exclude: the hypnotized witness who saw Laci walking her dog; the hair on the pliers, on the boat; the scent from the tracking dogs which led to where the body was found; the GPS tracking as inaccurate; and information from the wiretaps, as gotten with false information.
William Fallon, former prosecutor: To make a long preliminary hearing by the defense; maybe exclude hypnosis. [headline]: **EVIDENCE AGAINST SCOTT?**
Abrams: Can't ask her what she remembers after hypnosis; at trial, only before hypnosis.
Lady prosecutor: The prosecutor will want her to say it was her walking the dog and not Laci.
Abrams: Prosecutor says not now, but use her at trial.
John Burris, former prosecutor, attorney: The defense is worried about the DNA; the hair on the pliers.
Abrams: Sounds like the O.J. defense; now two hairs.
John Burris, former prosecutor, attorney: It is critical evidence for the prosecution.
Abrams: When it sounds like O.J., it makes me nervous.
Lady prosecutor: They'll do anything they can.
William Fallon, former prosecutor: They have to go after the investigation, it led to dead body and led to Scott Peterson.
John Burris, former prosecutor, attorney: Heart of case is DNA.

[Aren't the news corps forgetting that the tracking dog took the officer away from the house and towards the park, just as Scott and Laci's dog had done. The tracking dog went away from the house and then returned, which may indicate that Laci went that way, but, the scent was getting weaker, the farther away from the house and stronger in the other direction, so the dog turned around and came back to its original, its strongest, or its last, scent spot.]

Fox News Channel **Geraldo Rivera:** No preliminary Monday, other trial, maybe 27th.
Greta: Defense has alot to exclude from the preliminary, in the Scott Peterson case.
Bernie Grimm, Defense Attorney: Go over all, how died, when died.

Ted Williams, former D.C. police detective, attorney: So many questions, the preliminary hearing is necessary.
Jayne Weintraub, Defense Attorney: Prosecutor will give Amber a dry run, put tapes on to stop rumors. Geragos would get to cross exam Amber.

10/17/03

Court TV ticker: Scott Peterson and his lawyers will appear in Modesto court today for a status hearing. Scott Peterson is accused of killing his pregnant wife, Laci, and their unborn son, Conner.

Court TV **Nancy Grace**, former prosecutor: Next we'll be delving into the Laci Peterson case, and what went down in court today; almost.
Stay tuned.
Beth Karas, of Court TV: The judge continues the preliminary hearing for November 28th. Geragos is in Los Angeles.
Jim Hammer, prosecutor: No more; it's put up or shut up for Geragos.
Nancy Grace, former prosecutor: Apparently the cadaver dog didn't 'hit' on Scott's boat.
Dr. Larry Koblinsky, forensic scientist: Dogs can do amazing things. If Scott transported the body to the Bay, obviously the body would be on the boat.
Jim Hammer, prosecutor: Could be in the back of the car and wrapped tightly.
Michael Weiner, M.D.: Alot of things lend guilt; don't know. The overwhelming evidence came by means of pushing Scott by the prosecutor.
Jim Hammer, prosecutor: Maybe they're waiting for the real killers. Ha, Ha.
Michael Mazzariello, attorney: He's on trial for murder, how much can you rush him.
Nancy Grace, former prosecutor: Now DNA from mother has shown up. Are we getting a DNA mixture here or some mishandling of evidence by police?
Beth Karas, of Court TV: Motion to suppress some wiretaps.
Nancy Grace, former prosecutor: Talk to Amber about Mexico and stripper to Mexico, girlfriend to Europe.
Dr. Larry Koblinsky, forensic scientist: Have to show motive; Amber's enough for that. Hair is critical evidence to case, reliable

science; admitted to twelve states now. Laci was never known to be on the boat Scott purchased the first of December.
Nancy Grace, former prosecutor: Hair found, wound in the pair of needle nosed pliers, hidden under the seat in the boat. [Shows Scott, in court, saying that he agrees with continuing the case to November 28th.]
Nancy: Do you think Geragos has a trick up his sleeve and won't let the prosecutor know if he's calling someone [as a witness]?
Jim Hammer, prosecutor: Don't know, I forget all the defenses Geragos has, I'd have to look on the O.J. website to remind me.
Michael Mazzariello, Attorney: Prosecutors are notorious for holding evidence until the last minute.
Jim Hammer, prosecutor: Prosecutor will pay Geragos back at the preliminary for all the tricks he's played.
Michael Mazzariello, Attorney: So the prosecutor is going to try the case in the media?
Jim Hammer, prosecutor: Won't be tried in Modesto. Prosecutor wanted transaction sealed, so it won't be tried in public.
[headline]: **LACI PETERSON MURDER CASE.**
Nancy Grace, former prosecutor: This time, no blonde look for Scott. The defense is arguing the state didn't give them exculpatory evidence; the dog did not 'hit' on the boat. If the prosecutor says it hit in the driveway, can't the defense deduct that it hit on the boat. [Only in Sherlock Holmes stories, and only then if we add a little magic to the words spoken. To deduce that the dog hit on the boat, there would need to be some evidence that allows that deduction, which in essence would mean the dog did hit on the boat. But, in order to 'deduct' that information, we'd first have to assume that the dog hit everywhere, and then we were told to 'deduct' that he did not hit on the boat.]
Jim Hammer, prosecutor: Judge won't throw out; should have disclosed to defense.
Michael Mazzariello, attorney: He's detached from the family, no dedication to them and no dedication to the investigation, so that's where you look. [Obviously this fellow hasn't been watching the same police investigation or TV inquisition that's been going on. How could Scott cooperate with an investigation that's targeting him with trickery and deceit?]

MSNBC ticker: Preliminary for Scott Peterson is continued till 10/28, Peterson charged with murder of wife Laci and unborn son.

[When Scott Peterson was shown today, sitting in court and answering the judge's two questions, he seemed focused, at ease, and confident, in the little body language shown, and, in the tone of his voice and the words he used. So he's gone from, in court, being a little pissed off at the prosecutor for withholding evidence and delaying the preliminary hearing and thus the trial, to being okay, with an attitude that we'll get this straight at trial, showing the prosecutor and the public at the preliminary hearing, that the prosecutors are making most of this stuff up. Seems like the spectrum of emotions that occurred when police accused him within forty-eight hours and the media condemned him; he was still confident in his innocence.]

Fox News Channel **Greta Van Susteren:** Scott Peterson was back in court today. Wait till you hear what he had to say. Stay tuned.
[headline]: **SCOTT IN COURT TODAY.**
Scott Peterson: Yea, the 28th is appropriate.
I do.
Stan Goldman, Fox News legal editor: Postponed cause Geragos in trial, may not make the 28th. When Scott walked in court, and out, the first time that he didn't look at family; not happy, not happy preliminary hearing isn't going on. Scott hasn't been around the legal system. Geragos ought to be there.
Greta: Dogs?
Stan Goldman, Fox News legal editor: Dogs, no trail at boat, no evidence body was in the boat. The prosecutor didn't tell the judge this; would he have signed warrants? Say for wiretaps? Don't know yet. Amber's conversations okay, she agreed to it. Defense says if dogs don't show the boat, then Scott's not the murderer; gives the defense the best defense to argue.
Greta: What if in plastic?
Stan Goldman, Fox News legal editor: None of that mentioned yet. No motions argued today. Search warrant issues come up right away. Up to Geragos to argue others at end of the preliminary.
Greta: 12/27, dog scent with police, so already on his trail by that point.

[Stan says, that if the judge would not have issued the wiretap warrant, if he'd known the dogs did not hit on Scott's boat, that that, is a technical thing. They focused on Scott from the beginning. Law schools throughout the country tell students that there is no such thing as a 'legal technicality', so remove that term from your vocabulary.]

Fox News Channel The No Spin Zone
Geraldo Rivera: In spite of mounting evidence, the judge allowed postponement of the preliminary hearing. The defense has adopted the traditional approach, to dismiss evidence; hair on pliers; no scent by dogs of the boat and didn't tell the defense; and has dropped the hypnotized witness. Far from a slam dunk as the California Attorney General said.
Michael Cardoza, attorney: Absence of scent, no big deal to the prosecution; but why hide it? Why not up front?
Geraldo Rivera: Hair, now two; attack cops.
Michael Cardoza, attorney: Won't be effective because of the O.J. case. Twelve jurors bought a portion of it. It will damage Geragos' case if he tries it.
Geraldo Rivera: Most telling of Scott is the Amber relation. No one night stand. He met her as a masseuse. Still courting her with Laci missing. She's above reproach here.
Michael Cardoza, attorney: Geragos could use that he offered the lie detector test. Cheating doesn't make a murderer. Put on an expert to explain.
Geraldo Rivera: Motive to kill?
Michael Cardoza, attorney: No, other affairs too. Why not kill before. Amber has a child. He won't jump from one fire to another. I'd go with the insurance money. They won't let if he said he'd take a polygraph, come in. That's not gonna come in.

<u>10/18/03</u>

Fox News Channel **Rita Cosby:** Alot of evidence in the Scott Peterson case; Is It tainted by police? Coming up. Will this damage the prosecutor's case and is this the break Scott Peterson was waiting for? [headline]: **TAINTED EVIDENCE?** [Shows Scott coming into court.]
Rita Cosby: Stan, you were in court yesterday. What do you think was the most important new development?
Stan Goldman, Fox News legal editor: Well nothing happened yesterday. Geragos not there and continued. Outside the courtroom there was talk of cadaver dogs, no hit at the boat.

Jared Lewis, former Modesto police officer: Interesting the defense wants to dismiss the dogs when they don't help them and use them when it does. He told Amber he knows who the killers are. Someone saw him that morning putting something wrapped up in his truck. The boat was stored in the warehouse.
Stan Goldman, Fox News legal editor: Hypnotized witness; the prosecution puts her use in jeopardy, she may not be allowed to testify.
Rita Cosby: She said she saw three men in a brown/tan van.
Stan Goldman, Fox News legal editor: Yea, and the defense can say that an important witness was blocked by the police.
Jared Lewis, former Modesto police officer: They'll follow all tips, till the end.
[headline]: **REVEALING RECORDS.**
Rita Cosby: Coming up, we'll give you more details from the tapes of Amber and Scott Peterson. Will this damage the defense's case? Scott's defense team has portrayed Amber as a sex temptress and pursued Scott, but Scott called her ... times. Told Frey he loved her, told TV interview he didn't.
Lis Wiehl, Fox News legal analyst, former federal prosecutor: Not good for Scott. Suppose he's innocent and wife missing. Doesn't make sense.
Stan Goldman, Fox News legal editor: Don't know how defense will play it.
Lis Wiehl, Fox News legal analyst, former federal prosecutor: Maybe one call, two, but not all these to keep her out of the way.
Mickey Sherman, former prosecutor, defense attorney: She's not a great motive, but does destroy his character. Allows the jury to take him out.
Rita Cosby: What of 'love tapes'?
Stan Goldman, Fox News legal editor: Haven't heard tape, but if he said 'I didn't do it, but I know who did', that may be damaging. Others say they saw Laci that morning.
Mickey Sherman, former prosecutor, defense attorney: Tell jury he's a cheater right away.
Lis Wiehl, Fox News legal analyst, former federal prosecutor: Dogs; can't wait, say credible, then not credible.
Mickey Sherman, former prosecutor, defense attorney: People love dog evidence in America.
Lis Wiehl, Fox News legal analyst, former federal prosecutor: Wiretaps are coming in.

Mickey Sherman, former prosecutor, defense attorney: He didn't say he did it; that he killed her.
Rita Cosby: First he said he did, said yes, then, Oh, Oh, no, but knew or thinks he knows who did, according to my sources. [Dirty and Skeeter must have eloped.]

Fox News Channel **Geraldo Rivera:** The public will hear the tape of Scott telling Amber that he loved her, just hours after attending a candlelight vigil in her honor, while missing. The lies he told provide motive to kill his wife. On 12/31, the call, after candlelight.
Tape: I don't know who did anything to Laci, but I know who did.
Lady from National Enquirer: We heard the tapes; good sources listened to tapes. [headline]: **THE 300 CALLS THAT WILL CONVICT SCOTT.**
Craig Silverman, former Colorado prosecutor, attorney: Calls will put him in jail for a long time.
Wendy Murphy, former federal prosecutor: Prosecutor will give the jury the information of him and his cavalier attitude; couldn't care less. [headline]: **POLICE ASK AMBER TO GET SCOTT TO TAKE POLYGRAPH TEST.**
Geraldo Rivera: How hurt is the prosecutor's case that dogs didn't pick up the scent in that boat? Police say he killed his wife, wrapped in plastic, put in boat, and dumped in Bay; Laci and her unborn son, Conner.
Dr. Michael Baden, Forensic Pathologist: Can clean boat, and if in plastic bags, not have scent, not decisive.
Craig Silverman, former Colorado prosecutor, defense attorney: This wasn't a leak, it was in a defense motion.
Wendy Murphy, former federal prosecutor: Hair, defense has tried so many theories, and the public doesn't buy any; then attack the government and a certain part of the public doesn't like government and will latch on to that.

<u>10/19/03</u>

[If the police found a pair of needle nose pliers under the seat of Scott's boat, since every fisherman and nearly every boat needs needle-nosed pliers, was this before or after the dog failed to recognize Laci's scent on the boat? When were the pliers found? When was the hair discovered? We know when the two hairs were discovered, by the two detectives who went in to look at the evidence. Is it the same hair, now in two pieces, or, are the two pieces of hair different altogether? Didn't somebody say that the hair would be more important if one end was pulled out, rather than a broken hair? Didn't someone before that also say it would be nice to find some DNA evidence in the boat? Was Laci's Mom's DNA found on the 'now two hairs' from the pliers?]

10/20/03

CNN Larry King Live
Ted Rowlands, KTVU TV Reporter: The defense says the prosecutor didn't provide all the evidence when they went to get search warrants from the judge, and goes against the prosecutor that Laci was in boat. Misconduct by the police detective; looked at evidence, the hair; came out, and two hairs. Prosecutors say the hair just broke in half.
Nancy Grace, of Court TV, former prosecutor: The prosecutor must turn over trial evidence and exculpatory. Now prosecutor says dog did go up to boat and barked, barked at the workbench, but heavy chemical smell in the warehouse. Bet they [defense] don't like that answer.
Jan Ronis, attorney: Not tough or impossible to get conviction. Defense just goes from one theory to another and worried.
Larry King: Why not divorce?
Chris Pixley, Defense Attorney: The prosecutors have to answer, when, where, why, how; and haven't. Why on Christmas eve? Media floats many of these theories.
Dr. Robi Ludwig, psychotherapist: Person who kills spouse isn't thinking clearly. Only takes a brief moment, an impulsive act; child could have provoked it.
Nancy Grace, of Court TV, former prosecutor: Amber is a motive; not a one night stand; wanted to marry her. Two dogs followed scent from home all the way to the San Francisco Bay. We know this from the prosecutor's filings.
Chris Pixley, Defense Attorney: Many of the phone calls from Amber are while she's working for the police.
Jeanine Pirro, prosecutor Westchester County, New York: Why tell a mistress that you're a widower? That's sick.
Jan Ronis, attorney: At that moment, men are known to say alot of things. Doesn't mean you're a murderer.

Ted Rowlands, KTVU TV Reporter: The preliminary hearing to take five days. Amber will testify, a full day, day and a half. Scott called Amber after the TV interview, he loves her.
Nancy Grace, of Court TV, former prosecutor: Amber a big witness, motive, he led her on to the polygraph, then no show.
Chris Pixley, Defense Attorney: The defense won't put up any witnesses; cross examine the prosecution's witnesses and learn.
Larry King: Fair trial?
Jeanine Pirro, prosecutor Westchester County, New York: We'll see trashing of law enforcement; very predictable.

[New bits and pieces, or changed bits? Now, it's two dogs, both showing Laci left home, in a car, was taken to the San Francisco Bay, and in Scott's boat. Up till now, the dog had shown Laci to be headed to the park, but came back to the driveway at the Peterson house and stopped there. There was a dispute as to if the dog hit, both towards the park and, or, at the driveway. The Peterson dog also went toward the park, stopped, and lingered in one spot.]

10/21/03

Court TV **ad:** We'll have new information on Scott Peterson tomorrow on Crier Live at five. See you then.

Fox News Channel **Greta Van Susteren:** Coming up, new evidence in the Laci Peterson murder case. Who did Amber ... and where did the cadaver dogs trace Laci's scent to? [Fox shows video of a German shepard dog on a boat dock.] Next, Amber Frey wages war in federal court over nude photos. Why didn't she do anything about it when they were taken? We'll talk to Gloria Allred. And why the defense says prosecutor is barking up the wrong tree about dogs tracing Laci's body to Scott's boat. Amber filed suit; turn over the pictures and negatives, plus damages.
Gloria Allred, Amber Frey's lawyer: Broker said on Fox he'd have a web site to sell the photos. He did and Amber filed suit. Two other lawyers represent her. She didn't pick up the photos; not interested in career; her wish they not be exploited; never sign a release. She signed a data sheet; what her vital information is, tattoos, piercing, but no release, to her understanding. I asked the broker for the original release and not provided. I've seen what he says is a copy of a release.

Greta: Dogs mild interest at the boat and containers under the bench at the warehouse, work.
Dr. Michael Baden, Forensic Pathologist: Odor from body, cadaver dogs vary in ability. Better at looking for a body, if body on move, hard to tell. Many people use plastic bags when fishing, when leave bags, odor leaves.
Ted Williams, Defense Attorney: No physical evidence; nothing. Scott not so well versed to do that.
Jayne Weintraub, Defense Attorney: Scent, would it have been there long enough? No alert, or the prosecutor would be jumping; as is, Geragos can....
Greta: Judge will decide if can use it or not.

[Nancy Grace says that the dogs had a definite hit or barking at, or in, the boat, workbench and underneath the workbench. Nancy names the dog, a female, and acts as though she knows the dog. Whereas, Greta Van Susteren merely says that the dog showed an interest in the boat and containers under the bench. Nancy says she got her information from the prosecutor's [court] filings.]

<u>10/23/03</u>

MSNBC **Dan Abrams:** Amber Frey came to police with information about Scott Peterson and now she's being repaid with nude photos on the internet. She filed suit in federal court.

Fox News Channel **Greta Van Susteren:** Coming up, the war over the nude photos of Amber. I'll ask the fellow who has them if he has a release for them when we come back.
Gloria Allred, Amber Frey's lawyer: [Amber] Not interested in a modeling career at that time.
Greta: Did Amber sign a release?
Schmidt, broker: It's on dot com, she signed it, original given to Amber at the signing.
Greta: Photographer says Amber signed the release; copied it; gave her the original. Why original?
Broker: No idea, he's a photographer, not a contractor.
Greta: Copy is as good as original. Handwriting sample?
Broker: Larry Flint already did that; forensics of driver's license and our copy.
Greta: Between Amber and the photographer?

Broker: Yea, well....
Bernie Grimm, Defense Attorney: Game, set, match. The story of Amber and the photographs will come out at the pretrial.
Geoffrey Fieger, attorney: Larry Flint said Amber's photos was a two-bagger. Geragos needs to waive Scott's preliminary hearing.
Ted Williams, Defense Attorney: No, No, Jeff, you've been drinking those tea leaves again.

Fox News Channel **ad:** Tune in to Fox tomorrow for the latest on the Scott Peterson case. Are all the delays a part of the defense strategy and preventing the Rocha family from justice? Stay tuned to Fox.

<u>10/24/03</u>

A&E CHANNEL Who Killed Laci Peterson? Aired 4/30/03. The Murder of a Young Woman and Her Unborn Son. Special. [headline]: **1/24/03 AMBER GOES PUBLIC. MET SCOTT 11/20/03.**
Commentator: Scott drove ninety minutes at least once a week to see Amber. In that instant, in the public, Scott became the sole suspect. Amber became a victim too. Amber's revelation ended the Rocha family support; turned the public against Scott. Four days after Amber went public, Scott did an interview with LA-TV; this cast more doubt. The family says Laci would have told them of an affair, if she'd known.
Video of **Scott:** A few days after 12/24 to tell Amber of Laci's disappearance. Told her I was married.
Interviewer: Amber says you called her 12/24 and said you told her you were going with your family to Brussels.
Scott: Won't waste media time answering that.
Commentator: The same day as the TV interview, Scott bought a car and talked to a realtor about selling their home. [A&E shows a shock-jock jerk with a bull horn in front of Scott's home, yelling.]
Commentator: Getting charged, tried, and sentenced in the media and this is a problem that's not gonna go away easily. The body was found and Scott was arrested. By the time he was arrested, the public already had him convicted. Case closed; maybe not. If a circumstantial case, maybe good news for Scott Peterson; jury will see facts. We know in a very different light; the house sale, Laci's car sale, most say guilty. Sounds to me like he needs a pickup truck. Fleeing as consciousness of guilt is easy for defense to

defend. If blood in house, tarp, boat, then Mr. Peterson has a very difficult case to fight.
Dr. Michael Baden, Forensic Pathologist: If dismemberment, tool marks left.
Commentator: Said he went fishing and that very Bay is where the body washed up; and if cement in his boat, it about locks up the case. Most say because of Amber, but could be a defense, Laci mad about the affair and then probably not a death penalty case. There's evidence we don't know about. We don't know of any evidence to say Scott did this. Some say two years to trial. Experts say the defense won't get a change of venue. Who hasn't heard of Scott Peterson and Laci. Just might take a little longer to find an impartial jury of twelve. [The commentators on A&E were a variety of people, sometimes showing their face and sometimes their name.]

Court TV ticker: A status hearing in Scott Peterson murder case is scheduled for today; the preliminary is scheduled for next week.

Court TV **Nancy Grace**, former prosecutor: The preliminary hearing is set for November 29th. Is his defense attorney telling the truth?
Beth Karas, of Court TV: This is the fifth date set for the preliminary hearing. Geragos is still at trial in Los Angeles. Wednesday is more realistic; Thursday or Friday.
Carl Fox: If the lead attorney isn't available, it won't go forward.
Ramon Magama, Defense Attorney: California law says Scott gets his choice of attorney and a one day delay isn't much.
Lisa Kaplan: Very difficult for Laci's family, to get started again after all these stops.
Beth Karas, of Court TV: Prosecutor won't go into the hypnotized witness, will call at trial. Not using GPS, leaning to not using, to not prolong the preliminary.
Carl Fox: Show probable cause. [Court TV shows video of Scott in court, with a lady attorney, while in an orange jumpsuit and handcuffs.]
Ramon Magama, Defense Attorney: Just show crime took place and is related to Scott. Surprised prosecutor isn't using all the evidence. Prosecutor said he wanted a preliminary hearing, rather than a grand jury so the public would know what's going on.
Carl Fox: Show enough to get the public on their side.

Nancy Grace, former prosecutor: Whew, there's Scott Peterson with blonde hair, a little different from his appearance in court today.
[headline]: **THE FACES OF SCOTT PETERSON.** [Shows four pictures of Scott.]
Nancy Grace, former prosecutor: Apprehended near Mexico.
Beth Karas, of Court TV: The defense wanted another delay today; sure the judge knew beforehand. One out-of-state DNA prosecution witness; money, just inconvenience.
Nancy Grace, former prosecutor: Plus they're tired and want to go home. The preliminary will be short and sweet.
Carl Fox: Scott's changed his appearance, and the jury will notice.
Nancy Grace, former prosecutor: Why is his appearance important, even at the preliminary, with no jury?
Ramon Magama, Defense Attorney: Dress affects demeanor.
Lisa Bloom, of Court TV, Civil Rights lawyer: Change in hair and dress is deceiving and hiding.
Nancy Grace, former prosecutor: He said hair was from a dip in a pool.
Carl Fox: Yea, his skin would be orange.
Nancy Grace, former prosecutor: If the prosecutor puts on too much at the preliminary, the defense gets a free, all expense paid shot at witnesses.
Beth Karas, of Court TV: The family didn't know Scott bought the boat three days before. Laci gets sea sick and probably never set foot in the boat. Many think Amber will testify.
Nancy Grace, former prosecutor: Oh boy, we can expect three to four days of cross exam and the nudie photos.

Court TV **Diane Dimond:** Why are the prosecutors calling Scott's father?
Beth Karas, of Court TV: Supposedly to say he didn't know Scott had bought the boat three weeks earlier.
Trent Copeland, defense attorney: Had some concerns about the defense, but it's getting better. It went in all directions at the beginning, shades of O.J. Simpson; now go to the heart of the prosecutor's evidence. The wiretaps may be gotten with false information by the police to the judge. This is a much better approach.
Diane Dimond: Not hearing of satanic cults and the brown van is better.

Yale Galanter, Defense Attorney: Geragos leveled the playing field; everyone thought Scott was guilty and now everyone's asking, where's the evidence.
Dr. Larry Koblinsky, forensic scientist: That hair puts Laci on the boat. Scott could have had it on his clothes and that got it onto the boat; but it was found on the pliers; now true, there's no root on it. There are some people with the same DNA. Was the hair tampered with? We can tell with forensics.
Marshall Hennington, Jury Consultant: Some do lie to get on a jury. Not all jurors will tell the truth. They'll tell what they think you want to hear during voir dire. [Voir dire is French for, to speak the truth.]
Gloria Allred, Amber Frey's lawyer: There's red paint found on the front of Scott's boat. The police are looking at Buoy #4, to see if Scott tied his boat to it, to dump the body.
Dr. Larry Koblinsky, forensic scientist: Police, with forensics, will be able to tell ID that's the exact same paint.
Diane Dimond: Why a hearing on the DNA?
Trent Copeland, defense attorney: The defense will probably put on some witnesses. Use a cost/benefit analysis to determine what to spend on the preliminary.
Marshall Hennington, Jury Consultant: Make sure you put your spin on it.
Beth Karas, of Court TV: Amber may testify for two days; the preliminary five to six days.

Fox News Channel **Dari Alexander:** Scott Peterson's preliminary hearing has been postponed for the fourth time. This time for one day. Peterson is charged with the murder of his wife Laci and their unborn son.

Fox News Channel [headline]: **LACI TRIAL UPDATE.**
Greta Van Susteren: Coming up, the latest details in the Laci Peterson case, new information released today by both the prosecutor and the defense. Stay tuned. [headline]: **TO FACE SCOTT?** Will Amber come face to face with Scott in court? **LEGAL MANEUVERS.** Up next, who is the defense flying in next week to testify? Stay tuned. The judge pushes the hearing to Thursday. The witness list; Amber will take the stand Wednesday.
Ron Sullivan, defense attorney: A gold mine for the defense to cross [examine] her.

Geoffrey Fieger, attorney: Preliminary is insane for Geragos, the evidence will kill Scott Peterson. I wouldn't put her on, but she'll bury Scott Peterson; jury will be polluted.
Jayne Weintraub, Defense Attorney: Don't need Amber to put on the tapes. The prosecutor here wants to show the world and not like the ones in the Kobe case.
Bernie Grimm, Defense Attorney: Geragos will question her till the judge says stop; bias, reward, pictures.
Jayne Weintraub, Defense Attorney: Photos; money; wants the right to sell them later. She's in it for the money.
Geoffrey Fieger, attorney: Somebody may feel negative about the photos.
Ron Sullivan, defense attorney: Judge won't allow the question, but ask it anyway.
Greta: But she's not selling them, the other guy is.

10/25/03

Fox News Channel **Geraldo Rivera:** The preliminary, five to seven days. The prosecutor promises big surprises. The defense attacks the forensics, hair. All Amber, all the time.
Rita Cosby: They'll have alot of hearings. Amber to testify for three days. A reporter, we'll talk to him tonight, spoke to an inmate who is neighbor's in jail with Scott. They drank some homemade wine and Scott confessed to hitting her over the head with a golf club. Scott asked him to move the golf clubs from the house; supposedly he hit her with a golf club; maybe hit in the neck in front and no blood spatter. Not much evidence in this case. Amber could play on the jury.
Geraldo Rivera: Blonde hair, girlfriend, most damaging evidence. It doesn't take much evidence to convict.

[So, with no physical evidence shown, that Scott killed Laci or that Laci was murdered, we have: Scott gave Laci a date rape drug, GHB, before strangling her; Scott hit Laci in the head with a hammer; Scott hired someone to kidnap Laci, didn't pay and Laci died during childbirth, or She was killed because Scott didn't pay; Scott killed Laci somehow, we don't know how, but it was because of Amber; Scott hit Laci in the throat with a golf club and killed her; and Scott didn't want to be married or have a child, so he killed Laci so he could be free and travel.]

Fox News Channel **Rita Cosby:** An inmate at the jail where Scott was; Scott confessed to the murder of Laci.

David Thompson, of Globe Republic: I talked to James a few months ago; said he had more on Scott, but couldn't tell cause there's a code of ethics in jail.

Rita Cosby: They had alcohol?

David Thompson, of Globe Republic: Pruno, with fruit, a few glasses. Scott confessed to James; incredible, vivid details. Hit his wife, Laci, with a club. [Fox shows a quote from the Globe of what Scott was supposed to have said.]

David Thompson: The comment was made while they were watching TV; three to four glasses of alcohol; then the confession. Scott told James that he snapped and hit her with a club; he didn't want children. There were several more confessions; most intense of were after the court date; Scott snapped and blamed Laci for being behind bars. His mind changed about Laci; from, didn't mean to do it, to now blaming her for his predicament.

Stan Goldman, Fox News legal editor: It's hard to disregard the story. Many are convicted on jailhouse snitches. Highly subject to impeachment by the defense.

Gloria Allred, Amber Frey's lawyer: Amber will be ready to testify. She'll tell the truth and not much to fear. She'll have confidence, cause telling the truth. [headline]: **SCOTT'S BIG DAY.**

Gloria Allred, Amber Frey's lawyer: If Geragos attacks her, it may boomerang on him. Won't be helpful to Scott on what he says.

Stan Goldman, Fox News legal editor: The judge made clear that the witness list not be given out. Alot of motions to exclude evidence by the defense at the preliminary.

Rita Cosby: Will we see any bomb shells in the Scott Peterson case when it goes to the preliminary hearing next week? The judge told both sides, this time, be ready to go; Wednesday.

Lis Wiehl, Fox News legal analyst, former federal prosecutor: It'll be a mini-trial. The prosecutors tell the defense to pony up and plea now.

Mickey Sherman, former prosecutor, defense attorney: Circumstantial case, can't take a chance of not enough evidence.

Geoffrey Fieger, attorney: Amber tapes are a bombshell. We'll hear Scott in his own voice. Why Geragos would have a preliminary is beyond me. A high profile preliminary only hurts.

Mickey Sherman, former prosecutor, defense attorney: Maybe the tapes are not harmful.
Lis Wiehl, Fox News legal analyst, former federal prosecutor: The defense wants to cross her now; for trial later.
Geoffrey Fieger, attorney: Public only remembers bad things.

Fox News Channel **Geraldo Rivera:** After being delayed so many times, preliminary will occur Wednesday, come hell or high water. What does the prosecutor have? They promised evidence weeks ago and haven't delivered so far. There's certainly no smoking gun. A source close to the defense doesn't know if Amber will testify. The defense doesn't believe any phrase in there, of, No, didn't murder. It does have the neighborhood break-in information on it.
Stan Goldman, Fox News legal editor: Both sides are calm and confident, both think win. We'll hear alot of tapes, forensics, and motions to exclude. All day Wednesday with admissibility of DNA; hair on pliers.
Geraldo Rivera: Heard the prosecutor will say that the hair split.
Dr. Henry Lee: Dogs; Can't put dog on stand, just handler, and some overstep bounds of science. Can't talk about case.
[headline]: **PROSECUTORS ISSUED SUBPOENAS TO PETERSON FAMILY.**

Court TV Hollywood At Large [A piece is done on Scott and Laci Peterson. One defense attorney said, You can be convicted of a crime, with bad press, before you ever step into the witness box at trial. The commentator says that many people still believe that the press serves the public with information, even if sometimes titillating it.]

10/26/03

[If there was some sinister plan by Scott to have someone steal Laci's car for the insurance money, why then, after police took Scott's truck, was it so easy for Scott to merely trade Laci's car in for the pickup truck Scott needed to continue working. His motions and decisions concerning business seem entirely normal, considering his wife was missing and the world believes he was at fault.]

10/27/03

Court TV [Shows Scott in court, in an orange jumpsuit, blonde hair, and in handcuffs.]
Catherine Crier, former judge: He told Amber that he'd be traveling in Maine with family during Christmas.
Annika Pergament, Court TV News: Hair?
Catherine Crier: Reported that Laci was never in the boat; no root on the hair. Two hairs instead of one; or two pieces; probably won't keep it out of evidence.
Annika Pergament, Court TV News: As far as defense strategies, we've heard everything from satanic cults to neo-nazi bikers. What will be the defense?
Catherine Crier: Preliminary, probably a week at minimum; thirty-five to forty witnesses on the state's list. Probably won't call all of them at the preliminary hearing.

Court TV Catherine Crier Live
Bob Tanenbaum, author: Want as much information as possible; preliminary a waste, why not indict.
Bob McNeill, defense attorney: Can be a down side if prosecutor puts out damning evidence.
James Curtis, of Court TV, former prosecutor: It's time for the prosecutor to put up the evidence. Won't see alot of evidence, just enough to bind over.
Candice DeLong, retired FBI: Would think the police would have went after the clubs; see if they did. Scott loves to talk; we know that. Confession; three to four glasses of pruno, alcohol. Friends say they spent eighteen months to get Laci pregnant. [headline]: **SCOTT PETERSON WILL BE PERMITTED TO DRESS IN CIVILIAN CLOTHES.**
Bob Tanenbaum, author: One cell mate says confession, and another says he hired someone.
Bob McNeill, Defense Attorney: It's necessary to contest the hair DNA; mitochondria can have two people with the same DNA, it's not the same as nuclear DNA test.
Catherine Crier: Still can say it doesn't deviate from hers and it'll come in.
James Curtis, of Court TV, former prosecutor: Right, and a scientific method.
Bob McNeill, Defense Attorney: But, can't exclude wife and then can't exclude girlfriend, so what does it say?

James Curtis, former prosecutor: Yea, but he'll be convicted anyway, with what the prosecutor told me they have. [Court TV shows a tabloid paper with Scott confessing to killing Laci.]
Catherine Crier: Dogs, wiretap, sightings of Laci and van.
Bo Dietl, retired N.Y. detective: If killed in the house, there should be more evidence from inside the house. Challenge the wiretaps if not turned off when not investigating the case.
Catherine Crier: Dog showed interest, I guess, at boat and workbench.
Elizabeth Faulkner, Research Analyst: All evidence should be shown.
Bo Dietl, retired N.Y. detective: Ammonia content in fertilizer and the prosecutor argues this took alot of evidence away.
Candice DeLong, retired FBI: Living scent isn't the same as cadaver scent. Could it be a transferred scent or on someone's clothing naturally?
Bo Dietl, retired N.Y. detective: Could be alot of other evidence that won't be shown, or I hope so. I love this jail bit; yea, he goes to jail and wants to confess. Yea, right, these bozos always want the prosecutor to cut them a break. Somebody may get him in jail for the baby, the little boy, and see God.
James Curtis, former prosecutor: No need to put Amber on, can use tapes and hearsay.
Elizabeth Faulkner, Research Analyst: Research the background, public records, something to impeach her character.
Bo Dietl, retired N.Y. detective: Take away credibility; falsehoods in life.
James Curtis, former prosecutor: Prosecutor will do this ahead of the defense and take away the surprise by the defense.

Fox News Channel [headline]: **SCOTT'S COURT DATE.**
Greta Van Susteren: What or who will be waiting for Scott Peterson in court Wednesday? [Fox shows Scott in court, with a suit and tie.] Will Scott Peterson come face to face with his lover on Wednesday? **COURT PREVIEW.** Scott Peterson is less than forty-eight hours from being in court and prosecutors plan to say how he killed Laci. [Fox shows pictures of Scott and Laci.] Less than forty-eight hours to the preliminary.
Gloria Allred, Amber Frey's lawyer: We'll see if the prosecution calls her [Amber]. Geragos will be surprised, if, and when.

Bernie Grimm, Defense Attorney: Geragos won't be surprised; he's good. Be nice to have more facts.
Geoffrey Fieger, attorney: Use Amber to introduce the tapes. A known liar; says he told police of the affair earlier. Now we'll find out. [headline]: **MODESTO MYSTERY.**
Geoffrey: We'll see forensics, whatever the prosecutor lets us see.
Gloria Allred, Amber Frey's lawyer: Hair, the prosecutor says it's Laci's and if DNA test is scientific enough.
Ted Williams, former D.C. police detective, attorney: Amber will be called; desperation by the prosecutor and if centered on Amber, they're desperate.
Geoffrey Fieger, Defense Attorney: Purpose is to prejudice public more.
Ted Williams, former D.C. police detective, attorney: You're right. Don't need Amber to introduce the tapes.
Gloria Allred, Amber Frey's lawyer: Unfair to say prosecutors would sway public opinion; Hollywood is on the other side of this.
Bernie Grimm, Defense Attorney: His conduct hurts him more than anything; but, if that's all they have. They need more to tell us how and why.

<u>10/28/03</u>

Fox News Channel [headline]: **TRIAL OF EVIDENCE.** Scott Peterson's preliminary hearing begins tomorrow.

Court TV Catherine Crier Live
Catherine Crier, former judge: Experts say Amber Frey will testify in the Scott Peterson preliminary hearing.
Gloria Gomez, KOVR TV Reporter: Good tip; will she testify, end of week or early next week. Mr. Peterson called by the prosecutor; he didn't know of the boat Scott bought. Found red paint mark on the front of boat. Three miles away from Berkley Marina, looking at Buoy. Don't know if results back yet. Tie to buoy to stable the boat to throw the body over; two to three foot waves. Fishermen said body, if dumped there, currents take it to where found.
Candice DeLong, retired FBI: If he said he wasn't there, and it's found he was.
Gloria Gomez, KOVR TV Reporter: Industrial paint.
Nancy Grace, of Court TV, former prosecutor: Amber's testimony is the tapes, turn the jury upside down when they hear them. She dated a married man in the past. [headline]: **PROSECUTOR**

SAYS HE'LL BEGIN PRELIMINARY WITH DNA EVIDENCE.

Catherine Crier: Why not get wife swapping, etc., out in the open and let the public chew on it?

Nancy Grace, former prosecutor: Why let the defense have a free ride, just go with the tapes.

Catherine Crier: What about witnesses seeing him in the middle of the night?

Gloria Gomez, KOVR TV Reporter: Neighbor saw Scott that morning; other neighbor suspicious that the blinds were closed on Christmas eve morning, always open. He said he was fishing at Brooks Island, near the buoy. A fourteen foot aluminum boat, with a thirteen horsepower engine, takes two hours to get to the buoy. He showed up around 5pm at home, looked for Laci, then quickly made phone calls.

Candice DeLong, retired FBI: The FBI stopped hypnotizing witnesses twenty years ago and they can't testify in court, in federal court. We didn't hypnotize anyone, except maybe for a license plate number, but not if we needed them to testify down the road somewhere.

Gloria Gomez, KOVR TV Reporter: The neighbor came to police and said she saw him loading or unloading something. They also ask her about the brown van.

Brian Wice, attorney: Paint won't show alot. Hair on pliers, the defense claims it's tampered with. They'll lay the ground work to criticize the police.

Geoffrey Fieger, attorney: He'll be bound over, activity won't come into the preliminary; but his conduct afterward will prejudice the jury so much they won't favor anything in his favor.

Catherine Crier: Jailhouse snitch.

Nancy Grace, former prosecutor: Yea, drinking pruno, don't believe it. Scott is not available to the other inmates and don't believe he opened up to other inmates. Geragos would have told him not to. I disagree with Wice that the prosecutor has to prove motive; never have, never will. And with Geragos condemning other attorneys for being on cable TV, come on, talk about the kettle calling the skillet black; Hello!

Catherine Crier: Trying to get Scott to take a polygraph.

Geoffrey Fieger, attorney: Those part of the tapes won't come in. Amber was controlling him with police help.

Catherine Crier: Scott attempted to delay the search of his workplace, said no electricity there.
Brian Wice, attorney: Consciousness of guilt; I must have done something wrong.
Geoffrey Fieger, attorney: Geragos would be doing his client a disservice if he shows his hand at the preliminary hearing and goes into a full fledged defense.
Catherine Crier: You're right about that. Tune in tomorrow evening and we'll chat live with viewers about the Laci Peterson murder case.

MSNBC **Dan Abrams:** Prosecutors are pulling out the evidence stacking up against Scott Peterson, but it's nothing compared to what Amber Frey will say. Tomorrow Scott Peterson will be in court for the first time with the evidence laid out against him. Tonight we'll tell you what will happen. Tomorrow, finally, the murder case of Laci Peterson in court. Amber expected to be the star witness for the prosecution. [MSNBC shows the video of Amber saying Scott told her he wasn't married. Shows a video of Scott's interview with him saying that the told Laci and told Amber after Laci's disappearance. Scott says he told police earlier, but said not to talk about dates of affair with Amber, so they could investigate.]
John Burris, former prosecutor, attorney: Depends on what Amber says. If admissions of murder, yea, but affair, no.
Gloria Allred, Amber Frey's lawyer: The prosecutor hasn't said if Amber's a witness.
Paul Pfingst, former prosecutor: Can't say Scott loved his wife.
Dan Abrams: Why kill Laci, pregnant, yet with Amber who has a child.
Paul Pfingst, former prosecutor: He didn't want a child, his own.
Jan Ronis, attorney: Only lurid details make her an interesting witness.
Gloria Allred, Amber Frey's lawyer: There's proof she's not gonna be there to provide lurid or salacious testimony.
John Burris, former prosecutor, attorney: Yea, what is the evidence Amber has? Has to be other evidence.
Dan Abrams: One point on the tape, Scott said he didn't know who did it, but he knows who did.
Paul Pfingst, former prosecutor: Too easy to focus on one point of evidence; alot we don't know about.

Dan Abrams: We'll be surprised on how much we do know about. [MSNBC shows a video of Scott saying he left at 9-9:30am, the dog was returned by the neighbor, and that's all we know.]
Paul Pfingst, former prosecutor: One lie by husband whose wife is missing is enough for a jury to convict.
Jan Ronis, attorney: They didn't have anything until the bodies washed up.
Dan Abrams: Either he's guilty or someone framed him.
Jan Ronis, attorney: Could just have been killed and dumped in that area.
Gloria Allred, Amber Frey's lawyer: Well, no rush to judgment by the police on arresting him.
John Burris, former prosecutor, attorney: Bodies; difficult to overcome, must create doubt.
Dan Abrams: Satanic cult; we'll hear about it in the preliminary hearing?
Paul Pfingst, former prosecutor: Yes.
Gloria Allred, Amber Frey's lawyer: Don't know.
John Burris, former prosecutor, attorney: No.
Jan Ronis, attorney: No.

Fox News Channel **Greta Van Susteren:** Coming up, Scott Peterson's preliminary hearing starts tomorrow. Who will be the surprise witness against him and what evidence will the prosecutor show? We're in front of the Modesto courthouse and tomorrow, for the very first time we'll hear the prosecutor's evidence against Scott Peterson. [headline]: **PETERSON MURDER.** Still ahead, Scott's in court tomorrow and we'll hear the evidence. [Fox shows Geragos saying Scott is looking forward to prove his innocence.] Up next, how will prosecutors say Laci was killed and what role will Amber play in that evidence?
Ted Rowlands, KTVU TV Reporter: The first of five days, prosecutor says mitochondria DNA first thing. May bring in investigators to say hair broke in to. Both want to win the court of public opinion. Hair is important, puts Laci in the boat that she knew nothing about. Defense says they're married and it came from Scott's clothes. Seems as though Amber's been practicing for testifying.
Gloria Allred, Amber Frey's lawyer: There's nothing to practice.
Dr. Michael Baden, Forensic Pathologist: Mitochondria DNA has been established one out of 100; 150. If on pliers and pliers came

from home, or on his clothes, that explains it, and not much that Laci was in boat. Prosecutor still must concede, no cause of death yet.
Geoffrey Fieger, attorney: Not important at preliminary or trial. But Geragos could make more of it at trial.
Bernie Grimm, Defense Attorney: Hair, depends if fallen hair or pulled hair, with root or not. [headline]: **SURPRISE EVIDENCE.**
Greta: Witness and evidence for the first time, up next.
Ted Williams, former D.C. police detective, attorney: Geragos' strategy tomorrow is the court of public opinion. Go after Amber some; book deal; called TV stations. Got to do it.
Gloria Allred, Amber Frey's lawyer: Geragos has a choice, attack her and it'll boomerang.
Ted Rowlands, KTVU TV Reporter: The Peterson's believe no evidence against Scott, and this may even bring the Rocha family over.
Gloria Allred, Amber Frey's lawyer: Right decision for judge to exclude both families from the witness exclusion rule. [So both families could stay in the courtroom and not be sequestered from talking to other witness.]

[Bernie says that it'll make a difference if the hair on the pliers has a root or not, meaning that it could have been pulled out, as opposed to breaking off, but it really makes no difference at all. Either type of hair can be found in a hair brush and from softly running your fingers through your hair, but the reason it makes no difference in this case is because of the media. Either way it'll be used to propagate guilt.

If Scott was hiding the fact that he bought a boat, why did he immediately say he went fishing? Didn't the media immediately say he was lying.]

10/29/03

MSNBC: 12/24 Missing; 1/24 Frey goes public; 4/13 Conner; 4/14 Laci; 4/18 Arrest, identify bodies; 4/24 Scott pleads guilty. [Huh?]

SCOTT'S PRELIMINARY HEARING BEGINS

Court TV [headline]: **STATE: NO WIRETAP EVIDENCE AT PRELIMINARY.**
Beth Karas, of Court TV: Geragos says can't cross exam on some DNA, because of late, recently received discovery [from prosecutor].
James Curtis, of Court TV, former prosecutor: No GPS, no wiretaps, what else?
Lisa Bloom, of Court TV, Civil Rights lawyer:
Geragos asked the judge that Gloria Allred be excused from the courtroom; Gloria Allred being my mother. [The preliminary hearing is being told to us by the news corps, so what's the use? They're only gonna give us what they want it to be.]
Beth Karas, of Court TV: Judge says Gloria Allred can stay, but she can't tell Amber what's said. She can advise her.
James Curtis, former prosecutor: Age of fetus to help the defense?
Beth Karas: Compare the development of Conner in pristine shape, and developed more than he was on December 24th.
Lisa Bloom, Civil Rights lawyer: Case hangs on the hair for the prosecution.
Beth Karas: No reason to believe that Laci was ever on the boat, he bought it three weeks earlier. No follicle attached to hair; no blood on the pliers; hair transfers all the time with spouses.

Fox News Channel Dayside with Linda Vester
Claudia Cowan: Prosecutors say they will not introduce wiretaps or GPS. Both sides with DNA expert on hair. Don't know if, or when Amber to testify.
Jim Hammer, former prosecutor: Maybe use Amber to relay tapes. Suggests some problem with the wiretaps, might have to play on the Spice Channel.
David Wise, defense attorney: Maybe a problem with the warrant and not helpful to the prosecution, or hide their cards till later.
Jim Hammer, former prosecutor: Trial won't be in Modesto. None of us really know what evidence the prosecutor has. Computer with flow charts and possibly date rape drug. Physical evidence can't lie.
Linda Vester: Physical evidence that could be a bombshell in this case, with Dr. Baden when we come back.

Dr. Michael Baden, Forensic Pathologist: Mitochondria DNA comes from the Mom. Her, Laci; and siblings of both will have the same mitochondria DNA. The pliers could have come from the home, the hair from Scott's clothes. Laci could have also committed suicide. All the defense needs is one juror with reasonable doubt.

[If when there is a death penalty charge, voir dire in the choosing of a jury must include their view on the death penalty, so that those who don't believe in the death penalty are excluded from the jury, while only those that believe in the death penalty are kept on the jury. Aren't these people more prosecutorial than those excluded, and is this fair? The jury has a choice of death or life, guilty or not guilty; as does each individual juror. We don't have an individual society of death penalty persons, but have many societies with an undeterminable mixture. Does this particular legislative law require special treatment from the judiciary for a conviction? And does this law require a special jury to determine guilt or non-guilt? Certainly, no law deserves it.]

Court TV **Jean Casarez**: First witness on the stand.
Beth Karas, of Court TV: FBI employee; mitochondria DNA; a Kelly hearing to find if new evidence is to be permitted into evidence. [Mitochondria DNA is not accepted in California courts, yet. Notice that it doesn't require scientific proof, just that it's accepted in other courts.]
Beth Karas: The defense says negligence in handling the hair and that mitochondria DNA is not scientifically accepted in the scientific community.

[Guess excluding witnesses from the courtroom will be as successful as telling Gloria Allred not to tell Amber, when either one can tune in and hear more than they'd ever want to hear.]

CNN Headline News [headline]: **PRELIMINARY HAS BEEN POSTPONED FOUR TIMES.** Geragos tried to have Allred thrown out of the courtroom. **SCOTT PETERSON CHARGED WITH KILLING WIFE AND UNBORN SON.**

Court TV **Vinnie Politan**: Scott seems thinner, happened when in jail, longer hair. The judge to decide if mitochondria DNA testing will be accepted.
Beth Karas, of Court TV: Gloria Allred said at a press conference; Geragos seems threatened by my appearance; the gag order; he tried contempt of court; today to exclude me from the courtroom; and you'd think after three failed attempts he'd focus attention on Scott Peterson and not me. [headline]: **ACCUSED OF KILLING WIFE AND FETUS. LACI PETERSON MURDER CASE.**
Beth Karas: Scott seemed relaxed, but when the testimony began, he took notes and stayed focused.

Court TV **Nancy Grace**, former prosecutor: Why are they fighting the DNA evidence when it has been accepted for twenty years, and even the ABA [American Bar Association] has thrown up their hands and accepted it.
Dr. Jeffrey Gardere, psychologist: Yea, it's been accepted in all jurisdictions for years and just a defense ploy.
Vinnie Politan, of Court TV: Well, mitochondria DNA is relatively new science and trying to get it accepted. [Nancy and Dr. Jeff continue as if mitochondria DNA testing is years old and widely accepted.]
Nancy Grace, former prosecutor: How will they explain the GPS system shows he returned to where the bodies washed up numerous times? [Court TV shows Scott in an orange jumpsuit, with leg irons and handcuffs.]

CNN Larry King Live
Larry: Gloria Allred made headline today.
Ted Rowlands, KTVU TV Reporter: Mitochondria DNA; long day. Prosecutor won't use wiretap in the preliminary hearing. Allred wanted out of court; next witness, the Peterson maid.
Brian Melley, Associated Press: DNA 101; Allred dozing off at one point. Not a high level of probability on DNA; one in hundred, and one in a hundred-fifty with hispanics.
Nancy Grace, of Court TV, former prosecutor: The judge in the neighboring county says hair DNA is okay. The hair was wound around in to the pliers.
Chris Pixley, Defense Attorney: No case law in California with mitochondria DNA; not an appellate court. Why not; the prosecutor's own brief says thirty-eight states don't allow it.

[headline]: **BODIES OF LACI, UNBORN SON, CONNER, FOUND IN LATE APRIL.**

Dr. Robi Ludwig, psychotherapist: Originally people thought Scott guilty and that's hard to change, but some believe what's most recently revealed.

Ted Rowlands, KTVU TV Reporter: Yea, he'll be bound over; both sides playing to the jury pool.

Brian Melley, Associated Press: Want to introduce evidence now.

Nancy Grace, of Court TV, former prosecutor: Constitutional right to a preliminary hearing, every safeguard or the defense attorneys will be screaming. Now thirty-four states don't allow [mitochondria DNA], or rather haven't said yes or no. [CNN shows a video of Geragos saying: glad to be underway and the truth coming out in this matter. CNN's volume was off while Chris Pixley talked about headlines.]

Laci's sister: Cut Scott's hair Friday and he and Laci were very happy.

Ted Rowlands, KTVU TV Reporter: Last one to see Scott and Laci together, saw her the night before; maybe same pants on when found washed up; time line. February 13th, 2003 interview with Nancy Grace, Laci's sister: Black top, maternity, cream colored pants, scarf.

Nancy Grace, of Court TV, former prosecutor: Jury ain't gonna buy that Laci wore the same clothes two days; and abducted by a satanic cult with the same clothes on. Okay to show trial on live TV, cause jury's already picked and they don't watch TV. Laci's Mom only wanted Laci's wedding dress, so Geragos will play down the break-in. He doesn't want to open that can of worms.

Caller: A simple motive, in that he just grew to hate Laci, for her take charge personality.

Nancy Grace, former prosecutor: Never heard that Laci was bossy.

Chris Pixley, Defense Attorney: No history of violence in their lives.

Larry King: Why does Amber need you there to advise her?

Gloria Allred, Amber Frey's lawyer: I need to be there to understand the case and advise her. I'm there as her support, her advisor. She's neutral on guilt or innocence. She's a victim of Scott Peterson's deception. No plans to sue Scott Peterson.

Chris Pixley, Defense Attorney: Still didn't get an answer from Gloria why she's in court; book deals.

Dr. Robi Ludwig, psychotherapist: Allred helps Amber look fragile and vulnerable.
Brian Melley, Associated Press: Laci's name was barely mentioned today.
Ted Rowlands, KTVU TV Reporter: The defense began its cross [examination] today; has own expert.
Caller: Do experts testify, no matter what they find?
Chris Pixley, Defense Attorney: No, you don't have to use them.
Caller: Never seen Scott's support from his brothers.
Ted Rowlands, KTVU TV Reporter: Inaccurate. The brothers have come out and are very supportive.
Caller: The emphasis has been on the hair; pregnant women lose hair. All indicators on Scott is that he's well balanced; yet media says behavior's not right.
Nancy Grace, former prosecutor: He picked up fliers, but instead, played golf. He was going to a vigil, but on the phone with Amber one hour before, wanting Amber to have his baby.
Chris Pixley, Defense Attorney: Nothing Nancy said is in evidence; not in any filing in court. It's disgraceful to go on national TV and say things like that.
Nancy Grace, former prosecutor: Phone calls Chris.
Chris Pixley, Defense Attorney: We've read the transcripts and not in there.
Nancy Grace, former prosecutor: It's in official court filing.
Caller: Selling home [Scott]?
Ted Rowlands, KTVU TV Reporter: Peterson's staying there, when up from Modesto; can't sell it yet.
Caller: Why not Laci tell her Mom Scott went fishing, and why wasn't he working since his wife was pregnant and what about that boat?
Nancy Grace, former prosecutor: Nobody knew about the boat; none of the family.
Ted Rowlands, KTVU TV Reporter: The defense says she did know of the boat and witness to say they saw Laci at the warehouse looking at the boat.

Fox News Channel **Greta Van Susteren:** Defense wants the hair thrown out; mishandled by police and tests not reliable.
Gloria Allred, Amber Frey's lawyer: Don't know why Geragos is fixated on me.

Stan Goldman, Fox News legal editor: Gloria agreed not to discuss the case with Amber and Amber is public, so Gloria may not be able to discuss the case on TV.
Gloria Allred, Amber Frey's lawyer: She doesn't watch TV.
Stan Goldman, Fox News legal editor: Housekeeper maybe on the bleach smell when the police got there. Things cleaned up that the housekeeper didn't.
Gloria Allred, Amber Frey's lawyer: FBI experts testified today on hair. [Fox shows the TV interview of Scott saying: when people accuse me of her disappearance, and people still do, I reply the same way, thank you for being aware of Laci missing and please do what you can to help find her.]
Dr. Michael Baden, Forensic Pathologist: Mitochondria DNA not as precise as nuclear DNA. If same as Mom, sister, then it has some value.
Geoffrey Fieger, attorney: Why mitochondria DNA first?
Ted Williams, Defense Attorney: Not Allred versus Geragos, that's the problem with court today, no reason for Gloria to be there.
Gloria Allred, Amber Frey's lawyer: I need to be there; to help her.
Geoffrey Fieger, Defense Attorney: To intimidate Geragos; to harass him.
Gloria Allred, Amber Frey's lawyer: Why is it the defense has the only right to spin it his way?
Bernie Grimm, Defense Attorney: The prosecutor uses Act IV to begin, put Amber on the stand, sexy.
Greta: It's not drama to the prosecutor.
Geoffrey Fieger, attorney: The prosecutor in this case isn't brilliant.
Ted Rowlands, KTVU TV Reporter: Prosecutor thinks he killed her in the house, wrapped her up, tied to buoy, dumped. The defense says she went walking, have witnesses, picked up and kidnapped, dropped in water, in the Bay.
Dr. Michael Baden, Forensic Pathologist: She had a cup of coffee that morning, caffeine in Laci, not looked for in Conner. Coffee, hours before death.
Ted Williams, Defense Attorney: Wiretaps better than Frey; the defense may bring up the taps.
Geoffrey Fieger, attorney: Prosecutor doesn't want to go overboard now, use to shock jury at trial.

Ted Rowlands, KTVU TV Reporter: Prosecutor wants to cut things out, cause it's too long, and it'll take another day just on motions. [Fox shows a video of Scott saying: Called Amber a few days after Laci's disappearance and Amber contacted police shortly after the phone call.]
Bernie Grimm, Defense Attorney: Like Geoff said, bombshell at trial, with the tapes. I'd cross Amber with the tapes till the cows come home.
Stan Goldman, Fox News legal editor: You see why Geragos wants Gloria shut up; she's with the prosecutor's side.
Gloria Allred, Amber Frey's lawyer: Come on, how many husbands' wives' hair in their pliers?
Geoffrey Fieger, Defense Attorney: Just say DNA and the jury believes he's guilty. The layman doesn't know anything about DNA.
Greta: How did Laci and Conner die? Coming up.
Ted Rowlands, KTVU TV Reporter: Today's only day hair expert could be here.
Greta: The prosecutor asked a billion more questions than necessary.

[Ten thousand fishermen threw their needle nose pliers overboard today, two thousand men showed their wives the fishing boat they had secretly bought for those thinking days, five thousand men decided to put off purchasing a fishing boat till their wives have their babies, three men confessed to their wives that they used needle nosed pliers to pull hair from their own noses, and Ms. Grace bought stock in hardware.]

Court TV Special The Laci Peterson Nightly Update
Beth Karas, of Court TV: Hair match okay with Mom, but not with Scott's, includes all her relatives. We'll hear color and texture same as Laci's.
James Curtis, of Court TV, former prosecutor: Expert had to admit; he never testified in California, never accepted.
Gloria Allred, Amber Frey's lawyer: Geragos wanted alot; unsuccessful. Why are you threatened by me, Geragos? Why only a defense spin? Surprised today that the prosecutor wouldn't use the tapes.
Catherine Crier, of Court TV, former judge: How far would you go with the defense at the preliminary hearing?

Leslie Synder, former New York Supreme Court Justice: I don't know what the defense attorney here will do cause he's quite a character. Both are playing to the press.
Yale Galanter, defense attorney: PR campaign at this point, a media play. Biggest thing defense has for it is how and who did it.
Lisa Pinto, former prosecutor: Geragos is throwing out everything and see what sticks to the wall; the hair was wrapped in the pliers on the boat he bought the day before Christmas; Come On.
Leslie Synder, former New York Supreme Court Justice: Circumstantial case; a good one, is better than a direct case.
Kimberly Guilfole Newsom, Assistant District Attorney, San Francisco: No other physical evidence by the prosecution that has leaked out; no explanation of the hair in the boat.
Catherine Crier: Don't tell me the pliers weren't supposed to be in the kitchen drawer and she used them and then the pliers to the boat with her hair in it. I want evidence to tie Scott Peterson to the crime.
Yale Galanter, Defense Attorney: If dismembered in home and all they have is pliers, the prosecution is in trouble.
Lisa Bloom, of Court TV, Civil Rights lawyer:
You know if the housekeeper tells domestic violence, she'll lay out their marriage for us. Laci would have confided in her.
Leslie Synder, former New York Supreme Court Justice: The prosecution has going for it; Who else would have done this?
Catherine Crier: Doesn't that shift the burden of proof to the defense?
Leslie Synder, former New York Supreme Court Justice: No, no, no.
Lisa Bloom, of Court TV, Civil Rights lawyer:
Number one cause is by the partner; murder.
[Court TV shows an interview with Scott.
Question: She claims you called her December 24th. Scott: Informed Amber a few days after Laci's disappearance.]
Kimberly Guilfole Newsom, Assistant District Attorney, San Francisco: So many inconsistent statements out there. Shows motive to lie.
Yale Galanter, defense attorney: Lying is not a motive for murder. Inconsistent statements will haunt him.
Lisa Bloom, Civil Rights lawyer: Seventy-six phone calls; started nine days before the disappearance. Said he wasn't married; a makeover.

James Curtis, of Court TV, former prosecutor: Measure Amber's against Scott's credibility.
Catherine Crier: Why care whether a masseuse or not? Got tapes.
Yale Galanter, attorney: Evidence of flight or prepare to flight can be used.
Kimberly Guilfole Newsom, Assistant District Attorney, San Francisco: Very persuasive to a jury.
Leslie Synder, former New York Supreme Court Justice: What could be more powerful to a jury?
Catherine Crier: How similar to O.J.?
Yale Galanter, attorney: The prosecutor decided not to use the Bronco chase.
Lisa Bloom, Civil Rights lawyer: He played golf, ten thousand dollars in his pocket, while ten thousand people looked for his wife.
James Curtis, former prosecutor: Folks live down there, he was distraught. [All the ladies laugh and cackle.] HA HA HA COME ON HE HEE HE
Catherine Crier: I know darn well you don't believe that, James, but, Thank You. [Catherine said this while laughing.]
Catherine Crier: Why challenge mitochondria DNA?
Dr. Cyril Wecht, Forensic Pathologist: Not permitted to talk directly about the case, but can on mitochondria DNA. It's not scientifically precise, must be very careful, not all DNA labs can do it.
Catherine Crier: Eliminates large population.
Dr. Cyril Wecht, Forensic Pathologist: Sure, just as with blood.
Rockne Harmon, DNA Expert: Not just use for exclusion of people, if only one in one hundred and fifty-nine have the profile, and if only one of one hundred and fifty-nine in the boat, it's very powerful. [I sure hope this fellow tests DNA alot better than he analyzes statistics, facts, and logic.]
Candice DeLong, retired FBI: Puts her in vicinity of the boat.
Catherine Crier: Yea, how many know Scott Peterson, get in the boat, and go to the warehouse.
Candice DeLong, retired FBI: Or even knew the boat existed?
Gloria Gomez, KOVR TV Reporter: Sources say there's red paint on the bow of Scott's boat and similar to Buoy #4, three miles from the Marina.
Catherine Crier: Several trips back to the crime site?

Candice DeLong, retired FBI: Bay is a disposal site, and with information of him going there over and over; maybe to assure himself the body hasn't floated up.
Catherine Crier: Cement in the boat, making weights, and they're not there.
Gloria Gomez, KOVR TV Reporter: Found three to five cement markings, probably five boat anchors, but only one in the boat. Unusual cause cement residue in the boat and the salesman said not there when he sold it to Scott. Scott delayed the police search of the warehouse; said no electricity there. [Court TV shows a video of Scott's brother saying it'll be nice for the prosecution to show what they say Scott did; for the prosecution to show their hand.]
Catherine Crier: How old was Conner? Evidence of older than December 24th?
Dr. Cyril Wecht, Forensic Pathologist: Autopsy report by the medical examiner and others, the size is given, with the gestational age and a December 23rd sonogram, with a margin of error; thirty-four to thirty-eight weeks?
Catherine Crier: Doctor said No sonogram on December 23rd, None.
Dr. Cyril Wecht, Forensic Pathologist: If you say it, you're never wrong.
Catherine Crier: You're the witness in court.
Dr. Cyril Wecht, Forensic Pathologist: I don't know. You've just told me something I didn't know.
Catherine Crier: Most important evidence against Scott?
Candice DeLong, retired FBI: Scott put himself at the crime scene, ninety miles from home where both lived.

[All of Scott's and Laci's friends, both sides of their families, everyone who saw them and remembers them, plus all the photos and videos say that Scott and Laci were one of the happiest and most in love married couple they knew. No one has ever mentioned anger or disagreement, yet one former prosecutor says that when the housekeeper testifies, that we'll hear of the temper, violence, and spousal abuse. Even Laci's sister, who cut Scott's hair and talked to them where she works, said they were very happy.

We were led to believe that burglars saw Scott loading his pickup in the wee hours of the morning, but now it's said by police sources that the burglaries were on another day, with some of media stating it was on December 24th. We were led to believe that a neighbor saw Scott in the wee hours of the morning loading or unloading his truck, but Scott said he left to go fishing at about 9:30am and returned home around 5:30pm.

Some of the very same facts that are put in a light of Scott being guilty, but are then discredited by the police, are actually facts, that if true, would go to Scott's being innocent.]

<u>10/30/03</u>

CNN **Jeffrey Toobin**, CNN legal analyst, former federal prosecutor: The prosecution's theory is that Scott hit her on the head with the pliers, then dumped her body in the Bay. Neither Geragos or Mrs. Peterson said much, just that they're glad the proceedings are underway. With the gag order, they shouldn't have said anything, but gave no evidence.

Court TV **Vinnie Politan**: Court has started.
James Curtis, of Court TV, former prosecutor: What do you think about this hair; fight over mitochondria DNA, much to do about nothing?
Roger Ross, defense attorney: It's important to keep only scientific value to evidence, and not go beyond that. [Court TV shows Scott in court in an orange jumpsuit and handcuffs.]
Lisa Bloom, of Court TV, Civil Rights lawyer:
Scott said he told Laci in late November about Amber, but did Laci tell anyone?
Vinnie Politan: Be interesting to see of it comes up.
Lisa Bloom, Civil Rights lawyer: They always say the wife knew and had an open marriage, she was okay with it.
James Curtis, former prosecutor: When we return, we discuss wiretap evidence, dog evidence, and Amber Frey.
Lisa Bloom, Civil Rights lawyer: All the defense attorney has to do is show reasonable doubt, but, hosts like James and I, are gonna remember that Geragos said he'd find the real killer. [Lisa tries to slip one in, but that ain't how it goes. The government has the burden, throughout the process due a person accused of a crime. At trial, it's the prosecutor's burden to show guilt, on each and every element of the charged crime, beyond a reasonable doubt. The defendant has the burden of proving nothing. If you begin with the presumption of innocence, then the process takes its intended course.]

James Curtis, former prosecutor: Roger, play prosecutor for me and tell us about Amber.

Vinnie Politan: Laci Peterson's parents come and go out the back door of the court house and are allowed to leave the courtroom before anyone else can and are shielded from the media. Scott Peterson's parents come and go out the front door just like everyone else.

[The ladies of TV say that it's very possible that the nineteen year old accusing Kobe Bryant of rape, grabbed a pair of old underwear with semen in them, to put on to go to the police station and hospital for a rape evaluation kit, that women do this all the time, but they refuse to believe, and in fact say 'no way', that Laci put on the same pants and shirt, the maternity ones, from the day before, even though Scott said Laci planned to walk the dog and when the dog was found he was muddy, and it had been raining. Do they really think Laci would have put on fresh, clean clothes to go out and walk a dog in muddy conditions, but the nineteen year old would put on dirty underwear to go to a hospital for a rape examination.

It may be that the prosecution doesn't have enough evidence for the case to be given to the jury by the judge, but, if the defense, Geragos, has to put on a defense, Scott's character will be an issue, and will already be in issue before the court from within the jury, even though Scott's character cannot legally be in issue, unless and until the defense places the character in issue before the court. Character is most, if not ninety-nine percent, of the public talk of why Scott is thought to be guilty.

Kinda ironic that character is not allowed in court, unless the defense brings it up, for the very same reason that it is being used by the TV news corps to prosecute Scott. Ironic, that is, unless you're Scott.]

MSNBC [headline]: **PETERSON IS CHARGED WITH MURDERING HIS WIFE, AND THEIR UNBORN SON.**

Dan Abrams: They've gotta get this hair in cause it's the only physical evidence they have tying Laci to the Bay, tying Laci to the boat.

Keith Olbermann: Movie coming out about Scott Peterson, to end at the point he's arrested.

CNN Larry King Live

Cynthia McFadden, of ABC News: Old jail; tough living.

Ted Rowlands, KTVU TV Reporter: Aggressive cross exam by the defense, very important to the defense, end court at 1pm tomorrow for Halloween. We've heard Laci was very tired and probably not up for a walk, and maid. [Laci was out for the day and evening before this with Scott.]

Dr. Henry Lee: Mitochondria to show similarity, no ID.

Nancy Grace, of Court TV, former prosecutor: Before trial, they'll be fifty-two more issues to solve between Scott and Laci.

Chris Pixley, Defense Attorney: Negative publicity against Scott has been a problem since the beginning. The preliminary hearing may counter it some. The defense hasn't had a chance to respond. The paint on the boat is the latest leak and it didn't come from the defense, and for the police it's a real problem.

Ted Rowlands, KTVU TV Reporter: Letters were given, from Scott; life in jail, cell size, food, missing Laci on her birthday and their unborn son.

Cynthia McFadden, of ABC News: Someone sympathetic to the defense released them, want the public to know a normal guy grieving for his wife.

Ted Rowlands, KTVU TV Reporter: Won't say where gotten, not from the defense; they're just letters from jail to a friend.

Nancy Grace, of Court TV, former prosecutor: Self-serving statements and not allowed in a court of law. Don't know who is responsible for the leaks, it doesn't have to be the prosecutor that leaked there was paint on the boat.

Chris Pixley, Defense Attorney: We'll see more leaks and from those who have nothing to do with the case. The prosecutor will be forced to prove premeditation to kill his wife.

Nancy Grace, of Court TV, former prosecutor: Don't need history of violence to kill. Others convicted without hard evidence or a history of violence.

Dr. Henry Lee: Even if prove Laci's hair, doesn't prove Scott killed her; that's a quantum leap. Nancy mentioned those convicted, well then we look at jury and question why.

Nancy Grace, of Court TV, former prosecutor: Scott told Laci about the affair and says she was okay with it; I'll Stand on my head. If the hair means nothing, how'd it get on the pliers? Wound into them?

Dr. Henry Lee: Secondary transfer, lose fifty hair every day. Find hundreds, sometimes thousands hair at crime scene.
Caller: The missing student and Scott?
Nancy Grace, former prosecutor: They ruled Scott out, her boyfriend is the prime suspect.
Cynthia McFadden, of ABC News: It's a story because it's tragic; the defense has been effective, at the risk of bringing Nancy's wrath down on me.
Nancy Grace, former prosecutor: She's right; a four prong attack, not compared to Laci's bone, mitochondria DNA science, hair contaminated.
Caller: Psychic said Scott hit her with a hammer?
Nancy Grace, former prosecutor: They have the cell phone records. [Calls Nancy claims were made on December 24th, while at a vigil for Laci. Nancy says she read these things in official filings, but, if the calls weren't recorded, and they weren't, then what was said is up to the two flies on two different walls, and not Nancy, nor a court filing, nor Scott, nor Amber.]
Cynthia McFadden, of ABC News: The prosecution must prove, and link Scott to the death. Alot of people have girlfriends and they don't commit murder.
Gloria Allred, Amber Frey's lawyer: Geragos doesn't wasn't able to shake the DNA expert's conclusion.
Larry King: What about 'The Perfect Husband' movie coming up?
Gloria Allred, Amber Frey's lawyer: Don't know about the movie; don't know if they can do one. She'll tell the truth, so don't need to practice.
Chris Pixley, defense attorney: Amber gives the prosecution motive; still don't know anything about her, yet. How long was the relationship before the disappearance? How many times seen? Suppose she misled Scott to keep him in the relationship.
Nancy Grace, former prosecutor: Let's talk about what he may have said in those tapes, since we won't get to hear those.
Cynthia McFadden, of ABC News: One hair; two days. 2004-2005, trial.
Ted Rowlands, KTVU TV Reporter: Scott and family will urge quickness for trial.
Dr. Henry Lee: Don't know when trial, but give time for evidence and let evidence speak for itself.

Fox News Channel Hannity and Colmes
Lis Wiehl, Fox News legal analyst, former federal prosecutor: Hair is but one piece of evidence.
Alan Colmes: House cleaned the day before?
Mary Prevost, Defense Attorney: The prosecution will say to clean up the blood, but we don't know their cleaning habits.
Mark Fuhrman, former O.J. cop: Hair means everything; it puts Laci between the house and the Bay.
Sean Hannity: Get hair; and let's say bleach; and let's say sister says Laci said he's a monster; can you convict?
Mark Fuhrman, former O.J. cop: We're gonna have alot more.
Lis Wiehl, Fox News legal analyst, former federal prosecutor: Amber will testify, and if solid, Geragos won't want to face her again. [All guests say that the jury will say, guilty, except Mary Prevost, who says that if this is all they have, she'd say there's reasonable doubt. Again, it's not a question of reasonable doubt or not reasonable doubt. The question is, is there proof beyond a reasonable doubt? The doubt, in our American system of justice, remains, until so.]

Fox News Channel **Greta Van Susteren:** Coming up, Who was Scott's jailhouse lawyer and wait till you hear what he confessed to them in jail, and who will be the surprise witness against him?
Claudia Cowan: The defense says the hair tampered with and contaminated. Tomorrow the housekeeper; she cleaned before Christmas eve, if she used bleach, and into their marriage. Amy [sister] December 23rd saw Laci, and Scott told her he would go play golf, not fishing.
Stan Goldman, Fox News legal editor: The defense says one hair plus another one that fell in there; contamination.
Gloria Allred, Amber Frey's lawyer: Not fatal to case, but links Laci to the boat. Interesting how hard Geragos is trying to keep it out; He Thinks It's Important.
Greta: Housekeeper? Hard to get rid of blood.
Gloria Allred, Amber Frey's lawyer: The prosecution may have some evidence of blood. Does satanic cults use bleach?
Greta: Ninety bags of evidence from the house.
Gloria Allred, Amber Frey's lawyer: I know women who clean before the housekeeper comes, but not after.
Greta: Me. Do we know the bleach smell was there?
Gloria Allred, Amber Frey's lawyer: No.

Stan Goldman, Fox News legal editor: No, and of body chopped up in there. [Fox shows a video of the Bay area.]
Dr. Michael Baden, Forensic Pathologist: What's interesting is what brought police to Conner's body; a dog brought a femur bone [from someone else's body].
Man: Body found here behind the community, and Scott placed himself across there on that Island.
Greta: Letters from jail, tells alot about him and Laci.
Ted Rowlands, KTVU TV Reporter: Alot of letters, we were given seven from a person, has many more. [Fox shows excerpts, typed on the screen, of Scott's letters to a friend: Crying in grief for Laci and Conner; found out from the detective after the arrest that Laci was dead; only knew it was true the next day when saw the newspaper; Laci's birthday, want to hold and love her, in tears.]
Ted Rowlands, KTVU TV Reporter: A sense of humor about the food in jail, lost alot of weight.
Greta: Stay tuned, coming up, Will any of the evidence get tossed because of sloppy police work? [headline]: **APRIL 18TH ARRESTED.**
Greta: Boat?
Ted Williams, Defense Attorney: Have alot of problems with the boat; highly unlikely; fourteen foot long, and try to transport a body in it.
Greta: What if dismembered?
Ted Williams, Defense Attorney: Where dismembered? If in house, can't clean it.
Dr. Michael Baden, Forensic Pathologist: Hair; maybe when boat was at the house; police treated this as murder from the first day, before Amber. They had to have something from someone.
Greta: Spouse first one to suspect.
Dr. Michael Baden, Forensic Pathologist: Yes, but most come back. Police usually wait forty-eight to seventy-two hours on deciding murder with a disappearance.
Jayne Weintraub, Defense Attorney: May say bleach, but bleach won't clean blood.
Gloria Allred, Amber Frey's lawyer: Why release the letters now? Didn't know wife was dead, crying, OH Come On. I hear violins playing in the background. [Didn't Gloria say last night that she was neutral on guilt or innocence, and that she really didn't know.]
Ted Rowlands, KTVU TV Reporter: Had to release them sometime.

Gloria Allred, Amber Frey's lawyer: Scott Peterson trying to testify without being under oath.
Greta: Any mistakes?
Jared Lewis, former Modesto police officer: Modesto police has a ninety-six percentile, the rest have sixty percent, to solving homicides. It wouldn't take rocket scientist to focus on Scott.
Greta: Receipt, then bodies.
Stan Goldman, Fox News legal editor: Three to four things he did makes him look guilty.
Jayne Weintraub, Defense Attorney: Adulterer; gets caught; lies, but a big leap to murder. Hair has nothing to do with death or cause of death.
Dr. Michael Baden, Forensic Pathologist: Mitochondria DNA never rejected in a court, yet. But hair not important. Police were suspicious right away, so there's something else.
Stan Goldman, Fox News legal editor: Had to schedule the hair first; expert availability.
Greta: Yea, this ain't a made for TV trial. Maybe the prosecutor has who, how, where, and when.
Bernie Grimm, Defense Attorney: I'd rather watch paint dry than listen to mitochondria DNA. [The news corps are bored with a hair, but appear to be taking adrenalin while meditating. Headline]: **FAMILY FEUD.**
Rita Cosby: Could cut the tension; feel it between the families.
Greta: Amber will be on the stand for a long time.
Rita Cosby: Absolutely. Reporters passing notes to families in the courtroom.
Greta: Yes, gag order, they can't speak.
Rita Cosby: Yea, but the press tries anyway.
Greta: Oh no, it's your job to do that, to try.
[headline]: **AMY'S TESTIMONY.**
Greta: What will Amy say in court? [Fox shows a February 11th, interview of Amy [Laci's sister or half-sister] saying that if Scott knows anything, he should come forward and tell us.]
Ted Rowlands, KTVU TV Reporter: December 23rd last saw Laci; Amy. They brought her to the home during the search, to see if the clothes were there that she wore on December 23rd. Scott said Laci was wearing them.
Stan Goldman, Fox News legal editor: Rough in the preliminary hearing on cross exam; jury won't see it, not on TV. He can charm her also.

Ted Rowlands, KTVU TV Reporter: Long witness list. Not alot of physical evidence, unless police have a bombshell we don't know.
Stan Goldman, Fox News legal editor: This is a 'behavior of the defendant' circumstantial case, a little different that a 'circumstantial evidence' case.

Court TV Laci Peterson Nightly Update
Nancy Grace, of Court TV, former prosecutor: You'd think DNA was on trial. Geragos spent two days so far. Letters from jail.
Ted Rowlands, KTVU TV Reporter: Sure they're from Scott, didn't get them from the defense.
Nancy: He has love letters from all over the U.S.
Ted Rowlands: Don't know. Scott found out about the deaths when arrested.
Nancy Grace: Seems like he has a sense of humor? Another report says he's robust; he still looks good.
Vinnie Politan, of Court TV: Looks comfortable in court, longer hair, clearly lost weight.
Nancy Grace, former prosecutor: Shower only outlet from his cell? Yoga?
Ted Rowlands, KTVU TV Reporter: Two ninety minute workouts while shackled.
Nancy Grace, former prosecutor: Laci taking yoga, but the instructor never met Scott. [Nancy reads an excerpt from a letter, Laci's birthday.] Get in front of the jury?
Vinnie Politan, of Court TV: Don't see it coming in.
Nancy Grace, former prosecutor: Self-serving statements.
Kim Peterson, representative for Laci's family: Can't comment on the letters. Always talk about the defendant's rights, but the only one who didn't choose to be there, is the victim's family.
Nancy Grace, former prosecutor: It's their daughter's hair, wound into those needle nosed pliers. [Nancy uses her finger in a circular motion. Court TV shows Laci's brother saying that he stood beside Scott, but now it's time to come forward. Then Court TV shows Scott coming into the courtroom in a red jumpsuit, handcuffs, and leg irons, with blonde hair and with the lady attorney appointed by the court to represent Scott when he was first arrested.]
Nancy Grace, former prosecutor: Reports Scott bought the boat with intentions of killing Laci and Laci may have been unconscious in the boat and died there.

Mickey Sherman, former prosecutor, defense attorney: Good chance to keep out mitochondria DNA. Geragos is very informed.
James Hammer, assistant San Francisco prosecutor: Practices with his own expert.
Chris Pixley, Defense Attorney: Science may be okay, but one hair into two, contaminated or not, hair is very, very, strong; handled rough; if others mixed in?
Nancy Grace, former prosecutor: There you go, Johnnie Cochran.
James Hammer, assistant San Francisco prosecutor: Flying DNA. Ha, Ha. The defense can retest the hair.
Ted Rowlands, KTVU TV Reporter: Chain of custody issue; defense argues two detectives reexamined the hair, then there's two hairs. The defense says, well maybe something else happened here.
James Hammer, assistant San Francisco prosecutor: O.J. Simpson all over again. Different here cause O.J. had to do with race. Why plant evidence here?
Ted Rowlands, KTVU TV Reporter: Defense not say the hair is planted, just sloppy.
Nancy Grace, former prosecutor: When Amber comes in, everyone will forget DNA. The newspaper headlines, the Globe, help or hurt the prosecution?
Chris Pixley, Defense Attorney: So many stories floated; if a hair, dogs, is all they have, they're in trouble. If they have more, they've gotta show some.
Mickey Sherman, Defense Attorney: People believe it, without buying it, just read the headline.
Ted Rowlands, KTVU TV Reporter: Town mentality and all want to see what happens.
Mickey Sherman, Defense Attorney: Amber doesn't have a smoking gun, if so, Gloria would have told us and Scott would have been arrested sooner.
Nancy Grace, former prosecutor: Well I do, and I think it'll be a bombshell.
Dr. Robi Ludwig, psychotherapist: Geragos should have his very own reality show; he's very good and Scott is lucky to have him.
Nancy Grace, former prosecutor: No woman is gonna wear the same outfit two days in a row; had on what Amy saw her in at the hair salon.
Dr. Larry Koblinsky, forensic scientist: Impossible to tell time of death.

Nancy Grace, former prosecutor: Scott said she had on black pants, but she washed up with same ones she had on the day before. Scott has internet access, so he probably voted. Poll: 8% NO; 92% YES [Didn't catch the poll question. Court TV shows Scott in a red jumpsuit, handcuffs and leg irons in court.]

[The hair in the pliers, 'belonging to Laci' is an inference, at best. Because the mitochondria DNA shows the hair to be of the same type as Laci's, we can infer that it's Laci's because she was Scott's wife and therefore a link that could be foul play or could be innocence, but nonetheless, it's still an 'inference' that the hair even belongs to Laci.

If we were to the choose that it's innocent, that's a second inference; as it would be, to choose that it's a link to foul play. Since either of these second choices would be an inference upon an inference, the law does not allow such inferences to produce what's called 'evidence'.

If the hair could be identified as belonging to Laci, then either second inference could be chosen, since either would then become a first inference. But, we don't know if it's her hair.

Mr. Peterson, Scott's Dad, said early on that police were intimidating Scott and Laci's friends. Sounds a little like the O.J. scenario where the defense witnesses were also intimidated in that investigation, and, even on the witness stand.]

<u>10/31/03</u>

Court TV **Vinnie Politan**: Scott's Dad didn't know Scott bought the boat. Mrs. Rocha says Laci was tired, told her not to take walks cause almost passed out once, but Laci was strong headed and walked anyway. On December 23rd, about 8:30pm, she talked to Laci, made plans for a December 24th dinner with Mom. December 24th, Scott called Mrs. Rocha at 5:17pm, she talked to Scott, he asked if Laci there; Mom said no. Scott said Laci missing. Mom thought just walking dog, or at a neighbor's house and will be back. On December 23rd, Scott and Laci at Amy's work; to cut Scott's hair. Scott volunteered to pick up, on December 24th, between twelve and three, a package for Amy, cause he'd be golfing that day, nearby. The housekeeper, came four times. December 23rd, 8:30am to 2pm, used water and pine sol, used bleach to clean the bathroom. Laci not walk the dog, tired, went and got groceries and carried in house herself. Laid on sofa most of the time. She used towels to clean the door, put them in the mop bucket on the washer, and took the mop outside. The blinds in the living room and bedroom were shut on December 23rd.

MSNBC **Dan Abrams:** Housekeeper, blinds generally down when she arrives, in living room and bed room.

Fox News Channel **Shepard Smith:** Family testifies; but where's the evidence?
Laura Ingle, KFI Radio Reporter: No real evidence to speak of; sister, Mom, housekeeper. Amy said Scott was to go golf, not fish. Mom said Scott never mentioned boat; her husband loves to talk fish. December 23rd, she heard from Laci, Amy at the salon, 8:30 talk to Mom. The housekeeper cleaned the floors with a touch of pine sol, but police say they smelled bleach.
Shepard Smith: So the housekeeper doesn't use any bleach.
Judge Politano: Not enough to bind over yet.

Court TV **Catherine Crier**, former judge: In court today.
Vinnie Politan, of Court TV: Housekeeper from 8:30 to 2pm on December 23rd, Laci there; she didn't walk the dog. Used bleach in the bathroom. Mop and bucket outside, cement wet around the mop on December 24th; you'd think it'd be dry. Prosecution says second cleanup.
Catherine Crier: Cleanup later than Laci's last sighting.
Vinnie Politan: Two mops, housekeeper not clear if two mops or one.
Gloria Gomez, KOVR TV Reporter: Mrs. Rocha thinks, that when Scott called and said Laci missing, Mrs. Rocha went to the park and Scott was there looking, the dog with the leash on. A couple weeks before, Laci got sick in the park walking the dog.
Catherine Crier: Both said Laci tired all the time.
Gloria Gomez, KOVR TV Reporter: The housekeeper said Laci was tired, on the sofa with her feet up.
Vinnie Politan: Amy; haircut on December 23rd; gift basket Amy needed to pick up and Scott volunteered, cause he'd be golfing in the area.
Lisa Bloom, of Court TV, Civil Rights lawyer:
Not knowing of the boat by Dad, but the defense showed Scott had a number of vehicles Dad didn't know about.

Catherine Crier: Laci trying to sell inherited jewelry? If money problems, why buy a boat?
Lisa Bloom, of Court TV, Civil Rights lawyer:
Yea, if so.
Catherine Crier: Different outfit on Laci.
Gloria Gomez, KOVR TV Reporter: Defense trying to question Amy's memory on the pants, but what Laci was found in seems to match what Amy says she wore the day before. [Court TV shows a video of **Gloria Allred**, Amber Frey's lawyer: No one but Scott knew he bought the boat. Why keep big purchase a secret?]
Catherine Crier: Use term 'missing'?
Candice DeLong, retired FBI: Not heard it before; depends on what you think of guilt or not.
Dr. Jordon Casey: I agree Catherine, family doesn't use those words, always positive words.
Catherine Crier: Too cold to golf, so I went fishing? Mistake to tell police no lights in the warehouse, when Scott went there with them?
Candice DeLong, retired FBI: They looked anyway. Was Scott wrong, or mistaken about the lights?
Mickey Sherman, Defense Attorney: No smoking gun out there; just assume he did it and go from there.
Catherine Crier: Couldn't tell cops what kind of fish he went after. Said too cold to golf.
Mickey Sherman, Defense Attorney: Need a little more for murder.
Catherine Crier: Rumor Amber has real bombshells with her personal recordings.
Mickey Sherman, Defense Attorney: Gloria said Amber doesn't think guilt or innocence, and he'd been arrested earlier.
Marshall Hennington, Jury Consultant: No emotion from Scott that his wife is dead. Makes him look guilty.
Catherine Crier: Letter excerpts; cried, told by police she was dead.
Dr. Casey: Scott's behavior is bizarre from the beginning. Not typical behavior.
Catherine Crier: Mop wet on December 24th?
Candice DeLong, retired FBI: Ask maid what she did with the mop; I leave the wet part, sponge up, not down.

Fox News Channel Greta Van Susteren

Claudia Cowan: Scott told Amy he was to play golf at the Club he and Laci just joined. Mom said she thought the world of Scott. Scott's Dad said he didn't know about the boat, motorcycle, or truck. Mrs. Rocha said Scott told her Laci was missing, rather than not at home.

Stan Goldman, Fox News legal editor: Housekeeper was nervous, trouble remembering some details. Four times; clean every two weeks.

Gloria Allred, Amber Frey's lawyer: Amy tried Scott's cell phone on December 24th and couldn't get him; about the gift basket. Laci would have told Amy about the affair.

Laura Ingle, KFI Radio Reporter: No marriage problems, Mrs. Rocha liked Scott. When she called Scott and Laci, and Scott answered, she'd have long conversations with him, very pleasant. She was supposed to have lunch with Laci the next day; planned it with her Mom.

Gloria Allred, Amber Frey's lawyer: If Laci knew of the boat, she'd have told her Mom.

Greta: Why did the prosecution call Scott's Dad today to testify and what did Scott's Dad say that night to help put his son behind bars?

Stay tuned.

Jayne Weintraub, Defense Attorney: Don't know why they'd call the sister.

Greta: Bought boat and didn't tell anyone.

Ted Williams, Defense Attorney: The prosecutor hasn't made a case against Scott Peterson. Prosecutor is trying to make a case in public opinion with emotionalism.

Dr. Michael Baden, Forensic Pathologist: Marina; not lighted, can't do it at night; in day, people could see what's going on. People come and go from the marina unexpectedly.

Stan Goldman, Fox News legal editor: Had Scott told his own father of the boat; also, catamaran, motorcycle, auto; he doesn't tell me what he buys. The prosecutor is trying to string together twenty things to create suspicion.

Greta: How will the maid's testimony affect the case? Stay tuned. [Fox shows a video of Scott saying that he left at 9:30am or so, Laci still in the house, the dog returned at 10:30am.]

Greta: Maid didn't use bleach in the kitchen, some in the bathroom. [headline]:

BLEACH AND BLOOD STAINS.

Ted Yeshion, forensic serologist: Can't clean blood, it leaves a pattern, even if use bleach. One part blood plus millions of liquid; still detect blood. Two hundred scenes and is some residue, even in bleach.
Laura Ingle, KFI Radio Reporter: Did mention cleaned the back bathroom with bleach and had bleach rags on the bucket on top of the washer.
Dr. Michael Baden, Forensic Pathologist: Some people smell bleach easy, some not.
Laura Ingle, KFI Radio Reporter: Neighbor said the blind closed on December 24th and Laci opens them early, but the maid said the blinds were closed on December 23rd.
Gloria Allred, Amber Frey's lawyer: Cleaning with bleach after the maid doesn't make sense.
Greta: The expert just said you can still find blood.
Ted Williams, Defense Attorney: Blinds closed with Laci there helps the defense. [While Gloria is still talking in the background.]
Dr. Michael Baden, Forensic Pathologist: Don't know what's in the ninety bags of evidence from the house.
Greta: May only be hair. Coming up, Amber on the witness stand. Are we finally gonna hear what Scott said to her? Stay tuned.
[headline]: **WILL AMBER TESTIFY?**
Stan Goldman, Fox News legal editor: With Geragos and Mrs. Rocha wasn't somber; it was lite and smiling about Laci. Interesting mood in court today; families cordial.

Fox News Channel **John Kasich:** The families of Laci and Scott gave tearful testimony today. We'll have the latest. Stay tuned.
[headline]:
LACI'S FAMILY SPEAKS.
John Kasich: We'll tell you what they said when we come back.
Laura Ingle, KFI Radio Reporter: Very important witness today. The housekeeper, December 23rd, used water and a tad of pine sol; bleach in the back bathroom. Amy didn't know of the boat; said golf, not fishing.
Bob McNeill, Defense Attorney: Strong case of suspicion, not a yacht, why tell in-laws. Can't say the hair belongs to Laci Peterson. Where'd the maid put the cleaning rags and mops.
Laura Ingle, KFI Radio Reporter: Scott wiped tear away when his Dad on the stand. Laci's friends crying. The detective said when first reported, went to the park and Mrs. Rocha asked where he was

and said went fishing; too cold for golf. She couldn't understand, cause Mr. Rocha loves fishing.
Bob McNeill, Defense Attorney: If call Amber, they don't know where, how, or who. They lack the smoking gun.

[So, Scott said 'fishing', right away to the detective and to Ms. Rocha.]

<u>11/1/03</u>

CNN **Ted Rowlands**, KTVU TV Reporter: Scott called the Rocha house to find if Laci there, then said missing.
Laura Ingle, KFI Radio Reporter: Scott got home, hungry, got a slice of pizza, took a shower, washed clothes, and started calling to look for Laci.
Chris Pixley, Defense Attorney: The prosecutor hasn't shown a common theme. The defense just keeps poking holes in the bits on information.
Jeanine Pirro, prosecutor Westchester County, New York: Don't agree; December 24th, Scott's Dad said he talked to him, around 2pm or so, and this would have been while Scott was fishing and Scott should have told his Dad he was fishing and not golf.
Chris Pixley, Defense Attorney: Your time line is wrong; that's not what his ticket says.
Dr. Cyril Wecht, Forensic Pathologist: Mitochondria DNA, much less exclusion ratio. I've heard many billions used and not that many people ever populated the Earth.
[headline]: **LACI'S MOM: I WAS REALLY SCARED WHEN SCOTT SAID 'MISSING'.**
Nancy Grace, of Court TV, former prosecutor: What Laci wearing?
Ted Rowlands, KTVU TV Reporter: Amy says beige pants, may get tape at the salon and see. Scott didn't call Amy to say he couldn't pick up the gift.
Dr. Robi Ludwig, psychotherapist: Not with Laci's personality to wear clothes two days. Some of Scott's lies are bigger than others. Went out in a small boat, wrong time of the day to fish.
Laura Ingle, KFI Radio Reporter: Dad said other things Scott bought and not told him.
Nancy Grace, of Court TV, former prosecutor: Clearly Geragos had the Dad prepared for testifying.

Chris Pixley, Defense Attorney: Don't know if Laci saw the boat, it ain't a house, other purchases. Amy said different clothes than what other eyewitnesses saw her in the next day. Sure, say poor witnesses, but they are credible. Mom says Laci active.
Jeanine Pirro, prosecutor Westchester County, New York: You're wrong.
Chris Pixley, Defense Attorney: You're wrong.
Jeanine Pirro, prosecutor Westchester County, New York: So she had to go grocery shopping, December 23rd, pregnant, while husband fishes on December 24th.
Dr. Robi Ludwig, psychotherapist: There's a pattern of deception here.
Chris Pixley, Defense Attorney: How such a poor liar, get away with such a clean murder? He's either a mastermind or he didn't do it.
Nancy Grace, of Court TV, former prosecutor: We understand there is no blood DNA from the home. What about paint?
Ted Rowlands, KTVU TV Reporter: Don't know yet; prosecutor will fill in the blanks. With Amber we'll learn more about lies Scott told.
Nancy Grace, of Court TV, former prosecutor: Takes one hour to get to the buoy and one hour to get back and Scott went fishing for two hours. So Where Was The Fishing? Stay tuned.
Gloria Allred, Amber Frey's lawyer: Interested Amy and Mom said didn't know of Amber Frey relation. The Mom, December 23rd, talked to Laci. Scott says he told Laci; hard to believe Laci be okay with it and hard that she didn't tell her mother. Beginning to unmask Scott Peterson, it's Halloween. Geragos will be aggressive, dog style, in her face, but it will boomerang.
Greta: Did Amber pass a polygraph?
Gloria Allred, Amber Frey's lawyer: Can't comment.
Greta: Why not call? Tapes?
Gloria Allred, Amber Frey's lawyer: If Amber, cause the prosecutors think she has something.
Greta: Naked photos with Geragos?
Gloria Allred, Amber Frey's lawyer: Try to beat her up; but won't be successful. Never good to watch a man beat up on a woman.
Laura Ingle, KFI Radio Reporter: Laci's Mom solid on the stand. Laci was headstrong.
Nancy Grace, former prosecutor: Significant?

Laura Ingle, KFI Radio Reporter: December 15th dinner with Scott and Laci. Ron Grantsky loves to fish, boat never came up. December 12th [23rd], 8:30pm phone call, Laci called, to have brunch the next day. December 24th Scott called, said Laci missing, right away. When she went to the Park, Scott was thirty feet away and she yelled Scott, Scott, and he never acknowledged her.
Nancy Grace, former prosecutor: First day out with the boat.
Laura Ingle, KFI Radio Reporter: Don't know, could be true.
Jeanine Pirro, prosecutor Westchester County, New York: Mom says close relationship. Mom says if Laci knew of Amber, Laci would have told her. Detective says two mops outside and a bleach smell on December 24th; it wouldn't be there a day later.
Chris Pixley, Defense Attorney: Mom also said Laci was active and Scott was active in the pregnancy with Laci.
Dr. Robi Ludwig, psychotherapist: Future jurors are watching on TV.
Nancy Grace, former prosecutor: Potential jurors will have on their minds pictures of the Rocha family that day. [Quote of the day: Nancy said she was just sitting in for Larry King as host and not there as a former prosecutor.]
Kelly Huston, spokesperson for Stanislaus County Sheriff's Department: Two visits per week; maximum security cells, individual, quite a chore to remove someone from a cell, chains, etc., he gets alot of mail.
Nancy Grace, former prosecutor: Letters from Scott, read them, outgoing mail.
Kelly Huston: Yes, but for security, contraband, key words.
Nancy Grace, former prosecutor: What if crime in a letter?
Kelly Huston: Don't know, sometimes alert attention if needed.
Jeanine Pirro, prosecutor Westchester County, New York: Letters are self-serving; he looks better now than before. Letters are what he wants to get out to the public.
Dr. Robi Ludwig, psychotherapist: Women writing him are desperate.
Laura Ingle, KFI Radio Reporter: Looks pretty good, nice haircut, suit.
Nancy Grace, former prosecutor: We gotta take a break.

Fox News Channel **Geraldo Rivera:** 'Missing' is not a word I'd use if my wife wasn't home at 5:17pm. How do you go fishing for a five foot fish, a sturgeon, in a fourteen foot boat?
Page Hopkins, of Fox News: Cops detect Clorox in the kitchen. You don't think Scott came home and bleached the kitchen?
Geraldo Rivera: That's what the detective says, but I wish it was someone else who doesn't have an axe to grind against Scott.
Page Hopkins: Like Simpson case, where you attack the police?
Geraldo Rivera: Simpson is the most innocent guilty person on Earth.

Fox News Channel **Rita Cosby:** Coming up, find out who will testify in the Scott Peterson trial. [headline]: **WHO WILL TALK?** Several people close to Amber tell me Amber will testify next week.
Dr. Larry Koblinsky, forensic scientist: Hair important, defense won't win.
Lis Wiehl, Fox News legal analyst, former federal prosecutor: As the prosecutor I'd ask why in the world is this hair on these pliers.
Mickey Sherman, Defense Attorney: Easy to explain; married.
Dr. Larry Koblinsky, forensic scientist: There's alot of other evidence; duct tape may have a fingerprint; paint on boat.
Rita Cosby: Bleach, maid used in the bathroom, but not in the kitchen.
Lis Wiehl, Fox News legal analyst, former federal prosecutor: Yea, and Scott wasn't a neat guy.
Rita Cosby: Yea, never did laundry, never cook.
Mickey Sherman, Defense Attorney: Boat's not the smoking gun.
Lis Wiehl, Fox News legal analyst, former federal prosecutor: But all things add up, jury maybe can forget one thing, but not all these.
[Rita Cosby reads that Mrs. Rocha said that Scott didn't say Laci wasn't there or couldn't find her, but said she was missing. Also that the prosecution doesn't have much, but forensics is important. Dr. Koblinsky says yes, Geragos has a tough row to hoe and the prosecutor is in good shape.]

<u>11/3/03</u>

Court TV: Alot of DNA evidence being heard in the Scott Peterson case today. [Court TV shows Scott on video saying

he had an affair, but it had absolutely nothing to do with Laci's disappearance.]
Lisa Bloom, of Court TV, Civil Rights lawyer:
His lies went on for months, until the bodies of Laci and her unborn son they named Conner, washed up in the Bay.
Vinnie Politan, of Court TV: DNA expert for the defense says really can't match mitochondria DNA, can only say the two samples are similar.
Lisa Bloom, Civil Rights lawyer: The prosecution says that the hair found wound around the tip of the needle nosed pliers.
[headline]: **LACI MET SCOTT IN 1995. LACI MARRIED SCOTT PETERSON IN 1997.**
Lisa Bloom, Civil Rights lawyer: No one knowing he bought the boat shows a level of premeditation.
Vinnie Politan: Scott didn't tell Dad that he was fishing in the Bay while talking on the phone to his Dad.
John Schick, attorney: Did they go water skiing in the boat? Take others out? I'd want to know these things.
Lisa Bloom, Civil Rights lawyer: Very interesting, me too. Sharon Rocha spoke to Laci at 8:30pm, December 23rd. Sharon said Laci was a private person.
Vinnie Politan: When asked by the detective, 'Did you go play golf?' Scott said, 'No, too cold', and Ron [Sharon Rocha's companion] said that, 'You go fishing either early morning or afternoon and weren't you a little late to go fishing'? Scott said he tried to call Laci twice from his cell phone while fishing, went home, dog in backyard with the back door unlocked, he ate two slices of pizza and took a shower, then started calling to look for Laci. Scott asked Sharon Rocha if Laci was at her house and then, at some point, said Laci was missing. And when Sharon went to the Park to look for Laci, Scott wasn't there looking.
Lisa Bloom, Civil Rights lawyer: The detective did say Scott was upset that day, right?
Vinnie Politan: Oh yea, that testimony is there and he was active in the search for Laci.

Fox News Channel: Supposedly the duct tape on Laci was the same tape Scott used to put up 'Laci missing' posters.
Dr. Michael Baden, Forensic Pathologist: Well that would be compelling evidence. We've heard of people putting the tape in their mouth to tear it and leaving DNA on the tape.

Court TV ticker: Scott Peterson's defense attorney is supposed to call a witness today in a California court to attempt to discredit forensic science.

Court TV ticker: Prosecutors are trying to show that a hair found wrapped into a pair of pliers belongs to Laci, who Scott is accused of murdering.

Court TV **Beth Karas**: The defense has a DNA expert, a New York University professor states that contamination with mitochondria DNA is highly probable and that the way in which the percentage rates of probability are made up is highly questioned within the science fields. The detective says Scott didn't know what type of fish he was after on that day. Some have suggested it was sturgeon.

CNN Headline News: The defense DNA expert today; the prosecution was able to get the professor to admit that twenty to sixty percent of his income is from testifying about DNA for defendants, and therefore take away some of his credibility with the judge. The prosecution never really extracted DNA to test it.

MSNBC **Dan Abrams:** The prosecutor claims the hair found on the boat belongs to Laci. [MSNBC shows a video of Amber Frey saying she had an affair with Scott, and another video of her saying that she will probably be called to testify.]
Gloria Allred, Amber Frey's lawyer: What she has to say will be important.
Dan Abrams: I'm told Amber will be called.
Paul Pfingst, former prosecutor: In a domestic murder, which this is.
Mary Fulginiti, Defense Attorney: Ninety percent of guys with an affair, leave the marriage and divorce, not murder. Friends say the marriage was the greatest.
Mark Carlos, Defense Attorney: The prosecution wants to dirty up Peterson with past relation, but nothing in the past and it may backfire on them.
Gloria Allred, Amber Frey's lawyer: Geragos will try to dirty up Amber and it'll boomerang.

Paul Pfingst, former prosecutor: It'd be malpractice as a prosecutor not to call Amber, at least at this stage.
Dan Abrams: Scott Peterson's former girlfriend may become the star witness against him and will the defense tell us who the real killer is; they told us they would. Coming up.
Remember when Geragos wanted the preliminary hearing closed. [Abrams continues by reading what Geragos said, 'it would give the real killers clues'.]
Mark Carlos, Defense Attorney: Better have it, but don't use at the preliminary.
Dan Abrams: Does that mean he doesn't have it?
Mary Fulginiti, defense attorney: Means he didn't mean it.
Dan Abrams: No satanic cults?
Mark Carlos, defense attorney: Do theories to get people out of woodwork with information.
Gloria Allred, Amber Frey's lawyer: The defense better produce, if not, his credibility is on the line; and if his is on the line, so is his client's. Can't have it both ways. Jurors will remember promises.
Dan Abrams: Not okay to do this.
Mary Fulginiti, defense attorney: If used in an opening statement, it could be problems.
Gloria Allred, Amber Frey's lawyer: When's the last time you heard an affirmative defense? My client didn't do it and here's the one who did?
[Sounds like the defense attorney is on trial, in the media.]

CNN Larry King Live
Larry King: Scott's parents aren't poor.
Bill Kurtis: Scott's a very successful fertilizer salesman.
Jeanine Pirro, prosecutor Westchester County, New York: His father would have known; 12-2pm phone call; Scott said he was at the pier at twelve noon.
Caller: Insurance? When did he put it on wife and unborn son?
Bill Kurtis: It'll come up. On wife; don't know about the child. Sometime before the incident.

Fox News Channel **Greta Van Susteren:** Bombshell evidence in the Scott Peterson case.
Claudia Cowan: Investigators say similarities between the tape next to Laci's body and the same roll Scott used to put up posters

for Laci. They won't use this at the preliminary hearing, but will wait and use at trial.
Laura Ingle, KFI Radio Reporter: Nobody says that Laci knew of the boat.
Gloria Allred, Amber Frey's lawyer: Some say he was going to present the boat to Laci for Christmas.
Laura Ingle, KFI Radio Reporter: He has a work warehouse and one in Modesto for the boat, boat never at their home.
Vinnie Politan, of Court TV: The defense expert didn't do a mitochondria DNA test. Testified one hundred-fifty times for the defense, and six times for the prosecution.
Greta: Yea, but prosecution experts always testify for the prosecution; they're paid to.
Gloria Allred, Amber Frey's lawyer: Mitochondria DNA used to ID Vietnam vets.
Greta: ID, or exclude?
Laura Ingle, KFI Radio Reporter: The judge pays attention.
Vinnie Politan, of Court TV: The prosecution has a rebuttal DNA expert. [headline]: **DUCT TAPE CLUE. HAIR LINK TO BOAT.** [Fox shows a video of Scott saying: I had nothing to do with Laci's disappearance. Even if you think I did, think about Laci and help bring her home.]
Greta: Does the hair definitely link Laci to the boat? Stay tuned. Will a single strand of hair be the smoking gun?
Bernie Grimm, Defense Attorney: Three days splitting a hair; can't ID the hair.
Geoffrey Fieger, attorney: The prosecution has more. Hair only thing ties Laci's body to Scott and the water. Judge will accept it; need it to bind over.
Greta: The defense expert said; it's biased against the defendant and it's wrong.
Dr. Michael Baden, Forensic Pathologist: Still don't know where the hair came from.
Geoffrey Fieger, attorney: Amber tapes will prejudice the jury and the rest will be believed. [headline]: **HANGING ON BY A HAIR?**
FORENSIC BOMBSHELL.
Greta: Fingerprint on tape?
Dr. Michael Baden, Forensic Pathologist: [Fox shows Dr. Baden, standing by the dock of the Bay.] Very difficult to launch a boat from here and not be seen.

Greta: Unconfirmed reports on the duct tape. A TV station reports Scott's fingerprint on the tape. Compare, and same roll?
MacFarland, Duct Tape Man: Look at pattern, cloth, and adhesive. Can determine manufacturer of the tape; different manufacturers; different cloths; adhesive.
Greta: From a particular role?
MacFarland: Would be similar in the whole roll. Analyze for similarity, reasonable certainty; can't give a percentage of odds.
Dr. Michael Baden, Forensic Pathologist: Difference in science and criminal justice system. Mitochondria DNA isn't one hundred percent, but can use with Amber [Laci], duct tape and circumstance; then likely hair is someone else's and how it got there is something else.
Greta: Unreliable pieces?
Bernie Grimm, defense Attorney: MacFarland said if from 3M, then it's 3M, that's all. The jury will despise Scott and convict with no evidence.
Gloria Allred, Amber Frey's lawyer: The tape is just another piece. Won't be any smoking gun; won't be more prejudicial than probative.
Geoffrey Fieger, Defense Attorney: Judge may exclude if they say the tape is the same as the other tape. Remember, used to be convictions on blood type.
Laura Ingle, KFI Radio Reporter: Don't think we'll hear of the tape at the preliminary.
Greta: Did Amber dump Scott Peterson just hours before Laci went missing? Stay tuned. [headline]: **FISHY ALIBI?**
Greta: Cops say Scott said fishing, but didn't know what kind. [Now you know, many times, fishin' ain't for fishing, it's for thinkin'.]
Vinnie Politan, of Court TV: Big problem, Ron Grantsky, an avid fisherman.
Gloria Allred, Amber Frey's lawyer: Fish for two hours and come back; sounds fishy.
Dr. Michael Baden, Forensic Pathologist: Impossible after dark to launch a boat and if body in the boat, would have been seen. Maybe establish alibi and. Can't do it in the dark; can't, I've been there.
Laura Ingle, KFI Radio Reporter: Amy says look at the surveillance tape to see what Laci had on. She told them right away; cream pants.

Greta: Scott said he saw her going off to walk the dog.
Bernie Grimm, Defense Attorney: You're looking for missing wife and someone asks about fish.
Geoffrey Fieger, attorney: No one talked to Laci after December 23rd evening.
Vinnie Politan, of Court TV: Geragos will be in Los Angeles tomorrow and McAllister will take over tomorrow.
Gloria Allred, Amber Frey's lawyer: Just for first officer. [Fox shows Scott coming into court, with Geragos and with a suit and tie.]
Laura Ingle, KFI Radio Reporter: Scott Peterson's side of court kinda thin today.
Vinnie Politan, of Court TV: Brutal for the parents of the families when Amber testifies.
Gloria Allred, Amber Frey's lawyer: Amber had no knowledge; if the prosecutor uses her for motive.
Laura Ingle, KFI Radio Reporter: Scott lost alot of weight, still tanned, natural.
Gloria Allred, Amber Frey's lawyer: Scott is very involved with defense.

11/4/03

CNN Larry King Live [Well, almost live, since this is the 12midnight show, and only the first few minutes, that was missed at 9pm on 11/3.]
Dr. Henry Lee: Be interesting to see if find Scott's fingerprint on poster or tape and then if find fingerprint on tape from being in water long time, and see if tape match up. Fiber could be same, adhesive sometime change. Can't comment on evidence of case.

Court TV **Vinnie Politan**: The defense says one in nine that could be Laci's hair. Well, the prosecution could turn that around and say, well, it's not Scott's hair, so whose hair is it? Tell us. [headline]: **FREY FIRST CONTACTED POLICE December 30TH. FREY FIRST MET PETERSON November, 2002.**

CNN Larry King Live
Larry King: The defense thinks police may have planted evidence in Scott's house the day after Laci disappeared.
Ted Rowlands, KTVU TV Reporter: Detective said Scott couldn't or didn't answer what he was fishing for. No smell of bleach or

cleaning smell in the house. No wet floors. Scott took them to the warehouse and either Scott, or someone, said no lights. Scott was cooperative the entire process. Police took the pail and mops when they came to the house.
Nancy Grace, of Court TV, former prosecutor: The defense takes a page from Cochran's book; DNA hair planted in the pliers; defense expert never extracted DNA; sex on wolves expert.
Chris Pixley, Defense Attorney: Detective debunked the bleach theory; significant for the defense, no freshly sanitized crime scene. Mitochondria DNA evidence; major questions of one hair into two hairs; who was there? How'd the hair get on the boat?
Ted Rowlands, KTVU TV Reporter: More for public opinion; both sides.
Nancy Grace, of Court TV, former prosecutor: Geragos trying to set a record for a preliminary hearing; both sides. Want Amber, she'll put the lid on the pot. To suggest the hair was planted, police already said the hair broke.
Chris Pixley, Defense Attorney: Hair is awfully strong, and just broke? The defense still wins, cause the hair could get in the boat in a thousand ways; no blood or vomit on the mop, no cleanup. Where's all the evidence? [Larry has to tell Nancy not to interrupt.]
Larry King: Why is the preliminary hearing so long?
Nancy Grace, of Court TV, former prosecutor: The defense cross exam of the witnesses; all over one little hair.
Gloria Allred, Amber Frey's lawyer: Concern over Amber's security when she testifies; if I tell you now. I'll be informed, if she testifies. She's never testified before, and to face Geragos as an attack dog.
Nancy Grace, former prosecutor: Amber will testify, main jest of relation, what did Scott say about Laci? Involved statement? Goes to what Scott said; Amber asked if he had anything to do with it, and he said, No, uh, uh, but....
Larry King: Hold it, stop it, you don't know that. This is what we get into.
Gloria Allred, Amber Frey's lawyer: If the defense attacks her, she'll tell the truth, do the right thing.
Johnnie Cochran: Difficult to defend someone that the public believes guilty. Scott is already guilty and Geragos is under a gag order. He has to cross exam, he must plant the seeds of doubt.
Larry King: Speculation.

Johnnie Cochran: Planting evidence is possible. Mitochondria DNA pass the test? May not be enough. Longer preliminary, the defense has to question the evidence. The prosecutor also wants the jury to know they have evidence. If a break in the prosecutor's chain, Peterson may go free. One mistake and a client could end up on death row. Amber; no confession, a spurned lover, rejected, maybe he lied to her. Doesn't make him a killer. Circumstances; only to guilt, or to innocence?
Johnnie Cochran: Dr. Lee is the best forensic expert on Earth.
Dr. Henry Lee: Maybe not testify.
Vinnie Politan, of Court TV: No big evidence yet.
Ted Rowlands, KTVU TV Reporter: Lead detective tomorrow; figured Scott was guilty from the first.
Nancy Grace, former prosecutor: Detective in the Kobe Bryant case waffled and here, Geragos will have both guns blazing; planted evidence.
Chris Pixley, Defense Attorney: Reason here to question police motives, police aren't infallible, not god-like as on TV. They're human beings.
Johnnie Cochran: Same bias as others, once they make a judgment, they go after him. Police never back up and say they're wrong.
Dr. Henry Lee: Need open mind, objective; doesn't matter who hires me, tell them what I find. Once, Johnnie [Cochran] going to strangle me in O.J. case, cause I say DNA okay and I almost became a prosecution witness. [Against Johnnie, kiddingly.]
Nancy Grace, former prosecutor: The defense leaks theories; satanic cult, Donnie and the brown van.
Johnnie Cochran: Once a gag order, always comes from the prosecution.
Nancy Grace, former prosecutor: Why prosecution, why not the defense.
Johnnie Cochran: Geragos wouldn't hurt his own defense would he?
Vinnie Politan, of Court TV: Somebody's talking; smell of bleach, don't know where come from. No bleach or smell with the first officer in the house; No Mr. Clean, or anything else.
Nancy Grace, former prosecutor: I've heard that; an article in the Enquirer; take with a box of salt.
Caller: The defense team, the tennis shoes missing? How, if Laci walking?

Nancy Grace, former prosecutor: The defense attorney says they're the key, the sandals, but not in the case. The defense theories evaporate in air.
Johnnie Cochran: There are potential jurors watching.
Vinnie Politan, of Court TV: The dog in the back yard, with the leash. Prosecutor says, Scott's master plan, that Laci walked the dog.
Nancy Grace, former prosecutor: The dog was found at 10:30am by a neighbor. Scott left at 9:30, and Laci had on black pants. In one hour it was over, Laci gone, dog in back yard.
Dr. Henry Lee: Other witness saw Laci walking, 10am to 10:30.
Chris Pixley, Defense Attorney: The dog's not strong for the prosecution; between 9 and 10:30; plenty of time for all the witnesses to be right, it's a common story and it fits.
Nancy Grace, former prosecutor: A witness has a glass eye.
Johnnie Cochran: I have a glass eye; everybody has a spin, depends on own thoughts. No eyewitness here.
Caller: Why is not the accused able to proclaim their innocence?
Larry King: Why not jump up, holler.
Johnnie Cochran: Plead not guilty, and sit down.
Nancy Grace, former prosecutor: The defendant's demeanor is important. Larry, you keep showing the shot of Scott, Squeezing Out That One Little Tear; he managed to cry once, through all of this.
Johnnie Cochran: Perception becomes reality.
Ted Rowlands, KTVU TV Reporter: Scott was active today; passed notes during the cross exam.
Johnnie Cochran: If the officer is saying things, not so, well, the defendant was there, so he knows, and help is welcomed from the defendant.
Chris Pixley, Defense Attorney: There's no jury now, so you can do more on cross exam with Amber, now. For thirty days they know each other; see each other maybe five times; no promises from Scott; no future with Scott.
Dr. Henry Lee: Ninety-six bags of evidence; one thousand pieces, but how many link suspect to case is crucial.
Caller: Fishing equipment used? Polygraph?
Nancy Grace, former prosecutor: Amber is most important. On December 24th, couldn't say what he was fishing for.
Johnnie Cochran: Amber is not that relevant; speculation, relation not important, unless he told her something.

Fox News Channel **Claudia Cowan:** The detective said no bleach smell, but that's funny, cause other detectives said they smelled bleach. The prosecutor may play the tape and not have Amber testify.
Vinnie Politan, of Court TV: With the detective; on defense, the bleach issue, no smell. On prosecution side, the fish story, Scott not know what for; rug out of place, jammed up against the door, but, in cross exam, the detective said this was not in the police report.
Laura Ingle, KFI Radio Reporter: The defense; no bleach. The prosecution; when they talked to Scott, the way he handled the questions.
Gloria Allred, Amber Frey's lawyer: For the prosecution; the rug caught in the door; a struggle? Body dragged out? The detective said he told another detective.
Greta Van Susteren: Not a supplemental report though?
Gloria Allred, Amber Frey's lawyer: Bucket outside? Maid said in the laundry room.
Laura Ingle, KFI Radio Reporter: Scott was interested today in the testimony.
Gloria Allred, Amber Frey's lawyer: He was also distracting his own attorney, during the warehouse testimony.
Vinnie Politan, of Court TV: Scott was there, so he can be very helpful to his attorney.
Gloria Allred, Amber Frey's lawyer: Annoying to an attorney for a client to talk to him. Maybe Scott can't control himself.
[headline]: **COP CLUES. RUG RAISES FLAGS.** [Fox shows Scott saying: No, I didn't have anything to do with Laci's disappearance. Please help bring her home.]
Greta: What the defense says about tainted evidence, and why some say a shag rug throws up red flags. Stay tuned. What about the bucket on the washer by the maid and police find it outside? [Maybe because Scott washed his clothes that evening and set the bucket outside.]
Vinnie Politan, of Court TV: The maid may not remember where she put the bucket.
Ted Williams, Defense Attorney: Why not Laci herself move the bucket? She was there. What piece of puzzle?
Gloria Allred, Amber Frey's lawyer: Maid there on December 23rd, and a tired, pregnant woman ain't gonna clean house.

Greta: Why did police take a throw rug and why search Scott's warehouse on December 24th?
[headline]: **WAREHOUSE CLUES.**
Dr. Michael Baden, Forensic Pathologist: Weights would stay in place, body would sway and free itself.
Greta: The detective, at the warehouse, a dispute over the electricity.
Vinnie Politan, of Court TV: Not clear if electricity, Scott said no, others said theirs was on; maybe he didn't pay the bills.
Greta: There was a fax there, received a fax that day.
Laura Ingle, KFI Radio Reporter: They looked in the dark, with flashlights.
Greta: Date; December 23rd?
Gloria Allred, Amber Frey's lawyer: He didn't want full light for the detective to see.
Dr. Michael Baden, Forensic Pathologist: To look on the boat. Scott talking to his attorney in court, not a good idea.
Bernie Grimm, Attorney: The client wants a thousand Perry Mason questions asked. Usually says the policeman is lying.
Ted Williams, former D.C. police detective, attorney: Clearly Scott was a suspect; first one to look at. Why not go back the next day to look at the warehouse?
Greta: If police look at the warehouse and suspect Scott on December 23rd, then they suspected she's dead, right away?
Gloria Allred, Amber Frey's lawyer: Turns out their suspicions were right. [headline]: **PET QUESTIONS. JAIL LIFE EXCLUSIVE.**
Greta: Scott blamed the dog and cat playing for the rug against the door.
Vinnie Politan, of Court TV: Think they had a cat; rug moved back by Scott with his foot; easily.
Laura Ingle, KFI Radio Reporter: He didn't think much of it; moved with his toe.
Gloria Allred, Amber Frey's lawyer: Red herring; no gun under it. Was the body drug through it?
Greta: What does 'scrunched' mean? Fibers?
Dr. Michael Baden, Forensic Pathologist: Rug should be looked at; blood, hairs, maybe police have it.
Ted Williams, Defense Attorney: Critical that he didn't write it in his report. Gloria said drug body; no evidence of that.

Greta: One officer told another, that night, that he didn't know what he saw fishing for.
Gloria Allred, Amber Frey's lawyer: Later he said sturgeon, and can't catch them with his boat.
Greta: There was whispering that night by the police, maybe go to the warehouse, suspected Scott from the beginning.
Vinnie Politan, of Court TV: That night.
[headline]: **JAILHOUSE EXCLUSIVE. COP CONTROVERSY.**
Greta: Why does the defense say that he planted evidence? What does Scott have hanging on his wall in prison and why does he have ear plugs? What does the hair mean? Stay tuned. [headline]: **4/18 SCOTT ARRESTED.**
Rita Cosby: Reading behind bars, toothpaste sculptures, photos of Laci on the wall, colored photo of Laci; Laci photos, all of them. In a single cell; he can only see others when he's out of his cell. No one else is out, when Scott is removed from his cell. He was next to the drunk tank at first, so he made his own earplugs. Nice jail [HUH?], Scott is polite, courteous. One million dollars cost to his parents; with ninety-five percent already paid. Dr. Wecht was fifty thousand alone and they'd already paid McAllister before Geragos. The prosecutor believes the hair is the key; the pliers are the key. Friends say Laci always used these particular type of pliers. [Fox shows Scott saying: Police have done a wonderful job. They were out here that night with helicopters and police dogs. Detective Brocchini, they want to find her and bring her home].
Laura Ingle, KFI Radio Reporter: Probably hear different on the smell of the house from Brocchini.
Vinnie Politan, of Court TV: There's always a villain, like on the TV shows.
Greta: Same detective who went back to the hair? And broke?
Vinnie Politan, of Court TV: Yes, and the evidence technician. The defense say the hair is mixed up; now two. Got to find one person to put on trial by the defense.
Greta: Sometimes police don't do it right.
Gloria Allred, Amber Frey's lawyer: You played Scott's statements and he thinks the officers doing a Wonderful Job. How self-serving are the photos on the wall? He knew it would get out. Won't rule out a plot by Scott.
Laura Ingle, KFI Radio Reporter: Scott knew full well the information; the photos would get out, on purpose.

Greta: Why go ninety miles from home, with a receipt to show this? Why are the clothes different?
Vinnie Politan, of Court TV: We may hear from the lead detective; the big pieces.
Greta: If I were the prosecutor, I'd subpoena Diane Sawyer and all the tapes.
Gloria Allred, Amber Frey's lawyer: He says the clothes are different on December 24th. [So Laci had on black pants that morning and decided to wear other clothes to jog or walk the dog. Have you ever changed your clothes to cut grass, work outside, go for a walk, play, work, go to the store, or to go next door?]

11/5/03

Fox News Channel **Greta Van Susteren:** Coming up; Why were police whispering in Scott Peterson's kitchen the night Laci went missing and why it may be a key piece of evidence.

[Has anyone thought that Scott doesn't know alot about fishing? Sometimes there can be nothing worse than an expert and a novice, or even worse, a beginner. Maybe Scott would like a little experience with the boat before inviting someone to go out. I doubt that an expert would want to go out in a small boat.]

Fox News Channel [headline]: **EVIDENCE QUESTIONED AT PETERSON HEARING.**
Linda Vester, of Fox News: What did the detectives find when they first visited the house after Laci went missing? Did police really plant evidence? That's what the defense claims.
Claudia Cowan: No court today, Geragos in Los Angeles with a murder trial. The Peterson's are livid about this. They've already paid nearly one million dollars. There were three other affairs; a sexual problem. Amber Frey was purely a physical relation. Amber won't testify; prosecutor to play one tape. The controversial detective; was the second to arrive on the scene, the defense says tampered with evidence.
Linda Vester: Plant evidence?
Audience: Yes; No.
Allison Nelson, California prosecutor: What motive is there to plant evidence by the police? [Probably the same one that makes the donkey pull the cart.]

John Burris, former District Attorney, Defense Attorney: They develop an interest in a person and then police credibility is on the line. Evidence throughout the country that police plant evidence.
Allison Nelson, California prosecutor: The affairs shows Scott wanted to get rid of his wife and baby; get them out of the way.
Linda Vester: A fish story; Christmas Eve; Boat too dangerous? Too small to go in the Bay?
Allison Nelson, California prosecutor: The prosecution's case is based on common sense; Christmas Eve fishing?
John Burris, former prosecutor, attorney: This is strong evidence, I agree.

Court TV [headline]: **SHE WAS EIGHT MONTHS PREGNANT WITH A BOY.**
Beth Karas, of Court TV: The maid says she always put the buckets on the washer and set the mop outside to dry.

Fox News Channel Hannity and Colmes
Mark Fuhrman, former O.J. cop: They tried it in the O.J. trial and it didn't work. Not one lie by the police and no planted evidence. It didn't work then and Geragos should learn, cause it ain't gonna work now.
Peter Johnson, Fox News legal analyst: If all the defense Scott has, is that there was no smell of bleach, he's headed down the creek.
Debra Opri, attorney: Scott Peterson will convict Scott Peterson. A ball and chain around his neck and he wanted out. He didn't count on the Modesto Police being the best there is.
Alan Colmes: Reasonable doubt?
Lis Wiehl, Fox News legal analyst, former federal prosecutor: At trial, hundreds of pieces of evidence will build a story and convict Scott Peterson.
Sean Hannity: Geragos clearly catering to the potential jury pool.
Debra Opri, attorney: Need a psychological profile of Scott Peterson; agree with Fuhrman.
Peter Johnson, Fox News legal analyst: Could go to the home and find Laci's hair right now in the closet. The only defense Geragos has, is that the police framed Scott. [headline]: **4/13 BODY OF MALE FETUS FOUND ON SHORE.**

Fox News Channel **Greta Van Susteren:** The first detective may be on the stand for several days.
Gloria Allred, Amber Frey's lawyer: Obviously Scott gave Geragos permission to go to Los Angeles and not be here.
Vinnie Politan, of Court TV: 8:30am, the housekeeper, the blinds down; 2pm, cleaned the blinds. The translator is a problem. Scott was at home sometime during the day and don't know if Laci at home then or not. She put bucket on the washer, mop outside.
Laura Ingle, KFI Radio Reporter: December 23rd, Scott got a haircut at 5 to 5;30 with Amy. Talking about brunch, pick up gift, no problem, a lovely evening.
Vinnie Politan, of Court TV: The housekeeper; no problems. Four times been there.
Laura Ingle, KFI Radio Reporter: 8:30pm, Laci called; Sharon, brunch the next day.
Gloria Allred, Amber Frey's lawyer: Scott never picked up the gift on December 24th, nor call Amy; something change his plans?
Laura Ingle, KFI Radio Reporter: Amy said there's a surveillance video of what Laci wore that evening.
Greta: Only a rug out of place on December 24th; no sign of a struggle.
[headline]: **CLUES IN THE HOUSE?**

[If Sharon Rocha talked to Laci on December 23rd, about having brunch on December 24th, wouldn't Sharon be calling Laci around that time to confirm and then begin to wonder where Laci was? Yet when Scott called to see if Laci was at her Mom's, Sharon simply replied that it's okay and that Laci would be home soon. Would this have tipped Scott off that Laci may still be at her Mom's, after having brunch with her, and if he sounded concerned, maybe Sharon would tell him Laci was there?]
Jayne Weintraub, Defense Attorney: Zero on the bucket and pail, yet they already said they smell bleach, it's in the warrant. Four days of evidence, equals no murder by Scott Peterson.
Greta: Even if bleach, luminal can detect blood.
Bernie Grimm, Defense Attorney: A soap opera or a murder investigation? You gotta open the door to get the body out, so that didn't cause a Scrunched rug.
Vinnie Politan, of Court TV: The prosecution says a master plan, but if so, why make a commitment to pick up the gift.
Gloria Allred, Amber Frey's lawyer: Assumes a perfect murder; ain't none. Piece by piece of the prosecution's case.

Greta: What if Amber is not the only mistress? Help or hurt Scott? Stay tuned.
[headline]: **EXCLUSIVE VIDEO.**
Claudia Cowan: Say that Laci came home early one day, not long after marriage, and caught Scott Cheating. Scott told Amber that he was going to Paris with his family for Christmas.
[headline]: **SCOTT'S LIFE AND LOVES. THE AMBER AFFAIR.**
Gloria Allred, Amber Frey's lawyer: Attempts by the defense to say what; a sex addict? A question of whether the defense theory is grounded in fact or not.
Bernie Grimm, Defense Attorney: Why not just say the marriage is over?
Greta: Why not kill Laci when he had other affairs? Kind of destroys the prosecution's motive.
Vinnie Politan, of Court TV: How do you prove affairs in court?
Dr. Michael Baden, Forensic Pathologist: No cause of death; don't know where murdered; neighbors saw her after the prosecution says the murder occurred. [headline]: **AMBER'S TESTIMONY.**
Laura Ingle, KFI Radio Reporter: December 24th, the house next door broken into.
Greta: So nothing to do with Laci's murder?
Laura Ingle, KFI Radio Reporter: No. [Fox shows the bedroom blinds that face the street, and they're closed; about forty feet estimated. Then shows two spotlights on the facia corner of the house; two on each side, pointing towards the driveway.]
Greta: So if loading something at night, you could see it?
Laura Ingle, KFI Radio Reporter: Yea. Scott and Laci had a cat, see it on the fence, the roof; friends have it now. You could see them, played all the time. [headline]: **LACI'S TRIP TO THE PARK. FISHING QUESTIONS.**
Greta: Scott goes on the record about Amber, and Laci knowing of the affair. Stay tuned.
[headline]: **SCOTT'S ALIBI.**
Dr. Michael Baden, Forensic Pathologist: He could fish for sturgeon, towards Brooks Island, where he told police he was going. [Fox shows the Bay.]
Aaron Hunger: There's sturgeon in the river also.
Greta: What if a non-fisherman?
Aaron Hunger: Scott said he was an experienced fisherman, in his own words.

Dr. Michael Baden, Forensic Pathologist: The baby was found a day earlier than Mom.
Aaron Hunger: He could launch a boat by self; that size. A polar front brings rough water; when Scott said he was fishing.
Dr. Michael Baden, Forensic Pathologist: Wash up near each other, so it takes away the theory of being born. [headline]: **THE AMBER AFFAIR.**
PRELIMINARY PREVIEW.
Greta: What did the cop see when he first visited the house? [headline]: **IN HIS OWN WORDS.** [Fox shows a video of Scott]: Glad that Amber came forward in the press. Told Laci in early December. Called Amber shortly after Laci went missing and shortly after that, Amber had a meeting with the police. The affair had nothing to do with Laci's disappearance.
Question: Are you angry at police?
Scott: At first, with the accusations, but they were here that night and here the next day with hundreds of officers looking for Laci. They're looking for bodies, but also following all leads to find them. Think what you want of me, I'm not media savvy and I've made some mistakes, but I hope we find Laci, and pray to God we do, and bring her home. [headline]: **AMBER'S ANNOUNCEMENT.** [Fox shows a video of Amber]: When I was introduced to Scott, I was told he was not married.
Gloria Allred, Amber Frey's lawyer: What Scott said is a laugh; he's glad Amber told police?
Vinnie Politan, of Court TV: Little pieces of the TV interview were used by the prosecutor. A common theme in a wife murder case, the husband says the wife knew of the affair. The lead investigator tomorrow; maybe the real meat of the case.
Gloria Allred, Amber Frey's lawyer: See Geragos attack the police too; someone has to be the villain.
Greta: He went to see the hair, then two hairs.
Vinnie Politan, of Court TV: The same detective went to the warehouse with Scott on December 24th, when Scott said no lights.
Gloria Allred, Amber Frey's lawyer: How's the fax working if electricity is out.

[The fax, if there is one, would not verify nor negate Scott telling the police that there wasn't any lights or electricity, whichever one he may have said or may not have said, about the warehouse, since Scott would only know that to be true when Scott was there before. Whether there were lights, apparently not, when the police were there would be up to the police. If he was lying, did police flip on a switch? The fax machine is plugged into a wall socket, and the lights are hooked to a wall switch, each usually on a separate circuit breaker.]

11/6/03

Court TV ticker: Preliminary hearing for Scott Peterson is underway in California. Peterson is charged with killing his wife, and their unborn child.

Court TV **Amand:** Vinnie, you've been in court this morning. What's going on?
Vinnie Politan: The detective testified that Scott said he woke up at 8am, had cereal with Laci and they watched Martha Stewart. Said it was too cold to play golf. This was the first time the boat was in the water; bought it two weeks ago, paid four hundred dollars in cash. Laci's plans, to clean the kitchen on December 24th, mop the kitchen. She asked Scott to bring the mop in. To have brunch and walk the dog. Barefoot, pregnant, and mopping the kitchen when he left home. He went two miles north of the landing dock. Tried to call Laci on her cell phone twice on the way home; message, can't get home in time to pick up Amy's gift basket. Laci's number is on his cell phone. He stopped to get gas on the way back. Laci's cell phone was in her car, plugged in, but dead out of power. The prosecutor beginning of picking apart Scott Peterson's alibi of fishing. Came home and mop and bucket inside, afraid cat would knock over, so he put them outside. Towels found on the washing machine and the bucket outside. Leads the prosecution to believe some sort of cleanup in the house and the defense wants us to believe that somehow the kitchen got dirty between December 23rd with the maid and December 24th morning.

Court TV: What do you have Beth?
Beth Karas, of Court TV: Alot of good stuff. The detective, on December 30th, talked to Amber. Amber met Scott on November 20th, and on December 9th, learned he was married. Scott said his wife was dead. On December 26th, 27th, and 28th, Scott called her. Said he was out of the country for Christmas. Amber taped these calls, even before the police recorded calls. On December 9th, he bought the boat and was with Amber that day. Scott taking it out

in salt water for the first time on.... Scott said they'd be together around January 20th. Scott bought a 84 Mercedes; the prior owner says five thousand dollars, but that Peterson paid thirty-six hundred in one hundred dollar bills. Scott said he had a Florida license and gave his Mom's name as his name. On December 24th, he was brought to the police station and videotaped. 9:30 to 9:45, Scott left, Laci asked him to remove the mop and when he left, Laci was mopping the kitchen, a dark blouse and pants on. At the Marina, people were laughing at him trying to get the boat out of the water. He called police at 3am, cause the police took his gun from his truck. Called again to ask if they were using cadaver dogs at the Park; Interesting. Scott said no problem with a [gunpowder] residue test on him, cause there's a spent cartridge in the semi-automatic weapon. Scott said no power. A fax from New Jersey on December 24th, at 2pm; 11am, New Jersey time? Scott said maybe he read it before fishing or maybe after. At 5:17, he called the Rochas, to tell her Laci was missing, didn't say out walking, or maybe at a neighbor's, or....

Court TV [headline]: **DETECTIVE AL BROCCHINI**
Vinnie Politan: Alot of highlights; McAllister doing the cross exam. The prosecutor went after the alibi; many little problems. In house, Scott said he left, pregnant barefoot wife mopping floor; went to warehouse; did some work; then went fishing, cause too cold to golf.
Nancy Grace, former prosecutor: He already had his bait with him, uh?
Vinnie Politan: He bought two lures, but not opened. Two poles in the boat.
Ronnie, lady psychologist: Scott lying, lying, lying; just shows arrogance. When he called Laci's Mom and the first thing said was Laci missing; didn't even ask if Laci was there.
Michael Griffith, Defense Attorney: Big deal, so he used an inappropriate word; not guilty and send him home.
Nancy Grace, former prosecutor: Missing, is the first word he used. The blackout not only in New York, but reached a California warehouse.
Vinnie Politan: 14:28 [2:28pm] time on the fax. Detective says New Jersey time and Scott had read the fax; 11:28 California time, but Scott said he left home, got the boat, and went fishing. Don't know if the lights out, the detective didn't try to turn on the switch.

Went to the country club, Del Rio. Scott said he'd pick up Amy's gift by 4pm.
Greta: A twenty-five thousand dollar membership fee.
Vinnie Politan: Scott's business doing well. Scott said he called Laci on cell phone; he left message; ask Laci to pick up gift for Amy.
Greta: Probably can't triangulate from the cell call, where Scott was. Odd, he didn't tell Dad he was fishing when Dad called him.
Vinnie Politan: Purchased a Mercedes after he dyed his hair and grew a goatee. He does use Peterson as a last name to buy the car.
Greta: Scott purchased the boat the day that Amber questions him if married and he tells her that day, that they'll be together. A virgin boat voyage on the same day that Laci disappears.
Ronnie, lady psychologist: He's making too many changes in his life to make rational decisions.

Court TV Catherine Crier
Vinnie Politan: The detective said Scott told him no martial problems.
Catherine Crier, former judge: The National Enquirer reports that Scott gave Amber some of Laci's jewelry.
Vinnie Politan: Detective thought Scott hedging a bit on taking a gun residue test.
Catherine Crier, former judge: Isn't this a lake boat and not a salt water one; too small?
[So, if Amber began taping her phone calls with Scott, beginning a day or so after Christmas, we could assume that Amber saw Scott and Laci's picture on TV, and, or, that Amber began taping as soon as Scott told her he was married. That is, if Amber did any taping at all.]
Leslie Synder, former New York Supreme Court Justice: Scott said strange things. So much circumstantial evidence here.
Trent Copeland, Defense Attorney: Circumstantial evidence can equal direct evidence, but not surpass it or be stronger. One hair, now two hairs, raises questions.
Leslie Synder, former New York Supreme Court Justice: Who's the logical person to do it? Are we gonna look at satanic cults.
Catherine Crier, former judge: Scott always has an answer to explain everything; becomes suspicious after a while.
Trent Copeland, Defense Attorney: Fact is, Scott has an answer to this point.

Bob Tanenbaum, former prosecutor: Strand of hair? Mops and a bucket misplaced? Need linkage to the defendant.
Leslie Synder, former New York Supreme Court Justice: When you were a prosecutor, that'd been enough for you.
Catherine Crier, former judge: If he strangles her, there'd be no blood.
Leslie Synder, former New York Supreme Court Justice: How about the self-serving phone call to the cell phone?
Bob Tanenbaum, former prosecutor: Need more linkage to the defendant.
Leslie Synder, former New York Supreme Court Justice: The prosecutors say there's no other reasonable inference to make.
Catherine Crier, former judge: Color his hair, grow a goatee, buy car and head south; it just keeps getting better and better. Stay tuned.

CNN Larry King Live
Johnnie Cochran: Both sides are playing to jurors.
Ted Rowlands, KTVU TV Reporter: A couple of [fishing] lures in the truck; poles in the boat, wet. A cement weight, solid. The previous owner kept the anchor, so Scott made one.
Chris Pixley, Defense Attorney: Scott's lies focus around the affair with Amber and he didn't trust police if they knew that. Police rummaging through his home.
Jim Hammer, San Francisco prosecutor: Glad Johnnie's here, he wrote the book on planted evidence. Scott lied to police; critical.
Jeanine Pirro, prosecutor Westchester County, New York: Affair is relevant. Said yes, then no, to knowing of her disappearance. If he told Amber that he'd be free to be with her in January, he's got alot of explaining to do.
Caller: Know if they put luminal in the house and boat? [To look for blood residue.]
Chris Pixley, Defense Attorney: Believe so, but not testified about yet. Presumably, police don't have blood DNA or they would have arrested earlier.
Johnnie Cochran: The FBI taped Scott and that's not turned over yet [to defense]. Geragos made a motion today.
Jim Hammer, San Francisco prosecutor: Hope there's more evidence. I'd like to take a shot at Johnnie; with another jury, of course. [Jim needs to read the Constitution; ya only get one whack at it.]

Caller: Can the judge order Scott to take a lie detector or a truth serum? [Yea, and they're on the way to your house now to give some to your spouse.]
Jeanine Pirro, prosecutor Westchester County, New York: No.
Johnnie Cochran: The defense could use it to go to the prosecution and say, look, you've got the wrong man here.
Chris Pixley, Defense Attorney: The defense told Scott not to take a polygraph, they're unreliable throughout the country.
Caller: On December 24th, Scott did his own laundry?
Ted Rowlands, KTVU TV Reporter: Both Scott and Laci are clean people, and wouldn't think his wife was missing when he walked through the door, so.
Johnnie Cochran: Amber may have more than we thought. [CNN shows a video of Geragos in front of the courthouse.]
Question: How would you rate the prosecution's case today?
Geragos: If I did that, I'd violate the court order. Let me say this. Today was a very good day.
Larry King: Prosecutors choose not to speak today to the press. We always try to be fair and balanced.
Gloria Allred, Amber Frey's lawyer: I know if she'll testify [Amber].
Larry King: Can't Amber watch the news and know what's going on?
Gloria Allred, Amber Frey's lawyer: She's not interested in the news in this case. [headline]: **January: SCOTT TOLD ABC TV HE TOLD POLICE OF AFFAIR "IMMEDIATELY".**
Gloria Allred, Amber Frey's lawyer: Geragos may attack her and we learned today on what that might be. The detective said that Amber called the tip line; she said that Scott indicated that he lost his wife and this is the first holiday without her; just couple weeks before Laci missing.
Larry King: You were convinced O.J. was guilty before the jury came back.
Gloria Allred, Amber Frey's lawyer: No.
Larry King: Yes you did, I used to hear you on the radio.
Gloria Allred, Amber Frey's lawyer: Civil trial said responsible.
Johnnie Cochran: Test her now, without a jury, memory, etc.
Gloria Allred, Amber Frey's lawyer: Tell Geragos to bring it on.
Jeanine Pirro, prosecutor Westchester County, New York: Don't want to take her apart, if the tapes are in Scott's own words.

Johnnie Cochran: True, but different than when a jury is there. Geragos knows Gloria will have her client ready, not telling her what to say, but ready.
Caller: Odd she was abducted, and found exact same place as fishing?
Johnnie Cochran: Not exact same place.
James Hammer, assistant San Francisco prosecutor: Good for the prosecutor.
Gloria Allred, Amber Frey's lawyer: If he loved her, he'd have told the truth. Lied about affair.
Chris Pixley, Defense Attorney: If Scott is innocent and being questioned on December 24th, what relevance is the affair? Nothing to do with the disappearance and he didn't want police to know of the affair.
Gloria Allred, Amber Frey's lawyer: Why did Scott ask police about the cadaver dogs in the Park.
Ted Rowlands, KTVU TV Reporter: True, according to detective Brocchini, Scott called and asked.
Jeanine Pirro, prosecutor Westchester County, New York: Weeks before, Amber confronts him of marriage, so why not tell the police? He had three cell phones, told police one. Buys boat same day Amber confronts him; planning going on here.
Caller: A theory that Scott mopped up after Laci's water broke?
Ted Rowlands, KTVU TV Reporter: He'd have said that. Nothing in the mop or water. Just location.
Gloria Allred, Amber Frey's lawyer: The bucket; the maid left it on the washer, and mysteriously outside. The defense asks to suppress the bucket; asked the detective if he had permission to take the bucket.
James Hammer, assistant San Francisco prosecutor: They been watching Martha Stewart and became excessive cleaners.
[headline]: **SCOTT PETERSON CHARGED WITH KILLING WIFE LACI, UNBORN SON.** [CNN shows a video of a detective saying]: Scott denied having an affair the day after Laci went missing.
Johnnie Cochran: He was being surveillanced by the FBI, knows he's being followed, so change of appearance means nothing.
Caller: Pliers with hair, from inside house, mop with bucket, pregnant and wanted them outside, maybe something spilled during breakfast.

James Hammer, assistant San Francisco prosecutor: Yea, we need more evidence.
Caller: Objective jury?
Johnnie Cochran: Very difficult, voir dire and questionnaires, get to know them the best you can.

Fox News Channel Greta Van Susteren
Claudia Cowan: Detective said Laci's wallet and keys in a closet and Scott's fishing clothes in the washer. A .22 caliber in the glove box of Scott's truck. A December 30th call, Scott said a widower on December 9th. The defense showed that the detective was out of site of the others while in the Peterson home.
Vinnie Politan, of Court TV: Detective said Scott decided to buy a boat on December 8th, and picked up money for it on December 9th, the same day Amber happened to ask if Scott is married.
Greta: Detective asked Scott to take a residue test, after getting the gun and when the detective went to get the kit, Scott asked if fumes from the boat would produce false positives and the detective said no. Swabs were never tested. Police aren't interested in the gun.
Jayne Weintraub, Defense Attorney: Police may have tested to see if fired; not in evidence at all.
Vinnie Politan, of Court TV: Doesn't help the defense.
Greta: Judge let it in?
Gloria Allred, Amber Frey's lawyer: It may not be legal.
Greta: Why not arrest him?
Jayne Weintraub, Defense Attorney: Illegal to have locked in glove box, without a permit; not an illegal gun.
Greta: What did Scott call police and ask the next day? [headline]: **HIS COP QUESTIONS. LACI'S LAST WALK. CLUES LEFT AT HOME. SEEKING JUSTICE**. [Fox shows Laci's Mom, crying, she hopes the killer hears her voice begging for her life.]
Ted Williams, former D.C. police detective, attorney: If he called, and asked about the cadaver dogs the next day; troubling. If he came home, and wife missing and he takes a shower and eats, something's wrong.
Jayne Weintraub, Defense Attorney: We don't know what went on, we're guessing.
Gloria Allred, Amber Frey's lawyer: Watch the defense try to exclude the bucket. He set that up today; if detective had permission to take it.

Ted Williams, Defense Attorney: The bucket excludes itself.
Ted Rowlands, KTVU TV Reporter: Simple, Scott said he took the bucket out, cause he didn't want the cat tipping it over.
Dr. Michael Baden, Forensic Pathologist: Need evidence on the bucket. Cadaver dogs good at living people also.
Laura Ingle, KFI Radio Reporter: It was a random statement from Scott during a conversation.
Gloria Allred, Amber Frey's lawyer: Scott said 'missing'.
Jayne Weintraub, Defense Attorney: The prosecutor is asking the judge to bind Scott over without showing a murder.
Gloria Allred, Amber Frey's lawyer: Prosecutor wasn't the one grandstanding today. Geragos went to the microphones. [Fox shows a video of Scott saying]: It was a conscious decision by the family, Peterson, Rocha, etc., that I not speak to media, on purpose, to keep media coming back to ask me to talk and therefore keep attention on finding Laci. I wouldn't speak until absolutely necessary. This caused alot of accusations against me. [headline]: **5/5/03: GERAGOS ANNOUNCES DEFENSE OF SCOTT.** [Fox shows Geragos in flashes of different shows, three to four, saying: People in prison with alot less evidence than against Scott, and....]
Greta: Does the warehouse make or break Scott's timeline? Stay tuned. Power Company; no record of outage that day. [headline]: **WAREHOUSE WOES**. [Fox shows the interior photo of warehouse; the one next to Scott's.]
Vinnie Politan, of Court TV: 14:28 fax, Scott said New Jersey time and said he read the fax, couldn't be on way to fish, would have to be when he got back.
Gloria Allred, Amber Frey's lawyer: Scott also said he went back to the warehouse and read e-mails. Didn't want employer to know boat stored there.
Dr. Michael Baden, Forensic Pathologist: Any duct tape at the warehouse, bags, fibers in the boat? Where did pliers come from?
Ted Williams, Defense Attorney: Detective should know of electricity, if off or on, from his investigation. [headline]: **DOG CLUES.**
Greta: What did the Peterson dog do, and does it give any clues as to where Laci may have been killed? Stay tuned. Very large Park. [Fox shows a video of a dirt path.]
Laura Ingle, KFI Radio Reporter: Huge, a full scale search began at daylight.

Greta: This would scare me, it's isolated and no one here.
Laura Ingle, KFI Radio Reporter: A lot of nooks and crannies in there.
Greta: I'd walk around a nice neighborhood if eight and a half months pregnant, rather than go down the incline at the entrance to the Park.
Laura Ingle, KFI Radio Reporter: Cold and muddy that week.
Greta: Maybe she felt secure in that Park cause she knew it. Rumors Scott gave Laci's jewelry to Amber?
Gloria Allred, Amber Frey's lawyer: If so, see if testifies.
Laura Ingle, KFI Radio Reporter: The loaded gun surprising, but don't think it's the cause of death.

[As soon as Greta's show goes off].
Fox News Channel: Very damaging evidence in the Scott Peterson hearing. The second detective to reach the scene, said he found Laci's pocketbook and keys in the closet, Scott's wet clothes in the laundry room and that Scott had told Amber that his wife was already dead, two weeks before Laci's disappearance.

11/7/03

[It would appear that Amber knew, possibly was told, or she suspected from intuition and experience, that Scott was married on or before December 8th. That's the day Amber questioned Scott about being married. Amber has a child and the media reports that she dated a married man before. Even if no one told her Scott was married, she would know enough of the signs to alert her; and she did ask.]

Court TV Poll Question: Will Scott Peterson's defense team be successful in discrediting the police?
Gloria Gomez, KOVR TV Reporter: The defense, McAllister, using a line of questions that the detective may have left an opening to plant evidence. [Remembering of course, that Mr. McAllister also defends police officers who are accused of abuse.]
Diane Dimond: Dye hair, fake passport from brother, six girlfriends.
Man: Now there appears a motive. [headline]: **BROCCHINI: PETERSON SAID HE WAS NOT MARRIED, HE WAS A WIDOWER.** [No, the detective says that Amber says that Scott said this.]

Gloria Allred, Amber Frey's lawyer: Scott told Amber this would be the first holiday without wife, on December 9th. [headline]: **WILL GERAGOS DISCREDIT MODESTO POLICE?**
Gloria Gomez, KOVR TV Reporter: Back in court on Wednesday. May hear secretly recorded calls by Amber next week.

MSNBC [headline]: **TRUTH OR CONSEQUENCES.**
Sumi Das: Live in Modesto at the courthouse, the Modesto detective brings out some untruths Scott Peterson told. Stay tuned.
Chris Jansen: New information coming out of the Laci Peterson case. Boy, it's a blockbuster. Stay tuned. The courtroom is dark today. The defense got more than they asked for yesterday.
Sumi Das: The detective said Scott said Laci mopping the floor when he left to go fishing. Detective found gun in Scott's truck. November 20th began dating, said single, later a widower and could be with her in January.

Fox News Channel **Greta Van Susteren:** Could Scott have been framed? Hair?
Dr. Michael Baden, Forensic Pathologist: Hair could break; lab could tell. Measure when first come in, if mitochondria DNA same, it's same. What's the difference in two hairs or one hair? Question is, did the detective pick up the hair on clothes from homes and get deposited there.
Stan Goldman, Fox News legal editor: If detective, like he said, dropped his keys in the boat and had to go back and get them.
Greta: Left his keys in Scott's truck and later, left his folder in Scott's boat. He didn't even put the pliers in his police report.
Ted Williams, former D.C. police detective, attorney: Keystone Cops mentality. If cops set up, then they'd use more evidence than we have here. [Huh?]
Gloria Allred, Amber Frey's lawyer: Didn't put in his report, but does have photo of pliers in the boat. The defense can test the residue swabs if want.
Ted Williams, Defense Attorney: Gloria is shifting the burden to the defendant.
Jayne Weintraub, Defense Attorney: The prosecutor could have tested the swabs; should have; have separate test to see if the gun was fired, on the gun itself. [headline]: **WAS SCOTT FRAMED?**
Henry Lee, of San Francisco Chronicle: The defense asked the police, see him leave anything in the boat? Opportunity to leave

anything incriminating? Detective says an honest mistake on leaving his keys at the home and his folder at the warehouse. The prosecution tried to link the boat purchase and telling Amber that he's a widower the same day.

Greta: But the defense showed that the deal to buy the boat was a day earlier.

Henry Lee, of San Francisco Chronicle: The day may not be important. Scott used his own name to buy the boat. [headline]: **IN HIS OWN WORDS.** [Fox shows a January interview of Scott saying]: It's easier to look for Laci with Amber out in the open. Told Laci about the affair in early December. It's not right to defend myself on the affair while Laci is missing and take attention away from looking for her. Every tip is important. Left the house about 9:30am, the dog was returned at 10:30am by the neighbor, with the leash on. **THE AMBER AFFAIR.**

Greta: Why did Scott tell Amber he was a widower, just weeks before Laci disappeared?

[Fox shows one of Amber's press announcements.]

Greta: Dog leash?

Dr. Michael Baden, Forensic Pathologist: Could find prints on the strap, soil on leash and tell where been. Police are forced to retire from homicide; age fifty or so. Younger ones learn from own mistakes. Very little planting of evidence by police. [headline]: **THE FREY FACTOR.**

Stan Goldman, Fox News legal editor: The prosecutor should go easy with the Amber motive, many affairs. One; did he kill her? Must prove for murder. Two; plan in advance? Must prove for premeditation. The prosecution doesn't have alot of physical evidence, and alot of stupid behavior by Scott. The defense says the officers didn't do their job.

Gloria Allred, Amber Frey's lawyer: Shouldn't wait for bombshells in the case. Only the beginning of prosecution's case; alot more to come. The detective said that Amber told him that Scott said the first Christmas without his wife, and he and Amber could be together in January. Very compelling; why'd he say that? [headline]: **SCOTT'S INDISCRETIONS.**

Greta: Will Scott's indiscretions help him in court?

[Maybe Scott didn't want to be bothered by Amber during the holidays and his wife was due to have a baby, so maybe January would be a better time to continue the affair, maybe.]

[headline]: **MODESTO MURDER.**

Ted Williams, Defense Attorney: Seven days, a hair, rotten police work. Where's the When, and How?
Greta: Marina, receipt, bodies?
Jayne Weintraub, Defense Attorney: The defense's only concern now to overcome, how do objects travel in the Bay. Just because they end up there, doesn't mean where the bodies started from.
Greta: Unless the defense shows retaliation against Scott; hard to sell. [headlines]:
POLICE HAVE NOT DISCLOSED HOW LACI AND CONNER WERE KILLED. DETECTIVE SAID THEY TOOK PHOTOS OF SCOTT'S BOAT. THE FREY FACTOR. LACI'S REACTION.
Greta: Later, hear what Scott says on how Laci handled the news of his affair with Amber.
[headline]: **IN HIS OWN WORDS.**
Greta: Coming up, hear what Scott says how Laci handled the affair. Stay tuned. [headline]:
SCOTT SPEAKS. Coming up.

[So, the same detective who Scott's friends and parents have said was abusive and intimidating people, is the same detective who's the case lead detective, and the one who was whispering in the Peterson home on December 24th, was alone in the home at times, left his keys in Scott's truck where he found a gun in the glove box while parked at the home, and left his folder in Scott's boat at the warehouse, where he found the pliers, which later was found to have a hair in them, which later changed to two hairs when this same detective visited the evidence room, and the same detective who says that Amber talked to him first about the affair, and the same detective who says Amber told him that Scott told her that he was a widower and could be with Amber in January. Well, it's Wyatt Erupt and Dick Tracy all rolled into one.]
Greta: Exclusive Fox interview. [Fox shows a January interview with Scott saying]: Nothing to do with Laci's disappearance.

<u>11/8/03</u>

Fox News Channel
Rick: FBI had video surveillance equipment planted outside the Peterson home and Geragos says it may help clear Scott.
William Daily, former FBI agent: No evidence that police are trying to cover this up.

[headlines]: **DEPUTY D.A. SAYS THEY'LL PROVIDE TAPES TO DEFENSE.**
DEFENSE: FBI TAPES COULD CLEAR SCOTT PETERSON.
Rick: The D.A. says they don't have the tapes and don't know anything about it.

11/10/03

Court TV **Diane Dimond:** In California, it is illegal to tape a conversation, unless both parties know about it. [Does this include the Amber taped tapes?]

11/11/03

Court TV [headline]: **TOP STORY: ROSIE, LACI, KOBE.**
Gloria Gomez, KOVR TV Reporter: Took dogs to the warehouse and detected her scent and also down the boat ramp within forty-eight hours of her disappearance.
Yale Galanter, attorney: Very damning evidence, if true.
Marshall Hennington, Jury Consultant: Very difficult to pick a jury for him.
Gloria Allred, Amber Frey's lawyer: They're going over her secret calls that Amber recorded and they'll be used in the hearing; getting her prepared to testify.

11/12/03

MSNBC [MSNBC shows an interview with Scott. Listening to Scott Peterson talk in an interview, he is solid, convincing, expressive, and impressive, all with confidence and no arrogance or hiding. Scott says that several days after Laci's disappearance, he and the family, all families, decided that Scott would not talk to media, in order to keep media focused on Laci, because from experience, the families knew that it was up to them to keep the media publicity focused on Laci's disappearance. Scott: But unfortunately, the accusations against me became so numerous and speculative, that I had to come forward and talk to the media. My affair with Amber had nothing, absolutely nothing, to do with Laci's disappearance. Many times the husband or boyfriend is suspected, or not a suspect, but looked at first, and then it's found out they didn't do it.]

Dan Abrams: Will Scott Peterson's own words come back to haunt him, and why is his defense team saying the police planted evidence? Does this sound like a case we all remember, like O.J., and we'll talk to Johnnie Cochran about that.
Johnnie Cochran: Remember, Fuhrman or the other detective, pled guilty to perjury from the O.J. trial, and he was effectively off that case as lead detective by the time the gloves were even found. He leaves, and magically he finds a glove at O.J.'s? That case was entirely different than this one and don't say it doesn't happen; happens all the time.
Mary Fulginiti, Defense Attorney: Go back to DNA tomorrow, then another detective.
Gloria Allred, Amber Frey's lawyer: Let the judge give weight to testimony.
James Hammer, assistant San Francisco prosecutor: Like to have a shot at Johnnie to try the O.J. case again. The lie he told, that wife was dead, is a bombshell.
Johnnie Cochran: If Scott had said, missing or lost, on December 9th, that would be devastating.
Gloria Allred, Amber Frey's lawyer: Detective did say that Amber said that Scott said she was missing and damning for the jury to hear.
[headline]: **AMBER GOES TO CHURCH.**
Mary Fulginiti, Defense Attorney: Amber does want the limelight; two press conferences [announcements] and hires a high caliber media savvy attorney to go on all the talk shows and keep Amber in the public light.
Gloria Allred, Amber Frey's lawyer: ....
James Hammer, assistant San Francisco prosecutor: O.J. should have been a slam dunk. Here, one strand of hair. Boat, fish on December 24th and body shows up. Hard to believe a coincidence.
Johnnie Cochran: We haven't heard Geragos yet. A good shot at reasonable doubt.
James Hammer, assistant San Francisco prosecutor: They're trying to make it O.J. II.
Dan Abrams: I agree; sounds like it.
Gloria Allred, Amber Frey's lawyer: The pliers were in the boat, cause there's a picture of them in boat.

[Nancy Grace has said that the pliers were hidden under the seat of the boat, with the hair wound around down inside of the pliers. Since the pliers aren't in the police report, we can assume that the photo of the pliers wasn't taken during the first visit by the detective. The detective left his folder in the boat, so is his folder in the photo also? Was the photo taken when he went back? The detective is said to have went back the next day to get his folder, probably on his way to the Peterson home to retrieve his keys from Scott's truck after spending the night out in the cold, not being able to drive home or get into his front door.]

Court TV **Beth Karas**: On January 3rd, 2003, surveillance equipment installed by the FBI across from the Peterson home, in a neighbor's home, and recorded video, but the FBI says it's not a party to the case and doesn't have to comply with the defense subpoena. Sometime between January 16th and January 19th, the Peterson home was burglarized and the defense says maybe the camera caught the burglar. Also a neighbor's home burglarized the night of December 23rd or early morning December 24th. Testimony continues today on DNA of a single hair which the prosecution says ties the murder of Laci to Scott Peterson. The defense says the FBI camera is gone, but the equipment is still on the pole across the street from the Peterson home.

CNN **ad:** For the latest on the Scott Peterson preliminary hearing, tune in to Larry King Live, tonight at 9.

Court TV **Amanda Grove:** Testimony centers on a single hair wrapped in pliers found on Peterson's boat.
Beth Karas, of Court TV: Geragos said in court that he subpoenaed tapes from the FBI and the FBI failed to comply. The prosecutor said he's not aware of the tapes. Now it's found the police do have a tape, but the prosecutor says he didn't know. They say the FBI didn't install the equipment to survey, it was the DEA [Drug Enforcement Agency]. Peterson's home burglarized in mid-January and the prosecutor says the surveillance was to keep tabs on Scott and not to survey home.

MSNBC: Coming up, Will Amber testify? **WILL AMBER TESTIFY?** Will Amber testify and will her testimony send Scott Peterson to trial for murder?

[According to Gloria Allred last night on Dan Abrams, when Allred took a hypothetical, put forth by Johnnie Cochran; that if Scott told Amber on December 9th, that he was a widower, that that is mostly irrelevant, but, that if Scott had told Amber on December 9th that Laci was missing or would be missing, then that would be very damning; and Gloria turned immediately and said that detective Brocchini did testify that Amber told him that Scott told Amber on December 9th that his wife was missing or would be. At first Gloria said that Amber said that Scott told her he was a widower and this would be his first Christmas by himself. So how could Scott also tell Amber that Laci was missing, at the same time he said he was a widower?]

MSNBC **Kirby Clements**, former prosecutor: Rich get to buy, hire better lawyers.
Sumi Das: The prosecution has a rebuttal DNA witness on now; says mitochondria DNA accepted, disagrees with the defense's expert testimony. Geragos complains that the prosecutor's expert won't answer his questions asked. Geragos says mitochondria DNA doesn't have enough spectrum of identifiers to ID a person.
Kirby Clements, former prosecutor: I wouldn't want the defense to get a crack at Amber.
Brian Wice, attorney: The defense is happy as kids on Christmas morning, to get to cross exam Amber. Unless Amber says Scott told her he would kill Laci, she has no relevance to probable cause.
Kirby Clements, former prosecutor: With a jury, DNA makes jurors eyes glaze over and they say, just tell me who the DNA says it is.

Court TV **Diane Dimond:** Why the DEA [Federal Drug Enforcement Agency] had Scott Peterson under security surveillance; coming up. Back in court for Scott Peterson as his attorneys examine evidence with a fine tooth comb. The preliminary hearing that Just Doesn't Go Away.
Beth Karas, of Court TV: Expert rebuts the defense on contamination of DNA by the defense. They will finish him [expert] today and maybe the detective back on the stand; a little bobbling; December 24th left his keys and notebook at the warehouse, careless.
Diane Dimond: Well, Colombo left his coat and still did pretty good.

John Kelly, former prosecutor: Even without hair, the case would be bound over; the hearing means nothing.
Diane Dimond: Say the dogs followed the scent all the way to the boat ramp.
Kimberly Guilfole Newsom, Assistant District Attorney, San Francisco: Still could be appealed, if convicted, on the hair DNA. It's the most powerful evidence so far for the prosecution.
John Kelly, former prosecutor: The prosecutor selected the hair to put Laci in the boat and get her out to the Bay.
Diane Dimond: DEA?
Beth Karas: Probably cause the DEA has good equipment and not involved with Scott. January 3rd, 2003 they started, and the Modesto police had, has one hour of the recording.
Diane Dimond: Scott had affairs in airplanes, took trips abroad, Mercedes, motorcycle, boat, joined Country Club; I'm thinking where's the money coming from. Wouldn't Geragos say, like in the O.J. case, drugs involved and Laci was killed that way?
Kimberly Guilfole Newsom, Assistant District Attorney, San Francisco: The prosecution must turn over the tapes. Can't take a risk on the judge sanctioning them, fines, or throw out the case.
Diane Dimond: Coming up, We'll get into the mind of Scott Peterson and tell what he's thinking. Stay tuned.
Diane Dimond: Goes fishing on Christmas Eve, leaves convenient messages on wife's answering machine, eats, showers, and calls mother-in-law and first thing he says is Laci's missing.
Pat Brown, criminal profiler: Scott never mentions his son, always Laci, never the child.
Roger Diamond, Defense Attorney: Need evidence, can't speculate. Look at the Durst case.
Kimberly Guilfole Newsom, Assistant District Attorney, San Francisco: Idea of people when committing homicide, is to get away with it, so won't have alot of evidence. Amber will sink him.
Roger Diamond, Defense Attorney: It's not evidence of guilt, by the way a person acts. It must be guilt beyond a reasonable doubt.
Kimberly Guilfole Newsom, Assistant District Attorney, San Francisco: A jury can consider consciousness of guilt.
Diane Dimond: I don't see alot of evidence here.
John Kelly, former prosecutor: Don't need Amber to testify. If he strangled his wife and wrapped in plastic, there won't be much evidence.

Roger Diamond, Defense Attorney: You say that you don't give the benefit of the doubt to the defendant, well you're wrong. Of course you presume innocence until proven guilty.
John Kelly, former prosecutor: You're right, I misspoke, but....
Diane Dimond: Amber taped calls on her own. You'd think if too cold to golf, it'd be too cold to fish. He called the police officer, at 2am, and said he wish he hadn't let him take his gun; asked it they used cadaver dogs, and said, by the way, will fuel exhaust from the boat skew the gun test results?

[Diane knows that California law requires that both parties know that a tape or recording of the conversation is occurring, or it is illegal to do so, but Diane says nothing of this fact. Wonder why, when Diane has a segment on this show about her being bugged/taped by a private investigator, without her knowledge.]

Fox News Channel **Bill O'Reilly:** Up next, the Scott Peterson scandal, and meet the man who could get him off? [headline]: **WILL HE GET OFF.**
Rita Cosby: Ferrous battle over DNA. All over one piece of hair found in Scott Peterson's boat and people say Laci never in that boat. Scott lied about everything.
Bill O'Reilly: Durst lied about everything and he got off.
Rita Cosby: The prosecutor is not showing his hand. Scott's boat said not to have salt water on it, so he may not even have been in the Bay, so that's another lie there. The financial situation with Scott looking for money, Amber, boat, Country Club. Amber taped secretly and asked, Did you have anything to do with your wife's disappearance, and he said, Yes, well uh, uh, no, but I know who did.

CNN Larry King Live **Larry King:** More drama in Scott Peterson's hearing. Did Amber tape phone calls a week before police?
Ted Rowlands, KTVU TV Reporter: More DNA, the police used the Rocha's, Sharon and son, to tape Scott on the phone, also friends of Scott to call Scott and pump him for information. The detective said he had no knowledge of Amber's taped calls.
Johnnie Cochran: Difficult to get anything from the FBI; judge said to go pound sand. The prosecutor will have to respond.

Nancy Grace, of Court TV, former prosecutor: Feds is like pulling teeth. Surveillance didn't start until January, so nothing to do with Laci's disappearance.
Johnnie Cochran: Don't know yet.
Chris Pixley, Defense Attorney: Peterson's home broken into, police stalling on that; was evidence taken? Ten months after the incident and the defense still doesn't have all the discovery from the prosecutor.
Jeanine Pirro, prosecutor Westchester County, New York: Don't know if it was the FBI. The Supremacy Clause says the feds don't have to cooperate. Was it about Laci or about drugs; he used cash and he's a fertilizer salesman.
Ted Rowlands, KTVU TV Reporter: McAllister said he was aware of the Amber tapes. The detective said, No, Absolutely no knowledge of tapes beforehand.
Johnnie Cochran: Probably illegal to tape. Ask Gloria if her client illegally taped.
Nancy Grace, of Court TV, former prosecutor: One party consent rule.
Johnnie Cochran: No, no, no.
Nancy Grace, former prosecutor: Why are we suspicious of her taping Scott? HELLO, he was married.
Johnnie Cochran: She's taping him; and says something about her character.
Jeanine Pirro, prosecutor Westchester County, New York: What?
Johnnie Cochran: Don't know, we'll have to hear it.
Chris Pixley, Defense Attorney: Means the relation wasn't so strong with Amber; by her anyway. [The ladies laugh. CNN shows a video of Geragos today, outside of the courthouse, saying]: We don't know what the documents say, cause we have to subpoena them. Once we get them, so we can read them. Then we'll know what they say. At some point, somebody's got to get on the stand and explain the equipment. [The surveillance equipment placed outside of the Peterson home.]
Dr. Cyril Wecht, Forensic Pathologist: Mitochondria DNA comes from the Mom. Only seven or eight labs in the U.S. set up for mitochondria DNA. Only fifteen states accept. If done properly, can/has been used. Different mitochondria DNA results from the same hair; depends on where the sequence begins. See if Scott Peterson is held over, before thinking of testifying.

Nancy Grace, former prosecutor: Feds; Geragos will get the tapes, takes a long time. He'll get pictures of Scott's home, sitting there. We know about the neighbor coming over to get Laci's dress; no burglary. Get Scott talking on his cell phone while dumping the trash. GEE, I Wonder Who He Was Talking To.
Johnnie Cochran: Don't agree; it puts the prosecution on the defense.
Chris Pixley, Defense Attorney: He'll get it quickly; Modesto police with the equipment. The prosecutor says he didn't know about it, so what other exculpatory evidence may be out there. You said a drug issue; No, the DEA was involved because they have good equipment.
[headline]: **DEFENSE SUGGESTS AMBER TAPED SCOTT'S CALLS BEFORE LACI VANISHED.** [CNN shows a video of Geragos saying]: The burglary took place after cameras were set up and before the search warrant was issued in this case. Obviously, if it shows what was being carried in and what was being carried out.
Caller: How did she die?
Nancy Grace, former prosecutor: Don't know, mostly cause the head is missing. Conner in tact.
Caller: Psychiatric testing?
Nancy Grace, former prosecutor: Don't know, more interested if he had a polygraph exam.
Caller: On December 23rd the hair salon, the next day coming home from golf, what of the gift?
Nancy Grace, former prosecutor: 2:15pm on December 24th, Scott called Laci and said; Hi beautiful, on the way home from Berkley.
Ted Rowlands, KTVU TV Reporter: The story does fit; fished only a short while, came back and called Laci and said not time to pick up the gift.
Nancy Grace, former prosecutor: What about paint on the boat?
Johnnie Cochran: Good likelihood he'll take the stand.
Jeanine Pirro, prosecutor Westchester County, New York: He'll have to admit all those lies; Don't think so.
Johnnie Cochran: Alot of people said that this fellow Durst, shouldn't testify either, and look what happened.
Chris Pixley, Defense Attorney: Tend to think he won't take the stand, but that's because I don't believe that they have a very strong case. [CNN shows a video of Geragos saying]: They're trying to put my client to death.... [Geragos is cut off, the TV

screen goes black for five seconds, and then a commercial. Pirro then gives us her list of Scott's lies, her list, and as Ted Rowlands said that the message on Laci's machine says Scott didn't have time to pick up the gift for Amy, Pirro says, How?]
Larry King: The Amber story in People's Magazine.
Gloria Allred, Amber Frey's lawyer: She didn't cooperate in the story.
Larry King: She dated a male, married stripper; she knew he was married. Lived with a male stripper.
Gloria Allred, Amber Frey's lawyer: Story's out of context; the defense fears her. The defense didn't present any evidence of private phone tapes by Amber and his statement isn't evidence. Can't comment on, if tapes or not. [Did someone tell Gloria that those tapes would be against the law?]
Nancy Grace, former prosecutor: Amber will be dragged through the mud. I made the decision years ago to never, ever, be a defense attorney and do that kind of stuff. She'll be carved up like a Thanksgiving turkey.
Johnnie Cochran: Her background does matter. Have to test her memory. Defense attorneys defend people and the Constitution, you should try it sometime, Nancy.
Jeanine Pirro, prosecutor Westchester County, New York: Larry, you've been showing these clips of Geragos at the microphone, every time we go to break. The last I heard, there was a gag order. Why is Geragos talking to media?
Chris Pixley, Defense Attorney: He can make reference to matters of public record and not to the weight of the evidence.
Jeanine Pirro, prosecutor Westchester County, New York: Why isn't the prosecutor doing it?
Chris Pixley, Defense Attorney: They have, with leaks.
Ted Rowlands, KTVU TV Reporter: Break-in of the Peterson home; a woman, supposedly broke the glass, went in, stole some things, draped in Laci's wedding dress and laid on their bed. [CNN shows Geragos and Scott in court, as a still picture, with music only, no words.]
Larry King: On December 9th, told wife dead?
Dr. Robi Ludwig, psychotherapist: Not good, says he likes the idea of being a widower; free from marriage to go to extent of murdering wife? Not grieving like one would. He's quite happy, calls girlfriend.
Larry King: What if bi-polar or not, as you say is normal?

Dr. Robi Ludwig, psychotherapist: Suppose possible, but it says something about his character. Fantasize about killing wife, beforehand.
Johnnie Cochran: Character is a two edged sword.
[headline]: **DETECTIVE LAST THURSDAY: SCOTT TOLD AMBER LACI WAS DEAD; THREE WEEKS BEFORE DISAPPEARANCE.**
Nancy Grace, former prosecutor: He told Amber, that he knows who did have something to do with Laci's disappearance.
Jeanine Pirro, prosecutor Westchester County, New York: What if said, How do you defend it?
Johnnie Cochran: Very difficult. Let's see if it exists.
Chris Pixley, Defense Attorney: By the time Scott had this conversation, the investigator of the attorney hired by Scott already suspected Laci was dead.
Nancy Grace, former prosecutor: Less than twenty-four hours, Scott asked about cadaver dogs. Same day as missing occurred, he got a secret mailbox.
Caller: If brunch with Mom, why not Mom worried?
Nancy Grace, of Court TV, former prosecutor: Brunch or dinner, night of December 24th; there was no brunch. Scott says he left at 9:30am with her mopping, while wearing a diamond necklace and earrings.
Caller: Heard Scott involved in drugs?
Nancy Grace, former prosecutor: It would be out there, if true.
Caller: Was Frey given a polygraph exam?
Nancy Grace, former prosecutor: She has and passed, before ever making first public appearance.
Chris Pixley, Defense Attorney: Understand she is right. Why does she have counsel?
Jeanine Pirro, prosecutor Westchester County, New York: Why wouldn't Scott tell police of Amber, so the police could check her out.
Chris Pixley, Defense Attorney: When he first talked to the police, Scott didn't want an affair public. Why not that Laci was passed out somewhere, or Laci was with friends and would return?
Nancy Grace, former prosecutor: From what I see, Scott Peterson is the only choice.
Chris Pixley, Defense Attorney: The prosecution has to prove it, and the physical evidence isn't there. The prosecutor is trying

to ride on the 'why' evidence, and right now, that's Amber Frey. They're not telling us how, or when.

Fox News Channel **Greta Van Susteren:** Exclusive new information today.
Claudia Cowan: How Amber was coached by the police; the detective took her to get the tape recorder and slipped her notes with questions to ask him. The detective said, he kind of remembers, that Scott said he felt sorry for Amber if police suspected her. Can't figure out why three hours of surveillance tape was lost. [The why is obvious; it's the where and who that demands figuring to be applied. Fox shows Geragos asking]: Where are the tapes? Why weren't we told? **WHERE ARE THE TAPES?** The burglary was before the time the second search warrant issued. The burglary was after the camera was put up and before the second search warrant.
Stan Goldman, Fox News legal editor: Police put the camera on pole; never turned over to the defense. Wasn't supposed to be taped, just surveillance to see when he left, but accidentally got three hours taped.
Greta: Neighbors said the box taken down only a couple days ago, after Geragos filed the complaint.
Laura Ingle, KFI Radio Reporter: Alot of boxes out there to transmit, so we wonder which box they put the camera in and what information was gathered.
Gloria Allred, Amber Frey's lawyer: Detective Brocchini testified that he didn't know about the tape. An attempt to vilify prosecution; anything they can.
Greta: Obligation on the prosecutor to turn it over, without stumbling on it?
Stan Goldman, Fox News legal editor: Probably so, yes, and.... [Fox shows Scott coming into court with a suit on. Then shows a video of Scott saying]: Now's the time to come out and speak, to get Laci's picture out there and get someone to find her. Now's the time for me to come out and ask for help. I've learned to do that over the past month.
Greta: Tapes show up on the detective's desk when he returned from vacation.
Ted Williams, former D.C. police detective, attorney: DEA may have been looking at Scott without Modesto. Scott had been to Mexico and back. Left hand doesn't know what the right hand is

doing. Geragos trying to show police overzealous and it happens, as with other cases. [headline]: **EYES ON SCOTT.**

Dr. Michael Baden, Forensic Pathologist: The defense wants to know who went in, who rolled around on the bed.

Jayne Weintraub, Defense Attorney: The prosecution intentionally misled the court with the tapes. Geragos asked for the tapes, and the prosecutor said he didn't have them and said not aware of any testimony before a federal grand jury. The prosecutor has an obligation under *Brady* [U.S. Supreme Court decision] to look.

Gloria Allred, Amber Frey's lawyer: Unfair to attack ethics of the prosecution in this case. It was recorded by accident.

Greta: Difference between stupidity and negligence.

Stan Goldman, Fox News legal editor: Police knew of the tapes, knew they had to turn over and didn't.

Greta: Why is the prosecutor making the defense jump through hoops in this case? Coaching Amber; gotten from the cops?

Dr. Michael Baden, Forensic Pathologist: Mitochondria DNA never bounced from court yet. May be hair from Mom or sister, all kinds of ways it got there.

Laura Ingle, KFI Radio Reporter: Cops coached her, DOJ [Department of Justice] helped with the questions. Scott said in Europe; cops said to encourage this point.

Greta: False reports that Amber taped phone calls before cops?

Gloria Allred, Amber Frey's lawyer: It was just a question by the defense. No evidence yet presented. I didn't hear the detective say Amber was coached, today in court.

Greta: McAllister asked; Do you remember getting questions...

Jayne Weintraub, Defense Attorney: I'd say it's coaching, putting words in her mouth. They are getting her to act as a agent of the state; a scorned woman.

Greta: I don't agree.

Stan Goldman, Fox News legal editor: The defense argument is that they rushed to judgment. [headline]: **COPS COACHING AMBER. COPS TRAILING SCOTT.**

Greta: We've done some digging on detective Brocchini. Stay tuned.

Jayne Weintraub, Defense Attorney: They don't need Amber.

Greta: I bet the prosecution does, no way.

Ted Williams, Defense Attorney: Amber will testify. November 20th, they meet. December 30th, goes to police. December 9th, Scott

said lost his wife, but from November 20th to December 9th, wife doesn't come up?
Greta: Amber investigating, in early December, of the marriage?
Laura Ingle, KFI Radio Reporter: Heard she hired investigators.
Stan Goldman, Fox News legal editor: Will testify.
Gloria Allred, Amber Frey's lawyer: Amber not in Modesto, not testify tomorrow.
Dr. Michael Baden, Forensic Pathologist: All prosecution is working on, is how Scott got rid of the body and not how killed. Not a slam dunk.
Stan Goldman, Fox News legal editor: People don't understand, one-quarter of a million people in California have the same DNA in their hair. Geragos is arguing two million people in California.
Gloria Allred, Amber Frey's lawyer: Body washes up where his boat was.
[headline]: **WHO IS Brocchini?**
Greta: Up next, Who is detective Brocchini? Who is the detective in the Scott Peterson case that's under fire from the defense? Stay tuned.
Claudia Cowan: Eighteen years, eight years with Alameda, ten years in Modesto. A master detective, forty-five years old. First to arrive on December 24th, found gun in the truck, on hand when Amber called the tip line, drove ninety minutes to Fresno to interview Amber. The detective testified that Scott told Amber he could be with her after January 25th, 2003. The defense suggests the detective planted evidence in the pliers. The two hairs; sloppy. Brocchini still on cross exam tomorrow. Some say he's a rouge cop.
Stan Goldman, Fox News legal editor: We'll never know how Laci died.
Laura Ingle, KFI Radio Reporter: Two key neighbors; across the street; blinds. Next door; found dog on December 24th.
Greta: And the housekeeper disputes the neighbor on the blinds.
Stan Goldman, Fox News legal editor: If the prosecutor had more, we thought it'd come from the lead detective, but not yet.
Gloria Allred, Amber Frey's lawyer: How many of us have forgotten our keys? Suggesting he was alone to plant evidence, but defense hasn't presented any evidence to show that, so their case is weak.

11/13/03

Court TV ticker: Scott Peterson is charged with killing his pregnant wife Laci, and their unborn son.

Court TV ticker: Detective testified that Amber agreed to tape Scott Peterson phone calls. Detective testified that he enlisted fellow officers, friends, family members, neighbors, and mistress of Scott Peterson to try and snare Scott Peterson. Scott Peterson is charged with the murder of his pregnant wife Laci, and their unborn son.

MSNBC: Coming up, whether police used her to trap Scott. Stay tuned.
Host: Surveillance testimony?
Jeralyn Merritt, Defense Attorney: The prosecutor didn't disclose it to the defense. He's on trial for his life. State wants to put him to death.
William Sullivan, former federal prosecutor: His behavior wasn't of a grieving husband and I agree with Jeralyn that the tapes must be turned over to the defense.
Jeralyn Merritt, Defense Attorney: Don't think they'll put Amber on. Not relevant to probable cause.
William Sullivan, former federal prosecutor: Not sure she's needed. Doesn't make sense from a strategy viewpoint.

Court TV **Beth Karas**: Detective Brocchini on the stand. Police; on January 5th, 6th, and 9th, followed Scott to Berkley Bay, he'd stay at the Marina, stare, then leave. A lady fixed Scott up with Amber and promised not to tell Amber that Scott was married.

Court TV [headline]: **SHOCKING EVIDENCE IN SCOTT PETERSON HEARING TODAY.**
Diane Dimond: Wait till you hear about Scott Peterson's behavior just days after Laci's disappearance, cops know, cause they tailed him.

[Did police put out the idea that Scott should be down in southern California with the group that's searching for Laci, so Scott would be embarrassed and go out of town with the searchers? The news corps kept asking, Why wasn't Scott out of town with the others looking for Laci? And who said Laci could be found out of town? It was when Scott was gone, that someone broke into the

Peterson home, stole some things and rolled around in his bed. Was it the lady neighbor, or ...? It was shortly after this break-in at the Peterson home, that a second search warrant was issued, served, and many, many, items were removed from the home by police.]

Diane Dimond: Bombshell testimony today. Detective Brocchini; Scott returned to the Bay, two to three times in a rental car and lost the police tail; sometimes making u-turns and quick turns to lose them. Sometimes he did lose them. Each time, he went directly to the Marina and didn't stop anywhere. He even went to the cops tailing him, and asked if they'd like a cup of coffee or a donut at the Marina.
Ernie Riso, private detective: Either the worst liar in history, or a very smart killer.
Diane Dimond: Shows how much pressure Scott was under.
Mickey Sherman, former prosecutor, defense attorney: Depends on whether it was felony driving or misdemeanor driving.
Diane Dimond: Scott's friends? Shawn?
Beth Karas, of Court TV: Shawn, Amber's friend in October, 2002, she was Amber's friend and introduced him to Amber. Shawn asked Scott if he knew anyone available.
Ernie Riso, private detective: If didn't know it was a murder and listen to both sides, there'd be nothing wrong here; talking about dates, etc.
Beth Karas: Shawn confronted Scott on December 8th, and Scott begged her not to tell Amber he was married.
Ernie Riso, private detective: Again, we're talking about what we're gonna hear.
Beth Karas: Dogs alerted at the house, warehouse, boat, and ramp.
Ernie Riso, private detective: I'm waiting for the dogs to testify.
Diane Dimond: Lied to own attorneys?
Mickey Sherman, former prosecutor, defense attorney: They're clients, that's what they do.
Ernie Riso, private detective: You have to lie to your lawyers.
Diane Dimond: Detective bought the recorder from Radio Shack for Amber.
Ernie Riso, private detective: And want her to lie to Scott, yet the police complain Scott is lying to her. Police want both sides to lie, yet get evidence to convict, somehow.
Diane Dimond: Police asked Amber to lie and say, tell Scott she was part of Laci's disappearance?

Beth Karas: Don't think it got to Amber, but police did kick it around some.
Diane Dimond: Geragos says the police surveillance tapes were withheld from the defense on purpose.
Lisa Pinto, former prosecutor: So far, no harm.
Diane Dimond: Police denied their existence.
Lisa Pinto, former prosecutor: Just didn't think it was relevant. I'm more interested in what's going on; hamper full of dirty clothes, but Scott just washes own clothes. That's not how people do clothes.
Trent Copeland, defense attorney: Not a strong case, but it's coming together. Prosecutor misplaces the case on the rug, buckets and mops, and hair. The prosecutor doesn't have the discretion on whether to turn over *Brady* information or not. The prosecutor, earlier, also said not aware of the audio tapes that were found.
Lisa Pinto, former prosecutor: If late on the tapes, it's no harm, no foul, to the defense. Trial hasn't started. What about Geragos floating all these theories. With the prosecutor out of line here, it's okay, it's tit for tat here.
Ernie Riso, private detective: Cults do happen. Cut a baby out of a woman's stomach, after he got her pregnant and the baby lived. It happens.
Lisa Pinto, former prosecutor: The defense own expert says the baby came out in the water.
Ernie Riso, private detective: The baby had tape on his neck.
Diane Dimond: The detective called the Peterson tip line himself.
Beth Karas: Pretended he was a tipster, and said on December 24th, he saw the boat with a big blue blanket in Scott's truck, but the Peterson tip line never called the police tip line to report that.
Diane Dimond: Do you think Scott Peterson can beat this rap?
Trent Copeland, defense attorney: Yes.
Lisa Pinto, former prosecutor: Lies, DNA, cash; he's going down.

MSNBC ticker: Amber Frey's attorney says she will not be called to testify at Scott Peterson's preliminary hearing.

MSNBC **Keith Olbermann:** Scott Peterson's eighth day. The detective says Scott trying to establish an alibi with Amber, feeding her a story he would be in Europe over Christmas. Amber's attorney, Gloria Allred, said Amber will Not be called to testify.

CNN Larry King Live
Ted Rowlands, KTVU TV Reporter: Gloria Allred said the prosecutor said he's not going to utilize Amber. Scott Peterson made trips to the Marina, in early January, peer into the Bay and drive home. Told Amber his wife dead and Amber's friend. Pants, cream colored, same as on December 23rd. Neighbor testified Scott came to her house and ask if seen Laci and told her he'd played golf all day.
Nancy Grace, of Court TV, former prosecutor: Amber at trial. Enough evidence today to bind over. Geragos would go on a fishing expedition with her.
Johnnie Cochran: Prosecutor doesn't have what they thought she has.
Jeanine Pirro, prosecutor Westchester County, New York: Twenty-seven years a judge and prosecutor, and don't need any more testimony. Cream pants, clear she disappeared on December 23rd.
Chris Pixley, Defense Attorney: Agree; keep her off the stand. With Amber, the prosecution's case goes south if she didn't hold up. Prosecutor has no major smoking gun; alot of inference.
Nancy Grace, of Court TV, former prosecutor: Pants; huge, huge. Rocha family on your show, Amy said creamed colored outfit. Police got Amy, took her into the Peterson home, and Amy came out crying. All those who claim they saw her on December 24th are wrong.
Johnnie Cochran: What kind of police wouldn't follow up eye witnesses.
Nancy Grace, former prosecutor: ....
Larry King: Don't interrupt.
Johnnie Cochran: Reported all over, that Scott went fishing and where. He knew he was being followed; proved it by talking to the cops.
Jeanine Pirro, prosecutor Westchester County, New York: If detective Brocchini said he didn't question the eye witnesses, doesn't mean police didn't.
Chris Pixley, Defense Attorney: Pants most compelling evidence so far. Prosecution doesn't have any more that Scott's behavior with Amber Frey and not much physical evidence.
Gloria Allred, Amber Frey's lawyer: She's ready and willing. Won't comment on how she feels about not being called. She's been a victim of Scott Peterson's and may try again.

Larry King: You're speculating on the defense treatment of her, so why not speculate on your client, on how she feels?
Gloria Allred, Amber Frey's lawyer: Prosecution has enough evidence.
Larry King: On December 16th, the Amber tapes began?
Gloria Allred, Amber Frey's lawyer: Won't give the defense a preview of what she has, on TV.
Larry King: People's Magazine says friends say Amber says don't believe or never said Scott is guilty?
Gloria Allred, Amber Frey's lawyer: I've read the article. I won't further invade her privacy, like others have. An unauthorized article, can't prevent it. She doesn't watch the news or read articles about her.
Nancy Grace, former prosecutor: Yes, Gloria is serving Amber well. Think if she wasn't protected. Hope you're listening, Geragos. There's a gag order.
Johnnie Cochran: Remember, the detective testified that they had been giving Amber theories and questions to ask; almost like she was an agent. Called Peterson tip line to see if Peterson reported it. These are why Amber may not have been called to testify.
Jeanine Pirro, prosecutor Westchester County, New York: He said she was missing, not dead, before she went missing. Agent doesn't matter, if Scott called her. If he refused to talk to the police, then police can't use an agent. [headline]: **DETECTIVE POSED AS TIPSTER ON PETERSON HOTLINE.** [CNN shows a video of Geragos saying]: There's another detective for them to call, a couple uniformed officers, the medical examiner, and I guess, a forensic pathologist.

[Why would Scott report a tip that he knows to be a lie, or mistake. He's looking for his wife, not writing a movie script.]
Dr. Robi Ludwig, psychotherapist: If Amber recorded calls as of December 16th, 2002, she's suspicious. Has a history of dating married men, so she was protecting herself, maybe.
Larry King: Geragos said that Scott went to the Marina three times, cause the Modesto Bee reported the police had divers there. I might drive to the Marina, if I thought my wife was there.
Dr. Robi Ludwig, psychotherapist: Could be consciousness of guilt. Different story, depends on who hears it, and who's saying it; depends on how it's interpreted. [headline]: **GERAGOS SAYS SCOTT WENT TO MARINA, AFTER NEWSPAPER REPORTED DIVERS WERE THERE.**

Caller: The man walking the dog on December 24th, why not hypnotize him?
Nancy Grace, of Court TV, former prosecutor: I spoke with him, glasses and a glass eye. Says saw dog at a distance, went home and said, Saw Laci's dog; never said he saw Laci.
Johnnie Cochran: I love Nancy's objectivity.
Larry King: Yea, Right down the middle.
Johnnie Cochran: Police want to exclude everybody and they haven't done it yet.
Caller: Let's hope Nancy's followers don't get selected for the jury. Thank You Chris, for being objective and not convicting everyone.
Chris Pixley, Defense Attorney: Nothing yet has opened my eyes.
Jeanine Pirro, prosecutor Westchester County, New York: Already met the threshold to bind over. You agree, if beige pants, that's a connection to Scott Peterson.
Chris Pixley, Defense Attorney: It's important.
Caller: What did Scott get Laci for Christmas?
Ted Rowlands, KTVU TV Reporter: A wallet.
Caller: To Johnnie Cochran, wasn't it confirmed by another lady walking dog? He never asked the divers if they found anything?
Johnnie Cochran: Don't know of other lady.
Nancy Grace, former prosecutor: Scott went to the Bay, but not to the police dive station. Rented a car to go and then high tail it out of there.
Jeanine Pirro, prosecutor Westchester County, New York: Day bodies found, he'd have been there. Instead he chose to play golf.
Caller: Her purse and keys in the closet at home?
Chris Pixley, Defense Attorney: Evidence jurors can seize on; when she walked the dog, she left the door open, but, if Scott is guilty, then it means alot. The man who saw the dog is a wonderful witness.
Nancy Grace, of Court TV, former prosecutor: Yea, if you're looking for a dog.
Chris Pixley, Defense Attorney: Others saw Laci too, and can't find the other woman who's pregnant that walked her dog.
Nancy Grace, former prosecutor: Scott said she was mopping floor when he left.
Chris Pixley, Defense Attorney: And Scott said Laci said she was gonna walk the dog.

Larry King: Remember, none of this is evidence. We're just talking about what might be.
Nancy Grace, former prosecutor: The preliminary hearing is evidence, what Scott told the detective.
Caller: Golf outing; did he have reservations or someone to play with?
Jeanine Pirro, prosecutor: Don't know.
Caller: Has the prosecutor looked for the other women of Scott's?
Ted Rowlands, KTVU TV Reporter: Other affairs; some say six. Likely interviewed by the police.
Larry King: Benefit the defense?
Johnnie Cochran: Possibly, just because he's a cat, doesn't mean he's a murderer.
Caller: With circumstantial evidence, if the judge throws it out, can he be recharged?
Johnnie Cochran: Immediately, plus everything else.
Caller: With the media hype about Amber, how will it be kept from the jury?
Johnnie Cochran: Wonderful question. Serious voir dire process; open mind?; and honest about it? Very careful, if someone is not honest, the whole system falls apart.
Caller: What about Scott giving away Laci's jewelry?
Chris Pixley, Defense Attorney: Not in evidence, heard that, but the prosecutor makes statements through the press, or the press does it on their own, and it proves not to be true later. This has happened many times in this case so far.

Fox News Channel Greta Van Susteren [headline]: **AMBER WON'T TESTIFY.**
Claudia Cowan: Either Laci died in the clothes she wore on December 23rd, or she wore the same clothes two days in a row. [Fox shows a video of Gloria Allred in front of the microphones, saying: I don't think it's necessary for her to testify. And then Geragos saying: Very good day; looks like they're winding up. Every day's been a Very Good day.]
Gloria Allred, Amber Frey's lawyer: I never like talking about what I discuss with the prosecution.
Greta: What's the point in you being here?
Gloria Allred, Amber Frey's lawyer: I don't want to give a preview to the defense.
Greta: They've got the tapes. You're not tipping off the defense.

Gloria Allred, Amber Frey's lawyer: A good argument for testifying and for not testifying. The defense re-victimized her for doing the right thing.
Stan Goldman, Fox News legal editor: The bind over standard so low in California. The suspicious behavior of Scott, bodies where fishing, the lies; may not be enough to convict, but okay to bind over.
Greta: Then, what's the point.
Stan Goldman, Fox News legal editor: Six months until trial, may find more evidence.
Laura Ingle, KFI Radio Reporter: Detective said how Scott and Amber got together. Scott ask her to hook him up with a friend. It keeps adding layers to his deception.
Gloria Allred, Amber Frey's lawyer: And second time Scott said that he lost his wife. He said lost before she even went missing.
Greta: Yea, well, we could do the whole hour on lies, but.... [So, now we have layers of deception. From which side? Last night, 'lost' was 'missing', and before last night, it was 'I'm a widower'. Lost would mean widower, and widower would mean lost, so missing means, 'someone's imagination'?]
Greta: One hair, or did police plant a second hair? Test for the same hair?
Dr. Michael Baden, Forensic Pathologist: Would have to do that first, cause mitochondria DNA destroys the hair. Amazing that a detective can go to an evidence locker, without signing in, and take the hair out of the evidence seal, and look at. He doesn't know what he's looking at with a magnifying glass.
Greta: And police reports say 'hair', not 'hairs'. The missing person report says, black pants. When found, tan pants.
Bernie Grimm, Defense Attorney: Compelling evidence to the prosecution; the chain of custody on the hair is now shot. Accelerated decomposition of the pants, don't know how to tell the color.
Jayne Weintraub, Defense Attorney: Pregnant, you can change clothes, put on what she wore the night before isn't that unusual.
Greta: Coming up, learn about the frantic phone call Scott made. Amber's friend found out that Scott was married in early December and he begged her not to tell Amber. The detective went to Scott's employer and wanted to check his expense account, and the employer faxed it to the detective, and he said the expense account was okay.

Gloria Allred, Amber Frey's lawyer: No evidence the detective wanted Scott to get fired.
Greta: Surveillance; January 5th, 6th, and 9th.
Laura Ingle, KFI Radio Reporter: There were reports in the Modesto Bee on those days that divers were looking for the body. A long way to drive for five minutes looking in the Bay.
Stan Goldman, Fox News legal editor: Not if you're a grieving husband.
Gloria Allred, Amber Frey's lawyer: He didn't know police were following him. If he did, why didn't he change cars or something. [Huh?]
Bernie Grimm, defense attorney: Problem that he told the neighbor that he went to play golf. Little lies that don't mean anything, but the jury may think he's lying about murder.
Dr. Michael Baden, Forensic Pathologist: No single way for people to grieve, seen hundreds, and all different. [headline]: **STATE'S TACTICS.**
Greta: Why is the prosecution shy about putting Amber on the stand? [Fox shows a video of Scott, saying: Told Laci a couple weeks earlier about Amber.]
Claudia Cowan: Amber, born in Los Angeles in 1975, has a two year old daughter, parents divorced when five, earned a degree in child development. 1978, Hart; married with a pregnant wife. Amber confronted his wife and played the tapes she'd recorded of hubby, with negative comments about his wife. [So, is this why Amber recorded Scott? A scorned woman with a vengeance and a history of experience. If she lied about the other married man having slapped her, for revenge, and played tapes of hubby to his wife, for vengeance, what would she do to Scott and Laci? Is it de ja vu all over again?]
Jayne Weintraub, Defense Attorney: The prosecution had nothing to gain with putting Amber on.
Bernie Grimm, Defense Attorney: There's good prosecutors, who later become great defense attorneys. Both you'll cut me off like you're judges here. [Gloria and Greta].
Gloria Allred, Amber Frey's lawyer: Likely she'll testify at trial. Strong witness. Be an ugly experience for the defense and not her.
Greta: I'd use her for information, and get on her side on the stand.

Jayne Weintraub, Defense Attorney: Good idea, but won't work here, with her. Not on tape, that Amber says Scott said he's a widower; it's hearsay. Geragos' job to show her as not credible.
Gloria Allred, Amber Frey's lawyer: Jayne doesn't have access to the tapes. Detective said that Scott said, he lost his wife.
Dr. Michael Baden, Forensic Pathologist: Cross exam of the medical examiner interesting; different age of Laci and baby idea. No known cause of death. [Dr. Baden goes on to give a scenario of Scott disposing of the body after an accidental death of Laci.]
Stan Goldman, Fox News legal editor: I'd try this case as soon as possible, cause the prosecution isn't ready. [Maybe by the time this case gets to the California Supreme Court on appeal, the prosecutor will have handed over everything that Discovery Laws require it to give to the defendant.]
Laura Ingle, KFI Radio Reporter: Testified that duct tape found around Laci's groin area.
Gloria Allred, Amber Frey's lawyer: Geragos said he'd prove Scott's innocence. Is he gonna put on evidence at this hearing, or what? I Don't Think So.
Stan Goldman, Fox News legal editor: Dogs not able to trace Laci's body to the boat and that may be a problem for the prosecution. Were able to say the dogs traced body from the home to car and then all the way to the Bay; I don't know how they're gonna prove that; but then at the docks.

[Gloria is again trying to snooker us. The detective said that Amber's friend, Shawn, told the detective that she confronted Scott on December 8th, about Scott being married and that Scott asked Shawn not to tell Amber. Obviously, Shawn did tell Amber. The detective testified that Amber told him that she confronted Scott on December 9th about being married, and that Amber says Scott told her that he was a widower. All this from a police detective. Gloria went from 'widower' being told to Amber only, to 'missing' being told to Amber only, to 'lost' being told to Amber and Shawn. Judge Pirro remains on 'missing'.]

MSNBC **Karen Russell**, Defense Attorney: The prosecutor doesn't want to unleash Geragos on Amber.
William Fallon, former prosecutor: Mistake not to put Amber on. Lies, dead wife, widower.

Karen Russell, Defense Attorney: Isn't on tapes; she's practically an agent of the state.
Host: There's talk that Geragos may call her and put her on.
William Fallon, former prosecutor: I would in Massachusetts, let me tell you...

Court TV **Diane Dimond:** I can't believe that police found the pliers and took into evidence, then, when looking at a photo of the pliers, police saw a hair in the pliers?
Bob McNeill, Defense Attorney: One piece of hair is said to be Amber's and one piece to be from the Peterson dog.
Man: Alot of evidence reported by the press isn't showing up; like the blood and vomit in the mop.
Beth Karas, of Court TV: In the report, a single piece of hair, but, when taken out of the evidence bag, says two pieces of hair. Colors not the same; texture not the same.
Bob McNeill, Defense Attorney: Prosecutor said never tested the other piece of hair.
Diane Dimond: December 20th, Scott bought a fishing license for December 24th and December 25th, but when questioned, said it was a snap decision to go fishing.
Bob McNeill, Defense Attorney: Maybe Laci changed her pants; who knows, and if it's the dog's hair, it could get on the pliers and boat, the same way Laci's did, if it's Laci's hair.
Lynn Bikin, attorney: It's cheaper to kill her, than to divorce her. He didn't want to pay child support. Evidence shows he didn't want the baby.

11/14/03

Fox News Channel **Bill O'Reilly:** Judge already said there's enough evidence to bind Peterson over.
Mary Attridge, Defense Attorney: The judge would rule that Amber's testimony not applicable.
Rita Cosby: The defense scenarios; defense team did autopsy, maybe baby born alive, cult, taken hostage and baby born. The detective said that a couple witnesses said they saw two guys with Laci and arguing in the Park and maybe Laci knew them. On redirect, the detective said maybe not arguing with Laci, but talking, discussing something.
Bill O'Reilly: Devil worshipper thing?
Greta: Not brought out in court yet.

Bill O'Reilly: America tired of stuff these guys throw out there with no evidence.
Mary Attridge, Defense Attorney: The prosecution has a really bad case against Scott and trying him with dirt. There's a duty to defend your client.
Bill O'Reilly: Oh! Bull! Once do this, you're a disgrace to the court. You don't lie in a courtroom, to deflect. Don't be condemning to me, Counselor. [Both Mary and Bill talk at same time.] We're not letting lawyers lie in the courtroom. Period. We're gonna keep a watch on It Here.

[Within days of Laci's disappearance, the police have: Scott left home at 9:30am; the dog, muddy with a leash on him, is put into the Peterson yard at 10:30am by a neighbor; a man neighbor, who knows dogs, saw the Peterson dog in the Park with Laci, or a lady who was pregnant, with black pants on; a woman neighbor who saw Laci walking a dog in the neighborhood; a woman neighbor who saw a brown or beige van near the Peterson home that morning; and, two witnesses who say they saw Laci in the Park walking with two guys, and either arguing or discussing something. Yet, the police aren't looking for Laci alive, but are trying to catch, set up, snare, trick, conspire, and lie their way into getting Scott Peterson to either commit suicide or break down and confess to killing his wife and unborn son; from the very moment that the first Modesto Police Department detective came to the Peterson home.]

Fox News Channel Hannity & Colmes
Claudia Cowan: The prosecutor called the hair fiber analyst; the hair consistent with Laci's hair. The defense shifts from cult killers to sloppy police work.
Alan Colmes: Conner born alive?
Claudia Cowan: Would help the defense. Geragos said today, full term. If so, Scott had nothing to do with the death.
Sean Hannity: Detective Brocchini didn't follow up the tip from the neighbor, who saw Laci. With tan pants on when washed up and not black, as Scott said.
Claudia Cowan: Would mean she wore the same pants two days.
Sean Hannity: Don't know of any women who do that.
Debra Opri, Defense Attorney: Lackadaisical not to check out the lead by the police.

Peter Johnson, Fox News legal analyst: Mistake of law and fact.
Debra Opri, Defense Attorney: In what way?
Peter Johnson, Fox News legal analyst: Wait and I'll tell you. Ooh, Ooh. Different accounts when Laci last seen. Not a Christmas gift to the defense.
Debra Opri, Defense Attorney: Early Christmas gift to the defense. Can't just focus on Amber.
Sean Hannity: Her information conflicted with other information police had.
Lisa Bloom, of Court TV, daughter of Gloria Allred, Amber Frey's lawyer: With thousands of tips, can't follow each one; priority.
Sean Hannity: As a defense attorney, Debra, you'd love for this to be a block buster.
Debra Opri, Defense Attorney: It is! [Lisa Bloom tries to over talk Debra.] As a defense attorney, you have to defend.
Sean Hannity: Well, you're not gonna do it here.
[Seems like O'Reilly and Hannity got the same memo.]
Peter Johnson, Fox News legal analyst: The defense has to establish an alibi and an alternate theory of death.
Sean Hannity: Dog walk at 10:25, but lady says the dog alone at 10:18am.
Lisa Bloom, of Court TV, Civil Rights lawyer:
10:18am, the tip has credibility; dog with a dirty leash.
Sean Hannity: Not black pants, as Scott says, but tan as Amy says.
Peter Johnson, Fox News legal analyst: Puts all witnesses in conflict, if killed December 23rd, No, on saw her, and no, on returned the dog to the yard. [Peter asks Debra a question.]
Debra Opri, defense attorney: [Colmes interrupts.]
Alan Colmes: Police let out information all along, that turns out not to be true. Insurance policy, etc.
Debra Opri, Defense Attorney: Do this all the time...[Lisa Bloom interrupts Debra.]
Lisa Bloom, of Court TV, Civil Rights lawyer:
Husband always the first suspect. He rents a car; Why?; Not even his own car, and goes to the Bay and looks out over the water.
Alan Colmes: Pattern of behavior by the police; the detective called people to give the impression Scott was guilty.
Peter Johnson, Fox News legal analyst: Common to go to family and friends, and say something bad and see what response he gets. Maybe they'll agree.

Alan Colmes: But the detective said; to plant seeds of suspicion in the family and friends.
Debra Opri, Defense Attorney: It's important, but take it all together and look at it.
Peter Johnson, Fox News legal analyst: Not supposed to do discovery in a preliminary hearing, but that's what we got here. Not premeditation by Scott, if it was, Amber would be involved.
Lisa Bloom, Civil Rights lawyer: Geragos not proving what he said he would. He's trying to deflect.
Debra Opri, defense attorney: The subpoena of Amber will probably be quashed. He's a sleazy womanizer. [Says Debra, after being overcome, on two shows.]
Sean Hannity: It was premeditation and Amber is important, can't impeach her credibility. Who, what, man would say he's a widower?
Peter Johnson, Fox News legal analyst: He's a serial cheater.
Debra Opri, Defense Attorney: There's a reason for all he said.
Lisa Bloom, Civil Rights lawyer: Why secretly buy a boat? Amber will be a bombshell.
Debra Opri, Defense Attorney: Won't be the straw that breaks the camel's back.
Sean Hannity: It's gotta pass the smell test, Debra.
Lisa Bloom, of Court TV, Civil Rights lawyer, Gloria Allred's daughter: A month before he met Amber, he was out trolling for a mistress.
Peter Johnson, Fox News legal analyst: Who saw him carry her body to the boat?; or dispose of it? [Peter said this in a very quiet voice.]
Everybody: Nobody, Nobody, Nobody, Nobody.
Debra Opri, Defense attorney: The people who saw Laci and Scott looking at the boat, is Very important.

CNN Larry King Live
Nancy Grace, of Court TV, former prosecutor: Laci had a sonogram in September and the baby fine; talked to the doctor.
Caller: Why did Scott say Laci was missing so fast? Why not Laci out on errands?
Ted Rowlands, KTVU TV Reporter: That's from Mrs. Rocha and said she was surprised, but Scott did come home and take care of errands before calling, so maybe not so concerned, at first.
Johnnie Cochran: Affairs won't come in unless relevant.

Nancy Grace, of Court TV, former prosecutor: Geragos tried to say Scott's marriage fine and no problems, and we know better.
Jeanine Pirro, prosecutor Westchester County, New York: Proves we have a man who can pull the wool over everybody's eyes.
Johnnie Cochran: Of murder though?
Chris Pixley, Defense Attorney: Eyewitness testimony is very important here. Not a conspiracy with them; nobody got together to tell a lie here.
Ted Rowlands, KTVU TV Reporter: The Peterson family wants the trial in a hurry. [headline]: **SCOTT PETERSON CHARGED WITH KILLING WIFE, LACI AND UNBORN SON CONNER.**
Dr. Cyril Wecht, Forensic Pathologist: Can't look at two hairs and tell if from same person. If a witness says so, it's absolutely false. [headline]: **DEFENSE QUESTIONS RELIABILITY OF MITOCHONDRIA DNA.**
Larry King: If rust on the pliers, mean not used for a while?
Dr. Cyril Wecht, Forensic Pathologist: Have to ask those experts. Contact between people causes transfer of DNA. [headline]: **JUDGE LEANS TOWARDS ALLOWING MITOCHONDRIA DNA EVIDENCE.**
Caller: Possibly Laci didn't discuss affairs, cause painful?
Chris Pixley, Defense Attorney: Absolutely, it'll be interesting to see how much of her private life she shared with others.
Nancy Grace, of Court TV, former prosecutor: Circumstantial case is real, all relevant. When Laci went missing, families stuck by him and said nothing wrong with the marriage and Laci was close with Mom.
Caller: Why did Amber tape the calls?
Jeanine Pirro, prosecutor Westchester County, New York: She was suspicious. Called him December 9th, and asked him. Don't know if this says... Scott had a license for December 23rd and December 24th, and if so, even before December 23rd he knew, so is it premeditated?
Johnnie Cochran: He had a two day fishing license... Is it relevant? Two hairs, are two different colors; was overlooked? Someone needs to explain it.
Jeanine Pirro, prosecutor: Explain his golfing; check with the golf club, and if their rules say he has to sign up earlier, and he didn't, then he never planned to play golf. [Okay fellows, now you know

how much trouble you can get into, if you say you're gonna go play basketball, but instead play softball.]

Chris Pixley, Defense Attorney: A California resident can only purchase a yearly, or a two day license in California. He bought the license two days within purchasing the boat; on December 20th, okay, during the holidays, I'll go use the boat.

Caller: Amber said she did not know Scott was married, did she call the Peterson home?

Nancy Grace, former prosecutor: ... [headline]: **ALLRED: DEFENSE HAS NOT DECIDED IF IT WILL CALL FREY.**

Johnnie Cochran: Listen how different people on shows interpret facts, think how the jury will feel.

Fox News Channel Greta Van Susteren

Claudia Cowan: The detective didn't follow the witness tip. A woman said she saw Laci walking the dog, and two men yelling at her to shut up her dog. The defense, Geragos, says they might call Amber. The prosecutor will object.

Greta: We timed the walk to the Park.

Gloria Allred, Amber Frey's lawyer: Geragos will decide by Monday if he wants to subpoena Amber. He has to show important to an 'affirmative defense', which he doesn't have.

Greta: He'll get it, cause the prosecutor opened it up with the detective's testimony. Pliers rusty?

Stan Goldman, Fox News legal editor: Yea, could be salt water, but if rusty as suggested, hair would be there a long time; tough road for the prosecution.

Greta: Two hairs; the defense says the second hair planted.

Laura Ingle, KFI Radio Reporter: Expert said he opened the bag; said hair like Laci's.

Greta: One fragment darker than other.

Laura Ingle, KFI Radio Reporter: Yea, he said that too.

Nola Foulston, prosecutor Wichita, Kansas: The defense counsel is doing all the talking. Mistakes by law enforcement; What else do they have to poke holes in.

Jeanine Pirro, prosecutor Westchester County, New York: Not following up the lead; is much to do about nothing. Police prioritize. Geragos spins in the courtroom, with inflammatory questions, knowing they'll be sustained.

Greta: A hospital worker saw; the prosecutor says at 10:45, and the defense says 9:45; men talking to Laci, while she was on a smoke break.
Gloria Allred, Amber Frey's lawyer: Maybe the detective put down the wrong time in report.
Greta: The defense has 9:45 on tape and the prosecutor didn't investigate.
Nola Foulston, prosecutor Wichita, Kansas: Can't chase all leads, some come from thin air. How many golden retrievers in California? Can't go on a wild goose chase.
Jayne Weintraub, Defense Attorney: Independent witnesses and police didn't follow up, and say they didn't focus on Scott right away.
Greta: Detective said the hospital worker's story didn't go in their [police] direction, so not follow up.
Geoffrey Fieger, Defense Attorney: Prosecution's case incredibly weak. No evidence Scott killed his wife. Where's the evidence? At this point, Scott would be acquitted.
Jayne Weintraub, Defense Attorney: They want to execute him, but don't want to follow up on a lead. [headline]: **NEW DOG STORY.**
Greta: How long for the dog to get home from the Park? Stay tuned. [That would seem to depend on which way he took, walk or run, trot, stop and smell anything, or use the bathroom,...]
Nola Foulston, prosecutor Wichita, Kansas: The prosecution doesn't need Amber for the preliminary hearing. Then the defense gives a subpoena.
Stan Goldman, Fox News legal editor: Amber may not be directly linked to an affirmative defense.
Geoffrey Fieger, attorney: If they play the Amber tapes, judge may allow the defense to call her. He'd be crazy to do it, Crazy, Crazy to do it. [headline]: **DOG MYSTERY. SPLITTING HAIRS.**
Greta: Wait'll you hear the breaking news in the courtroom today that had both sides dropping their jaws in disbelief. Stay tuned. Color, cuticle and rust.
Stan Goldman, Fox News legal editor: Judge said he'd let the hair in, but don't know, if 'one in a hundred', or 'consistent with Laci's'.
Gloria Allred, Amber Frey's lawyer: He's a hard working judge. Terrific judicial demeanor.

Jayne Weintraub, Defense Attorney: Pliers and hair are a non-issue, to prove murder of Laci. December 9th, whatever words by Amber, if wife dead, lost, or missing, as the detective says that Amber says, but, not on the tape.
Geoffrey Fieger, Defense Attorney: They're saying the hair in the pliers says murder, but I haven't seen any evidence of murder.
Stan Goldman, Fox News legal editor: No evidence, or they'd have arrested him earlier.
Gloria Allred, Amber Frey's lawyer: They didn't know what she was wearing till the bodies washed up.
Geoffrey Fieger, Defense Attorney: Still not.
Nola Foulston, prosecutor Wichita, Kansas: Oh, my God! You guys sound like a bunch of goofs out there. My God; you need to listen to the prosecutor and stop taking pot shots at the prosecution. You're taking all that slop that the defense is throwing out and using it to talk.
Geoffrey Fieger, Defense Attorney: Where's the proof, or Amy evidence, that Scott killed his wife?
Greta: Is there an eyewitness to back up Scott's story that Laci was walking her dog on the morning of December 24th, and do police have the wrong man? Stay tuned.
Greta: December 23rd? Twenty-three weeks pregnant when examined by the doctor on September 23rd?
Dr. Cyril Wecht, Forensic Pathologist: Pathologist can make determination of fetus age, within couple weeks of age. Read the autopsy report on size of baby, and how the medical examiner characterizes the baby.
Dr. Michael Baden, Forensic Pathologist: If died after Laci, means the child was alive after Laci. Some five pounds, some nine pounds; the same age. My evaluation, Conner in excellent condition, and Laci in very bad condition.
[headline]: **WALK IN THE PARK.**
Greta: Could the dog make it back home within the time the lady says she saw the dog? Stay tuned. [Fox shows a video of where the hospital worker was smoking a cigarette. The area looks out and down over a parking lot, and the Park beyond that, where the lady saw two men in dirty clothes.]
Greta: The men said, Tell your dog to shut the f... up.
Laura Ingle, KFI Radio Reporter: Lady got out of her car, took the dog to the yard, didn't see Laci or Scott; in the 10 o'clock hour.

Greta: Police say the hospital worker; 10:45. The defense says, 9:45. If 10:45, can't put the dog in the yard at 10:18. The walk, twenty minutes from the Park, at a pretty good clip. 10:18, Karen says the dog in the street.
Laura Ingle, KFI Radio Reporter: Parks, grabs the leash, gate was open, saw no one, left dog, closed gate.
Greta: Detective says 10:45am on the tape of the hospital woman. The defense says 9:45am on the tape of the hospital woman, and we found another, easier way for a pregnant lady to enter the Park.
Nola Foulston, prosecutor Wichita, Kansas: Go to the scene, good work, Greta. Police report says 10:45, and dog at 10:18, so it doesn't work. The defense says now, there's a time discrepancy; Incredible.
Geoffrey Fieger, attorney: I'd say it was 9:45, and it was Skeeter and Dirty leading her to her death. Lack of evidence; if at trial, judge shouldn't allow it to go to the jury.
Laura Ingle, KFI Radio Reporter: Others say they saw these two men also.
Greta: Yea, while we were in the Park, two guys accosted our lady camera people, saying horrible things to them.
Gloria Allred, Amber Frey's lawyer: However you cut it, they got her on tape. When did the defense tape her? How much has she heard before that?
Laura Ingle, KFI Radio Reporter: Yea, someone jogging that day, had someone jump out of the bushes at her. Christmas morning, three neighbors called in on suspicious people, but no one called back, and, said they saw Laci and no one called them back.
Gloria Allred, Amber Frey's lawyer: Why aren't we focusing on that shady character called Scott Peterson.
Stan Goldman, Fox News legal editor: Cause you're on TV every day doing that. You don't want to execute someone, cause someone else couldn't tell the difference between black and tan pants.

Fox News Channel **Bill O'Reilly:** Is the lawyer representing Scott Peterson turning the hearing into a sham? Coming up.

11/15/03

Fox News Channel [headline]: **PETERSON EXCLUSIVE.**
Rita Cosby: Shocking news about Scott Peterson's plans to go play golf. Was it that he went fishing on spur of the moment or

was it planned? Stay tuned. [Fox shows a video of Scott in court with a suit and tie.]

Rita Cosby: Case is forensically weak; the experts say. [Fox shows a video of Geragos, saying]: May be end of next week, trial? First, he has to be held over. Trial? Early summer. Allred? Yesterday, said she wouldn't accept service, today, she said she would, you'll have to ask her. Scott? Great. Lost weight? Jail food.

Howard Breur, New York Post reporter: He had a round at 9am, at the Club, didn't show, didn't cancel. A good golfer. Don't know if he never cancelled before. Jury will wonder what he intended to do. Don't know, couple of ways to interpret it. Either side can spin it, but neither side has it yet.

Rita Cosby: Scott told Amber he's a widower the same day he bought the boat, then soon after he got a fishing license for December 23rd and December 24h, but, you have a golf date at the Club.

Howard Breur, New York Post reporter: December 9th, just an unlucky day for Scott. Friends say that Scott told women sometimes that he's married and sometimes widower.

David Wright, of National Enquirer: Scott told real whoppers and now lying to his defense team. The Amber lie, when he hired attorneys, and told them he never called Amber after Lai's disappearance and she had called him, but he called her up to two months later. [headline]: **2/18 POLICE BEGIN SEARCHING PETERSON'S HOME. 3/6 POLICE CONSIDERED THE CASE A HOMICIDE. 4/18 SCOTT ARRESTED.**

Rita Cosby: A sex addict? Something set out by the defense.

David Wright, of National Enquirer: Prosecution says motive is Amber. The defense leaks he's a sex addict. [headline]: **AMBER'S TESTIMONY.**

Rita Cosby: Will Amber have to testify, after the prosecution decides not to call her, and the defense subpoena's her, and what does the defense have on her? Stay tuned. [headline]: **SCOTT'S LEGAL MOVES.** Amber was subpoenaed by the defense. Geragos wanted Amber for himself.

Mickey Sherman, Defense Attorney: Absolutely, she won't be a smoking gun and may be exculpatory.

Lis Wiehl, Fox News legal analyst, former federal prosecutor: Can't help the defense, It's Wrong! It's not his time to put her on. Probable cause and that's it.

Geoffrey Fieger, attorney: Just don't do that as a defense attorney. California law; only calls for affirmative defenses. If the prosecutor puts on Amber tapes; maybe so.
Rita Cosby: Scott had a golf tee time.
Lis Wiehl, Fox News legal analyst, former federal prosecutor: Doesn't help him.
Rita Cosby: Premeditation?
Lis Wiehl: Maybe.
Mickey Sherman, former prosecutor, defense attorney: Not unlikely to book a tee time and do something else.
Geoffrey Fieger, attorney: Peterson a number one member of scum bag club, but no evidence against him. Prosecutor is supposed to eliminate all other possibilities and hasn't.
Rita Cosby: Forensically weak case. [headline]: **DEFENSE STRATEGY: ATTACK DETECTIVE, BABY BORN ALIVE/ CULT THEORY, SEVERAL SUSPICIOUS PEOPLE IN PARK.**
Lis Wiehl, Fox News legal analyst, former federal prosecutor: Beyond reasonable doubt is at trial, not here. [All talk at once, yak, yak, yak.]
Geoffrey Fieger, Defense Attorney: No probable cause at this point!

11/17/03

Court TV **Amy Atkins:** The coroner in the Scott Peterson preliminary hearing.
Vinnie Politan: Both sides refer to 'the baby' and 'Conner'. Expert said the baby nine months old in his opinion. Thirty-three to thirty-eight weeks old from the bones and other expert opinion said could have been born. Decomposition, tidal effects, and animal feeding. Laci, from the waist up, no flesh, no organs. Uterus there. Tape around thc baby's neck and around chest or under arm. Two centimeters of space between the tape and the baby's neck. The judge asked, how did the tape get over the head and around his neck; could the head collapse to allow the tape? A bag found, baby wrapped in a bag? And later come out, with tape around neck? Scott waived his presence for this testimony and not have to sit there and listen to this type of stuff. Mitochondria DNA is considered, but not certain aspects of it. May make hearing shorter, at this point. Judge will consider the mitochondria DNA in his ruling.

Fox News Channel **Claudia Cowan:** Geragos theory; Conner in a plastic bag and thrown in the water. Mitochondria DNA is in, and prosecution can use it for a solid foundation to put Laci in the boat.

Fox News Channel **Jane Skinner:** Judge ruled the hair found in Scott Peterson's boat will come in.

Court TV [Shows a video of Mrs. Rocha at press announcement, saying; hope they hear her voice.]
Vinnie Politan: The medical examiner; the state of each body, Laci at one stage and baby at; Waist up, no flesh on Laci, no extremities.
Nancy Grace, former prosecutor: Cutting marks?
Vinnie Politan: No, no tool marks or bite marks. Tidal effects; washed around.
Nancy Grace, former prosecutor: No evidence of vaginal birth?
Vinnie Politan: No evidence of vaginal birth, no evidence of a C-section. Separated bodies by tidal effects, animal feeding. Baby in the water only a few days.
Nancy Grace, former prosecutor: Medical examiner said he couldn't rule out a vaginal birth.
Michael Cardoza, attorney: Born before death? This shows it's not true.
Nancy Grace, former prosecutor: Doesn't have to be true for the defense to use it. Couldn't rule out a live birth. [headline]:
SCOTT PETERSON IS 31 YEARS OLD.
Nancy Grace, former prosecutor: Why did Scott leave the courtroom?
Lisa Borton?, prosecutor: It's a show. He's so cynical; a ploy.
Nancy Grace, former prosecutor: It saves him from analysis by others on how he reacted.
Vinnie Politan: Everyone speculates on how he reacts.
Nancy Grace, former prosecutor: Oh, he managed to squeeze out one little tear so far, so don't go get your bucket for his tears yet, Vinnie.
[Court TV shows a video of Mrs. Rocha at the press announcement.]
Nancy Grace, former prosecutor: They searched for Laci, but she came home on her own.

Vinnie Politan: Duct tape on Laci. Clear tape on Conner, neck, tightly on neck. Prosecutor says; no injuries to the neck, no sign of strangled. Defense says; impossible for the tape to float onto the neck. The medical examiner says the brain decompressed and the head shrunk to allow the tape on the baby. The defense says they found a plastic bag near Conner's body and the baby in it. Duct tape found in the bag, on Laci, but don't know if it matched.
Nancy Grace, former prosecutor: Duct tape used to put up Laci flyers.
Michael Cardoza, attorney: Fingerprints can survive in water on duct tape. California law; if circumstantial evidence can be interpreted both ways, jury must choose innocent. Geragos is turning each piece of evidence and explaining it innocently.
Nancy Grace, former prosecutor: Reasonable! Killed by a satanic cult, or by her husband.
Michael Cardoza, attorney: Peterson out of the courtroom will get alot of coverage. Judge may say it's an act. His actions depends on who's interpreting it.
Nancy Grace, former prosecutor: All these conflicting theories. Jury will never know he followed his lawyer's advice and not take a polygraph.
Vinnie Politan: The hearing is still going on.

Court TV **James Curtis**, former prosecutor: Is there enough circumstantial evidence to convict Scott Peterson of murder? Gruesome testimony of condition of the bodies. Prosecutors hope the hair will prove Laci was in Scott's boat. [Court TV shows a video of Gloria Allred, saying: Hope the D.A. will object to Amber's testimony and make Geragos prove affirmative defense so to use her.]
Vinnie Politan: Evidence for the defense; testimony of tape around the baby's neck, one and a half times around the neck, with one centimeter of space, tight. Age, state's expert, nine months. Thirty-three weeks to thirty-eight weeks, another state expert.
James Curtis, former prosecutor: Age of fetus?
Candice DeLong, retired FBI: A problem with a sonogram to determine age. Also should see swelling of baby's body, if in the water very long.
Steve Cron, defense attorney: Don't know what Geragos is up to with Amber. Her statement probably sealed, but the judge may say he wants to hear it.

James Hammer, assistant San Francisco prosecutor: O.J. case was rich with DNA evidence compared to this one. I'd like to see a smoking gun, but don't believe there is one. I believe he's guilty, but hard to prove.
Steve Cron, defense attorney: Prosecutor has to be aware of public opinion. Prosecution already said a slam dunk...
James Curtis, former prosecutor: Wait a minute. Scott went out of court during testimony of the medical examiner.
Candice DeLong, retired FBI: Maybe he had a golf date. [Laughter.] Who knows? It was a show! It was a show!
Vinnie Politan: Maybe if mitochondria DNA had been let in earlier, we'd be through with the preliminary.
Alan Peacock, private eye, former Modesto policeman: The lead investigator is a Cowboy, but he's been removed from the lead position and taken apart by the defense attorney. He's a fine officer, detective Brocchini, but gets tunnel vision and goes out of the textbook. Centered on Scott Peterson within hours, searched home, warehouse, all without search warrants. Say he's not a suspect, but has surveillance cameras. Took Scott's gun from the truck, but didn't want Scott to see him take it.
Candice DeLong, retired FBI: Detective confirmed, on a show I was on, detective said want to look around, and Scott said get a search warrant and this put red flags on self.
James Hammer, assistant San Francisco prosecutor: Long couldn't be on this jury. [Laughter.] To say they need a search warrant makes it suspicious. Geragos has moved to Idaho. Trying the O.J. defense. Detective said woman who saw Laci walking, didn't fit his theory.
Steve Cron, Defense Attorney: Took gun shot residue from Scott's hand and police misplaced them; Sloppy. Can't trust the case with missteps and mistakes.
Vinnie Politan: Duct tape on Laci, kaki pants, tape on baby and plastic bag with duct tape in it. Prosecutor says just debris washed ashore. Defense says maybe the baby in the bag, bag comes open, and tape goes onto baby's neck.
Alan Peacock, private eye, former Modesto policeman: Brocchini, Grogan, all did a good job, but they have a history of quick to judgment. Twenty percent of husbands don't kill wife. If center too soon on a suspect, you lose the forest for the trees.

MSNBC [headline]: **DNA MYSTERY? Keith Olbermann:** Prosecutors in Mrs. Peterson's murder mystery won a single strand victory today. Judge ruled hair is admissible and can use it at trial. Mitochondria DNA is a round about way to identify the hair as belonging to Laci, through her family. Prosecutors hope to use the hair to link Laci to Scott Peterson's boat.

CNN Larry King Live [headline]: **JUDGE ALLOWS MITOCHONDRIA DNA TEST OF HAIR FROM SCOTT'S BOAT.**

Ted Rowlands, KTVU TV Reporter: The forensic pathologist's autopsy; decomposition of Laci, severe. Conner, in tact; about two days in the water. On cross exam, the forensic pathologist admits it could be a bag that preserved the baby. The tape on the neck, pulled tight, only allowed one centimeter of space. Even the judge asked, How could the tape come over the baby's head? The pathologist said the head shrinks. The detective was questioned on the chain of custody, not much on the concrete blocks.

Nancy Grace, of Court TV, former prosecutor: The defense grabbing at straws. Cervix in tact and no birth. Impossible for baby to be in a bag; scientifically impossible.

Johnnie Cochran: Two men, seen with Laci. Baby, maybe born, don't know. Mitochondria DNA, the defense will argue, not reliable.

Jeanine Pirro, prosecutor Westchester County, New York: No vaginal delivery, the cervix was in tact. If Conner had air or water in lungs, then it's a sign born alive. [What if born deceased?]

Chris Pixley, Defense Attorney: Not a defense team's job to confuse everyone; It's to rebut the prosecution's theory. The prosecutor is grabbing at straws with the theory of the tape on the baby's neck. The pathologist said can't rule out born alive. The pathologist says, thirty-three to thirty-eight weeks, and is a week older than on December 25th, but yet saying he was protected by the womb until a couple of days before being washed up. They can't be both ways. They have to go one way or the other.

Johnnie Cochran: The defense has two of the greatest experts in the world, as to all of these matters. The doctor, today, said can't say wasn't born alive, and the defense has witnesses that saw her alive.

Nancy Grace, of Court TV, former prosecutor: No doctor report of over thirty-two weeks, and remember, fetus grows twice as fast after thirty-two weeks. Don't be fooled by a sonogram.
Jeanine Pirro, prosecutor Westchester County, New York: Pathologist should know if born dead or alive. Maybe the prosecution should use another pathologist, and not this one.
Chris Pixley, Defense Attorney: Geragos will decide tomorrow if he'll put on witnesses. Mitochondria DNA took majority of the time.
Johnnie Cochran: Scott will be bound over. Once DNA allowed, he'll be bound over.
Nancy Grace, former prosecutor: Lose/lose for Geragos if he puts anything up. The BS meter is off the chart here tonight. The woman either had to have a C-section or birth, she had neither.
Johnnie Cochran: Nancy ain't testifying. The pathologist expert said he can't say if born alive or not.
Jeanine Pirro, prosecutor: Johnnie's right, he said he couldn't tell if born alive or not.
Chris Pixley, Defense Attorney: Nancy's effective; the witness testifies, and Nancy says it's not true.
Nancy Grace, former prosecutor: Then tell me how it got out, if no C-section and no vaginal delivery. Then only thing left is from tissue breakdown and baby is expelled underwater.
Dr. Cyril Wecht, Forensic Pathologist: With no cause, no mechanism, no time, no place, of death, so it's almost impossible to determine the manner of death; generically speaking. I get a kick out of an attorney taking a possibility and a non-probability and making it so. It's a difficult case. The forensic pathologist was there, he's an excellent doctor. They have past sonograms; science, as opposed to what's being argued by some on the panel.
Caller: Why doesn't Scott look at the cameras in court, is it because he's guilty?
Johnnie Cochran: Well, on trial for life, lost wife and baby.
Nancy Grace, former prosecutor: Just a show. Don't know why he left the courtroom today. A no win situation.
Caller: Scott request viewing his child?
Jeanine Pirro, prosecutor: He went and played golf that day; not sure if he asked. [headline]: **SCOTT PETERSON CHARGED WITH MURDER OF PREGNANT WIFE LACI, AND UNBORN SON, CONNER.**

Ted Rowlands, KTVU TV Reporter: Everyone expects the hearing to be over tomorrow.
Dr. Robi Ludwig, psychotherapist: Agree; Scott choreographed his out of courtroom. He'd be talked about. He's not a great actor. It keeps his character in tact. Needs to rehabilitate his image.
[headline]: **ONE HAIR FOUND ON BOAT, BECAME TWO HAIRS WITH POLICE.**
Dr. Robi Ludwig, psychotherapist: Amber is the star witness, show how she was a victim and she just happened to survive to tell about it.
Caller: Any other woman come forward?
Chris Pixley, Defense Attorney: Haven't seen any at the preliminary. The defense doesn't want to trash their own client. Depends on how the prosecutor uses Amber for motive.
Nancy Grace, former prosecutor: Six other women and a stripper. Maybe he killed her over many women, a Lifestyle; move to Europe.
Johnnie Cochran: Still have divorce, don't we.
Caller: The weight of Conner?
Nancy Grace, former prosecutor: It's in the autopsy report, but didn't hear it in court.
[headline]: **PATHOLOGIST: BABY'S EXACT AGE OBSCURED BY LONG EMERSON.**
Caller: Was the pathologist asked if there was air and water in the lungs? Question for anyone who's actually read the court transcripts.
Johnnie Cochran: Don't think so.
Jeanine Pirro, prosecutor: Didn't see it.
Chris Pixley, Defense Attorney: The prosecutor didn't ask, cause they don't like the answer. Still no evidence of a murder in the home. Just a hair they're saying puts her in the boat.
Nancy Grace, former prosecutor: Didn't see the question. Conner's insides had begun liquefying. May not be able to tell. Defense didn't ask either. So Hold On, Don't Call The Kettle Black. Make of it what you want.
Gloria Allred, Amber Frey's lawyer: Geragos told me he would decide on whether to call Amber, after the prosecutor closes his case. Still have to show an affirmative defense to call her. The prosecution has enough evidence without Amber testifying. No thoughts on the People's Magazine story, but she wasn't portrayed right. She'll just have to suffer through all the unauthorized stuff.

Caller: A man came forward, in prison, heard Laci was kidnapped, and met Scott to kidnap Laci, but instead Scott asked him to murder Laci?
Nancy Grace, former prosecutor: Insurance, kidnap, to murder; if it exists, we'd hear more.
Caller: Detective testimony tipping hand on Amber?
Johnnie Cochran: Be interesting to see how it goes.
Caller: Scott and Laci, he was a gentleman and never cheated, now an affair? Yet parents say they never argued? How?
Ted Rowlands, KTVU TV Reporter: Amber saw Scott on TV and called the detective that was on the case, so that's how the affair news got started. Nancy said, pathologist said no evidence of a C-section, but the pathologist said the flesh was gone, so there wouldn't be any evidence.
Nancy Grace, former prosecutor: Uterus in tact.
Ted Rowlands, KTVU TV Reporter: Pathologist said part of the uterus missing.
Caller: What if the family runs out with the jury there? Laci's Mom?
Chris Pixley, Defense Attorney: Don't expect it to happen at trial. [CNN shows a video of Scott wiping tears away with a tissue, in court, in a suit.]
Johnnie Cochran: Bodies washed up near where he said fishing. If on December 9th, said to Amber that wife missing or lost, that would be a major problem.

Fox News Channel **Greta Van Susteren:** Exclusive photos from inside the Peterson home.
Claudia Cowan: Dr. Lee Peterson, no relation, no cause of death. Hair will be allowed into evidence. Test okay to show a likely match. Computer expert; the day before bought the boat, downloaded information on the Bay and alot of other fishing spots.
Greta: Police not investigate the tip of the hospital worker. She said the woman was wearing a white blouse. At 9:53am; forty-three degrees in California.
Laura Ingle, KFI Radio Reporter: It would be chilly. Imagine pregnant woman with a jacket or sweater. Heard of Scott making anchors, so the jury will be interested in how many he made and how many found.
Greta: Any evidence?
Gloria Allred, Amber Frey's lawyer: Don't think so.

James Hammer, assistant San Francisco prosecutor: Not follow leads, but if dead on December 23rd, then December 24th not important. Lady had already seen Laci on TV at that point. Why have an anchor factory in the warehouse. Four or five places with outlines on floor of where made anchors.
Bernie Grimm, Defense Attorney: Anchors could be damning, but the judge can let in that he had concrete in his warehouse, to show he made anchors, to show he used them to weigh the body down, to show he killed her?
James Hammer, assistant San Francisco prosecutor: Don't have to show where, or how killed, but she was murdered. Very damning case against Scott.
Gloria Allred, Amber Frey's lawyer: Look at all the evidence, as accumulative effect.
Greta: That's exactly what a circumstantial case is, but just cause can't find anchors, that doesn't make a case. [Fox shows a video of Scott talking about the things that he and Laci had done to prepare for the baby; the room, bed, toys, little clothes.]
Fox ticker: Judge allows mitochondria DNA test of hair found in Scott Peterson's boat, even though it cannot show a definitive match.
Dr. Michael Baden, Forensic Pathologist: No way to tell if Conner had air in his lungs, decomposition. I agree with doctor that the baby in the uterus womb until couple days of being washed up. Defense will raise baby's age, if lived past December 24th, Scott couldn't have done it. Too much overlap and imprecise tools to determine age.
Greta: Some fractured ribs on Laci.
Dr. Michael Baden, Forensic Pathologist: Water, debris, fish, boats. Durst case had alot more evidence than here. Where'd she die? Jurisdiction issue? Legal issue? And if prosecution can't prove death occurred in his county?
Laura Ingle, KFI Radio Reporter: Wonder if mop was left at the side of one door by the maid and Laci asked Scott to bring it in, and set back out on the other side of the door. [Fox shows a photo of a door, then the kitchen floor.]
Greta: Hard to clean up blood?
James Hammer, assistant San Francisco prosecutor: Could be a soft kill; no blood.
Gloria Allred, Amber Frey's lawyer: Didn't have head or neck either, so we wouldn't know.

James Hammer, assistant San Francisco prosecutor: Jurisdiction where found. No evidence where occurred.
Laura Ingle, KFI Radio Reporter: The detective said he looked at all the rooms, saw Laci's pocketbook hanging in the closet.
Greta: Could a scrunched up rug be trouble and how about those rags and mop? Stay tuned.
Ted Williams, former D.C. police detective, attorney: Rug, that's a narrow door.
Dr. Michael Baden, Forensic Pathologist: Blood in bathtub is easily gotten rid of; just keep....
Greta: No sign of cutting.
Dr. Michael Baden, Forensic Pathologist: Separate the joints. Nobody noticed a body in the boat, cause it was in separate bags.
James Hammer, assistant San Francisco prosecutor: Gonna be hard to prove that. Maybe he loaded the body in the truck, went to the warehouse, and loaded in the boat at the dock.
Bernie Grimm, Defense Attorney: Closed blinds is a wash.
Gloria Allred, Amber Frey's lawyer: Neighbor testified blinds always up in the morning. Maid only there a couple of times.
Greta: Yea, but she was there a couple of days before.
Laura Ingle, KFI Radio Reporter: Scott said he put his clothes in the washer, before taking a shower. Scott was seen carrying a large wrapped object from the house and he said in an interview it was lawn umbrellas.
Greta: Maid said she put the mop where the washer is and the bucket with the rags on top of the washer. The detective said Scott told him he washed clothes, maybe he moved the bucket. Show you where cops found Laci's purse. Stay tuned.
James Hammer, assistant San Francisco prosecutor: If he lied about using bleach in the kitchen, the first detective said he didn't smell bleach, so I'm not sure where that came from. [Fox shows a photo of the bathroom on the side of the kitchen.]
Laura Ingle, KFI Radio Reporter: Bathroom is close to the kitchen, didn't realize that. If the maid cleaned that closely, I don't know.
Gloria Allred, Amber Frey's lawyer: Issue, if to believe; Laci pregnant, would be cleaning, tired, and just after the maid there.
Greta: They've got a dog, kitchen is so small.
Gloria Allred, Amber Frey's lawyer: He said black pants and found in tan pants.
Bernie Grimm, Defense Attorney: They have a dog and cat.

Ted Williams, former D.C. police detective, attorney: Laci could have used the mop. Washer is problem, wife missing and he washes clothes?
Dr. Michael Baden, Forensic Pathologist: Mop could have been cleaned, but may be blood on the handle, if there.
Laura Ingle, KFI Radio Reporter: You're right, kitchen floor is so small, so she could have been mopping.
Greta: We'll show you where police found Laci's wallet. Stay tuned.
Claudia Cowan: Police served the first warrant on Scott December 26th, just two days after Laci was reported missing. [Claudia goes through a time line of events.] A cut or tear on Conner's body; the leaks were confirmed by the autopsy.
Greta: Next, where police found Laci's wallet.
[Fox shows a fellow at the Bay shore saying: With the body weighted down and shifting currents, it pulls on the joints and dislodges them. Fox then shows a photo of where police say they found the purse.]
Laura Ingle, KFI Radio Reporter: Police said, hanging there in the closet, with keys.
James Hammer, assistant San Francisco prosecutor: Seems Laci was killed in this house, but which theory will the prosecutor use?
Dr. Michael Baden, Forensic Pathologist: Some convicted with less evidence and some found not guilty with more evidence.
Gloria Allred, Amber Frey's lawyer: Conner information, not born by vaginal or C-section; most important evidence.

11/18/03

CNN [headline]: **JUDGE IN MODESTO ALLOWS DNA TEST RESULTS IN AS EVIDENCE.**
Lady: The prosecution won a victory in the Scott Peterson hearing with DNA test results allowed in as evidence.
Jeffrey Toobin, CNN legal analyst, former federal prosecutor: Hair not that incriminating, since they were married. One issue, was whether the fetus was murdered separately? The prosecutor shot that down, so that took all that away. The prosecutor said they died together.
Bill Hemmer: Okay, so it'll be winding down soon.

AFTER SCOTT'S PRELIMINARY HEARING

Court TV **James Curtis**, former prosecutor: Scott Peterson's hearing has come to a close. Will he stand trial for the murder of his wife and baby? Stay tuned. [Court TV shows Geragos saying: The standard in California is; Is the defendant breathing?]
James Curtis, former prosecutor: Scott bound over shortly after the prosecution closed its case. A December 3rd hearing.
Beth Karas, of Court TV: Judge immediately ruled at close of the evidence. Not much asked about Amber by the prosecutor, so probably couldn't call her. The case is very light in forensic evidence. Mostly Scott's behavior.
James Curtis, former prosecutor: The defense chose not to make a stand.
Gary Casimir, former prosecutor, Attorney: No strong case or evidence by the state. The insurance turns out to be purchased two years before.
Lou Palumbo, former police detective: I agree with the last guest, circumstantial evidence.
Gary Casimir, former prosecutor, attorney: No smoking gun here.
James Curtis, former prosecutor: What about Amber Frey?
Gloria Allred, Amber Frey's lawyer: Happy Amber not called.
[headline]: **INVESTIGATOR TESTIFIED: 240 CALLS MADE BETWEEN SCOTT AND AMBER.**
Beth Karas: Police evacuated the lot, caller said a bomb. The prosecutor built a premeditated timeline; Scott introduced to Amber in late..., then Amber found out he's married.
Ted Williams, Defense Attorney: The strand of hair; can't prove. Bleach; ain't none. Weights; bought boat, without an anchor. Scott could walk out of court.
Gary Casimir, former prosecutor, attorney: Case is weak. The boat never made it to the San Francisco Bay.
James Curtis, former prosecutor: John, help me out with all the defense people.
John Kelly, former prosecutor: These guys can buy me dinner when Scott's convicted. Opportunity; last seen with wife, fishing where wife washes up.
James Curtis, former prosecutor: Christmas Eve and wife pregnant and you go fishing? Come On!
John Kelly, former prosecutor: Motive! Shakel was convicted. Just put him at the scene.

Gary Casimir, former prosecutor, attorney: Cause the public thought he was guilty. In court it wasn't proven.
Lou Palumbo, former police detective: Different verdict, if in different location. Instinct and institution, and depends on how you think.
[headline]: **SCOTT MADE CALLS 80 MILES AWAY FROM BERKLEY AFTER 2PM.**
Gary Casimir, former prosecutor, attorney: What's gonna kill Scott is...
James Curtis, former prosecutor: Sorry, gotta go.

Fox News Channel ad: As Scott Peterson goes to trial, has the media made it so he will go free? Watch Greta Van Susteren tonight.

Fox News Channel **Bill O'Reilly:** Scott Peterson will stand trial for Two murders and he Could get the death penalty. Stay tuned. Scott Peterson faces execution if he's found guilty.
Surprised Geragos no witnesses.
Greta Van Susteren: The defense usually doesn't call witnesses at the preliminary hearing; just learn the prosecution's case as much as possible to determine strategy.
Bill O'Reilly: We heard Geragos say he'll do this, that, etcetera.
Greta: Geragos was at dinner and said, maybe call Amber and the media there seized on it.
Bill O'Reilly: Geragos uses the media.
Greta: So did the prosecutor.
Bill O'Reilly: Yea, they all do it.
Greta: No cause of death, etcetera. Strongest, fishing where the bodies found. A December 3rd hearing, Geragos will push for a speedy trial as the prosecution doesn't have much; no weapon, no scene. Without alot of cards in his pocket, the prosecutor is in trouble. A call to Sharon Rocha, and said Laci missing. There's an explanation for each piece the prosecutor says.
Bill O'Reilly: I'm waiting for satan to show up at the trial.

MSNBC **Dan Abrams:** Scott Peterson will stand trial for the murders of his wife, Laci and their unborn child. Why did the judge give his ruling so quickly? As soon as the prosecution rested its case? In the transcripts of Scott's phone calls with Amber, well, let's just say the word 'sweetie' comes up alot.

Fox News Channel Hannity and Colmes
Sean Hannity: [Shows photos that Sean says are of the inside of the Peterson home.]
Mark Fuhrman, former O.J. cop: The prosecutor asked questions of the mop, but may be forensic evidence there, we don't know. Scott probably said, wife never in the boat, yet they find hair in the pliers and they have something of Laci's where she's not supposed to be.
Jeanine Pirro, prosecutor Westchester County, New York: The medical examiner says homicide. The hair connected to Laci; other owner didn't leave the pliers on the boat. It shows she was on the boat. With the shades, the maid put the blinds up.
Jeralyn Merritt, Defense Attorney: Hair in pliers, well, they're married. Could have gotten there a million ways.
Alan Colmes: Why be surprised about this? They're married.
Mark Fuhrman, former O.J. cop: Okay, everyone go out to your toolbox and get your needle nose pliers and see how many have your wife's hairs in it. [Everyone laughs.] He engaged with police, but at some point he stopped and that caused suspicion.
Jeanine Pirro, prosecutor Westchester County, New York: Circumstantial evidence is subject to interpretation.
Sean Hannity: Alot of fishermen don't know what they're fishing for.
Jeanine Pirro, prosecutor: You gotta know your Pole, Line, Bait, where you're going.
Jeralyn Merritt, Defense Attorney: The prosecutor wants premeditation because of Amber, but also believe he wanted to and planned to kill his unborn child. He'd get a divorce first.
Jeanine Pirro, prosecutor: Husbands killing pregnant wife isn't unusual.
Mark Fuhrman, former O.J. cop: Parents kill their children and there's nothing in their history either.
Jeanine Pirro, prosecutor: Homicide just doesn't make sense anytime.

MSNBC **Dan Abrams:** The defense says he lied to the police; didn't want the affair known.
Roy Black, Defense Attorney: Police certainty coached Amber, tried to get her to get Scott to confess.

Dan Abrams: [Dan reads from a transcript of phone calls, with Scott saying: If you think I had anything to do with my wife's disappearance, that's silly. And Amber saying:...]
Jayne Weintraub, Defense Attorney: Not one shred of evidence to show premeditation. The tapes will help Scott.
Paul Pfingst, former prosecutor: Anyone thinks these tapes will help Scott is insane.
Roy Black, Defense Attorney: The prosecutor still needs a confession or some fact to tie him to murder.
Paul Pfingst, former prosecutor: I agree, but the tapes will set the entire tone with the jury.
Jayne Weintraub, Defense Attorney: Take care of that in voir dire of the jury and let them know there's an affair.
Roy Black, Defense Attorney: Yea, him sitting there while holding hands with Amber and crying over his missing wife is damaging.

CNN Larry King Live
Ted Rowlands, KTVU TV Reporter: Enough evidence to hold over. A December 3rd arraignment. Two hundred and forty-one times, in three months, the detective said Scott and Amber calls. Scott had brother's driver's license and Scott's own license; the first time we've heard this, and Scott said he had brother's license so he could get a discount at the Club for the family.
Nancy Grace, of Court TV, former prosecutor: Expect a change of venue; probably bus the jurors in.
James Hammer, assistant San Francisco prosecutor: Evidence yesterday of the weight factory he had is a bombshell. Good thing Johnnie's in retirement, cause this'd be a tough case to defend.
Nancy Grace, of Court TV, former prosecutor: Where's those concrete blocks, six, he made. And these transcripts of phone calls are ridiculous. They're set up.
Dr. Robi Ludwig, psychotherapist: Phone calls damning, yes, lying to another woman and his wife. [headline]: **DETAILS OF SCOTT TELLING AMBER LACI DIED BEFORE LACI DISAPPEARED. HEARING ENDED TODAY.**
Gloria Allred, Amber Frey's lawyer: Never thought the defense would call her. The prosecution had enough evidence. Calls after Laci's disappearance, people will be curious. December 9th, Scott said he lost his wife.
Ted Rowlands, KTVU TV Reporter: Five separate weights made on a trailer in the warehouse, but, Scott said one weight, and he

moved it around to dry. And a look at the photos, it doesn't show five separate marks, just concrete around the trailer.
James Hammer, assistant San Francisco prosecutor: Why'd he lie about the concrete and say the pool people using it?
Johnnie Cochran: The defense forensic experts very important. The prosecution expert couldn't say 'not born'. Has to be beyond a reasonable doubt.
Nancy Grace, former prosecutor: If anything saves Scott Peterson's skin, it'll be Dr. Henry Lee. Looked up Bay currents, went and bought the boat, and then went on his maiden voyage in the Bay. And the detective said, Five Distinct, Five Distinct, concrete patterns on that trailer.

Fox News Channel **Greta Van Susteren:** New information on what Scott told Amber in those tapes when Laci went missing. Stay tuned. New revelations surface about his calls to Amber. How many were there and what did he say? Stay tuned. [Fox shows a video of Scott saying that he told Laci of the affair a couple of weeks before disappearance, and told Amber of Laci's disappearance a couple to three days after Laci disappeared. Every time this video is shown, no matter the news corp, Scott is still saying the same thing. Headline]:
AMBER BOMBSHELL.
Greta: What did Scott tell Amber on December ?, and is it a bombshell? Up next.
Claudia Cowan: Big news, January 6th Scott had something to hide. On a cell phone, he told Amber that Laci was alive and in Modesto. We listened to the secret call of Amber's; Scott comforting her of his being married. Another, Scott said, She's alive Amber. Amber: Where? Scott: In Modesto. Amber: Visitation with the new child?
Laura Ingle, KFI Radio Reporter: Looked like the same photos you had last night on the show. One in the warehouse showing where the anchors were made, very distinct markings. Flatbed trailer, on piece of wood, just round deposits of cement. A bucket nearby, looks like he used it to make those concrete blocks.
Greta: Scott said alive and in Modesto on January 6th.
Claudia Cowan: The tape entered into evidence, not played, but the transcript is available to the press. The defense may jump on this explosive piece of evidence.

Greta: What's fueling the feud between Scott's parents and Laci's parents? Stay tuned. [Fox shows a video of Mrs. Peterson saying someone killed Laci and Conner, and they're still out there.]
Greta: Detective said two hundred and forty-one times; calls. Didn't talk on December 24th, and Easter.
Dr. Michael Baden, Forensic Pathologist: Locate cell phone, even if just on, and no calls made, as it passes cell phone towers. Only evidence is the hair, very weak evidence. The prosecution must use the evidence, and not passion.
Gloria Allred, Amber Frey's lawyer: No idea of the January 6th phone call. Why didn't Scott tell the police she's alive. Just another lie?
Ted Williams, former D.C. police detective, attorney: Just one of many, many, lies. The trial; won't get over that hurdle.
Gloria Allred, Amber Frey's lawyer: Disagree with you Ted. Disrespectful to the judge, to say no evidence.
Ted Williams, Defense Attorney: Gloria, They Met The Standard, now must get ready for trial. Tell me who, what, when, where.
Gloria Allred, Amber Frey's lawyer: Ted, Ted, Ted, Ted, Ted, Ted. [Gloria said this while Ted's talking.]
Bernie Grimm, Defense attorney: We're all liars. How about Amber deceiving people years ago with the married man and a pregnant wife?
Gloria Allred, Amber Frey's lawyer: That's unfair. That's unfair.
Nola Foulston, prosecutor Wichita, Kansas: He wants sympathy. Disagree with Dr. Baden. We have mitochondria DNA test of the hair.
Greta: Dr. Baden, I know you want to respond to that. [headline]: **A FAMILY DIVIDED.** Coming up; an inside scoop on the e-mail between the families when we come back. Stay tuned. Up next; why are the parents sending e-mails and why one e-mail from ?? caused a lawsuit. Stay tuned. **A FAMILY TORN APART. RIFT BETWEEN FAMILIES BEGAN WITH EXPOSURE OF AMBER FREY AFFAIR.**
Claudia Cowan: When Sharon Rocha tried to enter the Peterson house, the locks and alarm had been changed. Attorney for Peterson said that even evidence may have been planted when the Rocha's broke into the Peterson home. [headline]:
9/05 SHARON ROCHA FILES LAWSUIT TO BLOCK MONEY FROM BOOK DEAL OR MOVIE TO SCOTT.
Greta: Is change of venue.

Dr. Michael Baden, Forensic Pathologist: A hundred and thirty exonerations: first, false eyewitnesses; second, hair evidence. Hair of Mom, sister, have same hair. The detective could have brought it there on his clothes. The detective broke the chain of evidence by not having a lab person there, in the evidence room.
Greta: The former mayor of Modesto says Scott can't get a fair trial there.
Laura Ingle, KFI Radio Reporter: Most people here do know about this case. They did talk in court today of busing in jurors.
Gloria Allred, Amber Frey's lawyer: Dr. Baden, there are millions of viewers out there. Go and see if hair of spouse is in your pliers. It's ridiculous.
Bernie Grimm, Defense Attorney: The prosecution's on their heels. I'd push for a speedy trial.

[Again, if Laci is wrapped in plastic before leaving the home, how'd her hair get in the pliers which are in the boat, rusty, so rusty that they don't show use; and if the hair got there while at the warehouse, why not more DNA. Why leave the concrete weight mess, but clean up all other evidence, without a trace of DNA? If a hair got out of the plastic, where's the DNA?]

NBC 12 News Richmond, Virginia, **Sabrina Squire**: The judge has ruled Scott Peterson will stand trial for the murders of his wife and their unborn child. The judge found there was enough probable cause to hold the case over for trial.

[So, it appears that Amber did know Scott was married, before December 8, 2002, and when Scott continued saying he wasn't married, or for some other unknown reason, Amber began taping her phone calls and who knows what else. Amber took revenge on a pregnant woman whose husband she was seeing, so why wouldn't she dislike Laci. This hatred is also a trait of the 'usual' mistress.

After December 24th, with Scott knowing Amber already knew of his marriage, he would also know not to trust Amber. The widower story, the missing story, and the lost story, would each have been a fallacy to both of them after December 8th, even if the tape exists.]

11/19/03

NBC 12 News Richmond, Virginia: Judge ruled there's enough evidence to prosecute Scott Peterson.

NBC News Today **Katie Couric:** Secret tape recordings by Amber Frey of Scott Peterson have been released. [NBC shows a video of Scott in court, in a suit and tie.]
Ann: The arraignment set for two weeks. Judge rules enough evidence to stand trial.
Katie: Here's NBC legal analyst, Dan Abrams.
Dan Abrams: Only moments after the prosecution rested, the judge ruled enough evidence. The defendant refused to concede defeat. Now his lawyers want the case out of Modesto. Scott and Amber two hundred and forty-one times; twenty-three times between December 25th and December 27th, just two days after Laci's disappearance. Amber said, You told me you lost your wife. And Scott said, She's alive. And Amber asked, Where? And Scott replied, Modesto. On another tape Scott said, I never cheated on you. And Amber laughed, Ha ha ha, you're married.

Fox News Channel **Lauren Green:** Scott Peterson is going to trial. The judge ruled there's enough evidence for Scott Peterson to go to trial. His arraignment is scheduled for two weeks.

MSNBC **Valarie:** Scott Peterson will stand trial for the murder of his wife Laci and their unborn child. Tapes also released, with Amber saying, You told me on December 9th, that you lost you wife and now you're telling me she's missing. [How'd Amber know the date, December 9th?]

MSNBC **Sumi Das:** A seventeen page transcript of a twenty minute Amber taped phone call on January 6th, 2003. The transcript wasn't released to the press, but we were allowed to view it. Scott says he can't explain it to Amber now, wish he could, but can't.

Fox News Channel **Greta Van Susteren:** Coming up, is Scott Peterson running out of cash? Hear what his legal team has to say. Stay tuned. [Fox shows a video of Scott jogging with his dog, with the headline]: **RUNNING OUT OF CASH?**

What's this about Scott asking cops for a pickup truck? **LACI'S MURDER?** Up next, news from the Scott Peterson murder trial. Word Scott needs cash for his defense. Wants fifteen thousand back and pickup.
James Hammer, assistant San Francisco prosecutor: Should give it back, judge will say.
Ted Williams, Defense Attorney: Pickup, unless evidence, should give it back.
James Hammer, assistant San Francisco prosecutor: Trial within sixty days, if Scott wants to push it.
Bernie Grimm, Defense Attorney: With circumstantial evidence against Scott, which Scott produced, Geragos has the prosecution on its heels. Can't say how, when, where.
James Hammer, assistant San Francisco prosecutor: Everyone in Modesto knows every single detail we've talked about. Jurors won't like being bused in, but the venue will change.
Ted Williams, Defense Attorney: Especially with the former mayor coming out and saying Scott can't get a fair trial there.
Greta: And the prosecutor would much rather have the trial there, where everything is, the police, detectives, etcetera.
James Hammer, assistant San Francisco prosecutor: The prosecutor said he may not fight he motion. Why spend alot of money on something you're gonna lose.

11/21/03

Court TV **Lisa Bloom**, of Court TV, Civil Rights lawyer, daughter of Gloria Allred, Amber Frey's lawyer: [Commenting on a case, *Wisconsin versus Beck.*] Yea, he shoots his girlfriend and then flees. We saw it in the Scott Peterson case; fleeing, where he was headed for Mexico. Andrew Luster fled. Scott Peterson, arguably, fled, with the hair, money, and ID. [Actually, Lisa, Scott was said to be headed NORTH from his parents house and to the golf course, so they would have had to wait and stop him on his way back to his parents home, to say that he was headin' south.]

11/24/03

MSNBC Imus in the Morning
Imus: Have you seen that new video of Nancy Grace?
Voice: Yes I have.

Nancy Grace, of Court TV, former prosecutor, on the telephone: Since Geragos has been representing Michael Jackson since March, all the evidence will be gone, videos, photos, etcetera.
Imus: Why would anyone want to be represented by someone who's representing this garbage in Modesto, Scott Peterson? Who's clearly guilty.
Nancy Grace, former prosecutor: Just like when Johnnie Cochran walks into a courtroom; Geragos is the same way; you know that somebody has done something really, really, bad. Geragos is like a snake charmer, when he wants to be. Amber Frey has a hearing set to block her nude photos. Wonder if Scott Peterson is following the Amber Frey nudie case?

11/26/03

Fox News Channel **Laurie Dhue:** Amber Frey is said to be four months pregnant and has plans to marry a chiropractor.

Fox News Channel **Greta Van Susteren:** New developments in the Scott Peterson case. Who did he just ask for one hundred thousand dollars? Stay tuned. [Fox shows a video of Scott in court, with a suit and tie.] Who did Scott Peterson just get one hundred thousand dollars from, and is the transaction legal? Stay tuned. Scott put up the house, so his parents could take out a one hundred thousand dollar loan to pay for Scott's defense. [A rerun of a report on Scott Peterson?]
Claudia Cowan: They met....Scott cheated on her early in the relation. Tried to get pregnant for a year. Amber said Scott broke down in tears to tell her he was a widower. Amber hired a private investigator to find Scott was married and found out Laci was pregnant and was missing, so she went to the cops. [Fox shows a video, from January, 2003, of Scott saying: Affair with Amber very inappropriate....I was angry at first, at the Modesto police, for thc accusations. But, I think they've done a very good job.]
Greta: Did she suspect he was married?
Gloria Allred, Amber Frey's lawyer: Met November 20th, confronted him of marriage 9th of December.
Claudia Cowan: We heard so much abut the bleach smell in the house, but heard nothing about it at the preliminary hearing, so everyone was saying that's because the bathroom was so far from the kitchen and the maid said she only used bleach in the

bathroom, so you wouldn't smell bleach, but, when you look at these pictures, the bath is right next to the kitchen.

12/1/03

Fox News Channel
Gloria Gomez, KOVR TV Reporter: Experienced fishermen say the day Scott says fishing; two to four foot waves in a fourteen foot boat, and the wrong fishing pole for sturgeon, would snap the pole, some equipment gear never used in salt water. Amber began dating in January, with the guy she's four months pregnant by and plans to marry.
Catherine Crier, of Court TV, former judge: With a man that's not married, and has never been married. We want to make that perfectly clear. [Catherine just made millions of wives across the country feel much safer.]

12/2/03

Fox News Channel: Arraignment expected in the Scott Peterson case tomorrow. Scott Peterson's defense team is crying foul. They say he can't get a fair trial unless it's moved.

12/3/03

CNN [headlines]: **PROSECUTORS SAY PICKUP TRUCK IS PART OF CRIME SCENE. PETERSON IS CHARGED WITH MURDERING WIFE, UNBORN SON.** [CNN shows a video of Scott coming into court wearing an orange/red jumpsuit, with LIVE in the upper left corner.]
Ernie Norries, former assistant prosecutor: Hundreds of pieces of circumstantial evidence; uh, uh, the locale, fishing alone in the boat.
[CNN shows a video of Scott in court wearing a suit and tie.]
CNN **reporter:** Judge says police had the truck for a year and could have done all the testing they need, take pictures, etcetera, so the defense gets the truck back.

Court TV [Shows a 'just released video' of Scott in court for his arraignment.]
Judge: Change of venue motion first?
Geragos: Yes.

Judge: If the court grants change of venue now, will all pretrial motions be handled here.
Geragos: Yes sir, my opinion is only the trial be moved.
Dave Harris, prosecutor: We'd like the court to look over the questionnaire first, if not, we'd proceed with the phone survey. Case law says appropriate to delay the ruling till the jury be polled first.
Judge: I'd want to see some information first, but with questionnaire, it may pollute other trial jury pools.
Geragos: Court may see alot of others coming in and wanting a change of venue because of a survey.
Judge: Defense has it's finger on the court's thoughts on that, so you may want to consider that, Mr. Harris.
Dave Harris, prosecutor: December 12th for motions and a..., and January ?, for a full blown hearing on change of venue?
Judge: Correct. What about jury surveys?
Geragos: I believe....[Court TV cuts Geragos off, even though it's on a video tape, and goes to commercial.]
Judge: January 7, a 995 hearing.
[headlines]: **1/7 MOTION HEARING TO DISMISS. CHANGE OF VENUE HEARING 1/6. CHANGE OF VENUE FILINGS ON 12/15. TRIAL DATE SET FOR January 26.**
Judge: Reconsider protective order?
Geragos: Yes, wrong information abound, theories, facts abounding that aren't true. Maybe a safe-harbor provision, so a statement can be put out saying it's not true. Maybe prosecution and defense statement together or not, to respond positively. Tracks law and case law; something where we can respond.
Prosecutor: Safe harbor is to respond to other side. A release was given to media, but they still can't get it right. Two experts at the preliminary hearing and TV still couldn't get it right, with lawyers on TV shows repeatedly.
Judge: Findings still valid, even if media competition continues, even with other profile cases, the truth will come out at trial and they can even misquote that if they want. But the Order continues and going directly to media is prohibited.
Lisa Bloom, of Court TV, Civil Rights lawyer:
Strange, Geragos wanted the gag order relaxed so he could respond to the media. Prosecutor said no, and the judge said no.
James Curtis, of Court TV, former prosecutor: Yea, that's right. If you want to know the latest on this case, just tune in to Court

TV. [James said this as they went to another commercial. Another commercial when the media attorney begins to speak in court.]
Geragos: No reason anyone needs to see these photos, it's sick. Contrary to what Miss Kinney says.
Judge: What's different, Charity Kenyon, in looking at autopsy photos and telling what they see, as opposed to saying what a witness says the photo shows?
Kenyon: Parties don't control evidence, court does, and it's public information. Principle is what we're concerned about. Not for parties to control, but for the court to control. Public has a right to access.
Judge: I've viewed photos, and there's an overriding interest to keep closed. For family and others. Will cause harm and damage to others. I'm ruling it's going to stay sealed. Media wants warrants sealing revisited, but I'm not going to do that.
Kenyon: The case has changed. A plea may be entered. Changed circumstances would require the court to revisit the issue. The court now knows of informants and potential witnesses and what they've said.
Prosecutor: No Change. Parties do have the right to control evidence at the preliminary and have. Have done it, and will continue to do it, so no change in circumstances. Fifth Judicial District said parties have right to control.
Geragos: If the court said it won't revisit it, the defense has nothing to say.
Kenyon: ....[Commercial].
Geragos: They've had the truck for a year.
Prosecutor: Disagree; truck is important. Witnesses say they saw the truck and important that jurors see the truck. What? It's just a couple more payments made till trial. Samples already taken, blood found in the truck that matches defendant's, on the door and visor, or door jam.
Judge: Thousands of cases tried with photos and tapes. Why not here?
Prosecutor: Important for jurors to see how body loaded and taken.
Judge: If unique vehicle, maybe, but this is a Ford F-150.
Prosecutor: Defense challenges photos taken. I'd prefer actual items. Where did detective leave his keys? Okay, I left them here.
Judge: I'll grant motion. I'll give you two weeks to take more photos or whatever. Court orders return of truck, December 18th.

Geragos: I'll fly up and drive it back. Money will be returned?
Judge: Yes?
Prosecutor: By Friday.
Judge: December 12th at 9:30, next appearance.
Vinnie Politan, of Court TV: One year ago no one knew of Scott Peterson, now nearly everyone has heard of him and has an opinion. [Court TV shows a video of Scott, in court today, saying: That's correct, Your Honor, I'm innocent.]
Beth Karas, of Court TV: They're not waiving the speedy trial. A different judge to decide on the motion by the defense to dismiss for lack of evidence. A January 6th change of venue hearing. The prosecutor says the trial to be three to six months in length.
Vinnie Politan: Survey to be taken?
Beth Karas: December 12th, argue on if a survey can be used. Other attorneys may fear that the survey may affect their case.
Beth Karas: Many in Modesto know the Rocha family personally or participated in the search for Laci.
Jay Alpert, former sheriff: Many times items are given back.
Vinnie Politan: Could sheriff's department purchase the truck?
Jay Alpert, former sheriff: Why should they? They've got evidence in it. Why pay for evidence?
John Lakin, Defense Attorney: The key is forensic value. Why do they need it?
Vinnie Politan: Wonder what value the truck would have on e-Bay and auction it off?
Beth Karas: Fetus is not considered a person, but yet it's murder.
John Goold, Chief Deputy D.A., Stanislaus County, on the Peterson case: No pretrial date, trial date January 26th. Defense will file motion to challenge the preliminary hearing. A change of venue motion will be filed by the defense. We've asked the judge to survey the jurors. We'll argue that on December 12th. Judge expressed concern we may be polluting the jury pool here. The defendant has a right to trial in sixty days. If change of venue, may punch trial date back.
Roger Ross, defense attorney: Sixty day time limit can be met here. If the defense says sixty days, then attorneys have to. If the defense attorney then needs more time, he can ask the judge and may get it.

Fox News Channel **Stan Goldman**, Fox News legal editor: This tells me that the defense believes their case is only going to get

worse with more time. The prosecution is building its case with time. Geragos made hints that Scott and family is going broke here, with wanting release of the truck and money.
Laura Ingle, KFI Radio Reporter: Defense wants to hurry and try the case, maybe before more witnesses show up.

[Maybe Geragos wants to try the case, since the Constitution states the accused is guaranteed a speedy trial, not as fast or in the manner of media, but in a court of law. More time in the media does advantage the press trial and the prosecution, since the defense is keeping quiet, as per the gag order. A prosecutor cannot file charges against a person, without, in his own mind, believing that the person is guilty beyond a reasonable doubt. He must also have the evidence to prove this, since, if he doesn't, how can he believe guilt beyond a reasonable doubt. To say, well, we'll charge you now, throw you in jail, and when we figure the time is right, we'll either try you in court, or turn you loose, that is, if we ever get a round to-it, is one of the exact reasons that 'speedy trial' was written into the Constitution.]

CNN: Scott Peterson pled not guilty to murder charges in court today. His defense attorney is asking for a January 26th trial date.

Court TV **Nancy Grace**, of Court TV, former prosecutor: Judge makes rulings that Hurt the State's case today.
Beth Karas, of Court TV: Tentative trial date set for January 26th.
Nancy Grace, former prosecutor: Prosecutor said, Judge, don't give the truck back to the defense, we need it for a couple months. There's blood on the glove compartment, door, visor, and who knows where else. Rare for a judge to do this.
Michael Hardy, defense attorney: Not rare to give stuff back. They can show this with other trucks.
Lauren Howard, clinical social worker: The prosecutor didn't make a very strong case. What if they had removed the staircase in the Michael Peterson case. Yea, like we have to live here, so we'll clean it up.
Nancy Grace, former prosecutor: Defense already questioned the state's photos.
Michael Hardy, defense attorney: Photos of vehicle, and murder weapon, are two different things.

Nancy Grace, former prosecutor: In a TV interview, Scott said he bleeds all the time. Wouldn't be surprised if my blood or Laci's blood in truck.

Beth Karas: Well, he went fishing....

Nancy Grace, former prosecutor: He went fishing in a boat, Beth, not his truck. Why would he mention Laci's blood? Do you bleed at a golf game? Scott's a golfer, fisher, outdoorsman; he's a nature lover as well. Why he bought a Mercedes under a different name. Stay tuned. The prosecutor fought tooth and nail to keep the truck and the fifteen thousand dollars from Geragos. [Court TV shows four different photos of Scott.]

Beth Karas: Fifteen thousand dollars, four cell phones, brother's drivers license, alot of clothes, alot of camping gear, but no mention of golf clubs in the car. Clothes came out at the preliminary hearing. Said using brother's license at Club, to get a discount.

Nancy Grace, former prosecutor: When and where the camping gear purchased?

Beth Karas: Police are looking, and everything checked out.

Michael Hardy, Defense Attorney: He knew the FBI and police were following him. He said, what the heck, take a weekend off, have some fun.

Nancy Grace, former prosecutor: What about golf?

Michael Hardy, Defense Attorney: Well, we'll play a little golf first.

Nancy Grace, former prosecutor, and **Lauren Howard**, clinical social worker: OH, Come ON! Ha Ha Ha.
[At the same time.]

Lauren Howard, clinical social worker: So, where are the golf clubs?

Michael Hardy, Defense Attorney: I liked what Scott said, not only pled not guilty, but said he's innocent. Clearly if Amber's pregnant, it ain't by Scott and surely he didn't kill for Amber.

Beth Karas: Laci's stepfather and mother, Mrs. Rocha there.

Nancy Grace, former prosecutor: When you look at Scott Peterson in the courtroom, he looks like he doesn't have a care in the world.

Lauren Howard, clinical social worker: Yea, let's forget he's a liar and a smug person.

Michael Hardy, Defense Attorney: The fact that he's relaxed, shows me he's innocent.

Court TV **Catherine Crier**, former judge: Prosecution wants to keep Scott's alleged get away truck. Some say a great loss? I disagree.
Beth Karas: Geragos said hardship on Scott, with seven hundred dollars a month truck payment.
Catherine Crier, former judge: People betting Geragos won't try this case, won't go to trial with Scott.
Victor Sherman, defense attorney: I understand Mark [Geragos] quoted a price at the beginning and was paid.
Jack Ford, former prosecutor: It leads to other business, so he won't quit. Not too many would walk away here.
Gloria Allred, Amber Frey's lawyer: Not important if Amber is pregnant. No impact on her credibility. She will be called to testify at trial.
Beth Karas: Geragos wanted right to issue statement to correct bad information out there. Said many things reported are not true, but the judge denied it.
Catherine Crier, former judge: We're not in a courtroom under oath.
Victor Sherman, defense attorney: Simple way is to say nobody's talking on the outside. [Court TV shows a video of Geragos in court today, saying that if someone wants to look at Laci's autopsy photos, then take them over to a therapist first.]
Catherine Crier, former judge: I've seen the photos and they are gross. I wouldn't allow the photos out. What about keeping arrest and search warrants sealed? Think Geragos would try to beat the USA movie of Scott Peterson with the trial?
Victor Sherman, defense attorney: Don't think so, unless he thinks he'll win.
Jack Ford, former prosecutor: Speed by the defense in the Zodiac trial, hurt the prosecution's case. Once in a while, it happens. Client in jail and needs to be resolved.
Catherine Crier, former judge: Report says Scott went to neighbor, looking for Laci, and said he'd been golfing.
Gloria Allred, Amber Frey's lawyer: Not a rumor, just another lie. Why say golfing, if he didn't have anything to hide, and say he'd been golfing? Why lie?
Victor Sherman, defense attorney: Terrible evidence, if the jury hears he lied that day, to create an alibi.
Catherine Crier, former judge: Scott's arrogant, lies, what if on the stand?

Jack Ford, former prosecutor: Some clients demand to take the stand and say they didn't do it.
Gloria Allred, Amber Frey's lawyer: I disagree, he's too much of a liar to take the stand.

Fox News Channel **Rita Cosby:** Scott Peterson is a liar and cheater. There's one guy, Mark Geragos, that was very happy when Durst was acquitted.

MSNBC **Keith Olbermann:** He pleaded innocent, and an indication that Scott Peterson was injured a year ago. New information out of Modesto in the Scott Peterson hearing. Stay tuned. Court documents that Scott was injured during the crime.
Dan Abrams: Prosecutor responded yesterday with filing in court that Scott's blood was, during crime. In TV interview, Scott said there'd be blood in his truck, he's a fertilizer salesman. Prosecution may not have a sense of when it happened, December 23rd or December 24th. They believe they can explain after the fact. Laci in truck, but we haven't heard any evidence of that.
Keith Olbermann: If evidence of Laci's dead body in the truck, would the judge give it back?
Dan Abrams: Usually see photos, but the prosecutor wanted to show the jury where the blood was. The defense says they need the truck to pay for the defense. Prosecutor estimated the trial to take three to six months in length.

MSNBC **Gloria Allred**, Amber Frey's lawyer: Geragos with Scott in jail and not a happy camper. Maybe he's not ready.
Dan Abrams: Bet Geragos won't use the words Michael Jackson in Modesto court.
Howard Weitzman, attorney: Maybe there's something we don't know, but hard to believe Mr. Geragos has the cards in his hip pocket to go ahead with this.
Dan Abrams: Prosecutor said cement-like material found in the bed of the truck.
Gloria Allred, Amber Frey's lawyer: Surprised Geragos made motion, cause now blood is out in public.
Dan Abrams: [Abrams reads, says Scott says, my hands are rough and cut, I'm out on farms all the time.]
Howard Weitzman, attorney: Can be devastating to the defense, assuming it's Scott's blood.

[Beth Karas of Court TV has said earlier that it wasn't alot of blood, just a couple of specks. Since it's Scott's truck, why would it be devastating to find Scott's blood in his own truck? It may, or may not, be devastating to find someone else's blood in the truck.]

MSNBC **Dan Abrams:** Problem isn't the media and its reporting; it's the arguments made by the lawyers themselves. I'm not gonna let 'em get away with those cheap shots.

[Dan is having a tizzy because of what the judge and prosecutor said in court; that they can give media a transcript, yet media still can't report it accurately. The prosecutor had said at one hearing, possibly this one, that he had even heard that one witness has been referred to as a 'star witness' [Amber Frey], which brought a moment of laughter from the judge, prosecutors, and defense attorneys.]

Fox News Channel **Stan Goldman**, Fox News legal editor: Scott looked relaxed. Defense seems confident.
James Hammer, assistant San Francisco prosecutor: Could happen by January 26th, maybe February. Entirely up to the trial judge as to where it goes with a change of venue.
Laura Ingle, KFI Radio Reporter: Scott's hair grown, still losing weight. Prosecutor really laid it on thick to keep the truck. Surprised judge gave it back. Said they'd had their time with the truck.
Bernie Grimm, Defense Attorney: No such plea as innocent. Maybe with Mark's encouragement. I don't let my client speak at an arraignment. Who knows what the hell will come out of their mouth. [headline]: **SPEEDY TRIAL?**
Ted Williams, Defense Attorney: One way for Geragos to throw the prosecution off stride. Geragos will tell the jury, not one piece of evidence.
James Hammer, assistant San Francisco prosecutor: The prosecutor will tell the jury; he won't tell them alot, cause Scott killed the only witness to the murder.
Stan Goldman, Fox News legal editor: Sirens, cause Geragos pays them to do it when Gloria Allred is on. [Laughter by all.] Priority

under California law goes to the child abuse case, the Michael Jackson case.
Greta: Prosecutors say Scott's blood is in the truck, so why did the judge release it?
Bernie Grimm, Defense Attorney: I can say, same as the prosecutor, with no evidence, that Amber called, Laci answered and then confronted Scott, argued, she fell, unconscious, he panicked and finished her off.
Greta: There's no evidence of that.
Bernie Grimm, Defense Attorney: Better than what the prosecutor is saying.
James Hammer, assistant San Francisco prosecutor: Big problem with no blood in the house.
Laura Ingle, KFI Radio Reporter: The prosecution could have alot more. No hard evidence, that we've been told of.
[headline]: **SCOTT: "I'M INNOCENT".**
Stan Goldman, Fox News legal editor: Geragos said if no truck and money, he'd have to ask the court to fund the defense. I was stunned the truck was given back. Can use pictures.

12/4/03

CNN Larry King [12 midnight]
Nancy Grace, of Court TV, former prosecutor: Judge gave away state's physical evidence.
Chris Pixley, Defense Attorney: There wasn't any blood evidence at the preliminary hearing.
Nancy Grace, former prosecutor: Yes there was, today.
Chris Pixley, Defense Attorney: If they had blood evidence, they'd have shown it. There wasn't a shred of blood evidence presented at the prelim.
Nancy Grace, former prosecutor: There was blood in several places in that car. And what about neighbors and police saying they saw cuts on Scott's hands.
Adam Stewart, Sharon Rocha's civil attorney: Alot of Laci's assets are being encumbered; house, a hundred thousand dollars; truck and money given to Scott; photos that someone paid a very high price for. Photos shown on TV taken recently, wondered who did this. Laci still has an interest in that home. Ms. Rocha feels they're using Laci's assets to finance Scott's defense.

Nancy Grace, former prosecutor: If the defense camp gave access to the media to take the photos in exchange for money. The state can appeal judge giving the truck back.
Chris Pixley, Defense Attorney: Laci's family does have an interest, but that's putting the cart before the horse and assuming he'll be convicted. Adam would have to show that Scott is responsible.
Dr. Robi Ludwig, psychotherapist: Not right for Scott to profit off anything relating to the crime. Makes him look really criminal with the jury. [CNN shows a video of the Stanislaus County Deputy D.A., **Rick Distaso**, in court yesterday, saying, blood in door pocket and over visor.]
Nancy Grace, former prosecutor: On his computer was found where he was looking at various waterways.
Larry King: Do you need a motive?
Chris Pixley, Defense Attorney: Practically speaking, yes.
Dr. Robi Ludwig, psychotherapist: Amber a woman who is driven to men. She's going to present a problem to the jury.
Nancy Grace, former prosecutor: Why judge someone's morals? What about Scott running around?
Chris Pixley, Defense Attorney: Well, whose morals do you want to judge, Nancy?
Nancy Grace, former prosecutor: I don't care who's sleeping with whom.
Ted Rowlands, KTVU TV Reporter: Haven't seen state's whole case. Don't know where they're going with it.
Nancy Grace, former prosecutor: Haven't heard any evidence of Laci being alive December 24th. Geragos didn't question about used dishes, coffee cup, etcetera. If it existed, we'd have heard about it from Geragos. Scott had four cell phones with him when caught. No golf clubs with him that day.
Dr. Robi Ludwig, psychotherapist: His behavior is unusual. Behavior adds up to mischief. [CNN shows a video of Geragos in court, stating]: I'll stipulate to the money and denominations. I guess they'll photocopy it, but I don't want to stipulate and lose the right to question the detective on the seizure of it, the manner, or motive, or the location.
Caller: Amy embryo fluid on Scott's clothes?
Ted Rowlands, KTVU TV Reporter: All kinds of tests.

Caller: They wonder about Scott getting a sixty pound fish in the boat, but yet prosecutors say he carried a hundred and sixty pound body in it.
Chris Pixley, Defense Attorney: If paint on Scott's boat, why didn't the divers go down there immediately; They didn't.
Nancy Grace, former prosecutor: You're the only one reporting that Chris.
Chris Pixley, Defense Attorney: It was on TV just a week before the preliminary.
Nancy Grace, former prosecutor: Yea, Geragos brought it up in cross [exam].
Dr. Robi Ludwig, psychotherapist: Could Laci swim? Would she follow Scott?
Caller: Has Scott been tested for being a psychopath?
Dr. Robi Ludwig, psychotherapist: There's a test, but they can trick the test.

<u>12/11/03</u>

Court TV **Catherine Crier**, former judge: Has a cause of death finally been determined in the Laci Peterson case? Stay tuned. National Enquirer has the cause.
David Wright, of National Enquirer: Laci died while sleeping in bed and smothered with a pillow by Scott. Alot of evidence from the bed, during the February 18th, second search; sheets, cover, blankets. Police went to Laci's family and told them right after the search. A missing pillow case from the bed, perhaps stains on it and had to get rid of it.
Gloria Gomez, KOVR TV Reporter: A pregnant woman would release bodily fluids if strangled. But not sure if anything like that was found.
Catherine Crier, former judge: Mop; blood?
Gloria Gomez, KOVR TV Reporter: Never any evidence of vomit or blood on the mop.
David Wright, of National Enquirer: Police believe a struggle before he went to bed and Scott was injured with his blood on the comforter on the bed. Scott talked to Sandy, a friend of her Mom's, and said if blood found, it's okay cause I bleed all the time.
Catherine Crier: Clothing on Laci?
Gloria Allred, Amber Frey's lawyer: Confirmed Amy's story; kaki pants found on Laci's torso.

12/12/03

Court TV **Catherine Crier:** Scott Peterson's back in court, claiming Modesto's no place to get a fair trial. Today at 5, stay tuned.

Court TV **Vinnie Politan**: Case will stay on for January 26th, and jury to be ready. Looks like it'll go forward. Geragos asked for two more days, prosecutor wanted two more weeks, judge says two days, to file for change of venue motions. Compare polls here and surrounding counties and Los Angeles, where Geragos wants it. The defense, eight thousand exhibits, put on a disk. Accounts of all media coverage of the case on a disk to the judge. The truck, the prosecutor wanted more time, judge said no. The prosecutor offered to buy, Geragos said to make an offer. The judge wanted no parts of it. Between them. The prosecution will want to try and pick a jury first, before moving. The judge ordered a jury list of 2003, given to the prosecutor, to make calls for survey. Mrs. Peterson passed two detectives in the court hallway this morning and said, shame on you, shame on you both. [headline]: **PETERSON ACCUSED OF KILLING WIFE AND FETUS. PARTIES AGREE POTENTIAL JURORS SHOULD BE POLLED.** [Court TV shows a video tape from the courtroom.]
Prosecutor: Would like two more weeks for jury survey, holidays, not many jurors in the court house. We'll still argue to try and pick jury first, after survey done.
Geragos: We would like to exceed fifteen page maximum on motion, to twenty pages. Eight thousand pages of exhibits and put them on disk for the court. If we go past the 8th, we'll be pushing the defendant's right to a speedy trial with no way to do anything. During Christmas, more people will be home.
Judge: Why would I want to look at eight thousand pages?
Geragos: We've summarized it to twenty pages from different media outlets.
Judge: Relevance of media outside of Stanislaus County?
Geragos: More media in this case in comparison to others in other counties.
Prosecutor: We respond to defense motion, which we still don't have. Jury selection won't happen here in this case in a couple days, like most cases. Best way is to put it to January 20th.

Judge: We'll go with two days more; December 15th, defense to prosecutor motion. January 2, 04, for.... Reply by January 6th. January 6, vacated to January 8. You're in court on January 7.
Prosecutor: Discovery date January 7? Prefer January 7, over January 8.
Judge: Discovery on January 8, won't take much time.
Prosecutor: Can people use phone list?
Geragos: Same problem, don't think they can have access to that. Prosecution also wants L.A. surveyed, and judge there, will probably throw it at the receptacle. He won't honor it. Would pollute the jury pool there. Jurors from 2003 may be the ones sitting in 2004. Don't need a juror list to do a phone survey. [Commercial.]
Court Administrator: Excused jurors would be hard to list.
Judge: Yea, make it those not served.
Court Administrator: We have seventeen hundred per week, but may only summon four hundred a week.
Geragos: And some called, can't serve, but that isn't found out until they come in.
Court Administrator: Right, cause we can't eliminate those not eligible from the Master List.
Geragos: Like L.A., the juror list draws on other data bases.
Judge: Isn't a form sent out?
Court Administrator: They're only called again, if they send in the survey. [Commercial.]
Judge: You'll can submit samples of the survey and I'll look them over, with corrections or so forth.
Prosecutor: People willing to pay fair market vale of truck. We can negotiate with the defense.
Geragos: He's a used truck salesman this morning.
Prosecutor: Or change the date we return it. A couple of weeks?
Geragos: Court stated ten days. I won't dispose of it, but it should be turned over Monday and not keep it one minute longer that court ordered.
Judge: I gave my order and I'm sticking by it. I won't get involved in a sale. People had the truck long enough. Sounds like defense won't get rid of it. [Commercial, and we miss alot during commercials, which makes it impossible to know what some of the arguments are about or which issues they concern. Kinda neat how that happens, even when it's on tape. The prosecution tried to delay, on each point, and on each issue.]

Nancy Grace, of Court TV, former prosecutor: Geragos is fighting for a fair trial and the prosecutors agree.
Judge: For court to certify the transcript records, change: variance to variants; exhibit 37, is 38; question 11, is question 1.1; Perkin and Elmer, is Perkin-Elmer; B, is A; November 1, is November 3; cases referred, to not as cases; some cases referred, to not actually cases, as spelled here, phonic name spelling; understand, is under oath; J., is CD; .25 Caliber, is .22 Caliber. No one said .25 caliber. They were, is he was; great, is greater; state, is side; Sec.62.64, is Sec. 62.64, and remove [sic]. See you again on January 8th. Defendant's remanded and no bail set.
Nancy Grace, former prosecutor: Defense is delay, delay, delay.
Vinnie Politan: I don't know. The defense looks ready.
Nancy Grace, former prosecutor: Yea, but it can be the day of the trial, and defense says, Your Honor, our rights have been violated and we need more time.
Vinnie Politan: But it looks like it's the prosecution that keeps asking for more time on each and every issue, want more time to poll jurors, more time to keep the truck.
Eddie Hayes, of Court TV: It may be the defense wants to go quickly cause they're afraid with more time, that the prosecution will come up with more damaging evidence.
Nancy Grace, former prosecutor: Look at Scott, sitting there smug and smiling. Where's The Hanky, Scott? Where's The Tears Today?
Eddie Hayes, of Court TV: Where's the hanky? Ha, Ha.
Vinnie Politan: No; on ask for delay of the trial. Defense asked for extra time to file change of venue; granted. Prosecutor wanted two weeks extra; not granted. January 8th change of venue motion. Prosecutor wanted truck held longer; not granted. Twenty to twenty-five thousand dollar value on truck. Judge wants no part of negotiation on truck. Laci and Conner First Annual Blood Drive; fliers with picture of Laci and message from the Rocha family. December 21st through December 23rd blood drive.
Gerry Spence, Defense Attorney: If you're gonna bus in jurors, from where?
Nancy Grace, former prosecutor: Next county.
Gerry Spence, Defense Attorney: Well you might as well bring them in from Tim Buck Too. Everyone in America knows the facts of this case. It's been tried in the media over and over.

Vinnie Politan: Mrs. Peterson passed two detectives and said shame on you and shame on you too.
Nancy Grace, former prosecutor: Funny, we haven't heard of such outbursts from the Rocha family. [Court TV shows a video of Mrs. Rocha crying, asking to bring Laci home, at a press announcement.]
Nancy Grace, former prosecutor: Laci's body may have been transported in that truck and Geragos and Scott are smiling and laughing about the truck in court.
Michael Cardoza, attorney: Yes, I heard that and it may hurt them if jurors find out about this. They'll show him as a liar from the start. Oh, they'll kill 'em, they'll kill 'em. The jury will want to know why he lied, why he walked across the street and told his neighbor he'd been playing golf.
Nancy Grace, former prosecutor: No blood from Laci. It's mostly Scott saying stuff that messes him up.
Vinnie Politan: Why hair changing color? Why fifteen thousand dollars? Why fishing on Christmas Eve? These will be stressed by the prosecutor. But, the other side will ask, where's the evidence? So it cuts both ways.
Nancy Grace, former prosecutor: I reacted completely different than Scott Peterson did as a victim of crime. [Huh?]

Court TV Catherine Crier Live
Gloria Gomez, KOVR TV Reporter: We have information that the prosecutor will subpoena Amber Frey's father, mother, and sister, for information Amber may have told them.
Vinnie Politan: Seems like the defense is pushing forward and the prosecution is stalling for time.
Angelo MacDonald, former prosecutor: Defense may be trying to attack, figuring the prosecution isn't ready, but it may backfire on them.
Catherine Crier, former judge: Laci's torso showed the clothes she was wearing the night before. [If the prosecutor says Laci was murdered in bed, wouldn't she have on night clothes, or a gown?]

<u>12/13/03</u>

Fox News Channel **Geraldo Rivera:** National Enquirer quotes sources from close inside the case, Laci was suffocated. [headline]: **LACI WAS SUFFOCATED.**

Dr. Michael Baden, Forensic Pathologist: Entirely speculative. Pillow case found two months later. No cause of death. Suffocation probably the hardest cause to name.
Geraldo Rivera: Scott Peterson's defense now asks to be moved out of Modesto. Northern California seems guilty, southern California seems not guilty.
Stan Goldman, Fox News legal editor: Defense wants it moved and prosecution wants to try and pick a jury first.

12/16/03

Fox News Channel **Shepard Smith:** Lawyer says Scott has been demonized. [headline]:
LAWYER SAYS SCOTT HAS BEEN DEMONIZED.

Court TV **Nancy Grace**, former prosecutor: Scott Peterson slipped up the next day. He couldn't keep his story straight for twelve hours. He told a neighbor that he golfed, after he had told police that he went fishing on Christmas Eve.
Dr. Caryn Stark, psychologist: He told Amber his wife was missing and then....
Nancy Grace, former prosecutor: BOOM, his wife his found dead. Why would you put yourself up to be a liar?
Gerald Boyle, Defense Attorney: Maybe he's innocent.
Nancy Grace, former prosecutor: OH, OH.

Fox News Channel **Greta Van Susteren:** Breaking news in the Scott Peterson murder. Gloria Allred, Amber Frey's lawyer, says she has an announcement to make and she'll make it here on Fox. Stay tuned. We have news about a slashed tire and a confrontation at a restaurant. Stay tuned.
Laura Ingle, KFI Radio Reporter: Geragos doesn't want bused in jurors.
Greta: An attorney's car tire slashed. Attorney accosted in restaurant. The Mayor said he didn't believe Scott get a fair trial.
Geoffrey Fieger, attorney: Judge won't grant change of venue. Where's he gonna go? Simpson case had as much publicity and he was acquitted.
Greta: Survey says seventy-five percent of Stanislaus County has prejudged it.
James Hammer, assistant San Francisco prosecutor: Geragos didn't compare Stanislaus County to another county.

Bernie Grimm, Defense Attorney: Question is, can you put aside your prejudgment and try this defendant fairly?
Greta: Coming up, Gloria Allred has breaking news.
Gloria Allred, Amber Frey's lawyer: Nude photos of Amber; federal judge issued a temporary order not to publish on website. And, next time I warn someone, they'd better heed the advice. [Sure got me scared.]
Ted Williams, Defense Attorney: It's a preliminary injunction and not a final one. It's all still up in the air.
Geoffrey Fieger, attorney: I thought Gloria was gonna tell us that she was gonna adopt Amber's baby.
Greta: We were all betting that Amber was going to get married.
James Hammer, assistant San Francisco prosecutor: Amber's credibility may be at issue in trial, cause it came out later that she had made recordings before she really did and Geragos is going to go after that. Did she try to do more against Scott than what she really had and what motive for that.
Gloria Allred, Amber Frey's lawyer: Her credibility won't be in trouble. Let it rest.

[Even the prosecutor, at Scott Peterson's hearing, said some were even on TV saying they had a 'star' witness, that the prosecutor didn't know about. The judge said, yea, when they have cameras here, they still can't get it right. Gloria's riding the coattails of Scott Peterson's woes, and she's creating alot of those woes all on her own, just like she's doing with Michael Jackson. Isn't publicity wonderful for business, especially when you're paid for the publicity you're creating.]

<u>12/17/03</u>

Court TV **James Curtis**, former prosecutor: Scott Peterson's lawyer says Modesto is a lynch mob and trial must be moved.
Gloria Gomez, KOVR TV Reporter: Defense team at restaurant and people saying shame on you, how could you defend a murderer. Thirty-seven percent on prosecution survey say guilty, down from fifty-four percent. Geragos would like the trial in Los Angeles where he's based. I'm hearing Santa Clara County alot, and prosecutor here pinches pennies, so he wants to keep it here.
Gloria Allred, Amber Frey's lawyer: Federal court judge decided on preliminary injunction on releasing nude photos of Amber. He published them on his web site, despite my warning not to.

Christine Grillo, prosecutor Brooklyn, New York: Great that some kind of precedent is now set on not allowing photos like this to be published, where someone becomes known or famous and someone will go back and find photos and try to profit off it.

12/24/03

Fox News Channel **Laurie Dhue:** Scott Peterson's lawyers file new motions against police officers in the case, and could this mean charges will be dropped? Stay tuned.
Scott Peterson's lawyer attacks police, judge style, and could this mean charges against Scott could be dropped; when we come back. New information in the Scott Peterson case. Did police mishandle this case from the beginning, about one year ago today. Scott's lawyer files motion to have the charges dismissed, there is no circumstantial or physical evidence to link Scott to the crime. A January 14, 2004 hearing.
Ted Williams, former D.C. police detective, attorney: Geragos drank some of the water at the Michael Jackson party the other day.
Laurie Dhue: Has the prosecution fallen short here?
Bernie Grimm, defense Attorney: Common sense says it's Scott and if not, who? Legal sense, they can't any of who, when, why, how.
Mickey Sherman, former prosecutor, defense attorney: We had all this buildup to Amber, yet she didn't even show up, and now she's pregnant with someone else's child.
Ted Williams, Defense Attorney: Police need a nexus, a connection to this death. Jury won't send him to death cause he had an affair.
Mickey Sherman, former prosecutor, defense attorney: Yea, we ran Condit out of office and town, and now we find out he didn't do it. So it's not that much of a stretch of the imagination to happen here.
Bernie Grimm, Defense Attorney: Jury here could convict Scott, just because they despise him.
Laurie Dhue: And Laci's Mom has filed two wrongful death suits against Scott. [What happened to the lead-in headline of police mishandling the case? Viewers got worried Scott would be set free, with one liners leading up to the story, but never fear, cause the show was to elate those fears with a story about Scott being convicted; because he had an affair, he's a liar, and the jury will despise him. And all this from, supposedly, defense attorneys.]

12/27/03

ABC News Good Morning America [ABC shows a video of some of the TV interview between Diane Sawyer and Scott Peterson. Scott said that he told Laci of his affair with Amber and that Laci was not okay with it, and that no one knows a relationship but the two people involved. Scott said he told Laci because it was the right thing to do. He also said that he saw Amber again, but did not tell Amber that he had told Laci of the affair.]

12/30/03

Fox News Channel **Greta Van Susteren:** Up next, Scott Peterson's Christmas surprise. What special treat did he receive while behind bars? [Fox shows Scott coming into court wearing an orange jumpsuit, in handcuffs and leg irons.]

1/2/04

Fox News Channel Greta Van Susteren
[Fox shows a rerun of an earlier show, on Scott talking about Laci missing; the Modesto police, at first, made allegations, but did a fantastic job; a special by Claudia Cowan on Amber Frey's background and Amber's previous boyfriend who was also married.] Either Greta or Claudia: On January 6th, 2003, Scott calls to tell Amber of Laci, and Amber records it. Amber says, what about a newborn baby? Wouldn't you want visitation? And Scott says, Honey, I can't tell you. Amber: Why not? Scott: It would hurt too many people.

1/5/04

Court TV **James Curtis**, former prosecutor: Lady here, just like Amber Frey, says she didn't know he was married.
Lisa Bloom, of Court TV, Civil Rights lawyer, daughter of Gloria Allred, Amber Frey's lawyer: Just like Amber Frey and Scott Peterson, she, Amber, never knew that Scott was married until after the death of Laci.

1/7/04

Court TV **Jean Casarez**: Scott Peterson's lawyer has filed papers saying that Los Angeles is the best place to try Scott Peterson.

MSNBC
Catherine Crier, of Court TV, former judge: I'd change venue, if still on the bench.
Dan Abrams: Bus in jurors?
Catherine Crier, former judge: Easier to move court personnel.
Paul Pfingst, former prosecutor: People have heard of the case, but most of the time they haven't made up their mind yet. Judge shouldn't rely on experts and polls, but call jurors in and ask them.
John Burris, former prosecutor, attorney: High profile case, jurors will say they're fair, but they want to be on the jury. There was a lynch attitude when Scott was arrested. [headline]: **PETERSON CASE MOVED?**
Dan Abrams: They found a jury in the O.J. Simpson civil case. Why is it that, in high profile cases, the defense attorneys don't want cameras in the courtroom? What are they afraid of; the information will come out eventually, anyway. If the media reports evidence that isn't allowed in court, because of some legal technicality, that doesn't mean that it didn't happen, it just means it wasn't allowed to be shown to the jurors in court. That goes for the Kobe Bryant case, the Scott Peterson case, and the Michael Jackson case.

1/8/04

ABC World News Now: Jury selection for the Scott Peterson trial is set to begin January 21st.

Fox News Channel Dayside with Linda Vester
Claudia Cowan: Judge issued a temporary ruling, agreeing with defense attorney, that his client can't get a fair trial here in Modesto, citing the media reports of over eight thousand exhibits. He says too much adverse publicity to have a fair trial here. Almost certainly they'll be a delay in the trial.

Court TV **Jean Casarez**: Judge in the Laci Peterson case is inclined to grant a change of venue.
Beth Karas, of Court TV: Witness on the stand, called by Geragos, an expert who did a survey. Apparently he wasn't hired by Geragos, but he had done a survey early in January, and, just recently. This expert has testified in trials before and familiar with the judge and justice system. He said he wasn't hired by anyone,

but he lives in the area and was concerned. He did a study with his students, where 75% believed Scott guilty, with only 2.7%, not guilty.
Jean Casarez: Defense says they don't agree with busing in jurors.
Beth Karas: Judge didn't say he's considering that, with Geragos saying the surrounding counties are basically the same, so busing in jurors won't work. Court took a ten minute recess and the judge told the prosecutor that if he had any witnesses to call, he'd better call them, cause this hearing was ending at twelve noon, which is 3pm eastern standard time. The prosecutor was still crossing the professor who did the juror survey on his own. [While Beth is talking of the hearing, Court TV shows Scott wearing an orange jumpsuit.] The prosecution's expert says eighty percent of Stanislaus County residents can set aside any information and decide fairly. Geragos brought out on cross that this expert has always testified for the prosecution. Judge says the prosecutor relied on some questions in the questionnaire, that would not have been permitted in voir dire. Prosecution may appeal the judge's decision and that would delay the proceedings.
Nancy Grace, of Court TV, former prosecutor: If a juror states on the record, that he or she can return a true verdict in this case, based on the truth, then that person is qualified to be a juror. Geragos may end up like Burr Rabbit and say, please don't throw me in the briar patch. [Nancy, Nancy, Nancy. The rabbit wanted to be thrown into the briar patch, because that's a part of his home. Scott Peterson's hearing begins, a 3:20pm feed, with video, but no audio, so, a commercial. Court TV shows a video of Scott coming into court today, wearing a suit and tie, then a video of the hearing.]
Judge: I have received and reviewed the following briefs:.... I've scrolled enough through articles to see there are at least three Scott Peterson's, and the attorneys connection with Michael Jackson. Many articles are on the front page. It would be impossible to seat a fair jury. I must conclude, that without a change of venue, the defendant would not receive a fair trial. Agree with defense, that it's better to grant change of venue, before voir dire, and thereby poison the jury pool. Five to six factors to analyze and weigh each factor, if it favors change of venue, not, or is neutral. One: Nature and gravity of offense; murder, death penalty, national media and a Christmas disappearance; heavily favors change. Two: Size of community; slightly favors change with five hundred thousand

population. Three: Political or controversial factors; neutral, even with Attorney General comments and other politicians running for... Four: Status of defendant in community; prior to the case, no publicity and an upstanding citizen, not a public figure, not a 1960's hippy, crowd at jail when brought in to custody; slightly favor change. Five: Status of victims in community; slightly favor change; some jurors may view victims as their own. Six: Nature and extent of news coverage; most heavy factor; substantially favor change, not seen in my career, the amount and nature of the coverage. Some factual, many speculative and inflammatory in nature. Coverage here, not typical for a crime of this type. Jurors may base decision on what they learned outside of the courtroom. We have sixteen other venues, larger than ours, available to us. Evidence presented by the defense shows other communities aren't biased. Weighs heavily on change of venue. Media will continue to cover this, even today, on their front page. Almost impossible, without sequestering the jury. Media doesn't report what they hear in court. Without sequestering jury, they'll be comments from those in the case, friends of the family, and those who were in the search.

Prosecutor: I've never been provided with a Declaration by Professor S....

Geragos: Would the court okay a brief recess to discuss the tentative order?

Judge: Yea, okay, a ten minute recess.

Nancy Grace, of Court TV, former prosecutor: State wants venue to remain in Modesto and Geragos wants a change, but the judge came down with a ruling, before arguments ever began.

Geragos: Your Honor is treating the affidavit by Professor S. as a Declaration and we'd like to submit that to the court now.

Prosecutor: We understand there's a Declaration by Dr. ..., but not Professor ....

Judge: Okay, we'll call Dr. ... to the stand. Geragos, you can lay foundation first.

Geragos: Spell name.

Stephen J. Schoenthaler: I teach Sociology and Criminal Justice at California ....

Defense never paid me a dime; first time I met you [Geragos] was 8:30 this morning. I quit looking back in March, when the count was three hundred articles about the case.

Prosecutor: Your PhD in nutrition? Your thesis?

Professor Schoenthaler: No, it's on plea bargaining and affect on sentencing. What happens? Why? And where they end up, to determine effects of plea bargaining. The University awarded me for research in nutrition and change of venue effects.
Prosecutor: You indicated you know some of the law in area of change of venue?
Professor Schoenthaler: Not really.
Prosecutor: Don't you have a legal conclusion in your report?
Professor Schoenthaler: Yes, in the earlier report, that I turned in to your office in March?
Judge: I'm not worried about his legal conclusions, just his statistical data. The legal conclusions are my job.
Professor Schoenthaler: Law in California, decisions, show alot of bias from media on cases. So during a sabbatical, I studied cases. It peaked in 1992, with the justice system allowing an undue influence and prejudice against defendants.
Prosecutor: That's not what I asked you.
Geragos: Objection.
Judge: Sustained.
Prosecutor: ....
Geragos: Objection, asked and answered.
Judge: Sustained.
Prosecutor: Didn't you testify in a case where change of venue wasn't granted. So, let's talk a little bit about that case.
Geragos: Excuse me, but the case he's [prosecutor's] talking about is ..., but the facts he's [prosecutor's] saying are from another case, ... [Court TV takes a commercial.]
Nancy Grace, of Court TV, former prosecutor: Like a ping pong match, every time Geragos objects, the judge sustains it.
Prosecutor: ....
Geragos: Objection.
Judge: Overruled.
Prosecutor: You gave your survey to the Modesto Bee [newspaper]?
Professor Schoenthaler: Yes.
Prosecutor: And then you came down to the courthouse and gave interviews with media?
Professor Schoenthaler: Yes.
Prosecutor: And this was two months after you stopped looking at articles?
Professor Schoenthaler: Yes.

Prosecutor: And you had students call with a survey?
Professor Schoenthaler: Yes.
Prosecutor: How many? Sixty to seventy here? One hundred seventy...?
Professor Schoenthaler: End of November and beginning of December.
Prosecutor: How many were called more than once?
Professor Schoenthaler: Probably none, cause each had different instructions on how to choose numbers.
Prosecutor: You exclude unlisted numbers?
Professor Schoenthaler: Yes.
Prosecutor: Can't they exclude themselves, with an unlisted number?
Professor Schoenthaler: That's a strange defense, but yes. We compare these figures with other surveys and polls to find if there's a difference.
Prosecutor: So, fifty percent of possible jurors are excluded from your survey?
Professor Schoenthaler: Results don't vary with which method you use, they're identical.
Prosecutor: [After a long answer by Professor Schoenthaler.] That's all fine and dandy, but..
Geragos: Objection, to comments by prosecutor.
Judge: Sustained. [Commercial.]
Nancy Grace, of Court TV, former prosecutor: Aren't you surprised the judge gave his ruling, up front, without any arguments?
Jack Furlong: No, as you know, these are based on the briefs filed.
Dr. Jeffrey Gardere, psychologist: Very disrespectful, without hearing the arguments.
Jack Furlong: He [judge] has the thought-out arguments, on paper.
Nancy Grace, former prosecutor: Whatever Geragos objects to is being sustained, and I find that very disturbing. Maybe Geragos is correct. Let's go back in and see.
Prosecutor: So you get a bunch of students, who do this for a grade in your class, to go out and make phone calls to see if this case should have a change of venue?
Professor Schoenthaler: No.
Prosecutor: You DO look for outliers, don't you? [Out of ordinary, or individual.]

Professor Schoenthaler: Yes.
Prosecutor: With raw data, no outliers; were there?
Professor Schoenthaler: Yes.
Prosecutor: So there's wrong data in the survey?
Professor Schoenthaler: No.
Prosecutor: You don't know if they're telling the truth or not, do you?
Geragos: Objection, calls for speculation.
Judge: It's the same on your side Mr. [prosecutor], so it's apples for apples here. So let's finish this up today, Mr. [prosecutor]. [Most of the court laughs.]
Professor Schoenthaler: Our surveys show great predictability with other cases, when compared to, before and after conclusions by the surveys, and what was asked and decided in court. This survey will prove to be accurate also.
Nancy Grace, of Court TV, former prosecutor: If bus in jurors, can Geragos object?
Michael Cardoza, attorney: Yes, but it'll fall on deaf ears, if already decided. Judicial Council decides on which county, and, or, if to bus in jurors. Thirty years, I haven't seen busing in jurors.
Nancy Grace, former prosecutor: All the witnesses, court personnel, everybody. A mad exodus.
Michael Cardoza, attorney: Politics and economics will decide where it ends up.
Jack Furlong: Well, I wouldn't give Kudos to the doctor, since change of venue is the right thing to do, and I wouldn't give Kudos to the prosecutor, for all the stupid questions he was asking, or the judge for rightly stopping the prosecutor from doing that.
Nancy Grace, former prosecutor: I'm always disturbed when the judge decides objections in favor of the defense attorney and gives his ruling, even before the arguments.
Prosecutor: There are several counties that believe the defendant is guilty, more so than Stanislaus County, correct?
Professor Schoenthaler: You can't go by what one response was in a survey...
Prosecutor: Aren't some people in certain counties presupposed to find a defendant guilty?
Professor Schoenthaler: Yes.
Prosecutor: Did you include those in your survey?
Professor Schoenthaler: No, the information is there, but the survey tell current attitude.

Prosecutor: Aren't they also different on the death penalty?
Professor Schoenthaler: Yes.
Prosecutor: But you didn't break that statistic down, so the court could exclude that?
Professor Schoenthaler: No, cause the court can't factor that in, the penalty... [Commercial]
[headline]: **LACI PETERSON MURDER CASE.**
Beth Karas, of Court TV: Geragos has gone on record to request Los Angeles County.
Nancy Grace, former prosecutor: Any other reason, beside being closer to Hollywood? [Laughter.]
Beth Karas: Nothing other than it is the largest county.
Nancy Grace, former prosecutor: Judge sustains Geragos' objections, even though they're not legal objections. The law books say they're not valid unless objected to correctly.
Michael Cardoza, attorney: The prosecutor had the task of changing the judge's mind, but the judge didn't say which areas concerned him. Suppose jurors did that, and then you had to change their minds. [Waala! Michael may have just exposed the plot, with many sequels to follow. Wonder why Jack Furlong wasn't around anymore, and no mention or thank you from Nancy at the end of the show.]

Court TV **Catherine Crier**, former judge: Geragos can claim a victory. [Court TV shows a video clip of the judge saying that because it's a double homicide case; that weighs heavily on a change of venue.]
Beth Karas: Judge didn't allow prosecutor's last witness. He had two, but the judge hasn't allowed the second. They're in there arguing now, discussing the issue.
Catherine Crier, former judge: Let's listen to what the judge says about Laci being well known. [Court TV shows a video clip of the judge saying, the searches, blood drive, and media coverage changed Laci from ordinary citizen to being well known.]
Catherine Crier: I agree with moving the trial and have said so all along.
Gloria Gomez, KOVR TV Reporter: Judge said alot of articles, especially in Modesto, were biased against Scott Peterson. The Modesto Bee even compared the time line and events with Laci's disappearance and Scott fishing and so forth. The media was split on their articles on whether Scott should get a change of

venue. Many believe that twelve jurors could be found here in this community.
Catherine Crier, former judge: No doubt they could be found, but....
Catherine Crier: [Court TV shows a video of Geragos objecting to the prosecutor saying that the doctor didn't know if responders lied or not, and Geragos objects, with, it's speculative and borders on ludicrous. Shows Geragos' facial expressions, laughing a little, as did everyone else, as the judge tells the prosecutor that it would be the same with his survey, in that he wouldn't know if the responders lied or not. Catherine then says that the state can't get high profile experienced prosecutors, and that there is a young guy for the state against a veteran defense attorney.]
[headline]: **JUDGE GRANTS CHANGE OF VENUE IN PETERSON CASE.**
Beth Karas, of Court TV: Judge granted change of venue, and he indicated he may not stay with the case. We'll know where, next Wednesday.

Fox News Channel **Greta Van Susteren:** Up next, Scott Peterson scored a major victory in court today and will an inmate be forced to testify at his trial? Stay tuned.
Greta: Scott Peterson scored a major victory.
Claudia Cowan: Judge says no way Scott could get a fair trial in Modesto. [Fox shows a video with the judge saying, Despite the court's best efforts, the media coverage....]
Stan Goldman, Fox News legal editor: Judge gave preliminary ruling, unless you can talk me out of it. Felt coverage hadn't cooled down, although he hinted he didn't want to move it out of driving range.
Gloria Allred, Amber Frey's lawyer: Doesn't affect Amber, although Geragos took a cheap shot at the prosecutor and me today.
Geoffrey Fieger, Defense Attorney: Don't think this will change things. Jury pool is contaminated all over United States. It'll be delayed and hurt the defense.
James Hammer, assistant San Francisco prosecutor: Up to Council to tell the judge which counties are available and then a hearing on January 20th, and the judge will say which county.
Greta: Up next, will an inmate be forced to testify, and is he involved in Laci's death? Stay tuned. [Later, Fox shows a video of

Geragos saying: It's a very, Very, good day, today, with headline]: **VICTORY FOR THE DEFENSE.**
Ted Williams, Divorce Attorney: I can't wait for Gloria and Geragos to get married.
Greta: I'm surprised it got moved. Judge could say everyone in California is biased.
Ted Williams, former D.C. police detective, attorney: Smart judge and he doesn't want to leave these issues for appeal.
Greta: Suddenly the prosecutor, is just like the defense attorney and a visitor.
Stan Goldman, Fox News legal editor: Under evidence rules, Geragos has the right to see ABC's entire interview with Scott and not just the edited part on TV, if not, interview may not be allowed in court.
Gloria Allred, Amber Frey's lawyer: Why would prosecution want ABC interview? If....[Gloria ifs alot.]
Stan Goldman, Fox News legal editor: Gloria, why would the defense want something that then the prosecutor could use against the defense; No, they want the tape cause there may be something there to help the defense.
Greta: Does the inmate who burglarized Scott Peterson's neighbor, hold the key to the answer? Stay tuned.
James Hammer, assistant San Francisco prosecutor: Could be a powerful piece of evidence. Maybe, if...[James ifs alot.]
Geoffrey Fieger, attorney: Could be like Jim says, could be he saw Laci and what happened and help Scott, or hurt Scott.
Gloria Allred, Amber Frey's lawyer: What if one of the women testifies that Scott Peterson didn't want children in his life?
Greta: You got a tip?
Gloria Allred, Amber Frey's lawyer: No idea what those other women will say, but, if so, that's powerful.
Greta: We still don't have a murder scene.
[headline]: **WHEN IS THE TRIAL. 1/14 MOTION TO DISMISS. 1/20 CHANGE OF VENUE. 1/26 TRIAL START.**
[Fox shows a video of the prosecutor saying, The defendant has right to speedy trial and hasn't waived those rights, so we're ready to go ahead with trial right away.]
Geoffrey Fieger, Defense Attorney: Total lack of physical evidence, minus two hairs, and rest is based on what Scott said.

Stan Goldman, Fox News legal editor: If they had other physical evidence to connect Scott Peterson to this death, they'd have arrested him earlier. No bombshells in this case.
James Hammer, assistant San Francisco prosecutor: I've said even a junior prosecutor could have won the O.J. case anywhere, except in Los Angeles. Scott is felony stupid with what he's said and done.
Gloria Allred, Amber Frey's lawyer: Remember, four hundred witnesses on the prosecutor's witness list.
Greta: Four hundred witnesses and four months to try by the prosecution; talk about felony stupid. How long Bernie? In D.C.?
Bernie Grimm, Defense Attorney: Eight days.
Greta: Ted?
Ted Williams, former D.C. police detective, attorney: Two weeks.
Greta: Geoffrey. In Michigan?
Geoffrey Fieger, attorney: Eight days to two weeks.

1/9/04

Court TV **Beth Karas**: Some students in University of California stated that they made up poll results for a survey they performed as part of their class grade for the Professor who testified in the Scott Peterson hearing yesterday, and with the judge issuing a tentative order to change venue. The judge may reconsider.

Court TV ticker: Judge agrees to move the Scott Peterson murder trial from Scott Peterson's hometown of Modesto, California, after the defense argued pretrial publicity clouded the potential jury pool.

Court TV ticker: Judge grants change of venue request for Scott Peterson's trial.

Court TV **Jean Casarez**: It's six of seventy-two students who said they made up poll results.
Nancy Grace, of Court TV, former prosecutor: It could be grounds to open up old cases, that relied on polls.
Jean Casarez: Santa Clara County has had other high profile cases.

Court TV Catherine Crier Live

James Hammer, assistant San Francisco prosecutor: Prosecution has a right to appeal the decision, but the judge was right to move the trial, cause you still have all the pretrial publicity.
Richard Greene, jury consultant, body language expert: We see Scott Peterson sitting there smiling and laughing with Geragos, and I think he hurts his chance with a jury, when he wasn't even able to work up an emotion or tear for his wife while she was missing. [Whoa. Sounds like Richard has been with Scott for over a year now. The smiling they are talking about, was when the prosecutor told Professor Schoenthaler that the responders to the survey could have lied, and the judge told the prosecutor that his survey could have the same results, and, the courtroom had a moment of laughter.]
Catherine Crier, former judge: Do you think that a prosecutor would go for the death penalty, knowing they'll get a life sentence verdict, but with the knowledge they'll be getting a jury willing to give the death penalty?
James Hammer, assistant San Francisco prosecutor: Absolutely. That knocks out alot of jurors, and won't be a liberal jury.

1/11/04

Fox News Channel [headline]: **FOX POLL: 72% THINK SCOTT PETERSON WAS INVOLVED IN LACI'S DEATH. 3/5/03 BECOMES HOMICIDE INVESTIGATION.**
Geoffrey Fieger, attorney: Judge did the right thing to grant change of venue; problem is, he's not gonna find a place any less prejudicial than he's got now.

1/13/04

Court TV ticker: Hearing to discuss charges against Scott Peterson to be held tomorrow.

Court TV ticker: Scott Peterson is charged with killing his wife, Laci, and their unborn child.

CNN **Linda Fairstein**, former N.Y. City sex crimes prosecutor, author: Extraordinary amount of information in the Scott Peterson case, and when all said and done, we'll see alot more evidence. Michael Jackson; probably guilty. Kobe Bryant; never should have been charged. Maybe dismissed before going to trial, or if trial, acquitted. Scott Peterson; the easiest for the prosecution to try and will be found guilty. I'd love to be in the middle of this.

MSNBC Dan Abrams [Michael Jackson case]
Jeanine Pirro, prosecutor Westchester County, New York: Absolutely gagged by the judge [Geragos]. Every time Geragos comes out of the courtroom in the Scott Peterson case, he talks to the cameras.
Karen Russell, Defense Attorney: Yes.
Dan Abrams: I think so, and a sweeping gag order, which may be unconstitutional.

Fox News Channel [headline]: **COPS UNDER FIRE?**
Greta Van Susteren: Is Scott Peterson's lawyer, Mark Geragos, going after the cops in the Scott Peterson case? Stay tuned. Up next, did the cops in the Scott Peterson case violate the judge's gag order and does his lawyer have a secret document to prove it? And, why is Scott going back to court tomorrow? Will the charges be dropped against him? Stay tuned. Up next, did the police in the Scott Peterson case violate the gag order and slip a top secret document to a supermarket tabloid and can Mark Geragos prove it? Stay tuned. The Modesto Bee reports the prosecutor leaked document to tabloid. Transcript of a statement Scott Peterson gave to police.
Bernie Grimm, Defense Attorney: Yea, a violation, but won't dismiss charges.
Ted Williams, former D.C. police detective, attorney: Leaks could have come from anywhere.
James Hammer, assistant San Francisco prosecutor: Won't find where leak came from. Geragos is more skilled with the media than the prosecutor.
Ted Williams, Defense Attorney: Jim sounds like a prosecutor. More than likely the prosecutor leaked it.
Greta: It'll be shown to the jury anyway.
James Hammer, assistant San Francisco prosecutor: Not a huge secret at this point. Won't be dismissed tomorrow. Saddam Hussein has better chance to be released, with an apology from the American people. Rather thin physical evidence. Be interesting to see what theory prosecution uses. Geragos will use the O.J. defense. [Seems like Jim and James keep waffling.]

Bernie Grimm, Defense Attorney: GPS puts Scott a couple miles from where bodies found.
James Hammer, assistant San Francisco prosecutor: There's a window of time, where Scott wasn't answering his phone and calls went to voice mail, so there's some explaining to do there. [Wonder how many phony phone calls were made to the Peterson tip line, saying that bodies were floating in the Bay? Or was one of these calls, true?]

1/14/04

MSNBC ad: Tune in to Dan Abrams to find out why Abrams says Scott Peterson may be free sooner than you think.

Court TV **Beth Karas**: Different judge has to hear motion to dismiss, since Judge G. was the one with probable cause. [headline]: **JUDGE DENIES REQUEST OF SCOTT PETERSON TO DISMISS CHARGES.** [Court TV shows a video tape of Geragos saying]: If he dumped the body in the Bay on the morning of December 24th, then the baby could not have been three to four weeks older than that day.
Christine Grillo, prosecutor Brooklyn, New York: Geragos is putting too much weight on the baby's age.

Fox News Channel Greta Van Susteren [Fox shows a video of today, in court.]
Prosecutor: The defendant says he went fishing on Christmas Eve and that in itself is ludicrous, for anyone to think or say that they bought a small aluminum boat and went fishing, is, in and of itself, to suspect murder. [Scott is looking at the prosecutor, while the prosecutor is saying this, and looks in wonderment, what the hell kind of person could be saying such nonsense.]
Greta: Still there's no murder scene.
James Hammer, assistant San Francisco prosecutor: Right, and it's something for people to think about. The scene, blood; it's stuff you see on CSI and people expect to find it.
Greta: December 24th, one call to Laci and one to his Dad. Wouldn't you want to know where Scott was when he made those calls; but, for some reason the cops can't, or won't, say.
Bernie Grimm, Defense Attorney: Yea, if I was Geragos, I'd file a motion just to find out.

Greta: From what I heard, police say they don't know, or for some reason, that can't be determined.

1/15/04

CNN Larry King [12 midnight, CNN shows a video tape of the prosecutor today in court.]
Prosecutor: People don't wrap themselves up in plastic, or duct tape, and go jump in the Bay. If that's not a corpus delicti of homicide, I don't know what is.
Jo-Ellen Dimitrius, Jury Consultant: Farther away; less exposure.
Nancy Grace, of Court TV, former prosecutor: Prosecution will want it within driving distance.
Beth Karas, of Court TV, former prosecutor: We're all hoping it's in ..., cause there's nice hotels there.
Caller: Thanks, Chris Pixley, for being on the side of the defense, a much needed position. What one we mostly hear ..., and lies.
Larry King: What's your question?
Nancy Grace, of Court TV, former prosecutor: No, Court TV does not take a position.
Beth Karas, of Court TV, former prosecutor. No, Court TV does not take a stand and I'm not either. Mark Geragos wouldn't even talk to me if I took a stand; No.
Caller: Think Scott will testify?
Johnnie Cochran: Remains to be seen.
[headline]: **JUDGE DENIES DEFENSE MOTION TO DISMISS CASE: TRIAL STARTS 1/26.**
Nancy Grace, former prosecutor: No way, no way. Has to explain too much. Amy ..., his neighbor, he told December 24th he'd been golfing.
Chris Pixley, Defense Attorney: Two words why not testify; Weak case.
Larry King: Media wants him to testify.
Beth Karas: Oh, yes, as a former prosecutor, I'd love to cross examine him.
Caller: You are awesome Nancy, and Chris, this isn't a weak case at all. Why didn't he take someone with him fishing?
Beth Karas: Don't think it'll start January 26th.

MSNBC Dan Abrams [MSNBC shows a video of the January 14th hearing.]

Prosecutor: If you listen to the defense, Laci Peterson would have had to finish mopping the floor, change into tan pants, take the dog walking far enough away from the house to be abducted, and the dog come back home, all in a span of ten minutes. We know that couldn't happen, and therefore, this man, Scott Peterson, [prosecutor points his finger at Scott] is guilty of murder.
Prosecutor: People don't wrap themselves in duct tape and then go throw them self in the Bay during the winter.
Geragos: Case is nothing more than, from early on, this man having an affair and don't bother me with the facts, don't let that get in his way. And let's convict this man cause he had an affair and went fishing.

1/19/04

Fox News Channel Geraldo Rivera [Fox shows a video of the hearing to dismiss charges.]
Geragos: Prosecution gives the court three possibilities; killed by Scott, suicide, or accident. Thirty-two weeks pregnant on December 23rd doctor visit; thirty-three weeks by the doctors on view of the baby's body. The prosecutor wants the court to decide on wild speculation. Those aren't the only possibilities. Being abducted is the most likely, and with Scott not having anything to do with that.
Jeanine Pirro, prosecutor Westchester County, New York: No cause of death, but we have manner; homicide. Have girlfriend, neighbors, lies, says golfing, when he was fishing, license to fish on December 23rd and December 24th, no one knew he had boat, a deliberate liar, lied to Diane Sawyer on TV.
Man: Probable cause is to determine if crime has occurred and if this defendant committed that crime. No crime shown and no connection of defendant to a crime.
Jeanine Pirro, prosecutor Westchester County, New York: She didn't commit suicide; she didn't jump off the boat.

1/20/04

Court TV **Beth Karas**: Judge first heard motion to reconsider change of venue. He'll announce his venue at ten till the hour. The prosecutor wants Santa Clara, San Mateo, ... The defense wants Orange, Alameda, ...
Lisa Bloom, of Court TV, Civil Rights lawyer:

Funny how various counties are making a pitch to get the trial, with all the revenue from media, etc.

Beth Karas: Judge says Orange County is a consideration since half of the prosecution witnesses have to be flown in anyway. Judge heard motion to reconsider from the prosecution, and to put Sacramento back on the list. Judge said he didn't rely on the survey alone to decide change of venue. The professor is in court, but no testimony taken from him. Judge says media isn't using the nine students' names and ain't going to come forward anyway and risk expulsion from school, but if the prosecutor wants to investigate, go ahead, but he doubted if he'd get very far.

Lisa Bloom, Civil Rights lawyer: There should be severe consequences for bringing this into a court of law.

James Curtis, former prosecutor: Yea, even if Schoenthaler didn't know, he should have known.

Beth Karas: Geragos said, if moved to Orange County, he won't apply for public funds for defense and save over a hundred thousand dollars for the state. Says savings on busing witnesses will save defense alot of money.

Former prosecutor: It's unethical for Geragos to say he can save the money if in one place and not another. Either he needs the money for a fair trial or he doesn't.

Lisa Bloom, Civil Rights lawyer: Stick around and we'll have that court tape for you as soon as the hearing is over.

Beth Karas: Judge has selected San Mateo for the Scott Peterson case, eighty miles away. Courthouse is five miles from San Jose airport, so that helps.

Jean Casarez, of Court TV: San Mateo did send an ad to the court?

Beth Karas: Yes. Scott Peterson hasn't waived time, yet, so it's going to begin January? We'll learn Friday if this judge will move with the case to San Mateo. He had said he didn't want to travel with it. Judge G. said if he's on the case, he won't allow any electronic media in the hearings, but that doesn't cover the trial. Alot of suppression motions to hear, along with that television issue. [The hearing begins without audio.]

Judge: People's motion to reconsider change of venue. Mr. Harris.

Mr. Harris, prosecutor: [Somebody's music phone is playing in the background.] Nine students came forward and survey may be fraudulent, and played role in change of venue.

Judge: Also concerned about type of media coverage also.

Mr. Harris, prosecutor: Professor Schoenthaler survey saying different in Counties ..., and ours says ..., so if judge strikes Professor Schoenthaler, then decision may change. We have Professor Schoenthaler's statement that he didn't verify the survey.
Judge: What are you gonna do, subpoena those sixty-five students and bring them all in to testify. What makes you think the students will tell the sheriff who they are.
Mr. Harris, prosecutor: They will come in and say the professor said the survey was for class and not to come into court. I think they will come in and testify. The professor or University won't turn over the list to us. We have one student who says he falsified information in the past.
Judge: Don't have enough legal grounds to strike Professor Schoenthaler statement or testimony, but my decision isn't solely on that. The media base is the same with Channels [TV stations], and I don't need a survey to tell me that. What's shown here is shown on Channels [TV stations] also. Don't think it's a University issue and why should the courts get involved? I'm not going to order that. Survey and testimony are not given much weight in court's final decision and as far as that goes, if the court throws out this and other survey and testimony, the decision would be the same, based on media reports. Your choices of venue. Let's start with you, Mr. Harris.
Mr. Harris, prosecutor: ...County, San Mateo second, and ..., Orange County should be court's last choice.
Judge: Well, let's discuss that point, since Orange seems to be Mr. Geragos' first choice. [Commercial. Later, Court TV comes back with Geragos talking.]
Judge: Sorry, Mr. Geragos, but I can't consider costs in court's decision.
Geragos: Orange County seems to be the choice of AAOC. If you're looking for a place with less media and Orange County seems to be that choice here. You just fly into Orange County and boom you're there at the courthouse.
Mr. Harris, prosecutor: Orange County airport closes at different times. Court can look at court costs.
Judge: Maybe convenience to witnesses, but not costs.
Mr. Harris, prosecutor: Can't look at costs to deny change, but okay on where to change to. Funny how defense counsel comes up with money if he doesn't get his way. There will be alot of witnesses in this case. Orange County may be an abuse

of discretion, for four hundred people to caravan to southern California. Santa Clara is our first choice, resources there, availability of courtroom.
Judge: Says they'd need time to renovate courtroom, sorry wrong County.
Mr. Harris, prosecutor: San Jose also has a wonderful courthouse. San Mateo is our second choice; within driving distance.
Judge: I'm moving it mainly on amount of media coverage, and part in the community involvement in the case. Proceed to trial on the 26th?
Geragos: That's correct. This trial takes precedent over the other, since he's free on bond and this is a capital case. [Commercial.]
Judge: Try to keep potential juror list from public, so they'll be more forthcoming. If I do it, I will say, I won't let the electronic media in. So, you'll may want to discuss that among yourselves. As soon as we have the name of a judge who will take it, I'll let you know.
Geragos: Well, we're still hoping you'll travel with us.
Judge: Well, I've already said I don't want to travel, if there's a judge that will take it.
Geragos: I need the certified record of January 8th.
Judge: Yea, you'll need that for your brief.
Geragos: You'd be surprised if you knew how we did that. [The TV disk of 8,000.]
Judge: Page 41, line 1, is Mr. Geragos speaking, not Mr. Harris. [Court TV shows a close-up of Scott Peterson, for thirty seconds or more, as he drinks water and stands up to leave the court. The view that we see on TV is a camera view, with capabilities different from our eyes, and from a view that the public doesn't get to see in a courtroom.]
Professor Schoenthaler, professor of Criminology: Students knew it would be used in court, would be reimbursed, had twenty days to do twenty surveys, but some students went outside the University to claim the limelight and have themselves viewed as the good guys.
Jennifer: And you've testified and qualified as an expert in court.
Professor Schoenthaler: Yes, and also outside of the University. Very sound ruling, cause Scott Peterson would have gotten nothing short of the death penalty here. Two pockets, Los Angeles Bay and San Francisco Bay, that are okay and not much difference and judge did exactly that with San Mateo.

Beth Karas, of Court TV, former prosecutor: Prosecutor's last choice was San Mateo. [Well Beth, actually it was his second choice.]
Michael Cardoza, attorney: San Mateo is very conservative.
Beth Karas: How did they vote, and it counts?
Michael Cardoza, attorney: Republican, so be careful Mark, on what you ask for, cause you might just get it. What's interesting is that Geragos almost threatened the judge to get him to move it. He tried to use it as a club. [I could feel the judge just a shakin' all the way over here in Virginia, Mike.]
Nancy Grace, of Court TV, former prosecutor: Leslie, how do you feel about Geragos using the argument that Mrs. Peterson is sick and not able to travel?
Leslie Austin, psychotherapist: Arguing that Scott's Mom is sick and while Laci's Mom sits there suffering every day is disingenuous.
[Court TV shows a video of Geragos saying]: I think both sides would like Judge G. to stay on the case.
Nancy Grace, former prosecutor: Geragos, please don't try to speak for both sides on wanting to keep Judge G. It began with the truck, which was covered on the inside, with Scott's blood, Judge G. gave it back to Geragos.
Michael Cardoza, attorney: Each side has one challenge, to say they don't like the judge picked.
Nancy Grace, former prosecutor: Professor Schoenthaler has a fraudulent survey and this judge says whatever.
Beth Karas: San Mateo hasn't had a death penalty case since 1991, and in that case they gave the death penalty.
Nancy Grace, former prosecutor: Will the trial go, on January 26th?
Beth Karas: So far, yes. Prosecution is expected to ask for two weeks to get ready and move stuff to San Mateo. [headlines]: **SAN MATEO ABOUT 90 MILES FROM MODESTO. SAN MATEO HAS LOBBIED COURT TO HOST TRIAL.**
Richard Gabriel, jury consultant: Makes a difference on where it is. It's a better move for Geragos. Conservative area, different venue from Modesto itself.
Gary Casimir, former prosecutor, attorney: Jury selection will take longer, cause millionaires don't have time to sit on a jury.
Beth Karas: Officials are democrats and area voted for Gore in last election.

Richard Gabriel, jury consultant: Excellent choice; given other areas. Alot more democrats up there. Very reluctant to dole out the death penalty.

1/21/04

MSNBC **Dan Abrams:** Up next, the Scott Peterson case. The trial's leaving its hometown of Modesto and moving to a small community in north California. What will that mean? Stay tuned.
Dan Abrams: Today the judge moved the trial ninety minutes west to San Mateo. [MSNBC shows a video of Geragos saying]: As long as two weeks to hear motions in limine. [in limine, is Latin and means, at the outset.]
Jennifer London, of MSNBC: Geragos says it would be a waste of resources to have another judge come in.
Dan Abrams: Less than 700,000; 49% male, 59% white; median income, $80,000; professionals, 42%.
Gary Casimir, former prosecutor, attorney: Liberal side out there. Defense may think they have a good jury pool. Jury will look beyond speculation.
John Burris, former prosecutor, attorney: Not a jurisdiction that's necessarily friendly to defendants or defense lawyers.
Dan Abrams: San Mateo officials sent material to Modesto to get the trial.
Anne Leclair, San Mateo Visitors Center: We did not solicit the trial, but did send information sheet telling what we had available.
Dan Abrams: Are you worried San Mateo may be seen in a bad light if Scott Peterson isn't convicted? That the rest of the country will think your community turned loose a murderer?
Anne Leclair: Not at all. [MSNBC shows a video of Michael Nevin, San Mateo Board of Supervisors saying: The family won't be left behind. We'll do what justice requires. We'll make sure Laci gets justice.]
Anne Leclair: We did not lobby.

Fox News Channel Greta Van Susteren
Laura Ingle, KFI Radio Reporter: Geragos said Scott is ready to go; wants the trial to begin, and Geragos is ready to go with it.
Stan Goldman, Fox News legal editor: If there's trouble in picking a jury, then California law allows for Geragos to apply for another venue change. [Fox shows a video of Geragos saying: I'd like to thank the Modesto Bee, because without them, this change

of venue would never have been possible. Professor Schoenthaler is shown saying, The University and myself are doing separate investigations to find out what happened and who did it. We're calling the numbers back to see who did this. Headline]: **VENUE SURVEY SCANDAL.**

Ernie Spokes, Professor Schoenthaler's attorney: Geragos did a good job on filing his response to the prosecutor's motion to quash the survey, cause the prosecutor used hearsay testimony for his survey.

Greta: Mayor, what have you heard about the Laci Peterson case?

Jeff Ira, Mayor of Redwood City, California: Not much, just what we see on the nightly news. Just generalizations, not many specifics at all.

Greta: Do you get cable there?

Mayor: Oh yes.

James Hammer, assistant San Francisco prosecutor: Today was a big win for the prosecution. Doesn't have police mistrust the way others do.

Geoffrey Fieger, Defense Attorney: This could scare the Jesus out of him. They solicited for the trial. They won't want to be the community who set Scott Peterson free, but the place that hung Scott Peterson.

Bernie Grimm, Defense Attorney: This is one of those where, be careful what you ask for, cause you might just get it.

James Hammer, assistant San Francisco prosecutor: He's gonna get a jury that he's not very happy with.

CBS The Early Show: The Scott Peterson trial has been moved from Modesto. The judge said that Scott Peterson could not get a fair trial in Modesto, due to all the pretrial publicity. [CBS shows a video, while the lady is saying this, but, this is not a video of Scott Peterson in court yesterday, but rather a video of Scott looking, very concerned and somewhat in defiance, at the prosecutor. The prosecutor, in this particular video, was saying that Scott Peterson murdered his wife and unborn son, and was taking place at the hearing to dismiss charges against Scott Peterson. A little bit of mix and match, that'll show Scott as being defiant, in nearly every TV news story.]

CNN Headline News: Scott Peterson's trial was moved yesterday and now it has a new judge, Judge Richard A. will preside over the Scott Peterson case.

1/23/04

Fox News Channel [headline]: **JUDGE REMOVAL.**
Stan Goldman, Fox News legal editor: Prosecutor has objected to the judge, Geragos plans to challenge that in court. Under California law, each side gets one objection to the judge. Geragos can call the prosecutor to the stand, says he waited too long to object. The prosecutor already talked to the judge and discussed the case. The judge is eighty-two years old.
Greg: We heard a prosecutor's secretary made a remark that the judge was biased against the prosecutor.
Stan Goldman, Fox News legal editor: I'm relishing the idea of one cross examining the other. They were both students of mine. [Geragos and the prosecutor.]

Fox News Channel **Uma Pemmarjau:** The Scott Peterson murder case has a hearing today. Meanwhile the trial has been delayed, as the prosecutor has refused to accept the appointed judge in that case.
Voice: A new judge in the Scott Peterson case becomes history. What happened? Stay tuned, we'll explain.

Court TV **Beth Karas**: Last thing before Judge G.. Just yesterday, the prosecution exercised its challenge against this judge. [Court TV shows a video of Scott looking at the prosecutor, during the hearing that the prosecutor was saying that Scott murdered Laci and their baby. This is the TV news corps' favorite video of Scott now, but they don't ever put it into context for us. They say he never shows any emotion for Laci, but it's because they use these videos for other purposes.]
Beth Karas: Another judge will be appointed and the process will begin again. Scott Peterson has not waived his right to a speedy trial, so come hell or high water, the case is scheduled to begin next week. [headline]: **COURT TV TRIAL DATES: SADDAM HUSSEIN: NO TRIAL DATE SET.**

Court TV Vinnie Politan and Kimberly Newsome
[Court TV shows a video of the hearing, already begun.]

Court Administrator: AAOC will get back with us Tuesday or Wednesday on another judge.
Jean Casarez, of Court TV: Scott Peterson back in court today.
Beth Karas: Two and a half hours ago; two recesses. Last time before Judge G.. Geragos challenging the prosecutor's choice to take the judge off. Geragos said to Judge G., that he doesn't have authority over this case anymore and that he shouldn't even. [Court TV shows a video of Geragos saying, already determined who is the judge. Issue is, whether prosecutor timely filed to challenge judge.]
Beth Karas: Prosecutor met with the judge, talked, and agreed to meet next Monday, then filed this challenge.
Jean Casarez: Judge may not have had authority to change date?
Beth Karas: Judge G. said, look, time is running out. And that it was the defense who filed motion for change of venue, so a two week continuance should be okay, and Geragos then responded with, look judge, you may not even have jurisdiction to be handling this trial.
Geragos told the judge not a proper motion for him to hear, since he's not on the case. Judge agreed and put it over till February 1st. Trial must begin that day. Prosecutor says the appointed judge is biased towards the defense, to be more compassionate. On February 1st, this issue will be settled and judge said to be ready to begin motions in limine, two weeks of hearings on evidence; dogs, GPS, eavesdropping on Scott's phone call errors, and Amber's testimony. [headline]: **HEARING SET FOR 2/1 IN SAN MATEO, CALIF.** [Court TV shows this headline, with Kobe Bryant's, and Scott Peterson's picture, side by side.]
Mickey Sherman, former prosecutor, defense attorney: It's a sham by the prosecutor. If the defense did this, they'd be roasted.
Michael Cardoza, attorney: It's an unwritten rule in California that prosecutors don't do that.
Beth Karas: I know the background of the chosen judge, and he's sympathetic to defendants. Just months ago, the judge took away a jury decision of the death penalty.
Michael Cardoza, attorney: It was an arson case. But here, nobody can say how Laci died.
Nancy Grace, former prosecutor: We'll let me...
Michael Cardoza, attorney: Okay, go ahead Nancy, go ahead.

Dr. Larry Koblinsky, forensic scientist: Let's remember the O.J. case. That case set the tone for a judge. The judge is critical to the outcome of the case.
Mickey Sherman, Defense Attorney: So he overturned a death penalty case. That's why he was chosen as a judge, cause he can overturn a sentence when he knows the facts don't support it. That's the kind of judge we want in there.
Gloria Gomez, KOVR TV Reporter: The prosecutor held onto the tool box from the back of Scott's truck and plan to test it to see if Laci was transported to the warehouse from the house. From what I've heard, someone Laci's size, Was able to fit into that box.
Chris Pixley, Defense Attorney: Geragos is correct to preserve this for the record. The judge will be recused, but the prosecutor doesn't have the same strike for the next judge and he'll have to accept whoever's chosen.
Catherine Crier, former judge: Couldn't the prosecutor strike for just cause.
Chris Pixley, Defense Attorney: Well, as you know, that's very difficult. When Judge G. was chosen, Geragos went to him and said, look, you know you shouldn't be on this case.
Beth Karas: If the motions begin on February 1st, alot of motions. If the defense gets just one evidence thrown out, then it's a victory.
Catherine Crier, former judge: It's interesting, cause we'll get back to the facts, the best part, and that's the part I like.

CNN Larry King Live
Chris Pixley, Defense Attorney: You get one strike, without challenge, but what Geragos is saying, is that the prosecutor filed it too late, that Judge G. was already off the case and that the prosecutor filed with the wrong judge.
Rick Distaso, prosecutor: If the defense hadn't made motion for change of venue, we'd be having it here, but that was his choice.
Jo-Ellan Dimitrius, jury consultant: Wealthy, somewhat liberal, tends to vote republican.
Nancy Grace, of Court TV, former prosecutor: I've never used a jury consultant. I like to use my gut feeling, look them in the eye. It wasn't that long ago that Geragos wanted the prosecutor removed, the judge removed, and said the cops were ganging up on him. [headline]: **DEFENSE WANTS JUDGE GIROLAMI TO CONTINUE PRESIDING OVER THE CASE.** [CNN shows a video of Geragos in court saying: I don't know if this court still has

jurisdiction, and in fact the Chief Justice of the California Supreme Court stepped in and made the decision on which judge and that's not according to procedure or law. I guess, he's the Chief Justice, and he can do what he wants, but so far, no one is following the statutes or law. I don't even know if any court in California, now has jurisdiction of this case, then shows a video clip of Geragos outside of the courthouse saying: The judge has ordered that we go to ..., on February 1st, and then it'll be decided which judge we have.]

Ted Rowlands, KTVU TV Reporter: There's three civil cases against Scott Peterson, no profit to Scott, no $250,000 Laci insurance to Scott; put off for one hundred and twenty days.

Chris Pixley, Defense Attorney: This is a very interesting case, alot of circumstantial evidence, but nothing physical to show he killed her, and after investigating and talking to the families, there's just no way he's guilty.

Nancy Grace, of Court TV, former prosecutor: Uh, that's the Peterson family, right, Chris.

Chris Pixley, Defense Attorney: Naturally, just like you've talked to the Rocha's and the other side, that's natural.

Caller: They should let you handle it, Nancy.

Larry King: Well, there'd never be any trials.

[Laughter from the guests.]

Ted Rowlands, KTVU TV Reporter: The prosecutor wanted some time and we'll see if this'll allow that.

Nancy Grace, former prosecutor: We all try to find someone guilty by how they act, but we don't know and it doesn't mean anything.

Ted Rowlands, KTVU TV Reporter: About sixty miles away; about an hour and a half drive.

Fox News Channel **Greta Van Susteren:** Coming up, Scott Peterson's lawyer, Mark Geragos says not so fast. Did the prosecutor wait too long and miss the window to get the judge tossed? Up next, Scott Peterson left Modesto for the first time since his arrest and did the judge leave the door open for him to stay on the case. [Fox shows a video of Geragos saying, Mrs. G. should pack her bags and go on vacation with your husband.] Will trial start Monday?

Stan Goldman, Fox News legal editor: Nah, no judge yet. February 1st issue is the judge, one appointed by Chief Justice of California Supreme Court? Scott Peterson and Geragos have every

right to start trial within 60 days of the arraignment, actually 62, since of weekend, unless good cause.
Greta: Good cause could be cause the change of venue wasn't decided until last week.
Stan Goldman, Fox News legal editor: There were three people today in the audience, three reporters. Geragos said the Chief Justice of California Supreme Court was like an 800 pound gorilla, despite law, like a dictator he chose the judge, and Judge G. said, well they might just tell me to stay on the case, and if that happens, I'll forget about all those nice things you've had to say about me.

1/28/04

MSNBC ticker: Retired judge is chosen to preside over the Scott Peterson murder case.

Court TV ticker: Retired judge ... has been chosen by the Chief Justice of the California Supreme Court to preside over the Scott Peterson murder trial.

Court TV **Beth Karas**: Only six of the twenty-two death penalty cases he's heard, was the death penalty handed down, and on one, he almost cried in handing down the death penalty, so, he is a bit defense orientated.
Walter Cannady, defense attorney: I'm rather surprised to hear that, cause he gave the death penalty to a client of mine, and there were no tears shed. Don't think he'll be receptive to cameras in his courtroom.
Beth Karas: He's been known to allow cameras in, for opening, closing, and the jury verdict. So what happens when Monday gets here and the first judge refuses to step aside or yet the prosecutor has asked for a two week extension for good cause determination, and yet the judge has been told to be ready for hearings Monday.
Rod Wheeler, former police detective, crime analyst: Remember, I was one of the first to say Scott Peterson was guilty, and low and behold, two months later, he was arrested and I think he'll be convicted.

2/2/04

Court TV **Jean Casarez**: Geragos wants the judge to distribute a questionnaire to about a thousand potential jurors, before the trial begins, so the venue issue may not be over yet.

Court TV ticker: Mark Geragos, Scott Peterson's lawyer, argues that the trial should be moved closer to his parent's San Diego home, as the Peterson's have spent one million dollars for the defense of Scott.

Court TV **Jean Casarez**: There will be no cameras in the courtroom in the Scott Peterson case. Mark Geragos stood up, first thing, and said, You Honor, we want you on this case and are satisfied with you stellar reputation. The judge replied, thank you for the confidence.
[headlines]: **A SCHEDULING HEARING IS SET FOR FEBRUARY 9. DEFENSE WITHDRAWS CHALLENGE CONCERNING NEW JUDGE.**

Court TV ticker: San Mateo courthouse is charging $51,000 for a parking space to park TV trucks at the courthouse.

Court TV **Jean Casarez**: The judge had to ask Scott Peterson if it was okay to continue the trial date a few days.
San Mateo Sheriff: Scott Peterson is cooperative, nice and no problem. He's in protective custody, in a cell by himself. He has access to talk to other prisoners and can communicate back and forth. [Court TV shows a video of when Scott was looking at the prosecutor, in court, saying that Scott murdered his wife and child. That hearing, to dismiss the charges, took place some time ago. Well, at least most of the news corps are beyond the orange jumpsuit, handcuffs, and leg irons, but then the jury hasn't been chosen yet.]

2/3/04

Court TV **David Wright**, of National Enquirer: Motive, Scott never wanted the baby. A few weeks after Laci disappeared, several of Laci's girlfriends said Scott was less than enthusiastic about the baby and left Laci sad about that. Started from the moment she took home pregnancy test, they'd been trying for two

years to have a baby, but when she told Scott, he was hung-over from a party the night before, and said he wanted no parts of it. Met Amber on a blind date. One of his girlfriends showed up at his house at dawn and accused Laci of running around with her boyfriend and then she found out it was the other way around.
Catherine Crier, former judge: Oh, Boy.

2/5/04

Court TV **Beth Karas**: A Peterson witness dies of natural causes. She is the Peterson neighbor who claimed she saw Laci walking her dog on the day she went missing.

2/6/04

Fox News Channel **Greta Van Susteren:** An important witness for the defense has died of natural causes. Said she saw Laci on December 24th, at 10:15am. [Fox shows a video of the now deceased lady saying: Washing dishes, looking out the window; a beautiful sight, a lady, walking her golden retriever down the street.]

2/9/04

Court TV **Gloria Gomez**, KOVR TV Reporter: Judge has said the witness list will remain sealed. GPS will be first hearing, a Fry hearing, to determine if accepted by scientific community. People are saying that the pollsters are asking questions about evidence; on three people seeing Laci walking her dog, and ...
Catherine Crier, former judge: This could potentially taint a jury pool, wouldn't it?
David Schwartz, former prosecutor: Geragos could take this poll anywhere, cause everybody has heard about the case, he'd get the same results anywhere he goes.
Catherine Crier, former judge: Where does it cross the ethical line?
Bob McNeill, Defense Attorney: Questioning several hundred potential jurors won't cross that line.
David Schwartz, former prosecutor: His fleeing, is consciousness of guilt.

Gloria Gomez, KOVR TV Reporter: Geragos has said to the judge that he doesn't want any media interviews involved or played in the trial. I had a twenty minute interview with Scott myself.
Catherine Crier, former judge: Yea, and during the interview, his cell phone rang and he failed to answer it, with his wife, Laci, still missing. There's a film coming out, this week, on Scott Peterson, called 'The Perfect Husband'.

Court TV ticker: Judge presiding over the Scott Peterson murder trial, orders that witness lists and names of potential jurors remains sealed, despite media protests.

2/14/04

Fox News Channel **Greta Van Susteren:** The Perfect Husband on the USA channel. [headline]:
THE PERFECT HUSBAND ON USA CHANNEL.
Gloria Allred, Amber Frey's lawyer: What Amber's concerned about is the effect on the potential jury.
Greta: Yea, that he knew she was dead before the bodies were found.
Bernie Grimm, Defense Attorney: Obviously, they put a spin on it that Scott was guilty.
Stan Goldman, Fox News legal editor: Used innuendo to distort with fact; I didn't kill her, but I know who did. No such statement has ever been found by anyone.
Gloria Allred, Amber Frey's lawyer: Example of inaccuracy; where Scott is appearing to tell Amber Laci is missing, and portrays it after Laci is missing, with where he said he had lost his wife.

[Sounds like the same ole, same ole, to me, or pretty much what these same people have been inventing for months.]

2/17/04

Court TV ticker: Scott Peterson's attorney is expected to be back on the attack today against global positioning deices.

2/18/04

Fox News Channel ticker: Judge rules that Global Positioning technology is generally accepted and fundamentally sound.

Authorities had placed GPS devices on several vehicles used by Peterson after his wife disappeared in December 2002.

Fox News Channel **Lauren Green:** Prosecutors say the GPS shows Scott went to the Bay, at least once, where the bodies were discovered.

Fox News Channel **Stan Goldman**, Fox News legal editor: Some bad news for the police today. The pregnant woman who police hypnotized, can't testify. She was the one prosecutors thought they could get to say it was her that the people saw walking her dog in the neighborhood that day.
Martha McCallum: Scott Peterson's attorney, Mark Geragos, now wants two juries to hear this case.
Stan Goldman, Fox News legal editor: Two separate juries, one to hear the case and one to for the death penalty, if convicted. Since no one could sit on a single jury, who doesn't believe in the death penalty, and therefore there'd be a pro-prosecution jury.

2/19/04

Fox News Channel **Lauren Green:** Prosecutors go to court today in the Scott Peterson case over wiretapped phone calls. Scott Peterson's phone was tapped for three weeks in January, and two days in.... Peterson's defense attorneys say the taps were illegal and that police listened to confidential calls between Peterson and his attorneys. Police say they did nothing wrong and followed the rules.

2/23/04

Court TV **Diane Dimond:** Up next, Scott Peterson's phone calls that his lawyers don't want you to hear. Sex, lies, and videotapes the defense wants tossed out. Four days of hearings.
Gloria Gomez, KOVR TV Reporter: Yea, the judge keeps listening to the recorded tapes between Scott Peterson and his former attorney, Kirk McAllister.
Lisa Pinto, former prosecutor: So what, a few tapes out of many. So toss those out and bring in the rest.
Dana Cole, Defense Attorney: Curiosity killed the cat and the cops just couldn't resist listening.

Diane Dimond: Geragos said the prosecutor hasn't given him all the evidence and Geragos is saying there's evidence in the 8,000 pages turned over that points to the person who killed Laci.
Gloria Gomez, KOVR TV Reporter: The police say the prosecutor is trying his best to get the information to the defense.
Dana Cole, Defense Attorney: There's Brady evidence, to exculpate, and must be turned over within a certain time and sanctions applied if the prosecutor doesn't comply.
Diane Dimond: Scott fixed a Christmas dinner and even invited his neighbor, with Laci missing.
Lisa Pinto, former prosecutor: Yea, and when police asked for something of Laci's so the dogs could track her scent, like sunglasses, Scott asked the police for a receipt. Come On! Your wife is missing and you want a receipt for the items that may help find her? [Remember, Lisa, you've got a detective on this case that forgot his keys in Scott's truck while he took Scott's gun, left his folder at the warehouse where he found the pliers which later turned up with a hair that magically turned into two hairs upon the detective's visit. I'd want carbon copies of the receipt also.]

2/26/04

Fox News Channel **Savannah Guthrie:** There's a new law on Capitol Hill that would protect the unborn fetus. It's called the Laci and Conner law.

Court TV ticker: Redwood, California judge rules [decides] that jurors in the Scott Peterson double murder trial will not be sequestered.

Fox News Channel **Claudia Cowan:** There will be but one jury in Scott Peterson trial, and not two. The dog evidence won't be allowed, as it's not reliable.

2/27/04

Fox News Channel: The judge has denied Scott Peterson's attorney's request that the jury be sequestered during the trial. Jurors will be allowed to go home in the evening. Peterson's attorney wants the jury sequestered so they wouldn't be exposed to media reports. Another blow to the defense is that there will only be one jury. Defense attorneys had requested one jury for the penalty phase.

Court TV **David Wright**, of National Enquirer: Scott said he saw Laci's image of her ghost in the mirror, while she was still missing. February 8th, police discovered he had rented a storage locker, a warrant on February 18th, and found in the garbage, the wedding album of Scott and Laci.
Wendy Murphy, former federal prosecutor: I'd want to know, as a juror, that he saw Laci's ghost, so as to get those guilty feelings off his mind.
Mickey Sherman, former prosecutor, defense attorney: I don't know if you heard or not, but the ghost is on Larry King tonight.
David Wright, of National Enquirer: Scott expressed 'micro fear' when asked about blood in his truck and 'micro anger' when asked about the bedroom blinds being pulled.
Wendy Murphy, former federal prosecutor: Who cares? He had $15,000 and on the Mexican border. He has a micro chance of being acquitted.
Mickey Sherman, former prosecutor, defense attorney: And a micro chance of getting a fair trial.

2/29/04

Fox News Channel [headlines]: **DOGS TRACKED LACI PETERSON'S SCENT TO SCOTT'S WAREHOUSE. DOGS PICKED UP LACI'S SCENT AGAIN ON THE INTERSTATE. SCOTT PETERSON TOOK THAT INTERSTATE TO THE SAN FRANCISCO BAY ON 12/24/03.**

3/1/04

Fox News Channel **Laura Ingle**, KFI Radio Reporter: Closed door proceedings today with the wiretap calls, to see if they violated attorney-client privilege. Ruling will be tomorrow, also about the tracking dogs, whether that evidence is admissible at trial.
Greta Van Susteren: 76 of 3,000 calls were to his lawyer.
Laura Ingle, KFI Radio Reporter: One call was released to the media; where Amber asked Scott if he had anything to do with Laci's disappearance.
Greta: Yea, and we know that one doesn't show or mean much.

3/3/04

Fox News Channel **Claudia Cowan:** Scott Peterson's defense attorneys are livid and may appeal the judge's ruling, allowing the taped phone calls to be admitted into evidence. So the jury will hear Scott's voice, and even though he won't take the stand and they'll hear all of the inconsistencies with Amber Frey.
Laura Ingle, KFI Radio Reporter: Alot of people here in Redwood have already made up their minds, with Scott going fishing and where the bodies washed up, but others say they can listen to the evidence and then make up their mind.
Greta Van Susteren: Up next, questioning the potential jurors. Will they have to air their dirty laundry in public? Stay tuned. [headline]: **JUROR QUESTIONNAIRE HAS 127 QUESTIONS TO ANSWER.**

3/10/04

Court TV: Scott Peterson's lawyer is asking for a change of venue, saying too many potential jurors already believe Scott Peterson is guilty, relying on juror questionnaires.

3/16/04

Fox News Channel [headline]:
LACI PETERSON CASE. "FUGITIVE DEFENSE".
Dr. Cyril Wecht, Forensic Pathologist: Police concentrate on a suspect and overlook evidence, sometimes on purpose, as with the knife in the Fugitive case, where a bloody knife was found in the water, not far from the murder scene.

3/22/04

Court TV **Savannah Guthrie:** What about the TV interviews Scott did before his arrest?
Rusty: All of them will be admitted at trial, in court. Prosecutor said that if Scott can get up and tell all these lies, then the jury has a right to hear it. [headline]:
OPENING STATEMENTS SCHEDULED FOR MAY 17.
Rusty: They've got 300 potential jurors to go through.
Savannah Guthrie: We understand the prosecutor's star witness, Amber Frey, is pregnant. Will this affect the trial date?
Rusty: We haven't heard.

Yale Galanter, defense attorney: The problem is, that Scott's going to hang himself with these statements.
Steve Cron, defense attorney: With Scott out there talking about blood in his truck, what do you say?
Gloria Gomez, KOVR TV Reporter: Each time I asked him about telling Amber that Laci was missing, he dodged the question and finally stopped the interview and said, Listen, I don't know how much of this you'll air, but this is irrelevant to Laci missing. The rest of the interview was fully rehearsed; he had all his other answers prepared.
Yale Galanter, defense attorney: Every thing he told TV, every rumor, every response will now come in [court] this way.
Gloria Gomez, KOVR TV Reporter: We asked Geragos, why he doesn't file his change of venue motion, cause alot of jurors think Scott is guilty, and Geragos replied sarcastically, well, we're just waiting for the evidence to build. Did you her the jurors' responses?
Steve Cron, defense attorney: The case has been so exposed to the media, the problem will continue, no matter where in California.
Catherine Crier, former judge: I agree, this is a bit of a delay tactic; we'll see.

3/23/04

CNN Headline News: Several California newspapers will not get to see completed juror questionnaires in the Scott Peterson trial.

[One of the most favorite ways in attempts to degrade defense attorneys, is to accuse them of delay. If the prosecutor and media can convince the public, that defense attorneys are delaying, then obviously, the defendant is guilty and doesn't want to go to trial; be convicted, and go to jail. To help this fallacy along, media files hundreds of briefs that the defense has to respond to, and the prosecutor withholds evidence from the defense attorneys, causing more briefs to be filed and hearings to be held, causing more delays in the defense getting to examine, learn, and analyze the government's evidence.

If successful in this misperception, media and government have taken one more step in swaying public opinion towards guilt with their own manufactured 'evidence' of suspicion and doubt placed upon the ethics and honesty of the people representing the defendant himself, to the court, in the court, and in front of the jury, which will be chosen from those being influenced.

Sorta takes all the wondering out of where the U.S. Constitution's Sixth Amendment, 'the accused shall have the right to a speedy trial, came from, and why.]

4/15/04

Court TV ticker: Scott Peterson's lawyers say they will perform DNA tests on blood found in a brown van.

[Yesterday, a potential juror was dismissed for not being truthful, to get into the jury pool.]

Court TV ticker: Prosecutor's in the Scott Peterson murder case say they will perform DNA tests on blood found in a van.

4/26/04

Fox News Channel **Greta Van Susteren:** A new eyewitness pops up in the Scott Peterson murder trial and what did she see that morning? Tonight, a new surprise witness.
Laura Ingle, KFI Radio Reporter: The 43 year old is breaking her silence on what she saw December 24th, early morning. Seven to seven-thirty, driving her car, and saw a truck with a boat, and a large object covered with a tarp. She tried to relay this to police, but it doesn't fit in their time line.
Greta: Why aren't police using this?
Laura Ingle, KFI Radio Reporter: They say it just doesn't sound like Scott. He wouldn't have been able to get to the Marina and back home to make the call from his home.
Geoffrey Fieger, attorney: Introduces doubt into the prosecution's case, but Geragos won't use her either.
Jayne Weintraub, Defense Attorney: Cases like this bring out loonies, like Skeeter and Dirty. Why not hypnosis, polygraph; police do others and not her?
Yale Galanter, defense attorney: Doesn't fit the prosecution's theory of their case. Geragos has his. It doesn't fit either.
Greta: I could come up with a theory, after sitting through the preliminary.
Bernie Grimm, Defense Attorney: Yea, at 7:30am, he could have been doing something.

Greta: Yea, like cleaning up. But then the defense would punch holes in it. The trial on May 17th?
Geoffrey Fieger, attorney: Yea, looks like it. After Peterson gets convicted, who's gonna want Geragos to come to Santa Barbara to defend them?
Greta: Judge in the Scott Peterson case gets another mystery letter, this one with evidence in it.
Laura Ingle, KFI Radio Reporter: Letter #2 contains some of the same evidence as the first one, with some hair and a fingerprint, that the person says belongs to the person responsible. The judge discussed it in open court and each side will get to test it.
Geoffrey Fieger, Defense Attorney: Who's got the money to test the hair?

4/27/04

[The media has a special internet site, established by government to alleviate the unusual burden created by media's publicizing of the case, and of the media's desire to obtain the documents filed with the Superior Court in this case. This site is not available, nor accessible to the public.

So, we have to trust that media will inform us of everything that government is telling media about what government is doing to Scott Peterson. That's hearsay on top of.... Is this special and targeted release of information about the case to media because media is an arm of the government, a corporation, a medium that is our surrogate, or a special branch of the government which knows best about what the people should and will hear?]

Court TV
Mike Fleeman: Cory Lee Carroll was in jail on a parole violation.
Muna: Dirty and Skeeter? Have tracked down Dirty, in a local prison. A background that he might be capable. They met in a local strip club.
Catherine Crier, former judge: Date they met?
Muna: I'd have to look in the file. Absolutely passed a polygraph by a former police captain. The police went to Fresno, bar, and other agencies checking. Modesto won't confirm it, but did verify it. Won't use at trial, since it conflicts with their evidence. They took a picture; found the lady. Someone saw Scott talking to Cory.
Mike Fleeman: If there is a picture, it'd be quite an asset. The date said they met; Scott was with his father.

Muna: Not November 29th; If you're so sure about your facts, but you're so far off. People have offered a great deal of money for it, but we're dealing with a very dangerous and notorious gang and no one wants to come forward.
Bob McNeill, Defense Attorney: If they could actually show they killed Laci, they'd come forward with it. You have to have a staff, as an attorney, to follow up on these leads.
Mike Fleeman: It's a question of manpower. We'll see if they have time to do it.

Court TV ticker: [Michael] Jackson suggested Geragos spending too much time on the Peterson case.

[If we allow jurors to be analyzed, criticized, dissected, and publicly humiliated by the TV news corps, aren't we allowing ourselves to be indoctrinated and conditioned to produce a certain jury verdict, which in essence is a verdict that has nothing to do with the evidence presented in a court of law. This makes it rather easy for community leaders and those with government positions to get rid of, or put behind bars, anyone who opposes them and anyone they suspect belongs behind bars, just merely by planting suspicion in the media or by filing charges against them. An American's life can be ruined merely by government suspicion, whether done so by government by deceit or trickery, as well as when done so with legitimaticy.]

4/30/04

Court TV **Kimberly Guilfole Newsom**, of Court TV, former prosecutor: WOW! An unbelievable verdict here in the Jayson William's trial.
Judge: [To the jurors] You know from walking through all the media equipment and trucks outside, that media will try to question you and you need to know you can say, No. You may have to repeat, No, cause they'll ask. You can talk to them, but what you'all discussed during deliberations, should remain in your mind only. What goes on in the jury deliberations is to remain there and not open for public comment.
Vinnie Politan, of Court TV: A mistrial on the second count.
[Within five minutes of the verdicts, Court TV hosts have given Jason Williams 364 days in jail and retried him on the second count, of course, with a guilty verdict. The prosecutor in

the case was found to have withheld critical evidence, had experts testify that aren't experts, and had other witnesses change their expert reports to the court.]

5/3/04

Court TV **Jean Casarez**: If there's enough of an outcry from the community, not only will Jayson Williams be retried, but the judge will be replaced if the letters are sent to the court.

Court TV ticker: Scott Peterson's attorney is expected to file a change of venue request for his client's double murder trial.

5/7/04

Fox News Channel **Greta Van Susteren:** A third letter to the judge in the Scott Peterson case; make a difference?
Ted Williams, former D.C. police detective, attorney: No.
Jeff Brown, Defense Attorney: Won't change the defense, not require any additional motions.
Greta: How'd a man, who's a future son in law get on the jury?
Jim Hammer, assistant San Francisco prosecutor: Shows how low the standard is in California.
Jeff Brown, Defense Attorney: I'm always afraid of the 'stealth' juror, the one who says they don't have an opinion.
Greta: Change of venue from Redwood? Zero percent chance.
Jim Hammer, assistant San Francisco prosecutor: No chance. Jury will be picked soon. Defense needs just one juror to say circumstantial evidence isn't enough to give death penalty and vote not to convict.
Greta: Ok, coming up soon, Opening statements in the Scott Peterson trial.

5/10/04

Fox News Channel **Greta Van Susteren:** Prosecutors in the Scott Peterson case strike back. [headline]: **VENUE CHANGE FIGHT.**

5/11/04

Fox News Channel ticker: Arguments today on moving Scott Peterson trial a second time. Geragos wants the case moved to Los

Angeles. Prosecutors say juror bias could be found anywhere in California.

Fox News Channel: Mark Geragos will be back in court today, arguing for another change of venue. He wants the judge to move the trial to Los Angeles, where the media saturation hasn't been so intense.

CNN
A prospective juror in the Scott Peterson case: With all the publicity, I don't know. It's hard to Not think he's guilty.
CNN: Six jurors have been picked already.
Former prosecutor: He's not really expecting to get another change of venue, he's just hoping he'll get more peremptory challenges [dismissed without having to give an explanation] of jurors.

<u>5/12/04</u>

MSNBC **Christy:** Judge has delayed opening arguments in the Scott Peterson murder case to June 1st, stating that selecting jurors has been a long process.

[If it's okay to lie, cheat, deceive, and make false allegations during an investigation, would this not make it an inquisition. Who teaches these people to switch back to honesty, and when? Are they able to? How then would the deceit, lies, and cheating be deleted to only leave the truth. Seems like it would be awfully hard to remember all that stuff.

Why do we allow these same people [the uniform] to come into our preschools and present a totally opposite presence on the unknowing, who will have that bubble burst in another setting. What kind of example does this create among a growing, aging, and replenishing society? Experience shows that once you create something, then you must deal with it.]

<u>5/21/04</u>

MSNBC ticker: Jury selection continues today in the Scott Peterson murder trial. Opening statements are scheduled for June 1.

MSNBC ticker: Laci Peterson murder case, Pool of 76 jurors selected for the Scott Peterson murder trial. Final selection begins next Thursday.

5/25/04

ABC News ticker: Defense argues that new evidence points away from Scott Peterson in the murder of his wife Laci and his unborn son.

Fox News Channel: In the Scott Peterson case, the defense says new evidence just turned over by the prosecutor, may clear his client.
[later]
Fox News Channel: Is the prosecutor in the Scott Peterson case breaking the rules? Scott's attorney, Mark Geragos seems to think so. [headline]:
DIRTY DEFENSE?
[Much later, Nothing.]

5/27/04

Court TV: Jury selection is supposed to wind up today in the Scott Peterson murder trial in Redwood City. The jury will consist of 12 jurors and 6 alternates. The trial is set to begin on Tuesday. Scott Peterson is charged with the murder of his pregnant wife, Laci and their unborn son. In related news, Laci's mother, Sharon, is trying to prevent Scott from selling Laci's items.

CNN: A jury has been selected and certified by the judge and lawyers. We're just getting word that the jury in the Scott Peterson double murder trial has been seated.

CNN: A jury of 6 men and 6 women have been seated as the jury in the Scott Peterson double murder trial. Opening statements are scheduled for Tuesday.

5/28/04

Fox News Channel: One juror in the Scott Peterson case has been replaced, after claiming extreme financial hardship if he served.

MSNBC Dan Abrams
Gloria Allred, Amber Frey's lawyer: The hypnosis expert [prosecution] wasn't licensed, but the police didn't know.
Jayne Weintraub, Defense Attorney: This was a [defense] witness, who knew Laci Peterson, their next door neighbor, and she came forward right away, no agenda, and said she saw...
Dan Abrams: Three dark skin people, not African American, in the Peterson yard, She came down that street, asked them what were they doing...
Jayne Weintraub, Defense Attorney: And the police didn't like what they heard, so they hypnotized her, and then now want her testimony thrown out.

CNN Headline News: The 16 jurors chosen for the Scott Peterson trial, 9 are white.

Fox News Channel **Greta Van Susteren:** A former police officer on the jury, but then again he's been charged with assault on a police officer. Both defense and prosecution chose him. These are 12 very important citizens willing to put in their best and I applaud them.
[later]
Greta: Don't forget to stay tuned live, Tuesday night, for opening statements in the Scott Peterson case.

Fox News Channel Bill O'Reilly [Fox shows Scott coming into the courtroom in handcuffs, leg irons, and a red jumpsuit.]

<u>5/29/04</u>

[Notes were not taken of what the TV news corps are saying about the jurors, but, as usual, the degradation begins, so when the jury gives a not guilty verdict, the TV news corps have a way out; blame the jury. The news corps continue to base their analysis from a 'guilty' Scott Peterson, and all it takes to acquit is one juror with reasonable doubt. This is just a bit backassward. The proper American thought process of our legal system, is that it takes 12 jurors to find guilt beyond a reasonable doubt, or it's not guilty, since the presumption of innocence continues.

Many legislatures have overridden this principle, where, without a unanimous jury verdict of 'not guilty', then the trials can continue for life. This greatly increases the probability of a life sentence, one way or another, once the trial begins. Where is it, that once the trial begins, that the presumption of innocence, disappears? This is in effect what happens, since the U.S. Constitutional prohibition on government trying an accused twice for the same crime, is nullified.]

5/31/04

MSNBC: It's almost time for the Scott Peterson double murder trial to get under way tomorrow with opening statements. We'll discuss both prosecution and defense strategies when we come back. Stay tuned in the upcoming hours.
[later]
Stay tuned. A year and a half after his pregnant wife, Laci, went missing, Scott Peterson is ready to stand trial.

[The actual story in the above statement, is that Scott was arrested over 14 months ago, has been sitting in jail every day, and his 'speedy trial' is ready to begin. The elongated trial is over, and the TV news corp 'cut, splice, and dice the video' trial now emerges.]

MSNBC
Paul Pfingst, former prosecutor: The jurors are pretty removed from the case publicity. [headline]: **2ND DEFENSE REQUEST TO CHANGE VENUE WAS DENIED**. There's no smoking gun piece of evidence. Tomorrow, for the first time, we'll hear what the prosecutor's circumstantial evidence is. Defense can lay back and say they don't add up; or pick a theory, like she was picked up by three people. [headline]: **MOST EVIDENCE AGAINST PETERSON IS CIRCUMSTANTIAL.**
Host: Laci's Mom lost her battle to keep Scott from selling his story.
Paul Pfingst, former prosecutor: Yea, but to keep items of the estate, and there really isn't much left, everything's pretty much gone, to pay for Scott's defense.
[later]
Paul Callan, former prosecutor: You'd think they could come up with jurors without a connection to the case.
Gary Casimir, former prosecutor, attorney: Geragos' strategy is that he doesn't have a burden to prove anything, irregular that most of America thinks Scott is guilty.

[later]

Lester Holt, of MSNBC: Not since the O.J. trial has the nation's attention been on a domestic homicide, like the Scott Peterson case. We'll go over the possible defense and prosecution legal strategies when we come back, with Court TV's legal analyst, Nancy Grace. Stay tuned.

Nancy Grace, of Court TV, former prosecutor: 6 men, 6 women. I think we have a pro-state jury. It's death qualified. If it was a soft kill, there'd be no DNA evidence.

Lester Holt: Geragos convinced the judge to allow in more witnesses.

Nancy Grace, former prosecutor: State must discredit them, they claim to have seen Laci.

[later]

Gloria Allred, Amber Frey's lawyer: If Amber turns out to be motive, that'll be important to the jury.

Robert Shapiro, Defense Attorney: A trial is full of emotions and to have a woman come forward, while he's married and his wife pregnant, will go to the heart of the jurors.

Gerry Spence, Defense Attorney: I don't know if Laci would tell her Mom or others about an affair. About 50% of males in the U.S. have committed adultery, and if you're gonna use that as evidence of murder, it's a pretty sad shape.

Jeanine Pirro, prosecutor Westchester County, New York: 50% don't have their wife end up murdered. He didn't just say he lost his wife, he said he'd be able to be with Amber after January 25th-26th.

Gloria Allred, Amber Frey's lawyer: Much of what Amber's testifying to, will be corroborated, by other witnesses. [Bolstering.] And don't believe Laci wouldn't tell her Mom of an affair, that's unbelievable; that's illogical; it's just not real.

6/1/04

MSNBC Dan Abrams [Plays a video of a January 29, 2004 interview:

Scott: It's been a while since suspicion has come to me and therefore some aren't looking for Laci.

[later]

Gerry Spence, Defense Attorney: We have other people who have seen her abducted and taken away. There's a circumstantial case here, with not a single, not a single, fact that ties Scott Peterson to murder.

Dan Abrams: Where the bodies were found, isn't the defense going to have to say he was set up?

Jeanine Pirro, prosecutor Westchester County, New York: We have location, location, location, and it isn't a coincidence.

Robert Shapiro, Defense Attorney: This case, from a defense view, won't be tried on a bit by bit basis. The flawed investigation, the hypnotized defense witness by the prosecutor, no place of death, etc.

Jeanine Pirro, prosecutor Westchester County, New York: We have a guy very comfortable with lying.

[later]

Dan Abrams: One hair, says Laci's in the pliers. One gallon concrete anchor from the boat, other concrete in the warehouse.

Gerry Spence, Defense Attorney: Emma Jean is with me everywhere, her hair is everywhere I go. That hair, turned out to be multiple hairs. These people are taking this trial back to the witch hunting days. He can't get a trial, if everything he does is tried in the media, and everything he does is seen as guilt.

Jeanine Pirro, prosecutor Westchester County, New York: Everything he's done and said is relevant. All these little knit-pickin issues, we can argue about.

Gerry Spence, Defense Attorney: If you, or Mother Theresa, is charged with murder, and everything you do or say is recorded; If you wash your clothes, you're guilty; if you play golf, you're guilty; if you mop the floor, you're guilty. Give me all this time and all this media, and both you and Mother Theresa will be convicted.

SCOTT PETERSON'S TRIAL BEGINS

Court TV shows Scott coming into the courtroom in an orange jumpsuit, handcuffs, and leg irons, with the lady lawyer appointed by the court in April, 2003.

Beth Karas, of Court TV, former prosecutor: The prosecutor's opening statement is continuing now, for 2 hours. He says Scott lied to police. Said Scott said he went fishing for about an hour and a half, but then it began to rain, but the Harbor Master said it

didn't rain at the docks on the 24th. Prosecutor said Scott said he and Laci were watching Martha Stewart that morning and there was something about marmalade on her show. But, when police pulled up the shows, the marmalade was on the December 23rd show and not the December 24th show. So what he remembered was from the day before. Scott also made 11 phone calls from 10am to 6pm on December 24th, which is unusual, cause he was doing something, like dumping the body.
[later]
Beth Karas, of Court TV, former prosecutor: One thing, Scott drove 90 miles to fish, instead of choosing one of the closer places to fish.
John Burris, Defense Attorney: We've had many people in this country who weren't guilty, but because of the intense media coverage, felt they couldn't get a fair trial and fled the country. Scott may have felt this. With the intense media coverage, he changed his appearance, but he was also out looking and searching for Laci.
[later]
Beth Karas, of Court TV, former prosecutor: The judge gave an hour and forty-five minute lunch break and the prosecutors are still giving their opening statement. They say Scott met Amber through a friend, who told Scott he'd better be serious about this, and of course she didn't know Scott was married. Scott told Amber that he didn't want kids, that Amber's little girl is enough for him; and all the while his wife, Laci, is 7 months pregnant at the time and 8 months or 8½ months, when she disappeared.

We expect to hear about the brown van in Geragos' opening statement, probably sometime tomorrow, as the prosecutor is methodically going through each piece of evidence against Scott Peterson. The judge reversed his decision on not allowing the testimony of a police hypnotized [defense] witness, since Geragos made a good argument last week, that another person, a man, corroborates her story, saying he saw three men forcing a pregnant woman into a van that morning. So he will allow that testimony at trial, even though it wasn't allowed at the preliminary hearing, mainly because these could be big issues on appeal.
Diane Dimond, of Court TV: Yea, and we don't know if Geragos will throw in the satanic cult with the brown van, but we'll see.
[later]

Beth Karas, of Court TV, former prosecutor: Five hours maximum on a courtroom day here.
[headline]: **PROSECUTION EXPECTED TO CALL HUNDREDS OF WITNESSES, THE DEFENSE 18**.
Bob McNeill, Defense Attorney: If he, the prosecutor, goes on and on, the jury may ask, where's the evidence.
Catherine Crier, of Court TV, former judge: It's his, the prosecutor's, chance to tell his story uninterrupted, as long as there's no objection.
Leslie Synder, former New York Supreme Court Justice: Not having any physical or forensic evidence in this case is very surmountable in this case with circumstantial evidence.
Gloria Gomez, KOVR TV Reporter: In an interview, Scott said he told friends that some doctored photos may come out with his picture, but don't believe them, cause it wasn't him, and today the prosecutor showed photos of Scott and Amber.
Beth Karas, of Court TV, former prosecutor: The tracking dog followed the scent from the parking lot, down to the boat ramp, so the jury just learned that. [Followed Scott's scent?]
Catherine Crier, former judge: Cause of death? Water alone?
Leslie Synder, former New York Supreme Court Justice: It's Geragos' job to cast doubt on the cause of death, [laughs], it's his job...
Catherine Crier, former judge: As a defense attorney, do you cast all these defenses out there; that she was seen being dragged into a van, that tape was over Conner's neck, that he looked older than 8½ months, or do you just choose one?
Gloria Gomez, KOVR TV Reporter: On December 28th, he saw Laci in the neighborhood, and they, the 2 men, held a blanket up, and she was urinating by a fence, they helped her back into the van.
Catherine Crier, former judge: Yea, I ain't believing this, three days after she went missing, seen in the same neighborhood.
Leslie Synder, former New York Supreme Court Justice: Yea, not credible.

CNN Headline News: The prosecutor today said that Scott lied about leaving home at 9:30am, since cell phone towers show he was still home. Prosecutors say his boat was covered in gasoline, which would make it almost impossible to find any trace evidence. They say he lied to investigators when they confronted him with photos of Scott and Amber at a Christmas party and yet, Laci, pregnant, attended a Christmas party that night, alone. We don't hear what Geragos has to say on the defense side until tomorrow.

[Remember, this is not evidence, it's just the prosecutors making statements about what they believe the witnesses and evidence will show, to the jury. Both the prosecutors and defense attorney, at some point in their opening statement, must tell the jury that what they say is not evidence.]

MSNBC **Dan Abrams:** He had just finished playing golf, the day he was arrested. He wasn't heading to Mexico.
Deborah Norville: There was a burglary, that day, in the Peterson neighborhood.
Dan Abrams: The prosecutor will question that, they say it was 2 days later. Some will say he went to the Bay, others will say because they were searching for the bodies. But, why rent a car? His behavior isn't normal for someone who lost their wife.

[The 6:30pm national news in Richmond, VA., shows Scott coming into the courtroom, in an orange jumpsuit.]

MSNBC plays a video tape of Scott leaving a message for Laci at 2:15pm: I'm at the Berkeley Marina and can't make it in time to pick up the basket for Papa. Thought you might get this message and someone go over there and pick it up. See you in a bit. Love you, Bye Sweetie.

Fox News Channel **Greta Van Susteren:** The prosecutor never said Scott murdered Laci.
Gloria Allred, Amber Frey's lawyer: Well, he was being a gentleman.
Greta: The prosecutor stated that the hairs in the pliers was wound down inside of them. What if he overstated that?

6/2/04

[The prosecutors' opening statements were discussed throughout 6/1/04 and into 6/2/04, but, so far, at 2:30pm EST, no defense opening statement on TV.]

Court TV shows Jackie Peterson, Scott's Mom: Today you're going to hear the truth.

Beth Karas, of Court TV, former prosecutor: One hour and forty-five minutes for Geragos' opening statement. Highlights; an effort to interrupt Scott's conduct. Scott tried to find his wife; many efforts. He didn't throw his life away, with Amber, they had two dates, not a motive for anything. Amy, Laci's sister, says the pants, the slacks, Laci was wearing are 'not' consistent with the slacks she had on while at her shop December 23rd. They're different altogether, the draw string, the color. Baby born alive, the size, medical exams, December 23rd Laci saw her doctor. The twine and tape not on Conner by accident. A witness says someone pulled Laci into a van.

Geragos was very effective on the items tested; and nothing found, in the house or the warehouse. He didn't say Scott would take the stand.

Vinnie Politan, of Court TV: Alibi; fishing and Laci found there? Framed? Coincidence?

Beth Karas: Didn't hear him deal with that. Alot of objections by the prosecutor to the defense's opening statement. Scott owned 4 boats in his lifetime, fishing since he was four years old, not a novice.

Kimberly Guilfole Newsom, of Court TV, former prosecutor: Compare the two openings.

Beth Karas: Geragos is charismatic, but people said they think the prosecutors' statement was better. Both effective, the van, baby born alive. I'm not criticizing anything Distaso does.

Kimberly Guilfole Newsom, of Court TV, former prosecutor: Okay, Beth, that's right, play it safe out there.

Robert Talbot, Professor of Law, San Francisco Law School: I'd like to see Geragos deal with why that body was found there in that Bay, the $64,000 question. He's going to have to appeal to the jury's common sense and have it make sense. The judge will instruct the jury to rely on their common sense.

[later]

Court TV shows a video of,

Gloria Allred, Amber Frey's lawyer: The leading cause of death for pregnant women, is the husband.

[later]

Beth Karas: Housekeeper will be the first witness, left dirty rags in the washer. Scott took the rags out and washed his clothes. Laci ready to mop the floor, 8½ months pregnant, when he was ready to go fishing.

Vinnie Politan: Won't witnesses say that Scott had 0% chance of catching a sturgeon and there were many places to fish, closer to home.

Beth Karas: Yes, some experts, the prosecutor said yesterday, that they will say Scott didn't have the right equipment to catch sturgeon. Also experts for Geragos will say a body like Laci, would tip over and capsize a boat this size and it couldn't be done.

[later]

Beth Karas: The judge will allow testimony from witnesses that say they saw Laci after she disappeared. Geragos had floated this theory and has stuck to it. You can't just point the finger at someone other than the defendant [Scott], it's called 3rd party culpability; without good cause, and the judge is going to allow it. Geragos said Scott didn't change his appearance for any reason other than that the media was hounding him everywhere he went and everything he did.

[later]

Michael Cardoza, attorney: The prosecutor said no marmalade on the Martha Stewart Show on December 24th, but the defense opened up with a video of the December 24th Martha Stewart Show with marmalade, so the prosecutor's credibility is open to question. The prosecutor also said Scott went to the Marina looking for bodies, but Geragos showed where the Police called Scott those mornings and said, "Hey, we'll be out there today searching." The prosecutor is open to question and reliability. At the end, Geragos said, not only is Scott not guilty, but he's stone cold innocent.

Jared Lewis, former Modesto police officer: I've been to so many missing person cases and never have I seen where the reporting person can't answer basic questions, like the kind of fish. Detective Brocchini seeks the truth, he's not out there to rush to judgment and make an arrest.

[later]

Court TV versus State of New York, cameras in the courtroom case.

Joe: The New York Court of Appeals said we can't even apply to the court to cover a trial, said there's nothing in the Constitution to permit it, and Court TV would have to file a lawsuit, so we did. [headline]: **NEW YORK IS ONE OF ONLY 11 STATES BANNING CAMERAS IN COURTROOM.**

Fox News Channel **Sean Hannity:** Geragos said that 3 days before Laci went missing, she visited the storage unit and sat in the boat. To me, if proven, the hair means nothing. We hadn't heard this before. It's just now coming out.
[later]
Lis Wiehl, Fox News legal analyst, former federal prosecutor: That's what we want to know, if Scott's going to take the stand.
Jack Levin, criminologist, Northwestern University: It's not enough to talk about womanizing.
Lis Wiehl, Fox News legal analyst, former federal prosecutor: People think they're so smart, that they can get away with murder.
Jack Levin, criminologist: Boyfriends think of abortion during the first month of a pregnancy, but a husband will wait until the last month, and say this is the last straw, and I've gotta get rid of it. That's gonna be the motive. He didn't want a kid.

Fox News Channel Greta Van Susteren
Claudia Cowan: Geragos introduced the Martha Stewart Show. No way Scott would kill his wife for a lady he had 2 dates with. The defense claims Conner was born alive. The maid took the stand today, and the prosecutor said he couldn't remember who he would call next.
Jim Hammer, assistant San Francisco prosecutor: That's Geragos' whole case, to go after the police. The prosecutor got caught in a lie, saying someone else was lying.
Laura Ingle, KFI Radio Reporter: Scott walked into the courtroom with an air of confidence. He wasn't shaken. We've seen this before. Scott is paying attention to Mark Geragos and as Geragos goes along, Scott is nodding his head in agreement. Mark Geragos' voice was louder, more confident, in a story telling way.
Geoffrey Fieger, attorney: Geragos has to make the jury believe that someone planted the body where he went fishing.
Greta: 96 phone calls, from December 24th to February, what do you do?
Yale Galanter, Defense Attorney: Geragos showed very little physical contact and alot of phone contact. Why kill over that?
Greta: Prosecutor forgot to tell the jury, there were several 2-day fishing licenses in Scott's truck, not just the one for December 23rd and 24th.

Ted Williams, former D.C. police detective, attorney: If Geragos can show the fetus was born, then that's reasonable doubt. He was out playing golf while his wife missing?
Geoffrey Fieger, attorney: You'd think he'd be camping out at the police station. And Geragos, he'll, he will get killed on the baby being born alive thing.
Greta: Twine around Conner's neck with a knot in it; born alive?
Dr. Michael Baden, Forensic Pathologist: If born alive, that would bolster it. Prosecution will say picked up in water and not done with human hands.
[Fox shows a video of a man, saying that this is where Laci's body was found, and Conner's across the Channel, 3 days later, behind a housing development. The housing development appears to be within 40-60 yards of the rock-bank of the Bay cove, with tall weeds between the development and the water.]
Dr. Cyril Wecht, Forensic Pathologist: Micro studies to find if baby died, or other natural process. These things are what the experts will get into in this case.
Greta: Medical Examiner wrote that the baby was full-term at the autopsy. Was that a mistake?
Dr. Michael Baden, Forensic Pathologist: It can be mistaken, when looking at height and weight measurements, but don't know about if when doing tests.
[later]
Greta: Will forensics free Scott Peterson? 160 bags of evidence and not a single piece of physical evidence.
Jim Hammer, assistant San Francisco prosecutor: Very seldom do you hear; this is what will convict him.
Geoffrey Fieger, attorney: The twine was around the arm and the tape around the neck. Has anyone asked why Dr. Wecht isn't testifying, he was hired by mark Geragos and gave Geragos some information he didn't like.
Greta: Was Scott Peterson's relation with Amber strong enough to kill?
Jim Hammer, assistant San Francisco prosecutor: The maid said every time she saw Laci, Laci had on black pants and a white shirt.
Bernie Grimm, Defense Attorney: If ya got 3 witness that saw Laci after she was supposed to be dead, that's enough reasonable doubt for me.
Greta: 4 dates with Amber? Two before December 25th and two after?

Gloria Allred, Amber Frey's lawyer: That's not really the issue. It was a relationship to Amber. He continued this long relationship on the phone with Amber. A prayer vigil for Laci, and he's on the phone with Amber. If Scott didn't have feelings for Amber, why would he continue the relationship.
Yale Galanter, Defense Attorney: Remember, what happens on the tapes, is Amber acting as an agent of the State, and nowhere on there does he say anything or confess. A 30-40 day relationship, 4 dates? This was a phone conversation relation.
Greta: December 14th, the prosecutor put up pictures, big ones, of Scott and Amber at her Christmas party and beside that, he put Laci in her dress, alone at a Christmas party.
[later]
Greta: Prosecution says Laci's scent found on the ramp. Why not the boat?
Joe D., dog handler: Without knowing the dog or handler, hard to comment. My dog is a scent dog and not a trail dog. Weather, humidity, heat, others, determine time of scent. I've had my dog confirmed by forensics testing, as well as people confessing to the crime.
Bernie Grimm, Defense Attorney: The expert said his dog was a scent dog, and he don't know if the dog would follow Greta for two blocks or one block. He couldn't answer why. Cause the dog don't know. Is the dog a liar? Any skeletons in his closet? Any affairs?
Jim Hammer, assistant San Francisco prosecutor: Bring on the family witnesses, show how he lied.
Greta: Do you believe he's guilty?
Jim Hammer, assistant San Francisco prosecutor: I'm like the prosecutor, I want the 'real' guy who's the killer.

Fox News Channel **Claudia Cowan:** The spa owner testified that the police wrote down things that she didn't say. Another blow to the prosecutor's credibility. The lady said Laci came in December 23rd, and unlike other wives at the spa, Laci never complained about her husband, nor ever said anything about his infidelity.

Court TV **Nancy Grace**, former prosecutor: We'll go out to the Redwood City courthouse at 4:30pm and we've got alot of questions to ask. Have you heard Geragos' defense theory? Stay tuned.

[later]
Beth Karas: Theme today, 5 witnesses, saw Laci on December 23rd, people who had contact with her. In the morning, to the grocer store; afternoon, the Spa; evening, with Scott to get a haircut. Four said, two different outfits that day, black pants with a white top. At the hair salon, tan pants and a dark top. A facial at the Spa, no complaints of her marriage.
Nancy Grace, former prosecutor: We know Laci was found with tan, drawstring pants.
John Burris, Defense Attorney: Clothes don't matter, people change clothes.
Nancy Grace, former prosecutor: You don't want Laci to be wearing those clothes.
John Burris, Defense Attorney: That's the problem with prosecutors, you only see it one way.
Beth Karas: Appointment, 1pm at the Spa, got there at 12:30.
John Burris, Defense Attorney: Everything we hear and see of what Scott did December 23rd, he was a loving and caring husband, in a positive way and Laci was the same way.
Dr. Caryn Stark, psychologist: He has different stories. Don't care much about loving. Said Amber's child will be enough for him and he didn't want a child. Doesn't sound very loving to me.
[Court TV shows the video of Sharon, Laci's Mom crying, saying, hope the person responsible hears her voice crying for her life...]
[later]
[Court TV shows a video of Mr. and Mrs. Peterson, with Nancy Grace saying: I thought there was a gag order.]
Nancy Grace, former prosecutor: Would you have your client smiling and laughing in the courtroom?
John Burris, former prosecutor, attorney: No, but there's no post script on how a defendant will act.
Beth Karas: Am Rocha is on the stand now. Maid been there 4 times to clean. 8:30am-2:30pm, dark pants, and white shirt, usually what Laci had on when she's there.
Nancy Grace, former prosecutor: One of them mopped the next day, Scott or Laci, and that's an issue for the defense to clear up.
John Burris, Defense Attorney: Alot of us can't recall where we were at, at a particular time of the day, especially when you're not thinking of an alibi or planning one.
[later]
Court TV Catherine Crier Live

Beth Karas: Amy is on the stand now, about 10 minutes ago. A big picture of Laci on the TV screen in the courtroom and it stays up there for the jury to see. [A production #.] Amy will say that the top Laci was wearing was on the top of the dirty clothes in the clothes hamper.

Jeanine Pirro, prosecutor Westchester County, New York: All waist bands are the same with pregnant pants, if they're tan, she was murdered on December 23rd and not December 24th. Where's the question on that?

Beth Karas: Yea, Maybe she went home, took off her blouse and put it in the hamper, and was standing at the closet; she had on a maternity bra, so maybe that's when it happened. The black pants are consistent with what the maid said she had on that day, December 24th, and what other witnesses say they saw her wearing that day.

Jeanine Pirro, prosecutor Westchester County, New York: With the blinds down, that shows Laci wasn't there on December 24th to raise them.

Catherine Crier: Amy's the seventh witness.

Jeanine Pirro, prosecutor Westchester County, New York: Geragos is a master of spin. *Here Laci is 8½ months pregnant and carrying $100 worth of groceries. That's alot of groceries, where's Scott?*

Beth Karas: The Peterson's were loud and openly like a pep-rally sometimes during the opening statement by Geragos when he spoke about the police rushing to judgment and not following leads.

Ernie Riso, private detective: I think he's guilty. What is she wearing, have to do with it? The location of the body. I'd have put several GPS devices in the water and let them float for four months and show the jury where they ended up.

Beth Karas: The paint on the boat apparently matches some paint in the police parking lot.

Catherine Crier: OH!

Mickey Sherman: OH!

Jeanine Pirro: OH!

Ernie Riso: OH!

Catherine Crier, former judge: That's the problem with listening to the media.

Ernie Riso, private detective: I can't see making six anchors, it'd take 3-4 days, No, Uhnt-uh, I ain't buying that. He'd use chains,

rocks, whatever. I don't throw too much weight on the Amber Frey thing; two dates. I can write you a whole book on pickup lines. It will get sympathy from the girl, immediately.
Catherine Crier: Geragos defense; he's gonna say the baby was born alive, umbilical cord cut.
Ernie Riso, private detective: Here in Chicago, within the last two years, people are in jail for cutting baby out of a pregnant woman's stomach.
Mickey Sherman, Defense Attorney: It's a common sense argument.
Catherine Crier: How do you show; Mom decomposed greatly, and Baby not decomposed and in relatively good shape? That the baby was born alive, if there's no physical evidence to show that he was alive?

Fox News Channel [headlines]: **AMY SAID BEIGE PANTS 12/23 EVENING. FOUND WITH KAKI PANTS. SPA OWNER SAID BLACK PANTS 12/23 NOON.**
Sean Hannity: Put 4 people on who saw Laci and the case is over, he goes home.
[later]
Laura Ingle, KFI Radio Reporter: Amy says Laci was wearing tan pants.
Jeanine Pirro, prosecutor Westchester County, New York: *Laci only bought a few groceries, which proves she was tired and didn't want to carry alot of stuff.*
Gloria Allred, Amber Frey's lawyer: The prosecutor is trying to show the chronology of Laci, right up to the point of Laci missing. If all Geragos has is marmalade, then all he has is hot air. [Uh, Gloria, the gag order, which covers Gloria as to the weight of the evidence, was reiterated by the Court of Appeals.]
Fox shows a video of Mr. and Mrs. Peterson:
Dad: He's upbeat.
Mom: He's eating more.
Dad: ....
Mom: A human being again.
[later]
Greta Van Susteren: 500 witnesses for the State?
Jeanine Pirro, prosecutor Westchester County, New York: Can't predict how a trial can go. May need them. The jury came out today with she was tired, she was tired, she was tired, witness after

witness. This shows that she was too tired to walk the dog the next day.

Jim Hammer, assistant San Francisco prosecutor: Geragos asked her if she [spa lady] was against Scott Peterson and she said no. But, it was in the police notes and report. She said they [police] lied. This is twice this has happened.

[later]

Greta: Seems like we have dueling liars in this case. What do you do when an officer writes something, changes it, or leaves something out?

Jeanine Pirro, prosecutor Westchester County, New York: It won't matter at the end of the day. The facts will be important and not whether it was taken down wrong.

Greta: How come if prosecutor's are so bad, they get so many convictions? [RED FLAG! And no bull with horns to chase it. Actually, Greta answered the question, with the facts of the question.]

Geoffrey Fieger, Defense Attorney: Cause juries are inclined to convict.

[later]

Jim Hammer, assistant San Francisco prosecutor: 1½ hours of questioning by the prosecutor [of Amy], destroyed by only 2 questions on cross-exam by Geragos, so far. The pants Laci was found in, were not the pants Laci had on at the Salon when Scott got his hair cut on December 23rd.

6/4/04

[Although TV news corps and the prosecutors compliment one another, it appears that in the Kobe Bryant inquisition, that the police fed the TV news corps with rumor and accusations, while in the Scott Peterson inquisition, that the TV news corps feed the public and police with rumor and accusations.

The TV news corps began their suspicion of Scott in Laci's disappearance, within a day or so of December 24th, which would be shortly before media asked the question, 'Why isn't Scott out of town, in ???, with the others, searching for Laci?' Did the TV news corps come up with this suspicion to get Scott out of Modesto, or did the police get media to ask the question to get Scott out of Modesto. It was during the time Scott was out of Modesto that his home was broken into.

The TV news corps say that the police say that it was just one of the next door neighbors who broke into the house and nothing of value was taken. Scott's home was searched by the police, shortly after the break-in. One thing, or rather two things, constant in this event, are the TV news corps and the police.]

6/7/04

Court TV **Beth Karas**: I don't think Amber's Dad was subpoenaed to testify, but he did write a letter to the judge, saying the trial should be moved back to Modesto, and that Geragos should be taken off the case since Geragos had gone on TV before being retained in this case and had talked about Scott being guilty. I don't think Amber's Dad wants to testify, or will be called to, but he is trying to inject himself into this case.

Fox News Channel
Aphrodite Jones, Crime Reporter: Amy testified that the jewelry given to them was worth hundreds of thousands of dollars and Laci liked to wear it around, and a theory by Geragos is she was abducted for the jewelry.
Stan Goldman, Fox News legal editor: For the prosecution, when the bodies washed up, Sharon called Scott and left a message, but he never called her back. Very strange behavior. For the defense, Amy did say to the defense that Scott would be the last person in the world who would hurt someone, and she, at first, denied saying it, but Geragos showed her the documents, and then Amy admitted that she said that.
Aphrodite Jones, Crime Reporter: At first Sharon said when she went to the Park to look for Laci, and she saw Scott and hollered for him but he didn't answer, but, on cross exam when Geragos asked her about this, he said isn't it true that Scott was over 40 yards away and talking to several police officers, is why he didn't answer.

6/8/04

MSNBC **Dan Abrams:** Amy says Laci was active in walking up to a week before her disappearance.
Jennifer London: Sharon's hardest testimony was while she was at the Park and Scott wasn't engaged in the search, almost distant. Says she never saw Scott the night of the vigil. Said she didn't get

a chance to talk to Scott about what Laci was doing December 23rd to the 24th. The prosecutor played a tape with Sharon and Scott, but the quality of the tape was so poor, that the prosecutor had to get her to fill in sometimes.
Dean Johnson, former San Mateo prosecutor: Geragos sounds like he's doing a very good job.
Joe Tacopina: Laci didn't know of Scott's affair.
Dan Abrams: Amy said she had been invited to Laci and Scott's to dinner for December 24th?
Jennifer London: Amy said Scott asked Amy if she wanted to come over for pizza, as Laci was on the phone ordering pizza, while Amy was cutting Scott's hair.

Court TV
Beth Karas, of Court TV, former prosecutor: Two brothers and step-Dad testified that while the families were up on stage, Scott stayed in the crowd talking to a friend.
Michael Moffetta, Defense Attorney: It was brought out on cross exam by Geragos, that Scott was talking to a friend, before, the vigil. The brothers also said that Scott wouldn't hurt anyone and that it may be Laci's former boyfriend, who had been abusive to her.
Beth Karas: Geragos also brought out that if Conner had been born, then Laci would receive over $100,000, which would go to her at age 30, or to Conner or Scott, but without Conner's birth, the inheritance goes to her siblings.
Nancy Grace, of Court TV, former prosecutor: Well for all we know Scott still did it, cause maybe he didn't know of the terms of the inheritance will.
Beth Karas: Mr. Grantsky said on Christmas day that Scott's fishing story sounds fishy and if Scott knows anything he should tell them.
Lady, attorney: He's the worst kind of a criminal defendant, and I wouldn't want him as a client.
Beth Karas: A conversation with Bret Grantsky, the recording was so bad that Bret didn't even recognize his own voice at first, where Scott told Bret that the blood and life insurance policy stories were a lie. Geragos asked Bret, if by December 29th the media suspected Scott, and Bret said well, not everyone thought Scott was guilty. Bret also admitted that one of his favorite days to go fishing was Christmas Eve.

Catherine Crier, former judge: Scott didn't hug his mother-in-law, wouldn't participate with the family; strange behavior.
Former San Mateo prosecutor: Ron Grantsky stated on cross exam, that he went fishing Christmas Eve at 11am, even later than Scott, yet Grantsky stated all along that he told Scott that 9:30am was too late to go fishing.
Beth Karas: Ron Frey [Amber's Dad] showed up yesterday, has a San Mateo lawyer, and he spoke today, read a letter from Gloria Allred, that if her Dad testifies, he could say something about Amber on cross exam that could damage the case. He doesn't want to be crossed by Geragos, if he does testify.
Dr. Cyril Wecht, Forensic Pathologist: Decomposition can remove any trace of the baby being alive.

1/9/04

Fox News Channel **Greta Van Susteren:** So the prosecutor subpoenaed Amber's Dad, Ron Frey, to keep him from talking in public? The prosecutor had over 500 people subpoenaed.
Laura Ingle, KFI Radio Reporter: Harvey Gimbel said that Scott told him he went to play golf and not fishing. He said he followed Scott twice, when Scott was supposed to be putting up fliers, and said he went to a parking lot once and to play golf the other time. When on cross exam, he was asked why he followed Scott, and Harvey said cause Scott showed more emotion over a burnt piece of chicken on the grill than over his wife missing.
Ted Rowlands, KTVU TV Reporter: Harris [Scott's attorney] got the jury to laugh when he asked Harvey why he was watching Scott for 45 minutes in a parking lot.
Jim Hammer, assistant San Francisco prosecutor: This is 4 witnesses so far, that testified that Scott told them he had played golf and not that he'd went fishing.
[later]
Ted Williams, Defense Attorney: The neighbor lady, who said she found the dog at 10:18am used a stop watch to go back and time herself to get these times, but, yet she couldn't get the times correct.
Jim Hammer, assistant San Francisco prosecutor: I disagree with Ted, she called back the police and told them she had got it wrong at first.

Ted Williams, Defense Attorney: She didn't look at her watch or clock when she found the dog; she went later, looked at a receipt, and then traced her steps to get the time.

6/10/04

Fox News Channel
Gloria Allred, Amber Frey's lawyer: This afternoon, it was sad, the only people there for Scott were his parents. There were empty seats. Susan [Scott's neighbor] said Scott cried when he came and talked to her about Laci. They didn't give a date this happened.
Jeanine Pirro, prosecutor Westchester County, New York: We know Laci disappeared by 10:18 and the time line. People want to know why Scott wasn't involved in the search.
Bernie Grimm, Defense Attorney: Are we ready to vote now?
Greta Van Susteren: No, we have to hear all the evidence first. They have his cell phone call at 10:08 and the dog at 10:18, so there's a window.
Bernie Grimm, Defense Attorney: With cell phone, it's hard to tell how far from home he was, cause that won't pinpoint it.
Laura Ingle, KFI Radio Reporter: Scott talks alot with Geragos and Harris. When Susan was asked to identify Scott today, she did look at Scott and nodded and gave a smile.
Gloria Allred, Amber Frey's lawyer: When the jury left the courtroom today, they did not look at Scott Peterson.
Jim Hammer, assistant San Francisco prosecutor: ***That's because they were embarrassed, cause we called them on it the other day when they did.***

[Which would, in effect, open the jury up to 'outside the jury room' influence and information, which in turn opens up the investigation to an open courtroom, rather than what an 'inside the jury room' conflict would entail in that the investigation is keep within the jurors only. Either way, whether the jurors saw this 'called on them' on TV, or if someone notified the jurors not to look at Scott because the TV was reporting it, it's outside influence on the juror's thoughts and responses to those thoughts.]
Jeanine Pirro, prosecutor Westchester County, New York: The last time Scott cried was December 9th when he sat down with Amber and said he lost his wife, so we know he can cry on demand.
Gloria Allred, Amber Frey's lawyer: The prosecutor will seek to introduce the interview of Scott with Diane Sawyer. A number of

people on the jury was taking notes when the testimony was that Scott wasn't....
Greta: A neighbor said she was awakened by the Peterson dog, McKenzie, at 10:38am.
Laura Ingle, KFI Radio Reporter: And a postal worker in the neighborhood from 10:35 to 10:50, and around the corner at 10:19, and said he heard different dogs barking, depending on which house he was at.
Jim Hammer, assistant San Francisco prosecutor: Geragos really got after the lady who changed her time from 10:3? to 10:18, and asked her if she thought Geragos was the one who sicked the Globe on her.

6/16/04

Fox News Channel Poll Question: Will Scott Peterson be convicted?
38% Yes; 22% No; 40% Not Sure

6/17/04

Fox News Channel **Stan Goldman**, Fox News legal editor: Juror leaned over earlier and said something to Geragos, which everyone probably saw. But today the same juror had an exchange with Laci's brother. Maybe he just doesn't understand, but if I was the judge, I'd go ahead and dismiss this juror and move on.

Court TV shows the video of Sharon Rocha saying that Laci keeps repeating to bring her home and hope the person responsible hears her voice..., several times during Court TV's update on Scott's trial.
Nancy Grace, of Court TV, former prosecutor: Juror No. 5 told Bret Rocha that it looks like you'll are gonna lose again today, uh.

Court TV Question: What do you think of Mark Geragos' behavior in court?
Catherine Crier, of Court TV, former judge: The name Conner wasn't chosen until the media stepped in, as the Peterson's had two choices for a name and hadn't decided.

Court TV ticker: Laci's doctor said she was 33 weeks along in her pregnancy on 12/24.

[The TV news corps are going after Juror No.5, just as they did in North Carolina with the Michael Peterson jurors. Those jurors the media feels are not convinced of guilt are publicly chastised and humiliated into excusing themselves from the jury before a verdict is voted upon.]

6/18/04

Fox News Channel: Stay tuned, new information coming out of Redwood City. Find out what the motive for murder was.
[later]
[headline]: **JUROR CONDUCT**
Stan Goldman, Fox News legal editor: It could have been anything, like it could be a bad day to loose today; the audio is so bad it's hard to tell. Some media says that this same juror came in one day and spoke to Mark Geragos, and Geragos turned and smiled. But, the defense says that the juror came into the courtroom and tapped on the railing as he passed the defense table and Geragos turned and smiled.
[later]
Fox shows the video: Bret Rocha turns and smiles and replies in a very nice manner, after the man speaks to him.
Fox: The look on Laci's brother's face doesn't appear as though the juror had said anything derogatory to him.
Richard Gabriel, American Society of Trial Consultants: The defense may want to be concerned, cause if one of the jurors is establishing a relation with one of the victim's brothers....

Court TV: The prosecution tried to establish a financial motive for Scott Peterson to murder his wife Laci, with the jeweler who appraised Laci's recently inherited jewelry, testifying that Laci told her when she went to get it appraised, it was Scott Peterson who wanted to know the value of the jewelry. [Which would be hearsay on top of double hearsay.]

CNN Headline News: Scott Peterson's defense attorney, Mark Geragos, showed the jewelry appraiser a receipt for an appraisal of a watch like Laci's, which was a week after Laci's disappearance. He wouldn't show her the name on the receipt, but did say it wasn't Scott Peterson's.

6/21/04

Court TV
Jim Johnson, former San Mateo prosecutor: It's been this way since the trial started, Geragos just keeps pointing out flaws in the prosecution's evidence, time after time.
James Curtis, of Court TV, former prosecutor: But what of this information, this appraiser's receipt, buried in the prosecution's evidence. No redirect of the appraiser on who or where the pawn ticket came from on December 31st. Was someone pawning Laci's watch, seven days after her disappearance?
Lisa Bloom, of Court TV, Civil Rights lawyer: Maybe Laci just needed some quick cash, so she went to the pawn shop [12/10] and picked up a few dollars to Christmas shop.
Jim Johnson, former San Mateo prosecutor: Even Laci called her doctor, after he told her not to exercise, and told him she got sick while walking.
James Curtis, former prosecutor: Let's go over the jurors in this case.
Beth Karas, of Court TV, former prosecutor: Juror No.4, a former police officer, who was charged with assault on a police officer. Another, a former fire fighter, said he's ashamed to be associated with some of those officers on the case. A lady who married a man while he was in jail.
Jim Johnson, former San Mateo prosecutor: This has to be the most defense orientated jury I've seen.
James Curtis, former prosecutor: Yea, I hate those 'former' police officers on a jury.

Court TV: Court TV uncovers some top secret information in the Scott Peterson case, stay tuned for Catherine Crier Live today.

[This is from the same corporation which applied to the judge, presiding over this criminal trial to decide whether an American will be put to death by government, to show this trial 'live'.]

Court TV: Juror controversy takes center stage.
Beth Karas: Judge called in Bret Rocha and then Juror No.5. The judge said no misconduct by Juror No.5 and that the media got it wrong; they reported it wrong. Bret said the media got it wrong. Bret said the word wasn't 'lose', but he wouldn't say what it was. Geragos got up and lambasted the media, but didn't name names.

One of Laci's third grade friends is on the stand and she said when she arrived on December 25th, that Scott was vacuuming in the laundry room area. They'll be a 402 Hearing, an evidentiary hearing, to decide on evidence and then Detective Brocchini will testify.

Court TV: Top secret information, the worst is out. Stay tuned for Catherine Crier live.
[With this ad, Court TV shows a short video of Scott and Laci's home, with police tape tied around objects to keep the public out.]

[The TV news corps are again, imposing themselves in a negative manner on the 'trial of Scott Peterson' by becoming a part of the trial itself, from the outside. Negative, since it's once again, rumor and talk. Once the trial began in a view that the legal prosecution of Scott Peterson was also basing their decisions on rumor and talk, the TV news corps went after the jurors.

Since the actual evidence could not be spun towards prosecution, even in the prosecutor's case-in-chief, and instead went towards the facts showing Scott may be innocent, the jurors are the only ones remaining that possibly could be influenced to make the decision of convicting Scott Peterson, since the evidence surely doesn't seem to be going in that direction.]

Court TV
[Shows a video of alot of media surrounding and following Bret Rocha into the courthouse.]
Beth Karas: Third witness on the stand now. One said Scott didn't want his picture shown to media with Laci's, since this was about Laci and not him.
Vinnie Politan, of Court TV: Did they clarify what the word was, with Juror No.5?
Robert Talbot, San Francisco Law School Professor: Yea, sounds like it wasn't much and the judge wouldn't take a chance on a mistrial if anything to it.
Kimberly Newsom, of Court TV, former prosecutor: Well what the Juror No.5 said, doesn't matter, it's the fact that he spoke.
Vinnie Politan: [Scott] Cleaning up the laundry room?
Beth Karas: Yea, about 5pm, December 25th, and she [friend] asked what he was doing, and Scott said he can't keep it clean; and

it's true, by 5pm, there had been alot of people in two days been through the house, with police, friends and all.
Robert Talbot, San Francisco Law School Professor: The more the prosecution puts out as a question, the more it may be pushing Scott Peterson to have to take the stand to explain.
Vinnie Politan: Well, none of his TV interviews came off very well, so why would Geragos want to put Scott on the stand.
Beth Karas: The first lady barely got out her first answer before crying. All were teary. The prosecutor wanted one lady to elaborate on the dog's bark and Geragos asked, You want her to bark? That was a bit much, even for Geragos, as the witness shot him a look.
Kimberly Newsom, of Court TV, former prosecutor: Yea, that's going a bit far, even for Geragos.
[later]
Beth Karas: Laci's last [yoga]class was December 20th. She was the only one, as the others had dropped out because of their pregnancies. [Friend] Her last conversation with Scott Peterson was December 23rd, Stacey, Scott called her and said he couldn't find Laci and some friends came over to help look, and Scott asked her if she knew anyone who drove a white truck.
Robert Talbot, San Francisco Law School Professor: These friends may be shown to place suspicion on Scott. His cold behavior may be what the jury wants him to explain that.
Kimberly Newsom, of Court TV, former prosecutor: Yea, the throwing away of the wedding albums will be coming into evidence.
Beth Karas: A different pawn shop, from the December 10th Laci visited, and the December 14th visit that Scott and Laci went to, but privacy prevents Geragos from showing where from, pawned watch on December 31st, same type as Laci's, same name as the one Laci owned.
Kimberly Newsom, of Court TV, former prosecutor: No foundation shown by Geragos. He just showed it.
Robert Talbot, San Francisco Law School Professor: He'll have to show it in court, cause it would be a problem for Geragos if he doesn't. He can't just throw it out and not explain, cause the jury will want to know.
Beth Karas: Geragos called for a 402 Hearing, cause the lady just said that Laci told her that the dog was probably mad at her cause she doesn't walk him anymore.

Kimberly Newsom, of Court TV, former prosecutor: Yea, that shows she wasn't walking on December 20th, so what, did someone come into the house and make her change her clothes and then take her? We've been saying all along she was too tired to walk.
[later]
Beth Karas: Both sides asking the court to ban the camera that got the shot of the juror the other day. The statement by the lady saying Laci didn't walk the dog anymore, wasn't in any police report.
Nancy Grace, of Court TV, former prosecutor: Here we have a witness, non-partial, who says Laci said she doesn't walk her dog, yet, we have Scott Peterson telling police Laci went to walk her dog.
John Burris, Defense Attorney: Sometimes there's statements that aren't on the police report and Geragos has every right to say 'surprise', but it doesn't mean she didn't walk the dog, so the dog 'wouldn't' be mad at her.
Nancy Grace, former prosecutor: Yea, but Scott was making her out to be an Olympian.
Trevor, Defense Attorney: Maybe the dog indicated he wanted to go out, and so Laci took him.
Beth Karas: Stacey talked to Laci at 4:45pm on December 23rd, just before Scott and Laci went to get his haircut. Scott told her he didn't want media at the volunteer center until 9:30, maybe cause he'd be gone by then.
Nancy Grace, former prosecutor: Why do you think Scott Peterson didn't want his photo in a wedding picture out in public. Could it be his affair?
John Burris, Defense Attorney: The ultimate conclusion here, is that he wanted to find his wife.
[Court TV shows a video of Sharon Rocha, crying, saying she keeps hearing Laci's voice, begging to please bring me home.]
[later]
Dean Johnson, lawyer, is shown in front of the San Mateo Court Complex Entrance: I don't think vacuuming the house is the first thing on your mind with your wife missing. What? If the bad guys turn her loose and she comes home, she's gonna be mad if the house is dirty?
Court TV: What about this stuff on his computer about sex....
Patricia S., psychologist: Research shows that 30% of guys are aroused by physical torture of women.

Catherine Crier, of Court TV, former judge: Did Laci get robbed that morning? Coming up.
[later]
Catherine Crier, former judge: We have never before released tapes between Detective Brocchini and Scott Peterson in the early hours of the investigation, December 25th. Many believe he'll be the Mark Fuhrman of this trial. He told Scott that he'd have to ask some questions that will make you not like me very much, but keep in mind, I'm just doing my job.
Beth Karas: Some friends say the jewelry Laci wore was gwaudy, alot of jewelry. All but the earrings and one watch is still there, on the dresser in pictures.
Gloria Gomez, KOVR TV Reporter: The defense is trying to show the jewelry was pawned off on December 31st, but never said who.
Catherine Crier: The french doors were unlocked? Walk dog with door unlocked?
Gloria Gomez, KOVR TV Reporter: Scott said door unlocked when he got home. Friends say Laci always take her purse with her and always lock the door.
Catherine Crier: So what evidence does Geragos have that someone went in and took Laci?
William Fallon, former prosecutor: I wouldn't want to be Geragos on this one. Maybe they cleaned the jewelry for the Peterson's while they were there. It's the small parts coming together; let's look at the Colombo moments.
Catherine Crier: What do you do with that?
Victor Sherman, Defense Attorney: Doesn't look like she was taken from the home.
Catherine Crier: At one point, the detective, Brocchini, asked Scott which jacket she had on. Scott said she usually wore his jacket. Where's the jacket she had on? No jackets are missing.
Victor Sherman, Defense Attorney: Did they actually do an inventory to see if a jacket is missing?
Beth Karas: We don't know how many jackets she had. One of the friends asked if her purse or jacket is missing? And Scott replied he didn't know.
Catherine Crier: Scott replied that Laci usually steals his stuff to wear, cause she's pregnant and his stuff fit better. Uh, em, bizarre. The officer said Scott told him when he came home, that the bucket was in the same place as it was when he left.
[later]

Court TV Question: Whose testimony will carry more weight with the jury?
Amber's? OR Detective Brocchini's?
Catherine Crier: Detective Brocchini, he could be their idea of Mark Fuhrman. That he could lie, that he could set up Scott Peterson.
Gloria Gomez, KOVR TV Reporter: He was in the 'gang unit', so he's used to dealing with.... The families were really turned off by him treating Scott as a suspect, leaving his keys in Scott's truck and trying to trick him, manipulating witness' statements, the hair in the lab.
Catherine Crier: The transcript doesn't look like he tried to snare Scott at first. Detective Brocchini has a 1999 sexual assault charge? The woman later said she lied. Where his testimony drew fire from the judge; attempt to cause a mistrial? Witness intimidation? And a coerced false confession from a high school student?
Gloria Gomez, KOVR TV Reporter: Well known he's aggressive. He even called the Peterson tip line and made false reports. He called Scott's friend and said there's a $250,000 life insurance policy on Laci, to get them to turn on Scott.
Catherine Crier: No one ever charged Detective Brocchini, so does it come in?
William Fallon, former prosecutor: Don't think so. You know, when you don't have a defense, you first go after the prosecutor, then the police, and then the judge.
Catherine Crier: Is the judge going to talk to the media?
Beth Karas: I guess it's settled, as the judge says there was no misconduct. I guess the subpoena he issued on media for Wednesday, he won't need now, as we just have to be 25' away from the security area.

Court TV Question: Whose testimony will carry more weight with the jury? Answer:
Amber's testimony, 76%.
Detective Brocchini's testimony, 24%.

Catherine Crier: Stick with us tomorrow and we'll give you a time line. We'll pin everyone down as to where they were and when.

Chapter Two

What They Said

The following sections, of TV news corp hosts, news corp guest prosecutors, guest experts, and guest defense attorneys are grouped according to their professions and true colors. The news corp and host section contains the information given by the TV news corps, hosts, and guests that did not fit into the other categories.

The guest prosecutors section contains those statements by prosecutors, former prosecutors, attorneys, lawyers, and a few who would like for us to think they are defense attorneys. The expert section, as the TV news corp section, was simple to merely place the experts into that section.

The guest defense of Scott Peterson was a bit more complicated. Some defense attorneys make a defense statement and then make a prosecutorial statement. Only a few Defense Attorneys actually maintained the defense mindset. A few former prosecutors also made the defense section, but rarely, and then also waffled on some statements.

Some may think that this is because no one is innocent, therefore there may be some evidence that can't be explained innocently or as guilt. However, there's another compounding factor that makes the above thunkconclusion a debacle from within our justice system.

While the confusion of what is evidence and what shows guilt and non-guilt begins with the complications of written law itself; law students, during the very time they are honing their skills with the learning process, are told which adversarial side to argue on any given issue. Some were excellent prosecutors, a couple were pretty good at defense, but many were confused, and didn't know it. One question would be to elicit a confession and the very next question from the same student would be to elicit an alibi.

Many times the plaintiff's lawyer gave the respondent's information to the court, and many times the respondent gave the plaintiff just the right information to win their suit. While viewing these same events as a youngster in a real court of law with real life defendants, I just thought those attorneys were drunk. Now I realize that the confusion is built into the system.

The following sections are 'what they said' without any outside comment.

Section One

TV News Hosts

The judge has released government taped conversations between the press and Scott Peterson to the news media. Why are Scott Peterson's lawyers afraid of a televised preliminary hearing?

Scott Peterson enters the courtroom, wearing a bright red jumpsuit, handcuffed and shackled.

Scott's lawyer doesn't want the preliminary hearing shown, so as to prejudice his client's jury pool and a fair trial.

The Constitution shrouds a defendant in unimaginable rights. When people like parents or a spouse begin to back off from police during questioning and suspicion of murdering their child or spouse, and refuse to take a lie detector exam or shout out loud for justice and instead hire a lawyer, they bring suspicion and doubt upon themselves.

Laci Peterson Investigation: Scott's house broken into? Scott was crying during a TV interview, and told his girlfriend that he didn't kill Laci, but knows who did. Stay tuned to find out why Scott Peterson turned down a plea bargain to avoid the death penalty, before he was charged. Stay tuned for Scott Peterson and why he turned down offer that could have saved his life. The prosecution offered Scott Peterson a deal three months before charges were filed. His lawyers say that he turned it down because he's innocent.

Scott is shown wearing an orange jumpsuit and handcuffs in the courtroom.

New info in the Scott Peterson case. He was offered a plea bargain. New information out on Scott Peterson. New court documents show Scott was offered a plea in early January, if he told where Laci's body was.

Pathologist say that the autopsy shows that the Peterson baby was at thirty-eight weeks of age and the sonogram was done a couple of days before 12/24, shows the baby at thirty-one weeks, with a plus or minus, of three weeks accuracy.

Scott Peterson hearing; the government prosecutor says that people do change their behavior and respond differently in public when being faced with a camera video taping them. In the Scott Peterson hearing, the public can only get accurate information of the court proceeding with live video coverage, not recounts of it. The defense attorney, Geragos, gives inconsistent pleadings in court. First, he wants the preliminary hearing closed to all, but when the judge denies that request, Geragos changes his mind and says he wants live TV coverage. What's up with that?

The photo in the newspaper of Scott Peterson's defense team going over evidence is staged and I bet everything that Laci Peterson was not killed by a satanic cult.

If Geragos even thinks Scott is guilty, he will shut it out completely and try everything he can to get this guy off. Completely inappropriate for the Peterson family to make statements of innocence to the press and in violation of the courts gag order. If the Rocha family did this, on how they believe Scott killed their daughter, they'd have their butts dragged into court in a heartbeat.

Maybe the reason the defense team got Dr. Lee and Dr. Wecht is so the prosecutor couldn't get them. Is there a smoking gun?

Judge bars cameras in the Scott Peterson's case; Will it help or hurt?

Scott Peterson is shown wearing an orange jumpsuit and handcuffs coming into the courtroom.

Does the judge in the Laci Peterson case really believe that the real killer is still on the loose?

Guess who got served with a subpoena when they showed up in court at the Scott Peterson's hearing? No cause of death by the defense team and not dismembered before put in water. Prosecutor uses hypnosis on prosecution [defense!] witness. The age of the baby is many weeks older than he was on 12/23/02. Prosecutor subpoenas Scott Peterson's family when they get to court.

We'll hear the spin and not the facts of the courtroom. Why are you sarcastically, about the judge saying the killer may still be loose? I have a First Amendment right. It's ridiculous, the perpetrator can't read the court papers. In the Simpson case; the jury was contrary to the public poll.

NO CAMERAS IN LACI CASE. The leaks began on the prosecution side. We have gotten a lot of information we received, but don't feel comfortable reporting on.

Even before they found the bodies and when they picked up Scott, he wasn't wearing his wedding ring. He knows he wasn't crying in court and he was faking a tear.

Why might a new doctor's x-ray in the Scott Peterson case get him off the hook? Scott Peterson spent alot of money, just weeks before Laci's death, and the feds are interested. Will new autopsy details set Scott free? Why a radiologist? Age of fetus. **SCOTT'S FINANCES. SCOTT'S MONEY MYSTERY**. The feds want to know Scott's finances and may be involved in drugs.

Scott Peterson, caught on tape; Did he incriminate himself? In a conversation with Amber Frey, on tape, he said, yes, he had something to do with it. We have two trials in America; American Public and Media, then the real trial. We need the context it was said in. **SCOTT PETERSON'S OWN WORDS.** Frey met Scott on November 20, 2002. Scott tells Amber on Valentine's Day that he pledges love forever to her. This shows he's cold and indifferent to his wife's death. **SELF-INCRIMINATION?**

Did Scott Peterson tell Amber Frey that he knew who was responsible for Laci's disappearance? Did Scott Peterson tell Amber Frey that he knew who was responsible for Laci's disappearance? Did Scott Peterson tell his girlfriend that he knows what happened to Laci? Reports have some people wondering. Did Scott admit to Amber he was involved in Laci's disappearance? New report on what Scott Peterson may have said to Amber Frey. We'll talk to Gloria Allred, Amber Frey's attorney.

How will this impact the cult theory? The tape says, I'll tell you later who did this. Why are you backing off from what Amber will say? Is it logical he killed her over his love for Amber? Is the defense on the run in the Scott Peterson case and was he caught on tape admitting he has details of Laci's disappearance? **DID SCOTT ADMIT GUILT?**

Shocking information on what Scott may have told his girlfriend and why does the age of the fetus matter. How old was Conner? Rita reported the tapes. If tapes exist? First we heard he denied it, now we hear it's changed. Quote is, "Yes, uh uh but no." If that's so, it's curtains.

The Appeals Court opens the preliminary hearing in the Scott Peterson case to the public on 9/9/03. In the Scott Peterson case, no cameras allowed. Cameras are a discretionary call by each judge. People's Magazine got ahold of Laci Peterson's file and discloses some sensitive information and photos of the crime scene. The Appeals Court opens the preliminary hearing in the Scott Peterson case.

What role will the condition of Laci Peterson's body play in the case against Scott Peterson? **WAS BABY BORN ALIVE**, new information in the Laci Peterson case. Access to photos, the body of the baby was up on the shore fifteen feet and different condition than Laci. There were tire tracts and foot prints around the baby. The decomposition; thirty-one weeks at disappearance; Conner at thirty-five to thirty-eight weeks. There was debris and plastic on the bodies. Yes, there was tape on the bodies; not known type of tape which had a knot in the tape around the neck of Conner.

There was a robbery in the area, which questions the prosecutor's view of the timeline. Eyewitness saw Laci at 10:30am, on 12/24/02. The prosecution's case is mainly circumstantial, with what we know of the facts. Will the article taint the jury pool;, we gave a balanced account and there is no gag on us. We don't' have a conclusion; not our job; it's not an opinion piece. The article comes out tomorrow.

Initially Scott Peterson blamed blond hair color on chlorine. The People's Magazine article says that the police claim that the break-in near Scott Peterson's home was a couple of days later; when it was the morning of 12/24/02. His hair was a professional dye job and not chlorine. All the defense has to do is poke holes in the prosecution's case. Exactly.

The National Enquirer says, no tool marks on Laci's body. Probably postmortem dismemberment by/after in the water. "Did you have anything to do with the disappearance?" He said "Yes".

Laci's autopsy is said to be bad news for Scott's defense. If the tabloid report is true, Scott Peterson's defense is in a world of hurt. Satanic cult theory in trouble. Report says body not severed before going in water. **NEW AUTOPSY DETAILS.** Prosecutor and defense agreed to stop accusing each other of violating the gag order in Scott Peterson case.

Laci laid to rest, finally. In People's Magazine, new information in an article. The unborn was older than previously thought; thirty-five to thirty-eight weeks old. Both the defense and the prosecutor say they both violated the gag order and both agree to drop the allegations.

The amount of coverage in the Laci Peterson case is enormous. Interesting to see what the judge will do about the People's Magazine article. The tape on the baby raises questions as to what happened. We'll see what the judge says about People's Magazine.

NEW EVIDENCE IN THE SCOTT PETERSON CASE. NEW INFORMATION FILTERS IN ON THE PETERSON CASE. NEW INFO FILTERS IN ON THE PETERSON CASE. How will it play? Laci Peterson may have had the baby when it was alive; how will it affect the case? Experts believe that the baby was born alive. There's a September 9th hearing. It's a circumstantial case, with no direct evidence against Scott. This makes the timing of the murder off, with a full term baby, and no umbilical cord. It's a bombshell; only need one reasonable doubt. Scott was under surveillance after December 24th, constantly. There's an ace in the hole; Scott was fishing at the same place. There's no evidence to say he's guilty, and why would he say that he was there, if guilty? We don't know what the evidence is. Gag order? Violation?

Were you involved? Well Yes, but no, I'll tell you later when I see you. Scott teared up in court when details of Laci's and their unborn child's autopsy details were read in court. Tune in for all the latest details on the Scott Peterson case. Scott Peterson due back in court tomorrow. We'll get a preview in a moment.

A hearing today in the Scott Peterson case; both sides say they aren't getting enough information from the other side to continue. The discovery phase in the Scott Peterson case is coming to a head today. The defendant hasn't had enough time and both sides need more information from the other.

PROSECUTION SHOWING ITS HAND. The prosecutor is showing his hand in the Scott Peterson case today. We'll have the legal lowdown coming up. Suppose experts come up with evidence to hurt the defendant? You better believe we will question them. The Scott Peterson preliminary hearing has been delayed to October 20th. Big surprise, the defense is delaying the hearing.

Judge: The defense's motion for discovery.

Defense Attorney: There's a mass volume of tapes on dog tracking, and therefore we're not ready to proceed. There are other items needed; the materials found near the body have not been turned over. I have another case in Los Angeles to last seven days and a murder case in Los Angeles and the judge there continued for this case, and probably won't again. Is 10/20 okay? The tapes of the dogs arrived Friday, to the defense, and the video tape of the hypnotized lady and we want a hearing on her testimony, a 402 motion; also on the GPS tracking device. The lions share of discovery is with other agencies that the prosecutor sends it to. There's fifteen hundred items in the property room to look at, some tested by the Justice Department, and they don't want us to view what they're testing, while they're testing it.
Prosecutor: We've complied completely with discovery, if we feel it's valid. We have no basis to object to 10/20 preliminary hearing.
Judge: What happens if the other case doesn't go?
Defense Attorney: The defendant is a deputy sheriff and both sides are ready to go. The other case is set in stone and ready to go. We estimate four weeks to try these and should not run longer.
Scott Peterson: I do agree. [To waiving the thirty day requirement for a preliminary hearing.]
Prosecutor: We haven't received discovery; thirty day before trial requirement. We need a witness list for the preliminary.
Defense Attorney: We haven't decided yet, but probably no witnesses.
Judge: Set the discovery hearing; 10/17 for discovery, as this one; if needed.
Defense Attorney: Witness list?
Prosecutor: Maybe a week or two from now.
Judge: Dog tracking?
Prosecutor: Yes.
Judge: Hypnosis?
Prosecutor: Yes.
Judge: GPS?
Prosecutor: Yes.
Judge: Okay, a 402 hearing on each. [Interruption].
Judge: Four, 402 hearings; DNA also. Insert >except' and >doing' should be >going', in the certified transcripts of the earlier hearing.

The judge thought the discovery issues could be handled by next week and gave continuance on Geragos' schedule of other trials. The strategy in the [Winona] Ryder case was delay, delay, delay; and we'll see more of this. May be another delay. There's other attorneys in Geragos' firm that can handle the prelim. Maybe he should take fewer cases. The judge has no control over an attorney taking cases, or if he's in another trial. The hypnosis was to determine if the other pregnant woman was the one neighbors saw walking her dog, and not Laci.

Prosecutor's Press conference:
John Goold: Questions? A 402 hearing allows either side to ask for a hearing to determine if evidence is admitted. The witness hypnosis, dog handler, DNA. It will be at the same time as the preliminary hearing. 10/17 is a control to see if we're ready to go. The defense said they'd comply with our request. I can't comment on evidence, as the order prevents that. [Interruption].

What does the delay say to you? Are you buying Geragos' excuse? The schedule is skeptical. Nothing wrong with other trials is it? Tune in at 4:30 for the Scott Peterson continuance. Scott looked good in court today. A new defense theory today at 4:30. Tonight at 10pm, we separate fact from fiction in the Scott Peterson murder trial, accused of murdering his beautiful wife, Laci.

The judge said to take note, that the preliminary hearing is highly unlikely to be continued again. **COMING UP, NEW LACI PETERSON DEVELOPMENTS.** Delay helps the prosecution. The prosecutor wants the hypnotized lady to be the one neighbors saw. The prosecution is desperate and may be trying to create a memory. One dog says Laci was taken away by car. The defense wants the veterinarian records and the dogs' hit and miss records. They are mini-investigators; prosecutors. I believe the GPS failed. It could be rock solid evidence. Ninety bags of evidence. We're talking mitochondria DNA and not just dogs, GPS, and hypnosis.

The Peterson's are lashing out at the Rocha's for not being allowed to attend the funeral. Mr. Peterson lashed out at the police investigation and that Scott is innocent. Mrs. Peterson lashed out at the Rocha family. You can't find a copy of that Magazine in Modesto; it's sold out; says Conner was thirty-five to thirty-eight weeks, much older than should be. Blood and vomit were not found in the house.

The defense gets a preview of what prosecutors have planned in the Scott Peterson case today. What do they have planned?

Isn't it strange, two Peterson's, both charged with murdering their wives. **NOVELIST ON TRIAL.** Scott walks into the courtroom with blonde shaggy hair. Wife and unborn child. Why delay, delay, delay? **Scott Peterson accused of killing wife and her fetus.** The defense would drag the Rocha's to court if they spoke. There's lots of discovery outstanding and we said we wouldn't see the preliminary hearing on the set date. The prosecutor has complied with discovery and even willing to give information earlier than the law requires.

What about hypnosis? The prosecutor wants to show that, or whether she saw the brown van in the area. Police officer who found Conner said it looked like he had been born alive. A woman ten blocks away and a man nearby saw Laci that morning. The woman hypnosis was to see if she saw the brown van. Dogs decided Laci got in a car, and not that she went for a walk. Prosecutors in the Laci Peterson case say they have DNA evidence that links Scott Peterson to the murder of Laci.

LACI, UNBORN SON, CONNER BURIED FRIDAY IN CALIFORNIA. Laci had Never been on Scott's boat and yet Her hair was on the pliers in thc boat. The bloodhound told his handler that Laci left by car and didn't walk away. It was reported several months ago that Scott told Amber he knew who did it. Has this been explored? Lee Peterson and his wife have violated the gag order but the judge won't do anything. If Scott had taken a polygraph, police could have focused on someone else. Most of the information leaked, was leaked before the gag order and really isn't new. We keep our sources by protecting them and not letting it be known who they are and continue to get information.

A plea was offered to Scott if he said where the bodies were, but they found the bodies before anything could happen on that. Police feared Scott Peterson may flee before the bodies were identified. Laci Peterson's doctor denies he did a sonogram on Laci the day before she died. Will this hurt the defense? Laci's obstetrician comes out and says that he did not perform a sonogram on December, 23rd.

Why is Amber Frey under surveillance? Why is Amber hiding and has twenty-four/seven security? Laci's doctor speaks up. Is he making a case for the defense? Laci's baby doctor is speaking up will he seal her husband's fate? The doctor is suggesting he didn't do a sonogram on December, 23rd. Breaking news in the Kobe Bryant case and the Laci Peterson case, tonight 7pm. Breaking News in the Scott Peterson case and women speak out on Kobe's infidelity today at 5pm.

Will the tactical errors in the GPS system be allowed in court in the Scott Peterson case? In the Scott Peterson case we have a forensic columnist. The GPS may say that Scott visited the Berkley marina quite often and the defense might want to exclude that. Like, why did he do that? What was in Scott's mind? There's a late January interview with Scott.

Police used a GPS system to track Scott Peterson, and couldn't this evidence be used in court, say, to show he was trying to escape to Mexico. Scott Peterson's defense may try to prove that the baby was born alive, and personally I don't believe that, to show the court that they have the wrong man. Up next, the Laci Peterson murder case.

Geragos may run beyond October with the other trial and the prosecutor in the Scott Peterson case has a lengthy trial coming up in November. The trial may be next summer; the preliminary hearing moved to January. The prosecution says maybe two years to trial. More time to get more bogus people who could have done it.

Experts lean toward who ever hires them, from my experience as a lawyer. They say what the one who hires them wants. Jailhouse informant talks about Scott Peterson. An interview with jailhouse mate of Scott Peterson. Scott had a magazine of Mexico in his car. His cell mate is in for domestic abuse, break-ins, no rewards from the Globe offered to him. Jail not easy for Scott, loner, sad, keeps to self. Scott is cold hearted, still obsessed with Amber, forced to have sex in jail, talks more about dog than Laci, didn't want child with Laci, wanted to travel. **Scott is cold hearted, still obsessed with Amber, forced to have sex in jail, talks more about dog than Laci, didn't want child with Laci, wanted to travel.**

Scott had a gay relation with a male bar pick up; forced to have oral sex with an inmate and consented to give oral sex to an inmate shortly after arriving in jail. There's no conformation of this [oral sex]. He continued to romance Amber after Laci's disappearance, he wanted mini-vacations with her. The hypnosis witness saw Scott loading his truck on 12/24 and talked to Scott that morning; he was in no hurry or rush. He was loading or unloading something. Don't know what. The lady was under hypnosis for three hours, about the brown van; Scott had began the conversation with her.

James Soares, the jailhouse informant, has a life sentence. According to James Soares, Scott had more than ten to fifteen thousand dollars, brother's ID, clothes, camping gear, and said he was going to Mexico and live off the land. He was going to buy a car with the money. He used the ID at the golf course that his brother belonged to, for a discount. Scott talked to James Soares, he wanted James to remove the golf clubs from his house; that he could have them and don't tell anyone. **SCOTT PETERSON IS CHARGED WITH MURDER OF WIFE AND UNBORN SON.**

SCOTT PETERSON, NEW CLUE REVEALED! Wait till you hear what cops found in Scott's car. Is it a new clue? **SCOTT PETERSON, SMOKING GUN FOUND? UP NEXT, CLUES IN SCOTT'S CAR?** New information found in Scott's car. Is there an innocent explanation or is this a conviction? KSN TV reports a map found in car, may be an escape to Mexico.

Another affair in the Scott Peterson case. New legal strategy; a parade of women, seven, may take the stand. Will this help Scott? How seven women? Sources familiar with the defense strategy say he may admit to seven. Laci found Scott with a woman. Laci ignored Scott and never told her family about the women. Amber says Scott said his wife was never around. The defense says he said this to three others. No big deal. Laci did not tell her family about number one, so why say anything about Amber.

The real motive may be that he didn't want a child; responsibility as husband and father. The leading cause of pregnancy death is murder.

FIRST AFFAIR RIGHT AFTER BEING MARRIED.

Almost impossible to get a neutral jury. He said it'll change in three weeks and a child with Amber on the tapes.

CHARGED WITH HOMICIDE OF LACI AND CONNER.

Why was another women hypnotized in the Laci Peterson case and what will she say. Coming up, new development in the Laci Peterson case; another women was hypnotized. Will this hurt the prosecution? **UP NEXT, MODESTO MURDER**. Up next, police hypnotized another women in the Scott Peterson case. Stay tuned to hear what she said and if the prosecutor can use it in court. Tonight, new development in the Laci Peterson case. Two women are hypnotized. One pregnant lady was walking the dog on 12/24; to counter the defense that it was Laci. The second lady, claims she saw a brown van on 12/24 across from the Peterson home. The police say the van was there on 12/26, and robbing the home across from the Peterson home. Can't say what was said under hypnosis, only what was said before.

MURDER IN MODESTO. MURDER IN MODESTO. The National Enquirer claims the fingerprint of Scott Peterson was on a washed up tarp; day after the body was found. The Enquirer digs up good stuff. They do some hard work to get their stuff. The defense will say he wouldn't kill over Amber, cause he had seven others. It's been so over blown by the media; everything shown. [Laci never on the boat.] That's right, that's a very good point.

Up next, we have some stunning developments in the Laci Peterson case, new evidence. Will it convict Scott? **NEW EVIDENCE? NEW LACI EVIDENCE?** Up next, is there new evidence in Laci Peterson case? Up next, do prosecutors finally have the evidence that fingers Scott Peterson in the Laci Peterson case? New allegations in the Laci Peterson murder case. The National Enquirer; the bomb shell in the case; the fingerprint on duct tape on a black tarp found. They say duct tape was found on Laci's body.

If it's true no one has the same fingerprints. Even submerged, they can make a match. There can be eight-ten matches on a fingerprint; one-in-one million; one-in-eight million chances. If it's similar, it'll come in.

The National Enquirer says Scott Peterson's fingerprint found on black tarp which washed up in San Francisco Bay shortly after Laci Peterson's body was found. The National Enquirer, are probably as right as main stream press. Bomb shell allegation, very near the bodies, a big tarp of duct tape was found and a fingerprint on the duct tape and it's Scott's.

If a tarp was found, if a fingerprint on tape, if Scott purchased the tarp. Smoking gun here if correct. A fingerprint can be challenged in court. If it exists, I hate to defend Scott. I'd think someone else would have leaked this story sooner, if the evidence, the tarp and tape were found a day or so after the bodies were found. How do you defend against something like this, if it exist? Say it's real, what's the defense? A terrible problem for the defendant. A circumstantial case and even if it's weak, this evidence will become stronger.

The hypnosis of a witness was to question the story; is the prosecution desperate? The police were involved in the hypnosis, not the prosecutor. This looks bad on the prosecutor. It's about the woman who saw the van the next morning; this is a defense witness and hypnotic testimony isn't admissible, and everything before the hypnosis becomes suspect.

Were going to talk to Scott Peterson when we come back. The prosecution is putting forth satanic cult theory with hypnosis. Hypnosis puts the jury to believe there's prompting by the prosecutor and not a very strong case. The U.S. Supreme Court has condemned hypnosis. The public doesn't view it well. It's not a slam dunk case as they said early on.

We'll tell you about the fingerprint some thinks is Scott Peterson's. New hypnosis in the Scott Peterson case. National Enquirer reports Scott's fingerprint at the dumping place of Laci and Conner. Black tarp found near bodies with duct tape. If there is a fingerprint found on the tape, they better bargain.

The defense is still working on the cult theory in the death of Laci and her unborn son, Conner. The defense is testing the coat of a man arrested, who has been bragging he was involved in the murder of Laci and her unborn son, Conner. New evidence surfacing in the Laci Peterson case.

The Laci Peterson murder case, will a coat get Scott off the hook? The Laci Peterson murder case, the press is reporting a coat of a cult leader with Raider emblem. Four people executed with a ball bat, nine miles from Modesto. Why is a trench coat important to defense? **SCOTT'S DEFENSE.** Up next, the legal panel tells us what they'd do with the trench coat. Trench coat?

Today's top news stories. Scott Peterson; the National Enquirer magazine reports that police in Modesto say they believe they have found Scott Peterson's fingerprint on a piece of duct tape that washed up near where the bodies were found.

PLOT GONE AWRY. KIDNAPPING CLAIM. Scott's sister says no way, Scott couldn't drive the distance required in amount of time allowed. He was with family that day. Laci and unborn child. Disbelieve, he's a California inmate, but says he walked away cause he didn't want anything to do with it. The conservation with Amber and Scott; with the disappearance, "Yea, but no, I'll tell you later.

Coming up, new information on the Scott Peterson case, that he tried to hire a gang to kidnap Laci. Cory Lee Carroll says he met Scott to hire neo-nazis to kidnap Laci. He passed a polygraph. **TOXICOLOGY REPORT SHOWS CAFFEINE IN LACI'S SYSTEM. NOT PROOF CONNER WAS BORN BEFORE LACI'S DEATH. GERAGOS BEING INVESTIGATED BY SEC** [Securities and Exchange Commission]. **GERAGOS SAYS FEDS TRYING TO DISCREDIT HIM.**

PETERSON SNITCH. Apparently someone who met Scott in jail is telling on him. Stay tuned. New info. Made for a TV movie; he's in jail and wants to tell the truth. This happened about a month before the disappearance. He didn't know about the case while in jail. Did these guys know satan worshippers?

He saw the information about the case after he was out of solitary, and said he knows this guy. He met Scott and introduced him to two neo-nazi guys to steal Laci's car and when he walked away, he heard Scott ask the guys to kidnap Laci. The police are looking for the two guys and the inmate has passed a polygraph.

Scott is shown coming into court with handcuffs and wearing an orange jumpsuit.

LACI KIDNAPPING PLOT? I'll tell you why I don't believe it. Why not sooner? Scott has an alibi. You mean he left cause he didn't want to be involved? Could there be any truth to allegations that Scott talked to neo-nazis about Laci's death? Far fetched? Very dubious about this, unless corroborated.

TOXICOLOGY RESULTS, LACI PETERSON. Up next, wait till you hear who showed up Friday at the spot where Laci was found. The dive team returns, report shows caffeine in Laci but not in her unborn son, Conner. **FORENSIC CLUES.**

SCOTT'S DEFENSE. No GHB [date rape drug] found. **INMATE BOMBSHELL.** Inmate's lawyer joins us for an exclusive interview. Hear about Scott's lover in jail. **MODESTO MYSTERY. MORE CLUES IN THE BAY?** May be a new tip they received. Up next, new evidence and his attorney. Where was Scott on 11/29/02? An inmate says he introduced Scott to two neo-nazis; Cory Lee Carroll. Why won't you tell us exactly what was said? He would be implicated in kidnapping, and murder is a more serious charge. Met 11/29/02? More time? Is there cable [TV] in jail? Gag order, so Geragos hasn't said anything for months. **JAILBIRD TALL TALE?** His attorney just came on TV and told us what his client will say. Cory's story is almost unbelievable, except that he passed a lie detector test.

Rumors that Geragos will be replaced as attorney for Scott Peterson probably isn't true, at least not until after the preliminary hearing.

Was it a hired hit? And did it go wrong. **WAS IT A HIRED HIT?** Did you have anything to do with your wife's disappearance? No, but I know who did and I'll tell you later. **PETERSON KIDNAPPING PLOT?** You keep coming back with more information, as you get it. Scott's sister says meeting was impossible. Sister says Scott was in San Diego area where the baby shower was held. It's a seven hour drive to Modesto and one hour back to the meeting. **SCOTT'S ALIBI.** [Cory cut a deal with government?] Oh, there's one coming. I've seem it happen a million times as a lawyer.

More about the polygraph test in the Scott Peterson case. **MONEY TRAIL CLUES. LACI'S FEARS.**

A shocker, was Laci afraid of Scott's plans before she disappeared? But first, the man who administered the polygraph is here. Do you grade the polygraph test? Did they have a brown van?

We have the released phone numbers; twice a day, from Scott to Amber, before; and four times a day after the disappearance. The family not thrilled with Geragos; rumors. Sixty-five phone calls between Scott and Amber. Eighteen calls from Scott, nine days before Laci's disappearance. Forty-seven calls from Amber in the three weeks after Laci's disappearance. If they put her on and lock in her testimony, that's the prosecutor's problem.

The inmate's attorney says Laci died in childbirth after kidnapping, in retaliation for not being paid.

Scott Peterson now has one less attorney on his legal team to help with his defense. **LEGAL SHAKEUP. LACI PETERSON MURDER CASE.** Matthew Dalton quits the law firm, but no one will say why. He's off the Scott Peterson case.

I talked to the retired police officer who administered the polygraph to Cory and he says that Cory may believe he's telling the truth or he may be telling the truth, but either way, he passed.

The Rocha family [Laci's Mom] files a civil suit against Scott Peterson for the wrongful death of Laci, to prevent Scott from making any money from writing a book. The Rocha's want the money to go to the victim's beneficiaries.

Why is Amber fearing for her life? Did Amber ask for police protection? And why does Scott have one less lawyer on the defense team?

DALTON'S DEPARTURE. We don't know why he left.

Family unhappy with Geragos? Rumors? Scott Peterson is charged with the murder of Laci and their unborn son.

Laci's Mom files suit to prevent Scott from profiting from Laci's death. Could an artist's park bring clues to Laci's disappearance? **THE CULT THEORY. INSIDE THE LACI PETERSON MURDER.** Join us today at 5pm to get the inside latest scoop that's come out in the Laci Peterson murder.

Department of Corrections says that no prison Cory was in was under lock-down at any time and any inmates in lock-down can still see TV news. California Corrections Department doesn't believe Cory's story is true. A spokesman says Cory was not under lock-down and shows the institutions, with dates he was in jail. The low-rider gang is one of the most vicious and violent in California. People don't usually plead guilty to a crime they didn't commit, a second time. Muna, he says within twenty-four hours. **CORY'S LAWYER HOPES TO HAVE PROOF OF MEETING SOON.**

12/31 TWO TIMES TALK. 12/25 FOUR TIMES TALK. 12/26 AMBER CALL SCOTT THIRTEEN TIMES. 12/30 AMBER CALLS POLICE, TWENTY-TWO MINUTES. 2/14 AMBER CALLS SCOTT SEVENTEEN TIMES. WHO TO BELIEVE?

Is Scott Peterson trying to profit from Laci's death? According to Laci's Mom he is. They say in the suit filed against Scott that they have interviews, innuendo, and talk that suggests he is cutting a book or movie deal to tell his story and profit.

Exclusive new evidence in the Scott Peterson case. Learn what document was sent to police. Hired hit evidence? In the Scott Peterson case. **HIRED HIT EVIDENCE?** Cory has corroborating evidence of the meeting? Go get more info and come back and let us know. Why didn't Cory come forward sooner? If he hired them, then murder for Scott too. Phone calls. Be interesting to see how much ends up in court as to what we see on TV.

Bones found near where Laci Peterson was found; animal bones after testing. Diving, two weeks ago, for five days; a dive team from New York and ongoing. Low riders; well it isn't going away. Police knowledge. They talked to Cory several times. Still being checked into. Bones found near where Laci's body washed ashore, but investigators still don't know if human bones or not. What was just discovered where Laci's remains were found? Up next, Kobe Bryant rulings and startling discovery in the Laci Peterson case. **NEW EVIDENCE FOUND?**

New evidence found? Near where Laci's body found? **UP NEXT, MODESTO MYSTERY. GRUESOME NEW FIND.** Up next in the Laci Peterson case, find out what was just found and brought over to the coroner's office. The Costa County coroner examines the bones found; don't know if human or not. The woman found them weeks ago and took them home. **GRUESOME FIND.** Feel bad for the family.

SINISTER PLOT? In the Laci Peterson case; is there a sinister plot to profit from her death? Stay tuned and find out why some may think so. **MODESTO MYSTERY**. Up later, Cory and what he says about Dirty and Skeeter; and are police looking for them. **HIRED HIT THEORY.** Your story is getting larger. Where's Dirty and Skeeter?

NEW INFO ON PHONE CALLS BETWEEN SCOTT AND AMBER. We have new information on the recorded phone calls between Scott and Amber. **FREY FACTOR.** We're learning more about the Laci Peterson murder. **LACI PETERSON MURDER.** Much more lurid and complicated than we thought. The calls continued after the cops stopped taping. We reported alot of this before the conversations took place.

Amber and the polygraph; Melvin King; on 2/1/03, called him. Scott agreed to take a polygraph with Amber. King declined to comment. Law enforcement wanted to set up a sting, but Scott said the next day was not enough time. King called and thanked you for the respect shown to him. King says that no one has disproved the story yet. Alleges Cory has stayed in motel where the meeting took place. Like Scott is living in an alternate reality. Muna says corroborating evidence is the picture with the stripper and Cory just drops away. Club says it doesn't allow cameras in the Club, unless a celebrity.

EXCLUSIVE INFORMATION. Is there a bombshell in the Laci Peterson case. We have learned Scott offered to take a polygraph test. Amber kept asking if he had anything to do with Laci's disappearance and Scott said he'd take a lie detector test, but it was too early to get the police in to sting the polygraph. What could police have gotten? Why did Amber contact Lieutenant King? Apparently to ask him to give Scott a polygraph.

In the Scott Peterson case, the defense also wants to exclude evidence from hidden tracking devices. Scott Peterson's defense is trying to quash some hair evidence because of the way police handled it. Also the tracking devices in his vehicles. Scott Peterson, accused of murdering wife Laci and their unborn son, defense attorneys want to exclude strands of hair and other evidence and testimony from police hypnotized neighbor and tracking devices on vehicles.

SHADES OF SIMPSON TRIAL IN SCOTT PETERSON CASE? Are there shades of the Simpson trial in the Scott Peterson case? Mark Fuhrman coming up. **PETERSON ATTORNEYS SAY POLICE TAINTED SOME EVIDENCE.** Attorneys say police now have two hairs on pliers and that they put it there. Course they take a page out of the O.J. book. I hate to be here talking about hair. It's a three ring circus and might as well pick up as much as can on the way to acquittal. Don't defense attorneys do this to make it public and we talk about it. Scott Peterson, charged with killing his pregnant wife Laci, and their unborn son. Remember strand of hair on the pliers in the Scott Peterson case? Well the defense team now wants that evidence tossed.

THE RUNNING MAN? Scott is shown, behind bars in cuffs and leg irons, where he undressed and put on jail clothes.

Did Scott Peterson try to run and go on the lamb before police caught him? And what his defense team is up to with evidence.

Scott is shown, behind bars in cuffs and leg irons, where he undressed and put on jail clothes.

Was Scott Peterson planning to flee the United States shortly before his arrest? The National Enquirer reports he bought a used car using his mother's name. He knew police put a tracker on his truck; he found it; the GPS device. If they can prove he knew of it and other stuff.

Scott Peterson's lawyers are looking to push back his preliminary hearing. Stay tuned for the latest. Police looking for Dirty, confirmed by Muna, that he belongs to neo-nazis; forty-five years old; extensive criminal record; living with a blonde prostitute. This comes from Cory; so; remain skeptical of Cory; not in lock-down, lied about that; still they'll track it down.

Geragos in trial in Los Angeles; prosecutor delays; slam dunk for Geragos on delay, other trial, not my fault. Both sides told there may be a delay; week or maybe more.

If neo-nazi pans out; dispels prosecution's case; hair in boat, what if never in the boat. Playing the O.J. defense, go after the police.

Scott Peterson is charged with murdering his wife Laci and their unborn son. **COURT DELAY? STEAMY PHONE CALLS?** Something about phone calls and did police blotch some evidence in the beginning, intentionally? Or inadvertently? You'll be surprised; exclusive new info on who spent hours on the phone with Laci's family while she was missing.

MODESTO MYSTERY. New information; Amber Frey formed a relation on the telephone with the brother, father, and step-brother of Laci. Amber Frey tried to broker a deal to send Scott to take a lie detector test; but fell through.

Hair? Geragos will want that evidence suppressed; two hairs in the boat; initially, only one hair. Investigators went back and found another hair. Detective Brocchini; the Peterson family says he been aggressive from the beginning. He'll be the Mark Fuhrman of this case. Say dog hit at Scott's warehouse; they want that excluded. Scott in Berkley area alot; want that excluded, as GPS has inherent problems. Why go to Berkley to look for wife? He went to Berkley Manor the next day, when others were at the park where he said last seen. You get the last word.

Two reasons why Amber reached out: Amber wanted the Rocha family to know she didn't know Scott was married, and that Laci would be found safe and alive. This comes from a source close to the Rocha family and not from Amber herself.

Coming up; stunning news in the Scott Peterson case. Learn what he told Amber in those taped phone calls, just days after Amber went public.

Up next, why did police stop taping Amber and Scott Peterson? **MODESTO MYSTERY. AMBER'S AFFAIR.** Up next, you may be surprised who praised Amber, called her the next day for going public.

Rita gave details of relations days after 12/30, when Amber called the police. Amber kept the conversations going that day, 12/30, when Scott called her, and then Scott told her of the marriage. January 24th she went public. He called her, loved her, spend life with her; but public, saying affair a mistake. The preliminary, probably not Friday, maybe November 27th; to finish trial [Geragos] in Los Angeles.

No mishandling of evidence in the Scott Peterson case, say prosecutors, of the second hair found on the pliers that the defense wants tossed out. The dogs went to the car. Did Modesto police tamper with evidence from Scott's boat?

MODESTO MYSTERY.

Have police identified 'Dirty' and located him? **DIRTY IDENTIFIED? MODESTO MYSTERY.** Up next, one hair on Scott Peterson's boat could be key evidence, but did someone mess with it? Have cops tampered with evidence? Another herring by the defense. Like the satanist theory. Attack the evidence, the hair, as to a break in the chain of custody. Officers review evidence after being booked into evidence; is routine throughout the United States. One five-to-six inch hair, a single strand; next it appears as two; a one inch and a four inch, with damage on both ends and maybe damaged while in police custody. **MISHANDLED EVIDENCE?** Could be negligence? Two of the finest, Modesto police have on this case; top notch investigator. Could be negligence? See when go to court.

Speaking of spousal abuse, it'll come up in the Laci Peterson case, with the death of Laci and her son, Conner. Most of you know, most abuse happens when the woman is pregnant.

New information in the Laci Peterson case.

Witnesses hypnotized in the Laci Peterson case, wait till you hear as they prepare to testify in that case. The preliminary hearing is next week. The defense motions to exclude: the hypnotized witness who saw Laci walking her dog; the hair on the pliers, on the boat; the scent from the tracking dogs which led to where the body was found; the GPS tracking as inaccurate; and information from the wiretaps, as gotten with false information.

EVIDENCE AGAINST SCOTT? Can't ask her what she remembers after hypnosis; at trial, only before hypnosis. Prosecutor says not now, but use her at trial. Sounds like the O.J. defense; now two hairs. When it sounds like O.J., it makes me nervous.

No preliminary Monday, other trial, maybe 27th. Defense has alot to exclude from the preliminary, in the Scott Peterson case. Scott Peterson and his lawyers will appear in Modesto court today for a status hearing. Scott Peterson is accused of killing his pregnant wife, Laci, and their unborn son, Conner.

Next we'll be delving into the Laci Peterson case, and what went down in court today; almost. The judge continues the preliminary hearing for November 28th. Geragos is in Los Angeles. Apparently the cadaver dog didn't 'hit' on Scott's boat. Now DNA from mother has shown up. Are we getting a DNA mixture here or some mishandling of evidence by police?

Motion to suppress some wiretaps. Talk to Amber about Mexico and stripper to Mexico, girlfriend to Europe. Hair found, wound in the pair of needle nosed pliers, hidden under the seat in the boat. Do you think Geragos has a trick up his sleeve and won't let the prosecutor know if he's calling someone?

LACI PETERSON MURDER CASE. This time, no blonde look for Scott. The defense is arguing the state didn't give them exculpatory evidence; the dog did not 'hit' on the boat. If the prosecutor says it hit in the driveway, can't the defense deduct that it hit on the boat. Preliminary for Scott Peterson is continued till 10/28, Peterson charged with murder of wife Laci and unborn son.

Scott Peterson was back in court today. Wait till you hear what he had to say. **SCOTT IN COURT TODAY.** Postponed cause Geragos in trial, may not make the 28th. When Scott walked in court, and out, the first time that he didn't look at family; not happy, not happy preliminary hearing isn't going on. Scott hasn't been around the legal system. Geragos ought to be there.

Dogs? Dogs, no trail at boat, no evidence body was in the boat. The prosecutor didn't tell the judge this; would he have signed warrants? Say for wiretaps? Don't know yet. Amber's conversations okay, she agreed to it. Defense says if dogs don't show the boat, then Scott's not the murderer; gives the defense the best defense to argue. What if in plastic? None of that mentioned yet. No motions argued today. Search warrant issues come up right away. Up to Geragos to argue others at end of the preliminary. 12/27, dog scent with police, so already on his trail by that point.

In spite of mounting evidence, the judge allowed postponement of the preliminary hearing. The defense has adopted the traditional approach, to dismiss evidence; hair on pliers; no scent by dogs of the boat and didn't tell the defense; and has dropped the hypnotized witness. Far from a slam dunk as the California Attorney General said. Hair, now two; attack cops.

Most telling of Scott is the Amber relation. No one night stand. He met her as a masseuse. Still courting her with Laci missing. She's above reproach here. Motive to kill?

Alot of evidence in the Scott Peterson case; Is It tainted by police? Will this damage the prosecutor's case and is this the break Scott Peterson was waiting for? **TAINTED EVIDENCE?**

You were in court yesterday. What do you think was the most important new development? Well nothing happened yesterday. Geragos not there and continued. Outside the courtroom there was talk of cadaver dogs, no hit at the boat. Hypnotized witness; the prosecution puts her use in jeopardy, she may not be allowed to testify. She said she saw three men in a brown or tan van. Yea, and the defense can say that an important witness was blocked by the police.

REVEALING RECORDS. Coming up, we'll give you more details from the tapes of Amber and Scott Peterson. Will this damage the defense's case? Scott's defense team has portrayed Amber as a sex temptress and pursued Scott, but Scott called her ... times. Told Frey he loved her, told TV interview he didn't. Not good for Scott. Suppose he's innocent and wife missing. Doesn't make sense. Don't know how defense will play it. Maybe one call, two, but not all these to keep her out of the way. What of 'love tapes'? Haven't heard tape, but if he said 'I didn't do it, but I know who did', that may be damaging.

Others say they saw Laci that morning. Dogs; can't wait, say credible, then not credible.

Wiretaps are coming in. First he said he did, said yes, then, Oh, Oh, no, but knew or thinks he knows who did, according to my sources. The public will hear the tape of Scott telling Amber that he loved her, just hours after attending a candlelight vigil in her honor, while missing. The lies he told provide motive to kill his wife. On 12/31, the call, after candlelight. Tape says, I don't know who did anything to Laci, but I know who did. We heard the tapes; good sources listened to tapes. **THE 300 CALLS THAT WILL CONVICT SCOTT. POLICE ASK AMBER TO GET SCOTT TO TAKE POLYGRAPH TEST.**

How hurt is the prosecutor's case that dogs didn't pick up the scent in that boat? Police say he killed his wife, wrapped in plastic, put in boat, and dumped in Bay; Laci and her unborn son,

Conner. The defense says the prosecutor didn't provide all the evidence when they went to get search warrants from the judge, and goes against the prosecutor that Laci was in boat. Misconduct by the police detective; looked at evidence, the hair; came out, and two hairs. Prosecutors say the hair just broke in half. The prosecutor must turn over trial evidence and exculpatory. Now prosecutor says dog did go up to boat and barked, barked at the workbench, but heavy chemical smell in the warehouse. Bet they [defense] don't like that answer.

Why not divorce? Amber is a motive; not a one night stand; wanted to marry her. Two dogs followed scent from home all the way to the San Francisco Bay. We know this from the prosecutor's filings. The preliminary hearing to take five days. Amber will testify, a full day, day and a half. Scott called Amber after the TV interview, he loves her. Amber a big witness, motive, he led her on to the polygraph, then no show.

Fair trial? We'll have new information on Scott Peterson tomorrow on Crier Live at five. See you then.

Coming up, new evidence in the Laci Peterson murder case. Who did Amber ... and where did the cadaver dogs trace Laci's scent to? Next, Amber Frey wages war in federal court over nude photos. Why didn't she do anything about it when they were taken? We'll talk to her lawyer. And why the defense says prosecutor is barking up the wrong tree about dogs tracing Laci's body to Scott's boat. Amber filed suit; turn over the pictures and negatives, plus damages. Dogs mild interest at the boat and containers under the bench at the warehouse, work. Judge will decide if can use it or not.

Amber Frey came to police with information about Scott Peterson and now she's being repaid with nude photos on the internet. She filed suit in federal court. Coming up, the war over the nude photos of Amber. I'll ask the fellow who has them if he has a release for them when we come back. Did Amber sign a release? It's on dot com, she signed it, original given to Amber at the signing. Photographer says Amber signed the release; copied it; gave her the original. Why original? No idea, he's a photographer, not a contractor. Copy is as good as original. Handwriting sample? Larry Flint already did that; forensics of driver's license and our copy. Between Amber and the photographer? Yea, well.

Tune in tomorrow for the latest on the Scott Peterson case. Are all the delays a part of the defense strategy and preventing the Rocha family from justice?

Who Killed Laci Peterson? The Murder of a Young Woman and Her Unborn Son. Special. **1/24/03 AMBER GOES PUBLIC, MET SCOTT 11/20/03.** Scott drove ninety minutes at least once a week to see Amber. In that instant, in the public, Scott became the sole suspect. Amber became a victim too. Amber's revelation ended the Rocha family support; turned the public against Scott.

Four days after Amber went public, Scott did an interview with LA-TV; this cast more doubt. The family says Laci would have told them of an affair, if she'd known.

Scott: A few days after 12/24 to tell Amber of Laci's disappearance. Told her I was married.

Question: Amber says you called her 12/24 and said you told her you were going with your family to Brussels.

Scott: Won't waste media time answering that.

The same day as the TV interview, Scott bought a car and talked to a realtor about selling their home. Getting charged, tried, and sentenced in the media and this is a problem that's not gonna go away easily. The body was found and Scott was arrested. By the time he was arrested, the public already had him convicted. Case closed; maybe not. If a circumstantial case, maybe good news for Scott Peterson; jury will see facts. We know in a very different light; the house sale, Laci's car sale, most say guilty. Sounds to me like he needs a pickup truck. Fleeing as consciousness of guilt is easy for defense to defend. If blood in house, tarp, boat, then Mr. Peterson has a very difficult case to fight.

Said he went fishing and that very Bay is where the body washed up; and if cement in his boat, it about locks up the case. Most say because of Amber, but could be a defense, Laci mad about the affair and then probably not a death penalty case. There's evidence we don't know about. We don't know of any evidence to say Scott did this. Some say two years to trial. Experts say the defense won't get a change of venue. Who hasn't heard of Scott Peterson and Laci. Just might take a little longer to find an impartial jury of twelve.

A status hearing in Scott Peterson murder case is scheduled for today; the preliminary is scheduled for next week. The preliminary hearing is set for November 29th. Is his defense attorney telling the truth? This is the fifth date set for the preliminary hearing. Geragos is still at trial in Los Angeles. Wednesday is more realistic; Thursday or Friday. Prosecutor won't go into the hypnotized witness, will call at trial. Not using GPS, leaning to not using, to not prolong the preliminary.

Scott is shown in court, wearing an orange jumpsuit and in handcuffs, with a lady attorney.

Whew, there's Scott Peterson with blonde hair, a little different from his appearance in court today. **THE FACES OF SCOTT PETERSON**. Apprehended near Mexico. The defense wanted another delay today; sure the judge knew beforehand. One out-of-state DNA prosecution witness; money, just inconvenience. Plus they're tired and want to go home. The preliminary will be short and sweet.

Why is his appearance important, even at the preliminary, with no jury? Change in hair and dress is deceiving and hiding. He said hair was from a dip in a pool. If the prosecutor puts on too much at the preliminary, the defense gets a free, all expense paid shot at witnesses. The family didn't know Scott bought the boat three days before. Laci gets sea sick and probably never set foot in the boat. Many think Amber will testify. Oh boy, we can expect three to four days of cross exam and the nudie photos.

Why are the prosecutors calling Scott's father? Supposedly to say he didn't know Scott had bought the boat three weeks earlier. Not hearing of satanic cults and the brown van is better. Why a hearing on the DNA? Amber may testify for two days; the preliminary five to six days.

Scott Peterson's preliminary hearing has been postponed for the fourth time. This time for one day. Peterson is charged with the murder of his wife Laci and their unborn son.

LACI TRIAL UPDATE. Coming up, the latest details in the Laci Peterson case, new information released today by both the prosecutor and the defense. **TO FACE SCOTT?** Will Amber come face to face with Scott in court? **LEGAL MANEUVERS.** Up next, who is the defense flying in next week to testify? The judge pushes the hearing to Thursday. The witness list; Amber will take the stand Wednesday. [nudie photos] But she's not selling them, the other guy is.

The preliminary, five to seven days. The prosecutor promises big surprises. The defense attacks the forensics, hair. All Amber, all the time. They'll have alot of hearings. Amber to testify for three days. A reporter, we'll talk to him tonight, spoke to an inmate who is neighbor's in jail with Scott. They drank some homemade wine and Scott confessed to hitting her over the head with a golf club. Scott asked him to move the golf clubs from the house; supposedly he hit her with a golf club; maybe hit in the neck in front and no blood spatter. Not much evidence in this case. Amber could play on the jury. Blonde hair, girlfriend, most damaging evidence. It doesn't take much evidence to convict.

An inmate at the jail where Scott was; Scott confessed to the murder of Laci. I talked to James a few months ago; said he had more on Scott, but couldn't tell cause there's a code of ethics in jail. They had alcohol? Pruno, with fruit, a few glasses. Scott confessed to James; incredible, vivid details. Hit his wife, Laci, with a club. The comment was made while they were watching TV; three to four glasses of alcohol; then the confession. Scott told James that he snapped and hit her with a club; he didn't want children. There were several more confessions; most intense of were after the court date; Scott snapped and blamed Laci for being behind bars. His mind changed about Laci; from, didn't mean to do it, to now blaming her for his predicament.

It's hard to disregard the story. Many are convicted on jailhouse snitches. Highly subject to impeachment by the defense.

SCOTT'S BIG DAY. The judge made clear that the witness list not be given out. Alot of motions to exclude evidence by the defense at the preliminary. Will we see any bomb shells in the Scott Peterson case when it goes to the preliminary hearing next week? The judge told both sides, this time, be ready to go; Wednesday. It'll be a mini-trial. The prosecutors tell the defense to pony up and plea now.

The defense wants to cross her [Amber] now; for trial later. Public only remembers bad things.

After being delayed so many times, preliminary will occur Wednesday, come hell or high water. What does the prosecutor have? They promised evidence weeks ago and haven't delivered so far. There's certainly no smoking gun.

A source close to the defense doesn't know if Amber will testify. The defense doesn't believe any phrase in there, of, No, didn't murder. It does have the neighborhood break-in information on it.

Both sides are calm and confident, both think win. We'll hear alot of tapes, forensics, and motions to exclude. All day

Wednesday with admissibility of DNA; hair on pliers. Heard the prosecutor will say that the hair split. **PROSECUTORS ISSUED SUBPOENAS TO PETERSON FAMILY.**

Scott is shown in court, wearing an orange jumpsuit, blonde hair, and in handcuffs.

He told Amber that he'd be traveling in Maine with family during Christmas. Hair? Reported that Laci was never in the boat; no root on the hair. Two hairs instead of one; or two pieces; probably won't keep it out of evidence.

As far as defense strategies, we've heard everything from satanic cults to neo-nazi bikers. What will be the defense? Preliminary, probably a week at minimum; thirty-five to forty witnesses on the state's list. Probably won't call all of them at the preliminary hearing.

Want as much information as possible; preliminary a waste, why not indict. It's time for the prosecutor to put up the evidence. Won't see alot of evidence, just enough to bind over. **SCOTT PETERSON WILL BE PERMITTED TO DRESS IN CIVILIAN CLOTHES.**

[DNA] Still can say it doesn't deviate from hers and it'll come in. Right, and a scientific method. Yea, but he'll be convicted anyway, with what the prosecutor told me they have.

Dogs, wiretap, sightings of Laci and van. Dog showed interest, guess, at boat and workbench. No need to put Amber on, can use tapes and hearsay. [Amber's lack of credibility] Prosecutor will do this ahead of the defense and take away the surprise by the defense.

SCOTT'S COURT DATE. What or who will be waiting for Scott Peterson in court Wednesday? Will Scott Peterson come face to face with his lover on Wednesday? **COURT PREVIEW.** Scott Peterson is less than forty-eight hours from being in court and prosecutors plan to say how he killed Laci. Less than forty-eight hours to the preliminary. **MODESTO MYSTERY. TRIAL OF EVIDENCE.** Scott Peterson's preliminary hearing begins tomorrow.

Experts say Amber Frey will testify in the Scott Peterson preliminary hearing. Good tip; will she testify, end of week or early next week.

Mr. Peterson called by the prosecutor; he didn't know of the boat Scott bought. Found red paint mark on the front of boat. Three miles away from Berkley Marina, looking at Buoy. Don't know if results back yet. Tie to buoy to stable the boat to throw the body over; two to three foot waves. Fishermen said body, if dumped there, currents take it to where found. Industrial paint.

Amber's testimony is the tapes, turn the jury upside down when they hear them. She dated a married man in the past. **PROSECUTOR SAYS HE'LL BEGIN PRELIMINARY WITH DNA EVIDENCE.** Why not get wife swapping, etc., out in the open and let the public chew on it? Why let the defense have a free ride, just go with the tapes.

What about witnesses seeing him in the middle of the night? Neighbor saw Scott that morning; other neighbor suspicious that the blinds were closed on Christmas eve morning, always open. He said he was fishing at Brooks Island, near the buoy. A fourteen foot aluminum boat, with a thirteen horsepower engine, takes two hours to get to the buoy. He showed up around 5pm at home, looked for Laci, then quickly made phone calls. The neighbor came to police and said she saw him loading or unloading something. They also ask her about the brown van.

Jailhouse snitch. Yea, drinking pruno, don't believe it. Scott is not available to the other inmates and don't believe he opened up to other inmates. Geragos would have told him not to.

I disagree that the prosecutor has to prove motive; never have, never will. And with Geragos condemning other attorneys for being on cable TV, come on, talk about the kettle calling the skillet black; Hello! Trying to get Scott to take a polygraph. Scott attempted to delay the search of his workplace, said no electricity there.

[Geragos shouldn't put on defense] You're right about that. Tune in tomorrow evening and we'll chat live with viewers about the Laci Peterson murder case.

Prosecutors are pulling out the evidence stacking up against Scott Peterson, but it's nothing compared to what Amber Frey will say.

Tomorrow Scott Peterson will be in court for the first time with the evidence laid out against him. Tonight we'll tell you what will happen.

Tomorrow, finally, the murder case of Laci Peterson in court. Amber expected to be the star witness for the prosecution. Why kill Laci, pregnant, yet with Amber who has a child. One point on the tape, Scott said he didn't know who did it, but he knows who did. We'll be surprised on how much we do know about.

Either he's guilty or someone framed him. Satanic cult; we'll hear about it in the preliminary hearing? Scott Peterson's preliminary hearing starts tomorrow. Who will be the surprise witness against him and what evidence will the prosecutor show? We're in front of the Modesto courthouse and tomorrow, for the very first time we'll hear the prosecutor's evidence against Scott Peterson. **PETERSON MURDER.**

Still ahead, Scott's in court tomorrow and we'll hear the evidence. Up next, how will prosecutors say Laci was killed and what role will Amber play in that evidence? The first of five days, prosecutor says mitochondria DNA first thing. May bring in investigators to say hair broke in two. Both want to win the court of public opinion. Hair is important, puts Laci in the boat that she knew nothing about. Defense says they're married and it came from Scott's clothes. Seems as though Amber's been practicing for testifying.

SURPRISE EVIDENCE. Witness and evidence for the first time. The Peterson's believe no evidence against Scott, and this may even bring the Rocha family over. 12/24 Missing; 1/24 Frey goes public; 4/13 Conner; 4/14 Laci; 4/18 Arrest, identify bodies; 4/24 Scott pleads guilty.

STATE: NO WIRETAP EVIDENCE AT PRELIMINARY.

Geragos says can't cross exam on some DNA, because of late, recently received discovery. No GPS, no wiretaps, what else? Geragos asked the judge that Amber's lawyer be excused from the courtroom. Judge says Amber's lawyer can stay, but she can't tell Amber what's said. She can advise her.

Age of fetus to help the defense? Compare the development of Conner in pristine shape, and developed more than he was on December 24th. Case hangs on the hair for the prosecution. No reason to believe that Laci was ever on the boat, he bought it three weeks earlier. No follicle attached to hair; no blood on the pliers; hair transfers all the time with spouses.

Prosecutors say they will not introduce wiretaps or GPS. Both sides with DNA expert on hair. Don't know if, or when Amber to testify.

Physical evidence that could be a bombshell in this case, with Dr. Baden when we come back.

SCOTT'S PRELIMINARY HEARING BEGINS

First witness on the stand. FBI employee; mitochondria DNA; a Kelly hearing to find if new evidence is to be permitted into evidence.

The defense says negligence in handling the hair and that mitochondria DNA is not scientifically accepted in the scientific community.

PRELIMINARY HAS BEEN POSTPONED FOUR TIMES. Geragos tried to have Allred thrown out of the courtroom. **SCOTT PETERSON CHARGED WITH KILLING WIFE AND UNBORN SON.**

Scott seems thinner, happened when in jail, longer hair. The judge to decide if mitochondria DNA testing will be accepted. Gloria Allred said at a press conference; Geragos seems threatened by my appearance; the gag order; he tried contempt of court; today to exclude me from the courtroom; and you'd think after three failed attempts he'd focus attention on Scott Peterson and not me. **ACCUSED OF KILLING WIFE AND FETUS. LACI PETERSON MURDER CASE.**

Scott seemed relaxed, but when the testimony began, he took notes and stayed focused. Why are they fighting the DNA evidence when it has been accepted for twenty years, and even the ABA [American Bar Association] has thrown up their hands and accepted it. Well, mitochondria DNA is relatively new science and trying to get it accepted.

How will they explain the GPS system shows he returned to where the bodies washed up numerous times?

Scott is wearing an orange jumpsuit, with leg irons and handcuffs.

Gloria Allred made headline today. Mitochondria DNA; long day. Prosecutor won't use wiretap in the preliminary hearing. Allred wanted out of court; next witness, the Peterson maid. DNA 101; Allred dozing off at one point. Not a high level of probability on DNA; one in hundred, and one in a hundred-fifty with hispanics. The judge in the neighboring county says hair DNA is okay. The hair was wound around in to the pliers.

BODIES OF LACI, UNBORN SON, CONNER, FOUND IN LATE APRIL. Yea, he'll be bound over; both sides playing to the jury pool. Want to introduce evidence now. Constitutional right to a preliminary hearing, every safeguard or the defense attorneys will be screaming. Now thirty-four states don't allow [mitochondria DNA], or rather haven't said yes or no.

I Cut Scott's hair Friday and he and Laci were very happy.

Last one to see Scott and Laci together, saw her the night before; maybe same pants on when found washed up; time line. February 13th, 2003 interview with Nancy Grace, Amy said, She had on a black top, maternity, cream colored pants, scarf. Jury ain't gonna buy that Laci wore the same clothes two days; and abducted by a satanic cult with the same clothes on.

Okay to show trial on live TV, cause jury's already picked and they don't watch TV. Laci's Mom only wanted Laci's wedding dress, so Geragos will play down the break-in. He doesn't want to open that can of worms.

A simple motive, in that he just grew to hate Laci, for her take charge personality. Never heard that Laci was bossy. Why does Amber need you there to advise her? Laci's name was barely mentioned today.

The defense began its cross [examination] today; has own expert. Never seen Scott's support from his brothers. Inaccurate, the brothers have come out and are very supportive. The emphasis has been on the hair; pregnant women lose hair. All indicators on Scott is that he's well balanced; yet media says behavior's not right.

He picked up fliers, but instead, played golf. He was going to a vigil, but on the phone with Amber one hour before, wanting Amber to have his baby. Phone calls Chris. It's in official court filing. Selling home? Peterson's staying there, when up from Modesto; can't sell it yet. Why not Laci tell her Mom Scott went fishing, and why wasn't he working since his wife was pregnant and what about that boat? Nobody knew about the boat; none of the family. The defense says she did know of the boat and witness to say they saw Laci at the warehouse looking at the boat.

Defense wants the hair thrown out; mishandled by police and tests not reliable. Gloria agreed not to discuss the case with Amber and Amber is public, so Gloria may not be able to discuss the case on TV.

Housekeeper maybe on the bleach smell when the police got there. Things cleaned up that the housekeeper didn't. It's not drama to the prosecutor. Prosecutor thinks he killed her in the house, wrapped her up, tied to buoy, dumped. The defense says she went walking, have witnesses, picked up and kidnapped, dropped in water, in the Bay.

Prosecutor wants to cut things out, cause it's too long, and it'll take another day just on motions. You see why Geragos wants Gloria shut up; she's with the prosecutor's side. How did Laci and Conner die? Today's only day hair expert could be here. The prosecutor asked a billion more questions than necessary. Hair match okay with Mom, but not with Scott's, includes all her relatives. We'll hear color and texture same as Laci's. Expert had to admit; he never testified in California, never accepted.

How far would you go with the defense at the preliminary hearing? Don't tell me the pliers weren't supposed to be in the kitchen drawer and she used them and then the pliers to the boat with her hair in it. I want evidence to tie Scott Peterson to the crime. You know if the housekeeper tells domestic violence, she'll lay out their marriage for us. Laci would have confided in her. Doesn't that shift the burden of proof to the defense? Number one cause is by the partner; murder.

Seventy-six phone calls; started nine days before the disappearance. Said he wasn't married; a makeover. Measure Amber's against Scott's credibility. Why care whether a masseuse or not? Got tapes. How similar to O.J.? He played golf, ten thousand dollars in his pocket, while ten thousand people looked for his wife. Folks live down there, he was distraught. HA HA HA, COME ON, HE HEE HE. I know darn well you don't believe that, but, Thank You.

Why challenge mitochondria DNA? Eliminates large population. Yea, how many know Scott Peterson, get in the boat, and go to the warehouse. Sources say there's red paint on the bow of Scott's boat and similar to Buoy #4, three miles from the Marina. He made several trips back to the crime site? Cement in the boat, making weights, and they're not there. Found three to five cement markings, probably five boat anchors, but only one in the boat. Unusual cause cement residue in the boat and the salesman said not there when he sold it to Scott. Scott delayed the police search of the warehouse; said no electricity there.

How old was Conner? Evidence of older than December 24th? Doctor said No sonogram on December 23rd, None. You're the witness in court. Most important evidence against Scott?

The prosecution's theory is that Scott hit her on the head with the pliers, then dumped her body in the Bay. Neither Geragos or Mrs. Peterson said much, just that they're glad the proceedings are underway. With the gag order, they shouldn't have said anything, but gave no evidence.

Court has started. What do you think about this hair; fight over mitochondria DNA, much to do about nothing?

Scott is shown in court wearing an orange jumpsuit and handcuffs.

Scott said he told Laci in late November about Amber, but did Laci tell anyone? Be interesting to see of it comes up. They always say the wife knew and had an open marriage, she was okay with it.

When we return, we discuss wiretap evidence, dog evidence, and Amber Frey. All the defense attorney has to do is show reasonable doubt, but, hosts like us, are gonna remember that Geragos said he'd find the real killer. Roger, play prosecutor for me and tell us about Amber.

Laci Peterson's parents come and go out the back door of the court house and are allowed to leave the courtroom before anyone else can and are shielded from the media. Scott Peterson's parents come and go out the front door just like everyone else.

PETERSON IS CHARGED WITH MURDERING HIS WIFE, AND THEIR UNBORN SON. They've gotta get this hair in cause it's the only physical evidence they have tying Lacy to the Bay, tying Laci to the boat. Movie coming out about Scott Peterson, to end at the point he's arrested. Old jail; tough living. Aggressive cross exam by the defense, very important to the defense, end court at 1pm tomorrow for Halloween. We've heard Laci was very tired and probably not up for a walk, and maid.

Before trial, they'll be fifty-two more issues to solve between Scott and Laci. Letters were given, from Scott; life in jail, cell size, food, missing Laci on her birthday and their unborn son. Someone sympathetic to the defense released them, want the public to know a normal guy grieving for his wife. Won't say where gotten, not from the defense; they're just letters from jail to a friend. Self-serving statements and not allowed in a court of law.

Don't know who is responsible for the leaks, it doesn't have to be the prosecutor that leaked there was paint on the boat. Don't need history of violence to kill. Others convicted without hard evidence or a history of violence. Scott told Laci about the affair and says she was okay with it; I'll Stand on my head. If the hair means nothing, how'd it get on the pliers? Wound into them?

The missing student and Scott? They ruled Scott out, her boyfriend is the prime suspect. It's a story because it's tragic; the defense has been effective, at the risk of bringing Nancy's wrath down on me. She's right; a four prong attack, not compared to Laci's bone, mitochondria DNA science, hair contaminated.

Psychic said Scott hit her with a hammer? They have the cell phone records. The prosecution must prove, and link Scott to the death. Alot of people have girlfriends and they don't commit murder.

What about 'The Perfect Husband' movie coming up? Let's talk about what he may have said in those tapes, since we won't get to hear those. One hair; two days. 2004-2005, trial. Scott and family will urge quickness for trial. Hair is but one piece of evidence. House cleaned the day before? The prosecution will say to clean up blood, but we don't know their cleaning habits. Get hair; and let's say bleach; and let's say sister says Laci said he's a monster; can you convict? Amber will testify, and if solid, Geragos won't want to face her again.

Who was Scott's jailhouse lawyer and wait till you hear what he confessed to them in jail, and who will be the surprise witness against him? The defense says the hair tampered with and contaminated. Tomorrow the housekeeper; she cleaned before Christmas eve, if she used bleach, and into their marriage. Amy, December 23rd saw Laci, and Scott told her he would go play golf, not fishing.

The defense says one hair plus another one that fell in there; contamination. Housekeeper? Hard to get rid of blood. Ninety bags of evidence from the house. [Who cleans after the housekeeper?] Me. Do we know the bleach smell was there? No, and of body chopped up in there.

Letters from jail, tells alot about him and Laci. Alot of letters, we were given seven from a person, has many more. A sense of humor about the food in jail, lost alot of weight.

Will any of the evidence get tossed because of sloppy police work? **APRIL 18TH ARRESTED.** Boat? What if dismembered? Spouse first one to suspect. [Letters] Had to release them sometime. Any mistakes? Receipt, then bodies. Three to four things he did makes him look guilty. Had to schedule the hair first; expert availability. Yea, this ain't a made for TV trial. Maybe the prosecutor has who, how, where, and when.

FAMILY FEUD. Could cut the tension; feel it between the families. Amber will be on the stand for a long time. Absolutely. Reporters passing notes to families in the courtroom. Yes, gag order, they can't speak. Yea, but the press tries anyway. Oh no, it's your job to do that, to try.

AMY'S TESTIMONY. What will Amy say in court? December 23rd last saw Laci; Amy. They brought her to the home during the search, to see if the clothes were there that she wore on December 23rd. Scott said Laci was wearing them. Rough in the preliminary hearing on cross exam; jury won't see it, not on TV. He can charm her also.

Long witness list. Not alot of physical evidence, unless police have a bombshell we don't know. This is a 'behavior of the defendant' circumstantial case, a little different that a 'circumstantial evidence' case. You'd think DNA was on trial. Geragos spent two days so far.

Letters from jail. Sure they're from Scott, didn't get them from the defense. He has love letters from all over the U.S. Don't know. Scott found out about the deaths when arrested. Seems like he has a sense of humor? Another report says he's robust; he still looks good. Looks comfortable in court, longer hair, clearly lost weight. Shower only outlet from his cell? Yoga? Two ninety minute workouts while shackled. Laci taking yoga, but the instructor never met Scott. Get in front of the jury? Don't see it coming in. Self-serving statements.

It's their daughter's hair, wound into those needle nosed pliers.

Scott comes into the courtroom wearing a red jumpsuit, handcuffs and leg irons, with blonde hair, and a lady attorney.

Reports Scott bought the boat with intentions of killing Laci and Laci may have been unconscious in the boat and died there. There you go, Mr. Defense Attorney. Chain of custody issue; defense argues two detectives reexamined the hair, then there's two hairs. The defense says, well maybe something else happened here. Defense not say the hair is planted, just sloppy. When Amber comes in, everyone will forget DNA. The newspaper headlines, the Globe, help or hurt the prosecution? Town mentality and all want to see what happens. Well I do, and I think it'll be a bombshell.

No woman is gonna wear the same outfit two days in a row; had on what Amy saw her in at the hair salon. Scott said she had on black pants, but she washed up with same ones she had on the day before. Scott has internet access, so he probably voted. Poll: 8% NO; 92% YES.

Scott is shown in court wearing a red jumpsuit, handcuffs and leg irons.

Scott's Dad didn't know Scott bought the boat. Mrs. Rocha says Laci was tired, told her not to take walks cause almost passed out once, but Laci was strong headed and walked anyway. On December 23rd, about 8:30pm, she talked to Laci, made plans for a December 24th dinner with Mom. December 24th, Scott called Mrs. Rocha at 5:17pm, she talked to Scott, he asked if Laci there; Mom said no. Scott said Laci missing. Mom thought just walking dog, or at a neighbor's house and will be back. On December 23rd, Scott and Laci at Amy's work; to cut Scott's hair. Scott volunteered to pick up, on December 24th, between twelve and three, a package for Amy, cause he'd be golfing that day, nearby.

The housekeeper, came four times. December 23rd, 8:30am to 2pm, used water and pine sol, used bleach to clean the bathroom. Laci not walk the dog, tired, went and got groceries and carried in house herself. Laid on sofa most of the time. She used towels to clean the door, put them in the mop bucket on the washer, and took the mop outside. The blinds in the living room and bedroom were shut on December 23rd. Housekeeper, blinds generally down when she arrives, in living room and bed room.

Family testifies; but where's the evidence? No real evidence to speak of; sister, Mom, housekeeper. Amy said Scott was to go golf, not fish. Mom said Scott never mentioned boat; her husband loves to talk fish. December 23rd, she heard from Laci, Amy at the salon, 8:30 talk to Mom. The housekeeper cleaned the floors with a touch of pine sol, but police say they smelled bleach. So the housekeeper doesn't use any bleach. Not enough to bind over yet.

In court today. Housekeeper from 8:30 to 2pm on December 23rd, Laci there; she didn't walk the dog. Used bleach in the bathroom. Mop and bucket outside, cement wet around the mop on December 24th; you'd think it'd be dry. Prosecution says second cleanup. Cleanup later than Laci's last sighting. Two mops, housekeeper not clear if two mops or one.

Mrs. Rocha thinks, that when Scott called and said Laci missing, Mrs. Rocha went to the park and Scott was there looking, the dog with the leash on. A couple weeks before, Laci got sick in the park walking the dog. Both said Laci tired all the time. The housekeeper said Laci was tired, on the sofa with her feet up. Amy; haircut on December 23rd; gift basket Amy needed to pick up and Scott volunteered, cause he'd be golfing in the area.

Not knowing of the boat by Dad, but the defense showed Scott had a number of vehicles Dad didn't know about. Laci trying to sell inherited jewelry? If money problems, why buy a boat? Yea, if so. Different outfit on Laci. Defense trying to question Amy's memory on the pants, but what Laci was found in seems to match what Amy says she wore the day before.

Use term 'missing'? Too cold to golf, so I went fishing? Mistake to tell police no lights in the warehouse, when Scott went there with them? Couldn't tell cops what kind of fish he went after. Said too cold to golf. Rumor Amber has real bombshells with her personal recordings.

[Scott] Letter excerpts; cried, told by police she was dead.

Mop wet on December 24th? Scott told Amy he was to play golf at the Club he and Laci just joined. Mom said she thought the world of Scott. Scott's Dad said he didn't know about the boat, motorcycle, or truck. Mrs. Rocha said Scott told her Laci was missing, rather than not at home. Housekeeper was nervous, trouble remembering some details. Four times; clean every two weeks.

No marriage problems, Mrs. Rocha liked Scott. When she called Scott and Laci, and Scott answered, she'd have long conversations with him, very pleasant. She was supposed to have lunch with Laci the next day; planned it with her Mom.

Why did the prosecution call Scott's Dad today to testify and what did Scott's Dad say that night to help put his son behind bars? Bought boat and didn't tell anyone. Had Scott told his own father of the boat; also, catamaran, motorcycle, auto; he doesn't tell me what he buys. The prosecutor is trying to string together twenty things to create suspicion.

How will the maid's testimony affect the case? Maid didn't use bleach in the kitchen, some in the bathroom. **BLEACH AND BLOOD STAINS.** Did mention cleaned the back bathroom with bleach and had bleach rags on the bucket on top of the washer. Neighbor said the blind closed on December 24th and Laci opens them early, but the maid said the blinds were closed on December 23rd. The expert just said you can still find blood.

May only be hair. Coming up, Amber on the witness stand. Are we finally gonna hear what Scott said to her? **WILL AMBER TESTIFY?** With Geragos and Mrs. Rocha wasn't somber; it was lite and smiling about Laci. Interesting mood in court today; families cordial.

The families of Laci and Scott gave tearful testimony today. We'll have the latest. **LACI'S FAMILY SPEAKS.** We'll tell you what they said. Very important witness today. The housekeeper, December 23rd, used water and a tad of pine sol; bleach in the back bathroom. Amy didn't know of the boat; said golf, not fishing. Scott wiped tear away when his Dad on the stand. Laci's friends crying.

The detective said when first reported, went to the park and Mrs. Rocha asked where he was and said went fishing; too cold for golf. She couldn't understand, cause Mr. Rocha loves fishing. Scott called the Rocha house to find if Laci there, then said missing. Scott got home, hungry, got a slice of pizza, took a shower, washed clothes, and started calling to look for Laci. **LACI'S MOM: I WAS REALLY SCARED WHEN SCOTT SAID 'MISSING'.**

What Laci wearing? Amy says beige pants, may get tape at the salon and see. Scott didn't call Amy to say he couldn't pick up the gift.

Dad said other things Scott bought and not told him. Clearly Geragos had the Dad prepared for testifying. We understand there is no blood DNA from the home. What about paint? Don't know yet; prosecutor will fill in the blanks. With Amber we'll learn more about lies Scott told.

Takes one hour to get to the buoy and one hour to get back and Scott went fishing for two hours. So Where Was The Fishing? Did Amber pass a polygraph? Why not call? Tapes? Naked photos with Geragos?

Laci's Mom solid on the stand. Laci was headstrong. Significant? December 15th dinner with Scott and Laci. Ron Grantsky loves to fish, boat never came up. December 12th [23rd], 8:30pm phone call, Laci called, to have brunch the next day. December 24th Scott called, said Laci missing, right away. When she went to the Park, Scott was thirty feet away and she yelled Scott, Scott, and he never acknowledged her. First day out with the boat. Don't know, could be true. Potential jurors will have on their minds pictures of the Rocha family that day.

Letters from Scott, read them, outgoing mail. What if crime in a letter? Looks pretty good, nice haircut, suit [Scott]. We gotta take a break.

'Missing' is not a word I'd use if my wife wasn't home at 5:17pm. How do you go fishing for a five foot fish, a sturgeon, in a fourteen foot boat? Cops detect Clorox in the kitchen. You don't think Scott came home and bleached the kitchen? That's what the detective says, but I wish it was someone else who doesn't have an axe to grind against Scott. Like Simpson case, where you attack the police? Simpson is the most innocent guilty person on Earth.

Coming up, find out who will testify in the Scott Peterson trial. **WHO WILL TALK?** Several people close to Amber tell me Amber will testify next week. As the prosecutor I'd ask why in the world is this hair on these pliers. Bleach, maid used in the bathroom, but not in the kitchen. Yea, and Scott wasn't a neat guy. Yea, never did laundry, never cook. But all things add up, jury maybe can forget one thing, but not all these.

Alot of DNA evidence being heard in the Scott Peterson case today. His lies went on for months, until the bodies of Laci and her unborn son they named Conner, washed up in the Bay. DNA expert for the defense says really can't match mitochondria DNA, can only say the two samples are similar. The prosecution says that the hair found wound around the tip of the needle nosed pliers.

LACI MET SCOTT IN 1995. LACI MARRIED SCOTT PETERSON IN 1997. No one knowing he bought the boat shows a level of premeditation. Scott didn't tell Dad that he was fishing in the Bay while talking on the phone to his Dad. Very interesting, me too. Sharon Rocha spoke to Laci at 8:30pm, December 23rd. Sharon said Laci was a private person.

When asked by the detective, 'Did you go play golf?' Scott said, 'No, too cold', and Ron [Sharon Rocha's companion] said that, 'You go fishing either early morning or afternoon and weren't you a little late to go fishing'? Scott said he tried to call Laci twice from his cell phone while fishing, went home, dog in backyard with the back door unlocked, he ate two slices of pizza and took a shower, then started calling to look for Laci. Scott asked Sharon Rocha if Laci was at her house and then, at some point, said Laci was missing. And when Sharon went to the Park to look for Laci, Scott wasn't there looking. The detective did say Scott was upset that day, right? Oh yea, that testimony is there and he was active in the search for Laci. Supposedly the duct tape on Laci was the same tape Scott used to put up 'Laci missing' posters.

Scott Peterson's defense attorney is supposed to call a witness today in a California court to attempt to discredit forensic science. Prosecutors are trying to show that a hair found wrapped into a pair of pliers belongs to Laci, who Scott is accused of murdering. The defense has a DNA expert, a New York University professor states that contamination with mitochondria DNA is highly probable and that the way in which the percentage rates of probability are made up is highly questioned within the science fields.

The detective says Scott didn't know what type of fish he was after on that day. Some have suggested it was sturgeon.

The defense DNA expert today; the prosecution was able to get the professor to admit that twenty to sixty percent of his income is from testifying about DNA for defendants, and therefore take away some of his credibility with the judge. The prosecution never really extracted DNA to test it. The prosecutor claims the hair found on the boat belongs to Laci.

I'm told Amber will be called. Scott Peterson's former girlfriend may become the star witness against him and will the defense tell us who the real killer is; they told us they would. Remember when Geragos wanted the preliminary hearing closed, 'it would give the real killers clues'. Better have it, but don't use at the preliminary. Does that mean he doesn't have it? Means he didn't mean it. No satanic cults? Do theories to get people out of woodwork with information. Not okay to do this. If used in opening statement, it could be problems.

Scott's parents aren't poor. Scott's a very successful fertilizer salesman. Insurance? When did he put it on wife and unborn son? It'll come up. On wife; don't know about the child. Sometime before the incident.

Bombshell evidence in the Scott Peterson case. Investigators say similarities between the tape next to Laci's body and the same roll Scott used to put up posters for Laci. They won't use this at the preliminary hearing, but will wait and use at trial. Nobody says that Laci knew of the boat. He has a work warehouse and one in Modesto for the boat, boat never at their home.

The defense expert didn't do a mitochondria DNA test. Testified one hundred-fifty times for the defense, and six times for the prosecution. Yea, but prosecution experts always testify for the prosecution; they're paid to. [Use mito DNA] ID, or exclude? The judge pays attention. The prosecution has a rebuttal DNA expert.

DUCT TAPE CLUE. HAIR LINK TO BOAT. Does the hair definitely link Laci to the boat? Will a single strand of hair be the smoking gun? The defense expert said; it's biased against the defendant and it's wrong. **HANGING ON BY A HAIR? FORENSIC BOMBSHELL.**

Fingerprint on tape? Unconfirmed reports on the duct tape. A TV station reports Scott's fingerprint on the tape. Compare, and same roll? From a particular role? Unreliable pieces? Don't think we'll hear of the tape at the preliminary.

Did Amber dump Scott Peterson just hours before Laci went missing? **FISHY ALIBI?** Cops say Scott said fishing, but didn't know what kind. Big problem, Ron Grantsky, an avid fisherman. Amy says look at the surveillance tape to see what Laci had on. She told them right away; cream pants. Scott said he saw her going off to walk the dog.

Geragos will be in Los Angeles tomorrow and McAllister will take over tomorrow. Scott Peterson's side of court kinda thin today. Brutal for the parents of the families when Amber testifies. Scott lost alot of weight, still tanned, natural. The defense says one in nine that could be Laci's hair. Well, the prosecution could turn that around and say, well, it's not Scott's hair, so whose hair is it? Tell us. **FREY FIRST CONTACTED POLICE December 30TH. FREY FIRST MET PETERSON November, 2002.**

The defense thinks police may have planted evidence in Scott's house the day after Laci disappeared. Detective said Scott couldn't or didn't answer what he was fishing for. No smell of bleach or cleaning smell in the house. No wet floors. Scott took them to the warehouse and either Scott, or someone, said no lights. Scott was cooperative the entire process. Police took the pail and mops when they came to the house.

The defense takes a page from Cochran's book; DNA hair planted in the pliers; defense expert never extracted DNA; sex on wolves expert. More for public opinion; both sides. Geragos trying to set a record for a preliminary hearing; both sides. Want Amber, she'll put the lid on the pot. To suggest the hair was planted, police already said the hair broke. Why is the preliminary hearing so long? The defense cross exam of the witnesses; all over one little hair.

Amber will testify, main jest of relation, what did Scott say about Laci? Involved statement? Goes to what Scott said; Amber asked if he had anything to do with it, and he said, No, uh, uh, but....Hold it, stop it, you don't know that. This is what we get into. Speculation. No big evidence yet. Lead detective tomorrow; figured Scott was guilty from the first. Detective in the Kobe Bryant case waffled and here, Geragos will have both guns blazing; planted evidence.

The defense leaks theories; satanic cult, Donnie and the brown van. [Prosecution.] Why prosecution, why not the defense. Somebody's talking; smell of bleach, don't know where come from. No bleach or smell with the first officer in the house; No Mr. Clean, or anything else. I've heard that; an article in the Enquirer; take with a box of salt.

The defense team, the tennis shoes missing? How, if Laci walking? The defense attorney says they're the key, the sandals, but not in the case. The defense theories evaporate in air. The dog in the back yard, with the leash. Prosecutor says, Scott's master plan, that Laci walked the dog. The dog was found at 10:30am by a neighbor. Scott left at 9:30, and Laci had on black pants. In one hour it was over, Laci gone, dog in back yard. A witness has a glass eye.

The defendant's demeanor is important. You keep showing the shot of Scott, Squeezing Out That One Little Tear; he managed to cry once, through all of this. Scott was active today; passed notes during the cross exam.

Fishing equipment used? Polygraph? Amber is most important. On December 24th, couldn't say what he was fishing for. The detective said no bleach smell, but that's funny, cause other detectives said they smelled bleach. The prosecutor may play the tape and not have Amber testify.

With the detective; on defense, the bleach issue, no smell. On prosecution side, the fish story, Scott not know what for; rug out of place, jammed up against the door, but, in cross exam, the detective said this was not in the police report. The defense; no bleach. The prosecution; when they talked to Scott, the way he handled the questions. Not a supplemental report [scrunched rug] though? Scott was interested today in the testimony. Scott was there, so he can be very helpful to his attorney.

COP CLUES. RUG RAISES FLAG. What the defense says about tainted evidence, and why some say a shag rug throws up red flags. What about the bucket on the washer by the maid and police find it outside? The maid may not remember where she put the bucket. Why did police take a throw rug and why search Scott's warehouse on December 24th?

WAREHOUSE CLUES. The detective, at the warehouse, a dispute over the electricity. Not clear if electricity, Scott said no, other said theirs was on; maybe he didn't pay the bills.

There was a fax there, received a fax that day.

They looked in the dark, with flashlights. Date; December 23rd? If police look at the warehouse and suspect Scott on December 23rd, then they suspected she's dead, right away?

PET QUESTIONS. JAIL LIFE EXCLUSIVE. Scott blamed the dog and cat playing for the rug against the door. Think they had a cat; rug moved back by Scott with his foot; easily. He didn't think much of it; moved with his toe. What does 'scrunched' mean? Fibers? One officer told another, that night, that he didn't know what he saw fishing for. There was whispering that night by the police, maybe go to the warehouse, suspected Scott from the beginning. That night.

JAILHOUSE EXCLUSIVE. COP CONTROVERSY. Why does the defense say that he planted evidence? What does Scott have hanging on his wall in prison and why does he have ear plugs? What does the hair mean? **4/18 SCOTT ARRESTED.** Reading behind bars, toothpaste sculptures, photos of Laci on the wall, colored photo of Laci; Laci photos, all of them. In a single cell; he can only see others when he's out of his cell. No one else is out, when Scott is removed from his cell. He was next to the drunk tank at first, so he made his own earplugs. Nice jail, Scott is polite, courteous.

One million dollars cost to his parents; with ninety-five percent already paid. Expert was fifty thousand alone and they'd already paid McAllister before Geragos. The prosecutor believes the hair is the key; the pliers are the key. Friends say Laci always used these particular type of pliers.

Probably hear different on the smell of the house from Brocchini. There's always a villain, like on the TV shows. Same detective who went back to the hair? And broke? Yes, and the evidence technician. The defense say the hair is mixed up; now two. Got to find one person to put on trial by the defense. Sometimes police don't do it right.

Scott knew full well the information; the photos would get out, on purpose.

Why go ninety miles from home, with a receipt to show this? Why are the clothes different? We may hear from the lead detective; the big pieces. If I were the prosecutor, I'd subpoena Diane Sawyer and all the tapes. Why were police whispering in Scott Peterson's kitchen the night Laci went missing and why it may be a key piece of evidence. **EVIDENCE QUESTIONED AT PETERSON HEARING.** What did the detectives find when they first visited the house after Laci went missing? Did police really plant evidence? That's what the defense claims.

No court today, Geragos in Los Angeles with a murder trial. The Peterson's are livid about this. They've already paid nearly one million dollars. There were three other affairs; a sexual problem. Amber Frey was purely a physical relation. Amber won't testify; prosecutor to play one tape. The controversial detective; was the second to arrive on the scene, the defense says tampered with evidence. Plant evidence? Yes. No. A fish story; Christmas Eve; Boat too dangerous? Too small to go in the Bay?

SHE WAS EIGHT MONTHS PREGNANT WITH A BOY. The maid says she always put the buckets on the washer and set the mop outside to dry. If all the defense Scott has, is that there was no smell of bleach, he's headed down the creek. Reasonable doubt? At trial, hundreds of pieces of evidence will build a story and convict Scott Peterson. Geragos clearly catering to the potential jury pool. Could go to the home and find Laci's hair right now in the closet. The only defense Geragos has, is that the police framed Scott.

4/13 BODY OF MALE FETUS FOUND ON SHORE. The first detective may be on the stand for several days. 8:30am, the housekeeper, the blinds down; 2pm, cleaned the blinds. The translator is a problem. Scott was at home sometime during the day and don't know if Laci at home then or not. She put bucket on the washer, mop outside.

December 23rd, Scott got a haircut at 5 to 5;30 with Amy. Talking about brunch, pick up gift, no problem, a lovely evening. The housekeeper; no problems. Four times been there. 8:30pm, Laci called; Sharon, brunch the next day. Amy said there's a surveillance video of what Laci wore that evening.

Only a rug out of place on December 24th; no sign of a struggle. **CLUES IN THE HOUSE?** Even if bleach, luminal can detect blood. The prosecution says a master plan, but if so, why make a commitment to pick up the gift.

What if Amber is not the only mistress? Help or hurt Scott? **EXCLUSIVE VIDEO.** Say that Laci came home early one day, not long after marriage, and caught Scott Cheating. Scott told Amber that he was going to Paris with his family for Christmas. **SCOTT'S LIFE AND LOVES. THE AMBER AFFAIR.** Why not kill Laci when he had other affairs? Kind of destroys the prosecution's motive. How do you prove affairs in court? **AMBER'S TESTIMONY.**

December 24th, the house next door broken into. So nothing to do with Laci's murder? No. So if loading something at night, you could see it? Yea. Scott and Laci had a cat, see it on the fence, the roof; friends have it now. You could see them, played all the time.

LACI'S TRIP TO THE PARK. FISHING QUESTIONS. Scott goes on the record about Amber, and Laci knowing of the affair. **SCOTT'S ALIBI.** There's sturgeon in the river also. What if a non-fisherman? Scott said he was an experienced fisherman, in his own words. He could launch a boat by self; that size. A polar front brings rough water; when Scott said he was fishing.

THE AMBER AFFAIR. PRELIMINARY PREVIEW. What did the cop see when he first visited the house? **IN HIS OWN WORDS.**

AMBER'S ANNOUNCEMENT. Little pieces of the TV interview were used by the prosecutor. A common theme in a wife murder case, the husband says the wife knew of the affair.

The lead investigator tomorrow; maybe the real meat of the case. He went to see the hair, then two hairs. The same detective went to the warehouse with Scott on December 24th, when Scott said no lights.

Preliminary hearing for Scott Peterson is underway in California. Peterson is charged with killing his wife, and their unborn child. You've been in court this morning. What's going on? The detective testified that Scott said he woke up at 8am, had cereal with Laci and they watched Martha Stewart. Said it was too cold to play golf. This was the first time the boat was in the water; bought it two weeks ago, paid four hundred dollars in cash. Laci's plans, to clean the kitchen on December 24th, mop the kitchen. She asked Scott to bring the mop in. To have brunch and walk the dog. Barefoot, pregnant, and mopping the kitchen when he left home.

He went two miles north of the landing dock. Tried to call Laci on her cell phone twice on the way home; message, can't get home in time to pick up Amy's gift basket. Laci's number is on his cell phone. He stopped to get gas on the way back. Laci's cell phone was in her car, plugged in, but dead out of power.

The prosecutor beginning of picking apart Scott Peterson's alibi of fishing. Came home and mop and bucket inside, afraid cat would knock over, so he put them outside. Towels found on the washing machine and the bucket outside. Leads the prosecution to believe some sort of cleanup in the house and the defense wants us to believe that somehow the kitchen got dirty between December 23rd with the maid and December 24th morning.

What do you have? Alot of good stuff. The detective, on December 30th, talked to Amber. Amber met Scott on November 20th, and on December 9th, learned he was married. Scott said his wife was dead. On December 26th, 27th, and 28th, Scott called her. Said he was out of the country for Christmas. Amber taped these calls, even before the police recorded calls.

On December 9th, he bought the boat and was with Amber that day. Scott taking it out in salt water for the first time on.... Scott said they'd be together around January 20th. Scott bought a 84 Mercedes; the prior owner says five thousand dollars, but that Peterson paid thirty-six hundred in one hundred dollar bills. Scott said he had a Florida license and gave his Mom's name as his name. On December 24th, he was brought to the police station and videotaped.

9:30 to 9:45, Scott left, Laci asked him to remove the mop and when he left, Laci was mopping the kitchen, a dark blouse and pants on. At the Marina, people were laughing at him trying to get the boat out of the water. He called police at 3am, cause the police took his gun from his truck. Called again to ask if they were using cadaver dogs at the Park; Interesting. Scott said no problem with a [gunpowder] residue test on him, cause there's a spent cartridge in the semi-automatic weapon.

Scott said no power. A fax from New Jersey on December 24th, at 2pm; 11am, New Jersey time? Scott said maybe he read it before fishing or maybe after. At 5:17, he called the Rochas, to tell her Laci was missing, didn't say out walking, or maybe at a neighbor's, or....

DETECTIVE AL BROCCHINI. Alot of highlights; McAllister doing the cross exam. The prosecutor went after the alibi; many little problems. In house, Scott said he left, pregnant barefoot wife mopping floor; went to warehouse; did some work; then went fishing, cause too cold to golf. He already had his bait with him, uh? He bought two lures, but not opened. Two poles in the boat. Missing, is the first word he used. The blackout not only in New York, but reached a California warehouse. 14:28 [2:28pm] time on the fax. Detective says New Jersey time and Scott had read the fax; 11:28 California time, but Scott said he left home, got the boat, and went fishing. Don't know if the lights out, the detective didn't try to turn on the switch.

Went to the country club, Del Rio. Scott said he'd pick up Amy's gift by 4pm. A twenty-five thousand dollar membership fee. Scott's business doing well. Scott said he called Laci on cell phone; he left message; ask Laci to pick up gift for Amy. Probably can't triangulate from the cell call, where Scott was. Odd, he didn't tell Dad he was fishing when Dad called him.

Purchased a Mercedes after he dyed his hair and grew a goatee. He does use Peterson as a last name to buy the car. Scott purchased the boat the day that Amber questions him if married and he tells her that day, that they'll be together. A virgin boat voyage on the same day that Laci disappears. The detective said Scott told him no martial problems. The National Enquirer reports that Scott gave Amber some of Laci's jewelry. Detective thought Scott hedging a bit on taking a gun residue test. Isn't this a lake boat and not a salt water one; too small?

Scott always has an answer to explain everything; becomes suspicious after a while. If he strangles her, there'd be no blood. Color his hair, grow a goatee, buy car and head south; it just keeps getting better and better. A couple of [fishing] lures in the truck; poles in the boat, wet. A cement weight, solid. The previous owner kept the anchor, so Scott made one.

On December 24th, Scott did his own laundry? Both Scott and Laci are clean people, and wouldn't think his wife was missing when he walked through the door, so.

Prosecutors choose not to speak today to the press. We always try to be fair and balanced. Can't Amber watch the news and know what's going on? **January: SCOTT TOLD ABC TV HE TOLD POLICE OF AFFAIR "IMMEDIATELY".**

You were convinced O.J. was guilty before the jury came back. No. Yes you did, I used to hear you on the radio. Civil trial said responsible.

[Cadaver dogs] True, according to detective Brocchini, Scott called and asked. What of theory that Scott mopped up after Laci's water broke? He'd have said that. Nothing in the mop or water. Just location. **SCOTT PETERSON CHARGED WITH KILLING WIFE LACI, UNBORN SON.**

Detective said Laci's wallet and keys in a closet and Scott's fishing clothes in the washer. A .22 caliber in the glove box of Scott's truck. A December 30th call, Scott said a widower on December 9th.

The defense showed that the detective was out of site of the others while in the Peterson home. Detective said Scott decided to buy a boat on December 8th, and picked up money for it on December 9th, the same day Amber happened to ask if Scott is married.

Detective asked Scott to take a residue test, after getting the gun and when the detective went to get the kit, Scott asked if fumes from the boat would produce false positives and the detective said no. Swabs were never tested. Police aren't interested in the gun. Doesn't help the defense. Judge let it in? Why not arrest him? What did Scott call police and ask the next day? **HIS COP QUESTIONS. LACI'S LAST WALK. CLUES LEFT AT HOME. SEEKING JUSTICE.**

Simple, Scott said he took the bucket out, cause he didn't want the cat tipping it over.

It was a random statement from Scott during a conversation. **5/5/03: GERAGOS ANNOUNCES DEFENSE OF SCOTT.**

Does the warehouse make or break Scott's timeline? Power Company; no record of outage that day. **WAREHOUSE WOES.** 14:28 fax, Scott said New Jersey time and said he read the fax, couldn't be on way to fish, would have to be when he got back.

DOG CLUES. What did the Peterson dog do, and does it give any clues as to where Laci may have been killed? Very large Park. Huge, a full scale search began at daylight. This would scare me, it's isolated and no one here. A lot of nooks and crannies in there. I'd walk around a nice neighborhood if eight and a half months pregnant, rather than go down the incline at the entrance to the Park. Cold and muddy that week. Maybe she felt secure in that Park cause she knew it.

Rumors Scott gave Laci's jewelry to Amber? The loaded gun surprising, but don't think it's the cause of death. Very damaging evidence in the Scott Peterson hearing. The second detective to reach the scene, said he found Laci's pocketbook and keys in the closet, Scott's wet clothes in the laundry room and that Scott had told Amber that his wife was already dead, two weeks before Laci's disappearance.

Will Scott Peterson's defense team be successful in discrediting the police? The defense, McAllister, using a line of questions that the detective may have left an opening to plant evidence.

Dye hair, fake passport from brother, six girlfriends. Now there appears a motive.

BROCCHINI: PETERSON SAID HE WAS NOT MARRIED, HE WAS A WIDOWER. WILL GERAGOS DISCREDIT MODESTO POLICE? Back in court on Wednesday. May hear secretly recorded calls by Amber next week.

TRUTH OR CONSEQUENCES. Live in Modesto at the courthouse, the Modesto detective brings out some untruths Scott Peterson told. New information coming out of the Laci Peterson case. Boy, it's a blockbuster. The courtroom is dark today. The defense got more than they asked for yesterday. The detective said Scott said Laci mopping the floor when he left to go fishing. Detective found gun in Scott's truck. November 20th began dating, said single, later a widower and could be with her in January.

Could Scott have been framed? Hair? If detective, like he said, dropped his keys in the boat and had to go back and get them. Left his keys in Scott's truck and later, left his folder in Scott's boat. He didn't even put the pliers in his police report. **WAS SCOTT FRAMED?** The defense asked the police, see him leave anything in the boat? Opportunity to leave anything incriminating? Detective says an honest mistake on leaving his keys at the home and his folder at the warehouse.

The prosecution tried to link the boat purchase and telling Amber that he's a widower the same day. But the defense showed that the deal to buy the boat was a day earlier. The day may not be important. Scott used his own name to buy the boat. **IN HIS OWN**

WORDS. THE AMBER AFFAIR. Why did Scott tell Amber he was a widower, just weeks before Laci disappeared?

Dog leash? **THE FREY FACTOR.** The prosecutor should go easy with the Amber motive, many affairs. One; did he kill her? Must prove for murder. Two; plan in advance? Must prove for premeditation. The prosecution doesn't have alot of physical evidence, and alot of stupid behavior by Scott. The defense says the officers didn't do their job.

SCOTT'S INDISCRETIONS. Will Scott's indiscretions help him in court? **MODESTO MURDER.** Marina, receipt, bodies? Unless the defense shows retaliation against Scott; hard to sell. **POLICE HAVE NOT DISCLOSED HOW LACI AND CONNER WERE KILLED. DETECTIVE SAID THEY TOOK PHOTOS OF SCOTT'S BOAT.**

THE FREY FACTOR. LACI'S REACTION. Later, hear what Scott says on how Laci handled the news of his affair with Amber. **IN HIS OWN WORDS.** Hear what Scott says how Laci handled the affair.

SCOTT SPEAKS.

FBI had video surveillance equipment planted outside the Peterson home and Geragos says it may help clear Scott. **DEPUTY D.A. SAYS THEY'LL PROVIDE TAPES TO DEFENSE. DEFENSE: FBI TAPES COULD CLEAR SCOTT PETERSON.** The D.A. says they don't have the tapes and don't know anything about it. In California, it is illegal to tape a conversation, unless both parties know about it.

TOP STORY: ROSIE, LACI, KOBE. Took dogs to the warehouse and detected her scent and also down the boat ramp within forty-eight hours of her disappearance. Very damning evidence, if true. Will Scott Peterson's own words come back to haunt him, and why is his defense team saying the police planted evidence? Does this sound like a case we all remember, like O.J. **AMBER GOES TO CHURCH.** I agree; sounds like it.

On January 3rd, 2003, surveillance equipment installed by the FBI across from the Peterson home, in a neighbor's home, and recorded video, but the FBI says it's not a party to the case and doesn't have to comply with the defense subpoena. Sometime between January 16th and January 19th, the Peterson home was burglarized and the defense says maybe the camera caught the burglar. Also a neighbor's home burglarized the night of December 23rd or early morning December 24th.

Testimony continues today on DNA of a single hair which the prosecution says ties the murder of Laci to Scott Peterson. The defense says the FBI camera is gone, but the equipment is still on the pole across the street from the Peterson home.

For the latest on the Scott Peterson preliminary hearing, tune in tonight at 9.

Testimony centers on a single hair wrapped in pliers found on Peterson's boat.

Geragos said in court that he subpoenaed tapes from the FBI and the FBI failed to comply. The prosecutor said he's not aware of the tapes. Now it's found the police do have a tape, but the prosecutor says he didn't know. They say the FBI didn't install the equipment to survey, it was the DEA [Drug Enforcement Agency]. Peterson's home burglarized in mid-January and the prosecutor says the surveillance was to keep tabs on Scott and not to survey home.

Will Amber testify? **WILL AMBER TESTIFY?** Will Amber testify and will her testimony send Scott Peterson to trial for murder?

The prosecution has a rebuttal DNA witness on now; says mitochondria DNA accepted, disagrees with the defense's expert testimony. Geragos complains that the prosecutor's expert won't answer his questions asked. Geragos says mitochondria DNA doesn't have enough spectrum of identifiers to ID a person.

Why the DEA had Scott Peterson under security surveillance. Back in court for Scott Peterson as his attorneys examine evidence with a fine tooth comb. The preliminary hearing that Just Doesn't Go Away. Expert rebuts the defense on contamination of DNA by the defense. They will finish him [expert] today and maybe the detective back on the stand; a little bobbling; December 24th left his keys and notebook at the warehouse, careless. Well, Colombo left his coat and still did pretty good. Say the dogs followed the scent all the way to the boat ramp.

DEA? Probably cause the DEA has good equipment and not involved with Scott. January 3rd, 2003 they started, and the Modesto police had, has one hour of the recording.

Scott had affairs in airplanes, took trips abroad, Mercedes, motorcycle, boat, joined Country Club; I'm thinking where's the money coming from. Wouldn't Geragos say, like in the O.J. case, drugs involved and Laci was killed that way? We'll get into the mind of Scott Peterson and tell what he's thinking.

Goes fishing on Christmas Eve, leaves convenient messages on wife's answering machine, eats, showers, and calls mother-in-law and first thing he says is Laci's missing. I don't see alot of evidence here. Amber taped calls on her own. You'd think if too cold to golf, it'd be too cold to fish. He called the police officer, at 2am, and said he wish he hadn't let him take his gun; asked if they used cadaver dogs, and said, by the way, will fuel exhaust from the boat skew the gun test results?

The Scott Peterson scandal, and meet the man who could get him off? **WILL HE GET OFF.** Ferrous battle over DNA. All over one piece of hair found in Scott Peterson's boat and people say Laci never in that boat. Scott lied about everything. Durst lied about everything and he got off. The prosecutor is not showing his hand. Scott's boat said not to have salt water on it, so he may not even have been in the Bay, so that's another lie there.

The financial situation with Scott looking for money, Amber, boat, Country Club. Amber taped secretly and asked, Did you have anything to do with your wife's disappearance, and he said, Yes, well uh, uh, no, but I know who did.

More drama in Scott Peterson's hearing. Did Amber tape phone calls a week before police? More DNA, the police used the Rocha's, Sharon and son, to tape Scott on the phone, also friends of Scott to call Scott and pump him for information. The detective said he had no knowledge of Amber's taped calls.

Feds is like pulling teeth. Surveillance didn't start until January, so nothing to do with Laci's disappearance. Don't know yet. McAllister said he was aware of the Amber tapes. The detective said, No, Absolutely no knowledge of tapes beforehand. One party consent rule. No, no, no. Why are we suspicious of her taping Scott? HELLO, he was married.

Feds; Geragos will get the tapes, takes a long time. He'll get pictures of Scott's home, sitting there. We know about the neighbor coming over to get Laci's dress; no burglary. Get Scott talking on his cell phone while dumping the trash. GEE, I Wonder Who He Was Talking To. **DEFENSE SUGGESTS AMBER TAPED SCOTT'S CALLS BEFORE LACI VANISHED.**

How did she die? Don't know, mostly cause the head is missing. Conner in tact. Psychiatric testing? Don't know, more interested if he had a polygraph exam.

On December 23rd the hair salon, the next day coming home from golf, what of the gift? 2:15pm on December 24th, Scott called Laci and said; Hi beautiful, on the way home from Berkley. The story does fit; fished only a short while, came back and called Laci and said not time to pick up the gift. What about paint on the boat?

The Amber story in People's Magazine. She dated a male, married stripper; she knew he was married. Lived with a male stripper. Amber will be dragged through the mud. I made the decision years ago to never, ever, be a defense attorney and do that kind of stuff. She'll be carved up like a Thanksgiving turkey.

Break-in of the Peterson home; a woman, supposedly broke the glass, went in, stole some things, draped in Laci's wedding dress and laid on their bed.

On December 9th, told wife dead? What if bi-polar or not, as you say is normal? **DETECTIVE LAST THURSDAY: SCOTT TOLD AMBER LACI WAS DEAD; THREE WEEKS BEFORE DISAPPEARANCE.** He told Amber, that he knows who did have something to do with Laci's disappearance. Less than twenty-four hours, Scott asked about cadaver dogs. Same day as missing occurred, he got a secret mailbox.

If brunch with Mom, why not Mom worried? Brunch or dinner, night of December 24th; there was no brunch. Scott says he left at 9:30am with her mopping, while wearing a diamond necklace and earrings. Heard Scott involved in drugs? It would be out there, if true. Was Frey given a polygraph exam? She has and passed, before ever making first public appearance. From what I see, Scott Peterson is the only choice.

Exclusive new information today. How Amber was coached by the police; the detective took her to get the tape recorder and slipped her notes with questions to ask him. The detective said, he kind of remembers, that Scott said he felt sorry for Amber if police suspected her. Can't figure out why three hours of surveillance tape was lost. **WHERE ARE THE TAPES?**

Police put the camera on pole; never turned over to the defense. Wasn't supposed to be taped, just surveillance to see when he left, but accidentally got three hours taped. Neighbors said the box taken down only a couple days ago, after Geragos filed the complaint. Alot of boxes out there to transmit, so we wonder which box they put the camera in and what information was gathered. Obligation on the prosecutor to turn it over, without stumbling on it? Probably so, yes, and. Tapes show up on the detective's desk when he returned from vacation. **EYES ON SCOTT.**

Difference between stupidity and negligence. Police knew of the tapes, knew they had to turn over and didn't. Why is the prosecutor making the defense jump through hoops in this case? Coaching Amber; gotten from the cops? Cops coached her, DOJ [Department of Justice] helped with the questions. Scott said in Europe; cops said to encourage this point. False reports that Amber taped phone calls before cops? McAllister asked; do you remember getting questions... [Amber an agent of State] I don't agree. The defense argument is that they rushed to judgment. **COPS COACHING AMBER. COPS TRAILING SCOTT.** We've done some digging on detective Brocchini.

They don't need Amber. I bet the prosecution does, no way. Amber investigating, in early December, of the marriage? Heard she hired investigators. Will testify.

People don't understand, one-quarter of a million people in California have the same DNA in their hair. Geragos is arguing two million people in California.

WHO IS Brocchini. Who is detective Brocchini? Who is the detective in the Scott Peterson case that's under fire from the defense? Eighteen years, eight years with Alameda, ten years in Modesto. A master detective, forty-five years old. First to arrive on December 24th, found gun in the truck, on hand when Amber called the tip line, drove ninety minutes to Fresno to interview Amber. The detective testified that Scott told Amber he could be with her after January 25th, 2003. The defense suggests the detective planted evidence in the pliers. The two hairs; sloppy. Brocchini still on cross exam tomorrow. Some say he's a rouge cop. We'll never know how Laci died.

Two key neighbors; across the street; blinds. Next door; found dog on December 24th. And the housekeeper disputes the neighbor on the blinds. If the prosecutor had more, we thought it'd come from the lead detective, but not yet. Scott Peterson is charged with killing his pregnant wife Laci, and their unborn son.

Detective testified that Amber agreed to tape Scott Peterson phone calls. Detective testified that he enlisted fellow officers, friends, family members, neighbors, and mistress of Scott Peterson to try and snare Scott Peterson. Scott Peterson is charged with the murder of his pregnant wife Laci, and their unborn son.

Whether police used her to trap Scott.

Surveillance testimony? Detective Brocchini on the stand. Police; on January 5th, 6th, and 9th, followed Scott to Berkley Bay, he'd stay at the Marina, stare, then leave. A lady fixed Scott up with Amber and promised not to tell Amber that Scott was married.

SHOCKING EVIDENCE IN SCOTT PETERSON HEARING TODAY. Wait till you hear about Scott Peterson's behavior just days after Laci's disappearance, cops know, cause they tailed him. Bombshell testimony today. Detective Brocchini; Scott returned to the Bay, two to three times in a rental car and lost the police tail; sometimes making u-turns and quick turns to lose them. Sometimes he did lose them. Each time, he went direct to the Marina and didn't stop anywhere. He even went to the cops tailing him, and asked if they'd like a cup of coffee or a donut at the Marina.

Either the worst liar in history, or a very smart killer. Shows how much pressure Scott was under. Scott's friends? Shawn? Shawn, Amber's friend in October, 2002, she was Amber's friend and introduced him to Amber. Shawn asked Scott if he knew anyone available. Shawn confronted Scott on December 8th, and Scott begged her not to tell Amber he was married.

Dogs alerted at the house, warehouse, boat, and ramp. I'm waiting for the dogs to testify. Lied to own attorneys? You have to lie to your lawyers.

Detective bought the recorder from Radio Shack for Amber. Police asked Amber to lie and say, tell Scott she was part of Laci's disappearance? Don't think it got to Amber, but police did kick it around some.

Geragos says the police surveillance tapes were withheld from the defense on purpose. Police denied their existence.

The detective called the Peterson tip line himself. Pretended he was a tipster, and said on December 24th, he saw the boat with a big blue blanket in Scott's truck, but the Peterson tip line never called the police tip line to report that.

Do you think Scott Peterson can beat this rap? Yes. Lies, DNA, cash; he's going down. Amber Frey's attorney says she will not be called to testify at Scott Peterson's preliminary hearing. Scott Peterson's eighth day. The detective says Scott trying to establish an alibi with Amber, feeding her a story he would be in Europe over Christmas. Amber's attorney, said Amber will Not be called to testify, said the prosecutor said he's not going to utilize Amber.

Scott Peterson made trips to the Marina, in early January, peer into the Bay and drive home. Told Amber his wife dead and Amber's friend. Pants, cream colored, same as on December 23rd. Neighbor testified Scott came to her house and ask if seen Laci and told her he'd played golf all day. Amber at trial. Enough evidence today to bind over. Geragos would go on a fishing expedition with her.

Pants; huge, huge. Rocha family on your show, Amy said creamed colored outfit. Police got Amy, took her into the Peterson home, and Amy came out crying. All those who claim they saw her on December 24th are wrong. Don't interrupt.

You're speculating on the defense treatment of her, so why not speculate on your client, on how she feels? On December 16th, the Amber tapes began? People's Magazine says friends say Amber says don't believe or never said Scott is guilty? Yes, Gloria is serving Amber well. Think if she wasn't protected. Hope you're listening, Geragos. There's a gag order.

DETECTIVE POSED AS TIPSTER ON PETERSON HOTLINE. Geragos said that Scott went to the Marina three times, cause the Modesto Bee reported the police had divers there. I might drive to the Marina, if I thought my wife was there. **GERAGOS SAYS SCOTT WENT TO MARINA, AFTER NEWSPAPER REPORTED DIVERS WERE THERE.**

The man walking the dog on December 24th, why not hypnotize him? I spoke with him, glasses and a glass eye. Says saw dog at a distance, went home and said, Saw Laci's dog; never said he saw Laci. [Objectivity?] Yea, Right down the middle.

What did Scott get Laci for Christmas? A wallet. Wasn't it confirmed by another lady walking dog?

Scott went to the Bay, but not to the police dive station. Rented a car to go and then high tail it out of there. [Wonderful witness] Yea, if you're looking for a dog. Scott said she was mopping floor when he left. Remember, none of this is evidence. We're just talking about what might be. The preliminary hearing is evidence, what Scott told the detective. Golf outing; did he have reservations or someone to play with? Has the prosecutor looked for the other women of Scott's? Other affairs; some say six. Likely interviewed by the police. Benefit the defense? **AMBER WON'T TESTIFY.**

Either Laci died in the clothes she wore on December 23rd, or she wore the same clothes two days in a row.

What's the point in you being here? They've got the tapes. You're not tipping off the defense. The bind over standard so low in California. The suspicious behavior of Scott, bodies where fishing, the lies; may not be enough to convict, but okay to bind over. Then, what's the point. Six months until trial, may find more evidence.

Detective said how Scott and Amber got together. Scott ask her to hook him up with a friend. It keeps adding layers to his deception. Yea, well, we could do the whole hour on lies, but.

One hair, or did police plant a second hair? Test for he same hair? And police reports says 'hair', not 'hairs'. The missing person report says, black pants. When found, tan pants. Learn about the frantic phone call Scott made.

Amber's friend found out that Scott was married in early December and he begged her not to tell Amber. The detective went to Scott's employer and wanted to check his expense account, and the employer faxed it to the detective, and he said the expense account was okay.

Surveillance; January 5th, 6th, and 9th. There were reports in the Modesto Bee on those days that divers were looking for the body. A long way to drive for five minutes looking in the Bay. Not if you're a grieving husband. **STATE'S TACTICS.**

Why is the prosecution shy about putting Amber on the stand? Amber, born in Los Angeles in 1975, has a two year old daughter, parents divorced when five, earned a degree in child development. 1978, Hart; married with a pregnant wife. Amber confronted his wife and played the tapes she'd recorded of hubby, with negative comments about his wife. I'd use her for information, and got on her side on the stand.

I'd try this case as soon as possible, cause the prosecution isn't ready. Testified that duct tape found around Laci's groin area. Dogs not able to trace Laci's body to the boat and that may be a problem for the prosecution. Were able to say the dogs traced body from the home to car and then all the way to the Bay; I don't know how they're gonna prove that; but then at the docks.

There's talk that Geragos may call her [Amber] and put her on.

I can't believe that police found the pliers and took into evidence, then, when looking at a photo of the pliers, police saw a hair in the pliers? In the report, a single piece of hair, but, when taken out of the evidence bag, says two pieces of hair. Colors not the same; texture not the same. December 20th, Scott bought a fishing license for December 24th and December 25th, but when questioned, said it was a snap decision to go fishing.

Judge already said there's enough evidence to bind Peterson over. The defense scenarios; defense team did autopsy, maybe baby born alive, cult, taken hostage and baby born. The detective said that a couple witnesses said they saw two guys with Laci and arguing in the Park and maybe Laci knew them. On redirect, the detective said maybe not arguing with Laci, but talking, discussing something. Devil worshipper thing? Not brought out in court yet. America tired of stuff these guys throw out there with no evidence.

Oh, Bull! Once do this, you're a disgrace to the court. You don't lie in a courtroom, to deflect. Don't be condemning to me, Counselor. We're not letting lawyers lie in the courtroom. Period. We're gonna keep a watch on It Here.

The prosecutor called the hair fiber analyst; the hair consistent with Laci's hair. The defense shifts from cult killers to sloppy police work.

Conner born alive? Would help the defense. Geragos said today, full term. If so, Scott had nothing to do with the death. Detective Brocchini didn't follow up the tip from the neighbor, who saw Laci. With tan pants on when washed up and not black, as Scott said. Would mean she wore the same pants two days. Don't know of any women who do that.

Mistake of law and fact. Wait and I'll tell you. Ooh, Ooh. Different accounts when Laci last seen. Not a Christmas gift to the defense. Her information conflicted with other information police had. With thousands of tips, can't follow each one; priority. As a defense attorney, you'd love for this to be a block buster. Well, you're not gonna do it here. The defense has to establish an alibi and an alternate theory of death.

Dog walk at 10:25, but lady says the dog alone at 10:18am. 10:18am, the tip has credibility; dog with a dirty leash. Not black pants, as Scott says, but tan as Amy says. Puts all witnesses in conflict, if killed December 23rd, No one saw her, and no one returned the dog to the yard. Police let out information all along, that turns out not to be true. Insurance policy, etc.

Husband always the first suspect. He rents a car; Why?; Not even his own car, and goes to the Bay and looks out over the water. Pattern of behavior by the police; the detective called people to give the impression Scott was guilty. Common to go to family and friends, and say something bad and see what response he gets. Maybe they'll agree. But the detective said; to plant seeds of suspicion in the family and friends.

Not supposed to do discovery in a preliminary hearing, but that's what we got here. Not premeditation by Scott, if it was, Amber would be involved. Geragos not proving what he said he would. He's trying to deflect. It was premeditation and Amber is important, can't impeach her credibility. Who, what, man would say he's a widower? He's a serial cheater. Why secretly buy a boat? Amber will be a bombshell.

It's gotta pass the smell test, Miss Defense Attorney. A month before he met Amber, he was out trolling for a mistress. Who saw him carry her body to the boat?; or dispose of it? Nobody, Nobody, Nobody, Nobody.

Laci had a sonogram in September and the baby fine; talked to the doctor. Why did Scott say Laci was missing so fast? Why not Laci out on errands? That's from Mrs. Rocha and said she was surprised, but Scott did come home and take care of errands before calling, so maybe not so concerned, at first.

Geragos tried to say Scott's marriage fine and no problems, and we know better. The Peterson family wants the trial in a hurry. **SCOTT PETERSON CHARGED WITH KILLING WIFE, LACI AND UNBORN SON CONNER. DEFENSE QUESTIONS RELIABILITY OF MITOCHONDRIA DNA.** If rust on the pliers, mean not used for a while? **JUDGE LEANS TOWARDS ALLOWING MITOCHONDRIA DNA EVIDENCE.**

Circumstantial case is real, all relevant. When Laci went missing, families stuck by him and said nothing wrong with the marriage and Laci was close with Mom. **ALLRED: DEFENSE HAS NOT DECIDED IF IT WILL CALL FREY.**

The detective didn't follow the witness tip. A woman said she saw Laci walking the dog, and two men yelling at her to shut up her dog. The defense, Geragos, says they might call Amber. The prosecutor will object. We timed the walk to the Park.

He'll get it, cause the prosecutor opened it up with the detective's testimony. Pliers rusty? Yea, could be salt water, but if rusty as suggested, hair would be there a long time; tough road for the prosecution. Two hairs; the defense says the second hair planted. Expert said he opened the bag; said hair like Laci's. One fragment darker than other. Yea, he said that too.

A hospital worker saw; the prosecutor says at 10:45, and the defense says 9:45; men talking to Laci, while she was on a smoke break. The defense has 9:45 on tape and the prosecutor didn't investigate. Detective said the hospital worker's story didn't go in their [police] direction, so not follow up. **NEW DOG STORY.** How long for the dog to get home from the Park? Amber may not be directly linked to an affirmative defense. **DOG MYSTERY. SPLITTING HAIRS.**

Wait'll you hear the breaking news in the courtroom today that had both sides dropping their jaws in disbelief. Color, cuticle and rust. Judge said he'd let the hair in, but don't know, if 'one in a hundred', or 'consistent with Laci's'. No evidence, or they'd have arrested him earlier.

Is there an eyewitness to back up Scott's story that Laci was walking her dog on the morning of December 24th, and do police have the wrong man? December 23rd? Twenty-three weeks pregnant when examined by the doctor on September 23rd? **WALK IN THE PARK.** Could the dog make it back home within the time the lady says she saw the dog? The men said, Tell your dog to shut the f... up.

Lady got out of her car, took the dog to the yard, didn't see Laci or Scott; in the 10 o'clock hour. Police say the hospital worker; 10:45. The defense says, 9:45. If 10:45, can't put the dog in the yard at 10:18. The walk, twenty minutes from the Park, at a pretty good clip. 10:18, Karen says the dog in the street. Parks, grabs the leash, gate was open, saw no one, left dog, closed gate.

Detective says 10:45am on the tape of the hospital woman. The defense says 9:45am on the tape of the hospital woman, and we found another, easier way for a pregnant lady to enter the Park. Others say they saw these two men also. Yea, while we were in the Park, two guys accosted our lady camera people, saying horrible things to them. Yea, someone jogging that day, had someone jump out of the bushes at her. Christmas morning, three neighbors called in on suspicious people, but no one called back, and, said they saw Laci and no one called them back.

Cause you're on TV every day doing that. You don't want to execute someone, cause someone else couldn't tell the difference between black and tan pants.

Is the lawyer representing Scott Peterson turning the hearing into a sham?

PETERSON EXCLUSIVE. Shocking news about Scott Peterson's plans to go play golf. Was it that he went fishing on spur of the moment or was it planned? Case is forensically weak; the experts say. He had a round at 9am, at the Club, didn't show, didn't cancel. A good golfer. Don't know if he never cancelled before. Jury will wonder what he intended to do. Don't know, couple of ways to interpret it. Either side can spin it, but neither side has it yet.

Scott told Amber he's a widower the same day he bought the boat, then soon after he got a fishing license for December 23rd and December 24h, but, you have a golf date at the Club. December 9th, just an unlucky day for Scott. Friends say that Scott told women sometimes that he's married and sometimes widower.

Scott told real whoppers and now lying to his defense team. The Amber lie, when he hired attorneys, and told them he never called Amber after Lai's disappearance and she had called him, but he called her up to two months later.

2/18 POLICE BEGIN SEARCHING PETERSON'S HOME.

3/6 POLICE CONSIDERED THE CASE A HOMICIDE.

4/18 SCOTT ARRESTED.

A sex addict? Something set out by the defense. Prosecution says motive is Amber. The defense leaks he's a sex addict. **AMBER'S TESTIMONY.** Will Amber have to testify, after the prosecution decides not to call her, and the defense subpoena's her, and what does the defense have on her? **SCOTT'S LEGAL MOVES.** Amber was subpoenaed by the defense. Geragos wanted Amber for himself. Can't help the defense, It's Wrong! It's not his time to put her on. Probable cause and that's it.

Scott had a golf tee time. Doesn't help him. Premeditation? Maybe. Forensically weak case.

DEFENSE STRATEGY: ATTACK DETECTIVE, BABY BORN ALIVE/CULT THEORY, SEVERAL SUSPICIOUS PEOPLE IN PARK. Beyond reasonable doubt is at trial, not here.

The coroner in the Scott Peterson preliminary hearing. Both sides refer to 'the baby' and 'Conner'. Expert said the baby nine months old in his opinion. Thirty-three to thirty-eight weeks old from the bones and other expert opinion said could have been born. Decomposition, tidal effects, and animal feeding. Laci, from the waist up, no flesh, no organs. Uterus there. Tape around the baby's neck and around chest or under arm. Two centimeters of space between the tape and the baby's neck. The judge asked, how did the tape get over the head and around his neck; could the head collapse to allow the tape? A bag found, baby wrapped in a bag? And later come out, with tape around neck? Scott waived his presence for this testimony and not have to sit there and listen to this type of stuff.

Mitochondria DNA is considered, but not certain aspects of it. May make hearing shorter at this point. Judge will consider the mitochondria DNA in his ruling.

Geragos theory; Conner in a plastic bag and thrown in the water. Mitochondria DNA is in, and prosecution can use it for a solid foundation to put Laci in the boat. Judge ruled the hair found in Scott Peterson's boat will come in.

The medical examiner; the state of each body, Laci at one stage and baby at; Waist up, no flesh on Laci, no extremities. Cutting marks? No, no tool marks or bite marks. Tidal effects; washed around. No evidence of vaginal birth? No evidence of vaginal birth, no evidence of a C-section. Separated bodies by tidal effects, animal feeding. Baby in the water only a few days. Medical examiner said he couldn't rule out a vaginal birth. Doesn't have to be true for the defense to use it. Couldn't rule out a live birth.

SCOTT PETERSON IS 31 YEARS OLD. Why did Scott leave the courtroom? It saves him from analysis by others on how he reacted. Everyone speculates on how he reacts. Oh, he managed to squeeze out one little tear so far, so don't go get your bucket for his tears yet, Vinnie.

They searched for Laci, but she came home on her own. Duct tape on Laci. Clear tape on Conner, neck, tightly on neck. Prosecutor says; no injuries to the neck, no sign of strangled. Defense says; impossible for the tape to float onto the neck. The medical examiner says the brain decompressed and the head shrunk to allow the tape on the baby. The defense says they found a plastic bag near Conner's body and the baby in it. Duct tape found in the bag, on Laci, but don't know if it matched. Duct tape used to put up Laci flyers.

Reasonable! Killed by a satanic cult, or by her husband. All these conflicting theories. Jury will never know he followed his lawyer's advice and not take a polygraph.

The hearing is still going on. Is there enough circumstantial evidence to convict Scott Peterson of murder? Gruesome testimony of condition of the bodies. Prosecutors hope the hair will prove Laci was in Scott's boat.

Evidence for the defense; testimony of tape around the baby's neck, one and a half times around the neck, with one centimeter of space, tight. Age, state's expert, nine months. Thirty-three weeks to thirty-eight weeks, another state expert. Age of fetus? Wait a minute. Scott went out of court during testimony of the medical examiner.

Maybe if mitochondria DNA had been let in earlier, we'd be through with the preliminary. Duct tape on Laci, kaki pants, tape on baby and plastic bag with duct tape in it. Prosecutor says just debris washed ashore. Defense says maybe the baby in the bag, bag comes open, and tape goes onto baby's neck.

DNA MYSTERY? Prosecutors in Mrs. Peterson's murder mystery won a single strand victory today. Judge ruled hair is admissible and can use it at trial. Mitochondria DNA is a round about way to identify the hair as belonging to Laci, through her family. Prosecutors hope to use the hair to link Laci to Scott Peterson's boat. **JUDGE ALLOWS MITOCHONDRIA DNA TEST OF HAIR FROM SCOTT'S BOAT.**

The forensic pathologist's autopsy; decomposition of Laci, severe. Conner, in tact; about two days in the water. On cross exam, the forensic pathologist admits it could be a bag that preserved the baby. The tape on the neck, pulled tight, only allowed one centimeter of space. Even the judge asked, How could the tape come over the baby's head? The pathologist said the head shrinks. The detective was questioned on the chain of custody, not much on the concrete blocks.

The defense grabbing at straws. Cervix in tact and no birth. Impossible for baby to be in a bag; scientifically impossible. No doctor report of over thirty-two weeks, and remember, fetus grows twice as fast after thirty-two weeks. Don't be fooled by a sonogram. Lose/lose for Geragos if he puts anything up. The BS meter is off the chart here tonight. The woman either had to have a C-section or birth, she had neither. Then tell me out it got out, if no C-section and no vaginal delivery. Then only thing left is from tissue breakdown and baby is expelled underwater.

Just a show. Don't know why he left the courtroom today. A no win situation. **SCOTT PETERSON CHARGED WITH MURDER OF PREGNANT WIFE LACI, AND UNBORN SON, CONNER.** Everyone expects the hearing to be over tomorrow. **ONE HAIR FOUND ON BOAT, BECAME TWO HAIRS WITH POLICE.**

Any other woman come forward? Six other women and a stripper. Maybe he killed her over many women, a Lifestyle; move to Europe.

The weight of Conner? It's in the autopsy report, but didn't hear it in court. **PATHOLOGIST: BABY'S EXACT AGE OBSCURED BY LONG EMERSON.** Was the pathologist asked if there was air and water in the lungs? Didn't see the question. Conner's insides had begun liquefying. May not be able to tell. Defense didn't ask either. So Hold On, Don't Call The Kettle Black. Make of it what you want.

A man came forward, in prison, heard Laci was kidnapped, and met Scott to kidnap Laci, but instead Scott asked him to murder Laci? Insurance, kidnap, to murder; if it exists, we'd hear more.

Detective testimony tipping hand on Amber? Scott and Laci, he was a gentleman and never cheated, now an affair? Yet parents say they never argued? How? Amber saw Scott on TV and called the detective that was on the case, so that's how the affair news got started.

Nancy said, pathologist said no evidence of a C-section, but the pathologist said the flesh was gone, so there wouldn't be any evidence. Uterus in tact. Pathologist said part of the uterus missing.

Exclusive photos from inside the Peterson home.

Dr. Lee Peterson, no relation, no cause of death. Hair will be allowed into evidence. Test okay to show a likely match. Computer expert; the day before bought the boat, downloaded information on the Bay and alot of other fishing spots.

Police not investigate the tip of the hospital worker. She said the woman was wearing a white blouse. At 9:53am; forty-three degrees in California. It would be chilly. Imagine pregnant woman with a jacket or sweater.

Heard of Scott making anchors, so the jury will be interested in how many he made and how many found. Any evidence? Don't think so. That's exactly what a circumstantial case is, but just cause can't find anchors, that doesn't make a case.

Judge allows mitochondria DNA test of hair found in Scott Peterson's boat, even though it cannot show a definitive match. Some fractured ribs on Laci.

Wonder if mop was left at the side of one door by the maid and Laci asked Scott to bring it in, and set back out on the other side of the door. Hard to clean up blood? The detective said he looked at all the rooms, saw Laci's pocketbook hanging in the closet. Could a scrunched up rug be trouble and how about those rags and mop? No sign of cutting.

Yea, but she was there a couple of days before. Scott said he put his clothes in the washer, before taking a shower. Scott was seen carrying a large wrapped object from the house and he said in an interview it was lawn umbrellas. Maid said she put the mop where the washer is and the bucket with the rags on top of the washer. The detective said Scott told him he washed clothes, maybe he moved the bucket. Show you where cops found Laci's purse. Bathroom is close to the kitchen, didn't realize that. If the maid cleaned that closely, I don't know. They've got a dog, kitchen is so small. You're right, kitchen floor is so small, so she could have been mopping. We'll show you where police found Laci's wallet. Police served the first warrant on Scott December 26th, just two days after Laci was reported missing.

A cut or tear on Conner's body; the leaks were confirmed by the autopsy. Next, where police found Laci's wallet. Police said, hanging there in the closet, with keys.

JUDGE IN MODESTO ALLOWS DNA TEST RESULTS IN AS EVIDENCE. The prosecution won a victory in the Scott Peterson hearing with DNA test results allowed in as evidence. Hair not that incriminating, since they were married. One issue, was whether the fetus was murdered separately? The prosecutor shot that down, so that took all that away. The prosecutor said they died together. Okay, so it'll be winding down soon.

AFTER SCOTT'S PRELIMINARY HEARING

Scott Peterson's hearing has come to a close. Will he stand trial for the murder of his wife and baby? Scott bound over shortly after the prosecution closed its case. A December 3rd hearing. Judge immediately ruled at close of the evidence. Not much asked about Amber by the prosecutor, so probably couldn't call her. The case is very light in forensic evidence. Mostly Scott's behavior. The defense chose not to make a stand.

What about Amber Frey? **INVESTIGATOR TESTIFIED: 240 CALLS MADE BETWEEN SCOTT AND AMBER.** Police evacuated the lot, caller said a bomb. The prosecutor built a premeditated timeline; Scott introduced to Amber in late ..., then Amber found out he's married. John, help me out with all the defense people. Christmas Eve and wife pregnant and you go fishing? Come On! **SCOTT MADE CALLS 80 MILES AWAY FROM BERKLEY AFTER 2PM.** Sorry, gotta go.

As Scott Peterson goes to trial, has the media made it so he will go free? Watch tonight. Scott Peterson will stand trial for Two murders and he Could get the death penalty. Scott Peterson faces execution if he's found guilty.

Surprised Geragos no witnesses. The defense usually doesn't call witnesses at the preliminary hearing; just learn the prosecution's case as much as possible to determine strategy. We heard Geragos say he'll do this, that, etcetera. Geragos was at dinner and said, maybe call Amber and the media there seized on it. Geragos uses the media. So did the prosecutor. Yea, they all do it.

No cause of death, etcetera. Strongest, fishing where the bodies found. A December 3rd hearing, Geragos will push for a speedy trial as the prosecution doesn't have much; no weapon, no scene. Without alot of cards in his pocket, the prosecutor is in trouble. A call to Sharon Rocha, and said Laci missing. There's an explanation for each piece the prosecutor says. I'm waiting for Satan to show up at the trial.

Scott Peterson will stand trial for the murders of his wife, Laci and their unborn child. Why did the judge give his ruling so quickly? As soon as the prosecution rested its case? In the transcripts of Scott's phone calls with Amber, well, let's just say the word 'sweetie' comes up alot.

[hair] Why be surprised about this? They're married. Alot of fishermen don't know what they're fishing for. The defense says he lied to the police; didn't want the affair known. Enough evidence to hold over. A December 3rd arraignment. Two hundred and forty-one times, in three months, the detective said Scott and Amber calls. Scott had brother's driver's license and Scott's own license; the first time we've heard this, and Scott said he had brother's license so he could get a discount at the Club for the family.

Expect a change of venue; probably bus the jurors in. Where's those concrete blocks, six, he made. And these transcripts of phone calls are ridiculous. They're set up. **DETAILS OF SCOTT TELLING AMBER LACI DIED BEFORE LACI DISAPPEARED. HEARING ENDED TODAY**. Five separate weights made on a trailer in the warehouse, but, Scott said one weight, and he moved it around to dry. And a look at the photos, it doesn't show five separate marks, just concrete around the trailer.

If anything saves Scott Peterson's skin, it'll be Dr. Henry Lee. Looked up Bay currents, went and bought the boat, and then went on his maiden voyage in the Bay. And the detective said, Five Distinct, Five Distinct, concrete patterns on that trailer.

New information on what Scott told Amber in those tapes when Laci went missing. New revelations surface about his calls to Amber. How many were there and what did he say? **AMBER BOMBSHELL.** What did Scott tell Amber on December ?, and is it a bombshell? Big news, January 6th Scott had something to hide. On a cell phone, he told Amber that Laci was alive and in Modesto. We listened to the secret call of Amber's; Scott comforting her of his being married. Another, Scott said, She's alive Amber. Amber: Where? Scott: In Modesto. Amber: Visitation with the new child?

Looked like the same photos you had last night on the show. One in the warehouse showing where the anchors were made, very distinct markings. Flatbed trailer, on piece of wood, just round deposits of cement. A bucket nearby, looks like he used it to make those concrete blocks.

Scott said alive and in Modesto on January 6th. The tape entered into evidence, not played, but the transcript is available to the press. The defense may jump on this explosive piece of evidence. What's fueling the feud between Scott's parents and Laci's parents? Detective said two hundred and forty-one times; calls. Didn't talk on December 24th, and Easter.

A FAMILY DIVIDED. An inside scoop on the e-mail between the families when we come back. Why are the parents sending e-mails and why one e-mail from ?? caused a lawsuit. **A FAMILY TORN APART. RIFT BETWEEN FAMILIES BEGAN WITH EXPOSURE OF AMBER FREY AFFAIR.** When Sharon Rocha tried to enter the Peterson house, the locks and alarm had been changed. Attorney for Peterson said that even evidence may have been planted when the Rocha's broke into the Peterson home. **9/05 SHARON ROCHA FILES LAWSUIT TO BLOCK MONEY FROM BOOK DEAL OR MOVIE TO SCOTT.**

Is change of venue. The former mayor of Modesto says Scott can't get a fair trial there. Most people here do know about this case. They did talk in court today of busing in jurors. The judge has ruled Scott Peterson will stand trial for the murders of his wife and their unborn child. The judge found there was enough probable cause to hold the case over for trial. Judge ruled there's enough evidence to prosecute Scott Peterson.

Secret tape recordings by Amber Frey of Scott Peterson have been released.

The arraignment set for two weeks. Judge rules enough evidence to stand trial. Here's NBC legal analyst. Only moments after the prosecution rested, the judge ruled enough evidence. The defendant refused to concede defeat. Now his lawyers want the case out of Modesto.

Scott and Amber two hundred and forty-one times; twenty-three times between December 25th and December 27th, just two days after Laci's disappearance. Amber said, You told me you lost your wife. And Scott said, She's alive. And Amber asked, Where? And Scott replied, Modesto. On another tape Scott said, I never cheated on you. And Amber laughed, Ha ha ha, you're married.

Scott Peterson is going to trial. The judge ruled there's enough evidence for Scott Peterson to go to trial. His arraignment is scheduled for two weeks. Scott Peterson will stand trial for the murder of his wife Laci and their unborn child. Tapes also released, with Amber saying, You told me on December 9th, that you lost you wife and now you're telling me she's missing.

A seventeen page transcript of a twenty minute Amber taped phone call on January 6th, 2003. The transcript wasn't released to the press, but we were allowed to view it. Scott says he can't explain it to Amber now, wish he could, but can't.

Coming up, is Scott Peterson running out of cash? Hear what his legal team has to say. **RUNNING OUT OF CASH?** What's this about Scott asking cops for a pickup truck? **LACI'S MURDER?** Up next, news from the Scott Peterson murder trial. Word Scott needs cash for his defense. Wants fifteen thousand back and pickup. And the prosecutor would much rather have the trial there, where everything is, the police, detectives, etc.

Yea, he shoots his girlfriend and then flees. We saw it in the Scott Peterson case; fleeing, where he was headed for Mexico. Andrew Luster fled. Scott Peterson, arguably, fled, with the hair, money, and ID.

Have you seen that new video of Nancy Grace? Yes I have. Since Geragos has been representing Michael Jackson since March, all the evidence will be gone, videos, photos, etcetera. Why would anyone want to be represented by someone who's representing this garbage in Modesto, Scott Peterson? Who's clearly guilty. Just like when Johnnie Cochran walks into a courtroom; Geragos is the same way; you know that somebody has done something really, really, bad. Geragos is like a snake charmer, when he wants to be. Amber Frey has a hearing set to block her nude photos. Wonder if Scott Peterson is following the Amber Frey nudie case?

Amber Frey is said to be four months pregnant and has plans to marry a chiropractor.

New developments in the Scott Peterson case. Who did he just ask for one hundred thousand dollars? Who did Scott Peterson just get one hundred thousand dollars from, and is the transaction legal? Scott put up the house, so his parents could take out a one hundred thousand dollar loan to pay for Scott's defense.

They met. Scott cheated on her early in the relation. Tried to get pregnant for a year. Amber said Scott broke down in tears to tell her he was a widower. Amber hired a private investigator to find Scott was married and found out Laci was pregnant and was missing, so she went to the cops. Did she suspect he was married?

We heard so much abut the bleach smell in the house, but heard nothing about it at the preliminary hearing, so everyone was saying that's because the bathroom was so far from the kitchen and the maid said she only used bleach in the bathroom, so you wouldn't smell bleach, but, when you look at these pictures, the bath is right next to the kitchen.

Experienced fishermen say the day Scott says fishing; two to four foot waves in a fourteen foot boat, and the wrong fishing pole for sturgeon, would snap the pole, some equipment gear never used in salt water.

Amber began dating in January, with the guy she's four months pregnant by and plans to marry. With a man that's not married, and has never been married. We want to make that perfectly clear.

Arraignment expected in the Scott Peterson case tomorrow. Scott Peterson's defense team is crying foul. They say he can't get a fair trial unless it's moved.

PROSECUTORS SAY PICKUP TRUCK IS PART OF CRIME SCENE. PETERSON IS CHARGED WITH MURDERING WIFE, UNBORN SON.

Scott is shown coming into court wearing an orange/red jumpsuit, with LIVE in the upper left corner.

Judge says police had the truck for a year and could have done all the testing they need, take pictures, etcetera, so the defense gets the truck back.

SCOTT'S ARRAIGNMENT WITH COMMERCIALS AND MEDIA COMMENT

Judge: Change of venue motion first?
Geragos: Yes.
Judge: If the court grants change of venue now, will all pretrial motions be handled here.
Geragos: Yes sir, my opinion is only the trial be moved.
Dave Harris, prosecutor: We'd like the court to look over the questionnaire first, if not, we'd proceed with the phone survey. Case law says appropriate to delay the ruling till the jury be polled first.
Judge: I'd want to see some information first, but with questionnaire, it may pollute other trial jury pools.
Geragos: Court may see alot of others coming in and wanting a change of venue because of a survey.
Judge: Defense has it's finger on the court's thoughts on that, so you may want to consider that, Mr. Harris.
Dave Harris, prosecutor: December 12th for motions and a..., and January ?, for a full blown hearing on change of venue?
Judge: Correct. What about jury surveys?

Geragos: I believe....[commercial.]
Judge: January 7, a 995 hearing.

1/7 MOTION HEARING TO DISMISS. CHANGE OF VENUE HEARING 1/6. CHANGE OF VENUE FILINGS ON 12/15. TRIAL DATE SET FOR January 26.

Judge: Reconsider protective order?
Geragos: Yes, wrong information abound, theories, facts abounding that aren't true. Maybe a safe-harbor provision, so a statement can be put out saying it's not true. Maybe prosecution and defense statement together or not, to respond positively. Tracks law and case law; something where we can respond.
Prosecutor: Safe harbor is to respond to other side. A release was given to media, but they still can't get it right. Two experts at the preliminary hearing and TV still couldn't get it right, with lawyers on TV shows repeatedly.
Judge: Findings still valid, even if media competition continues, even with other profile cases, the truth will come out at trial and they can even misquote that if they want. But the Order continues and going directly to media is prohibited.

Strange, Geragos wanted the gag order relaxed so he could respond to the media. Prosecutor said no, and the judge said no. Yea, that's right. If you want to know the latest on this case, just tune in to Court TV.

Geragos: No reason anyone needs to see these photos, it's sick. Contrary to what Miss Kinney says.
Judge: What's different, Charity Kenyon, in looking at autopsy photos and telling what they see, as opposed to saying what a witness says the photo shows?
Kenyon: Parties don't control evidence, court does, and it's public information. Principle is what we're concerned about. Not for parties to control, but for the court to control. Public has a right to access.
Judge: I've viewed photos, and there's an overriding interest to keep closed. For family and others. Will cause harm and damage to others. I'm ruling it's going to stay sealed. Media wants warrants sealing revisited, but I'm not going to do that.

Kenyon: The case has changed. A plea may be entered. Changed circumstances would require the court to revisit the issue. The court now knows of informants and potential witnesses and what they've said.
Prosecutor: No Change. Parties do have the right to control evidence at the preliminary and have. Have done it, and will continue to do it, so no change in circumstances. Fifth Judicial District said parties have right to control.
Geragos: If the court said it won't revisit it, the defense has nothing to say.
Kenyon:[Commercial]
Geragos: They've had the truck for a year.
Prosecutor: Disagree; truck is important. Witnesses say they saw the truck and important that jurors see the truck. What? It's just a couple more payments made till trial. Samples already taken, blood found in the truck that matches defendant's, on the door and visor, or door jam.
Judge: Thousands of cases tried with photos and tapes. Why not here?
Prosecutor: Important for jurors to see how body loaded and taken.
Judge: If unique vehicle, maybe, but this is a Ford F-150.
Prosecutor: Defense challenges photos taken. I'd prefer actual items. Where did detective leave his keys? Okay, I left them here.
Judge: I'll grant motion. I'll give you two weeks to take more photos or whatever. Court orders return of truck, December 18th.
Geragos: I'll fly up and drive it back. Money will be returned?
Judge: Yes?
Prosecutor: By Friday.
Judge: December 12th at 9:30, next appearance.

One year ago no one knew of Scott Peterson, now nearly everyone has heard of him and has an opinion. They're not waiving the speedy trial. A different judge to decide on the motion by the defense to dismiss for lack of evidence. A January 6th change of venue hearing. The prosecutor says the trial to be three to six months in length. Survey to be taken? December 12th, argue on if a survey can be used. Other attorneys may fear that the survey may affect their case. Many in Modesto know the Rocha family personally or participated in the search for Laci.

Many times items are given back. Could sheriff's department purchase the truck? Wonder what value the truck would have on e-Bay and auction it off?

Fetus is not considered a person, but yet it's murder.

John Goold, Chief Deputy D.A., Stanislaus County, on the Peterson case: No pretrial date, trial date January 26th. Defense will file motion to challenge the preliminary hearing. A change of venue motion will be filed by the defense. We've asked the judge to survey the jurors. We'll argue that on December 12th. Judge expressed concern we may be polluting the jury pool here. The defendant has a right to trial in sixty days. If change of venue, may punch trial date back.

This tells me that the defense believes their case is only going to get worse with more time. The prosecution is building its case with time. Geragos made hints that Scott and family is going broke here, with wanting release of the truck and money. Defense wants to hurry and try the case, maybe before more witnesses show up. Scott Peterson pled not guilty to murder charges in court today. His defense attorney is asking for a January 26th trial date.

Judge makes rulings that Hurt the State's case today. Tentative trial date set for January 26th. Prosecutor said, Judge, don't give the truck back to the defense, we need it for a couple months. There's blood on the glove compartment, door, visor, and who knows where else. Rare for a judge to do this. Defense already questioned the state's photos. In a TV interview, Scott said he bleeds all the time. Wouldn't be surprised if my blood or Laci's blood in truck.

Well, he went fishing. He went fishing in a boat, not his truck. Why would he mention Laci's blood? Do you bleed at a golf game? Scott's a golfer, fisher, outdoorsman; he's a nature lover as well. Why he bought a Mercedes under a different name. The prosecutor fought tooth and nail to keep the truck and the fifteen thousand dollars from Geragos. Fifteen thousand dollars, four cell phones, brother's drivers license, alot of clothes, alot of camping gear, but no mention of golf clubs in the car. Clothes came out at the preliminary hearing. Said using brother's license at Club, to get a discount. When and where the camping gear purchased? Police are looking, and everything checked out. What about golf? OH, Come ON! Ha, Ha, Ha. So, where are the golf clubs?

Laci's stepfather and mother, Mrs. Rocha there. When you look at Scott Peterson in the courtroom, he looks like he doesn't have a care in the world.

Prosecution wants to keep Scott's alleged get away truck. Some say a great loss? I disagree. Geragos said hardship on Scott, with seven hundred dollars a month truck payment. People betting Geragos won't try this case, won't go to trial with Scott. Geragos wanted right to issue statement to correct bad information out there. Said many things reported are not true, but the judge denied it. We're not in a courtroom under oath.

I've seen the photos and they are gross. I wouldn't allow the photos out. What about keeping arrest and search warrants sealed? Think Geragos would try to beat the USA movie of Scott Peterson with the trial?

Report says Scott went to neighbor, looking for Laci, and said he'd been golfing. Scott's arrogant, lies, what if on the stand? Scott Peterson is a liar and cheater. There's one guy, Mark Geragos, that was very happy when Durst was acquitted.

He pleaded innocent, and an indication that Scott Peterson was injured a year ago. New information out of Modesto in the Scott Peterson hearing. Court documents that Scott was injured during the crime. Prosecutor responded yesterday with filing in court that Scott's blood was, during crime. In TV interview, Scott said there'd be blood in his truck, he's a fertilizer salesman.

Prosecution may not have a sense of when it happened, December 23rd or December 24th. They believe they can explain after the fact. Laci in truck, but we haven't heard any evidence of that. If evidence of Laci's dead body in the truck, would the judge give it back? Usually see photos, but the prosecutor wanted to show the jury where the blood was. The defense says they need the truck to pay for the defense. Prosecutor estimated the trial to take three to six months in length.

Geragos with Scott in jail and not a happy camper. Maybe he's not ready. Bet Geragos won't use the words Michael Jackson in Modesto court.

Prosecutor said cement-like material found in the bed of the truck.

Problem isn't the media and its reporting; it's the arguments made by the lawyers themselves. I'm not gonna let 'em get away with those cheap shots.

Scott looked relaxed. Defense seems confident. Scott's hair grown, still losing weight. Prosecutor really laid it on thick to keep the truck. Surprised judge gave it back. Said they'd had their time with the truck. **SPEEDY TRIAL?** Sirens, cause Geragos pays them to do it when Gloria Allred is on. Priority under California law goes to the child abuse case, the Michael Jackson case. Prosecutors say Scott's blood is in the truck, so why did the judge release it?

[made up story] There's no evidence of that. The prosecution could have alot more. No hard evidence, that we've been told of.

SCOTT: "I'M INNOCENT". Geragos said if no truck and money, he'd have to ask the court to fund the defense. I was stunned the truck was given back. Can use pictures. Judge gave away state's physical evidence. [no blood evidence] Yes there was, today. There was blood in several places in that car. And what about neighbors and police saying they saw cuts on Scott's hands. If the defense camp gave access to the media to take the photos in exchange for money. The state can appeal judge giving the truck back.

On his computer was found where he was looking at various waterways. Do you need a motive? Practically speaking, yes. Why judge someone's morals? What about Scott running around? I don't care who's sleeping with whom.

Haven't seen state's whole case. Don't know where they're going with it. Haven't heard any evidence of Laci being alive December 24th. Geragos didn't question about used dishes, coffee cup, etcetera. If it existed, we'd have heard about it from Geragos. Scott had four cell phones with him when caught. No golf clubs with him that day. Any embryo fluid on Scott's clothes? All kinds of tests. They wonder about Scott getting a sixty pound fish in the boat, but yet prosecutors say he carried a hundred and sixty pound body in it. You're the only one reporting that Chris. Yea, Geragos brought it up in cross [exam].

Has a cause of death finally been determined in the Laci Peterson case? National Enquirer has the cause. Laci died while sleeping in bed and smothered with a pillow by Scott. Alot of evidence from the bed, during the February 18th, second search;

sheets, cover, blankets. Police went to Laci's family and told them right after the search. A missing pillow case from the bed, perhaps stains on it and had to get rid of it. A pregnant woman would release bodily fluids if strangled. But not sure if anything like that was found.

Mop; blood? Never any evidence of vomit or blood on the mop. Police believe a struggle before he went to bed and Scott was injured with his blood on the comforter on the bed. Scott talked to Sandy, a friend of her Mom's, and said if blood found, it's okay cause I bleed all the time. Clothing on Laci? Scott Peterson's back in court, claiming Modesto's no place to get a fair trial.

Case will stay on for January 26th, and jury to be ready. Looks like it'll go forward. Geragos asked for two more days, prosecutor wanted two more weeks, judge says two days, to file for change of venue motions. Compare polls here and surrounding counties and Los Angeles, where Geragos wants it. The defense, eight thousand exhibits, put on a disk. Accounts of all media coverage of the case on a disk to the judge.

The truck, the prosecutor wanted more time, judge said no. The prosecutor offered to buy, Geragos said to make an offer. The judge wanted no parts of it. Between them.

The prosecution will want to try and pick a jury first, before moving. The judge ordered a jury list of 2003, given to the prosecutor, to make calls for survey.

Mrs. Peterson passed two detectives in the court hallway this morning and said, shame on you, shame on you both.

PETERSON ACCUSED OF KILLING WIFE AND FETUS.

PARTIES AGREE POTENTIAL JURORS SHOULD BE POLLED.

SCOTT'S HEARING: MOTION TO CHANGE VENUE WITH COMMERCIALS AND MEDIA COMMENT

Prosecutor: Would like two more weeks for jury survey, holidays, not many jurors in the court house. We'll still argue to try and pick jury first, after survey done.

Geragos: We would like to exceed fifteen page maximum on motion, to twenty pages. Eight thousand pages of exhibits and put them on disk for the court. If we go past the 8th, we'll be pushing the defendant's right to a speedy trial with no way to do anything. During Christmas, more people will be home.

Judge: Why would I want to look at eight thousand pages?

Geragos: We've summarized it to twenty pages from different media outlets.

Judge: Relevance of media outside of Stanislaus County?

Geragos: More media in this case in comparison to others in other counties.

Prosecutor: We respond to defense motion, which we still don't have. Jury selection won't happen here in this case in a couple days, like most cases. Best way is to put it to January 20th.

Judge: We'll go with two days more; December 15th, defense to prosecutor motion. January 2, 04, for.... Reply by January 6th. January 6, vacated to January 8. You're in court on January 7.

Prosecutor: Discovery date January 7? Prefer January 7, over January 8.

Judge: Discovery on January 8, won't take much time.

Prosecutor: Can people use phone list?

Geragos: Same problem, don't think they can have access to that. Prosecution also wants L.A. surveyed, and judge there, will probably throw it at the receptacle. He won't honor it. Would pollute the jury pool there. Jurors from 2003 may be the ones sitting in 2004. Don't need a juror list to do a phone survey. [Commercial].

Court Administrator: Excused jurors would be hard to list.

Judge: Yea, make it those not served.

Court Administrator: We have seventeen hundred per week, but may only summon four hundred a week.

Geragos: And some called, can't serve, but that isn't found out until they come in.

Court Administrator: Right, cause we can't eliminate those not eligible from the Master List.

Geragos: Like L.A., the juror list draws on other data bases.

Judge: Isn't a form sent out?

Court Administrator: They're only called again, if they send in the survey. [Commercial].

Judge: You'll can submit samples of the survey and I'll look them over, with corrections or so forth.

Prosecutor: People willing to pay fair market vale of truck. We can negotiate with the defense.

Geragos: He's a used truck salesman this morning.

Prosecutor: Or change the date we return it. A couple of weeks?
Geragos: Court stated ten days. I won't dispose of it, but it should be turned over Monday and not keep it one minute longer that court ordered.
Judge: I gave my order and I'm sticking by it. I won't get involved in a sale. People had the truck long enough. Sounds like defense won't get rid of it.

Geragos is fighting for a fair trial and the prosecutors agree.

Judge: For court to certify the transcript records, change: variance to variants; exhibit 37, is 38; question 11, is question 1.1; Perkin and Elmer, is Perkin-Elmer; B, is A; November 1, is November 3; cases referred, to not as cases; some cases referred, to not actually cases, as spelled here, phonic name spelling; understand, is under oath; J., is CD; .25 Caliber, is .22 Caliber. No one said .25 caliber. They were, is he was; great, is greater; state, is side; Sec.62.64, is Sec. 62.64, and remove [sic]. See you again on January 8th. Defendant's remanded and no bail set.

Defense is delay, delay, delay. I don't know. The defense looks ready. Yea, but it can be the day of the trial, and defense says, Your Honor, our rights have been violated and we need more time. But it looks like it's the prosecution that keeps asking for more time on each and every issue, want more time to poll jurors, more time to keep the truck. It may be the defense wants to go quickly cause they're afraid with more time, that the prosecution will come up with more damaging evidence.

Look at Scott, sitting there smug and smiling. Where's The Hanky, Scott? Where's The Tears Today? Where's the hanky? Ha, Ha. No, on ask for delay of the trial. Defense asked for extra time to file change of venue; granted. Prosecutor wanted two weeks extra; not granted. January 8th change of venue motion. Prosecutor wanted truck held longer; not granted. Twenty to twenty-five thousand dollar value on truck. Judge wants no part of negotiation on truck. Laci and Conner First Annual Blood Drive; fliers with picture of Laci and message from the Rocha family. December 21st through December 23rd blood drive.

[bus jurors from where?] Next county.

Mrs. Peterson passed two detectives and said shame on you and shame on you too. Funny, we haven't heard of such outbursts from the Rocha family.

Laci's body may have been transported in that truck and Geragos and Scott are smiling and laughing about the truck in court. No blood from Laci. It's mostly Scott saying stuff that messes him up. Why hair changing color? Why fifteen thousand dollars? Why fishing on Christmas Eve? These will be stressed by the prosecutor. But, the other side will ask, where's the evidence? So it cuts both ways. I reacted completely different than Scott Peterson did as a victim of crime.

We have information that the prosecutor will subpoena Amber Frey's father, mother, and sister, for information Amber may have told them. Seems like the defense is pushing forward and the prosecution is stalling for time.

Laci's torso showed the clothes she was wearing the night before. National Enquirer quotes sources from close inside the case, Laci was suffocated. **LACI WAS SUFFOCATED.**

Scott Peterson's defense now asks to be moved out of Modesto. Northern California seems guilty, southern California seems not guilty. Defense wants it moved and prosecution wants to try and pick a jury first.

Lawyer says Scott has been demonized. **LAWYER SAYS SCOTT HAS BEEN DEMONIZED.**

Scott Peterson slipped up the next day. He couldn't keep his story straight for twelve hours. He told a neighbor that he golfed, after he had told police that he went fishing on Christmas Eve. BOOM, his wife his found dead. Why would you put yourself up to be a liar? OH, OH.

Breaking news in the Scott Peterson murder. Gloria Allred, Amber Frey's lawyer, says she has an announcement to make and she'll make it here. We have news about a slashed tire and a confrontation at a restaurant. Geragos doesn't want bused in jurors. An attorney's car tire slashed. Attorney accosted in restaurant. The Mayor said he didn't believe Scott get a fair trial. Survey says seventy-five percent of Stanislaus County has prejudged it.

Coming up, Gloria Allred has breaking news. I thought Gloria was gonna tell us that she was gonna adopt Amber's baby. We were all betting that Amber was going to get married. Scott Peterson's lawyer says Modesto is a lynch mob and trial must be moved. Defense team at restaurant and people saying shame on you, how could you defend a murderer. Thirty-seven percent on prosecution survey say guilty, down from fifty-four percent. Geragos would like the trial in Los Angeles where he's based. I'm hearing Santa Clara County alot, and prosecutor here pinches pennies, so he wants to keep it here.

Scott Peterson's lawyers file new motions against police officers in the case, and could this mean charges will be dropped? Scott Peterson's lawyer attacks police, judge style, and could this mean charges against Scott could be dropped; when we come back. New information in the Scott Peterson case. Did police mishandle this case from the beginning, about one year ago today. Scott's lawyer files motion to have the charges dismissed, there is no circumstantial or physical evidence to link Scott to the crime. A January 14, 2004 hearing. Has the prosecution fallen short here?

And Laci's Mom has filed two wrongful death suits against Scott. Up next, Scott Peterson's Christmas surprise. What special treat did he receive while behind bars?

Scott is shown coming into court wearing an orange jumpsuit, in handcuffs and leg irons.

On January 6th, 2003, Scott calls to tell Amber of Laci, and Amber records it. Amber says, what about a newborn baby? Wouldn't you want visitation? And Scott says, Honey, I can't tell you. Amber: Why not? Scott: It would hurt too many people. Lady here, just like Amber Frey, says she didn't know he was married. Just like Amber Frey and Scott Peterson, she, Amber, never knew that Scott was married until after the death of Laci.

Scott Peterson's lawyer has filed papers saying that Los Angeles is the best place to try Scott Peterson. I'd change venue, if still on the bench. Bus in jurors? Easier to move court personnel. **PETERSON CASE MOVED?** They found a jury in the O.J. Simpson civil case.

Why is it that, in high profile cases, the defense attorneys don't want cameras in the courtroom? What are they afraid of; the information will come out eventually, anyway. If the media reports evidence that isn't allowed in court, because of some legal technicality, that doesn't mean that it didn't happen, it just means it wasn't allowed to be shown to the jurors in court. That goes for the Kobe Bryant case, the Scott Peterson case, and the Michael Jackson case.

Jury selection for the Scott Peterson trial is set to begin January 21st. Judge issued a temporary ruling, agreeing with defense attorney, that his client can't get a fair trial here in Modesto, citing the media reports of over eight thousand exhibits. He says too much adverse publicity to have a fair trial here. Almost certainly they'll be a delay in the trial.

Judge in the Laci Peterson case is inclined to grant a change of venue. Witness on the stand, called by Geragos, an expert who did a survey. Apparently he wasn't hired by Geragos, but he had done a survey early in January, and, just recently. This expert has testified in trials before and familiar with the judge and justice system. He said he wasn't hired by anyone, but he lives in the area and was concerned. He did a study with his students, where 75% believed Scott guilty, with only 2.7%, not guilty.

Defense says they don't agree with busing in jurors. Judge didn't say he's considering that, with Geragos saying the surrounding counties are basically the same, so busing in jurors won't work. Court took a ten minute recess and the judge told the prosecutor that if he had any witnesses to call, he'd better call them, cause this hearing was ending at twelve noon, which is 3pm eastern standard time. The prosecutor was still crossing the professor who did the juror survey on his own.

Scott is shown wearing an orange jumpsuit.

The prosecution's expert says eighty percent of Stanislaus County residents can set aside any information and decide fairly. Geragos brought out on cross that this expert has always testified for the prosecution. Judge says the prosecutor relied on some questions in the questionnaire, that would not have been permitted in voir dire. Prosecution may appeal the judge's decision and that would delay the proceedings.

If a juror states on the record, that he or she can return a true verdict in this case, based on the truth, then that person is qualified to be a juror. Geragos may end up like Burr Rabbit and say, please don't throw me in the briar patch.

SCOTT'S HEARING: CHANGE OF VENUE WITH COMMERCIALS AND MEDIA COMMENT

Judge: I have received and reviewed the following briefs:.... I've scrolled enough through articles to see there are at least three Scott Peterson's, and the attorneys connection with Michael Jackson. Many articles are on the front page. It would be impossible to seat a fair jury. I must conclude, that without a change of venue, the defendant would not receive a fair trial. Agree with defense, that it's better to grant change of venue, before voir dire, and thereby poison the jury pool. Five to six factors to analyze and weigh each factor, if it favors change of venue, not, or is neutral. One: Nature and gravity of offense; murder, death penalty, national media and a Christmas disappearance; heavily favors change. Two: Size of community; slightly favors change with five hundred thousand population. Three: Political or controversial factors; neutral, even with Attorney General comments and other politicians running for... Four: Status of defendant in community; prior to the case, no publicity and an upstanding citizen, not a public figure, not a 1960's hippy, crowd at jail when brought in to custody; slightly favor change. Five: Status of victims in community; slightly favor change; some jurors may view victims as their own. Six: Nature and extent of news coverage; most heavy factor; substantially favor change, not seen in my career, the amount and nature of the coverage. Some factual, many speculative and inflammatory in nature. Coverage here, not typical for a crime of this type. Jurors may base decision on what they learned outside of the courtroom. We have sixteen other venues, larger than ours, available to us. Evidence presented by the defense shows other communities aren't biased. Weighs heavily on change of venue. Media will continue to cover this, even today, on their front page. Almost impossible, without sequestering the jury. Media doesn't report what they hear in court. Without sequestering jury, they'll be comments from those in the case, friends of the family, and those who were in the search.
Prosecutor: I've never been provided with a Declaration by Professor S....
Geragos: Would the court okay a brief recess to discuss the tentative order?
Judge: Yea, okay, a ten minute recess.

State wants venue to remain in Modesto and Geragos wants a change, but the judge came down with a ruling, before arguments ever began.

Geragos: Your Honor is treating the affidavit by Professor S. as a Declaration and we'd like to submit that to the court now.
Prosecutor: We understand there's a Declaration by Dr. ..., but not Professor ....
Judge: Okay, we'll call Dr. ... to the stand. Geragos, you can lay foundation first.
Geragos: Spell name.
Stephen J. Schoenthaler: I teach Sociology and Criminal Justice at California .... Defense never paid me a dime; first time I met you [Geragos] was 8:30 this morning. I quit looking back in March, when the count was three hundred articles about the case.
Prosecutor: Your PhD in nutrition? Your thesis?
Professor Schoenthaler: No, it's on plea bargaining and affect on sentencing. What happens? Why? And where they end up, to determine effects of plea bargaining. The University awarded me for research in nutrition and change of venue effects.
Prosecutor: You indicated you know some of the law in area of change of venue?
Professor Schoenthaler: Not really.
Prosecutor: Don't you have a legal conclusion in your report?
Professor Schoenthaler: Yes, in the earlier report, that I turned in to your office in March?
Judge: I'm not worried about his legal conclusions, just his statistical data. The legal conclusions are my job.
Professor Schoenthaler: Law in California, decisions, show alot of bias from media on cases. So during a sabbatical, I studied cases. It peaked in 1992, with the justice system allowing an undue influence and prejudice against defendants.
Prosecutor: That's not what I asked you.
Geragos: Objection.
Judge: Sustained.
Prosecutor: ....
Geragos: Objection, asked and answered.
Judge: Sustained.
Prosecutor: Didn't you testify in a case where change of venue wasn't granted. So, let's talk a little bit about that case.
Geragos: Excuse me, but the case he's [prosecutor] talking about is ..., but the facts he's [prosecutor] saying are from another case, ...[Commercial.]

Like a ping pong match, every time Geragos objects, the judge sustains it.

Prosecutor: ....
Geragos: Objection.
Judge: Overruled.
Prosecutor: You gave your survey to the Modesto Bee [newspaper]?
Professor Schoenthaler: Yes.
Prosecutor: And then you came down to the courthouse and gave interviews with media?
Professor Schoenthaler: Yes.
Prosecutor: And this was two months after you stopped looking at articles?
Professor Schoenthaler: Yes.
Prosecutor: And you had students call with a survey?
Professor Schoenthaler: Yes.
Prosecutor: How many? Sixty to seventy here? One hundred seventy...?
Professor Schoenthaler: End of November and beginning of December.
Prosecutor: How many were called more than once?
Professor Schoenthaler: Probably none, cause each had different instructions on how to choose numbers.
Prosecutor: You exclude unlisted numbers?
Professor Schoenthaler: Yes.
Prosecutor: Can't they exclude themselves, with an unlisted number?
Professor Schoenthaler: That's a strange defense, but yes. We compare these figures with other surveys and polls to find if there's a difference.
Prosecutor: So, fifty percent of possible jurors are excluded from your survey?
Professor Schoenthaler: Results don't vary with which method you use, they're identical. **Prosecutor:** [After a long answer by Professor Schoenthaler.] That's all fine and dandy, but..
Geragos: Objection, to comments by prosecutor.
Judge: Sustained. [Commercial.]

Aren't you surprised the judge gave his ruling, up front, without any arguments? Whatever Geragos objects to is being sustained, and I find that very disturbing. Maybe Geragos is correct. Let's go back in and see.

Prosecutor: So you get a bunch of students, who do this for a grade in your class, to go out and make phone calls to see if this case should have a change of venue?
Professor Schoenthaler: No.
Prosecutor: You DO look for outliers, don't you? [Out of ordinary, or individual.]
Professor Schoenthaler: Yes.
Prosecutor: With raw data, no outliers; were there?
Professor Schoenthaler: Yes.
Prosecutor: So there's wrong data in the survey?
Professor Schoenthaler: No.
Prosecutor: You don't know if they're telling the truth or not, do you?
Geragos: Objection, calls for speculation.
Judge: It's the same on your side Mr. [prosecutor], so it's apples for apples here. So let's finish this up today, Mr. [prosecutor]. [Most of the court laughs.]
Professor Schoenthaler: Our surveys show great predictability with other cases, when compared to, before and after conclusions by the surveys and what was asked and decided in court. This survey will prove to be accurate also. [Interruption.]

If bus in jurors, can Geragos object? All the witnesses, court personnel, everybody. A mad exodus. I'm always disturbed when the judge decides objections in favor of the defense attorney and gives his ruling, even before the arguments.

Prosecutor: There are several counties that believe the defendant is guilty, more so than Stanislaus County, correct?
Professor Schoenthaler: You can't go by what one response was in a survey...
Prosecutor: Aren't some people in certain counties presupposed to find a defendant guilty?
Professor Schoenthaler: Yes.
Prosecutor: Did you include those in your survey?
Professor Schoenthaler: No, the information is there, but the survey tell current attitude.
Prosecutor: Aren't they also different on the death penalty?

Professor Schoenthaler: Yes.
Prosecutor: But you didn't break that statistic down, so the court could exclude that?
Professor Schoenthaler: No, cause the court can't factor that in, the penalty.[Commercial.]

LACI PETERSON MURDER CASE. Geragos has gone on record to request Los Angeles County. Any other reason, beside being closer to Hollywood? [Laughter] Nothing other than it is the largest county. Judge sustains Geragos' objections, even though they're not legal objections. The law books say they're not valid unless objected to correctly. Geragos can claim a victory. Judge didn't allow prosecutor's last witness. He had two, but the judge hasn't allowed the second. They're in there arguing now discussing the issue.

Let's listen to what the judge says about Laci being well known. I agree with moving the trial and have said so all along. Judge said alot of articles, especially in Modesto, were biased against Scott Peterson. The Modesto Bee even compared the time line and events with Laci's disappearance and Scott fishing and so forth. The media was split on their articles on whether Scott should get a change of venue. Many believe that twelve jurors could be found here in this community. No doubt they could be found, but. The State can't get high profile experienced prosecutors, and there is a young guy for the State against a veteran defense attorney.

JUDGE GRANTS CHANGE OF VENUE IN PETERSON CASE. Judge granted change of venue, and he indicated he may not stay with the case. We'll know where, next Wednesday.

Scott Peterson scored a major victory in court today and will an inmate be forced to testify at his trial? Scott Peterson scored a major victory. Judge says no way Scott could get a fair trial in Modesto. Judge gave preliminary ruling, unless you can talk me out of it. Felt coverage hadn't cooled down, although he hinted he didn't want to move it out of driving range.

Will an inmate be forced to testify, and is he involved in Laci's death? **VICTORY FOR THE DEFENSE.** I'm surprised it got moved. Judge could say everyone in California is biased. Suddenly the prosecutor, is just like the defense attorney and a visitor.

Under evidence rules, Geragos has the right to see ABC's entire interview with Scott and not just the edited part on TV, if not, interview may not be allowed in court. Gloria, why would the defense want something that then the prosecutor could use against the defense, No, they want the tape cause there may be something there to help the defense.

Does the inmate who burglarized Scott Peterson's neighbor, hold the key to the answer? You got a tip? We still don't have a murder scene.

WHEN IS THE TRIAL. 1/14 MOTION TO DISMISS. 1/20 CHANGE OF VENUE. 1/26 TRIAL START. If they had other physical evidence to connect Scott Peterson to this death, they'd have arrested him earlier. No bombshells in this case. Four hundred witnesses and four months to try by the prosecution; talk about felony stupid. How long Bernie? In D.C.? Eight days. Ted? Two weeks. Geoffrey. In Michigan? Eight days to two weeks.

Some students in University of California stated that they made up poll results for a survey they performed as part of their class grade for the Professor who testified in the Scott Peterson hearing yesterday, and with the judge issuing a tentative order to change venue. The judge may reconsider.

Judge agrees to move the Scott Peterson murder trial from Scott Peterson's hometown of Modesto, California, after the defense argued pretrial publicity clouded the potential jury pool. Judge grants change of venue request for Scott Peterson's trial.

It's six of seventy-two students who said they made up poll results. It could be grounds to open up old cases, that relied on polls. Santa Clara County has had other high profile cases.

Do you think that a prosecutor would go for the death penalty, knowing they'll get a life sentence verdict, but with the knowledge they'll be getting a jury willing to give the death penalty? Absolutely. That knocks out alot of jurors, and won't be a liberal jury.

FOX POLL: 72% THINK SCOTT PETERSON WAS INVOLVED IN LACI'S DEATH. 3/5/03 BECOMES HOMICIDE INVESTIGATION.

Hearing to discuss charges against Scott Peterson to be held tomorrow. Scott Peterson is charged with killing his wife, Laci, and their unborn child.

I think so, and a sweeping gag order, which may be unconstitutional. **COPS UNDER FIRE?** Is Scott Peterson's lawyer, Mark Geragos, going after the cops in the Scott Peterson case? Did the cops in the Scott Peterson case violate the judge's gag order and does his lawyer have a secret document to prove it? And, why is Scott going back to court tomorrow? Will the charges be dropped against him?

Did the police in the Scott Peterson case violate the gag order and slip a top secret document to a supermarket tabloid and can Mark Geragos prove it? The Modesto Bee reports the prosecutor leaked document to tabloid. Transcript of a statement Scott Peterson gave to police. It'll be shown to the jury anyway.

Tune in to Dan Abrams to find out why Abrams says Scott Peterson may be free sooner than you think. Different judge has to hear motion to dismiss, since Judge G. was the one with probable cause. **JUDGE DENIES REQUEST OF SCOTT PETERSON TO DISMISS CHARGES.**

Prosecutor: The defendant says he went fishing on Christmas Eve and that in itself is ludicrous, for anyone to think or say that they bought a small aluminum boat and went fishing, is, in and of itself, to suspect murder.

Still there's no murder scene. December 24th, one call to Laci and one to his Dad. Wouldn't you want to know where Scott was when he made those calls; but, for some reason the cops can't, or won't, say. From what I heard, police say they don't know, or for some reason, that can't be determined.

Prosecutor: People don't wrap themselves up in plastic, or duct tape, and go jump in the Bay. If that's not a corpus delicti of homicide, I don't know what is.

Prosecution will want it within driving distance. We're all hoping it's in ..., cause there's nice hotels there. Thanks, Chris, for being on the side of the defense, a much needed position. What one we mostly hear ..., and lies. What's your question? No, Court TV does not take a position. No, Court TV does not take a stand and I'm not either. Mark Geragos wouldn't even talk to me if I took a stand; No.

Think Scott will testify? **JUDGE DENIES DEFENSE MOTION TO DISMISS CASE: TRIAL STARTS 1/26.** No way, no way. Has to explain too much. Amy ..., his neighbor, he told

December 24th he'd been golfing. Media wants him to testify. Oh, yes, as a former prosecutor, I'd love to cross examine him. Don't think it'll start January 26th.

Prosecutor: If you listen to the defense, Laci Peterson would have had to finish mopping the floor, change into tan pants, take the dog walking far enough away from the house to be abducted, and the dog come back home, all in a span of ten minutes. We know that couldn't happen, and therefore, this man, Scott Peterson, [Prosecutor points his finger at Scott] is guilty of murder.
Prosecutor: People don't wrap themselves in duct tape and then go throw them self in the Bay during the winter.
Geragos: Case is nothing more than, from early on, this man having an affair and don't bother me with the facts, don't let that get in his way. And let's convict this man cause he had an affair and went fishing.

Geragos: Prosecution gives the court three possibilities; killed by Scott, suicide, or accident. Thirty-two weeks pregnant on December 23rd doctor visit; thirty-three weeks by the doctors on view of the baby's body. The prosecutor wants the court to decide on wild speculation. Those aren't the only possibilities. Being abducted is the most likely, and with Scott not having anything to do with that.

Judge first heard motion to reconsider change of venue. He'll announce his venue at ten till the hour. The prosecutor wants Santa Clara, San Mateo, ... The defense wants Orange, Alameda, ...

Funny how various counties are making a pitch to get the trial, with all the revenue from media, etc. Judge says Orange County is a consideration since half of the prosecution witnesses have to be flown in anyway. Judge heard motion to reconsider from the prosecution and to put Sacramento back on the list.

Judge said he didn't rely on the survey alone to decide change of venue. The professor is in court, but no testimony taken from him. Judge says media isn't using the nine students' names and ain't going to come forward anyway and risk expulsion from school, but if the prosecutor wants to investigate, go ahead, but he doubted if he's get very far. There should be severe consequences for bringing this into a court of law. Yea, even if Schoenthaler didn't know, he should have known.

Geragos said, if moved to Orange County, he won't apply for public funds for defense and save over a hundred thousand dollars for the state. Says savings on busing witnesses will save defense alot of money. Stick around and we'll have that court tape for you as soon as the hearing is over.

Judge has selected San Mateo for the Scott Peterson case, eighty miles away. Courthouse is five miles from San Jose airport, so that helps. San Mateo did send an ad to the court? Yes. Scott Peterson hasn't waived time, yet, so it's going to begin January? We'll learn Friday if this judge will move with the case to San Mateo. He had said he didn't want to travel with it. Judge G. said if he's on the case, he won't allow any electronic media in the hearings, but that doesn't cover the trial. Alot of suppression motions to hear, along with that television issue.

Judge: People's motion to reconsider change of venue. Mr. Harris.
Mr. Harris, prosecutor: [Somebody's music phone in the background.] Nine students came forward and survey may be fraudulent, and played role in change of venue.
Judge: Also concerned about type of media coverage also.
Mr. Harris, prosecutor: Professor Schoenthaler survey saying different in Counties ..., and ours says ..., so if judge strikes Professor Schoenthaler, then decision may change. We have Professor Schoenthaler's statement that he didn't verify the survey.
Judge: What are you gonna do, subpoena those sixty-five students and bring them all in to testify. What makes you think the students will tell the sheriff who they are.
Mr. Harris, prosecutor: They will come in and say the professor said the survey was for class and not to come into court. I think they will come in and testify. The professor or University won't turn over the list to us. We have one student who says he falsified information in the past.
Judge: Don't have enough legal grounds to strike Professor Schoenthaler statement or testimony, but my decision isn't solely on that. The media base is the same with Channels [TV stations], and I don't need a survey to tell me that. What's shown here is shown on Channels [TV stations] also. Don't think it's a University issue and why should the courts get involved? I'm not going to order that. Survey and testimony are not given much weight in

court's final decision and as far as that goes, if the court throws out this and other survey and testimony, the decision would be the same, based on media reports. Your choices of venue. Let's start with you, Mr. Harris.

Mr. Harris, prosecutor: ...County, San Mateo second, and ..., Orange County should be court's last choice.

Judge: Well, let's discuss that point, since Orange seems to be Mr. Geragos' first choice. [Commercial.]

Judge: Sorry, Mr. Geragos, but I can't consider costs in court's decision.

Geragos: Orange County seems to be the choice of AAOC. If you're looking for a place with less media and Orange County seems to be that choice here. You just fly into Orange County and boom you're there at the courthouse.

Mr. Harris, prosecutor: Orange County airport closes at different times. Court can look at court costs.

Judge: Maybe convenience to witnesses, but not costs.

Mr. Harris, prosecutor: Can't look at costs to deny change, but okay on where to change to. Funny how defense counsel comes up with money if he doesn't get his way. There will be alot of witnesses in this case. Orange County may be an abuse of discretion, for four hundred people to caravan to southern California. Santa Clara is our first choice, resources there, availability of courtroom.

Judge: Says they'd need time to renovate courtroom, sorry wrong County.

Mr. Harris, prosecutor: San Jose also has a wonderful courthouse. San Mateo is our second choice; within driving distance. [Commercial.]

Judge: I'm moving it mainly on amount of media coverage, and part in the community involvement in the case. Proceed to trial on the 26th?

Geragos: That's correct. This trial takes precedent over the other, since he's free on bond and this is a capital case. [Commercial.]

Judge: Try to keep potential juror list from public, so they'll be more forth coming. If I do it, I will say, I won't let the electronic media in. So, you'll may want to discuss that among yourselves. As soon as we have the name of a judge who will take it, I'll let you know.

Geragos: Well, we're still hoping you'll travel with us.

Judge: Well, I've already said I don't want to travel, if there's a judge that will take it.
Geragos: I need the certified record of January 8th.
Judge: Yea, you'll need that for your brief.
Geragos: You'd be surprised if you knew how we did that. [The TV disk of 8,000.]
Judge: Page 41, line 1, is Mr. Geragos speaking, not Mr. Harris.

Students knew it would be used in court, would be reimbursed, had twenty days to do twenty surveys, but some students went outside the University to claim the limelight and have themselves viewed as the good guys.

And you've testified and qualified as an expert in court. Yes, and also outside of the University. Very sound ruling, cause Scott Peterson would have gotten nothing short of the death penalty here. Two pockets, Los Angeles Bay and San Francisco Bay, that are okay and not much difference and judge did exactly that with San Mateo.

Prosecutor's last choice was San Mateo. San Mateo is very conservative. How did they vote, and it counts? Leslie, how do you feel about Geragos using the argument that Mrs. Peterson is sick and not able to travel?

Geragos, please don't try to speak for both sides on wanting to keep Judge G. It began with the truck, which was covered on the inside, with Scott's blood, Judge G. gave it back to Geragos.

Professor Schoenthaler has a fraudulent survey and this judge says whatever. San Mateo hasn't had a death penalty case since 1991, and in that case they gave the death penalty. Will the trial go, on January 26th? So far, yes. Prosecution is expected to ask for two weeks to get ready and move stuff to San Mateo. **SAN MATEO ABOUT 90 MILES FROM MODESTO. SAN MATEO HAS LOBBIED COURT TO HOST TRIAL.** Officials are democrats and area voted for Gore in last election.

Up next, the Scott Peterson case. The trial's leaving it's hometown of Modesto and moving to a small community in north California. What will that mean? Today the judge moved the trial ninety minutes west to San Mateo. Geragos says it would be a waste of resources to have another judge come in.

Less than 700,000; 49% male, 59% white; median income, $80,000; professionals, 42%. San Mateo officials sent material to Modesto to get the trial. We did not solicit the trial, but did send information sheet telling what we had available. Are you worried San Mateo may be seen in a bad light if Scott Peterson isn't convicted? That the rest of the country will think your community turned loose a murderer? Not at all. The family won't be left behind. We'll do what justice requires. We'll make sure Laci gets justice. We did not lobby.

Geragos said Scott is ready to go; wants the trial to begin, and Geragos is ready to go with it. If there's trouble in picking a jury, then California law allows for Geragos to apply for another venue change.

The University and myself are doing separate investigations to find out what happened and who did it. We're calling the numbers back to see who did this. **VENUE SURVEY SCANDAL.**

Mayor, what have you heard about the Laci Peterson case? Not much, just what we see on the nightly news. Just generalizations, not many specifics at all. Do you get cable there? Oh yes.

The Scott Peterson trial has been moved from Modesto. The judge said that Scott Peterson could not get a fair trial in Modesto, due to all the pretrial publicity. Scott Peterson's trial was moved yesterday and now it has a new judge, Judge Richard A. will preside over the Scott Peterson case.

JUDGE REMOVAL. Prosecutor has objected to the judge, Geragos plans to challenge that in court. Under California law, each side gets one objection to the judge. Geragos can call the prosecutor to the stand, says he waited too long to object. The prosecutor already talked to the judge and discussed the case. The judge is eighty-two years old. We heard a prosecutor's secretary made a remark that the judge was biased against the prosecutor. I'm relishing the idea of one cross examining the other. They were both students of mine. The Scott Peterson murder case has a hearing today. Meanwhile the trial has been delayed, as the prosecutor has refused to accept the appointed judge in that case. A new judge in the Scott Peterson case becomes history. What happened? Stay tuned, we'll explain.

Last thing before Judge G.. Just yesterday, the prosecution exercised its challenge against this judge. Another judge will be appointed and the process will begin again. Scott Peterson has not waived his right to a speedy trial, so come hell or high water, the case is scheduled to begin next week. **COURT TV TRIAL DATES: SADDAM HUSSEIN: NO TRIAL DATE SET.**

AAOC will get back with us Tuesday or Wednesday on another judge. Scott Peterson back in court today. Two and a half hours ago; two recesses. Last time before Judge G.. Geragos challenging the prosecutor's choice to take the judge off. Geragos said to Judge G., that he doesn't have authority over this case anymore and that he shouldn't even.

Prosecutor met with the judge, talked, and agreed to meet next Monday, then filed this challenge. Judge may not have had authority to change date? Judge G. said, look, time is running out. And that it was the defense who filed motion for change of venue, so a two week continuance should be okay, and Geragos then responded with, look judge, you may not even have jurisdiction to be handling this trial.

Geragos told the judge not a proper motion for him to hear, since he's not on the case. Judge agreed and put it over till February 1st. Trial must begin that day. Prosecutor says the appointed judge is biased towards the defense, to be more compassionate. On February 1st, this issue will be settled and judge said to be ready to begin motions in limine, two weeks of hearings on evidence; dogs, GPS, eavesdropping on Scott's phone call errors, and Amber's testimony. **HEARING SET FOR 2/1 IN SAN MATEO, CALIF.**

I know the background of the chosen judge, and he's sympathetic to defendants. Just months ago, the judge took away a jury decision of the death penalty. We'll let me...

The prosecutor held onto the tool box from the back of Scott's truck and plan to test it to see if Laci was transported to the warehouse from the house. From what I've heard, someone Laci's size, Was able to fit into that box.

Couldn't the prosecutor strike for just cause.

If the motions begin on February 1st, alot of motions. If the defense gets just one evidence thrown out, then it's a victory. It's interesting, cause we'll get back to the facts, the best part, and that's the part I like.

I've never used a jury consultant. I like to use my gut feeling, look them in the eye. It wasn't that long ago that Geragos wanted the prosecutor removed, the judge removed, and said the cops were ganging up on him. **DEFENSE WANTS JUDGE**

GIROLAMI TO CONTINUE PRESIDING OVER THE CASE.

There's three civil cases against Scott Peterson, no profit to Scott, no $250,000 Laci insurance to Scott; put off for one hundred and twenty days.

Uh, that's the Peterson family, right, Chris. They should let you handle it, Nancy. Well, there'd never be any trials.

The prosecutor wanted some time and we'll see if this'll allow that. We all try to find someone guilty by how they act, but we don't know and it doesn't mean anything. About sixty miles away; about an hour and a half drive.

Coming up, Scott Peterson's lawyer, Mark Geragos says not so fast. Did the prosecutor wait too long and miss the window to get the judge tossed? Scott Peterson left Modesto for the first time since his arrest and did the judge leave the door open for him to stay on the case. Will trial start Monday? Nah, no judge yet. February 1st issue is the judge, one appointed by Chief Justice of California Supreme Court? Scott Peterson and Geragos have every right to start trial within 60 days of the arraignment, actually 62, since of weekend, unless good cause. Good cause could be cause the change of venue wasn't decided until last week.

There were three people today in the audience, three reporters. Geragos said the Chief Justice of California Supreme Court was like an 800 pound gorilla, despite law, like a dictator he chose the judge, and Judge G. said, well they might just tell me to stay on the case, and if that happens, I'll forget about all those nice things you've had to say about me.

Retired judge is chosen to preside over the Scott Peterson murder case. Retired judge ... has been chosen by the Chief Justice of the California Supreme Court to preside over the Scott Peterson murder trial. Only six of the twenty-two death penalty cases he's heard, was the death penalty handed down, and on one, he almost cried in handing down the death penalty, so, he is a bit defense orientated. He's been known to allow cameras in, for opening, closing, and the jury verdict. So what happens when Monday gets here and the first judge refuses to step aside or yet the prosecutor has asked for a two week extension for good cause determination, an yet the judge has been told to be ready for hearings Monday.

Geragos wants the judge to distribute a questionnaire to about a thousand potential jurors, before the trial begins, so the venue issue may not be over yet. Mark Geragos, Scott Peterson's lawyer, argues that the trial should be moved closer to his parent's San Diego home, as the Peterson's have spent one million dollars for the defense of Scott.

There will be no cameras in the courtroom in the Scott Peterson case. Mark Geragos stood up, first thing, and said, You Honor, we want you on this case and are satisfied with you stellar reputation. The judge replied, thank you for the confidence. **A SCHEDULING HEARING IS SET FOR FEBRUARY 9. DEFENSE WITHDRAWS CHALLENGE CONCERNING NEW JUDGE.**

San Mateo courthouse is charging $51,000 for a parking space to park TV trucks at the courthouse. The judge had to ask Scott Peterson if it was okay to continue the trial date a few days.

San Mateo Sheriff: Scott Peterson is cooperative, nice and no problem. He's in protective custody, in a cell by himself. He has access to talk to other prisoners and can communicate back and forth.

Motive, Scott never wanted the baby. A few weeks after Laci disappeared, several of Laci's girlfriends said Scott was less than enthusiastic about the baby and left Laci sad about that. Started from the moment she took home pregnancy test, they'd had been trying for two years to have a baby, but when she told Scott, he was hung-over from a party the night before, and said he wanted no parts of it.

Met Amber on a blind date. One of his girlfriends showed up at his house at dawn and accused Laci of running around with her boyfriend and then she found out it was the other way around. Oh, Boy.

A Peterson witness dies of natural causes. She is the Peterson neighbor who claimed she saw Laci walking her dog on the day she went missing. An important witness for the defense has died of natural causes. Said she saw Laci on December 24th, at 10:15am. Judge has said the witness list will remain sealed.

GPS will be first hearing, a Fry hearing, to determine if accepted by scientific community. People are saying that the pollsters are asking questions about evidence; on three people seeing Laci walking her dog, and... This could potentially taint a jury pool, wouldn't it? Where does it cross the ethical line?

Geragos has said to the judge that he doesn't want any media interviews involved or played in the trial. I had a twenty minute interview with Scott myself. Yea, and during the interview, his cell phone rang and he failed to answer it, with his wife, Laci, still missing. There's a film coming out, this week, on Scott Peterson, called 'The Perfect Husband'.

Judge presiding over the Scott Peterson murder trial, orders that witness lists and names of potential jurors remains sealed, despite media protests.

The Perfect Husband on the USA channel. **THE PERFECT HUSBAND ON USA CHANNEL.** Yea, that he knew she was dead before the bodies were found. Used innuendo to distort with fact; I didn't kill her, but I know who did. No such statement has ever been found by anyone.

Scott Peterson's attorney is expected to be back on the attack today against global positioning deices. Judge rules that Global Positioning technology is generally accepted and fundamentally sound. Authorities had placed GPS devices on several vehicles used by Peterson after his wife disappeared in December 2002. Prosecutors say the GPS shows Scott went to the Bay, at least once, where the bodies were discovered.

Some bad news for the police today. The pregnant woman who police hypnotized, can't testify. She was the one prosecutors thought they could get to say it was her that the people saw walking her dog in the neighborhood that day.

Scott Peterson's attorney, Mark Geragos, now wants two juries to hear this case. Two separate juries, one to hear the case and one to for the death penalty, if convicted. Since no one could sit on a single jury, who doesn't believe in the death penalty, and therefore there'd be a pro-prosecution jury.

Prosecutors go to court today in the Scott Peterson case over wiretapped phone calls. Scott Peterson's phone was tapped for three weeks in January, and two days in.... Peterson's defense attorneys say the taps were illegal and that police listened to confidential calls between Peterson and his attorneys. Police say they did nothing wrong and followed the rules.

Up next, Scott Peterson's phone calls that his lawyers don't want you to hear. Sex, lies, and videotapes the defense wants tossed out. Four days of hearings. Yea, the judge keeps listening to the recorded tapes between Scott Peterson and his former attorney, Kirk McAllister.

Geragos said the prosecutor hasn't given him all the evidence and Geragos is saying there's evidence in the 8,000 pages turned over that points to the person who killed Laci. The police say the prosecutor is trying his best to get the information to the defense.

Scott fixed a Christmas dinner and even invited his neighbor, with Laci missing. There's a new law on Capitol Hill that would protect the unborn fetus. It's called the Laci and Conner law.

Redwood, California judge rules that jurors in the Scott Peterson double murder trial will not be sequestered. There will be but one jury in Scott Peterson trial, and not two. The dog evidence won't be allowed, as it's not reliable. The judge has denied Scott Peterson's attorney's request that the jury be sequestered during the trial. Jurors will be allowed to go home in the evening. Peterson's attorney want the jury sequestered so they wouldn't be exposed to media reports. Another blow to the defense is that there will only be one jury. Defense attorneys had requested one jury for the penalty phase.

Scott said he saw Laci's image of her ghost in the mirror, while she was still missing. February 8th, police discovered he had rented a storage locker, a warrant on February 18th, and found in the garbage, the wedding album of Scott and Laci.

Scott expressed 'micro fear' when asked about blood in his truck and 'micro anger' when asked about the bedroom blinds being pulled. **DOGS TRACKED LACI PETERSON'S SCENT TO SCOTT'S WAREHOUSE. DOGS PICKED UP LACI'S SCENT AGAIN ON THE INTERSTATE. SCOTT PETERSON TOOK THAT INTERSTATE TO THE SAN FRANCISCO BAY ON 12/24/03.**

Closed door proceedings today with the wiretap calls, to see if they violated attorney-client privilege. Ruling will be tomorrow, also about the tracking dogs, whether that evidence is admissible at trial. 76 of 3,000 calls were to his lawyer. One call was released to the media; where Amber asked Scott if he had anything to do with Laci's disappearance. Yea, and we know that one doesn't show or mean much.

Scott Peterson's defense attorney's are livid and may appeal the judge's ruling, allowing the taped phone calls to be admitted into evidence. So the jury will hear Scott's voice, and even though he won't take the stand and they'll hear all of the inconsistencies with Amber Frey.

Alot of people here in Redwood have already made up their minds, with Scott going fishing and where the bodies washed up, but others say they can listen to the evidence and then make up their mind. Up next, questioning the potential jurors. Will they have to air their dirty laundry in public? **JUROR QUESTIONNAIRE HAS 127 QUESTIONS TO ANSWER.** Scott Peterson's lawyer is asking for a change of venue, saying too many potential jurors already believe Scott Peterson is guilty, relying on juror questionnaires.

LACI PETERSON CASE. "FUGITIVE DEFENSE". What about the TV interviews Scott did before his arrest? All of them will be admitted at trial, in court. Prosecutor said that if Scott can get up and tell all these lies, then the jury has a right to hear it. **OPENING STATEMENTS SCHEDULED FOR MAY 17.** They've got 300 potential jurors to go through.

We understand the prosecutor's star witness, Amber Frey, is pregnant. Will this affect the trial date? We haven't heard. Each time I asked him about telling Amber that Laci was missing, he dodged the question and finally stopped the interview and said, Listen, I don't know how much of this you'll air, but this is irrelevant to Laci missing. The rest of the interview was fully rehearsed; he had all his other answers prepared.

We asked Geragos, why he doesn't file his change of venue motion, cause alot of jurors think Scott is guilty, and Geragos replied sarcastically, well, we're just waiting for the evidence to build. Did you her the jurors' responses? I agree, this is a bit of a delay tactic; we'll see. Several California newspapers will not get to see completed juror questionnaires in the Scott Peterson trial.

Scott Peterson's lawyers say they will perform DNA tests on blood found in a brown van. Prosecutor's in the Scott Peterson murder case say they will perform DNA tests on blood found in a van.

A new eyewitness pops up in the Scott Peterson murder trial and what did she see that morning? Tonight, a new surprise witness. The 43 year old is breaking her silence on what she saw December 24th, early morning. Seven to seven-thirty, driving her car, and saw a truck with a boat, and a large object covered with a tarp. She tried to relay this to police, but it doesn't fit on their time line.

Why aren't police using this? They say it just doesn't sound like Scott. He wouldn't have been able to get to the Marina and back home to make the call from his home. I could come up with a theory, after sitting through the preliminary.

Yea, like cleaning up. But then the defense would punch holes in it. The trial on May 17th?

Judge in the Scott Peterson case gets another mystery letter, this one with evidence in it. Letter #2 contains some of the same evidence as the first one, with some hair and a fingerprint, that the person says belongs to the person responsible. The judge discussed it in open court and each side will get to test it.

Cory Lee Carroll was in jail on a parole violation. Dirty and Skeeter? Have tracked down Dirty, in a local prison. A background that he might be capable. They met in a local strip club. Date they met? I'd have to look in the file. Absolutely passed a polygraph by a former police captain. The police went to Fresno, bar, and other agencies checking. Modesto won't confirm it, but did verify it. Won't use at trial, since it conflicts with their evidence. They took a picture; found the lady. Someone saw Scott talking to Cory. If there is a picture, it'd be quite an asset. The date said they met; Scott was with his father. Not November 29th; If you're so sure about your facts, but you're so far off. People have offered a great deal of money for it, but we're dealing with a very dangerous and notorious gang and no one wants to come forward.

It's a question of manpower. We'll see if they have time to do it. [Michael] Jackson suggested Geragos spending too much time on the Peterson case.

Scott Peterson's attorney is expected to file a change of venue request for his client's double murder trial.

A third letter to the judge in the Scott Peterson case; make a difference? No. How'd a man, who's a future son-in-law get on the jury? Change of venue from Redwood? Zero percent chance.

Ok, coming up soon, Opening statements in the Scott Peterson trial. Prosecutors in the Scott Peterson case strike back. **VENUE CHANGE FIGHT.** Arguments today on moving Scott Peterson trial a second time. Geragos wants the case moved to Los Angeles. Prosecutors say juror bias could be found anywhere in California.

Mark Geragos will be back in court today, arguing for another change of venue. He wants the judge to move the trial to Los Angeles, where the media saturation hasn't been so intense.

With all the publicity, I don't know. It's hard to Not think he's guilty.

Six jurors have been picked already.

Judge has delayed opening arguments in the Scott Peterson murder case to June 1st, stating that selecting jurors has been a long process. Jury selection continues today in the Scott Peterson murder trial. Opening statements are scheduled for June 1.

Laci Peterson murder case, Pool of 76 jurors selected for the Scott Peterson murder trial. Final selection begins next Thursday. Defense argues that new evidence points away from Scott Peterson in the murder of his wife Laci and his unborn son.

In the Scott Peterson case, the defense says new evidence just turned over by the prosecutor, may clear his client. Is the prosecutor in the Scott Peterson case breaking the rules? Scott's attorney, Mark Geragos seems to think so.

DIRTY DEFENSE?

Jury selection is supposed to wind up today in the Scott Peterson murder trial in Redwood City. The jury will consist of 12 jurors and 6 alternates. The trial is set to begin on Tuesday. Scott Peterson is charged with the murder of his pregnant wife, Laci and their unborn son. In related news, Laci's mother, Sharon, is trying to prevent Scott from selling Laci's items.

A jury has been selected and certified by the judge and lawyers. We're just getting word that the jury in the Scott Peterson double murder trial has been seated. A jury of 6 men and 6 women have been seated as the jury in the Scott Peterson double murder trial. Opening statements are scheduled for Tuesday.

One juror in the Scott Peterson case has been replaced, after claiming extreme financial hardship if he served.

Three dark skin people in the Peterson yard, She came down that street, asked them what were they doing...

The 16 jurors chosen for the Scott Peterson trial, 9 are white. A former police officer on the jury, but then again he's been charged with assault on a police officer. Both defense and prosecution chose him. These are 12 very important citizens willing to put in their best and I applaud them.

Don't forget to stay tuned live, Tuesday night, for opening statements in the Scott Peterson case.

Fox News Channel shows Scott coming into the courtroom in handcuffs, leg irons, and a red jumpsuit.

It's almost time for the Scott Peterson double murder trial to get under way tomorrow with opening statements. We'll discuss both prosecution and defense strategies when we come back. Stay tuned in the upcoming hours. Stay tuned. A year and a half after his pregnant wife, Laci, went missing, Scott Peterson is ready to stand trial.

2ND DEFENSE REQUEST TO CHANGE VENUE WAS DENIED.

MOST EVIDENCE AGAINST PETERSON IS CIRCUMSTANTIAL.

Laci's Mom lost her battle to keep Scott from selling his story.

Not since the O.J. trial has the nation's attention been on a domestic homicide, like the Scott Peterson case. We'll go over the possible defense and prosecution legal strategies when we come back, with Court TV's legal analyst. Stay tuned.

6 men, 6 women. I think we have a pro-state jury. It's death qualified. If it was a soft kill, there'd be no DNA evidence.

Geragos convinced the judge to allow in more witnesses. State must discredit them, they claim to have seen Laci. Where the bodies were found, isn't the defense going to have to say he was set up? One hair, says Laci's in the pliers. One gallon concrete anchor from the boat, other concrete in the warehouse.

SCOTT PETERSON'S TRIAL BEGINS

Court TV shows Scott coming into the courtroom in an orange jumpsuit, handcuffs, and leg irons, with the lady lawyer appointed by the court.

The prosecutor's opening statement is continuing now, for 2 hours. He says Scott lied to police. Said Scott said he went fishing for about an hour and a half, but then it began to rain, but the Harbor Master said it didn't rain at the docks on the 24th.

Prosecutor said Scott said he and Laci were watching Martha Stewart that morning and there was something about marmalade on her show. But, when police pulled up the shows, the marmalade was on the December 23rd show and not the December 24th show. So what he remembered was from the day before.

Scott also made 11 phone calls from 10am to 6pm on December 24th, which is unusual, cause he was doing something, like dumping the body. One thing, Scott drove 90 miles to fish, instead of choosing one of the closer places to fish.

The judge gave an hour and forty-five minute lunch break and the prosecutors are still giving their opening statement. They say Scott met Amber through a friend, who told Scott he'd better be serious about this, and of course she didn't know Scott was married. Scott told Amber that he didn't want kids, that Amber's little girl is enough for him; and all the while his wife, Laci, is 7 months pregnant at the time and 8 months or 8½ months, when she disappeared.

We expect to hear about the brown van in Geragos' opening statement, probably sometime tomorrow, as the prosecutor is methodically going through each piece of evidence against Scott Peterson. The judge reversed his decision on not allowing the testimony of a police hypnotized [defense] witness, since Geragos made a good argument last week, that another person, a man, corroborates her story, saying he saw three men forcing a pregnant woman into a van that morning. So he will allow that testimony at trial, even though it wasn't allowed at the preliminary hearing, mainly because these could be big issues on appeal.

Yea, and we don't know if Geragos will throw in the satanic cult with the brown van, but we'll see. Five hours maximum on a courtroom day here.

PROSECUTION EXPECTED TO CALL HUNDREDS OF WITNESSES, THE DEFENSE 18.

It's his, the prosecutor's, chance to tell his story uninterrupted, as long as there's no objection.

In an interview, Scott said he told friends that some doctored photos may come out with his picture, but don't believe them, cause it wasn't him, and today the prosecutor showed photos of Scott and Amber.

The tracking dog followed the scent from the parking lot, down to the boat ramp, so the jury just learned that. Cause of death? Water alone?

As a defense attorney, do you cast all these defenses out there; that she was seen being dragged into a van, that tape was over Conner's neck, that he looked older than 8½ months, or do you just choose one?

On December 28th, he saw Laci in the neighborhood, and they, the 2 men, held a blanket up, and she was urinating by a fence, they helped her back into the van. Yea, I ain't believing this, three days after she went missing, seen in the same neighborhood. Yea, not credible.

The prosecutor today said that Scott lied about leaving home at 9:30am, since cell phone towers show he was still home. Prosecutors say his boat was covered in gasoline, which would make it almost impossible to find any trace evidence. They say he lied to investigators when they confronted him with photos of Scott and Amber at a Christmas party and yet, Laci, pregnant, attended a Christmas party that night, alone. We don't hear what Geragos has to say on the defense side until tomorrow.

He had just finished playing golf, the day he was arrested. He wasn't heading to Mexico. There was a burglary, that day, in the Peterson neighborhood. The prosecutor will question that, they say it was 2 days later. Some will say he went to the Bay, others will say because they were searching for the bodies. But, why rent a car? His behavior isn't normal for someone who lost their wife.

The 6:30pm national news in Richmond, VA., shows Scott coming into the courtroom, in an orange jumpsuit.

The prosecutor never said Scott murdered Laci. The prosecutor stated that the hairs in the pliers was wound down inside of them. What if he overstated that?

Today you're going to hear the truth. One hour and forty-five minutes for Geragos' opening statement. Highlights; an effort to interrupt Scott's conduct. Scott tried to find his wife; many efforts. He didn't throw his life away, with Amber, they had two dates, not a motive for anything. Amy, Laci's sister, says the pants, the slacks, Laci was wearing are 'not' consistent with the slacks she had on while at her shop December 23rd. They're different altogether, the draw string, the color. Baby born alive, the size, medical exams, December 23rd Laci saw her doctor. The twine and tape not on Conner by accident. A witness says someone pulled Laci into a van.

Geragos was very effective on the items tested; and nothing found, in the house or the warehouse. He didn't say Scott would take the stand.

Alibi; fishing and Laci found there? Framed? Coincidence? Didn't hear him deal with that. Alot of objections by the prosecutor to the defense's opening statement. Scott owned 4 boats in his lifetime, fishing since he was four years old, not a novice.

Compare the two openings. Geragos is charismatic, but people said they think the prosecutors' statement was better. Both effective, the van, baby born alive. I'm not criticizing anything Distaso does. Okay, Beth, that's right, play it safe out there.

Housekeeper will be the first witness, left dirty rags in the washer. Scott took the rags out and washed his clothes. Laci ready to mop the floor, 8½ months pregnant, when he was ready to go fishing.

Won't witnesses say that Scott had 0% chance of catching a sturgeon and there were many places to fish, closer to home. Yes, some experts, the prosecutor said yesterday, that they will say Scott didn't have the right equipment to catch sturgeon. Also experts for Geragos will say a body like Laci, would tip over and capsize a boat this size and it couldn't be done.

The judge will allow testimony from witnesses that say they saw Laci after she disappeared. Geragos had floated this theory and has stuck to it. You can't just point the finger at someone other than the defendant [Scott], it's called 3rd party culpability; without good cause, and the judge is going to allow it. Geragos said Scott didn't change his appearance for any reason other than that the media was hounding him everywhere he went and everything he did.

NEW YORK IS ONE OF ONLY 11 STATES BANNING CAMERAS IN COURTROOM.

Geragos said that 3 days before Laci went missing, she visited the storage unit and sat in the boat. to me, if proven, the hair means nothing. We hadn't heard this before. It's just now coming out.

That's what we want to know, if Scott's going to take the stand. People think they're so smart, that they can get away with murder. Geragos introduced the Martha Stewart Show. No way Scott would kill his wife for a lady he had 2 dates with. The defense claims Conner was born alive. The maid took the stand today, and the prosecutor said he couldn't remember who he would call next.

Scott walked into the courtroom with an air of confidence. He wasn't shaken. We've seen this before. Scott is paying attention to Mark Geragos and as Geragos goes along, Scott is nodding his head in agreement. Mark Geragos' voice was louder, more confident, in a story telling way.

96 phone calls, from December 24th to February, what do you do?

[Prosecutor] Forgot to tell the jury, there were several 2-day fishing licenses in Scott's truck, not just the one for December 23rd and 24th.

Twine around Conner's neck with a knot in it; born alive? Medical Examiner wrote that the baby was full-term at the autopsy. Was that a mistake? Will forensics free Scott Peterson? 160 bags of evidence and not a single piece of physical evidence.

Was Scott Peterson's relation with Amber strong enough to kill? 4 dates with Amber? Two before December 25th and two after? December 14th, the prosecutor put up pictures, big ones, of Scott and Amber at her Christmas party and beside that, he put Laci in her dress, alone at a Christmas party.

Prosecution says Laci's scent found on the ramp. Why not the boat? Without knowing the dog or handler, hard to comment. My dog is a scent dog and not a trail dog. Weather, humidity, heat, others, determine time of scent. I've had my dog confirmed by forensics testing, as well as people confessing to the crime. Do you believe he's guilty?

The spa owner testified that the police wrote down things that she didn't say. Another blow to the prosecutor's credibility. The lady said Laci came in December 23rd, and unlike other wives at the spa, Laci never complained about her husband, nor ever said anything about his infidelity.

We'll go out to the Redwood City courthouse at 4:30pm and we've got alot of questions to ask. Have you heard Geragos' defense theory? Stay tuned.

Theme today, 5 witnesses, saw Laci on December 23rd, people who had contact with her. In the morning, to the grocer store; afternoon, the Spa; evening, with Scott to get a haircut. Four said, two different outfits that day, black pants with a white top. At the hair salon, tan pants and a dark top. A facial at the Spa, no complaints of her marriage. We know Laci was found with tan, drawstring pants.

You don't want Laci to be wearing those clothes. Appointment, 1pm at the Spa, got there at 12:30.

Would you have your client smiling and laughing in the courtroom? Amy Rocha is on the stand now. Maid been there

4 times to clean. 8:30am -2:30pm, dark pants, and white shirt, usually what Laci had on when she's there. One of them mopped the next day, Scott or Laci, and that's an issue for the defense to clear up.

Amy is on the stand now, about 10 minutes ago. A big picture of Laci on the TV screen in the courtroom and it stays up there for the jury to see. Amy will say that the top Laci was wearing was on the top of the dirty clothes in the clothes hamper. Yea, Maybe she went home, took off her blouse and put it in the hamper, and was standing at the closet; she had on a maternity bra, so maybe that's when it happened. The black pants are consistent with what the maid said she had on that day, December 24th, and what other witnesses say they saw her wearing that day. Amy's the seventh witness.

The Peterson's were loud and openly like a pep-rally sometimes during the opening statement by Geragos when he spoke about the police rushing to judgment and not following leads.

The paint on the boat apparently matches some paint in the police parking lot. OH! OH! OH! OH! That's the problem with listening to the media.

Geragos defense; he's gonna say the baby was born alive, umbilical cord cut. How do you show; Mom decomposed greatly, and Baby not decomposed and in relatively good shape? That the baby was born alive, if there's no physical evidence to show that he was alive?

AMY SAID BEIGE PANTS 12/23 EVENING. FOUND WITH KAKI PANTS. SPA OWNER SAID BLACK PANTS 12/23 NOON.

Put 4 people on who saw Laci and the case is over, he goes home. Amy says Laci was wearing tan pants. 500 witnesses for the State? Seems like we have dueling liars in this case. What do you do when an officer writes something, changes it, or leaves something out?

How come if prosecutor's are so bad, they get so many convictions? Cause juries are inclined to convict.

I don't think Amber's Dad was subpoenaed to testify, but he did write a letter to the judge, saying the trial should be moved back to Modesto, and that Geragos should be taken off the case since Geragos had gone on TV before being retained in this case and had talked about Scott being guilty. I don't think Amber's

Dad wants to testify, or will be called to, but he is trying to inject himself into this case.

Amy testified that the jewelry given to them was worth hundreds of thousands of dollars and Laci liked to wear it around, and a theory by Geragos is she was abducted for the jewelry.

For the prosecution, when the bodies washed up, Sharon called Scott and left a message, but he never called her back. Very strange behavior. For the defense, Amy did say to the defense that Scott would be the last person in the world who would hurt someone, and she, at first, denied saying it, but Geragos showed her the documents, and then Amy admitted that she said that.

At first Sharon said when she went to the Park to look for Laci, and she saw Scott and hollered for him but he didn't answer, but, on cross exam when Geragos asked her about this, he said isn't it true that Scott was over 40 yards away and talking to several police officers, is why he didn't answer. Amy says Laci was active in walking up to a week before her disappearance.

Sharon's hardest testimony was while she was at the Park and Scott wasn't engaged in the search, almost distant. Says she never saw Scott the night of the vigil. Said she didn't get a chance to talk to Scott about what Laci was doing December 23rd to the 24th. The prosecutor played a tape with Sharon and Scott, but the quality of the tape was so poor, that the prosecutor had to get her to fill in sometimes.

Amy said she had been invited to Laci and Scott's to dinner for December 24th? Amy said Scott asked Amy if she wanted to come over for pizza, as Laci was on the phone ordering pizza, while Amy was cutting Scott's hair.

Two brothers and step-Dad testified that while the families were up on stage, Scott stayed in the crowd talking to a friend. Geragos also brought out that if Conner had been born, then Laci would receive over $100,000, which would go to her at age 30, or to Conner or Scott, but without Conner's birth, the inheritance goes to her siblings. Well for all we know Scott still did it, cause maybe he didn't know of the terms of the inheritance will.

Mr. Grantsky said on Christmas day that Scott's fishing story sounds fishy and if Scott knows anything he should tell them.

A conversation with Bret Grantsky, the recording was so bad that Bret didn't even recognize his own voice at first, where Scott told Bret that the blood and life insurance policy stories were a lie. Geragos asked Bret, if by December 29th the media suspected

Scott, and Bret said well, not everyone thought Scott was guilty. Bret also admitted that one of his favorite days to go fishing was Christmas Eve.

Scott didn't hug his mother-in-law, wouldn't participate with the family; strange behavior.

Ron Frey [Amber's Dad] showed up yesterday, has a San Mateo lawyer, and he spoke today, read a letter from Gloria Allred, that if her Dad testifies, he could say something about Amber on cross exam that could damage the case. He doesn't want to be crossed by Geragos, if he does testify. So the prosecutor subpoenaed Amber's Dad, Ron Frey, to keep him from talking in public? The prosecutor had over 500 people subpoenaed.

Harvey Gimbel said that Scott told him he went to play golf and not fishing. He said he followed Scott twice, when Scott was supposed to be putting up fliers, and said he went to a parking lot once and to play golf the other time. When on cross exam, he was asked why he followed Scott, and Harvey said cause Scott showed more emotion over a burnt piece of chicken on the grill than over his wife missing. Harris got the jury to laugh when he asked Harvey why he was watching Scott for 45 minutes in a parking lot.

No, we have to hear all the evidence first. They have his cell phone call at 10:08 and the dog at 10:18, so there's a window.

Scott talks alot with Geragos and Harris. When Susan was asked to identify Scott today, she did look at Scott and nodded and gave a smile.

A neighbor said she was awakened by the Peterson dog, McKenzie, at 10:38am. And a postal worker in the neighborhood from 10:35 to 10:50, and around the corner at 10:19, and said he heard different dogs barking, depending on which house he was at.

Poll Question: Will Scott Peterson be convicted? 38% Yes

22% No

40% Not Sure

Juror leaned over earlier and said something to Geragos, which everyone probably saw. But today the same juror had an exchange with Laci's brother. Maybe he just doesn't understand, but if I was the judge, I'd go ahead and dismiss this juror and move on.

Juror No. 5 told Bret Rocha that it looks like you'll are gonna lose again today, uh. What do you think of Mark Geragos' behavior in court?

The name Conner wasn't chosen until the media stepped in, as the Peterson's had two choices for a name and hadn't decided. Laci's doctor said she was 33 weeks along in her pregnancy on 12/24.

Stay tuned, new information coming out of Redwood City. Find out what the motive for murder was.

JUROR CONDUCT. It could have been anything, like it could be a bad day to loose today; the audio is so bad it's hard to tell. Some media says that this same juror came in one day and spoke to Mark Geragos, and Geragos turned and smiled. But, the defense says that the juror came into the courtroom and tapped on the railing as he passed the defense table and Geragos turned and smiled. The look on Laci's brother's face doesn't appear as though the juror had said anything derogatory to him.

The prosecution tried to establish a financial motive for Scott Peterson to murder his wife Laci, with the jeweler who appraised Laci's recently inherited jewelry, testifying that Laci told her when she went to get it appraised, it was Scott Peterson who wanted to know the value of the jewelry.

Scott Peterson's defense attorney, Mark Geragos, showed the jewelry appraiser a receipt for an appraisal of a watch like Laci's, which was a week after Laci's disappearance. He wouldn't show her the name on the receipt, but did say it wasn't Scott Peterson's.

But what of this information, this appraiser's receipt, buried in the prosecution's evidence. No redirect of the appraiser on who or where the pawn ticket came from on December 31st. Was someone pawning Laci's watch, seven days after her disappearance?

Maybe Laci just needed some quick cash, so she went to the pawn shop [12/10] and picked up a few dollars to Christmas shop.

Let's go over the jurors in this case. Juror No.4, a former police officer, who was charged with assault on a police officer. Another, a former fire fighter, said he's ashamed to be associated with some of those officers on the case. A lady who married a man while he was in jail. Yea, I hate those 'former' police officers on a jury.

Court TV uncovers some top secret information in the Scott Peterson case, stay tuned Live today.

Juror controversy takes center stage. Judge called in Bret Rocha and then Juror No.5. The judge said no misconduct by Juror No.5 and that the media got it wrong; they reported it wrong. Bret said the media got it wrong. Bret said the word wasn't 'lose', but he wouldn't say what it was. Geragos got up and lambasted the media, but didn't name names.

One of Laci's third grade friends is on the stand and she said when she arrived on December 25th, that Scott was vacuuming in the laundry room area. They'll be a 402 Hearing, an evidentiary hearing, to decide on evidence and then Detective Brocchini will testify.

Top secret information, the worst is out. Stay tuned live. [With this ad, a short video of Scott and Laci's home, with police tape tied around objects to keep the public out.]

[Shows a video of alot of media surrounding and following Bret Rocha into the courthouse.]

Third witness on the stand now. One said Scott didn't want his picture shown to media with Laci's, since this was about Laci and not him.

Did they clarify what the word was, with Juror No.5? Well what the Juror No.5 said, doesn't matter, it's the fact that he spoke.

Cleaning up the laundry room? Yea, about 5pm, December 25th, and she asked what he was doing, and Scott said he can't keep it clean, and it's true, by 5pm, there had been alot of people in two days been through the house, with police, friends and all.

Well, none of his TV interviews came off very well, so why would Geragos want to put Scott on the stand.

The first lady barely got out her first answer before crying. All were teary. The prosecutor wanted one lady to elaborate on the dog's bark and Geragos asked, You want her to bark? That was a bit much, even for Geragos, as the witness shot him a look. Yea, that's going a bit far, even for Geragos.

Laci's last [yoga] class was December 20th. She was the only one, as the others had dropped out because of their pregnancies. Her last conversation with Scott Peterson was December 23rd, Stacey, Scott called her and said he couldn't find Laci and some friends came over to help look, and Scott asked her if she knew anyone who drove a white truck.

Yea, the throwing away of the wedding albums will be coming into evidence.

A different pawn shop, from the December 10th one Laci visited, and the December 14th visited by Scott and Laci, but privacy prevents Geragos from showing where from, pawned watch on December 31st, same type as Laci's, same name as the one Laci owned. No foundation shown be Geragos. He just showed it.

Geragos called for a 402 Hearing, cause it the lady just said that Laci told her that the dog was probably mad at her cause she doesn't walk him anymore. Yea, that shows she wasn't walking on December 20th, so what, did someone come into the house and make her change her clothes and then take her? We've been saying all along she was too tired to walk.

Both sides asking the court to ban the camera that got the shot of the juror the other day.

The statement by the lady saying Laci didn't walk the dog anymore, wasn't in any police report. Here we have a witness, non-partial, who says Laci said she doesn't walk her dog, yet, we have Scott Peterson telling police Laci went to walk her dog. Yea, but Scott was making her out to be an Olympian.

Stacey talked to Laci at 4:45pm on December 23rd, just before Scott and Laci went to get his haircut. Scott told her he didn't want media at the volunteer center until 9:30, maybe cause he'd be gone by then. Why do you think Scott Peterson didn't want his photo in a wedding picture out in public. Could it be his affair?

Shows a video of Sharon Rocha, crying, saying she keeps hearing Laci's voice, begging to please bring me home.

What about this stuff on his computer about sex....

Did Laci get robbed that morning? Coming up.

We have never before released tapes between Detective Brocchini and Scott Peterson in the early hours of the investigation, December 25th. Many believe he'll be the Mark Fuhrman of this trial. He told Scott that he'd have to ask some questions that will make you not like me very much, but keep in mind, I'm just doing my job.

Some friends say the jewelry Laci wore was gawdy, alot of jewelry. All but the earrings and one watch is still there, on the dresser in pictures. The defense is trying to show the jewelry was pawned off on December 31st, but never said who.

The french doors were unlocked? Walk dog with door unlocked? Scott said door unlocked when he got home. Friends say Laci always take her purse with her and always lock the door. So what evidence does Geragos have that someone went in and took Laci?

What do you do with that?

At one point, the detective, Brocchini, asked Scott which jacket she had on. Scott said she usually wore his jacket. Where's the jacket she had on? No jackets are missing. We don't know how many jackets she had. One of the friends asked if her purse or jacket is missing? And Scott replied he didn't know.

Scott replied [to Brocchini] that Laci usually steals his stuff to wear, cause she's pregnant and his stuff fit better. Uh, em, bizarre. The officer said Scott told him when he came home, that the bucket was in the same place as it was when he left.

TV Question: Whose testimony will carry more weight with the jury?

Amber's? OR Detective Brocchini's?

Detective Brocchini, he could be their idea of Mark Fuhrman. That he could lie, that he could set up Scott Peterson. He was in the 'gang unit', so he's used to dealing with.... The families were really turned off by him treating Scott as a suspect, leaving his keys in Scott's truck and trying to trick him, manipulating witness' statements, the hair in the lab.

The transcript doesn't look like he tried to snare Scott at first. Detective Brocchini has a 1999 sexual assault charge? The woman later said she lied. Where his testimony drew fire from the judge; attempt to cause a mistrial? Witness intimidation? And a coerced false confession from a high school student?

Well known he's aggressive. He even called the Peterson tip line and made false reports. He called Scott's friend and said there's a $250,000 life insurance policy on Laci to get them to turn on Scott. No one ever charged Detective Brocchini, so does it come in?

Is the judge going to talk to the media? I guess it's settled, as the judge says there was no misconduct. I guess the subpoena he issued on media for Wednesday, he won't need now, as we just have to be 25' away from the security area.

TV Question: Whose testimony will carry more weight with the jury? Answer:

Amber's testimony, 76%.

Detective Brocchini's testimony, 24%.

Stick with us tomorrow and we'll give you a time line. We'll pin everyone down as to where they were and when.

Section Two

TV Guest Prosecutors

The Constitution shrouds a defendant in tremendous rights and the prosecution can't get a fair trial with public attention. It's more of an intellectual exercise. The judge should open the court room if he really believes that and wants the real killer there. I agree, its a good intellectual exercise.

The judge made a better case for closure, with his holding on no cameras, than what Geragos did, on closing the preliminary hearing to the public.

Maybe he was supplying the chemicals to meth labs from his fertilizer business.

This is a confession. I won't confirm or deny the tape, but if it's true, it's damning. Anything Amber said to me is attorney-client privilege and I can't comment on that. Makes no difference. He said 'Yes'. He said he knew who was involved. The defense attorney needs to pull a rabbit out of his hat.

[Magazine article] Pokes some holes in the satanic cult theory. We'll have battling experts. Hope they dial down the theory. The report is pretty creditable. I like the evidence. This shows it wasn't a cult. I'd love it if they used the colt theory and I was prosecutor. I apologize to Laci's family, if they are watching. Geragos said he'd prove Scott's innocent and he'd show us who did it.

Were autopsy details leaked to the press? If so, who did it and which side will this help? Laci and Conner were buried today. He'll probably say someone else did it. Soddi defense; somebody else. But now the defense knows not to use the cult theory. They may still stick to it and attack everyone; the scene; the physical evidence; fluids; body fluids; burglary. When the judge issues a gag order, he should enforce it. A member of the defense team went on cable TV and talked of this case and judge should know about it. [Baby born?] Common sense show they washed up close to each other and this is a red herring.

There's ten thousand on him, the affair, the blonde hair doesn't prove anything. Are they winning the prehearing stage? The defense is bringing in hired guns. They won't be called [to testify]. They'll be sanctions against whoever leaked the autopsy photos. The defense is preparing as if this is a jury trial rather than a preliminary hearing.

The schedule [defense] is skeptical. Delay, delay, delay, helps the defense. They should have gone to a grand jury and indict. We'll see a O.J. scenario here with witnesses. The rules have changed to help exclude scientific evidence. Not hurt either. Delay tactic is common in defense attorneys. Let the public lose interest in the case. Any strong case, they try to delay. He may waive the preliminary, cause he doesn't want the public to know it's a very strong case. He'd be incompetent if he didn't stall.

[Hypnosis] It's successful because they can relax and clear their mind of clutter. What the public should focus on, is why the defense wants evidence suppressed that is against them. What do they want to hide? Hypnosis is questionable. The prosecution wants to show she looks like Laci and the defense wants to keep it out.

Geragos must be expecting a manslaughter conviction or he wouldn't leave Scott in jail all this time. The prosecutor must have a strong case. [Experts] They won't misstate science, but they also can't say Scott Peterson wasn't involved.

Geragos doesn't want the wiretaps admitted into evidence. So many smoking guns in the case. Scott's on fire. Being a liar goes to credibility and this may show what lead him to kill her. A circumstantial case is a good case.

If all come in, it's better than one. The prosecution shows a pattern, and went off, and killed her after a confrontation and fight.

We'll see with the wiretaps. What he did after his wife disappeared. May allow hypnosis, may lead to evidence that's admissible. Learn everything you can. The attorney general said it was a slam dunk, not the prosecutor, and he referred to the body identification of Laci. Amber is not a mistress, she didn't know he was married. We'll see later if the prosecution plans to call her.

There's circumstantial evidence that links him to the crime. Geragos has to do something else, within camera range, he does more damage than good. Both sides have uncleaned hands; unfortunate for Laci. Laci hadn't ever been on that boat; hair and pliers.

Nothing. They're not cults and didn't kill innocent people. Looking at the boogie man here. Was she killed in Modesto and carried ninety miles to frame Scott? No way. Come on.

Cory claims he met with Scott Peterson on 11/2/02, in strip club in Fresno, California. Cory says Scott met with two members of a neo-nazi gang to steal Laci's car, so he could buy her a new one. Peterson then wanted them to kidnap Laci, then murder her. The police interviewed Cory in jail this week. He took a polygraph; okay.

On 9/19/03, the police dive teams returned to Fresno Bay. Scott made a solicitation for kidnapping and it went awry. Cory told the story in June, cause he didn't know of Laci till then. This information ties Scott to what happened. I was there during the polygraph. Many with a criminal history tell the truth. He'll be believed when he takes the stand. There's no independent evidence to corroborate this; nothing; not what clothes; car; or anything Scott has. But, if true, it's devastating.

Scott solicited Cory to steal Laci's car. Cory introduced Scott to the two men. Scott asked if they'd kidnap Laci. Yes, and police are trying to locate the two fellows. Cory went back to jail on a parole violation and didn't hear of Scott's case. He gets discharged very soon. The prosecutor wants him to stay in jail for his own protection, since the two fellows tried twice already to kill him. These two fellows used a beige van; Dirty and Skeeter. Cory's been told he'd be called as a witness. This ties into Scott saying he knew about Laci's disappearance, to Amber. He [Cory] didn't get out till June.

Same happened to the O.J. lawyers, being investigated on where they got money.

He gave an approximate date, not clear of exact date [met with Scott]. He's trying to turn his life around. He was okay with meeting on car theft, but not kidnapping. I'd have left too. I was there, during the polygraph and interrogation. He's very level-headed and wants to turn life around. We've given more information [to police] than what's been released. There is corroborating evidence, what Scott did, clothes, etc. Cory couldn't have gotten this information from the news media. The polygraph was given by a retired police officer.

Very effective [polygraph], but not admissible. Good chance it's the truth. Easy to cross-check for a lie. Wonder if he had an agreement to talk with police. Criminals do stupid things, so I wouldn't discount it.

The doctor's explanation is very good. The defense is grasping at straws with caffeine not in Conner. The information was floated by the defense.

Scott's unsavory character. He met Scott, and Scott asked if he could find someone to steal Laci's car. Cory set up a meeting and went to a hotel room. When the kidnapping came up, Cory left. We don't want to impede the prosecutor's investigation. He passed a polygraph; much more information given there than I can say. More than one meeting; Cory, one or two days after Thanksgiving. The van, some say a camper, a small motor home with a van front. My client wrote letters to the parole board, the prosecutor, and other prosecutors, but no one called, so he contacted me two weeks ago. They said they had received the letters. TV in pot area, but I don't know what they play on it.

No more goofier than what Geragos has said for months. Geragos better pray he's a liar. If not true, prosecution won't use him. Need to establish the date that Scott met with Cory, cause Cory doesn't know.

Scott struck up the conversation with Cory. They didn't know each other before. Scott asked if he knew someone to steal Laci's car. Cory was maintenance at the motel, and met Skeeter and Dirty; Tony and Anthony are their real names. They met at a restaurant; Chili's, then at the motel later; a couple of days later. Not charged with conspiracy, but with murder. He didn't try to cut a deal.

Amber never gave or sold the right to sell photos of her. No legal right to do this. How do you know? She didn't do it to sell or give away.

Story parallels Geragos' defense, of two guys in a van. Geragos' defense dovetails the prosecution case, maybe. Motive, fishing, bodies, equals conviction. Up to the prosecutor to decide to call her [Amber] at the preliminary hearing. Yes, they'll call her. She'll testify at the prelim.

The kidnappers could have dumped the body in the Bay to frame Scott, cause they didn't get paid. It's just a theory.

[Amber] Never wise to comment on security. She's aware of the circumstances. I have concern for her security. Always should be careful, but not necessarily scared.

Must be something going on, or they'd tell us why he left. May not be giving case enough time. The defense hasn't been doing their homework, if they believe paintings are satanic cults. The currents in the Bay vary greatly from day to day and did so a couple days before the body was discovered.

I believe others are out there with information. Motive is to kill wife for Amber. In the initial interview, he said not a problem between he and wife. Police will use this. Use what King just said against Cory in court.

Yes, declaration submitted to the prosecutor that saw them together in Fresno. That person has agreed to be interviewed, a long-time friend of Cory's; can't question her character, she's right, either late November, Cory was doing work in her garage and Scott spoke to both of them, in Fresno. Cory was putting up shelves. Talked to both, small talk. This person, she liked Scott. No crime talk; small talk. Cory and Scott talked alone, probably set up a meeting. I spoke with her myself. Pretty, pretty reliable. Couldn't get her to lie, even if you pulled out her toenails. She was very clear about that. There may be other parties to say what occurred at the meeting; Scott, Cory, Dirty, and Skeeter. There were three to four meetings with Cory and Scott.

Muna is interesting, if he backs it up, materials, and dovetails with the theory by Geragos. Geragos wants this to be true cause killers are Cory, Dirty, and Skeeter. Jury pool polluted and guilty. Agree, not criminal conduct, but heartlessness conduct used to convict him.

The person didn't hear about hit or kidnap; Cory was fixing shelves or fixing a bicycle. Scott came over and had small talk with Cory and this person. This person knows Scott from pictures. Does she, the person, know of Cory's record? She signed a statement that her name not be released. No problem with Cory's background.

What about Scott trying to buy a car in his Mom's name and gave her name? What if that turns out to be true?

Cory heard Scott offer three thousand dollars to each, both Dirty and Skeeter, to kidnap and eight thousand dollars each to kill her. We have the phone records to show the calls. The story about someone buying his story for eight thousand dollars, by National Enquirer, Cory said no. No offers of seventy-five thousand. I'm obliged to convey offers to my client.

Cory told me right before talking to the police. I told him to answer their questions. If they didn't ask question, then he didn't answer one. The poly guy didn't ask for details. No, we give police first shot. What can we release without hurting the prosecution. We talk to them and fully cooperate. [Dirty and Skeeter] Don't know if they exist. Met several people who knew them; locals in area; still looking.

[polygraph] If guilty, the best thing to say is, of course, but you then just don't take it. He knows he'd fail it. He never expected it to go further than her, Amber, to convince her. I agree; it's further evidence of motive; to convince her and facilitate relations with her. Clouds the jury view and the defense is destroyed, without other evidence. Court of public opinion knows he said no and they'll be the jury. Jury will see through the defense argument that he offered to take it. You can trick a polygraph, but when police do it, much more likely to get results they are lying and that's why he refused. Better police didn't do it, may have backfired. Agree, better to offer, but never did.

Weak case, so attack the police, instead of factually innocent like Geragos said. Not talking about gun, bowling ball, etc., it's hair. They could find another one anywhere. The patrol officer and detective find evidence, and give it to the lab and processed according to standards they're using in the case. Police don't give evidence to the lab, then open bag and put another hair in.

The defense is getting around the gag order with motions; what he wants public to hear. Is blood on hair; pulled out; get rid of evidence using argument that splits hairs. Knock out GPS cause unreliable; Come On. Not sloppy work. They can go back and find another hair. Okay, if prove she's been in the boat.

Important is when he went south, when bodies were found, with money and fake ID. Amber is still most of his problems. Maybe he was looking for Dirty and Skeeter. Phone calls not consistent with the innocence of Scott Peterson. Dogs; critical evidence.

To make a long preliminary hearing by the defense; maybe exclude hypnosis. The prosecutor will want her to say it was her walking the dog and not Laci. The defense is worried about the DNA; the hair on the pliers. It is critical evidence for the prosecution. They'll do anything they can. They have to go after the investigation, it led to dead body and led to Scott Peterson. Heart of case is DNA.

No more; it's put up or shut up for Geragos. Could be in the back of the car and wrapped tightly. Maybe they're waiting for the real killers. Ha, Ha. Don't know, I forget all the defenses Geragos has, I'd have to look on the O.J. website to remind me. Prosecutor will pay Geragos back at the preliminary for all the tricks he's played.

Won't be tried in Modesto. Prosecutor wanted transaction sealed, so it won't be tried in public. Judge won't throw out; should have disclosed to defense. He's detached from the family, no dedication to them and no dedication to the investigation, so that's where you look. Won't be effective because of the O.J. case. Twelve jurors bought a portion of it. It will damage Geragos case if he tries it.

Geragos could use that he offered the lie detector test. Cheating doesn't make a murderer. Put on an expert to explain. I'd go with the insurance money. They won't let if he said he'd take a polygraph, come in. That's not gonna come in.

Interesting the defense wants to dismiss the dogs when they don't help them and use them when it does. He told Amber he knows who the killers are. Someone saw him that morning putting something wrapped up in his truck. The boat was stored in the warehouse. They'll follow all tips, till the end.

She's not a great motive, but does destroy his character. Allows the jury to take him out. Tell jury he's a cheater right away. People love dog evidence in America. Calls will put him in jail for a long time. Prosecutor will give the jury the information of him and his cavalier attitude; couldn't care less.

Hair, defense has tried so many theories, and the public doesn't buy any; then attack the government and a certain part of the public doesn't like government and will latch on to that. Not tough or impossible to get conviction. Defense just goes from one theory to another and worried.

Why tell a mistress that you're a widower? That's sick. We'll see trashing of law enforcement; very predictable.

Broker said he'd have a web site to sell the photos. He did and Amber filed suit. Two other lawyers represent her. She didn't pick up the photos; not interested in career; her wish they not be exploited; never sign a release. She signed a data sheet; what her vital information is, tattoos, piercing, but no release, to her understanding. I asked the broker for the original release and not provided. I've seen what he says is a copy of a release. Not interested in a modeling career at that time.

Very difficult for Laci's family to get started again after all these stops. Show probable cause. Scott's changed his appearance, and the jury will notice. Yea, his skin would be orange. It went in all directions at the beginning, shades of O.J. Simpson.

There's red paint found on the front of Scott's boat. The police are looking at Buoy #4, to see if Scott tied his boat to it, to dump the body. The defense will probably put on some witnesses. Use a cost/benefit analysis to determine what to spend on the preliminary. Preliminary is insane for Geragos, the evidence will kill Scott Peterson. I wouldn't put her on, but she'll bury Scott Peterson; jury will be polluted.

Somebody may feel negative about the photos. Amber will be ready to testify. She'll tell the truth and not much to fear. She'll have confidence, cause telling the truth. If Geragos attacks her, it may boomerang on him. Won't be helpful to Scott on what he says.

Circumstantial case, can't take a chance of not enough evidence. Amber tapes are a bombshell. We'll hear Scott in his own voice. Why Geragos would have a preliminary is beyond me. A high profile preliminary only hurts. Public only remembers bad things.

Can be a down side if prosecutor puts out damning evidence. Would think the police would have went after the clubs; see if they did. Scott loves to talk; we know that. Confession; three to four glasses of pruno, alcohol. Friends say they spent eighteen months to get Laci pregnant. One cell mate says confession, and another says he hired someone.

Ammonia content in fertilizer and the prosecutor argues this took alot of evidence away. Living scent isn't the same as cadaver scent. Could it be a transferred scent or on someone's clothing naturally? Could be alot of other evidence that won't be shown, or I hope so. Somebody may get him in jail for the baby, the little boy, and see God.

We'll see if the prosecution calls her [Amber]. Geragos will be surprised, if, and when. Use Amber to introduce the tapes. A known liar; says he told police of the affair earlier. Now we'll find out.

We'll see forensics, whatever the prosecutor lets us see. Hair, the prosecutor says it's Laci's and if DNA test is scientific enough. Unfair to say prosecutors would sway public opinion; Hollywood is on the other side of this. If he said he wasn't there, and it's found he was.

The FBI stopped hypnotizing witnesses twenty years ago and they can't testify in court, in federal court. We didn't hypnotize anyone, except maybe for a license plate number, but not if we needed them to testify down the road somewhere. They'll lay the ground work to criticize the police. He'll be bound over, activity won't come into the preliminary; but his conduct afterward will prejudice the jury so much they won't favor anything in his favor. Consciousness of guilt; I must have done something wrong.

Geragos would be doing his client a disservice if he shows his hand at the preliminary hearing and goes into a full fledged defense. Depends on what Amber says. If admissions of murder, yea, but affair, no. The prosecutor hasn't said if Amber's a witness. Can't say Scott loved his wife. He didn't want a child, his own. There's proof she's not gonna be there to provide lurid or salacious testimony.

Too easy to focus on one point of evidence; alot we don't know about. One lie by husband whose wife is missing is enough for a jury to convict. Well, no rush to judgment by the police on arresting him. Bodies; difficult to overcome, must create doubt.

There's nothing to practice. Geragos has a choice, attack her and it'll boomerang. Right decision for judge to exclude both families from the witness exclusion rule. Maybe use Amber to relay tapes. Suggests some problem with the wiretaps, might have to play on the Spice Channel.

Trial won't be in Modesto. None of us really know what evidence the prosecutor has. Computer with flow charts and possibly date rape drug. Physical evidence can't lie.

I need to be there to understand the case and advise her [Amber]. I'm there as her support, her advisor. She's neutral on guilt or innocence. She's a victim of Scott Peterson's deception. No plans to sue Scott Peterson.

Do experts testify, no matter what they find? No, you don't have to use them.

Don't know why Geragos is fixated on me. She doesn't watch TV.

FBI experts testified today on hair. Why mitochondria DNA first?

I need to be there; to help her. Why is it the defense has the only right to spin it his way? Prosecutor doesn't want to go overboard now, use to shock jury at trial. Come on, how many husband's wives' hair in their pliers? Geragos wanted alot; unsuccessful. Why are you threatened by me, Geragos? Why only a defense spin?

Surprised today that the prosecutor wouldn't use the tapes. I don't know what the defense attorney here will do cause he's quite a character. Both are playing to the press. Geragos is throwing out everything and see what sticks to the wall; the hair was wrapped in the pliers on the boat he bought the day before Christmas; Come On.

Circumstantial case; a good one, is better than a direct case. No other physical evidence by the prosecution that has leaked out; no explanation of the hair in the boat. The prosecution has going for it; Who else would have done this?

So many inconsistent statements out there. Shows motive to lie. Inconsistent statements will haunt him. Evidence of flight or prepare to flight can be used. Very persuasive to a jury. What could be more powerful to a jury? The prosecutor decided not to use the Bronco chase.

[hair] Puts her in vicinity of the boat. Or even knew the boat existed? Bay is a disposal site, and with information of him going there over and over; maybe to assure himself the body hasn't floated up. Scott put himself at the crime scene, ninety miles from home where both lived. Geragos doesn't wasn't able to shake the DNA expert's conclusion.

Don't know about the movie; don't know if they can do one. She'll tell the truth, so don't need to practice. Amber gives the prosecution motive.

Hair means everything; it puts Laci between the house and the Bay. We're gonna have alot more. Not fatal to case, but links Laci to the boat. Interesting how hard Geragos is trying to keep it out; He Thinks It's Important. The prosecution may have some evidence of blood. Does satanic cults use bleach? I know women who clean before the housekeeper comes, but not after. Body found here behind the community, and Scott placed himself across there on that Island.

Why release the letters now? Didn't know wife was dead, crying, OH Come On. I hear violins playing in the background. Scott Peterson trying to testify without being under oath. Modesto police has a ninety-six percentile, the rest have sixty percent, to solving homicides. It wouldn't take rocket scientist to focus on Scott. Can't comment on the letters. Always talk about the defendant's rights, but the only one who didn't choose to be there, is the victim's family.

Practices with his own expert. Flying DNA. Ha, Ha. The defense can retest the hair. It was found to be Laci's hair. O.J. Simpson all over again. Different here cause O.J. had to do with race. Why plant evidence here? No one but Scott knew he bought the boat. Why keep big purchase a secret?

[term 'missing'] Not heard it before; depends on what you think of guilt or not.

They looked anyway. Was Scott wrong, or mistaken about the lights? Ask maid what she did with the mop; I leave the wet part, sponge up, not down. Amy tried Scott's cell phone on December 24th and couldn't get him; about the gift basket. Laci would have told Amy about the affair. If Laci knew of the boat, she'd have told her Mom. Cleaning with bleach after the maid doesn't make sense.

Don't agree; December 24th, Scott's Dad said he talked to him, around 2pm or so, and this would have been while Scott was fishing and Scott should have told his Dad he was fishing and not golf. You're wrong. So she had to go grocery shopping, December 23rd, pregnant, while husband fishes on December 24th.

Interested Amy and Mom said didn't know of Amber Frey relation. The Mom, December 23rd, talked to Laci. Scott says he told Laci; hard to believe Laci be okay with it and hard that she didn't tell her mother. Beginning to unmask Scott Peterson, it's Halloween. Geragos will be aggressive, dog style, in her face, but it will boomerang. Can't comment. If Amber, cause the prosecutors think she has something. Try to beat her up; but won't be successful. Never good to watch a man beat up on a woman. Mom says close relationship. Mom says if Laci knew of Amber, Laci would have told her.

Detective says two mops outside and a bleach smell on December 24th; it wouldn't be there a day later.

Letters are self-serving; he looks better now than before. Letters are what he wants to get out to the public.

Did they go water skiing in the boat? Take others out? I'd want to know these things. What she has to say will be important. In a domestic murder, which this is.

Geragos will try to dirty up Amber and it'll boomerang. It'd be malpractice as a prosecutor not to call Amber, at least at this stage. The defense better produce, if not, his credibility is on the line; and if his is on the line, so is his client's. Can't have it both ways. Jurors will remember promises.

When's the last time you heard an affirmative defense? My client didn't do it and here's the one who did? His father would have known; 12-2pm phone call; Scott said he was at the pier at twelve noon. Some say he was going to present the boat to Laci for Christmas.

Mitochondria DNA used to ID Vietnam vets. The prosecution has more. Hair only thing ties Laci's body to Scott and the water. Judge will accept it; need it to bind over. Amber tapes will prejudice the jury and the rest will be believed. The tape is just another piece. Won't be any smoking gun; won't be more prejudicial than probative.

Fish for two hours and come back; sounds fishy. No one talked to Laci after December 23rd evening. Amber had no knowledge; if the prosecutor uses her for motive. Scott is very involved with defense.

Concern over Amber's security when she testifies if I tell you now. I'll be informed, if she testifies. She's never testified before, and to face Geragos as an attack dog. If the defense attacks her, she'll tell the truth, do the right thing.

For the prosecution; the rug caught in the door; a struggle? Body dragged out? The detective said he told another detective. Bucket outside? Maid said in the laundry room.

He was also distracting his own attorney during the warehouse testimony. Annoying to an attorney for a client to talk to him. Maybe Scott can't control himself.

Maid there on December 23rd, and a tired, pregnant woman ain't gonna clean house. He didn't want full light for the detective to see. The client wants a thousand Perry Mason questions asked. Usually says the policeman is lying. Clearly Scott was a suspect; first one to look at. Turns out their suspicions were right.

[rug] Red herring; no gun under it. Was the body drug through it?

Later he said sturgeon, and can't catch them with his boat. You played Scott's statements and he thinks the officers doing a Wonderful Job. How self-serving are the photos on the wall? He knew it would get out. Won't rule out a plot by Scott.

He says the clothes are different on December 24th . What motive is there to plant evidence by the police? The affairs shows Scott wanted to get rid of his wife and baby; get them out of the way. The prosecution's case is based on common sense; Christmas Eve fishing? This is strong evidence, I agree. They tried it in the O.J. trial and it didn't work. Not one lie by the police and no planted evidence. It didn't work then and Geragos should learn, cause it ain't gonna work now.

Scott Peterson will convict Scott Peterson. A ball and chain around his neck and he wanted out. He didn't count on the Modesto Police being the best there is. Need a psychological profile of Scott Peterson; agree with Fuhrman. Obviously Scott gave Geragos permission to go to Los Angeles and not be here.

Scott never picked up the gift on December 24th, nor call Amy; something change his plans?

Assumes a perfect murder; ain't none. Piece by piece of the prosecution's case. Attempts by the defense to say what; a sex addict? A question of whether the defense theory is grounded in fact or not. What Scott said is a laugh; he's glad Amber told police?

See Geragos attack the police too; someone has to be the villain. How's the fax working if electricity is out. Scott said strange things. So much circumstantial evidence here. Who's the logical person to do it? Are we gonna look at satanic cults. When you were a prosecutor, that'd been enough for you.

How about the self-serving phone call to the cell phone? The prosecutors say there's no other reasonable inference to make. Glad he's here, he wrote the book on planted evidence. Scott lied to police; critical. Affair is relevant. Said yes, then no, to knowing of her disappearance. If he told Amber that he'd be free to be with her in January, he's got alot of explaining to do.

Hope there's more evidence. I'd like to take a shot at him, with another jury of course. Can the judge order Scott to take a lie detector or a truth serum? No.

Amber may have more than we thought. I know if she'll testify. She's not interested in the news in this case. Geragos may attack her and we learned today on what that might be. The detective said that Amber called the tip line; she said that Scott indicated that he lost his wife and this is the first holiday without her; just couple weeks before Laci missing.

Tell Geragos to bring it on. Don't want to take her apart, if the tapes are in Scott's own words. Good for the prosecutor. If he loved her, he'd have told the truth. Lied about affair.

Why did Scott ask police about the cadaver dogs in the Park. Weeks before, Amber confronts him of marriage, so why not tell the police? He had three cell phones, told police one. Buys boat same day Amber confronts him; planning going on here. The bucket; the maid left it on the washer, and mysteriously outside. The defense asks to suppress the bucket; asked the detective if he had permission to take the bucket. They been watching Martha Stewart and became excessive cleaners. Scott denied having an affair the day after Laci went missing.

[Scott's gun] It may not be legal. If he called, and asked about the cadaver dogs the next day; troubling. If he came home, and wife missing and he takes a shower and eats, something's wrong. Watch the defense try to exclude the bucket. He set that up today; if detective had permission to take it.

Scott said 'missing'. Prosecutor wasn't the one grandstanding today. Geragos went to the microphones. Scott also said he went back to the warehouse and read e-mails. Didn't want employer to know boat stored there.

[Scott give Laci's jewelry to Amber?] If so, see if testifies. Scott told Amber this would be the first holiday without wife, on December 9th.

If cops set up, then they'd use more evidence than we have here. Didn't put in his report, but does have photo of pliers in the boat. The defense can test the residue swabs if want.

Shouldn't wait for bombshells in the case. Only the beginning of the prosecution's case; alot more to come. The detective said that Amber told him that Scott said the first Christmas without his wife, and he and Amber could be together in January. Very compelling; why'd he say that.

[surveillance tapes] No evidence that police are trying to cover this up.

They're going over her secret calls that Amber recorded and they'll be used in the hearing; getting her prepared to testify. Let the judge give weight to testimony. Like to take a shot at him to try the O.J. case again. The lie he told, that wife was dead, is a bombshell. If Scott had said, missing or lost, on December 9th, that would be devastating. Detective did say that Amber said that Scott said she was missing and damning for the jury to hear.

O.J. should have been a slam dunk. Here, one strand of hair. Boat, fish on December 24th and body shows up. Hard to believe a coincidence. They're trying to make it O.J. II. I agree, sounds like it. The pliers were in the boat, cause there's a picture of them in boat. Rich get to buy, hire better lawyers.

I wouldn't want the defense to get a crack at Amber.

Even without hair, the case would be bound over; the hearing means nothing. Still could be appealed, if convicted, on the hair DNA. It's the most powerful evidence so far for the prosecution. The prosecutor selected the hair to put Laci in the boat and get her out to the Bay.

The prosecution must turn over the tapes. Can't take a risk on the judge sanctioning them, fines, or throw out the case. Idea of people when committing homicide, is to get away with it, so won't have alot of evidence. Amber will sink him. A jury can consider consciousness of guilt. Don't need Amber to testify. If he strangled his wife and wrapped in plastic, there won't be much evidence.

Don't know if it was the FBI. The Supremacy Clause says the feds don't have to cooperate. Was it about Laci or about drugs; he used cash and he's a fertilizer salesman.

[Scott testify?] He'll have to admit all those lies; Don't think so.

[Amber magazine article] She didn't cooperate in the story. Story's out of context; the defense fears her. The defense didn't present any evidence of private phone tapes by Amber and his statement isn't evidence. Can't comment on, if tapes or not.

You've been showing these clips of Geragos at the microphone, every time we go to break. The last I heard, there was a gag order. Why is Geragos talking to media? Why isn't the prosecutor doing it?

[Scott said knows who did have something to do with Laci's disappearance?] What if said, How do you defend it? Why wouldn't Scott tell police of Amber, so the police could check her out.

[surveillance tape] Detective Brocchini testified that he didn't know about the tape. An attempt to vilify prosecution; anything they can. DEA may have been looking at Scott without

Modesto. Scott had been to Mexico and back. Unfair to attack ethics of the prosecution in this case. It was recorded by accident.

[Amber tape before cops?] It was just a question by the defense. No evidence yet presented. I didn't hear the detective say Amber was coached, today in court. Amber not in Modesto, not testify tomorrow.

Body washes up where his boat was. How many of us have forgotten our keys? Suggesting he was alone to plant evidence, but defense hasn't presented any evidence to show that, so their case is weak.

His behavior wasn't of a grieving husband. Not sure she's needed. Doesn't make sense from a strategy viewpoint. Lied to own attorneys? They're clients, that's what they do. You have to lie to your lawyers.

[surveillance tapes withheld] So far, no harm. Just didn't think it was relevant. I'm more interested in what's going on; hamper full of dirty clothes, but Scott just washes own clothes. That's not how people do clothes.

If late on the tapes, it's no harm, no foul, to the defense. Trial hasn't started. What about Geragos floating all these theories. With the prosecutor out of line here, it's okay, it's tit for tat here.

The defense own expert says the baby came out in the water. The baby had tape on his neck. Lies, DNA, cash; he's going down. Twenty-seven years a judge and prosecutor, and don't need any more testimony. Cream pants, clear she disappeared on December 23rd. If detective Brocchini said he didn't question the eye witnesses, doesn't mean police didn't. Pants most compelling evidence so far.

She's ready and willing. Won't comment on how she feels about not being called. She's been a victim of Scott Peterson's and may try again. Prosecution has enough evidence. Won't give the defense a preview of what she has, on TV. I've read the article. I won't further invade her privacy, like others have. An unauthorized article, can't prevent it. She doesn't watch the news or read articles about her. He said she was missing, not dead, before she went missing. Agent doesn't matter, if Scott called her. If he refused to talk to the police, then police can't use an agent.

Already met the threshold to bind over. You agree, if beige pants, that's a connection to Scott Peterson. Wasn't it confirmed by another lady walking dog? He never asked the divers if they found anything? Day bodies found, he'd have been there. Instead he chose to play golf.

I never like talking about what I discuss with the prosecution. I don't want to give a preview to the defense. A good argument for testifying and for not testifying. The defense re-victimized her for doing the right thing. And second time Scott said that he lost his wife. He said lost before she even went missing.

No evidence the detective wanted Scott to get fired. He didn't know police were following him. If he did, why didn't he change cars or something. Problem that he told the neighbor that he went to play golf.

Likely she'll testify at trial. Strong witness. Be an ugly experience for the defense and not her. She [defense attorney] doesn't have access to the tapes. Detective said that Scott said, he lost his wife. Geragos said he'd prove Scott's innocence. Is he gonna put on evidence at this hearing, or what? I Don't Think So. Mistake not to put Amber on. Lies, dead wife, widower. I would in Massachusetts, let me tell you.

It's cheaper to kill her, than to divorce her. He didn't want to pay child support. Evidence shows he didn't want the baby. The subpoena of Amber will probably be quashed. He's a sleazy womanizer. Proves we have a man who can pull the wool over everybody's eyes. She [Amber] was suspicious. Called him December 9th, and asked him.

Scott had a license for December 23rd and December 24th, and of so, even before December 23rd he knew, so is it premeditated? Explain his golfing; check with the golf club, and if their rules say he has to sign up earlier, and he didn't, the he never planned to play golf.

Geragos will decide by Monday if he wants to subpoena Amber. He has to show important to an 'affirmative defense', which he doesn't have. The defense counsel is doing all the talking. Mistakes by law enforcement; What else do they have to poke holes in. Not following up the lead; is much to do about nothing. Police prioritize. Geragos spins in the courtroom, with inflammatory questions, knowing they'll be sustained. Maybe the detective put down the wrong time in report. Can't chase all leads, some come from thin air. How many golden retrievers in California? Can't go on a wild goose chase.

The prosecution doesn't need Amber for the preliminary hearing. Then the defense gives a subpoena. He's a hard working judge. Terrific judicial demeanor.

They didn't know what she was wearing till the bodies washed up. Oh, my God! You guys sound like a bunch of goofs out there. My God; you need to listen to the prosecutor and stop taking pot shots at the prosecution. You're taking all that slop that the defense is throwing out and using it to talk. Go to the scene, good work.

Police report says 10:45, and dog at 10:18, so it doesn't work. The defense says now, there's a time discrepancy; Incredible. I'd say it was 9:45, and it was Skeeter and Dirty leading her to her death. However you cut it, they got her on tape. When did the defense tape her? How much has she heard before that? Why aren't we focusing on that shady character called Scott Peterson.

Just don't do that as a defense attorney. California law; only calls for affirmative defenses. Peterson a number one member of scum bag club.

Born before death? This shows it's not true. It's a show. He's so cynical; a ploy. Fingerprints can survive in water on duct tape. Peterson out of courtroom will get alot of coverage. Judge may say it's an act. His actions depends on who's interpreting it.

A problem with a sonogram to determine age. Also should see swelling of baby's body, if in the water very long. O.J. case was rich with DNA evidence compared to this one. I'd like to see a smoking gun, but don't believe there is one. I believe he's guilty, but hard to prove.

Maybe he had a golf date. Who knows? It was a show! It was a show! Detective confirmed, on a show I was on, detective said want to look around, and Scott said get a search warrant and this put red flags on self. To say they need a search warrant makes it suspicious. Geragos has moved to Idaho. Trying the O.J. defense. Detective said woman who saw Laci walking, didn't fit his theory.

No vaginal delivery, the cervix was in tact. If Conner had air or water in lungs, then it's a sign born alive. Pathologist should know if born dead or alive. Maybe the prosecution should use another pathologist, and not this one. He said he couldn't tell if born alive or not. Scott request viewing his child? He went and played golf that day; not sure if he asked. Didn't see it.

Geragos told me he would decide on whether to call Amber, after the prosecutor closes his case. Still have to show an affirmative defense to call her. The prosecution has enough evidence without Amber testifying. No thoughts on the People's Magazine story, but she wasn't portrayed right. She'll just have to suffer through all the unauthorized stuff.

Bodies washed up near where he said fishing. If on December 9th, said to Amber that wife missing or lost, that would be a major problem. Not follow leads, but if dead on December 23rd, then December 24th not important. Lady had already seen Laci on TV at that point.

Why have an anchor factory in the warehouse. Four or five places with outlines on floor of where made anchors. Don't have to show where, or how killed, but she was murdered. Very damning case against Scott. Look at all the evidence, as accumulative effect. Could be a soft kill; no blood. Didn't have head or neck either, so we wouldn't know. Jurisdiction where found. No evidence where occurred.

Gonna be hard to prove that. Maybe he loaded the body in the truck, went to the warehouse, and loaded in the boat at the dock. Neighbor testified blinds always up in the morning. Maid only there a couple of times. If he lied about using bleach in the kitchen, the first detective said he didn't smell bleach, so I'm not sure where that came from. Issue, if to believe; Laci pregnant, would be cleaning, tired, and just after the maid there. He said black pants and found in tan pants. Laci could have used the mop. Washer is problem, wife missing and he washes clothes? Seems Laci was killed in this house, but which theory will the prosecutor use? Conner information, not born by vaginal or C-section; most important evidence.

Happy Amber not called. The boat never made it to the San Francisco Bay. These guys can buy me dinner when Scott's convicted. Opportunity; last seen with wife, fishing where wife washes up. Motive! Shakel was convicted. Just put him at the scene. Different verdict, if in different location. Instinct and institution, and depends on how you think. What's gonna kill Scott is... The prosecutor asked questions of the mop, but may be forensic evidence there, we don't know.

Scott probably said, wife never in the boat, yet they find hair in the pliers and they have something of Laci's where she's not supposed to be. The medical examiner says homicide. The hair connected to Laci; other owner didn't leave the pliers on the boat. It shows she was on the boat. With the shades, the maid put the blinds up.

Okay, everyone go out to your toolbox and get your needle nose pliers and see how many have your wife's hairs in it. He engaged with police, but at some point he stopped and that caused suspicion. Circumstantial evidence is subject to interpretation. You gotta know your Pole, Line, Bait, where you're going. Husbands killing pregnant wife isn't unusual. Parents kill their children and there's nothing in their history either. Homicide just doesn't make sense anytime.

Anyone thinks these tapes will help Scott is insane. I agree, but the tapes will set the entire tone with the jury. Yea, him sitting there while holding hands with Amber and crying over his missing wife is damaging. Evidence yesterday of the weight factory he had is a bombshell. Good thing O.J.'s lawyer's in retirement, cause this'd be a tough case to defend. Never thought the defense would call her. The prosecution had enough evidence. Calls after Laci's disappearance, people will be curious.

December 9th Scott said he lost his wife. Why'd he lie about the concrete and say the pool people using it? No idea of the January 6th phone call. Why didn't Scott tell the police she's alive. Just another lie? Just one of many, many, lies. The trial; won't get over that hurdle. Disagree with you. Disrespectful to the judge, to say no evidence. We're all liars. That's unfair. That's unfair. He wants sympathy.

Disagree with the doctor. We have mitochondria DNA test of the hair. Doctor there are millions of viewers out there. Go and see if hair of spouse is in your pliers. It's ridiculous.

Met November 20th, confronted him of marriage 9th of December. Hundreds of pieces of circumstantial evidence.

Why should they? They've got evidence in it. Why pay for evidence?

It leads to other business, so he won't quit. Not too many would walk away here.

Not important if Amber is pregnant. No impact on her credibility. She will be called to testify at trial. Simple way is to say nobody's talking on the outside. Not a rumor, just another lie. Why say golfing, if he didn't have anything to hide, and say he'd been golfing? Why lie? Terrible evidence, if the jury hears he lied that day, to create an alibi. Some clients demand to take the stand

and say they didn't do it. I disagree, he's too much of a liar to take the stand.

Maybe there's something we don't know, but hard to believe Mr. Geragos has the cards in his hip pocket to go ahead with this. Surprised Geragos made motion, cause now blood is out in public. Can be devastating to the defense, assuming it's Scott's blood. Could happen by January 26th, maybe February. Entirely up to the trial judge as to where it goes with a change of venue.

No such plea as innocent. Maybe with Mark's [Geragos] encouragement. The prosecutor will tell the jury, he won't tell them alot, cause Scott killed the only witness to the murder.

Alot of Laci's assets are being encumbered; house, a hundred thousand dollars; truck and money given to Scott; photos that someone paid a very high price for. Photos shown on TV taken recently, wondered who did this. Laci still has an interest in that home. Ms. Rocha feels they're using Laci's assets to finance Scott's defense.

Confirmed Amy's story; kaki pants found on Laci's torso.

[Smiling in court] Yes, I heard that and it may hurt them if jurors find out about this. They'll show him as a liar from the start. Oh, they'll kill 'em, they'll kill 'em. The jury will want to know why he lied, why he walked across the street and told his neighbor he'd been playing golf.

Defense may be trying to attack, figuring the prosecution isn't ready, but it may backfire on them. Judge won't grant change of venue. Where's he gonna go? Simpson case had as much publicity and he was acquitted. Geragos didn't compare Stanislaus County to another county.

Nude photos of Amber; federal judge issued a temporary order not to publish on website. And, next time I warn someone, they'd better heed the advice. Her credibility won't be in trouble. Let it rest.

Federal court judge decided on preliminary injunction on releasing nude photos of Amber. He published them on his web site, despite my warning not to. Great that some kind of precedent is now set on not allowing photos like this to be published, where someone becomes known or famous and someone will go back and find photos and try to profit off it.

Geragos drank some of the water at the Michael Jackson party the other day. Common sense says its Scott and if not, who? Jury here could convict Scott, just because they despise him.

People have heard of the case, but most of the time they haven't made up their mind yet. Judge shouldn't rely on experts and polls, but call jurors in and ask them. Yes, but it'll fall on deaf ears, if already decided. Judicial Council decides on which county, and, or, if to bus in jurors. Thirty years, I haven't seen busing in jurors. Politics and economics will decide where it ends up.

The prosecutor had the task of changing the judge's mind, but the judge didn't say which areas concerned him. Suppose jurors did that, and then you had to change their minds. Doesn't affect Amber, although Geragos took a cheap shot at the prosecutor and me today. Up to Council to tell the judge which counties are available and then a hearing on January 20th, and the judge will say which county.

Why would prosecution want ABC interview. Could be a powerful piece of evidence. Maybe, if. Could be like he says, could be he saw Laci and what happened and help Scott, or hurt Scott.

What if one of the women testifies that Scott Peterson didn't want children in his life? No idea what those other women will say, but, if so, that's powerful.

The defendant has right to speedy trial and hasn't waived those rights, so we're ready to go ahead with trial right away.

I've said even a junior prosecutor could have won the O.J. case anywhere, except in Los Angeles. Scott is felony stupid with what he's said and done. Remember, four hundred witnesses on the prosecutor's witness list.

Prosecution has a right to appeal the decision, but the judge was right to move the trial, cause you still have all the pretrial publicity. [Death penalty jury?] Absolutely. That knocks out alot of jurors, and won't be a liberal jury.

Extraordinary amount of information in the Scott Peterson case, and when all said and done, we'll see alot more evidence. Michael Jackson; probably guilty. Kobe Bryant; never should have been charged. Maybe dismissed before going to trial, or if trial, acquitted. Scott Peterson; the easiest for the prosecution to try and will be found guilty. I'd love to be in the middle of this.

Absolutely gagged by the judge [Geragos]. Every time Geragos comes out of the courtroom in the Scott Peterson case, he talks to the cameras. Leaks could have come from anywhere. Won't find where leak came from. Geragos is more skilled with the media than the prosecutor.

Not a huge secret at this point. Won't be dismissed tomorrow. Saddam Hussein has better chance to be released, with an apology from the American people. Rather thin physical evidence. Be interesting to see what theory prosecution uses. Geragos will use the O.J. defense.

GPS puts Scott a couple miles from where bodies found. There's a window of time, where Scott wasn't answering his phone and calls went to voice mail, so there's some explaining to do there. Geragos is putting too much weight on the baby's age.

Right, and it's something for people to think about. The scene, blood; it's stuff you see on CSI and people expect to find it. No cause of death, but we have manner; homicide. Have girlfriend, neighbors, lies, says golfing, when he was fishing, license to fish on December 23rd and December 24th, no one knew he had boat, a deliberate liar, lied to Diane Sawyer on TV. She didn't commit suicide; she didn't jump off the boat.

It's unethical for Geragos to say he can save the money if in one place and not another. Either he needs the money for a fair trial or he doesn't.

[San Mateo] Republican, so be careful Mark, on what you ask for, cause you might just get it. What's interesting is that Geragos almost threatened the judge to get him to move it. He tried to use it as a club. Each side has one challenge, to say they don't like the judge picked.

Jury selection will take longer, cause millionaires don't have time to sit on a jury.

Liberal side out there. Defense may think they have a good jury pool. Jury will look beyond speculation. Not a jurisdiction that's necessarily friendly to defendants or defense lawyers.

Today was a big win for the prosecution. Doesn't have police mistrust the way others do. This could scare the Jesus out of him. They solicited for the trial. They won't want to be the community who set Scott Peterson free, but the place that hung Scott Peterson. This is one of those where, be careful what you ask for, cause you might just get it. He's gonna get a jury that he's not very happy with.

If the defense hadn't made motion for change of venue, we'd be having it here, but that was his choice.

His fleeing, is consciousness of guilt. [Movie about Scott] What Amber's concerned about is the effect on the potential jury. Example of inaccuracy; where Scott is appearing to tell Amber

Laci is missing, and portrays it after Laci is missing, with where he said he had lost his wife.

[Government tapes of Scott and his lawyer] So what, a few tapes out of many. So toss those out and bring in the rest. Yea, and when police asked for something of Laci's so the dogs could track her scent, like sunglasses, Scott asked the police for a receipt. Come On! Your wife is missing and you want a receipt for the items that may help find her?

I'd want to know, as a juror, that he saw Laci's ghost, so as to get those guilty feelings off his mind. I don't know if you heard or not, but the ghost is on Larry King tonight. Who cares? He had $15,000 and on the Mexican border. He has a micro chance of being acquitted.

Yea, looks like it. After Peterson gets convicted, who's gonna want Geragos to come to Santa Barbara to defend them?

[Jurors] Shows how low the standard is in California. No chance. Jury will be picked soon. Defense needs just one juror to say circumstantial evidence isn't enough to give death penalty and vote not to convict. He's not really expecting to get another change of venue, he's just hoping he'll get more peremptory challenges [dismissed without having to give an explanation] of jurors.

The hypnosis expert [prosecution] wasn't licensed, but the police didn't know. The jurors are pretty removed from the case publicity.

There's no smoking gun piece of evidence. Tomorrow, for the first time, we'll hear what the prosecutor's circumstantial evidence is. Defense can lay back and say they don't add up; or pick a theory, like she was picked up by three people.

[Sharon Rocha lost suit] Yea, but to keep items of the estate, and there really isn't much left, everything's pretty much gone, to pay for Scott's defense.

You'd think they could come up with jurors without a connection to the case. Geragos' strategy is that he doesn't have a burden to prove anything, irregular that most of America thinks Scott is guilty. If Amber turns out to be motive, that'll be important to the jury.

50% don't have their wife end up murdered. He didn't just say he lost his wife, he said he'd be able to be with Amber after January 25th-26th. Much of what Amber's testifying to, will be corroborated, by other witnesses. And don't believe Laci wouldn't tell her Mom of an affair, that's unbelievable; that's illogical; it's just not real.

We have location, location, location, and it isn't a coincidence. We have a guy very comfortable with lying. Everything he's done and said is relevant. All these little knit-pickin issues, we can argue about.

SCOTT PETERSON'S TRIAL BEGINS

Not having any physical or forensic evidence in this case is very surmountable in this case with circumstantial evidence. It's Geragos' job to case doubt on the cause of death, [laughs], it's his job... [Prosecutor didn't say Scott was guilty of murder.] Well, he was being a gentleman.

I'd like to see Geragos deal with why that body was found there in that Bay, the $64,000 question. He's going to have to appeal to the jury's common sense and have it make sense. The judge will instruct the jury to rely on their common sense. The leading cause of death for pregnant women, is the husband.

That's Geragos' whole case, to go after the police. The prosecutor got caught in a lie, saying someone else was lying. Geragos has to make the jury believe that someone planted the body where he went fishing. He was out playing golf while his wife missing? You'd think he'd be camping out at the police station. And Geragos, he'll, he will get killed on the baby being born alive thing.

Very seldom do you hear; this is what will convict him. The twine was around the arm and the tape around the neck. Has anyone asked why Dr. Wecht isn't testifying, he was hired by Mark Geragos and gave Geragos some information he didn't like.

The maid said every time she saw Laci, Laci had on black pants and a white shirt. That's not really the issue. It was a relationship to Amber. He continued this long relationship on the phone with Amber. A prayer vigil for Laci, and he's on the phone with Amber. If Scott didn't have feelings for Amber, why would he continue the relationship. Bring on the family witnesses, show how he lied.

I'm like the prosecutor, I want the 'real' guy who's the killer.

All waist bands are the same with pregnant pants, if they're tan, she was murdered on December 23rd and not December 24th. Where's the question on that? With the blinds down, that shows Laci wasn't there on December 24th to raise them.

Geragos is a master of spin. *Here Laci is 8½ months pregnant and carrying $100 worth of groceries. That's alot of groceries, where's Scott? Laci only bought a few groceries, which proves she was tired and didn't want to carry alot of stuff.*

The prosecutor is trying to show the chronology of Laci, right up to the point of Laci missing. If all Geragos has is marmalade, then all he has is hot air. Can't predict how a trial can go. May need them. The jury came out today with she was tired, she was tired, she was tired, witness after witness. This shows that she was too tired to walk the dog the next day.

It won't matter at the end of the day. The facts will be important and not whether it was taken down wrong.

Laci didn't know of Scott's affair. He's the worst kind of a criminal defendant, and I wouldn't want him as a client. This is 4 witnesses so far, that testified that Scott told them he had played golf and not that he'd went fishing.

I disagree with Ted, she called back the police and told them she had got it wrong at first.

This afternoon, it was sad, the only people there for Scott were his parents. There were empty seats. Susan [Scott's neighbor] said Scott cried when he came and talked to her about Laci. They didn't give a date this happened.

We know Laci disappeared by 10:18 and the time line. People want to know why Scott wasn't involved in the search.

When the jury left the courtroom today, they did not look at Scott Peterson. ***That's because they were embarrassed, cause we called them on it the other day when they did.***

The last time Scott cried was December 9th when he sat down with Amber and said he lost his wife, so we know he can cry on demand. The prosecutor will seek to introduce the interview of Scott with Diane Sawyer. A number of people on the jury was taking notes when the testimony was that Scott wasn't....

Geragos really got after the lady who changed her time from 10:3? to 10:18, and asked her if she thought Geragos was the one who sicked the Globe on her.

I don't think vacuuming the house is the first thing on your mind with your wife missing. What? If the bad guys turn her loose and she comes home, she's gonna be mad if the house is dirty?

[Broke into home and took Laci?] I wouldn't want to be Geragos on this one. Maybe they cleaned the jewelry for the Peterson's while they were there. It's the small parts coming together; let's look at the Colombo moments.

[Detective Brocchini and Mark Fuhrman effect?] Don't think so. You know, when you don't have a defense, you first go after the prosecutor, then the police, and then the judge.

Section Three

TV Guest Experts

People make mistakes, misinterpret things. It's rare for a satanic cult to kill someone, after all, if they did, we'd hear more about it. Why did it just stop with Laci Peterson?

Cameras distort the image to where is doesn't seem real. The camera affect depends on the personalities involved and may influence the jury. It may affect the jury's decision on what to decide, if they feel pressured because of the cameras. His action in court was bizarre and have people asking if this guy is innocent.

Thc prosecution expert says the baby was near term [nine months]. The x-ray shows growth points and then is compared to sonogram. Don't know if x-ray will show much if there's no external injury. 12/20 sonogram, and x-ray and they'll be a disagreement between the defense and prosecution on age; there are variations. Age would help corroborate eye witness accounts of seeing Laci. The x-ray is better age determinate and shows abnormalities. The autopsy; thirty-five to thirty -seven weeks old and this is by prosecution experts.

They [dogs] are wrong many times; sometimes no where near where the body is found. They're not as good at bodies, as drugs, and can't cross exam them.

Emotions fade and you get a trial without so much emotion. We know that a person's memory can be enhanced or changed by watching TV, so it may not be accurate. It concerns me that he's getting a public trial, and the effects on a fair trial.

It's far cry for help. He has a strained voice, but no water. There's no grief, nothing. No question from Scott on who did this. On January 24th, Amber claims Scott called her. Scott won't waste this time on a relevant question. He didn't defend himself. He's robo. He's asking the public to help, but he's not. It's what he doesn't say that counts. He didn't look at the cell phone when it rang, he just turned it off. He didn't flinch when it went off. He's a pro. Now that I know he had the questions before the interview; Oh, that makes a big difference.

They are the best there are. They won't say anything that isn't true. If she had a cup of coffee one hour or two before death, it would still show up in her and not necessarily in Conner. Can't tell when she had coffee, or chocolate or something with caffeine. A red herring on caffeine. Hard to find GHB, almost impossible with decomposition.

The dive team probably looking for weights, cinder blocks. Scott had a stack of cinder blocks at home, with some missing.

Did he mention $10,000 for murder? No. I met Cory, he had alot of information; in mid-November, later November, he met Scott and Scott wanted to know if there's anybody to steal a car? No problem. Yes, he exchanged phone numbers with Scott. Later in November, Scott called Cory, after 11/25 or 11/29. Any deception? He wasn't hooked up yet. He continued with the story. He met Dirty and Skeeter; met at the restaurant, then to Cory's motel room. Cory was paid $300 for introducing the men to Scott. First to steal car, then kidnap and Cory left; nothing to do with it.

Lie? No indication of lying. Did he lie about stealing car? Lie about introducing them? Lie about kidnapping? I believe he believes what he said is true. We report it to the police and let them do what is needed. Yes, he passed. Three grades: lie; pass; and deception. I wanted to clarify the names, but I didn't. Cory says he, Scott, and a female took a picture, but he said the girl kept it. Doesn't make sense. I didn't clarify this either. He gave names and addresses.

Autopsy rules that out. Came out after in water for months; out of womb. Wasn't tested for caffeine in fetus.

I didn't ask Cory if he was on lock-down while on the polygraph. Spent two and one-half hours with him; information needs to be investigated; don't know if truth or not, but he believes it. Satisfy yourself if true or not. It doesn't concern me if he was watching news or not; let's get to the truth, I'm not God, if polygraph was wrong, let's find out, recommend that another polygraph be given.

The lady who saw Laci and won't take a polygraph, yet police say Laci killed on 12/23-12/24, and yet lady may well pass polygraph.

There were no questions on money asked, no discussion of money offer. Every question, Cory had a logical answer. Two and one-half hours; everything I asked. He impressed me, in all my years, he's probably the only one I couldn't trip up.

Dogs can do amazing things. If Scott transported the body to the Bay, obviously the body would be on the boat. Alot of things lend guilt; don't know. The overwhelming evidence came by means of pushing Scott by the prosecutor. Have to show motive; Amber's enough for that.

Hair is critical evidence to case, reliable science; admitted to twelve states now. Laci was never known to be on the boat Scott purchased the first of December. Can clean boat, and if in plastic bags, not have scent, not decisive.

Person who kills spouse isn't thinking clearly. Only takes a brief moment, an impulsive act; child could have provoked it.

Odor from body, cadaver dogs vary in ability. Better at looking for a body, if body on move, hard to tell. Many people use plastic bags when fishing, when leave bags, odor leaves.

If dismemberment, tool marks left. That hair puts Laci on the boat. Scott could have had it on his clothes and that got it onto the boat; but it was found on the pliers; now true, there is no root on it. There are some people with the same DNA. Was the hair tampered with? We can tell with forensics.

Some do lie to get on a jury. Not all jurors will tell the truth. They'll tell what they think you want to hear during voir dire. [Voir dire is French for, to speak the truth.]

Police, with forensics, will be able to tell ID that's the exact same paint. Make sure you put your spin on it.

Dogs; Can't put dog on stand, just handler, and some overstep bounds of science. Can't talk about case. All evidence should be shown. Research the background, public records, something to impeach her character.

Mitochondria DNA has been established one out of 100; 150. If on pliers and pliers came from home, or on his clothes, that explains it, and not much that Laci was in boat. Prosecutor still must concede, no cause of death yet. Mitochondria DNA comes from the Mom. Her, Laci; siblings of both will have the same mito DNA. The pliers could have come from the home, the hair from Scott's clothes. Laci could have also committed suicide. All the defense needs is one juror with reasonable doubt. Yea, it's been accepted in all jurisdictions for years and just a defense ploy.

Originally people thought Scott guilty and that's hard to change, but some believe what's most recently revealed. Allred helps Amber look fragile and vulnerable.

Mitochondria DNA not as precise as nuclear DNA. If same as Mom, sister, then it has some value. She had a cup of coffee that morning, caffeine in Laci, not looked for in Conner. Coffee hours before death.

Not permitted to talk directly about the case, but can on mitochondria DNA. It's not scientifically precise, must be very careful, not all DNA labs can do it. Sure, just as with blood.

Not just use for exclusion of people, if only one in one hundred and fifty-nine have the profile, and if only one of one hundred and fifty-nine in the boat, it's very powerful.

Autopsy report by the medical examiner and others, the size is given, with the gestational age and a December 23rd sonogram, with a margin of error; thirty-four to thirty-eight weeks?

[No sonogram] If you say it, you're never wrong. I don't know. You've just told me something I didn't know.

Mitochondria to show similarity, no ID. Even if prove Laci's hair, doesn't prove Scott killed her; that's a quantum leap. She mentioned those convicted, well then we look at jury and question why. Secondary transfer, lose fifty hair every day. Find hundreds, sometimes thousands hair at crime scene. Don't know when trial, but give time for evidence and let evidence speak for itself.

What's interesting is what brought police to Conner's body; a dog brought a femur bone [from someone else's body].

Hair; maybe when boat was at the house; police treated this as murder from the first day, before Amber. They had to have something from someone. Yes, but most come back. Police usually wait forty-eight to seventy-two hours on deciding murder with a disappearance. Mitochondria DNA never rejected in a court, yet. But hair not important. Police were suspicious right away, so there's something else.

Geragos should have his very own reality show; he's very good and Scott is lucky to have him.

Impossible to tell time of death. Agree, family doesn't use those words, always positive words. No emotion from Scott that his wife is dead. Makes him look guilty. Scott's behavior is bizarre from the beginning. Not typical behavior.

Marina; not lighted, can't do it at night; in day, people could see what's going on. People come and go from the marina unexpectedly.

Can't clean blood, it leaves a pattern, even if use bleach. One part blood plus millions of liquid; still detect blood. Two hundred scenes and is some residue, even in bleach. Some people smell bleach easy, some not. Don't know what's in the ninety bags of evidence from the house. Mito DNA, much less exclusion ratio. I've heard many billions used and not that many people ever populated the Earth.

Not with Laci's personality to wear clothes two days. Some of Scott's lies are bigger than others. Went out in a small boat, wrong time of the day to fish. There's a pattern of deception here. Future jurors are watching on TV. Women writing him are desperate.

Hair important, defense won't win. There's alot of other evidence; duct tape may have a fingerprint; paint on boat. Well that would be compelling evidence. We've heard of people putting the tape in their mouth to tear it and leaving DNA on the tape. Still don't know where the hair came from.

Very difficult to launch a boat from here and not be seen. Look at pattern, cloth, and adhesive. Can determine manufacturer of the tape; different manufacturers; different cloths; adhesive. Would be similar in the whole roll. Analyze for similarity, reasonable certainty; can't give a percentage of odds. Difference in science and criminal justice system.

Mitochondria DNA isn't one hundred percent, but can use with Amber [Laci], duct tape and circumstance; then likely hair is someone else's and how it got there is something else. Impossible after dark to launch a boat and if body in the boat, would have been seen. Maybe establish alibi and. Can't do it in the dark; can't, I've been there.

Be interesting to see if find Scott's fingerprint on poster or tape and then if find fingerprint on tape from being in water long time, and see if tape match up. Fiber could be same, adhesive sometime change. Can't comment on evidence of case. Maybe not testify. Need open mind, objective; doesn't matter who hires me, tell them what I find. Once, Johnnie going to strangle me in O.J. case, cause I say DNA okay and I almost became a prosecution witness. Other witness saw Laci walking, 10am to 10:30. Ninety-six bags of evidence; one thousand pieces, but how many link suspect to case is crucial.

Weights would stay in place, body would sway and free itself. To look on the boat. Scott talking to his attorney in court, not a good idea. Rug should be looked at; blood, hairs, maybe police have it. No cause of death; don't know where murdered; neighbors saw her after the prosecution says the murder occurred.

He could fish for sturgeon, towards Brooks Island, where he told police he was going. The baby was found a day earlier than Mom. Wash up near each other, so it takes away the theory of being born.

Scott lying, lying, lying just shows arrogance. When he called Laci's Mom and the first thing said was Laci missing; didn't even ask if Laci was there. He's making too many changes in his life to make rational decisions.

Need evidence on the bucket. Cadaver dogs good at living people also. Any duct tape at the warehouse, bags, fibers in the boat? Where did pliers come from? Hair could break; lab could tell. Measure when first come in, if mito DNA same, it's same. What's the difference in two hairs or one hair? Question is, did the detective pick up the hair on clothes from homes and get deposited there.

Could find prints on the strap, soil on leash and tell where been. Police are forced to retire from homicide; age fifty or so. Younger ones learn from own mistakes. Very little planting of evidence by police.

Very difficult to pick a jury for him. Scott never mentions his son, always Laci, never the child.

Mitochondria DNA comes from the Mom. Only seven or eight labs in the U.S. set up for mito DNA. Only fifteen states accept. If done properly, can/has been used. Different mito DNA results from the same hair; depends on where the sequence begins. See if Scott Peterson is held over, before thinking of testifying.

Not good, says he likes the idea of being a widower; free from marriage to go to extent of murdering wife? Not grieving like one would. He's quite happy, calls girlfriend. Suppose possible, but it says something about his character. Fantasize about killing wife, beforehand. The defense wants to know who went in, who rolled around on the bed.

Mitochondria DNA never bounced from court yet. May be hair from Mom or sister, all kinds of ways it got there. All prosecution is working on, is how Scott got rid of the body and not how killed. Not a slam dunk.

If Amber recorded calls as of December 16th, 2002, she's suspicious. Has a history of dating married men, so she was protecting herself, maybe. Could be consciousness of guilt. Different story, depends on who hears it, and who's saying it; depends on how it's interpreted.

Would have to do that first, cause mitochondria DNA test destroys the hair. Amazing that a detective can go to an evidence locker, without signing in, and take the hair out of the evidence seal, and look at. He doesn't know what he's looking at with a magnifying glass.

No single way for people to grieve, seen hundreds, and all different. Cross exam of the medical examiner interesting; different age of Laci and baby idea. No known cause of death.

Can't look at two hairs and tell if from same person. If a witness says so, it's absolutely false. [Rusty pliers] Have to ask those experts. Contact between people causes transfer of DNA.

Pathologist can make determination of fetus age within couple weeks of age. Read the autopsy report on size of baby, and how the medical examiner characterizes the baby. If died after Laci, means the child was alive after Laci. Some five pounds, some nine pounds; the same age. My evaluation, Conner in excellent condition, and Laci in very bad condition. With no cause, no mechanism, no time, no place, of death, so it's almost impossible to determine the manner of death; generically speaking.

[No C-section, no vaginal birth, so only thing left is tissue breakdown and baby is expelled underwater.] I get a kick out of an attorney taking a possibility and a non-probability and making it so. It's a difficult case. The forensic pathologist was there, he's an excellent doctor. They have past sonograms; science, as opposed to what's being argued by some on the panel.

Agree; Scott choreographed his out of courtroom. He'd be talked about. He's not a great actor. It keeps his character in tact. Needs to rehabilitate his image. Amber is the star witness, show how she was a victim and she just happened to survive to tell about it.

No way to tell if Conner had air in his lungs, decomposition. I agree with doctor that the baby in the uterus womb until couple days of being washed up. Defense will raise baby's age, if lived past December 24th, Scott couldn't have done it. Too much overlap and imprecise tools to determine age.

Water, debris, fish, boats. Durst case had alot more evidence than here. Where'd she die? Jurisdiction issue? Legal issue? And if prosecution can't prove death occurred in his county?

Blood in bathtub is easily gotten rid of; just keep.... Separate the joints. Nobody noticed a body in the boat, cause it was in separate bags. Mop could have been cleaned, but may be blood on the handle, if there. Some convicted with less evidence and some found not guilty with more evidence.

Phone calls damning, yes, lying to another woman and his wife. Locate cell phone, even if just on, and no calls made, as it passes cell phone towers. Only evidence is the hair, very weak evidence. The prosecution must use the evidence, and not passion.

A hundred and thirty exonerations: first, false eyewitnesses; second, hair evidence. Hair of Mom, sister, have same hair. The detective could have brought it there on his clothes. The detective broke the chain of evidence by not having a lab person there, in the evidence room.

The prosecutor didn't make a very strong case. What if they had removed the staircase in the Michael Peterson case. Yea, like we have to live here, so we'll clean it up. OH, Come ON! Ha, Ha, Ha. So, where are the golf clubs? Yea, let's forget he's a liar and a smug person. Not right for Scott to profit off anything relating to the crime. Makes him look really criminal with the jury. Amber a woman who is driven to men. She's going to present a problem to the jury. His behavior is unusual. Behavior adds up to mischief.

Could Laci swim? Would she follow Scott? Has Scott been tested for being a psychopath? There's a test, but they can trick the test.

Entirely speculative. Pillow case found two months later. No cause of death. Suffocation probably the hardest cause to name. He told Amber his wife was missing and then....

[Tentative decision for change of venue.] Very disrespectful, without hearing the arguments. We see Scott Peterson sitting there smiling and laughing with Geragos, and I think he hurts his chance with a jury, when he wasn't even able to work up an emotion or tear for his wife while she was missing. Farther away; less exposure. Arguing that Scott's Mom is sick and while Laci's Mom sits there suffering every day is disingenuous. Makes a difference on where it is. It's a better move for Geragos.

Conservative area, different venue from Modesto itself. Excellent choice; given other areas. Alot more democrats up there. Very reluctant to dole out the death penalty. Let's remember the O.J. case. That case set the tone for a judge. The judge is critical to the outcome of the case. [San Mateo] Wealthy, somewhat liberal, tends to vote republican.

Remember, I was one of the first to say Scott Peterson was guilty, and low and behold, two months later, he was arrested and I think he'll be convicted.

Police concentrate on a suspect and overlook evidence, sometimes on purpose, as with the knife in the Fugitive case, where a bloody knife was found in the water, not far from the murder scene.

SCOTT PETERSON'S TRIAL BEGINS

I've been to so many missing person cases and never have I seen where the reporting person can't answer basic questions, like the kind of fish. Detective Brocchini seeks the truth, he's not out there to rush to judgment and make an arrest.

It's not enough to talk about womanizing.

Boyfriends think of abortion during the first month of a pregnancy, but a husband will wait until the last month, and say this is the last straw, and I've gotta get rid of it. That's gonna be the motive. He didn't want a kid.

If born alive, that would bolster it. Prosecution will say picked up in water and not done with human hands. Micro studies to find if baby died, or other natural process. These things are what the experts will get into in this case. It can be mistaken, when looking at height and weight measurements, but don't know about if when doing tests.

He has different stories. Don't care much about loving. Said Amber's child will be enough for him and he didn't want a child. Doesn't sound very loving to me.

I think he's guilty. What is she wearing, have to do with it? The location of the body. I'd have put several GPS devices in the water and let them float for 4 months and show the jury where they ended up.

I can't see making six anchors, it'd take 3-4 days, No, HUt-uh, I ain't buying that. He'd use chains, rocks, whatever. I don't throw too much weight on the Amber Frey thing; two dates. I can write you a whole book on pickup lines. It will get sympathy from the girl, immediately.

Here in Chicago, within the last two years, people are in jail for cutting baby out of a pregnant woman's stomach. Decomposition can remove any trace of the baby being alive.

The defense may want to be concerned, cause if one of the jurors is establishing a relation with one of the victim's brothers.... [Juror No.5] Yea, sounds like it wasn't much and the judge wouldn't take a chance on a mistrial if anything to it.

The more the prosecution puts out as a question, the more it may be pushing Scott Peterson to have to take the stand to explain. These friends may be shown to place suspicion on Scott. His cold behavior may be what the jury wants him to explain that.

[The pawn shop receipt] He'll have to show it in court, cause it would be a problem for Geragos if he doesn't. He can't just throw it out and not explain, cause the jury will want to know.

[Sex stuff on computer?] Research shows that 30% of guys are aroused by physical torture of women.

Section Four

TV Guest Defense

Suspicion and rumor will become charges and a conviction, with media coverage of pretrial events.

Well, if you don't look at them, you probably won't find it either. This puts them under the gag order. The baby can't live when the Mom's oxygen is cut off.

Your only slightly presumed innocent, and you have to prove your innocent. The prosecutor is hypnotizing witness to remember if they took a walk or not. Over fifty percent of the public believes he is guilty, without any evidence. Two people saw Laci after she's supposed to be dead.

[Amber tape] Can't take this out of context. If this was a real confession, he'd have been arrested immediately. We have two trials in America; American Public and Media, then the real trial.

Age is critical. Age is critical.

Amber's trying to put words in his mouth. Quote is, "Yes, uh uh but no."

[Magazine article] It doesn't mean Scott did it. Doesn't mean he did it. Discovery, He can't buy People's Magazine or the Enquirer. The gag order don't work. This may help his case; there may be evidence the baby was born. The only physical evidence is a hair on the pliers in the boat. Both were alive, four to five weeks after their abduction.

[Delay] No, not at all. You have to attend other trials.

[Dogs] You can't use the tools of investigation as evidence. We got dogs, GPS, hypnosis; Look at this, People. GPS goes blank when it can't see the satellite.

He's still alive; lost baby, lost freedom; what more could a man lose? A delay hurts Peterson. He's better served if the preliminary hearing is next week. The defense continues a case for good reason.

The dog tracked Laci three miles down the road, then backed up and followed to the car. The handler will say dog led him to Laci getting into the car.

Laci may have been alive two to six weeks after being abducted and police failed to follow up on leads that began coming in hours after she was missing. The police focused on Scott and didn't want anything to get in the way of their scenario.

The volume of discovery we just got from the prosecution prohibits us from going forward at this time.

He was on his way back; Headed North. He'd already been to Mexico and was back. Remember?

[Many affairs] Nobody wants this in. They want a better spin than just killing his wife. Many of us carry on affairs and don't kill our wife. It'll be more successful at keeping out seven affairs, than one.

The prosecution is trying to deflect what the defense says, and negate witness for the defense. Hypnosis tells you you're a dog and you bark. Hypnosis ain't a slam dunk case.

The article says it comes from the police. What harm to jury pool? This pollutes the jury pool; no cause of death; no time; no weapon, yet the majority thinks he's guilty. I didn't read the article as a fingerprint of Scott, but, so newspapers can say he's guilty. It was in the water for a long time; no creditability to the story. If, if, if, equals speculation; if they match the tape; if they match the tarp; if they match the fingerprint. They could match the duct tape to tape in your house. It has to be a one hundred percent match on a fingerprint. Very tough to believe; in the water for a long time.

The hypnosis will be challenged. Everybody wants to be a witness in this case. People under hypnosis can lie and be influenced.

The fingerprint is probably elongated and hard to connect. They found out in the last five years, fingerprinting is an invention of crime labs to get a conviction. Some countries don't allow fingerprints if there is one point difference; others say if there's one-in-five are different, can't use. Wait and see what evidence they find.

[Trench coat] It's inadmissible as evidence. No link to Laci or Scott.

How do you know she was killed in Modesto? The defense has an obligation to investigate it. It depends on what side your on, as to what's said in thought. This is a dead story. Who has the motive to leak this. The inmate wants police protection and be in the public media. This is as worthless as Enron stock.

Depends on information he has on Scott; could get it anywhere. Assume they met and Scott wanted to get rid of car. The story has changed since it first broke; first car, now kidnap, then two guys involved. I was told two weeks ago, by Muna, something would break, at a conference, but he said he was under a gag order. Why a gag order then, and not now. He said from a jailhouse snitch and he'll get something in return.

It's not a popularity contest. Experts will say it does pass on to the fetus. Pregnant women are told not to take caffeine. It may show separation from the Mom. We don't know how much caffeine was found. The suggestion is the child was born.

It's a floating junkyard in the Bay. They're desperate. Not a slam dunk case. Desperately diving for evidence.

Biggest con here. You know what happens to rats in prison. Jury would only take fifteen minutes on this one [acquit]. Story won't check out. It's stupid. Waits till now to come forward. If charged with conspiracy, Geragos would be delighted. Bring 'em in and let 'em testify. Scott didn't solicit them. Think you'd go to a bar and solicit murder of wife? There's a slew of jailhouse witnesses.

No credibility to story. Listen to lawyer. Tonight he said before 11/29, but before it was a couple of days after 11/29. Get the transcripts and compare them. This attorney gives lawyers a bad name. A neo-nazi gang? He's a dead man walking. He was in a jail house day room, saw the story and said this is my way out.

She [Amber] won't sue. Make his day. Gloria won't sue. He said he has the release. Amber thought somebody would look at them; she didn't take them so she could look at them herself.

You'd want him in on it before the murder, not after. Story parallels Geragos' defense, of two guys in a van. Geragos' defense dovetails the prosecution case, maybe. Content is missing ingredient; premise for motive. Other women he was involved with and didn't kill wife. She's not that big of an issue. Don't know if Amber will testify at the prelim.

Muna should take a polygraph himself. Maybe should check to see if this guy's really a lawyer. Sounds like these three guys killed Laci and trying to blame it on Scott. You can't disclose information, like Muna has about your client. You might as well go down and turn in your law license.

Natural to be stressful when family is facing Scott with death. Usually take it out on the attorney.

They'll have to put some evidence on at the prelim. Their theory is she was killed in the house on 12/23.

Scott was on TV for six days, 12/25-12/31, every day and hour. Amber called the police on 12/31, and yet she says she didn't know Scott was married. What? She didn't turn on the TV one time and she claims she didn't know. Scott called Amber four times on 12/25.

Can't imagine prosecutor using Cory's information, always looking for deal for self. Dangerous for prosecutor to use, cause it'll show they have other suspects. You have faith in Muna? Department of Corrections said Cory wasn't in lock-down. If she knew Scott, why didn't she come forward? All she knows is Scott met Cory.

We weren't light on Muna; he's a lunatic; said she was a she; said 11/29, then changed it. Why didn't she go to the police, instead of a declaration? Not giving the information early on, makes it unreliable. There's nothing physical to connect Scott with Fresno, and his family says he was with them; the sister.

No preservation of bones. Maybe show how separated. Doubt if they find any other evidence. Found bones in the Levy case much later. Okay to challenge evidence, if unscientific; must collect, store, and handle correctly; and patrol officer doesn't wear gloves.

File motions to question evidence and they become public. Not done for that, but to check evidence to see if reliable or not.

He didn't try to register it in Mom's name. He didn't want notoriety using his own name to buy a car.

Not desperation; doing what supposed to do. Hypnosis isn't reliable; all kinds of rules; it's a good motion. Everybody says one hair, lab, cops, etc., one hair. The two detectives pulled out the pliers without any company, and now there's two hairs. The original hair was five inches; and now if there's two hairs, two and a half inches, there's some explaining to do. May be in trouble. Move to suppress at the preliminary hearing; why one, now two; probably from hair brush. Pliers didn't kill her.

Scorned woman, Amber, she's more on the phone than affair.

Critical; no evidence he put her in the boat and dropped in the Bay; but the hair. Still won't carry the day. Hair not the lynchpin for anything; they were married. If this is all they have, then the prosecutor is in trouble.

Who said looking for wife? Maybe with family; sister. The criminal evidence against Scott wouldn't make it to a jury. They can't say how, when, where. Mark Geragos believes one hundred percent that Scott Peterson is innocent.

There are dog evidence standards in California; the defense questions this. Evidence of phone calls. Go over all, how died, when died. So many questions, the preliminary hearing is necessary. Prosecutor will give Amber a dry run, put tapes on to stop rumors. Geragos would get to cross exam Amber.

He's on trial for murder, how much can you rush him. Prosecutors are notorious for holding evidence until the last minute. So the prosecutor is going to try the case in the media? Absence of scent, no big deal to the prosecution; but why hide it? Why not up front?

No, other affairs too. Why not kill before. Amber has a child. He won't jump from one fire to another. He didn't say he did it; that he killed her. The prosecutors have to answer, when, where, why, how, and haven't. Why on Christmas eve? Media floats many of these theories. Many of the phone calls from Amber are while she's working for the police. At that moment, men are known to say alot of things. Doesn't mean you're a murderer.

The defense won't put up any witnesses; cross examine the prosecution's witnesses and learn. No physical evidence; nothing. Scott not so well versed to do that. Scent, would it have been there long enough? No alert, or the prosecutor would be jumping; as is, Geragos can....

Game, set, match. The story of Amber and the photographs will come out at the pretrial.

If the lead attorney isn't available, it won't go forward. California law says Scott gets his choice of attorney and a one day delay isn't much.

Just show crime took place and is related to Scott. Surprised prosecutor isn't using all the evidence. Prosecutor said he wanted a preliminary hearing rather than a grand jury so the public would know what's going on. Show enough to get the public on their side.

Dress affects demeanor. Now go to the heart of the prosecutor's evidence. The wiretaps may be gotten with false information by the police to the judge. Geragos leveled the playing field; everyone thought Scott was guilty and now everyone's asking, where's the evidence.

A gold mine for the defense to cross [examine] her. Don't need Amber to put on the tapes. The prosecutor here wants to show the world and not like the ones in the Kobe case. Geragos will question her till the judge says stop; bias, reward, pictures. Photos; money; wants the right to sell them later. She's in it for the money. Judge won't allow the question, but ask it anyway. Maybe the tapes are not harmful. Public only remembers bad things.

It's necessary to contest the hair DNA; mitochondria can have two people with the same DNA, it's not the same as nuclear DNA test. Can't exclude wife and then can't exclude girlfriend, so what does it say?

If killed in the house, there should be more evidence from inside the house. Challenge the wiretaps if not turned off when not investigating the case.

I love this jail bit; yea, he goes to jail and wants to confess. Yea, right, these bozos always want the prosecutor to cut them a break.

Take away credibility; falsehoods in life. Geragos won't be surprised; he's good. Be nice to have more facts.

Amber will be called; desperation by the prosecutor and if centered on Amber, they're desperate. Purpose is to prejudice public more. Don't need Amber to introduce the tapes. His conduct hurts him more than anything; but, if that's all they have. They need more to tell us how and why. Paint won't show alot. Hair on pliers, the defense claims it's tampered with.

Those part of the tapes won't come in. Amber was controlling him with police help. Only lurid details make her an interesting witness. Yea, what is the evidence Amber has? Has to be other evidence. They didn't have anything until the bodies washed up. Could just have been killed and dumped in that area.

Geragos could make more of it at trial. Hair, depends if fallen hair or pulled hair, with root or not.

Go after Amber some; book deal; called TV stations. Got to do it.

SCOTT'S PRELIMINARY HEARING BEGINS

Maybe a problem with the warrant and not helpful to the prosecution, or hide their cards till later. No case law in California with mitochondria DNA; not an appellate court. Why not; the prosecutor's own brief says thirty-eight states don't allow it.

No history of violence in their lives. Still didn't get an answer from Gloria why she's in court; book deals.

Nothing she said is in evidence; not in any filing in court. It's disgraceful to go on national TV and say things like that. We've read the transcripts and not in there.

Not Allred versus Geragos, that's the problem with court today, no reason for Gloria to be there. To intimidate Geragos; to harass him. The prosecutor uses Act IV to begin, put Amber on the stand, sexy. The prosecutor in this case isn't brilliant. Wiretaps better than Frey; the defense may bring up the taps. Like he said, bombshell at trial, with the tapes. I'd cross Amber with the tapes till the cows come home.

Just say DNA and the jury believes he's guilty. The layman doesn't know anything about DNA. PR campaign at this point, a media play. Biggest thing defense has for it is how and who did it. If dismembered in home and all they have is pliers, the prosecution is in trouble. It's important to keep only scientific value to evidence, and not go beyond that.

Negative publicity against Scott has been a problem since the beginning. The preliminary hearing may counter it some. The defense hasn't had a chance to respond. The paint on the boat is the latest leak and it didn't come from the defense, and for the police it's a real problem. We'll see more leaks and from those who have nothing to do with the case.

The prosecutor will be forced to prove premeditation to kill his wife. Still don't know anything about her, yet. How long was the relationship before the disappearance? How many times seen? Suppose she misled Scot to keep him in the relationship.

Have alot of problems with the boat; highly unlikely; fourteen foot long, and try to transport a body in it. Where dismembered? If in house, can't clean it. May say bleach, but bleach won't clean blood.

Hair has nothing to do with death or cause of death. Good chance to keep out mitochondria DNA. Geragos is very informed. Science may be okay, but one hair into two, contaminated or not, hair is very, very, strong; handled rough; if others mixed in?

So many stories floated; if a hair, dogs, is all they have, they're in trouble. If they have more, they've gotta show some. People believe it, without buying it, just read the headline. Amber doesn't have a smoking gun, if so, Gloria would have told us and Scott would have been arrested sooner. No smoking gun out there; just assume he did it and go from there. Need a little more for murder.

Gloria said Amber doesn't think guilt or innocence, and he'd been arrested earlier. Don't know why they'd call the sister. The prosecutor hasn't made a case against Scott Peterson. Prosecutor is trying to make a case in public opinion with emotionalism. Blinds closed with Laci there helps the defense.

Strong case of suspicion, not a yacht, why tell in-laws. Can't say the hair belongs to Laci Peterson. Where'd the maid put the cleaning rags and mops. If call Amber, they don't know where, how, or who. They lack the smoking gun. The prosecutor hasn't shown a common theme. The defense just keeps poking holes in the bits of information.

Your time line is wrong; that's not what his ticket says. Don't know if Laci saw the boat, it ain't a house, other purchases. Amy said different clothes than what other eyewitnesses saw her in the next day. Sure, say poor witnesses, but they are credible. Mom says Laci active. [You're wrong.] You're wrong. How such a poor liar, get away with such a clean murder? He's either a mastermind or he didn't do it.

Mom also said Laci was active and Scott was active in the pregnancy with Laci. Easy to explain; married. Boat's not the smoking gun. Ninety percent of guys with an affair, leave the marriage and divorce, not murder. Friends say the marriage was the greatest. The prosecution wants to dirty up Peterson with past relation, but nothing in the past and it may backfire on them. Three days splitting a hair; can't ID the hair.

MacFarland said if from 3M, then it's 3M, that's all. The jury will despise Scott and convict with no evidence. Judge may exclude if they say the tape is the same as the other tape. Remember, used to be convictions on blood type. You're looking for missing wife and someone asks about fish. Detective debunked the bleach theory; significant for the defense, no freshly sanitized crime scene.

Mito DNA evidence; major questions of one hair into two hairs; who was there? How'd the hair get on the boat? Hair is awfully strong, and just broke? The defense still wins, cause the hair could get in the boat in a thousand ways; no blood or vomit on the mop, no cleanup. Where's all the evidence?

Difficult to defend someone that the public believes guilty. Scott is already guilty and Geragos is under a gag order. He has to cross exam, he must plant the seeds of doubt.

Planting evidence is possible. Mito DNA pass the test? May not be enough. Longer preliminary, the defense has to question the evidence. The prosecutor also wants the jury to know they have evidence. If a break in the prosecutor's chain, Peterson may go free. One mistake and a client could end up on death row.

Amber; no confession, a spurned lover, rejected, maybe he lied to her. Doesn't make him a killer. Circumstances; only to guilt, or to innocence?

Dr. [Henry] Lee is the best forensic expert on Earth.

Reason here to question police motives, police aren't infallible, not god-like as on TV. They're human beings. Same bias as others, once they make a judgment, they go after him. Police never back up and say they're wrong. Once a gag order, always comes from the prosecution. Geragos wouldn't hurt his own defense would he? There are potential jurors watching.

The dog's not strong for the prosecution; between 9 and 10:30; plenty of time for all the witnesses to be right, it's a common story and it fits. I have a glass eye; everybody has a spin, depends on own thoughts. No eyewitness here.

Why is not the accused able to proclaim their innocence? Why not jump up, holler. Plead not guilty, and sit down. Perception becomes reality. If the officer is saying things, not so, well, the defendant was there, so he knows, and help is welcomed from the defendant.

There's no jury now, so you can do more on cross exam with Amber now. For thirty days they know each other; see each other maybe five times; no promises from Scott; no future with Scott. Amber is not that relevant; speculation, relation not important, unless he told her something.

Why not Laci herself move the bucket? She was there. What piece of puzzle? Clearly Scott was a suspect; first one to look at. Why not go back the next day to look at the warehouse? Critical that he didn't write it in his report.

Gloria said drug body; no evidence of that. They develop an interest in a person and then police credibility is on the line. Evidence throughout the country that police plant evidence.

Zero on the bucket and pail, yet they already said they bleach smell, it's in the warrant. Four days of evidence, equals no murder by Scott Peterson. A soap opera or a murder investigation? You gotta open the door to get the body out, so that didn't cause a Scrunched rug.

Why not just say the marriage is over? Big deal, so he used an inappropriate word; not guilty and send him home. Circumstantial evidence can equal direct evidence, but not surpass it or be stronger. One hair, now two hairs, raises questions.

Fact is, Scott has an answer to this point. Strand of hair? Mops and a bucket misplaced? Need linkage to the defendant. Need more linkage to the defendant.

Scott's lies focus around the affair with Amber and he didn't trust police if they knew that. Police rummaging through his home. Know if they put luminal in the house and boat? Believe so, but not testified about yet. Presumably, police don't have blood DNA or they would have arrested earlier.

The FBI taped Scott and that's not turned over yet [to defense]. Geragos made a motion today. [Polygraph] The defense could use it to go to the prosecution and say, look, you've got the wrong man here. The defense told Scott not to take a polygraph, they're unreliable throughout the country.

How would you rate the prosecution's case today? If I did that, I'd violate the court order. Let me say this. Today was a very good day.

Test her now, without a jury, memory, etc. True, but different than when a jury is there. Geragos knows Gloria will have her client ready, not telling her what to say, but ready.

[Odd she was abducted, and found exact same place as fishing?] Not exact same place. If Scott is innocent and being questioned on December 24th, what relevance is the affair?

Nothing to do with the disappearance and he didn't want police to know of the affair. He was being surveillance by the FBI, knows he's being followed, so change of appearance means nothing.

Pliers with hair, from inside house, mop with bucket, pregnant and wanted outside, maybe something spilled during breakfast. Yea, we need more evidence.

[Fair jury?] Very difficult, voir dire and questionnaires, get to know them the best you can.

Police may have tested to see if fired; not in evidence at all. [Illegal gun?] Illegal to have locked in glove box, without a permit; not an illegal gun.

We don't know what went on, we're guessing. The bucket excludes itself. The prosecutor is asking the judge to bind Scott over without showing a murder.

It was a conscious decision by the family, Peterson, Rocha, etc., that I not speak to media, on purpose, to keep media coming back to ask me to talk and therefore keep attention on finding Laci. I wouldn't speak until absolutely necessary. This caused alot of accusations against me.

Detective should know of electricity, if off or on, from his investigation. Keystone Cops mentality.

Gloria is shifting the burden to the defendant. The prosecutor could have tested the swabs; should have; have separate test to see if the gun was fired, on the gun itself.

It's easier to look for Laci with Amber out in the open. Told Laci about the affair in early December. It's not right to defend myself on the affair while Laci is missing and take attention away from looking for her. Every tip is important. Left house about 9:30am, the dog was returned at 10:30am by the neighbor, with the leash on.

Seven days, a hair, rotten police work. Where's the When, and How? The defense's only concern now to overcome, how do objects travel in the Bay. Just because they end up there, doesn't mean where the bodies started from.

Remember, [Mark] Fuhrman or the other detective, pled guilty to perjury from the O.J. trial, and he was effectively off that case as lead detective by the time the gloves were even found. He leaves, and magically he finds a glove at O.J.'s? That case was entirely different than this one and don't say it doesn't happen; happens all the time.

Go back to DNA tomorrow, then another detective. Amber does want the limelight; two press conferences [announcements] and hires a high caliber media savvy attorney to go on all the talk shows and keep Amber in the public light.

We haven't heard Geragos yet. A good shot at reasonable doubt. The defense is happy as kids on Christmas morning, to get to cross exam Amber. Unless Amber says Scott told her he would kill Laci, she has no relevance to probable cause.

With a jury, DNA makes jurors eyes glaze over and they say, just tell me who the DNA says it is. Need evidence, can't speculate. Look at the Durst case. It's not evidence of guilt, by the way a person acts. It must be guilt beyond a reasonable doubt. You say that you don't give the benefit of the doubt to the defendant, well you're wrong. Of course you presume innocence until proven guilty. You're right, I misspoke.

Difficult to get anything from the FBI; judge said to go pound sand. The prosecutor will have to respond. Surveillance didn't start until January, so nothing to do with Laci's disappearance. Don't know yet. Peterson's home broken into, police stalling on that; was evidence taken? Ten months after the incident and the defense still doesn't have all the discovery from the prosecutor.

Probably illegal to tape. Ask Gloria if her client illegally taped. [One party consent rule.] No, no, no. She's taping him; and says something about her character. Don't know, we'll have to hear it. Means the relation wasn't so strong with Amber; by her anyway.

[Surveillance equipment] We don't know what the documents say, cause we have to subpoena them. Once we get them, so we can read them. Then we'll know what they say. At some point, somebody's got to get on the stand and explain the equipment.

Don't agree; it puts the prosecution on the defense. He'll get it quickly; Modesto police with the equipment. The prosecutor says he didn't know about it, so what other exculpatory evidence may be out there. You said a drug issue; No, the DEA was involved because they have good equipment.

The burglary took place after cameras were set up and before the search warrant was issued in this case. Obviously, if it shows what was being carried in and what was being carried out.

Good likelihood he'll take the stand. Alot of people said that this fellow Durst, shouldn't testify either, and look what happened. Tend to think he won't take the stand, but that's because I don't believe that they have a very strong case.

They're trying to put my client to death....

Her background does matter. Have to test her memory. Defense attorneys defend people and the Constitution, you should try it sometime, Nancy. He can make reference to matters of public record and not to the weight of the evidence. They [prosecutors] have, with leaks. Character is a two edged sword.

[Scott said he knows of Laci's disappearance?] Let's see if it exists. By the time Scott had this conversation, the investigator of the attorney hired by Scott, already suspected Laci was dead.

Why does she have counsel? When he first talked to the police, Scott didn't want an affair public. Why not that Laci was passed out somewhere, or Laci was with friends and would return? The prosecution has to prove it, and the physical evidence isn't there. The prosecutor is trying to ride on the 'why' evidence, and right now, that's Amber Frey. They're not telling us how, or when.

Where are the tapes? Why weren't we told? The burglary was before the time the second search warrant issued. The burglary was after the camera was put up and before the second search warrant.

Now's the time to come out and speak, to get Laci's picture out there and get someone to find her. Now's the time for me to come out and ask for help. I've learned to do that over the past month.

Geragos trying to show police overzealous and it happens, as with other cases. The prosecution intentionally misled the court with the tapes. Geragos asked for the tapes, and the prosecutor said he didn't have them and said not aware of any testimony before a federal grand jury. The prosecutor has an obligation under *Brady* to look.

I'd say it's coaching, putting words in her mouth. They are getting her to act as a agent of the state; a scorned woman. They don't need Amber. November 20th, they meet. December 30th, goes to police. December 9th, Scott said lost his wife, but from November 20th to December 9th, wife doesn't come up?

[Surveillance] The prosecutor didn't disclose it to the defense. He's on trial for his life. State wants to put him to death. I agree that the tapes must be turned over to the defense.

Don't think they'll put Amber on. Not relevant to probable cause.

Either the worst liar in history, or a very smart killer. If didn't know it was a murder and listen to both sides, there'd be nothing wrong here; talking about dates, etc. Again, we're talking about what we're gonna hear. I'm waiting for the dogs to testify.

And want her to lie to Scott, yet the police complain Scott is lying to her. Police want both sides to lie, yet get evidence to convict, somehow. Prosecutor misplaces the case on the rug, buckets and mops, and hair. The prosecutor doesn't have the discretion on whether to turn over *Brady* information or not. The prosecutor, earlier, also said not aware of the audio tapes that were found.

Cults do happen. Cut a baby out of a woman's stomach, after he got her pregnant and the baby lived. It happens. The baby had tape on his neck.

Prosecutor doesn't have what they thought she has. Agree; keep her off the stand. With Amber, the prosecution's case goes south if she didn't hold up. Prosecutor has no major smoking gun; alot of inference.

What kind of police wouldn't follow up eye witnesses. Reported all over, that Scott went fishing and where. He knew he was being followed; proved it by talking to the cops. Prosecution doesn't have any more that Scott's behavior with Amber Frey and not much physical evidence.

Remember, the detective testified that they had been giving Amber theories and questions to ask; almost like she was an agent. Called Peterson tip line to see if Peterson reported it. These are why Amber may not have been called to testify.

Police want to exclude everybody and they haven't done it yet. Nothing yet has opened my eyes. Her purse and keys in the closet at home? Evidence jurors can seize on; when she walked the dog, she left the door open. The man who saw the dog is a wonderful witness. Others saw Laci too, and can't find the other woman who's pregnant that walked her dog. And Scott said Laci said she was gonna walk the dog.

Possibly, just because he's a cat, doesn't mean he's a murderer. If judge throws out, can he be recharged? Immediately, plus everything else. With media, how will Amber be kept from the jury? Wonderful question. Serious voir dire process; open mind?; and honest about it? Very careful, if someone is not honest, the whole system falls apart.

[Scott gave away Laci's jewelry?] Not in evidence, heard that, but the prosecutor makes statements through the press, or the press does it on their own, and it proves not to be true later. This has happened many times in this case so far.

Compelling evidence to the prosecution; the chain of custody on the hair is now shot. Accelerated decomposition of the pants, don't know how to tell the color. Pregnant, you can change clothes, put on what she wore the night before isn't that unusual.

The prosecution had nothing to gain with putting Amber on. Good idea, but won't work here, with her. Not on tape, that Amber says Scott said he's a widower; it's hearsay. Geragos' job to show her as not credible. The prosecutor doesn't want to unleash Geragos on Amber. Isn't on tapes; she's practically an agent of the state.

One piece of hair is said to be Amber's and one piece to be from the Peterson dog. Alot of evidence reported by the press isn't showing up; like the blood and vomit in the mop. Prosecutor said never tested the other piece of hair. Maybe Laci changed her pants; who knows, and if it's the dog's hair, it could get on the pliers and boat, the same way Laci's did, if it's Laci's hair.

The judge would rule that Amber's testimony not applicable. The prosecution has a really bad case against Scott and trying him with dirt. There's a duty to defend your client. Lackadaisical not to check out the lead by the police. As a defense attorney, you have to defend. Do this all the time.... It's important, but take it all together and look at it. There's a reason for all he said. [Secret boat?] Won't be the straw that breaks the camel's back. The people who saw Laci looking at the boat, is very important. Affairs won't come in unless relevant. Of murder though?

Eyewitness testimony is very important here. Not a conspiracy with them; nobody got together to tell a lie here.

[Laci not discuss affairs?] Absolutely, it'll be interesting to see how much of her private life she shared with others.

He had a two day fishing license. Is it relevant? Two hairs, are two different colors; was overlooked? Someone needs to explain it. A California resident can only purchase a yearly, or a two day license in California. He bought the license two days within purchasing the boat; on December 20th, okay, during the holidays, I'll go use the boat.

[Amber said not know Scott married, call his house.] Listen how different people on shows interpret facts, think how the jury will feel. Independent witnesses and police didn't follow up, and say they didn't focus on Scott right away.

Prosecution's case incredibly weak. No evidence Scott killed his wife. Where's the evidence? At this point, Scott would be acquitted. They want to execute him, but don't want to follow up on a lead.

If they play the Amber tapes, judge may allow the defense to call her. He'd be crazy to do it, Crazy, Crazy to do it. Pliers and hair are a non-issue, to prove murder of Laci. December 9th, whatever words by Amber, if wife dead, lost, or missing, as the detective says that Amber says, but, not on the tape.

They're saying the hair in the pliers says murder, but I haven't seen any evidence of murder. Still not. Where's the proof, or Amy evidence, that Scott killed his wife? Lack of evidence; if at trial, judge shouldn't allow it to go to the jury. Absolutely, she won't be a smoking gun and may be exculpatory. Not unlikely to book a tee time and do something else. No evidence against him. Prosecutor is supposed to eliminate all other possibilities and hasn't. No probable cause at this point!

California law; if circumstantial evidence can be interpreted both ways, jury must choose innocent. Geragos is turning each piece of evidence and explaining it innocently. Prosecutor has to be aware of public opinion. Prosecution already said a slam dunk...

The lead investigator is a Cowboy, but he's been removed from the lead position and taken apart by the defense attorney. He's a fine officer, detective Brocchini, but gets tunnel vision and goes out of the textbook. Centered on Scott Peterson within hours, searched home, warehouse, all without search warrants. Say he's not a suspect, but has surveillance cameras. Took Scott's gun from the truck, but didn't want Scott to see him take it. Took gun shot residue from Scott's hand and police misplaced them; Sloppy. Can't trust the case with missteps and mistakes.

Brocchini, Grogan, all did a good job, but they have a history of quick to judgment. Twenty percent of husbands don't kill wife. If center too soon on a suspect, you lose the forest for the trees. Two men, seen with Laci. Baby, maybe born, don't know. Mitochondria DNA, the defense will argue, not reliable.

Not a defense team's job to confuse everyone; It's to rebut the prosecution's theory. The prosecutor is grabbing at straws with the theory of the tape on the baby's neck. The pathologist said can't rule out born alive. The pathologist says, thirty-three to thirty-eight weeks, and is a week older than on December 25th, but yet saying he was protected by the womb until a couple of days before being washed up. They can't be both ways. They have to go one way or the other.

The defense has two of the greatest experts in the world, as to all of these matters. The doctor, today, said can't say wasn't born alive, and the defense has witnesses that saw her alive. Geragos will decide tomorrow if he'll put on witnesses. Mitochondria DNA took majority of the time.

Once DNA allowed, he'll be bound over. Nancy ain't testifying. The pathologist expert said he can't say if born alive or not. Nancy's effective; the witness testifies, and Nancy says it's not true.

[Why doesn't Scott look at cameras in court, is it because he's guilty?] Well, on trial for life, lost wife and baby.

[Other women?] Haven't seen any at the preliminary. Depends on how the prosecutor uses Amber for motive. Still have divorce, don't we.

[Air or water in lungs?] The prosecutor didn't ask, cause they don't like the answer. Still no evidence of a murder in the home. Just a hair they're saying puts her in the boat.

Anchors could be damning, but the judge can let in that he had concrete in his warehouse, to show he made anchors, to show he used them to weigh the body down, to show he killed her? Rug, that's a narrow door. Closed blinds is a wash. They have a dog and cat. Laci could have used the mop.

SCOTT'S PRELIMINARY HEARING ENDS

The standard [to bind over] in California is, is the defendant breathing? No strong case or evidence by the state. The insurance turns out to be purchased two years before. I agree, circumstantial evidence. No smoking gun here. The strand of hair; can't prove. Bleach; ain't none. Weights; bought boat, without an anchor. Scott could walk out of court. Case is weak. Hair in pliers, well, they're married. Could have gotten there a million ways.

The prosecutor wants premeditation because of Amber, but also believe he wanted to and planned to kill his unborn child. He'd get a divorce first. Police certainty coached Amber, tried to get her to get Scott to confess.

If you think I had anything to do with my wife's disappearance, that's silly.

Not one shred of evidence to show premeditation. The tapes will help Scott. The prosecutor still needs a confession or some fact to tie him to murder. The defense forensic experts very important. The prosecution expert couldn't say 'not born'. Has to be beyond a reasonable doubt.

I told Laci of the affair a couple of weeks before her disappearance, and told Amber of Laci's disappearance a couple to three days after Laci disappeared.

Tell me who, what, when, where. How about Amber deceiving people years ago with the married man and a pregnant wife? The prosecution's on their heels. I'd push for a speedy trial. Pickup, unless evidence, should give it back. Trial within sixty days, if Scott wants to push it. With circumstantial evidence against Scott, Geragos has the prosecution on its heels. Can't say how, when, where.

Everyone in Modesto knows every single detail we've talked about. Jurors won't like being bused in, but the venue will change. Especially with the former mayor coming out and saying Scott can't get a fair trial there. The prosecutor said he may not fight the motion. Why spend alot of money on something you're gonna lose.

The affair with Amber very inappropriate. I was angry at first, at the Modesto police, for the accusations. But, I think they've done a very good job. That's correct, Your Honor, I'm innocent.

[truck] The key is the forensic value. Why do they need it? Sixty day time limit can be met here. If the defense says sixty days, then attorneys have to. If the defense attorney then needs more time, he can ask the judge and may get it. Not rare to give stuff back. They can show this with other trucks. Photos of vehicle, and murder weapon, are two different things.

He knew the FBI and police were following him. He said, what the heck, take a weekend off, have some fun. Well, we'll play a little golf first. I liked what Scott said, not only pled not guilty, but said he's innocent. Clearly if Amber's pregnant, it ain't by Scott and surely he didn't kill for Amber. The fact that he's relaxed, shows me he's innocent. Client in jail and needs to be resolved.

One way for Geragos to throw the prosecution off stride. Geragos will tell the jury, not one piece of evidence. There wasn't any blood evidence at the preliminary hearing. If they had blood evidence, they'd have shown it. There wasn't a shred of blood evidence presented at the prelim.

Laci's family does have an interest, but that's putting the cart before the horse and assuming he'll be convicted. Adam would have to show that Scott is responsible. Do you need a motive? Practically speaking, yes. Well, whose morals do you want to judge, Nancy?

I'll stipulate to the money and denominations. I guess they'll want to photocopy it, but I don't want to stipulate and lose the right to question the detective on the seizure of it, the manner, or motive, or the location.

If paint on Scott's boat, why didn't the divers go down there immediately; They didn't. It was on TV just a week before the preliminary. If you're gonna bus in jurors, from where? Well you might as well bring them in from Tim Buck Too. Everyone in America knows the facts of this case. It's been tried in the media over and over. Maybe he's innocent. Question is, can you put aside you prejudgment and try this defendant fairly?

Amber's credibility may be at issue in trial, cause it came out later that she had made recordings before she really did and Geragos is going to go after that. Did she try to do more against Scott that what she really had and what motive for that.

Legal sense, they can't any of who, when, why, how. We had all this buildup to Amber, yet she didn't even show up, and now she's pregnant with someone else's child. Police need a nexus, a connection to this death. Jury won't send him to death cause he had an affair. Yea, we ran Condit out of office and town, and now we find out he didn't do it. So it's not that much of a stretch of the imagination to happen here.

I told Laci of the affair with Amber and Laci was not okay with it. No one knows a relationship but the two people involved. I told Laci because it was the right thing to do. I saw Amber again, but didn't tell Amber that I had told Laci of the affair.

High profile case, jurors will say they're fair, but they want to be on the jury. There was a lynch attitude when Scott was arrested.

[Tentative decision for change of venue.] As you know, these are based on the briefs filed. The judge has the thought-out arguments, on paper. Politics and economics will decide where it ends up. Don't think this will change things. Jury pool is contaminated all over United States. It'll be delayed and hurt the defense.

I can't wait for Gloria and Geragos to get married. Smart judge and he doesn't want to leave these issues for appeal.

Total lack of physical evidence, minus two hairs, and rest is based on what Scott said. Judge did the right thing to grant change of venue; problem is, he's not gonna find a place any less prejudicial than he's got now.

[Did government violate gag order?] Yea, a violation, but won't dismiss charges. Jim sounds like a prosecutor. More than likely the prosecutor leaked it.

If he dumped the body in the Bay on the morning of December 24th, then the baby could not have been three to four weeks older than that day. [Cops can't, or won't say where Scott was when he made December 24th phone calls.] Yea, if I was Geragos, I'd file a motion just to find out.

Two words why not [Scott] testify; Weak case. Probable cause is to determine if crime has occurred and if this defendant committed that crime. No crime shown and no connection of defendant to a crime.

San Mateo is very conservative. Geragos did a good job on filing his response to the prosecutor's motion to quash the survey, cause the prosecutor used hearsay testimony for his survey.

I'd like to thank the Modesto Bee, because without them, this change of venue would never have been possible. It's determined who is the judge. Issue is, whether prosecutor timely filed to challenge judge.

It's a sham by the prosecutor. If the defense did this, they'd be roasted. It's an unwritten rule in California that prosecutors don't do that. [Judge overturned death penalty.] It was an arson case. But here, nobody can say how Laci died. So he overturned a death penalty case. That's why he was chosen as a judge, cause he can overturn a sentence when he knows the facts don't support it. That's the kind of judge we want in there.

Geragos is correct to preserve this for the record. The judge will be recused, but the prosecutor doesn't have the same strike for the next judge and he'll have to accept whoever's chosen. [Remove judge for just cause.] Well, as you know, that's very difficult. When Judge G. was chosen, Geragos went to him and said, look, you know you shouldn't be on this case.

You get one strike, without challenge, but what Geragos is saying, is that the prosecutor filed it too late, that judge G. was already off the case and that the prosecutor filed with the wrong judge.

I don't know if this court still has jurisdiction, and in fact the Chief Justice of the California Supreme Court stepped in and made the decision on which judge and that's not according to procedure or law. I guess, he's the Chief Justice, and he can do what he wants, but so far, no one is following the statutes or law. I don't even know if any court in California, now has jurisdiction of this case.

This is a very interesting case, alot of circumstantial evidence, but nothing physical to show he killed her, and after investigating and talking to the families, there's just no way he's guilty.

I was washing dishes, looking out the window; a beautiful sight, a lady, walking her golden retriever down the street.

Geragos could take this poll anywhere, cause everybody has heard about the case, he'd get the same results anywhere he goes. Questioning several hundred potential jurors won't cross that [ethical] line.

[Movie about Scott] Obviously, they put a spin on it that Scott was guilty.

[Government taped Scott and his lawyer.] Curiosity killed the cat and the cops just couldn't resist listening. There's Brady evidence, to exculpate, and must be turned over within a certain time and sanctions applied if the prosecutor doesn't comply.

And a micro chance of getting a fair trial. Every thing he told TV, every rumor, every response will now come in [court] this way. The case has been so exposed to the media, the problem will continue, no matter where in California.

Introduces doubt into the prosecution's case, but Geragos won't use her either. Cases like this bring out loonies, like Skeeter and Dirty. Why not hypnosis, polygraph; police do others and not her? Doesn't fit the prosecution's theory of their case. Geragos has his. It doesn't fit either.

Who's got the money to test the hair? If they could actually show they killed Laci, they'd come forward with it. You have to have a staff, as an attorney, to follow up on these leads. Won't change the defense, not require any additional motions.

I'm always afraid of the 'stealth' juror, the one who says they don't have an opinion. This was a witness, who knew Laci Peterson, their next door neighbor, and she came forward right away, no agenda, and said she saw... And the police didn't like what they heard, so they hypnotized her, and then now want her testimony thrown out.

I don't know if Laci would tell her Mom about an affair. About 50% of males in the U.S. have committed adultery, and if you're gonna use that as evidence of murder, it's a pretty sad shape.

We have other people who have seen her abducted and taken away. There's a circumstantial case here, with not a single, not a single, fact that ties Scott Peterson to murder. This case, from a defense view, won't be tried on a bit by bit basis. The flawed investigation, the hypnotized defense witness by the prosecutor, no place of death, etc.

Emma Jean is with me everywhere, her hair is everywhere I go. That hair, turned out to be multiple hairs. These people are taking this trial back to the witch hunting days. He can't get a trial, if everything he does is tried in the media, and everything he does is seen as guilt.

If you, or Mother Theresa, is charged with murder, and everything you do or say is recorded; If you wash your clothes, you're guilty; if you play golf, you're guilty; if you mop the floor, you're guilty. Give me all this time and all this media, and both you and Mother Theresa will be convicted.

SCOTT PETERSON'S TRIAL BEGINS

We've had many people in this country who weren't guilty, but because of the intense media coverage, felt they couldn't get a fair trial and fled the country. Scott may have felt this. With the intense media coverage, he changed his appearance, but he was also out looking and searching for Laci.

If he, the prosecutor, goes on and on, the jury may ask, where's the evidence. The prosecutor said no marmalade on the Martha Stewart Show on December 24th, but the defense opened up with a video of the December 24th Martha Stewart Show with marmalade, so the prosecutor's credibility is open to question. The prosecutor also said Scott went to the Marina looking for bodies, but Geragos showed where the Police called Scott those mornings and said, "Hey, we'll be out there today searching." The prosecutor is open to question and reliability. At the end, Geragos said, not only is Scott not guilty, but he's stone cold innocent.

Geragos showed very little physical contact and alot of phone contact. Why kill over that?

If Geragos can show the fetus was born, then that's reasonable doubt. If ya got 3 witness that saw Laci after she was supposed to be dead, that's enough reasonable doubt for me.

Remember, what happens on the tapes, is Amber acting as an agent of the State, and nowhere on there does he say anything or confess. A 30-40 day relationship, 4 dates? This was a phone conversation relation.

Clothes don't matter, people change clothes. That's the problem with prosecutors, you only see it one way. Everything we hear and see of what Scott did December 23rd, he was a loving and caring husband, in a positive way and Laci was the same way.

The expert said his dog was a scent dog, and he don't know if the dog would follow Greta for two blocks or one block. He couldn't answer why. Cause the dog don't know. Is the dog a liar? Any skeletons in his closet? Any affairs?

No, but there's no post script on how a defendant will act. Alot of us can't recall where we were at, at a particular time of the day, especially when you're not thinking of an alibi or planning one. It's a common sense argument.

He's upbeat. He's eating more. A human being again.

Geragos asked her if she [spa lady] was against Scott Peterson and she said no. But, it was in the police notes and report. She said they lied. This is twice this has happened.

1½ hours of questioning by the prosecutor [of Amy], destroyed by only 2 questions on cross-exam by Geragos, so far. The pants Laci was found in, were not the pants Laci had on at the Salon when Scott got his hair cut on December 23rd.

Geragos sounds like he's doing a very good job. It was brought out on cross exam by Geragos, that Scott was talking to a friend, before, the vigil. The brothers [Laci's] also said that Scott wouldn't hurt anyone and that it may be Laci's former boyfriend, who had been abusive to her.

Ron Grantsky [Laci's step-Dad]stated on cross exam, that he went fishing Christmas Eve at 11am, even later than Scott, yet Grantsky stated all along that he told Scott that 9:30am was too late to go fishing.

The neighbor lady, who said she found the dog at 10:18am used a stop watch to go back and time herself to get these times, but, yet she couldn't get the times correct. She didn't look at her watch or clock when she found the dog; she went later, looked at a receipt, and then traced her steps to get the time. Are we ready to vote now? With cell phone, it's hard to tell how far from home he was, cause that won't pinpoint it.

It's been this way since he trial started, Geragos just keeps pointing out flaws in the prosecution's evidence, time after time. Even Laci called her doctor, after he told her not to exercise, and told him she got sick while walking.

This has to be the most defense orientated jury I've seen.

Sometimes there's statements that aren't on the police report and Geragos has every right to say 'surprise', but it doesn't mean she didn't walk the dog, so the dog 'wouldn't' be mad at her. Maybe the dog indicated he wanted to go out, and so Laci took him.

The ultimate conclusion here, is that he wanted to find his wife. Doesn't look like she was taken from the home. Did they actually do an inventory to see if a jacket is missing?

CHAPTER THREE

The Court Document List

The court documents listed are just that, a listing and not a record or court file. The list contains the documents filed in Stanislaus County, minus some of those that remain under seal. There were a few Stanislaus documents which were posted on the NBC Channel 11 website that appear from close scrutiny to be a copy of the court filed documents and those 16 documents are included in the list.

The list contains those documents filed in San Mateo County which are available to the public and the documents which can be gleaned from those documents.

No particular document was sought, nor any specific issue placed above another. The documents commented upon are those which were readily available from Stanislaus County without placing a burden on the court clerk's office, and those available from San Mateo.

The document list contains 400 listings, with 158 court orders. The prosecutor filed 61 documents listed, Scott filed 47, and media filed 114. Of the 158 court orders, 70 were directed to media issues only. Many of the remaining 88 orders dealt with media and publicity issues.

Amber filed 3 documents, the Coroner 1, and 17 of the listing are unknown authors.

This list was last updated with San Mateo documents on 4/19/04; and last updated with a Stanislaus documents list on 6/6/04. The comments are not meant to be exact reproductions of the briefs filed by the parties and non-parties, but rather to place the facts expressed in the particular document first and then the legal argument afterwards.

The chronological order of the listings are as important to the story told by the documents, as the decisions are on the individual issues. While many of the document dates are not available, their sequence is determined from the preceding and following documents.

??? ?, 200? **??'s Application** for an Order Authorizing the Interception of Wire Communications

??? ?, 200? **Order** of ?? Court Re: Wiretap No.1

There doesn't appear to be any listing or mention of wiretap No.1, but, there can't be a No.2 without being a No.1, just as if there's a B., then you know there's an A. out there somewhere.

??? ?, 2003 **Prosecutor's Application** for an Order Authorizing the Interception of Wire Communications

January 10, 2003 **Order** of Superior Court of Stanislaus County Re: Wiretap No.2

The prosecutor's application for wiretap No.2 to tap Scott's phones is granted.

February ?, 2003 **Prosecutor's Request** to Terminate Wiretap No.2

February 4, 2003 **Order** of Superior Court of Stanislaus County Re: Terminate Wiretap No.2

February 18, 2003 **Prosecutor Executes a Search Warrant on and in Scott's Home**

The date for this search was within the prosecutor's opposition to Scott's motion to suppress Scott's statements to the media.

??? ?, 2003 **Media Petition** to Release Pre-Arrest Search Warrants, Affidavits and Returns

Media consists of McClatchy Newspapers, Inc., joined by other media, and Contra Costa Newspapers, Inc., to have the investigation file [Materials] released.

April ?, 2003 **Superior Court of Stanislaus County**

The court holds a hearing in the judge's chambers as to the petition by media to release the Materials.

April 10, 2003 **Order** of Superior Court of Stanislaus County

The court denied media's petition to release the Materials, but then stated that the Materials would be released on July 9, 2003, or when a complaint was filed, whichever comes first.

The Findings of Fact by the court, with regard to the materials, become increasingly important as media aggressively files petitions to have the Materials released.

??? ?, 2003 **Prosecutor's Application** for an Order Authorizing the Interception of Wire Communications

April 15, 2003 **Order** of Superior Court of Stanislaus County Re: Wiretap No. 3

The prosecutor's application for wiretap No.3 to tap Scott's phones is granted.

April 17, 2003 **Detective Grogan's Complaint**

April 17, 2003 **Superior Court Order: Probable Cause Warrant of Arrest**

The Stanislaus County Superior Court judge, based upon the complaint given by Detective Grogan, finds probable cause to believe Scott Peterson committed two counts of homicide. The Order commands that Scott be arrested, and that no bail be allowed.

The warrant states that this warrant does not initiate a criminal proceeding; that all reports and copies of warrant and affidavit will be submitted to the District Attorney, who will review for a complaint. The original of the warrant and affidavit are to be retained as evidence.

The warrant lists Scott as 6'0", 200 pounds, brown hair, and brown eyes.

April 18, 2003 **Pre-Booking/Probable Cause Declaration**

This is a declaration by Detective Grogan, sworn before a magistrate on April 19, 2003, at 2:50pm, to establish probable cause that Scott, the arrestee, has committed a crime. The detective states that based on an outstanding warrant in San Diego County, he requested Department of Justice Special Agent Supervisor L., Special Agent S., and Officer J. to complete a felony traffic stop and arrest Scott. Scott was arrested at 11:10am, on

April 18th, with the location listed as Callas/Torrey Pines Road, San Diego. Scott's vehicle was released to J. Peterson.

Scott waived booking in San Diego County and was transported to Stanislaus County Jail for booking. Scott's clothing is listed as a blue sweater, white polo shirt, white shorts, and Nike tennis shoes.

April 19, 2003 **Booking Register**

The Stanislaus County Jail Register states that Scott was arrested by Detective Grogan at 11:10am, on April 18th, with the location listed as Callas/Trooey Pines Road, San Diego. The charges are listed as two counts of murder.

Scott's clothing is listed as a white shirt, Khaki shorts, blue/grey tennis shoes, and 'blue sweater' is written in and initialed.

What's interesting at this point is several possibilities. Apparently when Scott was arrested, he had on white shorts, etc. But, when he was booked into the Stanislaus jail, he had on Khaki shorts, and still wearing the blue sweater and tennis shoes.

So, either Scott changed his shorts, or, one of the people who wrote down his shorts' color was mistaken, in error, or colored blind, or, one of the officers who gave the shorts' color description to the person who wrote it down was one of the above, or any combination thereof.

April 18, 2003 **Prosecutor's** Petition for Writ of Mandate Re: Challenge to Superior Court Release of Materials

The prosecutor files this petition with the Court of Appeal for a mandate to tell the Superior Court not to release the Materials.

May 5, 2003 **Opinion of the Court of Appeal of the State of California, Fifth Appellate District**

The Court of Appeal grants peremptory relief in the first mandate proceeding, in that the trial court's Findings of Fact were thorough. Media failed to challenge the Findings and did not put them into issue before the court. Media failed to ask for a rehearing or to reconsider or review, so this opinion is final in the state of California.

April 21, 2003 **Prosecutor's Criminal Complaint**

The Stanislaus County District Attorney's Office complains and alleges that Scott committed the following crimes in Stanislaus County: Count I, a felony; murder, by willfully, unlawfully, and feloniously and with malice aforethought murder Laci Peterson. A special allegation is also made, that Scott acted intentionally, deliberately and with premeditation. An enhancement of the murder, is that during the murder of Laci, that the defendant, knowing Laci was pregnant, inflicted injury to Laci resulting in the termination of her pregnancy, a violation of Penal Code section 12022.9(a); and, Count II, a felony; by willfully, unlawfully, and feloniously and with malice aforethought murder Baby Conner Peterson, a fetus. A special allegation is also made, that the defendant acted intentionally, deliberately, and with premeditation.

An additional special allegation is made, that the defendant committed more than one murder in the 1st or 2nd degree in this proceeding, and is a special circumstance within Penal Code section 190.2(a)(3).

This Complaint prays that a warrant be issued for the arrest of the defendant and that defendant be dealt with according to law.

April ??, 2003 **Ramey Warrant**

April 21, 2003 **Minute Order** of Superior Court of Stanislaus County

April 28, 2003 **Superior Court Order:** Case Assignment

The case is assigned to Judge G. for all purposes, and is scheduled for bail review on May 6, 2003. A copy is sent to the District Attorney and the Public Defender.

April 29, 2003 **Minute Order** of Superior Court of Stanislaus County Re: Request for Court Appearance

The judge states that an informal request was received from the defense counsel to place the Peterson file on the court's calendar to vacate the Bail Review Hearing, scheduled for May 6th, and to request a substitution of counsel. So the matter is scheduled for May 2, 2003.

??? ?, 2003 **Substitution of Attorney**

May 2, 2003 **Minute Order** of Superior Court of Stanislaus County

May 3-4, 2003 **Order Re: To Retain Remains**

May ?, 2003 **Prosecutor's Motion** for a Section 170.6 Peremptory Challenge

May ?, 2003 **Scott Peterson's Reply** to Prosecutor's Motion for 170.6 Peremptory Challenge

May ?, 2003 **Prosecutor's** Points and Authorities in Support of Motion for 170.6 Challenge

May ?, 2003 **Scott Peterson's** Points and Authorities in Support of Reply to Prosecutor's Motion for 170.6 Peremptory Challenge

May ?, 2003 **Substitution of Attorney**

May 5, 2003 **Minute Order** of Superior Court of Stanislaus County

May ?, 2003 **??'s Motion** to Maintain Seal on Warrants

May ?, 2003 **Stipulation and Order Re: Release of Search Warrant**

May 6, 2003 **Minute Order** of Superior Court of Stanislaus County

May ?, 2003 **??'s Amended Motion** to Seal Documents

May ?, 2003 **??'s Opposition** to Prosecutor's Motion to Seal Search Warrant

??? ?, 2003 **Order** of Superior Court of Stanislaus County Re: All Media Performance

??? ?, 2003 **Media** CNN Request

??? ?, 2003 **Minute Order** of Superior Court of Stanislaus County Re: CNN Request Granted

??? ?, 2003 **Media Request** for Courtroom Artist

??? ?, 2003 **Minute Order** of Superior Court of Stanislaus County Re: Courtroom Artist Granted

May ?, 2003 **Media Request** to Permit Coverage of Hearing
Media consists of KCBA, NBC, CBC, CNN, and ABC.

May ?, 2003 **Order** of Superior Court of Stanislaus County Re: Media Coverage
The request of KCBA, NBC, CBC, CNN, and ABC is denied.

May ?, 2003 **Media** KOVR Request to Permit Coverage of Hearing

May ?, 2003 **Order** of Superior Court of Stanislaus County Re: Media Coverage
The request of KOVR is denied.

May ?, 2003 **Media** KRDN Request to Permit Coverage of Hearing

May ?, 2003 **Order** of Superior Court of Stanislaus County Re: Media Coverage
The request of KRDN is denied.

May ?, 2003 **Media** KTVU Request to Permit Coverage of Hearing

May ?, 2003 **Order** of Superior Court of Stanislaus County Re: Media Coverage
The request of KTVU is denied.

May 9, 2003 **Minute Order** of Superior Court of Stanislaus County

May 11, 2003 **Prosecutor's Notification** of Intercepted Communications

The prosecutor calls Scott's attorney, Mr. McAllister, to tell him that he would be receiving a letter informing him of the intercepted communications. Although Mr. McAllister states this phone call occurred on the 11th of May, a Sunday, the prosecutor disputes this date.

The prosecutor also tells Scott's lawyer that, while his communications were intercepted by the wiretap, they were not monitored.

May 14, 2003 **Prosecutor's Review** of the Wiretap Summary Log

The prosecutor notices that privileged conversations were recorded and directs the calls to be documented on a list and the recordings to be sealed and placed in a secure location.

May 19, 2003 **Minute Order** of Superior Court of Stanislaus County

Middle of May, 2003 **Prosecutor's Inventory** Pursuant to Penal Code Section 629.68; Re: Wiretaps No.2 and No.3

The prosecutor states that notification was sent to individuals whose calls were intercepted in the Stanislaus County Wiretaps. The date of this notification to Rita Cosby and Greta Van Susteren is May 2, 2003. Either the prosecutor's memory is a little off, or Rita and Greta got their notifications earlier than others.

??? ?, 2003 **Prosecutor Jacobson's Affidavit** Re: Wiretaps

May ??, 2003 **Media** Court TV Request for a Hearing

This is one of those media requests that media actually gets to be a part of.

May ??, 2003 **Order** of Superior Court of Stanislaus County Re: Court TV Request for a Hearing

Court TV's request for a hearing is granted, for 5/27/03.

May ??, 2003 **Media** KFBK Radio Request for a Hearing

May ??, 2003 **Order** of Superior Court of Stanislaus County Re: KFBK Radio Request for a Hearing

KFBK Radio's request for a hearing is granted, for 5/27/03.

May ??, 2003 **Media** KTUV 3 NBC Request for a Hearing

May ??, 2003 **Order** of Superior Court of Stanislaus County Re: KTUV 3 NBC Request for a Hearing

KTUV 3 NBC's request for a hearing is granted, for 5/27/03.

May ??, 2003 **Media** KCRA, NBC, CBS, CNN, and ABC Request for a Hearing

May ??, 2003 **Order** of Superior Court of Stanislaus County Re: KCRA, NBC, CNN, CBS, and ABC Request for a Hearing

KCRA, NBC, CBS, CNN, and ABC's request for a hearing is granted, for 5/27/03.

May ??, 2003 **Media** The Modesto Bee Request for a Hearing

May ??, 2003 **Order** of Superior Court of Stanislaus County Re: Modesto Bee Request for a Hearing

The Modesto Bee's request for a hearing is granted, for 5/27/03.

May 27, 2003 **Prosecutor's Request** for Release of Wiretap Recordings to Media from Stanislaus County Wiretap No. 2 and 3 Records

May 27, 2003 **Scott Peterson's Opposition** to Prosecutor's Request for Release of Audio Recordings from Stanislaus County Wiretap No. 2 and No.3 Records

May ?, 2003 **??'s Reply** to Prosecutor's 'Release of Wiretap Recordings'

??? ?, 2003 **Media Request** to Seal Records Re: Wiretap Recordings

??? ?, 2003 **??'s Objection** to Contra Costa Motion to Seal Affidavits

??? ?, 2003 **??'s Reply and Opposition** to Media Request to Seal Records

??? ?, 2003 **Prosecutor's Request** to Release of Wiretap Recordings to Media and Opposition to Media Request to Seal Records

??? ?, 2003 **Scott Peterson;** Declaration of Kirk McAllister Re: Wiretaps

May ?, 2003 **Stipulation and Order** Re: Release of Wiretap Information

May 27, 2003 **Minute Order** of Superior Court of Stanislaus County

May ??, 2003 **??'s Amendment** to Notice of Motion

June 2, 2003 **Scott Peterson's Motion** for Hearing on Sanctions Re: Eavesdropping

Scott motions the court for a hearing regarding sanctions over the government eavesdropping on privileged communications between Scott and his lawyer, Kirk McAllister, and between Scott and Mr. McAllister's investigator.

The prosecutor has admitted that they knew Scott had retained Mr. McAllister as his attorney, as of the first week of January 2003, as noted in Agent Jacobson's Affidavit which was filed with the prosecutor's request to release the audio recordings, and therefore the prosecutor knows that all communications between Scott and McAllister are totally privileged under California law. After knowing this for at least a week in advance, prosecutor Distaso prepared wiretap instructions and discussed them with the wiretap monitors and supervisors who would be doing the monitoring.

The prosecutor failed to instruct the monitors that all communications between Scott and Mr. McAllister were privileged, and instead, instructed them to intermittently listen in on the attorney-client communications. This illegal eavesdropping clearly constitutes grave prosecutorial misconduct. Unfortunately, the matter gets worse.

The monitors failed to heed the prosecutor's instruction, and chose instead to rely on a purported federal golden rule, that permits the eavesdropper to monitor the conversation four times as frequently as California law. This illegal eavesdropping clearly constitutes gross misconduct by the monitors. California law does not authorize monitoring when there is no possibility that the communication is not privileged.

Agent Jacobson states in his affidavit that he is certified by the California State Attorney General's Office in the practical, technical, and legal aspects of California State court ordered wiretaps.

The United States Supreme Court has stated that in cases of egregious prosecutorial misconduct resulting in prejudice to a criminal defendant, dismissal of a case, with prejudice [can't recharge], is appropriate. *United States v. Morrison*, 449 U.S. 361 (1981). The California Supreme Court states that the intrusion, through trickery, of the law enforcement agent into the confidential attorney-client conference, cannot be condoned. The right to confer privately with one's own attorney is one of the fundamental rights guaranteed by the American law; a right that no legislature or court can ignore or violate. The only effective remedy is the dismissal of the underlying charges. *Barber v. Municipal Court*, 24 Cal.3d 742, pp.759-760 (1979).

Many times the exclusion of illegally obtained information is inadequate to protect the defendant's rights and to deter future prosecutorial misconduct. As in *Barber*, at p.756, whether or not the prosecution has directly gained any confidential information which may be subject to suppression, the prosecution in this case has been aided by its agent's [mis]conduct. [The defendant] has been prejudiced in their ability to prepare their defense. They no longer feel they can freely, candidly, and with confidence discuss their case with their attorney.

As noted in *Barber*, at p.757, consider the prosecution witnesses who learn some of the illegally obtained information. Even if the witnesses do not divulge the information to the prosecutor, the witnesses will be in a position to formulate in advance answers to anticipated questions, and even to shade their testimony to meet expected defenses.

In order to enforce an exclusionary rule on the information illegally obtained, Scott would have to permit his confidential information rights to be violated, again; to protect that information, a hearing would be required with the judge then knowing the substance of the illegally obtained information, before he could decide. The prosecutor would also be required to be at this hearing, and therefore learn defense strategies, if not already known to him.

The exclusionary remedy does not create any incentive for State agents to refrain from such violations. The prosecution would proceed as if the unlawful conduct had not occurred. *Barber*, at p.759.

The California Supreme Court has stated that the attorney-client privilege applies to an investigator retained by defense counsel. An investigator is as reasonably necessary as a physician or psychiatrist, or a legal secretary, paralegal or receptionist. Because the investigator is a person encompassed by the privilege, he stands in the same position as the attorney for the purposes of the analysis and operation of the privilege; the investigator cannot disclose that which the attorney could not have disclosed.

There are more than three attorney-client calls that were intercepted and monitored by the prosecutor. There were more than fifty (50) privileged calls monitored, and are covered by the attorney-client privilege. For an offer of proof to be submitted by Scott, the defense will have to have an opportunity to fully review and analyze the recorded attorney-client communications.

Scott asks the court to impose one or more of the following sanctions for the improper monitoring of privileged communications:

1. Recusal of the Stanislaus County prosecutor's Office, and to totally screen a new prosecutor from any communications with the Stanislaus office, its agents, and the investigators involved in the eavesdropping.
2. Exclusion of the testimony of any investigators or attorneys involved in the eavesdropping.
3. Exclusion of any evidence that government cannot demonstrate was not the fruit of the eavesdropping.
4. Setting a hearing in the judge's chambers, during which Agent Jacobson, prosecutor Distaso, and others, may be questioned as to the circumstances of the improper monitoring and intrusion into the defense.

Mr. McAllister was told that the conversations were not recorded, and we would like to know who told this incorrect information to prosecutor Distaso, who then told it to Mr. McAllister. We would like to question the investigators, under oath, to determine the nature and scope of the privileged communications overheard by them.

In the event that the court does not dismiss the case or grant the relief sought as set forth in 1 through 4, inclusive, such a hearing will be necessary so that the defense can make an offer of proof as to the degree of prejudice the eavesdropping has caused so the court may properly determine the appropriate sanction(s); and, granting whatever other relief the court may deem necessary to further the ends of justice.

June 4, 2003 **Prosecutor's Opposition** to Motion for Sanctions and Opposition to Motion to Suppress Wiretap Audio Recordings

Over the course of approximately 30 days, through the conduct of two wiretaps, Stanislaus County Wiretap No. 2, authorized on January 10, 2003, and terminated on February 4, 2003, and Wiretap No. 3, authorized on April 15, 2003, and with 3,858 intercepted phone calls, Scott can only argue over three. The only appropriate sanction is suppression of these three calls. No one has communicated the content of the audio recordings at issue to any member of the prosecution.

The prosecutor has directed District Attorney Criminal Investigator Jacobson to seal the recordings of any monitored communications between Scott, Mr. McAllister [Scott's attorney], and Mr. Ermoian [Scott's attorney's investigator], and to place that information in a secure location. The prosecutor further directed D.A. Investigator Jacobson not to discuss the content of those recordings with the prosecuting attorneys, and for D.A. Investigator Jacobson to direct the two Stanislaus County Drug Enforcement Unit Agents to also not discuss the content of those recordings with the prosecuting attorneys.

On January 14, 2003, Agent H. inadvertently monitored a brief conversation between Mr. McAllister and Scott because he did not initially recognize Mr. McAllister's voice. When the Agent reentered the call for monitoring, he recognized the voice and minimized the remainder of the call. We concede the privilege nature of the call, but there was no violation of any minimization rule. Agent H. acted in good faith.

On January 15, 2003, Agent T. briefly monitored a conversation between Scott and Mr. McAllister [Scott's attorney], listening to the initial portion for six seconds, waited thirty-six seconds, then listened for six seconds, then waited for sixty-seven seconds and listened for six more seconds. Investigator Jacobson states that no substantive information was gained from either call. Sixty-nine calls were intercepted between Scott and his lawyer, with only short segments of two calls being recorded.

While Agent T.'s conduct might reflect a misunderstanding of the requirements of California's wiretap statute, it does not reflect any bad faith.

On January 29, 2003, Investigator Jacobson monitored a conversation between Scott and Gary Ermoian, Scott's attorney's investigator. The agent did not know Gary was an investigator or that he was employed by Scott's lawyer. This call simply involved Gary warning Scott about the media being present outside of his home. No substantive information was obtained as a result of that call being monitored.

While the attorney-client privilege does apply to an investigator retained by an attorney, every conversation involving that person and the attorney's client is not automatically privileged. At the heart of the matter regarding the attorney-client privilege is the fact that legal advice must be sought, or the communication must involve the attorney-client relationship. Letting Scott know that there was media outside, clearly does not involve information related to this relationship. If privileged, then the agents acted in good faith. To exclude Agent Jacobson as a witness would, in effect, suppress all evidence gained from Wiretap Nos. 2 and 3. Such an outcome is drastic and unnecessary, and clearly not an appropriate remedy.

The agents were properly instructed regarding attorney-client phone calls. No misconduct has occurred. The appropriate remedy has already occurred, as we do not intend to introduce any evidence from any call made to, or from, Scott and his attorney, or private investigator. There is certainly no conflict, let alone one that is so severe as to disqualify the prosecutor from acting.

The potential for prejudice to a defendant from a prosecutor's conflict of interest, or the likelihood the defendant will not receive a fair trial, articulates a two part test; whether there is a conflict of interest; and whether the conflict is so severe as to disqualify the prosecutor from acting. Prosecutor Distaso called Mr. McAllister to let him know a letter was coming to him to inform him of intercepted communications, in the middle of May, and also told Mr. McAllister that while his communications were intercepted by the wiretap, they were not monitored. That information was based on his recollection at the time of how the wiretap was conducted and not from any other source.

About May 14, 2003, the prosecutor reviewed the log of intercepted communications and noticed the log by Agent H. referencing the call between Scott and his attorney. Obviously, in hindsight, he should have reviewed the call log before speaking to the attorney, Mr. McAllister. No one has communicated the content on the audio recordings at issue to any member of the prosecution.

We request that the court review all of the calls at issue, independently, without either the prosecutor's or defense's input. After that, the prosecutor requests an opportunity to be heard on this motion.

California Penal Code Sections 629.50 to 629.98 provide the conduct for State run wiretaps. A judge may issue an order approving a wiretap, only if the following determinations can be made from the prosecutor's application; there is probable cause to believe that Scott has committed a specified offense, as murder; that there is probable cause to believe that communications regarding that offense will be obtained through the wiretap; that there's probable cause to believe the particular facility will be used by Scott; and a necessity requirement, that normal investigative procedures have been tried and have failed or reasonably appear either to be unlikely to succeed if tried or to be too dangerous.

The Code mandates periodic reports to the court regarding the conduct of the wiretap, showing the number of communications intercepted, the progress of the wiretap or lack thereof and an explanation for a need to continue, every six days. The court required Investigator Jacobson to report every three days. The prosecutor instigated the early termination of wiretap No. 2, because the prosecutor determined that further progress in the investigation would not be gained through additional interception.

There are numerous privileges that agents must be aware of, and make judgments about, as attorney-client, clergyman-parishioner, doctor-patient, husband-wife, and others. In order to make those judgments, agents must identify the parties speaking and determine that the call is privileged. Agents must make subjective judgments as to whether or not a call involves material that is pertinent to the investigation, or, is it related to the subject matter of the investigation? If so, and the call is not otherwise privileged, agents may monitor the call. If not, agents must minimize the call, or stop monitoring, regardless of who is speaking.

So, the prosecutor is saying that even though they're privileged conversations, which the term 'privileged' in and of itself seems to be from a dictatorial perspective, that government must listen to these privileged conversations to determine that they are privileged, then to listen some more to make sure that they remain 'privileged', and the to listen some more to find if there's any fraud involved in the conversations, and, or, if the conversation is about the case, or not. So, just who in this ordeal is really getting the privilege.

Many non-privileged calls contain elements of both pertinent and non-pertinent information and agents must make subjective judgments regarding when to minimize throughout the duration of the call. Monitoring agents are human beings, who must constantly make quick, subjective judgments regarding the information contained in each call. No special software or investigative tricks exist to allow agents to make perfect decisions at all times.

The defense refers to 'grave prosecutorial misconduct' throughout their brief, even stating that the prosecution 'orchestrated the eavesdropping'. While the defense apparently desires to influence the court with inflammatory language, noticeably lacking from their submission is any case relating to the conduct of wiretaps.

Based on the summary log, the prosecutor disputes that the call from Gary Ermoian involved privileged information. However, if the court finds that it does, it was only a brief call and did not involve any substantive information.

California Penal Code 629.80, Privileged Communications; all conversations involving any attorney shall be minimized unless the services of the attorney are being sought or obtained to enable or aid anyone to commit or plan to commit a crime of fraud. Failure to minimize phone calls involving an attorney or their telephone number may result in suppression of <u>all</u> pertinent phone calls seized during the establishment of the wiretap, and any evidence obtained as a result of information gathered during the wiretap. A client is anyone who seeks advice from a lawyer, whether or not the lawyer is actually assigned to, paid for, or appointed for, the person seeking advice.

The agent must cease listening, once a privileged call is intercepted, for a period of two minutes, then he may listen again for thirty seconds to determine if the nature of the communication is still privileged. The defense states that when there is no possibility that the communication is not privileged, no monitoring is permitted. The law does not require the agents to make such broad, subjective determinations. The defense tries to make this a personal issue regarding Mr. McAllister, stating that the prosecution intends to rely, at least in part, on the crime-fraud exception to justify improper monitoring.

The defense claims that in this case there was no chance that a communication between the defendant and his attorney did not involve privileged information. That might be true in this particular case. However, the court can not look at each individual case in a vacuum. The statute plainly states that the officer shall continue to go online and offline in this manner until the time that the communication is no longer privileged or the communication ends.

The prosecutor states, 'in this particular case', then something about vacuum cleaners. Individuality is the essence of a Republic government. Each State is guaranteed a Republic form of government by the U.S. President, who in turn is required to do so by the U.S. Constitution. At the very basis of Republic government, is the individual, which, or rather, who, that the government must operate upon; without such, it ain't a Republic form of government. The brief continues.

A motion to quash a wiretap requires the same principles as a search warrant. The duty of the reviewing court is simply to ensure that the magistrate had a substantial basis for concluding that probable cause existed. *Illinois v. Gates*, 462 U.S. 213, at pp.238-239 (1983). The defense carries the burden of overcoming the presumption of the wiretap's validity.

As to the conduct of the wiretap, the courts apply the standard of good faith. *United States v. Leon*, 468 U.S. 897(1984). In California, Penal Code Section 629.72, mandates that a motion to suppress a wiretap may be made, only on the basis that the contents or evidence were obtained in violation of the Fourth Amendment of the U.S. Constitution or of this Chapter [Code]. The clear intent of the California legislature, like that of the

U.S. Congress in drafting their 1986 revision, was to mandate the application of federal constitutional standards in evaluating motions to suppress wiretaps.

Thus, in California, as stated in the Federal District Court of Southern New York case, *United States v. Ambrosio*, 898 F.Supp. 177, at p.188(S.D.N.Y. 1995), when wiretap evidence is challenged because it was obtained pursuant to a warrant that lacked probable cause, a reviewing court is not limited to the statute's suppression remedy, but may also look to the good faith exception to the exclusionary rule. With good faith present, just as with a search warrant, the requirements to issue the warrant need not be met, as there are exceptions to government following procedure.

When it comes to minimizing a call, the courts use the standard of reasonableness; whether the minimizations effort was managed reasonably in light of the totality of the circumstances. *Scott v. United States*, 436 U.S. 128, at pp.137-140(1978). In *United States v. Hyde,* 574 F.2d 856, at p.870(5th Cir. 1978), the court stated, the defendants argue that calls between [defendant] and his attorney and physician were monitored, and that these calls should have been privileged...But the agents listened to these calls only long enough to determine that the doctor and lawyer were not participating in the conspiracy...It would be unreasonable to expect agents to ignore completely any call to an attorney or doctor; doctors and lawyers have been known to commit crimes.

Sounds like doctors and lawyers need some of that good ole boy, good cause. In essence, what the prosecutor has just led us through is the analysis path for finding that it is legally okay for government, illegally, to not follow the rules and prohibitions mandated to government by the very document that created government, the U.S. Constitution.

June ?, 2003 **Scott Peterson's** Motion for Setting of a Hearing on OSC Re: Contempt of Court

June ?, 2003 **Scott Peterson's** Supplement to Motion for Setting of a Hearing

June ?, 2003 **Gloria Allred's** Preliminary Opposition to Scott Peterson's Motion

June ?, 2003 **Stipulation and Order** to Continue Briefing Schedule and Hearing on Scott Peterson's Motion for Sanctions

??? ?, 2003 **Media Motion** for Order Authorizing Inspection of Intercepted Records

??? ?, 2003 **Media Motion** for Order Authorizing Inspection of Intercepted Communications

??? ?, 2003 **Media Motion** for Order Authorizing Inspection of Intercepted Communications

??? ?, 2003 **Media Declaration** of Stephen H. Johnson in Support of Motion for Order Authorizing Inspection of Intercepted Communications

June 4, 2003 **Media** Non-Party Journalists Motion for Order Authorizing Inspection of Intercepted Communications

June 4, 2003 **Non-Party Journalists** Reply to District Attorney's, Release of Wiretap Recordings to Media and Opposition to Media Request to Seal Records

Journalists, non-parties, Jodi Hernandez, Karen Brown, Dan Abrams, Sandy Rivera, Keith Morrison, Michael G. Mooney, Ty Phillips, Patrick Giblin, Judy Sly, Kimberly Culp, John Walsh, Chuck Rosenberg, Marvin Daye, Michael Reel, Gloria Gomez, Diane Sawyer, and Mark Robertson have filed a motion before the court to release the government wiretap tapes to the journalists only, so the respective journalists may inspect the tape recordings, and then take appropriate steps to continue keeping them sealed from the public, permanently. This Reply also requests the court to set a briefing schedule and hearing to hear their motions to permanently seal the records, or limit their release.

The journalists request that the court grant access to the tapes in the manner proposed by the prosecutor, and that the tapes not be released to anyone, including the prosecutor or the defendant. Neither the prosecutor or defendant oppose journalists' access to the tapes. The prosecutor does, however, ignore the First Amendment, which there can be no question that it gives non-party journalists a qualified privilege to refuse to disclose unpublished information.

The government should not be permitted to rely on the efforts of journalists, who by profession hold themselves out as having relevant information, to meet their burden of establishing Scott's guilt. The journalists who spoke with Scott Peterson believed, and had a right to believe, that their communications were protected and that disclosure could only be compelled if the parties demonstrated a significant need for those communications.

Other persons with whom Scott spoke also may have expected that their communications were private, but, their situation is very different. Other than Scott's attorneys, investigators, doctors or pastors, those individuals can be compelled to testify regarding the contents of their conversations with him. Journalists cannot be.

Wow! The journalist attorneys just gave government the authority to compel testimony from an American. Thanks, but no thanks.

When facts acquired by a journalist in the course of gathering the news becomes the target of discovery, a qualified privilege against compelled disclosure comes into play. *Shoen v. Shoen*, 5 F.3d 1289, at p.1292(9th Cir. 1993). The reporter's privilege protects confidential and non-confidential material. *Shoen I*, at p.1295; and *Shoen v. Shoen*, 48 F.3d 412, at p.414(9th Cir. 1995)(*Shoen II*).

The disclosure of non-confidential information obtained in the newsgathering process may be compelled only upon a showing that the requested material is; unavailable despite exhaustion of all reasonable alternative sources; non-cumulative; and, clearly relevant to an important issue in the case. *Shoen II*, at p.46. The party seeking to overcome the privilege must make a showing of actual relevance, not merely potential relevance. In *United States v. Ahn*, 231 F.3d 26, at p.37(D.C. Cir. 2000), the court stated that to overcome a journalist's rights in information sought, it must be essential and crucial to defendant's case.

The prosecutor has not made this showing, and therefore the communications should retain their privileged character. Government should have followed the procedure established by California statute law to ensure that communications of a privileged nature, such as that between a journalist and source, are not monitored. The prosecutor's suggestion that these communications are not privileged because, by analogy, the prosecutor would be entitled to use any tape they found while executing a search warrant, misses the point.

Here, the California statute expressly provides that privileged communications retain their character, notwithstanding the interception. The prosecutor's example is flawed. If the tape contained a conversation between Scott and his attorney, there can be little doubt that the conversation would remain privileged and the State would not be able to use it. Similarly, any non-consensual recording of communications between non-party journalists and Scott also retain their qualified privilege.

Non-party journalists respectfully request that they be given immediate access to their intercepted communications, in the manner proposed by the prosecutor, and that the court maintain the current seal on these records.

June ?, 2003 **Media's** Points and Authorities in Support of Media Request to Seal Records

May 2, 2003 **Prosecutor's Inventory** Pursuant to Penal Code Section 629.68 Re: Wiretap No.2

This notification was sent to Rita Cosby and Greta Van Susteren to inform them that during the period covered, 1/10/03-2/4/03, communications of theirs were intercepted.

June 4, 2003 **Media** Greta Van Susteren and Rita Cosby Notice of Motion and Motion for Order Authorizing Inspections of Intercepted Communications; Declaration of Amy M. Gallegos in Support Thereof

Rita and Greta want a copy of their intercepted communications so they can inspect them and determine if it is necessary for them to protect their rights pursuant to California Constitution, Article I, Section 2(b). The issue is whether there is a countervailing government interest in maintaining the confidentiality of the intercepted conversations.

Around January, 2003, Greta and Rita each made a number of phone calls to Scott, in the course of their duties as television journalists, concerning the disappearance of his wife, Laci. At the time these calls were made, Scott was under investigation by the police in connection with his wife's disappearance.

Penal Code § 629.68 states that the judge, when someone files a motion, may at his discretion, make available to the person or her counsel for inspection, the portions of the intercepted communications...that the judge determines to be in the interest of justice. Knowing what is in the tapes is essential for the determination by Greta and Rita, of whether to assert their rights under the California Shield Law; Article I, § 2(b), of the California Constitution.

A prosecutor cannot compel a journalist to reveal unpublished information 'obtained in the process of gathering, receiving, or processing information for communication to the public'. *Miller v. Superior Court*, 221 Cal.4th 883, at p.890(1999); California Constitution Article I, § 2(b). Greta's and Rita's conversations with Scott fall squarely within the protection of the Shield Law.

There is no compelling need to keep the contents of these conversations confidential. There is no ongoing investigation to protect, as the police investigation of Scott has presumably concluded. An order permitting Greta and Rita to receive a transcript of, or listen to, those portions that reflect their conversations with Scott would be in the interest of justice.

June 4, 2003 **Media** Notice of Motion and Motion; Request for Order Shortening Time Filed

The motion has an exhibit attached, which is the letter from the prosecutor informing those whose conversations were intercepted.

June 4, 2003 **Media** Declaration of Amy M. Gallegos Requesting Order Shortening Time for Hearing on the Motion of Rita Cosby and Greta Van Susteren for an Order Authorizing Inspections of Intercepted Communications

There is good cause for an order shortening the time for hearing of Greta's and Rita's motion for an order authorizing inspections of their conversations. The court is already scheduled, on June 6th, to hear identical issues raised by motions of other non-party journalists, thus it would be expedient for the court to address this motion also at that time.

June 4, 2003 **Order** of Superior Court of Stanislaus County Re: Inspections of Intercepted Communications

The court states that, with good cause appearing, it is ordered that the time for service of the notice authorizing inspection of intercepted communications is shortened, so that the motion, filed on 6/4/03 by Greta and Rita, may be heard on June 6, 2003.

Media wants what they said to Scott Peterson sealed from everyone, even though Scott is one of the people recorded in media's conversations. Scott also happens to be the one defending himself from being put to death, yet media wants all of the 'other' records and documents opened up to the public. It this because of what generally takes place during a deceitful and trickery conversation, which is used by police to gain an answer, although out of context and content, to fit their desire.

A person will compliment you to gain your trust, and in doing so, depending on whether they want a 'yes' or 'no' answer to their desire, they will have you agreeing either with that yes or no, using statements or questions which they know beforehand will get that particular yes or no. Once you're hooked, the 'out of context' statement or question will be slipped into the sequence of answers in order to get the desired answer, more so from repetition and trickery, than from reality and honesty.

It would appear from the very beginning that the questioner and the answeree would need a copy of the recording. The answeree to show just what was done, since he'll remember the event and how it happened. And the questioner to edit out all the deception and trickery that they won't remember unless they hear the tapes. Without the recordings, the questioners would not remember the conversation, since most of the sequence of entrusting questions and statements appear during the conversation itself, depending on how it's going, and may, in fact, negate, nullify, and be in complete opposition to the so-called incriminating statement or answer made by the 'suspect'. The second question usually depends on the answer to the first one. Remember, these are news reporters.

May ??, 2003 **Prosecutor's** Motion to Seal Search Warrant Records

May ??, 2003 **Media** Opposition to Prosecutor's Motion to Seal Search Warrant Records

May 27, 2003 **Prosecutor's Points and Authorities** in Support of Sealing Records

May 27, 2003 **Prosecutor's Addendum** to Points and Authorities in Support of Sealing Records

June 3, 2003 **Media** Motion to Unseal Search Warrant Records

Media, Contra Costa Newspapers, Inc., The Modesto Bee, the Los Angeles Times, and Hearst Communications, have motioned the court to unseal the search warrant records.

???? ?, 2003 **Scott Peterson's** Motion to Seal Search Warrant Records

???? ?, 2003 **Media** Newspapers' Opposition to Prosecutor's Motion to Seal Search Warrant Records

June 3, 2003 **Superior Court Minute Order** In Re: Sealed Search Warrants, Warrant Affidavits, and Returns, and Arrest Warrant Possible Cause Showing - Laci Peterson Investigation

Arguments were heard regarding media's motion to unseal the search warrant records from the prosecutor, David Harris; media, Charity Kenyon; and Scott Peterson, Matt Dalton.

The judge schedules a hearing in his chambers on June 6th, at the request of Scott's defense counsel, Matt Dalton. The court will make a written decision on June 12, 2003.

May 27, 2003 **Superior Court of Stanislaus Hearing**

The Court suggested to the prosecutor and Scott that the court would hold a hearing on June 6, 2003 concerning a Protective [gag] Order, and would like written comments from them. The court is concerned about the tremendous amount of pre-trial publicity in the case and the fact that there had been dissemination of information currently under seal. The court noted that the Rules of Professional Conduct 5-120 were not specific enough and that they only applied to the attorneys and not to other individuals.

June 4, 2003 **Prosecutor's Points and Authorities** in Support of Limited Protective Order

The prosecutor does not object to the court imposing a limited protective [gag] order as set out by the prosecutor, since, despite the court, on May 2, 2003, advising the parties to comply with California Rule of Professional Responsibility 5-120, which prohibits a member of the investigation, or litigation, from making any statement outside of the courtroom which they should reasonably know will have a substantial likelihood of materially prejudicing a judicial matter, and the parties arguing to keep the records sealed, information has repeatedly been leaked to the media.

Media identifies which side has leaked the information, but fails and refuses to identify its source. Media states that this court cannot impose a gag order, but the prosecutor disagrees. This court clearly can make an order that parallels the Rule of Professional Responsibility and can make the order binding, not only on the attorneys, but investigators, assistants, and others working on the case for them. The prosecutor would oppose an order any broader than that because it would only work to the detriment of the prosecutor.

Some of the sealed information has leaked to the media and has forced the prosecutor to respond to mitigate recent adverse publicity; a broader order would deprive the prosecutor of the right to protect its case. The person or persons who have leaked sealed information will not be deterred by a court imposed gag order, however, an order will prevent a party from announcing from the courthouse steps information in violation of the Rules of Professional Responsibility and the court's order.

It is the People's belief that once an order is put in place, responsible journalists will understand that leaked information violates the court's order and is being spewed forth with an intent to circumvent justice. And if justice cannot protect the defendant then who will protect the media in the future?

June 4, 2003 **Scott Peterson's Memorandum** in Response to Court's Inquiry Re: "GAG" or Protective Order

The court asked counsel for their arguments as to the issue of a protective order, and in response, Scott objects to the order on practical grounds. All that a gag order would do, is increase the breath and depth of misinformation and scurrilous accusations that swirl around this case, with no ability to mitigate the damage.

Here, Scott stands wrongly and falsely accused of the capital murder of his wife, Laci, and their son. Scott has no trepidation about the fair and accurate reporting of his case as it unfolds. Unless the media is permitted to properly and accurately report on developments as they occur, Scott will have no opportunity to remedy the prior avalanche of disinformation disseminated in the four months prior to his arrest.

As this court is indeed aware of, Scott has been relentlessly excoriated and vilified in the media. If the court were to impose a prior restraint on the participants, it would do no more than result in the unfair and inaccurate reporting of this case. Certainly, false reports can, and should, be dealt with appropriately. Because of the avalanche of disinformation that has already occurred in this case, any danger of prejudice to Scott is not just 'clear and present', but 'past and manifest'.

Although some, if not much, of what has been reported about this case has been pure sensationalism designed to appeal to the public's perceived more vile interests, a significant amount of the reporting has been fair and accurate. The media reports range from accurate reporting of factual or procedural matters to the patently absurd and often completely unfounded speculation.

The U.S. Supreme Court, in *Capital Cities Media, Inc. et al. v. Toole*, 463 U.S. 1303, at p.1304 (1983), stated, it is clear that even a short-lived 'gag' order in a case of widespread concern to the community constitutes a substantial prior restraint and causes irreparable injury to First Amendment interests as long as it remains in effect. The judicial system, and in particular our criminal justice courts, play a vital part in a democratic state, and the public has a legitimate interest in their operations. *Gentile v. State Bar of Nevada*, 501 U.S. 1030, at p.1035 (1991).

Public awareness and criticism have even greater importance where, as here, they concern allegations of police corruption, or where... the criticism questions the judgment of an elected public prosecutor. The press...guards against the miscarriage of justice by subjecting the police, prosecutors, and judicial processes to extensive public scrutiny and criticism.

The court requested that the parties' opinions as to the appropriate standard for issuance of a gag order, so Scott submits the three-prong *Hurvitz* approach. The California court states, that orders which restrict or preclude a citizen from speaking in advance are known as 'prior restraints', and are disfavored and presumptively invalid. Gag orders on trial participants are unconstitutional, unless; the speech sought to be restrained poses a clear and present danger or serious and imminent threat to a protected competing interest; the order is narrowly tailored to protect that interest; and, no less restrictive alternatives are available. *Hurvitz v. Hoefflin et al*, 84 Cal.App.4th 1232, at p.1241 (2nd Dist. 2000), review denied March 21, 2001.

Additionally, upon making such an order, the trial court must make express findings showing it applied this standard and considered and weighed the competing interests.

There is no clear and present danger or serious and imminent threat to a protected competing interest. No right ranks higher than the right of Scott to a fair trial. In the instant matter, no party has alleged as to the gag order, that potential jurors have been prejudiced or will be prejudiced, if the gag order does not issue. Where is the competing interest?

There is no way to narrowly tailor a gag order on this case. The imposition of a prior restraint in the form of a gag order is unlikely to deter those who traffic in the titillating and uniformly wrong disinformation that has plagued this case. Consequently, there simply is no way to narrowly tailor a gag order that would render it constitutionally permissible, while at the same time protecting Scott's right to a fair trial.

There are less restrictive alternatives in the event that certain information should not be disclosed. The parties have the option of filing documents under seal or requesting hearings in the judge's chambers. The court has the inherent authority to seal matters, order documents or filings to be sealed, or hold proceedings in its chambers. All of these procedures are more likely to protect the various interests and clearly represent a less restrictive alternative to a gag order.

June 4, 2003 **Amber Frey's Opposition** of Potential Witness, Amber Frey, To Proposed Gag Order Upon Her; Declaration of Gloria Allred

On May 27th, the court stated it would consider a gag order against parties to the case, their attorneys, and witnesses. Amber opposes a gag order as to her, since she would loose profoundly important First Amendment rights, and face further humiliation in the sense that she will be unable to answer those who would slander or libel her.

In contrast to the other parties, Amber has gone before the media only twice. She has not accused Scott of any crime, commented on the merits of the case, or disclosed what her potential testimony might be. Amber's first appearance at a press conference [announcement] was on January 24, 2003. Prior to this, media reports placed Amber in a false light and were damaging to her reputation. The press then sought out Amber and hounded her relentlessly.

After appearing in the company of police representatives at the press conference [announcement] and affirming that she had a romantic relationship with Scott while he was still married to Laci, which was unknown to Amber, she hoped the press would stop following her. She also hoped that the press would stop discussing her personal life. Instead, the press intrusion became so intense, that Amber hired Gloria Allred to act as her attorney and spokeswoman.

In addition, Amber also retained counsel to respond as necessary to unfair attacks on her reputation and to false statements about her private life. Amber appeared at a second press conference [announcement] on May 19, 2003 to announce the hiring of Gloria Allred and to state that she would not do interviews prior to testifying and would like to have her privacy respected. Since then, Amber has not given interviews to the press.

Unfortunately, the media continues to report rumors about Amber. Those rumors amount to an assault on her character and reputation. Because her information was deemed relevant by police, she is now expected to be a witness. Amber should not have to suffer unjustified attacks on her in the press without the ability to respond as the price of simply doing her duty as a citizen. A gag order against Amber would render her helpless in the face of a continued onslaught of rumor and innuendo. If the price a person may have to pay for providing police with evidence that may be relevant, in a high profile case, is that the person will be gagged and unable to respond to attacks on their character and reputation, then witnesses may be reluctant to step forward.

Scott is certainly entitled to a fair trial. Amber's conduct should be seen as protective of a fair trial. The question is whether Amber poses a clear and present danger to Scott's fair trial rights. She is not an eyewitness to the murders in question, and is not a witness for either side. It is crucial to note that she does not accuse Scott of murdering anyone.

Amber is entitled to have the court apply each of the three elements of the gag order test to her as an individual. As stated in *Saline v. Superior Court*, 100 Cal.App.4th 909, at p.915(2002), orders which restrict or preclude a citizen from speaking in advance are known as 'prior restraints', and are disfavored and presumptively invalid. Gag orders on trial participants are unconstitutional unless; the speech sought to be restrained poses a clear and present danger, or serious and imminent threat, to a protected, competing, interest; the order is narrowly tailored to protect that interest; and, no less restrictive alternatives are available.

The mere potential for prejudice is inadequate to justify a gag order. Where information might prejudice potential jurors, this does not constitute a finding that a risk of prejudice actually exists. Where a party contends their right to a fair trial has or will be compromised by pretrial publicity, the law imposes the burden on that party of producing evidence to establish the prejudice. It is not enough for a court to decide that the fair trial right may be affected by the exercise of free speech. *Hurvitz v. Hoefflin*, 84 Cal. App.4th 1232 at p.1242(2000).

If the court decides to gag the prosecutor and defense counsel, the court can easily carve Amber out of that order. In other words, the court can take measures which preserve Amber's rights of free speech, while at the same time addressing speech which the court finds to be more threatening to a fair trial.

Actually, it's 'free press', and not free speech. It's 'freedom of speech'. One means to be free of government regulation and, or, ownership. The other means to speak when you want, but it ain't necessarily free. Sometimes there are consequences, meaning that we may not have to be concerned so much about what we say, but more so on when we say it.

June 4, 2003 **Media Opposition** to a Protective "Gag" Order

June ?, 2003 **Prosecutor's Proposed Protective Order**

June ?, 2003 **Media** Request to Permit Coverage of 6/6/03 Hearing

June ?, 2003 **Minute Order** of Superior Court of Stanislaus County Re: Media Request to Permit Coverage of 6/6/03 Hearing

June ?, 2003 **Media** V.E. Behringer Request to Permit Courtroom Artist 7/9/03 Hearing

June ?, 2003 **Minute Order** of Superior Court of Stanislaus County Re: Request of Courtroom Artist Behringer

June ?, 2003 **Media** Court TV Request to Permit Coverage of 7/9/03 Hearing

June ?, 2003 **Minute Order** of Superior Court of Stanislaus County Re: Court TV Request to Permit Coverage of 7/9/03 Hearing

June ?, 2003 **Media** Request for Coverage....

June 6, 2003 **Superior Court of Stanislaus County Hearing**

The court heard oral arguments as to the gag order, among other things.

May 15, 2003 **Order** of Superior Court of Stanislaus County Re: Stipulation and Order for Sealing of Coroner's Reports and Release of Coroner's Reports Under Seal; Conditional Sealing of Contra Costa Reports

The court ordered that the Contra Costa Coroner's Office shall not release any reports involving Laci or Conner to any person, agency, or entity, except to the Stanislaus County District Attorney...pending further hearing on May 27, 2003.

May ??, 2003 **Media** Newspapers' Supplemental Opposition to Ex Parte Sealing of Coroner's Report

May ??, 2003 **Media** Declaration of Charity Kenyon in Support of Newspapers' Supplemental Opposition to Ex Parte Sealing

??? ?, 2003 **Scott Peterson's** Petition to Seal **Post-Arrest** Materials, Wiretap, and Autopsy Reports

This is Scott's third petition in the Superior Court to seal these Materials from the media.

??? ?, 2003 **Superior Court of Stanislaus County Hearing In-Camera**

May 30, 2003 **Minute Order** of Superior Court of Stanislaus County

The court stated that the autopsy reports of Laci and Conner were to be sealed in their entirety, that the prior orders remain in effect, and that all of these documents now in the possession of the prosecutor and defense shall not be released, conveyed, or disclosed to anyone outside of their respective trial teams without further order of the court.

June 4, 2003 **Prosecutor's Motion** to Release Autopsy Reports

June 4, 2003 **Contra Costa County Sheriff-Coroner Office's Response** to the People's Motion to Release Autopsy Reports

The Sheriff-Coroner defers to the court's judgment as whether to seal or unseal coroner records. The coroner wants to know which records are to be sealed or unsealed; if the order allows the coroner to share information with the prosecutor and investigators; whether it permits the coroner to file a death certificate for Laci and a fetal death certificate as to Conner; wants to redact personal information from the records that are unsealed; and, that the court order prohibits public disclosure of photographs, negatives, prints, copies, and reproductions.

Attached to the report may be coroner's findings, reports of autopsy, reports of toxicology examinations, associated forensic reports, and physical evidence examination reports. Photos may also exist. The court's 5/15/03 and 5/30/03 orders could be interpreted as prohibiting the Sheriff-Coroner from sharing the records and information with involved law enforcement agencies, so we request that the court issue an express order allowing us to share these records.

Since the manner and cause of death is required on the death certificates, the prior orders could be interpreted as prohibiting us from disclosing that information. Photographs by the coroner should only be unsealed according to court order in accord with Code of Civil Procedure, § 129; no image of the body shall be made, or portion of the body, of a deceased person, taken by the coroner or caused to be taken by the coroner, except for use in a criminal action which relates to the death of that person; except as a court permits by order after good cause has been shown and after written notification of the request has been served to the prosecutor in the county where the autopsy or examination occurred, at least five days prior to the court issuing the order.

June 6, 2003 **Minute Order** of Stanislaus County Re: Autopsy Reports

June 12, 2003 **Order** of Superior Court of Stanislaus County Re: Protective Order/Decision

The Court hereby finds as follows: That the amount and nature of the pre-trial publicity has been massive. The local print media rarely does not have a daily front page article on this matter. Besides extensive local television and radio coverage, the national television media has embraced this case with a passion providing frequent commentaries from notables like Larry King, Geraldo Rivera, and Katie Couric.

In addition, there have been a number of national programs where professionals involved in the criminal justice system have opined their views on the evidence and possible trial strategy. Even Defense Counsel was a regular commentator prior to the Scott's arrest and his being retained on the case. Also, Second Counsel gave a lengthy televised interview prior to the arrest.

During the investigation, the Modesto Police Department made a number of press releases covering various aspects of the investigation. Not only the families of both Scott and Laci but even Scott, prior to his arrest, was involved in a lengthy nationally televised interview with Diane Sawyer. The families also recently gained national attention over a dispute regarding the possession of personal belongings of the Decedent [Laci].

Following the filing of the Complaint, the Clerk's office of the Superior Court was inundated with calls and visits from the media requesting copies of the complaint and all other documents in the file. This problem, which impacted staff resources, was significantly reduced with a creation of a website specifically for the media where representatives can easily obtain copies of any unsealed paper filed in this action. From April 30, 2003 to the present date [June 12, 2003], there have been over 12,000 hits. The public did not have access to the website. In order to foster accuracy in reporting, the Court allowed cameras in the courtroom pursuant to Rules of Court 980.

The nature of the publicity is especially troubling as it often involves leaks of information that could be considered favorable for one side or the other. For example, even though the autopsy report had been sealed along with a specific protective order, information was publicized regarding facts contained only in that document.

Periodically, there have been reports of defense theories of a possible serial killer or a satanic cult being responsible in this case. On the prosecution side, there have been comments by the Attorney General regarding the weight of the evidence and by the District Attorney [prosecutor] comparing his capital case record against that of the original defense attorney. When the Defense fielded a comment regarding a brown van being possibly involved in the killing, the Prosecution subsequently made a public announcement that the investigation had cleared that van of any involvement in the killings.

Pre-complaint, there were a number of comments in the media that certain specific items had been found in searches of Scott's property even though the search warrants had been sealed by Court order. Also, pre-complaint, there were reports regarding the amount of cooperation or lack of cooperation on the part of Scott during the investigation. Post filing, there have been reports of information gleaned from an examination of Scott's computer.

Even though the main purpose of a Protective order is to allow Scott to have a fair trial, and at this time the Defense [Scott] is opposing such an order, the Court is mindful of the directions from *Sheppard v. Maxwell*, 384 U.S. 333, at p.359(1966): "[t]he Court should have made some effort to control the release of leads, information, and gossip to the press by the police officers, witnesses, and counsel for both sides. Much of the information thus disclosed was inaccurate, leading to groundless rumors and confusion."

The Court has reviewed the sealed documents and the wiretap evidence and much contained therein would likely be determined to be irrelevant and/or inadmissible. The *Sheppard* case gave further direction at page 360: "[i]t is obvious that the judge should have further sought to alleviate this problem by imposing control over the statements made to the news media by counsel, witnesses and especially the Coroner and police officers. The prosecution repeatedly made evidence available to the news media, which was never offered in the trial. Much of the "evidence" disseminated in this fashion was clearly inadmissible. The exclusion of such evidence in court is rendered meaningless when news media make it available to the public."

The Court has considered two different standards applicable to imposing a Protective Order. Specifically, there is the "clear and present danger of serious imminent threat to a protected competing interest", *Hurvitz v. Hoefflin*, 84 Cal.App.4th 1232 (2000), or the "reasonable likelihood of prejudicial news which would make difficult the impaneling of an impartial jury and tend to prevent a fair trial" standard, *Younger v. Smith*, 30 Cal.App.3rd 138 (1973). Even though *Hurvitz* is more recent and mentions the federal cases, it ignores the *Younger* case which the Court finds is more applicable in a criminal case.

If this case were to proceed to trial without a Protective Order in place until shortly before jury selection, all the statements by the witnesses, all of the rumors and gossip would be rehashed shortly before trial thereby making it extremely difficult to select a fair and impartial jury.

Even though the Court is applying the *Younger* standard, in the unique facts of this case, there is a clear and present danger because of the modern media's capability easily to store and recall bits of information in order to relate them at any time including during jury selection. Further compounded in this case is the fact that the publicity is nationwide and cannot be automatically cured by a change of venue or extensive voir dire.

If witnesses are allowed to discuss publicly their expected testimony or if trial counsel or their staff are allowed to comment on strategy or on the weight of the evidence, even if jurors can be found that are willing to be fair and impartial, it may never be known if a juror were to rely consciously or subconsciously on the out-of-court information.

Although the Court is extremely concerned with the due process and fair trial rights in this case, it is also keenly aware of the public's right of access to the proceedings herein and the right of free speech of the participants. However, after balancing these rights, and in order to protect against the disruption of the proper administration of justice, the Court finds that good cause exists for the issuance of a pre-trial Protective Order.

The Court has considered less restrictive alternatives. First, a change of venue and extensive voir dire are not especially helpful in this case because of the exceptional amount of publicity which has been broadcast throughout this state and country. Secondly, the Court has previously reminded the parties of the Rules of Professional Conduct, but the problem has persisted.

Being mindful of the necessity of narrowly tailoring such an order, the Court hereby orders:

ORDER

It is the Order of the Court that no attorney connected with this case as Prosecutor or Defense counsel, nor any other attorney working in those offices, nor their agent's, staff, or experts, nor any judicial officer or court employee, nor any law enforcement employee of any agency involved in this case, nor any persons subpoenaed or expected to testify in this matter, shall do any of the following:

1. Release or authorize the release for public dissemination of any purported extrajudicial statement of either Scott or witnesses relating to this case;
2. Release or authorize the release of any documents, exhibits, photographs, or any evidence, the admissibility of which may have to be determined by the Court;
3. Make any statement for public dissemination as to the existence or possible existence of any document, exhibit, photograph or any other evidence, the admissibility of which may have to be determined by the Court;
4. Express outside of court an opinion or make any comment for public dissemination as to the weight, value, or effect of any evidence as tending to establish guilt or innocence;
5. Make any statement outside of court as to the nature, substance, or effect of any statements or testimony that have been given;
6. Issue any statement as to the identity of any prospective witness, or the witness's probable testimony, or the effect thereof;
7. Make any out-of-court statement as to the nature, source, or effect of any purported evidence alleged to have been accumulated as a result of the investigation of this matter.
8. Make any statement as to the content, nature, substance, or effect of any testimony which may be given in any proceeding related to this matter.

Any violation of this order will result in a contempt action for any offender within the jurisdiction of this Court.

This order does not include any of the following:

1. Factual statements of Scott's name, age, residence, occupation and family status.
2. The circumstances of the arrest, namely, the time and place of the arrest, the identity of the arresting and investigating officers and agencies, and the length of the investigation.
3. The nature, substance, and text of the charge, including a brief description of the offenses charged.
4. Quotations from, or any reference without comment to, public records of the Court in the case, or to other public records or communications heretofore disseminated to the public.
5. The scheduling and result of any stage of the prejudicial proceedings held in open court in an open or public session.
6. A request for assistance in obtaining evidence.
7. Any information as to any person not in custody who is sought as a possible suspect or witness, nor any statement aimed at warning the public of any possible danger as to such person not in custody.
8. A request for assistance in obtaining of evidence or the names of possible witnesses.
9. Any witness may discuss any matter with any Prosecution or Defense Attorney in this action, or any agent thereof; and if represented may discuss any matter with his/her own attorney.

A copy of this order shall be provided to any prospective witness which a party intends to call for any proceeding in this action. If held to answer at the preliminary hearing, the Court will consider at the arraignment whether this order should be modified or terminated pending jury selection. Any objections or suggested modifications to the continuation of this order should be filed in writing five days prior to the arraignment.

June 13, 2003 **Minute Order** of Superior Court of Stanislaus County Re: Amendment to Protective Order/Decision

June ??, 2003 **News' Medias' Request** for Reconsideration of Protective "Gag" Order

June 16, 2003 **Minute** Order of Superior Court of Stanislaus County Re: Search Warrant Sealing

June ??, 2003 **Media** Consolidated Motion for Reconsideration of Court's Order, etc.

June 17, 2003 **Scott Peterson's Petition** for Writ of Mandate
Scott files another writ to prevent the sealed Materials of the case from being released to the media, and other relief.

June 17, 2003 **Media Petition** to Release Sealed Materials
This is media's second petition to release the sealed Materials.

June ??, 2003 **Prosecutor's** Request for Court Review of the Wiretap Recordings

June 25, 2003 **Minute Order** of Superior Court of Stanislaus County

June ??, 2003 **Scott Peterson's** Request to Continue the Briefing Schedule on Media Coverage of the Preliminary Hearing

June 26, 2003 **Minute Order** of Superior Court of Stanislaus County

June 26, 2003 **Media** Request of Courtroom Artist V.E. Behringer to Permit Coverage of Hearing

June 26, 2003 **Minute Order** of Superior Court of Stanislaus County Re: Request of Courtroom Artist

June 26, 2003 **Media** KTVU, FOX, and NBC Request to Permit Coverage of Hearing

June 26, 2003 **Minute Order** of Superior Court of Stanislaus County Re: Request of KTVU, FOX, and NBC Request to Permit Coverage of Hearing

June 26, 2003 **Media** Court TV Request to Permit Coverage of Hearing

June 26, 2003 **Minute Order** of Superior Court of Stanislaus County Re: Request of Court TV to Permit Coverage of Hearing

June 26, 2003 **Media** The Modesto Bee Request to Permit Coverage of Hearing

June 26, 2003 **Minute Order** of Superior Court of Stanislaus County Re: Request of Modesto Bee to Permit Coverage of Hearing

June 26, 2003 **Media** Fox News 40 Request to Permit Coverage of Hearing

June 26, 2003 **Minute Order** of Superior Court of Stanislaus County Re: Request of Fox 40 to Permit Coverage of Hearing

June 27, 2003 **Minute Order** of Superior Court of Stanislaus County

The court's third order grants media's second petition for release of the sealed Materials, after a hearing in the judge's chambers, on the first and third petitions.

June 27, 2003 **Opinion of Court of Appeal of the State of California, Fifth Appellate District**

The Court of Appeal stays the Stanislaus Superior Court's Order of June 12, 2003, as to any release of sealed Materials.

July 1, 2003 **Minute Order** of Superior Court of Stanislaus County Re: Amended Protective Order/Decision

The Court, having considered the Points and Authorities submitted and having heard the arguments of Counsel hereby amends the Protective order of June 12, 2003 as follows:

1. Scott is clearly specified as being subject to the order.
2. Those expected to testify are limited to those notified by the Prosecution or Defense.
3. Paragraph 2 of the prohibitions is modified to delete the last phrase and insert "that may be relevant to the guilt or innocence of Scott herein in that the document, exhibit, or photograph or any other evidence tends to either prove or disprove a material fact in issue in this matter.

4. Paragraph 3 of the prohibitions is modified in the same manner as paragraph 2. Also, "or authorize" is inserted after the first word.

August ?, 2003 **Stipulation and Order** Re: Allegations of Protective Order Violation

July 7, 2003 **Minute Order** of Superior Court of Stanislaus County

July 25, 2003 **Minute Order** of Superior Court of Stanislaus County Re: Continuing the 8/15/03 Motions to 9/9/03 Preliminary Hearing

July 30, 2003 **Opinion of the Court of Appeal of the State of California, Fifth Appellate District**

In his petition for writ of mandate, petitioner Scott Lee Peterson contends the trial court abused its discretion by authorizing upon certain conditions, the release to the media of pre-arrest warrants, affidavits and returns, [hereafter Materials], filed in connection with the police investigation into the deaths of Laci Peterson and her unborn son and currently under seal by order of the trial court. We agree and therefore issue the writ.

Therefore, let a peremptory writ of mandate issue directing the trial court to vacate its order filed on June 12, 2003, in Stanislaus County Superior Court action No. 1045188, and to enter a new and different order denying the petition of CCN, et al. [all media real parties] for disclosure of the Materials.

The order filed in this proceeding on June 27, 2003, staying the order filed on June 12, 2003, in action No. 1045188 of the Stanislaus County Superior Court shall remain in effect only until this opinion is final in all the courts of this state, the superior court complies with this disposition, or the Supreme Court grants a hearing herein, whichever shall first occur, thereafter the stay is dissolved.

Insofar as petitioner [Scott] requests relief in addition to that granted above, the request is denied.

The Materials were gathered after the victims' disappearance during December 2002. A petition (first petition) to release the Materials to the media was filed in the trial court, as action No. 1045098, by real party in interest McClatchy Newspapers, Inc. Other members of the media, including Contra

Costa Newspapers, Inc., another real party in interest in the instant proceeding, joined in the first opinion. All media real parties will be identified together as CCN.

After an in camera hearing on the first petition, the trial court entered an order (first order) on April 10, 2003, which denied the first petition "in its entirety" but then provided in effect that the Materials would be released on July 9, 2003, or alternatively on the date when "a criminal complaint is filed," whichever was earlier.

The first order was accompanied by detailed findings of fact (Findings), which included the following: "Testimony at the hearing [on the first petition] also established that revelation of confidential information contained in the [Materials] would irreparably harm the investigation. Investigation techniques, clues and focus on future avenues of inquiry by law enforcement personnel would unduly alert any potential suspect. Evidence would likely be destroyed and witnesses would be reluctant to provide information."

"Any information released at this time from any of the [Materials] would harm the reliability of information already gleaned and to be gleaned in the future. Furthermore, any information released to the public at this time would adversely impact future tips to law enforcement who must discern whether or not information provided to them by tipsters is based upon public information or independently verifiable." [¶]...[¶]

"The court also concludes that unsealing any of the [Materials] would likely impair any suspects' rights to a fair trial."

Shortly after the first order was filed, the bodies of Laci Peterson and her unborn were discovered and identified. Petitioner [Scott] was arrested and charged with their murders, in Stanislaus County Superior Court action No. 1056770.

On April 18, 2003, real party in interest the People [prosecutor], by the Office of the District Attorney of Stanislaus County, filed a petition for writ of mandate (first mandate) in this court (No. F042848) challenging those portions of the first order that authorized release of the Materials upon stated conditions. While this first mandate petition was pending, another petition (second petition) to release the Materials to media was filed in the trial court, in the existing action No. 1045188, by CCN. The trial court deferred action on the second petition until disposition by this court in the first mandate proceedings.

On May 5, 2003, this court granted peremptory relief (first opinion) in the first mandate proceeding. We concluded the trial court's Findings were "through, complete and unambiguously establish[ed] that the [trial] court carefully balanced all of the factors relevant under the case law, the provisions of Penal Code section 1534, and the California Rules of Court." We also pointed out that the media petitioners had not challenged the Findings, which manifested a determination by the trial court that both the People [prosecutor] and petitioner [Scott] would be prejudged by public disclosure of the Materials, and had not, in any opposition papers or in a separate writ petition, put the propriety of any of the Findings in issue. We therefore validated the trial court's Findings as fully supported by the record evidence.

After our first opinion was filed, the media petitioners neither asked this court to rehear or reconsider our opinion nor sought its review by the Supreme Court. The first opinion is now final in all the courts in this state.

Pursuant to requests of the parties, we take judicial notice of this court's file in the first mandate proceeding (No. F042848) and the exhibits attached to the pleadings in this proceeding.

However, we invalidated those provisions in the first order authorizing release of the materials upon the dates specified. We said in relevant part: "Though the portion of the trial court's order which sealed the Materials is legally sound, the portion of the order which requires disclosure of the Materials upon the filing of a criminal complaint and, in any event, by July 9, 2003, is so fundamentally inconsistent with the Findings as to constitute a manifest abuse of discretion. [Footnote omitted]. A criminal investigation does not automatically cease upon the filing of a complaint or upon the passage of a arbitrary period of time. The Findings themselves implicitly recognize that the investigation would likely continue for a substantial period, certainly more than the 11 days which elapsed before the complaint was filed."

"Moreover, the Findings expressly recognize that the disclosure of the '[i]nvestigation techniques, clues and focus on the future avenues of inquiry by law enforcement personnel would unduly alert any potential suspect. Evidence would likely be destroyed and witnesses would be reluctant to provide information.' These considerations would conceivably disappear only if the complaint was filed against the *actual* perpetrator or perpetrators, but an accurate identification of a perpetrator has yet to be made and legally will not be made by the filing of a complaint or the arrival of a specific date in the future based upon an erroneous assumption; that an arrest or the lapse of time would remove the possibility, among others, that a 'potential suspect' would be alerted, that evidence would be destroyed, or that witnesses would be discouraged." (See first Appellate Court Order).

A petition (third petition) to seal post-arrest warrant materials, wiretaps and an autopsy report (hereafter Materials II) was filed in the trial court, as action No. 1056770, by petitioner [Scott]. On May 30, 2003, the trial court entered an order (second order) sealing the Materials II. On June 12, 2003, the trial court entered an order (gag order) restricting the parties to the criminal action against petitioner [Scott] from making public comments about the case. Findings of fact accompanied the gag order.

Also on June 12, 2003, the trial court entered an order (third order) granting the second petition for release of the Materials, based upon the evidence presented during in camera hearings previously held in connection with the first petition and with the third petition. Among other things, the court noted that "the entire thrust of the People's evidence presented [at the hearing on the first petition] was directed toward preserving the integrity of the investigation <u>before an arrest was made</u> in order to avoid alerting any suspect," "[n]o evidence was presented at the in-camera hearing held on [the second petition]," and "The People have not produced any evidence since [defendant's] [Scott's] arrest to indicate they are investigating other suspects."

The trial court therefore directed release of the Materials based upon the court's findings that certain circumstances had changed. The changed circumstances identified by the court were the discovery and identification of the bodies, the arrest of petitioner [Scott] and charges of murder filed against him, and the representation of petitioner "by multiple and able defense counsel who can muster all available, legitimate means to assist the trial judge in ensuring their client [Scott] receives a fair trial." The court also concluded that the parties opposing the release of the Materials had not demonstrated a good reason to retain the Materials under seal.

The present petition for writ of mandate (second mandate) was filed on June 17, 2003.

In this second mandate proceeding CCN has not challenged the trial court's Findings contained in the first order or raised any issue about this court's first opinion. It follows then that good cause to maintain the Materials under seal existed when the trial court considered the second petition unless the circumstances upon which those Findings and that first opinion were based were shown to have materially changed since the entry of the first order. There is no conflict or dispute among the parties about the identity or nature of the specific changed circumstances relied upon by the trial court. The record discloses no such material change of circumstances.

Second, the arrest of petitioner [Scott] and the filing of the complaint against him are likewise irrelevant to the concerns addressed by the Findings. Our first opinion found that the filing of a complaint would not support an order unsealing the Materials, given the trial court's Findings about the practical realities of the investigation. If the filing of a complaint does not sanction release of the Materials, the fact that an arrest has been made provides no further justification, because the filing of a complaint virtually assures that an arrest of the subject of the complaint has been or ultimately will be made.

Third, **so far as we are aware, the presumption of innocence is still a fundamental constitutional right available to all criminal defendants**. The criminal action against petitioner [Scott] is yet in its early stages. A preliminary examination has not been held. When held it will not determine whether petitioner [Scott] is guilty or not guilty; it will only determine whether probable cause exists to try petitioner [Scott] under the complaint.

The investigation will continue during the likely substantial period of time between the preliminary hearing and any trial, should probable cause be found, and beyond the preliminary hearing, should probable cause not be found. If, at the time of the hearing on the first petition, it was unrealistic and speculative to assume that there could not be any other potential suspects, that all evidence had been developed and preserved, that all potential witnesses and informants had come forward, and that the investigation would not be compromised by the disclosure of the Materials, it is no less unrealistic and speculative to make the same assumptions now.

Put conversely, if, at the time of the hearing on the first petition, it was reasonable to conclude that disclosure of the

Materials might compromise the investigation and the search for the perpetrator, it is no less reasonable to come to the same conclusion now.

Fourth, the potential for prejudice from the release of the Materials is enhanced rather than diminished by the arrest of petitioner [Scott] and the filing of the complaint against him. The relationship of petitioner to the victims only serves to stimulate the public's appetite for the case, an appetite we would expect the media to satisfy. Release of the Materials would undoubtedly be followed by their widespread dissemination and dissection in every sort of media medium, including daily television with parades of "experts" endlessly commenting about likely prosecution and defense strategies, opining about the strengths, weaknesses and admissibility of the various factual tidbits disclosed by the Materials, and venturing predictions about the probable outcome of the trial against petitioner [Scott]. How a fair trial for both parties, and particularly how an untainted jury could be found anywhere, in the aftermath of such a frenzy escapes us.

CCN impliedly acknowledges the heightened degree of prolonged news coverage generated by this case but studiously ignores the potential for prejudice to the parties that might accompany release of the Materials. Instead, CCN addresses two other topics.

First, CCN claims that petitioner [Scott] has not provided an adequate record for review. We find the record satisfactory. No new evidence was presented at the in camera hearing on the second petition; the third order was based in part on the evidence presented at the hearing on the first petition which resulted in the first order, the order that included the critical Findings. As we have already pointed out, the third order on its face is inherently inconsistent with the import of the Findings. The third order was also based on evidence presented at the hearing on the third petition, which evidence led the trial court, in ruling on the third petition, to reach conclusions substantially equivalent to the conclusions reflected by the Findings.

Second, CCN argues that the prior disclosure of the Materials to petitioner and his counsel should have been considered by the trial court to be an additional changed circumstance warranting release of the Materials to the media. The third order expressly states that "The change in circumstances is discussed in Sections II and III above." "Sections II and III" articulate in detail the changed circumstances relied upon by the trial court, all of which we have already considered and none of which include the release of the Materials to petitioner. In fact, neither section II or section III even mentions that the Materials were made available to petitioner.

Even if CCN is correct that the particular event constitutes a changed circumstance, we would not find it a material one sufficient to unseal the Materials. The first order retained the Materials under seal because "...unsealing any of the documents in issue would likely impair any suspects' rights to a fair trial." Petitioner's [Scott's] position was then, as it is now, that the Materials should continue to be restricted. We will not entertain the unreasonable assumption that petitioner [Scott] will act against his own expressed interest in a fair trial by breaching the confidentiality of the Materials.

We also reiterate that all parties, including petitioner and his counsel, are subject to the gag order.

We recognize that evidence described in the Materials may be introduced, and perhaps made available to the public, during the preliminary hearing. But the extent and nature of the evidence presented at the hearing will be controlled by the parties, based upon their respective assessments of their own best interests and their pre-trial and trial plans. The right of each party to a fair trial is one of the concerns around which the issue of disclosure revolves.

Once the courts have determined that, under the relevant circumstances, that right [fair trial] prevails over any countervailing public right to disclosure, it is the parties who are entitled to decide whether to make a particular revelation and, by doing so, potentially work a change in the situation from which the then prevailing order of confidentiality derives and thus to likely invite a new challenge to all or part of that order.

CCN opposes peremptory relief, on a number of grounds. CCN argues there is no "temporal urgency" for peremptory relief. We disagree. A decision by this court without the delay that necessarily accompanies issuance of an order to show cause serves the interest of all parties, including CCN, which may now immediately seek review of this decision by the Supreme Court.

CCN also contends that petitioner's [Scott's] entitlement to relief is not "so obvious that no purpose could reasonably be served by plenary consideration of the issue..." (*Ng v. Superior*

Court (1992) 4 Cal. 4th 29, 35.) We have come to the opposite conclusion. This opinion is not based upon any disputed or questionable facts; it is based instead upon the Findings of the trial court in its first order and the conclusions reached in our first opinion, neither of which have ever been questioned by any party to this proceeding, CCN included, and both of which, as a matt of law, compel issuance of the relief sought by petitioner [Scott].

Finally, CCN had adequate notice of the current pendency before this court of the question whether the third order was improper in light of the unchallenged Findings underlying the first order, the conclusions expressed in the trial court's second order, and the rationale and disposition of our first opinion. The People's brief raised this precise issue. (*Palma v. U.S. Industrial Fasteners, Inc.*(1984) 36 Cal.3d 171, 180-181.)

For the reasons expressed above, Petitioner [Scott] is entitled to appropriate relief. (Code of Civ. Proc. Sec. 1085; see *Whitney's at the Beach v. Superior Court*(1970) 3 Cal.App.3d 258, 266.) A peremptory writ of mandate is proper and should issue. (Code Civ. Proc. Sec. 1088; *Palma v. U.S. Industrial-Fasteners, Inc., supra,* 36 Cal.3d at pp.180-181; *Goodenough v. Superior Court*(1971) 18 Cal.App.3d 692, 697.)

July ?, 2003 **Attorney for San Francisco** Motion to Quash Subpoena

July ?, 2003 **??'s Opposition** to City and County of San Francisco

??? ?, 2003 **Scott Peterson's Motion** to Close the Preliminary Hearing

??? ?, 2003 **Media's Opposition** to Scott Peterson's Motion to Close the Preliminary Hearing

??? ?, 2003 **Media** Non-Party Media Brief in Opposition to Scott Peterson's Motion to Close the Preliminary Hearing

??? ?, 2003 **Media** Non-Party Media Appendix on Non-California Points and Authorities in Support of Opposition to Scott Peterson's Motion to Close the Preliminary Hearing

??? ?, 2003 **Media** Non-Party Media Supplemental Appendix on Non-California Points and Authorities in Support of Opposition to Scott Peterson's Motion to Close the Preliminary Hearing

??? ?, 2003 **Media** Attorney for Non-Party Media Appendix of Exhibits, A-L, in Support of Opposition

??? ?, 2003 **Media** Media's Attorney Position Re: Media's Opposition to Scott Peterson's Motion to Close the Preliminary Hearing

??? ?, 2003 **Media** Attorney's Joinder in Brief in Support of Cameras in the Courtroom

??? ?, 2003 **Scott Peterson's Reply** to Media's Entities' Oppositions to Scott Peterson's Motion to Close the Preliminary Hearing

July ?, 2003 **Prosecutor's** Position Re: Media Coverage

July 9, 2003 **Hearing** in Superior Court of Stanislaus County

August 4, 2003 **Minute Order** of Superior Court of Stanislaus County

August 13, 2003 **Minute Order** of Superior Court of Stanislaus County

August ??, 2003 **Media** KFBK 1530AM Request for Coverage of 8/14/03 Hearing

August ??, 2003 **Minute Order** of Superior Court of Stanislaus County Re: KFBK Request for Coverage of Hearing

August ??, 2003 **Media** The Modesto Bee Request for Coverage of 8/14/03 Hearing

August ??, 2003 **Minute Order** of Superior Court of Stanislaus County Re: Modesto Bee Request for Coverage of Hearing

June 26, 2003 **Media** Ex Parte Application by Non-Party Media Organizations for Permission to File a Brief for 8/14/03 Hearing

August ??, 2003 **Order** of Superior Court of Stanislaus County Permitting Non-Party Organization to File Brief for 8/14/03 Hearing

August ??, 2003 **??'s** Notice of Lodging of Redacted Motion to Suppress

August ??, 2003 **Scott Peterson's Motion** to Suppress Illegally Obtained Wiretap Evidence

August ??, 2003 **Prosecutor's Opposition** to Motion to Suppress Wiretaps

August 14, 2003 **Order** of Superior Court of Stanislaus County Re: Defendant's Motion to Close the Preliminary Hearing; Media's Motion to Allow Television/Audio Coverage of the Preliminary Hearing; People's Motion for Venue Survey; People's Motion to Seal Part of the Opposition to Defendant's Suppression Motion

Scott's motion to close the preliminary hearing is denied. The court could not make the necessary findings required to find that a closure of the hearing would require, even in a death penalty matter. The court finds that the harm expected is speculative and not unlike that in other high publicity cases. The court will have control of the proceedings and the right to close specific portions of the hearing with appropriate findings, if necessary. The prosecutor takes no position on the matter.

Media's motion to allow television and audio coverage of the preliminary hearing is taken under submission and the court shall prepare a Statement of Decision. Scott did not file a written response, but orally states that based on the court's decision above in denying closure, he is for full coverage.

People's motion for a venue change is denied, without prejudice [he can bring it up again], as the prosecutor's motion is premature. In renewing any such motion, the court directs the People to include the experience of other counties in which such a survey has been conducted, and submit a proposed questionnaire for the court's review.

People's motion to seal part of the opposition to Scott's Suppression motion is granted, in that the portion of their opposition to the suppression motion, specifically 'Attachment A', shall remain sealed/confidential. Scott does not object and media has had their comments heard.

Scott files a motion in open court for discovery and a hearing is set for September 2, 2003 at 8:30am. If discovery is obtained prior to the above date, Scott shall notify the court to drop the hearing. Both sides represent they will be ready to proceed, subject to discovery issues being completed.

The court shall hold a hearing at the conclusion of the preliminary hearing, currently set on September 9, 2003, at 9:30am, as to the possible violation of the Protective Order by the defense. People are to review the issue to determine if they believe there is any merit, and file the appropriate documents within one week. Scott may file a reply prior to the scheduled hearing.

Counsel stipulate to an order authorizing additional limited examination of the remains and release of remains to next of kin, and is approved by the court.

Scott requests an order to allow defense to inspect the physical evidence in possession of the crime lab and, or, the police department. People represent a master list, re: evidence has been compiled by the Modesto Police Department, Detective Division, using the various property lists of items seized. A copy will be presented to the defense for review.

Scott requests a copy of all forensic reports and notes be provided to the defense forthwith. Based on People's representation, the court assumes informal discovery is adequate and any disputes will be addressed at the next hearing.

Scott is remanded to the custody of the Sheriff to appear on the date/time set for discovery motion of 9/2/03, as set forth above. Scott is held without bail.

August 15, 2003 **Minute Order** of Superior Court of Stanislaus County Re: Rule 980 Decision

August ??, 2003 **Media** The Modesto Bee Request for Coverage of Hearing

August ??, 2003 **Order** of Superior Court of Stanislaus County Re: Modesto Bee Request for Coverage of Hearing

August ??, 2003 **Media** Court TV Request for Coverage of Hearing

August ??, 2003 **Order** of Superior Court of Stanislaus County Re: Court TV Request for Coverage of Hearing

August ??, 2003 **Media** KXTV 10 Request for Coverage of Hearing

August ??, 2003 **Order** of Superior Court of Stanislaus County Re: KXTV Request for Coverage of Hearing

August ??, 2003 **Media** KFBF 1530 Request for Coverage of Hearing

August ??, 2003 **Order** of Superior Court of Stanislaus County Re: KFBF Request for Coverage of Hearing

August ??, 2003 **??'s Opposition** to Television Broadcast of Amber Frey's Testimony at the Preliminary Hearing

July ?, 2003 **Scott Peterson's Stipulation** to Continue Hearing on Suppression Motion

July ?, 2003 **Order** of Superior Court of Stanislaus County Re: Permitting Defense Experts to Examine Remains

August ?, 2003 **Order** Scott Peterson's Further Stipulation and Order Authorizing Defense Experts to Examine Remains

August ?, 2003 **Scott Peterson's Motion** for Discovery

August ?, 2003 **Prosecutor's Response** to Scott's Motion for Discovery

August ?, 2003 **Order** of Superior Court of Stanislaus County Re: Further Stipulation and Order Authorizing Additional Limited Exam/Release of Remains

August 25, 2003 **Scott Peterson's Petition for Writ of Mandate**

This document is not available, so I'm assuming from the Order below, and it having been attached to a media brief wanting cameras in the courtroom, that Scott's writ is requesting the Court of Appeal to tell the Stanislaus Superior Court to either close the preliminary hearing, or to allow cameras inside the courtroom, since the Stanislaus Order states that the judge will take the camera issue under advisement.

August 27, 2003 **Opinion of the Court of Appeal of the State of California, Fifth Appellate District**

Scott files petition with the Court of Appeal. The Court of Appeal states that, the 'Petition for Writ of Mandate' filed in this court on August 25, 2003, is denied.

The Writ isn't available, however; this particular document was attached to a media brief in objection to the prelim being closed in the Kobe Bryant case, filed in the Kobe Bryant case in Eagle, Colorado, along with a copy of the August 14, 2003, Stanislaus Superior Court's Order denying Scott's motion to close his preliminary hearing. This was in an effort by media, in the Kobe case, to gain camera access to Kobe's preliminary hearing, in part, by documenting to the Colorado court that Scott's prelim would be with cameras, so why not Kobe's too.

August ?, 2003 **Prosecutor's Motion** to Conduct Venue Survey

August ?, 2003 **Scott Peterson's Opposition** to Prosecutor's Motion to Conduct Venue Survey

August 28, 2003 **Minute Order** of Superior Court of Stanislaus County Re: Matters to be Heard on 9/2/03

August ??, 2003 **Media** V.E. Behringer Courtroom Artist Request for Coverage of 9/2/03 Hearing

August ??, 2003 **Order** of Superior Court of Stanislaus County Re: Behringer Request for Coverage of Hearing

August ??, 2003 **Media** Court TV Request for Coverage of 9/2/03 Hearing

August ??, 2003 **Order** of Superior Court of Stanislaus County Re: Court TV Request for Coverage of Hearing

August ??, 2003 **Media** KFBK 1530AM Request for Coverage of 9/2/03 Hearing

August ??, 2003 **Order** of Superior Court of Stanislaus County Re: KFBK Request for Coverage of Hearing

August ??, 2003 **Media** KTVU 2 and NBC 11 Request for Coverage of 9/2/03 Hearing

August ??, 2003 **Order** of Superior Court of Stanislaus County Re: KTVU 2 and NBC 11 Request for Coverage of Hearing

August ??, 2003 **Media** KTVU CH 2, NBC 11, NBC 3, and Fox Request for Coverage of 9/9/03 Hearing

August ??, 2003 **Order** of Superior Court of Stanislaus County Re: KTVU 2, NBC 11, NBC 3, and Fox Request for Coverage of Hearing

August ??, 2003 **Media** V.E. Behringer Courtroom Artist Request for Coverage of 9/9/03 Hearing

August ??, 2003 **Order** of Superior Court of Stanislaus County Re: Behringer Request for Coverage of Hearing

September 2, 2003 **Minute Order** of Superior Court of Stanislaus County

September 2, 2003 **Minute Order** of Superior Court of Stanislaus County No.2

September ?, 2003 **Media** KTVU CH 2, NBC 3, and Others Request for Coverage of 9/17/03 Hearing

September ?, 2003 **Order** of Superior Court of Stanislaus County Re: KTVU 2, NBC 3, and Others Request for Coverage of Hearing

The media request for coverage of the hearing is granted.

October 2, 2003 **Minute Order** of Superior Court of Stanislaus County Re: Sealed Search Warrant for Case #1045118

October ?, 2003 **Scott Peterson's Motion** to Conduct a Franks Hearing

October ?, 2003 **Prosecutor's Response** to Scott's Motion for "Franks" Hearing

October ?, 2003 **Scott Peterson's Motion** to Exclude Dog Trailing Evidence at the Preliminary Hearing

October ?, 2003 **Scott Peterson's Motion** and Motion in Limine to Exclude Mitochondrial DNA

October ?, 2003 **Scott Peterson's Motion** and Motion in Limine to Exclude GPS Tracking

October ?, 2003 **Media** The Modesto Bee Request for Coverage of 10/17/03 Hearing

October ?, 2003 **Order** of Superior Court of Stanislaus County Re: Modesto Bee Request for Coverage of Hearing

The request by The Modesto Bee is granted.

October ?, 2003 **Media** KFBK 1530AM Request for Coverage of 10/17/03 Hearing

October ?, 2003 **Order** of Superior Court of Stanislaus County Re: KFBK Request for Coverage of Hearing

October ?, 2003 **Media** Contra Costa Times Request for Coverage of 10/17/03 Hearing

October ?, 2003 **Order** of Superior Court of Stanislaus County Re: Contra Costa Times Request for Coverage of Hearing

The request by Contra Costa Times is denied.

October ?, 2003 **Media** The Modesto Bee Request for Coverage of 10/17/03 Hearing No.2

October ?, 2003 **Order** of Superior Court of Stanislaus County Re: Modesto Bee Request for Coverage of Hearing

The request by The Modesto Bee is granted.

October ??, 2003 **Scott Peterson's Motion** to Seal Search Warrant

October ??, 2003 **Prosecutor's Opposition** to Scott's Motion to Seal Search Warrant

October ??, 2003 **Prosecutor's Points and Authorities** in Support of Evidence

October ??, 2003 **Scott Peterson's Reply** to Prosecutor's Opposition to Scott's Motion to Seal Search Warrant

October 17, 2003 **Minute Order** of Superior Court of Stanislaus County

October ??, 2003 **Prosecutor's Response** to Scott's Motion to "Traverse" Wiretaps

October ??, 2003 **Media** KFBK Request for Coverage of Hearing

October ??, 2003 **Order** of Superior Court of Stanislaus County Re: KFBK Request for Coverage of Hearing

The request by KFBK is granted.

October ??, 2003 **Media** KTVU CH 2 Request for Coverage of 10/24/03 and 10/28/03 Hearings

October ??, 2003 **Order** of Superior Court of Stanislaus County Re: KTVU Request for Coverage of Hearings

The request by KTVU is granted.

October ??, 2003 **Media** KGO-TV CH 7 Request for Coverage of 10/24/03 Hearing

October ??, 2003 **Order** of Superior Court of Stanislaus County Re: KGO-TV Request for Coverage of Hearing

The request by KGO-TV is denied.

October ??, 2003 **Media** Court TV Request for Coverage of 10/24/03 Hearing

October ??, 2003 **Order** of Superior Court of Stanislaus County Re: Court TV Request for Coverage of Hearing

The request by Court TV is granted.

October 24, 2003 **Minute Order** of Superior Court of Stanislaus County

October 29, 2003 **Minute Order** of Superior Court of Stanislaus County

October 30, 2003 **Minute Order** of Superior Court of Stanislaus County

October 31, 2003 **Minute Order** of Superior Court of Stanislaus County

November 3, 2003 **Minute Order** of Superior Court of Stanislaus County

November 4, 2003 **Minute Order** of Superior Court of Stanislaus County

November 5, 2003 **Minute Order** of Superior Court of Stanislaus County

November 6, 2003 **Minute Order** of Superior Court of Stanislaus County

November ?, 2003 **??'s Application** for Subpoena duces tecum

November 12, 2003 **Minute Order** of Superior Court of Stanislaus County

November 13, 2003 **Minute Order** of Superior Court of Stanislaus County

November 14, 2003 **Minute Order** of Superior Court of Stanislaus County

November 17, 2003 **Minute Order** of Superior Court of Stanislaus County

November ??, 2003 **??'s** Exhibit List

November ??, 2003 **Order** of Superior Court of Stanislaus County Re: Mitochondria DNA Ruling [Decision]

November 18, 2003 **Minute Order** of Superior Court of Stanislaus County

November ??, 2003 **Media** Court TV Request for Coverage of 12/3/03 Hearing

November ??, 2003 **Order** of Superior Court of Stanislaus County Re: Court TV Request for Coverage of Hearing

The request by Court TV is granted.

November ??, 2003 **Media** The Modesto Bee Request for Coverage of 12/3/03 Hearing

November ??, 2003 **Order** of Superior Court of Stanislaus County Re: Modesto Request for Coverage of Hearing

The request by The Modesto Bee is granted.

November ??, 2003 **Media** KFBK 1530AM Request for Coverage of 12/3/03 Hearing

November ??, 2003 **Order** of Superior Court of Stanislaus County Re: KFBK Request for Coverage of Hearing

The request by KFBK 1530AM is granted.

November ??, 2003 **Scott Peterson's Motion** for Return of Property

November ??, 2003 **Prosecutor's Opposition** to Scott's Request for Return of Evidence [Property]

November ??, 2003 **Prosecutor's Motion** to Seal and Maintain Seal of Documents

November ??, 2003 **News' Media Opposition** to Seal and Maintain Seal of Documents

November ??, 2003 **Scott Peterson's Response** to "News Media's" Opposition

November ??, 2003 **Prosecutor's** "Information For" Document

December 1, 2003 **Minute Order** of Superior Court of Stanislaus County

December ?, 2003 **Media** CNN, NBC, ABC, CBS, KCRA, and Others Request for Coverage of 12/3/03 Hearing

December ?, 2003 **Order** of Superior Court of Stanislaus County Re: CNN, NBC, ABC, CBS, KCRA Request for Coverage of Hearing

The media requests for coverage of the hearing are granted.

December ?, 2003 **Media** NBCNC, Fox, KTVU-2, and NBC 11 Request for Coverage of 12/3/03 Hearing

December ?, 2003 **Order** of Superior Court of Stanislaus County Re: NBCNC, Fox, KTVU-2, and NBC 11 Request for Coverage of Hearing

The media requests for coverage of the hearing are granted.

December ?, 2003 **Media** Sketch Artist and The Modesto Bee Request for Coverage of 12/3/03 Hearing

December ?, 2003 **Order** of Superior Court of Stanislaus County Re: Sketch Artist and Modesto Bee Request for Coverage of Hearing

The media requests for coverage of the hearing are granted.

December 3, 2003 **Minute Order** of Superior Court of Stanislaus County

December 3, 2003 **Minute Order** of Superior Court of Stanislaus County No.2

December 5, 2003 **Minute Order** of Superior Court of Stanislaus County

December 5, 2003 **Minute Order** of Superior Court of Stanislaus County No.2

December ??, 2003 **Media** Court TV Request for Coverage of Hearing

December ??, 2003 **Order** of Superior Court of Stanislaus County Re: Court TV Request for Coverage of Hearing

The request by Court TV is granted.

December ??, 2003 **Prosecutor's** Informal Request for Discovery

December 11, 2003 **Minute Order** of Superior Court of Stanislaus County

December ??, 2003 **Media** The Modesto Bee Request for Coverage of Hearing

December ??, 2003 **Order** of Superior Court of Stanislaus County Re: Sketch Artist and Modesto Bee Request for Coverage of Hearing

The media requests for coverage of the hearing are granted.

December ??, 2003 **Media** Court TV Request for Coverage of Hearing

December ??, 2003 **Order** of Superior Court of Stanislaus County Re: Court TV Request for Coverage of Hearing

The request by Court TV is granted.

December ??, 2003 **Media** Sketch Artist Behringer Request for Coverage of Hearing

December ??, 2003 **Order** of Superior Court of Stanislaus County Re: Behringer Request for Coverage of Hearing

The request by Sketch Artist Behringer is granted.

December ??, 2003 **Media** KFBK Request for Coverage of Hearing

December ??, 2003 **Order** of Superior Court of Stanislaus County Re: KFBK Request for Coverage of Hearing

The request by KFBK is granted.

December ??, 2003 **Media** KUVS Request for Coverage of Hearing

December ??, 2003 **Order** of Superior Court of Stanislaus County Re: KVUS Request for Coverage of Hearing

The request by KVUS is denied.

December ??, 2003 **Media** Court TV Request for Coverage of 1/8/04 Hearing

December ??, 2003 **Order** of Superior Court of Stanislaus County Re: Court TV Request for Coverage of Hearing

The request by Court TV is granted.

December ??, 2003 **??'s** Receipt of Subpoenaed Records

December ??, 2003 **Prosecutor's** ?? and Order for Production of Inmate/Witness

December ??, 2003 **Prosecutor's Amended Motion** to Conduct Venue Survey

To be heard on 12/12/03.

December 15, 2003 **Scott Peterson's Motion** for Change of Venue, with Supporting Exhibits and Declarations

January 2, 2004 **Prosecutor's Opposition** to Motion for Change of Venue

It is the prosecution's position that Scott has not met his burden of establishing a "reasonable likelihood" that he cannot receive a fair trial in this county. The five factors break down as follows: (1)the nature of the crime, favors the defendant [Scott], but as a factor standing alone it would not support a change of venue, (2)publicity, when all of the factors are considered weighs against a change of venue and, favors the prosecution, (4)status of the victim weighs against a change of venue and, favors the prosecution, (5)status of the defendant [Scott] weighs against a change of venue and, favors the prosecution.

Scott has also not shown that moving his case will enable a jury to be chosen that has not heard all of the same pretrial publicity that a Stanislaus County jury has heard. This case is known worldwide and is indistinguishable from the Charles Manson case; when there has been this much publicity there is no point in a change of venue.

Rather than making a speculative pretrial determination that a change of venue is in order, the process of voir dire will allow the court to determine with accuracy whether a fair and impartial jury can be selected in this case. Several Supreme Court cases have approved the process of jury selection as a means of demonstrating the presence or absence of impartiality. Voir dire may demonstrate that pretrial publicity had no prejudicial effect.

Voir dire may also demonstrate that comments to the media from people who have no involvement with this case, such as the Sheriff's spokesman, have had little effect on jurors and only demonstrate that many people will go to great lengths to try and achieve their fifteen minutes of fame. These kinds of people exist everywhere and will be weeded out in court in the solemnity of legal proceedings and the voir dire process will ensure Scott's rights are protected.

Scott has pled not guilty. The prosecution strongly disputes the remainder of Scott's assertions of fact in his Motion for a Change of Venue. Scott has failed to substantiate any of the claimed facts by admissible evidence, except for one: this criminal prosecution has received widespread media attention. The term media, as used in this response will refer to radio, print and electronic forms of news coverage.

For the most part, the media has attempted to portray this case in a factual format. (See Scott's Exhibit A, the "allbundeled" file.) a few "tabloid" publications have exaggerated claims, or speculated on evidence but these publications are not accepted by the general public as legitimate news sources.

As for the claimed facts contained within footnotes 1 and 2, Scott's motion is devoid of evidence. However, similar claims have been made before in Scott's other cited cases, (See exhibits A, and Prosecutor's exhibit 4), and this court should not consider them as valid. As will be discussed below, jurors in Stanislaus County have not made up their minds and the defense's own survey says they will wait until they hear evidence in court. (See exhibits E, and Prosecutor's exhibit 1 and 1A.)

Scott, at pages 11-12 of his motion, makes generalized claims about the coverage of this case by the media and uses that to support a claim that only Stanislaus County jurors cannot be fair. However, Scott's exhibits demonstrate that this case has been a staple of the networks and cable TV (page 12 of Scott's motion) and has garnered international coverage. (See Scott's Exhibit A and prosecutor's exhibit 2, and 3.)

Even if this court were to assume that there has been widespread prejudicial or speculative media coverage, not caused by the defense, it would not make a difference in this case. As Scott's own motion shows, the case has been covered throughout the world, extensively in the United States and unrelentingly across the entire State of California. (See Scott's Exhibit A and prosecutor's exhibit 2, and 3.)

Scott has proven that "pretrial publicity has been geographically widespread and pervasive" and has failed to prove that jurors in any other county would view this case differently. The prosecutor, on the other hand, has taken that extra step to show that the attitudes of Stanislaus County jurors are no different from the attitudes of other jurors. (See prosecutor's exhibit 1, and 1A.)

The publicity in Scott's case has to a great extent been caused by and perpetuated by Scott, the defense attorney and the defense team. During the investigation Scott went before the national media, Good-Morning America, Prime-Time Live, etc., with his family to make pleas for the safe return of his wife and unborn child.

Early in the interviews Scott stirred the media's interest by dodging questions and speaking fondly of his mistress. (Scott's Exhibit A, #A7676, #A7643, etc.) Scott makes much of the fact that the media has referred to Scott as an adulterer, but it was Scott who admitted it on national television.

Scott's attorney, Mark Geragos, prior to becoming Scott's attorney of record, was a frequent panelist on television shows condemning Scott's behavior. (Scott's Exhibit A, #A7569, #A4959, etc.) After Mr. Geragos became counsel of record, he continued to appear on TV even holding press-conferences on the courthouse steps promising to prove Scott's innocence and produce the real killers. (Scott's Exhibit A, #A3255.)

The defense has fueled the interest of the media with accusations of satanist involvement and a "mystery woman" witness. (See Scott's Exhibit A, #A4336, #A4032, etc.) Mr. Geragos has recently referred to his client as "stone-cold innocent." (Exhibit 5.) The effect of this media grandstanding has resulted not only in increased media coverage, but also in changed attitudes about this case. (See exhibit 1 and 1A and Surveys, infra.)

To this day, the defense "team" of experts, jury consultant Jo-Ellan Dimitrius, Dr. Cyril Wecht, and Dr. Henry Lee, continue to violate this court's protective order and trumpet the defense theory and/or the innocence of Scott. (Exhibit 3.) It would be absurd to reward Scott by granting a change of venue for their conduct that has caused much of the publicity of which Scott complains.

Scott retained the services of Paul Strand to conduct a survey of jurors from Stanislaus County. Strand claims 39% believe that Scott is guilty. His data reports, in Question 1a, page A2 of Exhibit E, that 114 people said "did commit" out of 301 in the survey; that is 37.9%. He also says there is a 5.5% +/- error rate; this means that as little as 32.4% have prejudged Scott's guilt. Scott trumpets this as some divine sign that a change of venue is required, but other courts have said higher prejudgments aren't enough for a change of venue.

Scott has failed to test their survey across county lines. He has also failed to ask the next logical question and ask how many people could set their opinion aside and decide the case based on the evidence. The prosecutor's survey did both. (See prosecutor's exhibits 1 and 1A.)

Scott also makes use of a survey by Stephen Schoenthaler of California State University, Stanislaus; our survey disproves their point. As pointed out by our survey, time has changed the results from when Dr. Schoenthaler did his survey and the older survey did not take into account all jurors attitudes. (See prosecutor's exhibit 1.) Dr. Schoenthaler's survey isn't even in evidence.

In Scott's motion, he describes the population of Stanislaus County as "small." This is not true. He neglects to point out that the cases he cites are thirty years old. In those thirty years, society has changed from 8-track tapes to cd-roms, UHF to cable- satellite television, from punchcard computers to laptops and the Internet. Stanislaus County has also changed, and grown.

The court should consider that California is the most populous of our fifty United States and Stanislaus County is now ranked as the 16th largest out of 58 California counties. The City of Modesto where the crime occurred is ranked as the 15th largest city in the state. According to data collected by the United States 2000 census and available from the State of California, Department of Finance website, at http://www.dof.ca.gov/html/Demograp/druhpar.htm, Stanislaus County had a population of 481,600. (Exhibit 6.)

The court's analysis of this factor focuses on whether the size f the community neutralizes or dilutes the impact of news reports. The size of the community is not dispositive of the issue. Multiple cases have held that the prejudicial effect of news reports is considerably diminished in a community with a large metropolitan area. The larger the community, the less the chance that a change of venue will be requires.

With a diverse population of over 481,600, the routine local news reports documenting Scott's crime and the progress of the case through the court system have not transformed Scott's case into a "spectacular" or "notorious" case which would result in prejudice to Scott absent a change of venue.

In this case, Scott contends that the media has labeled him as an outsider, but fails to cite to a single article out of the 8319 documents attached as Exhibit A to his motion to prove this point. Instead, he cites to a single Modesto Bee article, #A99 of the Modesto Bee articles, which quotes a defense attorney saying Scott may have a hard time empaneling a fair jury. This is hardly competent evidence.

The article also quotes the former Modesto Mayor, but fails to mention that the former mayor was under investigation by the prosecutor's office at the time the comment was made and has subsequently been charged in a felony criminal complaint. (Stanislaus County Superior Court case #1061284, and of which this court may take judicial notice of pursuant to Evidence Code § 452(d).)

Nowhere in article #A99 does the press denigrate Scott. He has been described as an ordinary, nice and sociable person whom nobody suspected of responsibility for the crimes with which he is charged. (Exhibit A, "allbundled" file #A7151.) Although

Scott is not known outside a small circle of family and friends, he is a resident of Stanislaus County who has friends living in the community. There is nothing inherently unusual about Scott other than his commission of this crime and nothing prejudicial about his status in the community which supports a change of venue.

Scott stresses the "outpouring of sympathy" toward the murder victims in this case as a factor in favor of a change of venue. Any prominence achieved by a victim through news reports following the crime does not support a change of venue. Where the victim or the circumstances surrounding the victim's death generates a sympathetic response in the heart of a stranger, prospective jurors would sympathize with the victim and her family wherever the case is tried.

In this case, the status of the victims prior to their murders was exactly the same as Scott's. Laci Peterson was married to and lived in the same Modesto house as Scott; she had the same circle of acquaintances as Scott did. Conner Peterson was the unborn son of Laci Peterson and Scott; his status in the community was exactly the same as Scott's. the status of the victims in this case does not favor a change of venue.

There are no political overtones in this case; Scott confuses politicians making public statements about a case with trying to further their careers at the expense of an accused. Scott merely points to political events and tries to imply these events have affected his case; he has failed.

The Attorney General is not prosecuting this case and his comments cannot be said to be representative of this prosecution; that the Board of Supervisors has discussed this case amounts to nothing, in fact, Scott fails to even allege what was discussed; that the family has supported federal legislation again has no impact, directly or indirectly, on this case and Scott again fails to explain how it could possibly make a difference in his case; and lastly, the claim that legislators introduced legislation to reimburse costs incurred because of Scott's actions somehow injects "politics" into his case is wrong, it is what legislators do, and if this fact were proof of "political overtones" in this case, then the legislation should have passed, as the Legislation was vetoed by the Governor. (See exhibit #7.) as can be seen, the claimed "political overtones" in this case are a desperate stretch by Scott.

Wasn't it stated somewhere that the Governor should have veto power over the legislature to prevent political overtones from passing 'current' popular legislation, without contemplation.

Scott has submitted several declarations and the prosecution objects to them being considered by the court since they are hearsay and the prosecution is entitled to cross-examine their witnesses. The defense declarations are exactly the kind of inadmissible hearsay that is prohibited. The prosecution objects to the court's receipt of them as evidence. If the court is not inclined to strike the defense declarations, the prosecution demands the right to cross-examine the declarant(s) as essential to ensure the search for the truth.

Since the court has ruled [decided] on whether witnesses will be allowed to testify at the venue hearing, the prosecution has included declarations of its witnesses as well; the prosecution will have these witnesses available to testify on the date of the hearing.

As the *Manson* case prophetically predicted: "Modern means of news communication have taken away many of the reasons for the transfer of the cause celebre which may have existed fifty years ago." *People v. Manson*, 61 Cal.App.3d 102, at p.190(1976). Additionally, when jurors up and down the state hold the same feelings "in general," there is no point in moving venue. *People v. Venegas*, 25 Cal.App.4th 1731, at p.1738(1994).

The general rule of law is that there is a preference for trying felony cases in the country in which the crimes were committed. (See Penal Code § 777.) Penal Code § 1033 sets forth the court's responsibilities when considering a change of venue: "In a criminal action pending in the superior court, the court shall order a change of venue: (a) On motion of the defendant, to another county when it appears that there is a reasonable likelihood that a fair and impartial trial cannot be had in the county. When a change of venue is ordered by the superior court, it shall be for the trial itself. All proceedings before trial shall occur in the county of original venue, except when it is evident that a particular proceeding must be heard by the judge who is to preside over the trial. (b) On its own motion or on motion of any party, to an adjoining county when it appears as a result of the exhaustion of all of the jury panels called that it will be impossible to secure a jury to try the cause in the county."

Please note, under section 1033(b), that if it becomes apparent that a jury cannot be selected during the process of voir dire, a change of venue may be granted to an adjoining county at the time of trial, even when the motion has been denied pretrial, or the court on its own motion may move the case to an adjacent county even without the consent of the parties under such a circumstance.

The court should also consider the following Rule of Court before ordering a change of venue: Rule 4.160. Policies to be considered before ordering and transferring a criminal case on change of venue: (a) Before ordering a change of venue in a criminal case, the court should consider impaneling a jury that would give the defendant a fair and impartial jury.

Only Scott can move for a change of venue on the ground there is a "reasonable likelihood" that a fair trial cannot be had in the county in which the crimes were committed. *People v. Powell*, 87 Cal. 348, at p.360(1891); *Jackson v. Superior Court*, 13 Cal. App.3d 440, at p.443(1970). Scott bears the burden of proof since he is the party seeking the order granting a change of venue. *People v. Bonin*, 46 Cal.3d 659, at p.673(1988), citing *People v. Boyce*, 128 Cal.App.3d 850, at pp.856-859(1982); and *People v. Whalen*, 33 Cal.App.3d 710, at p.716(1973). *Bonin* was overruled on other grounds in *People v. Hill*, 17 Cal.4th 800 (1998).

The California Supreme Court has repeatedly set out what steps a trial court should follow when trying to determine if a change of venue motion should be granted. As the court has said: "To make that decision, we examine five factors: the nature and gravity of the offense, the nature and extent of the news coverage, the size of the community, the status of the defendant in the community, and the popularity and prominence of the victim." *People v. Weaver*, 26 Cal.4th 876, at p.905(2001).

The court is asked to take judicial notice of the fact that, in this county alone, numerous capital murder trials over the years have received extensive media attention and yet still were prosecuted here in the Stanislaus County. In this case, Scott is facing a potential sentence of death. The offenses with which he is charged, however, are not "spectacular", as much as the crimes charged in the *Corona* and *Harris* cases. This case does not concern any prominent public figures, mass murder, or community threats of race riots, and Scott's ability to select a fair and impartial jury in this case has not been compromised.

The term "nature of the offense" has been defined as those peculiar facts of the crime that bring it to the attention of the community. The gravity of a crime refers to the seriousness and potential consequences to the accused if he is found guilty. Since every capital case involves a serious crime, this factor is not dispositive [not something to base a decision on]. In fact, many capital cases have been tried in their counties of origin despite motions for change of venue demonstrating that the gravity and nature of the crime, standing alone, will not support a change of venue.

The extent of coverage in any given case, even if extensive and widespread, does not give rise to a presumption of prejudice to Scott. The *Harris* case, which resulted in Robert Alton Harris being executed, showed that widespread publicity does not automatically require a venue change. In the Harris case, 90% of the jurors had been exposed to publicity about the case. As the Harris case held, to require jurors to be ignorant of the case is not the law. "It is not required...that the jurors be totally ignorant of the facts and issues involved...It is sufficient if the juror can lay aside his impression or opinion and render a verdict based on the evidence presented in court." *People v. Harris*, 28 Cal.3d 935, at pp.949-950(1981), citing *Irvin v. Dowd*, 366 U.S. 717, pp.722-723(1961).

This was proven again in *Proctor*, where 80% of prospective jurors had heard about the case and 31% believed in the defendant's guilt. *Proctor* affirmed the denial of a change of venue from Shasta County, which, at that time, had a population of 122,100.

Am I missing something here, or wasn't Harris executed and Proctor given a life sentence!

The second part is the nature of the coverage. Scott fails to present any evidence of "prejudicial" press coverage. Apparently, it must be inferred that somewhere in defense Exhibit A, that an article or report contains some kind of prejudicial materials. This failure to specify the prejudicial feature of the evidence must be taken to mean that there is none.

In a case where there is so much publicity, a different rule applies: "In cases of pretrial publicity, a court may assume that the resulting prejudice is stronger in the locality of the offense, which is likely also to be the locality of the publicity; in those cases, the defendant need not necessarily show lack of prejudice in other counties. Where pretrial publicity has been geographically widespread and pervasive, however, a court may deny a change of venue on the sensible ground that it would do no good." *People v. Venegas*, 25 Cal.App.4th 1731, at p.1738(1994). (See *People v. Manson*, 61 Cal.App.3d 102, at pp.174-177(1976).

The Venegas case took place in Del Norte County, with a population of 27,300. The defendant was a Pelican Bay prison inmate and a defense survey showed that 82.5% believed that such an inmate could not be trusted. The trial court denied a change of venue and this was affirmed by the Court of Appeals. Both courts reasoned that "A change of venue, however, is by its very nature an effective remedy only for local bias or prejudice." *Venegas*, at p.1738.

In that case, the defendant failed to show that any other community would not feel the same bias against him as Del Norte County and therefore no venue change was warranted. The same is true in Scott's case.

The *Manson* case is legal precedent and a case of historical value in comparison to Scott's case. The Manson case, even more so than this case, involved horrendous crimes, massive publicity, aberrant/outcast defendants, and famous/prominent victims, and no change of venue was granted. A change of venue was denied because there was no place to go.

Well, you wouldn't think so with a curriculum vitae like that.

Dr. Ebbesen, whose curriculum vitae is on file with the court as an attachment to a prior motion found that: "Evidence from our survey suggests that potential jurors from Stanislaus can keep an open mind and set aside whatever they know and feel about this case. About 80% of the respondents from Stanislaus said that they could keep an open mind. The large majority, about 90%, said that they would be able to ignore comments and opinions from friends and relatives, were they selected as jurors. A little over 80% said that they would be able to follow judicial instruction to set aside what *they knew* and begin their services as potential jurors with the presumption that Scott was innocent.

Evidence from our survey suggests that potential jurors in Stanislaus do not harbor any greater or lesser degree of prejudice against Scott than potential jurors from Los Angeles or Sacramento...We found no evidence from our survey that moving to another venue would make any difference in the ability of Scott Peterson to receive a fair trial." (Prosecutor's exhibit 1A, conclusion.)

The prosecution requests that this court deny Scott's motion or, in the alternative, delay the ruling until such time as a venire demonstrably cannot be empaneled in this county.

January ?, 2004 **Scott Peterson's Reply** to the Prosecutor's Opposition to Scott's Motion for Change of Venue

January ?, 2004 **Prosecutor's Opposition** to Scott's Motion for Change of Venue; Rebuttal to Scott's Reply

January ?, 2004 **Media** Sketch Artist Behringer Request for Coverage of 1/8/04 Hearing

January ?, 2004 **Order** of Superior Court of Stanislaus County Re: Sketch Artist Behringer Request for Coverage of hearing

The request by Sketch Artist Behringer is granted.

January ?, 2004 **Media** The Modesto Bee Request for Coverage of 1/8/04 Hearing

January ?, 2004 **Order** of Superior Court of Stanislaus County Re: Modesto Bee Request for Coverage of hearing

The request by The Modesto Bee is granted.

January ?, 2004 **Media** NBC and Fox KTVU CH 2 Request for Coverage of 1/8/04 Hearing

January ?, 2004 **Order** of Superior Court of Stanislaus County Re: NBC and Fox Request for Coverage of hearing

The requests by NBC and Fox are granted.

January ?, 2004 **Media** Court TV Request for Coverage of 1/8/04 Hearing

January ?, 2004 **Order** of Superior Court of Stanislaus County Re: Court TV Request for Coverage of hearing

The request by Court TV is granted.

January ?, 2004 **Media** KFBK Request for Coverage of 1/8/04 Hearing

January ?, 2004 **Order** of Superior Court of Stanislaus County Re: KFBK Request for Coverage of hearing

The request by KFBK is granted.

January ?, 2004 **Scott Peterson's 995 Motion**

January ?, 2004 **Prosecutor's Opposition** to Scott's 995 Motion

January ?, 2004 **Scott Peterson's Reply** Memorandum of Points and Authorities in Support of Scott's 995 Motion

January ?, 2004 **??'s** Description of Exhibits

January ?, 2004 **Prosecutor's 190.3 Notice** Re: Aggravating Evidence

January 8, 2004 **Minute Order** of Superior Court of Stanislaus County Re: Change of Venue

The judge decided today to grant Scott's change of venue request.

January ?, 2004 **Prosecutor's Motion** to Reconsider Change of Venue

January ?, 2004 **Prosecutor's** Submission Re: Appropriate Venue and Motion for a McGowan Hearing

January ?, 2004 **Scott Peterson's Memorandum of Points and Authorities** in support of Transfer to Orange County

January ?, 2004 **Media** The Modesto Bee Request for Coverage of 1/14/04 Hearing

January ?, 2004 **Order** of Superior Court of Stanislaus County Re: Modesto Bee Request for Coverage of hearing

The request by The Modesto Bee is granted.

January 14, 2004 **Minute Order** of Superior Court of Stanislaus County

January 20, 2004 **Minute Order** of Superior Court of Stanislaus County Re: Venue Change

The judge orders the case to San Mateo County and that a different judge would be assigned to the case.

January 20, 2004 **Media Advisory; Judicial Council of California Re: Peterson Change of Venue**

Judge G., of the Superior Court of Stanislaus County, chose San Mateo County to hear the trial of Scott Peterson and that he will not serve as the trial judge in the case.

Chief Justice George will therefore assign a trial court judge to hear the Peterson case, in accordance with his assignment authority as set forth in Article VI, section 6, of the state Constitution. That order will be made public tomorrow morning on the California Courts Web Site.

January 21, 2004 **NEWS; Judicial Council of California Re: Chief Justice George Assigns Trial Judge in People v. Peterson**

San Francisco- Chief Justice George today assigned veteran Judge A. to preside over the trial of *People v. Scott Peterson.*

Well-known as a criminal law expert with extensive death penalty case experience, Judge A. served on the Superior Court of Contra Costa County for 31 years before his retirement in 1995. Shortly after, he joined the Chief Justice's Assigned Judges Program and has been assigned to preside over a number of criminal trials.

At the request of trial and appellate courts, the Assigned Judges Program provides temporary judicial assistance to courts throughout California for reasons such as vacancies, disqualifications, and calendar congestion. The program receives from 350 to 450 requests each month.

January 21, 2004 **Prosecutor Notifies Defense Counsel**

The prosecutor telephones Mark Geragos, Scott's lawyer, and they acknowledge that Judge A. has been assigned to the case. The prosecutor acknowledges that January 26, 2004 was the date he also desired the case be called for trial.

January 21, 2004 **Scott Peterson's Request** for Trial Date

Mark Geragos, Scott's lawyer, at the prosecutor's request, telephoned Judge A. and it was agreed that on January 26th the case would be called for trial.

January 22, 2004 **Prosecutor's Peremptory Challenge of Judge A.**

The prosecutor files this challenge under Code of Civil Procedure § 170.6, seeking to disqualify Judge A. The challenge is filed in Stanislaus County, even though the venue has been ordered to San Mateo County.

The prosecutor states that as a party to the action, the Honorable Judge A., the judge before whom the trial or hearing of the action is pending, is prejudiced against the interest of the party, so that I believe that I cannot have a fair and impartial hearing before said judge.

January 23, 2004 **Transcript of Hearing; Superior Court of Stanislaus County**

(9:00 a.m.)

The Court: Good morning.

Mr. Geragos: Good morning, Your Honor.

Mr. Pat Harris: Good morning, Your Honor.

The Court: Matter of Scott Lee Peterson, case number 1056770. Rick Distaso and Dave Harris appearing for the People, Mark Geragos and Pat Harris appearing for the defendant. The record reflect the defendant's present.

Court intended to do just some ministerial matters today, but obviously with the elimination of the first appointed judge we'll have some other matters to do, and I had Mike Tozzi coordinating with the AOC, and he'll bring us up to date.

What'd you want to say, Mr. Geragos?

Mr. Geragos: Well, before we go too far down the road on that I have an objection to and I want to make a record, if I can. I don't believe that the 170 sub (6) was timely filed. I believe, and I would proffer, either by way of stipulation or if Mr. Distaso and myself wants to testify, that in actuality what happened here is that the Chief Justice assigned Judge A., I believe that Mr. Distaso received a phone call from Judge A., who in turn asked Mr. Distaso to call me and have me call Judge A.

We did that process, Mr. Distaso and I agreed on a Monday court date in San Mateo at 9:00 a.m.. Shortly after that we were informed that they were also going to vacate today's date so that there was going to be no further proceedings.

I believe Mr. Distaso would agree with that rendition of the facts.

Mr. Distaso: (Nod of head).

Mr. Geragos: So that I have a record; and he's shaking his head yes.

Mr. Distaso: That's correct, Your Honor.

Mr. Geragos: I believe that if that is the case, under 170.6 sub (2), that at that point the time and place for the 170 sub (6) being exercised, if the People had a remaining 170 sub (6), is over. It's analogous to a master calendar court sending the matter out. If the court does that in such a fashion, sends you out for trial, once you leave that courtroom and go to the next courtroom, that's it, your peremptory challenge is lost, you no longer have the opportunity to exercise it.

In this case the peremptory challenge was exercised, I believe, the following day, after we had already set up the 9:00 o'clock appointment with the judge, or the court, scheduled the court date on Monday, the 26th, in San Mateo, in Department 2M.

At that point there is no peremptory challenge for the People to exercise. That's if the People had a peremptory challenge. This Court may remember back in May it was my argument that they had already exercised their one peremptory challenge, and I would point to 170.6 subdivision (3), which talks about under no circumstances shall a party or attorney be permitted to make more than one such motion in any one action or special proceeding pursuant to this section.

It's our position that there's already been one set; 170.6 that has been exercised in a special proceeding, which was the litigation surrounding the unsealing of the search warrant. If that is the case, and that was their 170.6 peremptory challenge that was exercised, they no longer have another 170.6 peremptory challenge to exercise, I would ask that the Court return to this matter; or strike the filing of the 170 sub (6), leave the date that was previously scheduled for 9:00 o'clock on Monday morning in Department 2M in San Mateo court.

In the alternative, if the Court does not do any of that, then I would ask the Court, under authority of California Rules of Court

4.161, which reads, "A criminal case in which a change of venue has been ordered should be tried in the court receiving the case be a judge from the court in which the case originated."

I would once again ask this Court to reconsider and, and travel with us and take the road trip. But I don't believe at this point that under either circumstance that it was timely nor did they have a peremptory challenge.

The Court: Well, let me cover one issue, the last issue regarding the previous 170.6 by the prosecution. Obviously I wouldn't be on this case if we held that that was the same action. So let's eliminate that one and not waste any time with it because of the fact that it is a totally separate action. That's the attitude we took, nobody writted on that, I think we're stuck with that regardless, and that's the law.

But the first issue regarding the 170.6 on Judge A., I don't even know if I should be considering that. One issue is that the matter was transferred, all I'm supposed to do is ministerial matters. The 170.6 on Judge A. probably should be considered by Judge A. or the AOC, I don't now, do you have anything on that, Mr. Geragos?

Mr. Geragos: Yes, I do. I think the Court is right, because I think that once; in my conversation with Mr. Tozzi, I hesitate to ever speak for Mr. Tozzi, but it's my understanding that once this, once that assignment was made that everything was being driven out of Judge A.'s court, including the vacating of the Friday; today's date. And that this was supposed to be ministerial.

So I believe, and; that the only way for this to be determined is that we're ordered in front of Judge A. on Monday morning at 9:00 o'clock in San Mateo, in Department 2M, to have this matter heard. Otherwise I think we're; it is a capital case, I think we're; it's fraught with danger in terms of time waivers and no time waivers, and I will give the Court advance notice. I'm not waiving time, we're not waiving time under any circumstances given the kind of state of flux that we are in at this point.

The Court: I might add, though, even though there's no time waiver, I think the court can easily find good cause to continue one or two more weeks due to the change of venue, then, as initiated by the defense.

Mr. Geragos: Except the problem is I think at this point I don't know that this Court has jurisdiction, I think that, I think we're in a situation where the person; apparently the Chief Justice has stepped in and has made the assignment, even though I don't, I don't even know that that's a lawful order. I realize he's the chief justice, it's like the 800-pound gorilla, he can do whatever he wants.

The fact of the matter is according to the California Rules of Court, if that's going to be done and the originating jurisdiction is not; or the judge from the originating jurisdiction is not going with it, the Rules of Court are very clear, it's not the chief justice who makes the assignment, it's the presiding judge of the county where you go.

So I'm not so sure that anybody has complied with any of the applicable statutes, Rules of Court, or case law at this point, and I don't know who could possibly make a finding of good cause at this point to waive time in a death penalty case, when it's my position that we don't even have a judge at this point or; or jurisdiction in any particular court.

The Court: Before we hear from Mr. Tozzi, Mr. Distaso, anything you'd like to add?

Mr. Distaso: No; I do, Your Honor, 'cause I disagree with pretty much the entire characterization. This Court said that they were not going to go on the change of venue, so then the AOC contacted, I guess Mr. Tozzi, who then was told that Judge A. was going to be assigned.

Judge A. called and we had about a 30-second or less phone call saying that, "I want to see you at 9:00 o'clock on Monday morning in San Mateo," and call Mr. Geragos. So I did that. Of course, I had no appearance before the judge, I've never even seen the judge, other than one picture in the Modesto Bee, I had no opportunity to file a paper at that time, and then--

The Court: He called you and you did not call him?

Mr. Distaso: That's correct. And I; and I believe then Mr., after I talked to Mr. Geragos, I believe just so the record's clear, he called the judge back and confirmed the 9:00 o'clock hearing. And I think he'd agree with that.

Mr. Geragos: I do with agree with that, that's exactly what happened, and then I called Mr. Distaso back and we had a conversation in which both agreed it would be 9:00 o'clock and--

Mr. Distaso: That's right. So then I had no opportunities, I've never appeared in front of that court, in fact, I've never even been in that court.

So then we decided, and we decided actually as a convenience to the, to the AOC, and to get this procedure going, well, we want to let everybody know we're going to exercise our, our challenge under 170.6, so we decided since we're still here and this particular court ordered us back here on Friday, we knew this would be the next hearing, we filed the 170.6 here, and we were told, or at least was passed on to me, that this court then; jurisdiction was returned to this court for the issue of dealing with that and getting a new judge assigned, and so that's the procedure that we believe that we were in, and I think it's completely proper.

So I think this Court has jurisdiction at this point to handle any matter that we do today, including contacting the AOC and getting another judge assigned, I don't think anything improper has happened. And regarding the good cause, we've done a little research, and Mr. Harris can talk to it if the Court wants to, but clearly there's good cause when the defense makes a motion to move this trial out to continue it.

Of course, if the defense hadn't made a venue motion he could have his trial on Monday in Stanislaus County. That's not where we're at.

So in this case I think everything is completely proper. I disagree completely with his characterization, and I believe that at this point the Court just needs to get another judge assigned by the AOC and that would be our position.

Mr. Geragos: I don't think that the court can hear at this point whether or not the 170 sub (6) is properly issued. I think that has to be done by Judge A. He's the one who it's directed towards, I don't care if it's filed here in Stanislaus County for convenience sake or anything else, there's nothing that I've seen, and I reviewed the code again this morning, that says for convenience sake you do it wherever, wherever it happens.

They; the fact of the matter is, and what has not been responded to by Mr. Distaso, is that as soon as Judge A. was assigned, that was the time to exercise the 170 sub (6). You don't at that point wait until you set up a court hearing, vacate the date here, and then say okay, I just read an article in the Modesto Bee and I'm now having second thoughts and therefore I'm going to exercise my peremptory challenge.

Mr. Distaso: Can I just make one additional comment? The case has been basically, I guess, transferred or accepted by the Chief Justice pursuant to his constitutional authority. He's not dealing with Rules of Court or any of the statutory things. According to the thing that we got, it said he was, I think pursuant to; I want to say Article VI, but I can't remember right off the top of my head, but he's doing this pursuant to the constitutional authority, he's not following the Rules of Court, as far as I can see, he's taking it right to the top.

So regarding the issues that were argued by Mr. Geragos, I think we're completely out of that. And I think he's just kind of reached down and grabbed ahold of it and that's what he's doing.

So anyway, I think I've made my argument.

The Court: Mr. Tozzi's been in contact with the AOC, what's the status, Mr. Tozzi?

Mr. Tozzi: The status, Your Honor, is that the AOC will get back to the Court next week some time around Tuesday or Wednesday.

The Court: That's for a second judge?

Mr. Tozzi: That's correct.

The Court: What about this Court's authority, did you discuss that with the AOC?

Mr. Tozzi: I was in San Mateo yesterday meeting with the presiding judge, the assistant presiding judge and staff on; just some logistical matters; media management, those kind of things.

I received a call in the afternoon, or at mid-morning, I'm sorry, from Brad Campbell, he said that the Chief was at the airport, he was flying out; that the Chief was taking his time with regard to looking at the second list of names, and that my notes say that you had the authority to act on all motions, and the recalendar motion, but on nothing that affects the conduct of the trial. Those were my notes from the conversation.

The Court: Anybody want to ask him any questions?

Mr. Geragos: Who was the gentleman who you spoke to?
Mr. Tozzi: Brad Campbell.
Mr. Geragos: And what was his position?
Mr. Tozzi: Brad Campbell, I believe, is the supervisor or the manager of the assignment section of the Administrative Office of the Courts.
Mr. Geragos: And he was relaying a hearsay statement from who in terms of what the judge's authority was?
Mr. Tozzi: The Chief Justice.
Mr. Geragos: Okay. So it was your understanding that the Chief Justice now is presiding over what's happening or not happening in this case?
Mr. Tozzi: No, my understanding was that Brad Campbell was in conversation with the Chief and he was telling me that we would be hearing from the AOC possibly next Tuesday or Wednesday, the Chief was considering a second list of names, and then he told me that; what I already said to the Court, that the Court still had the authority, I took notes on that, and there was some other conversation, but it wasn't pertinent to--

Mr. Geragos: What restaurants were in San Mateo. What was the--
Mr. Tozzi: Wasn't that, but that's okay.
Mr. Geragos: What was the specific statement as to what the authority of this Court was, at least as interpreted by the Chief Justice?

Mr. Tozzi: Actually, the interpretation would be by me, because I was taking notes of the conversation from Mr. Campbell, and what I wrote down, I wrote down, "Al, still authority to act on all motions. Recalendar motion, nothing that affects the conduct of trial."

Now, the conversation took place yesterday at around 11:30, so, you know, I can't recall the specifics of the conversation, but those are my notes. And I think that was the, the crux of the conversation of the court.

Mr. Geragos: Thank you, I have no further questions.

The Court: Mr. Distaso?

Mr. Distaso: I have no questions.

The Court: Any discussion regarding this court staying on the case, was that discussed at all?

Mr. Tozzi: Not with Mr. Campbell.

The Court: Okay. Not with the Chief Justice either?

Mr. Tozzi: No, I did not speak to the Chief Justice, this was all through Mr. Campbell.

The Court: Anything else?

Mr. Distaso: No, Your Honor.

Mr. Geragos: I -- yes, I think we've got a situation where -- that this Court should instruct Mr. Tozzi to call back and tell them that this Court, under 4.161, will stay with the case, and will recess until such time as he can run that up the flag pole. I think there's a -- I'm a little uncomfortable, obviously, I don't want to tangle with Chief Justice George, I don't think that there's any coin in that, so to speak, but the fact of the matter is I've never been in the position where the chief justice is micromanaging a special circumstance case which in the worst case scenario is going to be in front of him. And I don't think it's ever going to happen, but the fact of the matter is is that there's something I think untoward about the fact that we have the Chief Justice micromanaging this case. And it is micromanaging because I need to have a judge in which I can raise some issues, and obviously I've indicated under 4.161 I want

Your Honor, and I would like Your Honor to, to at least instruct Mr. Tozzi, I know it's presumptuous of me to ask, but to get involved once again and to say that you will take the case where we want to go and let's get on with it.

The -- as a practical matter, if you can't -- as of right now, as I understand what Mr. Tozzi just said, if you are not allowed to make any rulings that would affect the conduct of the trial, we're between a rock and a hard place, we can't decide the 170.6, we can't decide a good cause time waiver because we can't decide the 170.6, we also can't address my issue, which is if you make a -- or if somebody makes a good cause time waiver, I'm going to get snatched up and go into trial somewhere else and my client's going to sit here for another four months while I do a case or trial somewhere else. And I can't address any of these issues unless we recess, Mr. Tozzi calls the gentleman that he was speaking to, and the Court reconsiders and says that it will go with us to San Mateo and then we'll take the appropriate action and go from there.

Obviously I, I don't think if this Court takes the, takes the case back and puts its arms around it and we go forward with Your Honor as the presiding judge here, there's no issue on the 170.6, that solves the problem.

In terms of good cause, I assume that this Court could contact two of the other courts that are kind of nipping at my heels and we could set out a schedule. I can accommodate the prosecution, as I indicated I wanted to do, just as long as I don't go off into the ether on some other case, and we can handle this in an expeditious manner, and I think that's the best way to handle this thing. I understand that it's an inconvenience for everyone involved, but, you know, this is a case where everybody at least sitting in this courtroom has got a history with it, and I would hope that everybody would see it through.

The Court: Any further comments, Mr. Distaso?

Mr. Distaso: Only, Your Honor, that it appears to me that the Court has authority -- basically the conduct of the trial, in my opinion, means motions in limine, you know, the actual conduct of the trial, but it appears from what Mr. Tozzi says that the Court has the authority to act on the 170.6 and basically motions to continue and anything else other than the actual nuts and bolts of what we're doing in trial. I mean, that seems clear to me.

So, I know, with those comments, I'm going to submit it to the Court.

The Court: I'll take it under submission, we'll take a 15-minute recess.

(Short recess)
(9:20 a.m.)

(9:50 a.m.)
The Court: Record reflect everyone's present. Due to the change in circumstances, I think it's best to put the matter over for one week, not have an appearance in San Mateo County next Monday, the 26th, put it over 'til the 2nd of February, I find good cause to do that.

There's enough good cause merely on the change of venue. However, with the extra issue of the 170.6, I think that should be briefed and looked at in detail, and -- but that hearing will be in San Mateo County, it will be handled by either Judge A. or San Mateo County Superior Court judge, or whoever the Chief Justice assigns at that point in time.

But I don't feel comfortable handling that issue once I've changed venue and based on the type of hearsay we've had so far as the authority to speak. Or act.

Anybody have any trouble with that date, be February 2nd?

Mr. Geragos: The only, the only problem I have is what I'd indicated before, with the Court -- I don't even know if the Court's got the authority at this point.

What day would it make that, February 2nd? As of right now, I believe Monday is a 58-of-60 date.

The Court: It's actually within the 60th day. The 60th day, I believe, is February 1st.

Mr. Geragos: Okay.
The Court: And that's a Sunday.

Mr. Distaso: Well, Your Honor, I -- the Information was filed on December 1st. So I, I believe -- maybe I -- sometimes I --

The Court: It's -- December 3rd he's arraigned, it's 60 days from arraignment.

Mr. Geragos: Right. So --

The Court: In any event, there is good cause to continue it even beyond the 60 days, so --

Mr. Geragos: (Nod of head).

The Court: And at least the in limines will start that day, depending on what ruling is made on the 170.6.

That'll be 9:00 a.m., San Mateo County Superior Court.

Mr. Geragos: Department 2M?

The Court: I don't know what department, Mr. Tozzi, did you get a department?

Mr. David Harris: That is the department -- the courtroom they have available for us.

The Court: Okay. So you will have a judge there at that time and you'll know ahead of time from Mr. Tozzi or the AOC as to who that judge is going to be to handle the initial motion and the actual trial.

Did counsel meet as far as a list of the issues to be discussed during in limine?

Mr. Geragos: No.

Mr. Distaso: No. well, we -- you know, we've been discussing it, you know, I think the Court's list from the last time was fairly substantial. I didn't really have a whole lot more to add to it.

Mr. Geragos: Yeah, the only ones that I added were ones that I did at the end, which was the sequestration issue.

So I anticipate that what we'll do is confer between now and the 2nd and see if we can streamline. I believe that we understand what the issues are.

The Court: Well, first of all, the main issue that'll be done, the first thing on that Monday will be the 170.6 matter. I'm going to order that any papers by the defense be filed by Monday at 4:00 p.m. Any opposition by Wednesday at 4:00 p.m.

Mr. Geragos: And that would obviously be in the San Mateo clerk's office.

The Court: Be filed in the San Mateo County Clerk's Office. With copies here.

Mr. Geragos: Okay. They'll be ready to accept that, will they not, Your Honor?

Mr. Tozzi: Your Honor, you're saying county clerk, I think --

The Court: Court clerk.

Mr. Tozzi: Yeah, Superior Court, and I'll call them to make sure that they know all of this is coming.

The Court: Okay. And the numbers remain the same there? I assume they'll be using our number?

Mr. Tozzi: I'll get in contact with the presiding judge and if he changes the department I'll let the court know and I'll let counsel know.

The Court: In the event they have a similar numbering system, from now on, any filings in that county be prefaced with -- how about S-T-A-N? C-O. They will not have any problems with that.

Also, I'm going to order, by Wednesday of next week, to have on file an agreed order of the issues that are to be heard, unless you feel you can't have an agreement, then submit separate ones by Wednesday at 4:00 o'clock.

Is everybody in agreement the courthouse is in Redwood City?

Mr. David Harris: Yes.
Mr. Geragos: Yes.

The Court: The Court today will be transferring files, all the physical evidence and the transcripts to that court for their safekeeping. Also, I have work copies of all the motions that have been filed that will assist the judge, and I'll package those for that particular judge once we get to that point.

Mr. Geragos: Could the Court also issue an order for a laptop computer for my client so that -- the amount of discovery in this case is voluminous, we're approaching in excess of 35,000 pages, and I'm not able to give it to him or transport it to him by boxes. And subject, obviously, to the sher -- whatever security concerns the sheriff in that county has, but I would like to have an order for a laptop computer.

The Court: I'm not going to make that order, I think it will be something that should be on your list of in limines at that time that's covered by the trial judge, with input from the San Mateo County Sheriff's Office. I don't want to step on their toes.

Mr. Geragos: Okay.

The Court: I don't know what rules and regulations and problems that they may have as far as their custody arrangements.

That's the other thing, is when do you want him transported to San Mateo County?

Mr. Geragos: Forthwith transfer, as soon as possible is fine with me.

The Court: Probably be early next week unless they have somebody going today.

Mr. Geragos: Okay.

The Court: Any other issues before we do the certification of the record?

Mr. Distaso: Just, Your Honor, on -- regarding scheduling, you know, purposes, I'm trying to logistically, you know, figure out what's -- what our status is, I mean, do we need to be over there, you know, kind of living in San Mateo with the, with the understanding that we're going to be, you know, perhaps going from that date forward, or is this going to be just kind of pretrial in a couple weeks, I mean, we do need some of that information.

The Court: Well, I can't predict what that judge, or if it's up to me, what will happen at that point in time. It depends on all the circumstances. But at the very least you should be prepared to proceed with the in limines on that day.

Mr. Distaso: (Nod of head) Okay.

The Court: Certification of the record of January 8th? Does anyone have anything before page 206?

Mr. Geragos: No, Your Honor.
Mr. Distaso: I didn't have anything.
The Court: 206, line 12, the word "nothing" should be stricken and should be "un." Doesn't make sense otherwise. "Un." The word is "unless." Anybody have any problems with that? Any comments?
Mr. Geragos: No.
Mr. Distaso: No.
The Court: Anything else on that transcript?
Mr. Geragos: No.
Mr. Distaso: No.
The Court: Transcript of January 8th will be certified.
January 20th. Anyone have anything before page 250?

The court goes through several spelling changes with no objections.

The Court: On page 270, line six, where it says, "in or," those words should be stricken and I recall saying, "I mean the electronic media."

Mr. Geragos: No objection.

The Court: I'm sure if it's left -- if that's what I said, the press would have been here in arms. So line six, the "in or" are deleted, and "I mean," two words, is inserted therein.
Anyone have anything else on January 20th?

Mr. Geragos: No.
Mr. David Harris: On page 271, line 17, it indicates that I was the speaker. I believe that was the Court.

The Court: I believe that's correct. Any objection?

Mr. Geragos: No. That's fine.

The Court: That will be changed, "Mr. Harris" taken out and "The Court" inserted. Anything else?

Mr. David Harris: No.

The Court: That will be certified.

I'd like to close out the record today and have you certify today's record if you can stay around a little bit, let me find out from the clerk, we figured it would take twice as long as it did to take it in court to get a transcript ready, but I don't know how long it took here, Madam Clerk, or Madam Reporter, how long do you think it will take to prepare a transcript?

(Off the record discussion between the Court and reporter).

The Court: Any problem with meeting here at 11:30 --
Mr. Geragos: No.
The Court: -- closing this out here?
Mr. Geragos: That's fine.
Mr. Distaso: What about the 995 transcript?

The Court: In the meantime, I'm going to get another reporter and have to give Judge Silveira ten minutes' notice, so we'll do that at 10:15 here with Judge Silveira and a different reporter. Okay?

Mr. Geragos: That's fine.
Mr. Distaso: That's fine.

The Court: So that will conclude the proceedings in this county, other than the certification of the record for today's date and also for the 995. And the future hearing will be on February 2nd at 9:00 a.m. in Redwood City.

Mr. Geragos: Thank you, Your Honor.

(10:02 a.m.)
(End of proceedings)

(12:07 p.m.)
The Court: The record show everyone is present. The Court's received the transcript of the proceeding this morning, all parties have a chance to review that?

Mr. Geragos: Yes, Your Honor.
Mr. Distaso: We did, Your Honor.
The Court: Anyone have anything before page 279?
Mr. Distaso: I don't.

Mr. Geragos: Did the Court mean to say administerial matters or ministerial?

The Court: Ministerial, that's the one I had on line nine?
Mr. Geragos: 276, page -- or line 12.
The Court: Oh, it's also there, I missed that one. It's on 279, lines nine and 19, that should be "ministerial." Eliminating the A-D in both of those on page 276.
Mr. Geragos: Page 276, line 12.
The Court: That'll be stricken there also, the A-D. Anyone have anything prior to page 284?
Mr. Geragos: No.
Mr. Distaso: No.

The Court: Just to make more sense on line seven, the "to" should be stricken and I believe I said, "Did you discuss that with the AOC," so the words "did you" inserted therein.
Mr. Geragos: Okay.

The Court: Anyone have anything else?
Mr. Geragos: No.
The Court: Mr. Distaso?
Mr. Distaso: No, Your Honor.

The Court: So the Court will certify the record of the proceeding of the morning. And there'll be no further proceedings in this court.

One thing I failed to mention before, though, I'll add, is that the protective order is to continue until the new judge has an opportunity to reconsider that. So all protective orders are in effect until then.

Mr. Geragos: It is my understanding, though, that the Court is still awaiting to do a determination as to whether or not you're going to follow this case?

The Court: I'm awaiting for further orders from on high.
Mr. Geragos: Okay. Thank you, Your Honor.

The Court: But I'd say tentatively, I would suspect an 176 -- 170.6, in my opinion, would be granted, and very likely be a second judge on at that point, and I don't know who that's going to be.
Mr. Distaso: Thank you, Your Honor.
Mr. Geragos: Well, on behalf of my client and our staff, I'd like to thank the Court for all of -- everything that it's done in this case so far, you've been extremely patient, thoughtful, and we appreciate it.

The Court: In case I do it again, I will try not to remember that.
Mr. Geragos: Try to forget about that. Forget all about that, I'll insult you when you come back. Thank you, Your Honor.
Mr. Pat Harris: Thank you, Your Honor.
Mr. Distaso: Thank you, Your Honor.

The Court: Defendant's remanded to the custody of the sheriff, no bail is set.

(12:10 p.m.)
(End of proceedings)

January ??, 2004 **Notice of Change of Address**

SAN MATEO COUNTY SUPERIOR COURT FILED

DOCUMENTS

January 26, 2004 **Scott Peterson's Brief** Re: Untimeliness of People's Peremptory Challenge of Judge A.

Since the Stanislaus Superior Court ordered, on January 23, 2004, that Scott file a brief with both courts, San Mateo and Stanislaus, Scott asks the court to deny the prosecutor's challenge to the judge. Because the challenge was not immediate upon notification of the assignment of Judge A., it was not effective.

Code of Civil Procedure § 170.6, with its precise timing requirements, reflects a balance between a litigant's right to avoid judicial prejudice and the policy against judge-shopping.

On 1/20/04, the Stanislaus Court ordered venue to San Mateo, and that a different judge would be assigned. On 1/21/04, Chief Justice George, acting as ultimate master calendar judge, assigned Honorable Judge A. to the case in San Mateo. Neither defense or prosecution dispute that both received notice of the assignment on 1/21/04, communicated with Judge A. and each other, and agreed to appear in San Mateo Court on Monday, 1/26/04.

On 1/22/04, the prosecutor did an about-face and filed a peremptory challenge under Code of Civil Procedure § 170.6, seeking to disqualify Judge A. The challenge, however, was untimely. Any challenge would have to have been registered on 1/21/04, when the prosecutor received notice the case had been assigned for trial to Judge A. Any timely challenge under section 170.6 therefore had to be filed "not later than the time the cause is assigned for trial." Code Civ.Proc. § 170.6, subd.(2).

Scott maintains that, under the totality of the circumstances occurring in this case, the appointment of Judge A. by the Chief Justice was tantamount to an assignment for trial by a master calendar judge and therefore, should be governed by the master calendar exception of section 170.6, subdivision(2). The California Supreme Court, in *People v. Superior Court(Ravi)*, 4 Cal.4th 1164, at p.1175 (1993), defined a "true" master calendar assignment as being where '"a ready case is assigned to a ready department."' (Quoting *People v. Escobedo*, 35 Cal.App.3d 32, at p.38 (1973).

The California Supreme Court continued in (*Ravi*), explaining that a "ready" courtroom is one that is "available or reasonably expected to become available shortly so that the trial may commence." *Ravi*, at p.1177. The Court also stated that where a case is sent out from a so-called master calendar for some future trial date to be determined, the assigning department is not functioning as a master calendar for purposes of section 170.6, subdivision (2). Ravi had agreed that the parties were not ready for trial and no trial date had been set.

However, Scott does not, nor has he waived the time requirements for his trial to begin. The case was ready for trial. Judge A. and the San Mateo courtroom were ready to begin proceedings. The date for proceedings to begin had been set and agreed to by the parties and the Court. The prosecutor agreed to vacate the hearing set in Stanislaus County for 1/23/04. In essence, the Chief Justice stepped in and, functioning as a de facto master calendar department, assigned the case for trial forthwith. This confluence of factors satisfied the definition of a master calendar assignment set forth in *Ravi.*

The prosecutor, the next day, after agreeing to the 1/26/04 appearance in San Mateo County Courtroom 2M and seeing an article in the Modesto Bee newspaper, decided it wasn't in his best interest to have Judge A. try this case. Given, however, that what happened here was in effect a master calendar assignment, the prosecutor could not afford and in fact did not have the luxury of that extra day.

The "peremptory challenge is a creation of statute, lacking the constitutional underpinnings of a challenge for cause...." Therefore, its otherwise liberal availability is "strictly curtailed" by the statute itself, "which imposes on the litigant mandatory limitations with respect to [among other things] the time of making the challenge...." *Garcia v. Superior Court*, 156 Cal.App.3d 670, at p.684(1984).

Cognizant of this balance, and of the fact that the right to peremptorily disqualify a judge is neither absolute nor unlimited, "the courts of this state have been vigilant to enforce the statutory restrictions on the number and timing of motions permitted." *People v. Superior Court(Williams)*, 8 Cal.App.4th 688, at p.698(1992). Application of these stringent timing requirements is particularly crucial in a death penalty case such as the present one. Given that the statute permits the prosecution to disqualify without a showing of cause, a judge suitable to the defendant, in a case seeking a sentence of death, the controlling time frames within which it may do so must be narrowly construed and rigorously enforced.

The prosecution's challenge should be denied, as not effective.

This particular motion does not address the propriety of the Chief Justice's intervention at this time. We do note, however, that ordinarily the presumption will be that either the judge in the original venue will travel with the case to its new venue, or the presiding or master calendar judge in the new venue will assign the trial judge. (See, e.g., California Rules of Court, rules 4.154, 4.161.

This case is not like *Stevens v. Superior Court (Fridley)*, 52 Cal.App.4th 55 (1997). There, the court clerk, under the direction of an administrative "division manager", telephoned defense counsel's office and told his secretary that the case had been assigned to a particular judge for trial. By the time defense counsel received the message and instructed his secretary to inform the court he would be filing a peremptory challenge, the court was closed. Counsel therefore filed the challenge the next day, and it was denied as untimely.

The Fourth District held that the call by the clerk to the law office did not trigger the master calendar rule of Section 170.6, subdivision (2), in particular because the record did not show what authority the division manager would have had even if the attorney had been able to immediately voice his challenge at the time of the initial call.

Here, in contrast, the prosecution was apparently notified by means other than a phone call. Moreover, even assuming the phone call was the triggering event, the call was from Judge A. himself, not a clerk. Registering its challenge directly with the judge or, upon termination of the call, with the Chief Justice's office or the Stanislaus County Court, would have been an effective invocation of the prosecution's right to timely challenge the judge.

The prosecution's challenge should be denied as, not effective.

January 28, 2004 **Prosecutor's Reply** to Defendant's Brief Re: Untimeliness of People's Peremptory Challenge of Judge A.

Issue: Is the People's §170.6 challenge in this case timely?

The AOC announced Judge A.'s assignment on 1/21/04 and the People filed their challenge on 1/22/04. The provisions of the

Code of Civil Procedure § 170.6 require that within 10 days after notice of the judge's all purpose assignment the challenge must be made. Clearly, the next day is within ten days.

It is clear in the instant case that Judge G. had been assigned for all purposes. [Exhibit 3, Stanislaus Superior Case Assignment of Judge G. for all purposes]. After Judge G. granted the change of venue, he stated that he would go with the case unless another judge could/would be assigned to replace him. The Chief Justice assigned Judge A. to the case as Judge G.'s replacement; this assignment was for all purposes since the motions still had to be litigated as well as the trial.

The defense's sole contention is that the Chief Justice's appointment of Judge A. was "tantamount to an assignment by a master calendar judge" and the People therefore had to exercise their peremptory when Judge A. made a telephone call to the parties; this is certainly not the law. Since the statute is to be liberally construed in favor of allowing the challenge unless the "statute absolutely forbids it," the defense contention fails here. Otherwise, the court would be required to interpret the statute exactly opposite of the law and stretch the facts to fit the defense's "tantamount" theory. However, in order to assist the court, the People will address the defense's "tantamount" theory.

In the instant case, the Administrative Office of the Courts (AOC) announced the assignment of Judge A. through a press release. [See Exhibits 1 and 2.] The parties then received a subsequent telephone call from the judge. The master calendar rule clearly does not apply in this context. Even if the defense were to try and stretch this "tantamount" theory and denigrate the *Stevens* case as they have done, they cannot meet their burden.

Code of Civil Procedure § 170.6(2) states in part: "(2) Any party to or an attorney appearing in any action or proceeding may establish this prejudice by an oral or written motion without notice supported by affidavit or declaration under penalty of perjury or an oral statement under oath that the judge,...before whom the action or proceeding is pending or to whom it is assigned is prejudiced against any party or attorney or in the interest of the party or attorney so that [they] cannot or believes that he or she cannot have a fair and impartial trial or hearing before the judge,.... If directed to the trial of a cause that has been assigned to a judge for all purposes, the motion shall be made to the assigned judge or to the presiding judge by a party within 10 days after notice of the all purpose assignment,....

The court determined the standard of reviewing a peremptory challenge, saying: "As a remedial statute, section 170.6 is to be liberally construed in favor of allowing a peremptory challenge, and a challenge should be denied only if the statute absolutely forbids it. *Stephens v. Superior Court*, 96 Cal.App.4th 54, at pp.61-62(2002); quoting *People v. Superior Court(Williams)*, 8 Cal.App.4th 668, at pp.697-698(1992).

"The right conferred by...section 170.6... is a substantial right which is now part of the system of due process and judicial fair play in this state." *McCauley v. Superior Court*, 190 Cal. App.2d 562, at p.564(1961). "The purpose of the disqualification statute is...to promote fair and impartial trials..." *Williams*, at p.697.

Section 170.6 permits a party to obtain the disqualification of a judge for prejudice, upon sworn statement, without being required to establish it as a fact to the satisfaction of a judicial body. Thus, "where a disqualification motion is timely filed and in proper form, the trial court is bound to accept it without further inquiry." *Barrett v. Superior Court*, 77 Cal.App.4th 1, at p.4(1999).

The California Supreme Court interpreted the time limits for filing a section 170.6 peremptory challenge in *People v. Superior Court(Lavi)*, 4 Cal.4th 1164, at p.1171(1993). "As a general rule, a challenge of a judge is permitted under section 170.6 any time before commencement of a trial or hearing." However, the court recognized that section 170.6, subdivision(2) includes three express exceptions to the general rule: (1) the master calendar rule; (2) the all purpose assignment rule; and (3) the 10-day/5-day rule.

A court is a master calendar court within the meaning of section 170.6 if cases are assigned to trial by the following method: "a trial-ready case must be assigned to a court [department] that is ready and able to hear the case." *Levi*, at pp.1175, 1185. In master calendar courts, a peremptory challenge must be filed no later than the time the case is assigned for trial. Civ.Pro. §170.6, subd.(2).

"If the case is assigned from a master calendar court to a trial court for trial to begin that day, the challenge must be made to the judge supervising the master calendar not later than the time the case is assigned for trial." *Lavi*, at p.1176. As can be seen from the language of *Lavi*, an appointment by the Chief Justice, pursuant to Article VI, section 6, of the California Constitution, of Judge

A., was an "all purpose assignment" and not a "master calendar assignment" for a "trial to begin on that day."

Another case that examined what a master calendar assignment meant in context of section 170.6 is the case of *Sambrano v. Superior Court*, 31 Cal.App.3d 416, at p.419(1973); stating "A master calendar in criminal cases is a department to which all informations, accusations, and other criminal proceedings are, upon filing, automatically assigned, and from which, upon a plea other than a plea of guilty, the case is assigned a trial date and transferred to a trial department. (Rule 248, Cal. Rules of Court.) By the procedure applicable in the case at bench [Sambrano], the information was assigned directly to a trial department by a clerical rotation. Moreover, the memorandum establishing the method of assignment specifically provides that criminal matters will be so assigned 'rather than to a Master Calendar Court.'

Thus, the time limit for the filing of petitioner's [Sambrano case] motion to disqualify the trial judge is that established by Code of Civil Procedure section 170.6 for causes not appearing on a master calendar. Since the trial judge was known at least ten days before the date set for trial, the motion could be filed at any time up to and including five days before trial."

Another case that illustrates the fallacy of defendant's argument is *Stevens v. Superior Court(Fridley)*, 52 Cal.App.4th 55 (1997). Scott Peterson attempts to distinguish *Stevens* in a footnote. (See defense brief p.6, footnote 4.) The *Stevens* case, at p.60 noted: "when parties were not present before the court when the assignment was made by a clerk for trial to begin in a few days, the rationale for the master calendar rule does not apply."

First, *Stevens* says: "Although we need not decide this point, we also believe it is questionable whether the assignment on October 24, for trial to begin on October 28, can be considered an assignment for immediate trial within the meaning of the master calendar rule as explained by the Supreme Court in *Lavi*." (See *Stevens*, p.59, in footnote 6.)

Second, Scott's attempt to suggest that Los Angeles Superior Court Rules should control here is absurd, especially in light of the holding in *Lavi* regarding that Superior Court's rules and California Civil Procedure §170.6: "Given our holding herein, that for section 170.6's master calendar rule to apply, a trial-ready case must be assigned to a trial-ready courtroom, respondent's local policy in effect would improperly reduce the time within which the People or defendant may file a disqualification motion. Newly adopted Government Code section 68612, which comprises part of the Trial Delay Reduction Act, specifically provides that courts may shorten the statutory time for the performance of certain acts in civil cases. To our knowledge, there is no similar statute governing criminal cases. Thus, respondent's policy attempts to reduce the statutory time within which a litigant may file a section 170.6 challenge without authorization in another statute. The policy is therefore invalid." *Lavi*, at pp.1164, 1174. (See also, Gov.Code, § 68070 [local rules may not conflict with law]; *Wells Fargo Bank v. Superior Court*, 206 Cal.App.3d 918, at p.923(1988); *Estate of Brown*, 193 Cal.App.3d 612, at p.1619 [I think the prosecutor meant at p.619](1987); 2 Witkin, Cal. Procedure (3rd ed. 1985) Courts, §§ 154-155, pp.181-183 [local polices, to be valid, must not conflict with statutory law].) There can be no question that the master calendar exception does not apply in this instant [Scott Peterson] case.

The People will therefore address the second exception to the general rule of CCP §170.6, and that is the all purpose assignment rule. Under this rule, a peremptory challenge must be filed "'within 10 days after notice of the judge's all purpose assignment.'" *Lavi*, at p.1178. A trial court judge has an all purpose assignment if two criteria are met: (1) "the method of assigning cases must 'instantly pinpoint' the judge whom the parties can expect to ultimately preside at trial;" and (2) "that same judge must be expected to process the case 'in its totality.'" *Lavi*, at p.1180. (See also, *Pedus Services, Inc. v. Superior Court*, 72 Cal. App.4th 140, at p.145(1999).)

The *Lavi* court went on to discuss an all purpose assignment in a criminal case, stating: "We note that some cases have suggested that in an all purpose assignment, the specified judge processes the case 'from start to finish.' (See e.g., *Shipp v. Superior Court*, 5 Cal.App.4th (No page no. or date available.), at p.151. Such phraseology would indicate that a single judge must handle every matter in a given case. We believe that this language, especially in a criminal context, is overbroad and we decline to adopt such an impracticable standard for criminal cases in which the all purpose assignment rule is invoked.

Rather, if, at the time of the assignment, substantial matters remain to be processed in addition to trial, and the assigned judge is expected to process all those matters from that point on (thus allowing him or her [to] acquire expertise in, and familiarity with, the intricacies of the case), then the all purpose assignment rule may apply." *Lavi*, at p.1181, footnote 13.

The People have exercised their right to a peremptory challenge in this case pursuant to Code of Civil Procedure §170.6 in a timely manner and Scott's objection is unwarranted and should be overruled.

January 28, 2004 **Scott Peterson's Joint Discussion Proposal**

This brief is signed by both, Scott's attorney and the prosecutor.

Scott states that the parties present the following issues for discussion at the court hearing scheduled for February 2, 2004; (1) the parties have exchanged witness lists and jointly request that the lists provided to the Court remain confidential; (2) both parties desire that juror names be kept confidential from public disclosure; (3) both parties desire that cameras not be allowed in the courtroom at any hearing after February 2, 2004; (4) the People request that the jury not be sequestered, and Scott requests that the jury be sequestered; (5) parties request to continue allowing family member witnesses to be in the courtroom, despite the imposition of an exclusionary order; (6) parties agree that each party shall be entitled to the presence of two investigator witnesses, despite the exclusionary order, with the People's investigator witnesses being Detective Grogan and Investigator Bertolatto; (7) Scott requests to start the jury trial by distributing a jury questionnaire that will determine if a fair and impartial trial may be had in San Mateo County, and thereafter, hearings on motions in limine on February 17, 2004, and continue until completed, begin jury selection process and continue until completed, a one day break before Opening Statements, start witness testimony, and the parties request a Monday through Thursday trial week; the People oppose the distribution of a jury questionnaire prior to motions in limine, but otherwise agree with the schedule; (8) parties request the court to consider the motions in limine in the following order, GPS, wiretap, hypnotized witnesses, and dog tracking evidence; (9) Scott anticipates filing two additional motions in limine, a Motion for Separate Jury for Penalty Phase, and Motion to Exclude Scott Peterson's Statements to the Media; and (10) to discuss the continuation of the protective [gag] order.

January 28, 2004 **Order of Superior Court of San Mateo County**

Pursuant to CRC [California Rules of Court] 980(e)(4) and the authority as Presiding Judge, that during the pendency in San Mateo of the pre-trial proceedings, the trial, and the post-trial proceedings, if any, no person shall be permitted to possess and/ or bring any cameras, and other media and/or video equipment into any part of the San Mateo County Courthouse building located at 400 County Center, except for the first floor of that building. This order is to minimize interference with neighboring courtrooms, to minimize disruption of court proceedings, to provide unimpeded access to courtrooms for persons conducting regular court business, to protect the privacy rights of jurors and prospective jurors, and to enable the San Mateo Sheriff, who has been designated as the San Mateo Superior Court Security Officer, to enforce the provisions of this order.

January 30, 2004 **Scott Peterson's Notice** of Motion and Motion to Continue Trial

Scott states that he'd like to notify the court that on February 2nd, he will motion the court for an order continuing the trial date scheduled, to any date convenient with the court and counsel, as his attorney, Mark Geragos, was ordered to start trial, today, in Pasadena, California.

Every attempt was made to accommodate this court and to prevent an unnecessary expenditure of state resources, judicial and otherwise, necessitated by both the change of venue and the assignment of a new judge to preside over this trial. Mr. Geragos has made repeated requests to continue the Pasadena murder trial, involving an in-custody defendant, but the requests were denied.

By the time Mr. Geragos was released from the court and returned to his office, it was too late to file this motion to continue within the two-day period mandated by Penal Code § 1050. The Pasadena case is expected to last ten days.

January 30, 2004 **Non-Party Media** Newspapers' Brief Re: Witness Lists, Jury Selection Procedures, and Cameras in the Courtroom

San Francisco Chronicle, Contra Costa Times, McClatchy Newspapers, Inc., Los Angeles Times, and the San Jose Mercury

News submit this brief in support of the most basic principle, that what transpires in the courtroom is public property.

The parties' "Joint Discussion Proposal" suggests, without supporting authority, a trio of access restrictions which, singly and together, would significantly restrict the public and press' access to the trial proceedings in this case and inhibit the print media's ability to cover it for its readers.

Mr. Peterson's case has of course commanded significant public interest from the time his wife disappeared to the present. The public has a paramount interest in seeing that justice is done by a jury of his peers. That should not be done secretly, it should be done openly. The parties' suggestion that the witness list and juror names should be sealed, and that cameras should be excluded, strikes at the openness principles established so firmly in a California Supreme Court case, Rule 243.1, and the U.S. Supreme Court cases which gave rise to them. The sealing and closure requests should be denied.

The long search for Laci Peterson and the charges against her husband give rise to a "great and legitimate public interest" in the basis of the charges against Scott Peterson and the witnesses who will testify against him. This is not a secret or star chamber proceeding. It should be conducted openly. The electronic media is filing a brief on the same day as this one (January 30th) in support of television coverage. The print media will not repeat all of the arguments in favor of cameras made in that brief, although we join them.

It goes without saying that the media play a vital role in informing the public about what happens in judicial proceedings. The U.S. Supreme Court has regularly held that "representatives of the press and general public must be given an opportunity to be heard on the question of their exclusion" from judicial proceedings and records. (See, e.g., *Globe Newspapers Co. v. Superior Court*, 457 U.S. 596, at p.609 note 25(1982)(quotation omitted). Our own Supreme Court follows the nation's high court's lead in holding that the press and public must be given an opportunity to be heard on the question of exclusion. (*NBC Subsidiary(KNBC-TV), Inc. v. Superior Court*, 20 Cal.4th 1178, at p.1217, footnote 36(1999). Accordingly, it is clear that the print and other media have standing to oppose restrictions on their ability to cover this trial.

In *NBC Subsidiary*, pp.1217-1218, the California Supreme Court stated that, "before substantive courtroom proceedings are closed or transcripts are ordered sealed, a trial court must hold a hearing and expressly find that (i) there exists an overriding interest supporting closure and/or sealing; (ii) there is substantial probability that the interest will be prejudiced absent closure and/ or sealing; (iii) the proposed closure and/or sealing is narrowly tailored to serve the overriding interest; and (iv) there is no less restrictive means of achieving the overriding interest."

Those principles, which have since been written into law, California Rules of Court 243.1 and 243.2, as they apply to the requirements for sealing records, should be followed in examining any of the access restrictions suggested by the parties.

The parties' first proposal is to seal witness lists. The parties' sketchy submission on this point suggests, from the fact that the witness lists have been "provided to the court," that it is a public court document. As such, it should not be sealed unless the four requirements set forth in *NBC Subsidiary*, have been met. None can be.

The parties' have advanced no "overriding interest supporting closure and/or sealing" of a witness list. The public has a right to know which witnesses are likely to testify in this trial, which has received nationwide attention. The parties have failed to show that either their, or the witnesses', interests support closure and/or sealing of the simple witness list. Thus, under Rule of Court 243.1(d)(1), there is no overriding interest which overcomes the right of public access to the record.

In *Huffy Corp. v Superior Court*, 112 Cal.App.4th 97, at p.109(2003), the defendant argued that "documents which list witnesses to possible violations of federal and state pollution laws must be sealed." The Court of Appeal squarely rejected the sealing argument: "As noted..., no overriding public interest warrants sealing the identities of witnesses to such events." The court concluded that witness lists cannot be sealed. The same conclusion follows here.

"When that [public] interest is augmented by the strong presumption in favor of public access reflecting 'a first principle that the people have the right to know what is being done in their courts.'" *In re Providian Credit Card Cases*, 96 Cal.App.4th 292, at p.309(2002). Thus, under Rule 243.1(d)(2), no "overriding interest supports sealing the record."

Likewise, the parties have not shown a "substantial probability" that any interest in sealing a witness list would be "prejudiced absent closure and/or sealing." Rule 243.1(d)(3). The witness lists should not be confidential.

Any propose closure or sealing must also be "narrowly tailored to serve the overriding interest." Cal. Rule of Court 243.1(d)(4). As applied here, the wholesale sealing of a witness list cannot be justified even assuming, arguendo, that there might bc one witness as to whose identity a theoretical "overriding interest" in sealing could be shown. Accordingly, the parties have failed to show that their proposed sealing of the witness list is narrowly tailored and the request should be denied on that basis as well.

Finally, *NBC Subsidiary* requires express findings that "there is no less restrictive means of achieving the overriding interest" before any court records are sealed or hearings closed. (See also Cal. Court Rule 243.1(d)(5).) Again, the parties fail to discuss this or the other requirements for sealing. There is no showing that less restrictive means could not serve any theoretical interest which might be advanced by the parties on this point.

In short, the parties have failed to make any of the showings which would be required to seal witness lists. The witness lists provided to the Court should be public documents.

The Newspapers also oppose the parties' request that "juror names be kept confidential from public disclosure." The Newspapers hereby request access to juror names pursuant to California Code of Civil Procedure § 237(a).

The Supreme Court in *Richmond Newspapers, Inc. v. Virginia*, 448 U.S. 555, at p.577(1980), Chief Justice Burger stated that the First Amendment conveys an affirmative, enforceable right of public access to criminal proceedings, just as the right of association, right to travel, and right to be presumed innocent are implicit in other provisions of the Bill of Rights. In a capital murder case, *Press-Enterprise v. Superior Court of California*, 464 U.S. 501 (1984), the Court specifically extended this right to juror selection in a high profile criminal prosecution. "Public proceedings vindicate the concerns of the victims and the community in knowing that offenders are being brought to account for their criminal conduct by jurors fairly and openly selected." Id. at p.509. "The First Amendment of the United States Constitution guaranteeing public access to judicial proceedings overwhelms any countervailing privacy interests of prospective jurors." *Bellas v. Superior Court*, 85 Cal.App.4th 636, at pp.638-639(2000).

California has also recognized the importance of juror identification-both to the parties to the action and to the public in general. Pursuant to Cal. Code of Civil Procedure 237(a)(1), which applies to criminal and civil cases, the names of qualified jurors drawn from the qualified juror list "shall be made available to the public" upon request unless the court determines that a "compelling interest" requires that this information should be kept confidential. The "compelling" interest requirement is similar to the requirement of an "overriding" interest set forth in *NBC Subsidiary*. Under section 237(b), a compelling interest includes "protecting jurors from threats or danger of physical harm." There is no showing here, however, that any such threats or danger would confront prospective jurors as might be the case in a gangland slaying.

Section 237(a) provides that the court "shall" release the juror names unless a specific compelling interest has been identified. (See, e.g., *People v. Phillips*, 56 Cal.App.4th 1307, at pp.1309-1310(1997); where the trial court kept the names of prospective jurors confidential during voir dire but failed to make a showing that a compelling interest warranted confidentiality; "in absence of that determination, it was improper for the court to keep this information from the public, or the parties.") There is no compelling interest in these proceedings to justify sealing. There is absolutely no evidence that the jurors here, if named, would suffer threats or a danger of physical harm.

Moreover, the provision that provides for sealing of juror personal information, including name, address, and telephone number, § 237(a)(2), "[u]pon recording of a jury's verdict in a criminal proceeding", does not provide the court authority to seal juror names during voir dire or at any other time prior to verdict. In *Phillips*, at pp.1309-1310, "This postverdict provision [§237(a)(2)] cannot be used to justify the court's action during voir dire"; and in *Erickson v. Superior Court*, 55 Cal.App.4th 755, at p.758 & note 2, "The statute does not authorize sealing of juror information at any stage of a civil action or at any stage of a criminal action prior to return of jury verdict," and noting, "the impetus for the amendment to [section 237] was concern for the protection of jurors in criminal trials from post-verdict harassment."

Kinda like saying that you're gonna feed the horse some oats, hoping he won't sh....

It should be conducted openly, and as the U.S. Supreme Court held in *Press-Enterprise*, at pp.508-509, that openness extends to jury selection. It would be anomalous indeed if access to something basic like juror names or jury voir dire was restricted in those cases in which the public is most interested. The parties' proposal to seal juror names should be denied.

The parties have also stated their "desire" that cameras not be allowed in the courtroom after today's hearing. We will submit a few observations, and also point out that even if electronic media coverage is not allowed, and again, the print media supports the electronic media's brief on this point, there is no reason that one still "pool" camera should not be allowed at the trial for the print media.

As the U.S. Supreme Court, in *Richmond Newspapers*, at pp.572-573, observed, "[i]nstead of acquiring information about trials by firsthand observation or by word of mouth from those who attended, people now acquire it chiefly through the print and electronic media....In a sense, this validates the media claim of functioning as surrogates for the public."

Rule 980(e), sets forth 18 specific factors for the court to consider in ruling on a camera request, along with a catch-all 19th: "Any other factor the judge deems relevant." We will not address all 19 factors here, but briefly touch upon the most important considerations.

The first, and paramount, factor, is the "Importance of maintaining public trust and confidence in the judicial system." The public can and will benefit from seeing that the trial is conducted in a fair, impartial and orderly manner which affords dignity to the participants and fairness to the People and Scott Peterson.

The second factor is "Importance pf promoting public access to the judicial system." That factor, addressed in *NBC Subsidiary*, of course favors allowing cameras. As the U.S. Supreme Court observed in *Press-Enterprise*, at p.509, in quoting the *Richmond Newspapers* case, at p.472, "'People in an open society do not demand infallibility from their institutions, but it is difficult for them to accept what they are prohibited from observing.'"

That factor is of paramount importance here because even members of the press, who served as the eyes and ears of the public, may not be able to squeeze into the courtroom in this case.

Thus, there is the very real possibility that, without cameras in the courtroom, even accredited members of the major print media such as those submitting this brief may have to observe the proceedings in an auxiliary room. Without cameras in the courtroom, the ability of even major print media reporters to report on what happens in the courtroom may be severely inhibited; a fortiori, the vast majority of the public which can't come to the courtroom to observe these proceedings will lose an important component of their access to these proceedings.

The parties' opposition to cameras does not dictate a contrary conclusion. Two Courts of Appeal, in the similar context of sealing records under Rule 243.1, have concluded that settlement agreements should not be sealed "'merely upon the agreement of the parties without a specific showing of serious injury.'" *Huffy Corp.*, at p.106, quoting *Universal Studios, Inc. v. Superior Court*, 110 Cal.App.4th 1273, at pp.1281-1282(2003). Likewise, in the comparable context of the California Public Records Act, the courts have held that an assurance of confidentiality cannot transform a public record into a private one. *San Gabriel Tribune v. Superior Court*, 143 Cal.App.3d 762, at p.775(1984); also, *Register Div. Of Freedom Newspapers v. Superior Court*, 158 Cal.App.3d 893, at p.909(1984). Similarly, the parties' preference here to exclude cameras does not govern over the paramount interests of the public in being able to observe these proceedings.

Finally, while Rule 980(e)(vii) does not discuss the possible effect of cameras on the parties' ability to select a fair and impartial jury, we submit that the presence of a still pool camera, or a television camera, in the courtroom will not endanger Scott's right to a fair trial. The test is whether 12 impartial jurors can be found in San Mateo County. This County is large enough so that that question can be answered affirmatively whether or not cameras are allowed. *Press-Enterprise*, at p.503.

One important step in that direction has been taken by moving the trial from Stanislaus to San Mateo County. Scott Peterson, himself, has suggested other ways to ensure a fair trial, including sequestration and/or the distribution of a jury questionnaire. There is no reason to sacrifice the public right of access promoted by cameras to the speculative possibility that it will make it more difficult to empanel a jury. "Through voir dire, cumbersome as it is in some circumstances, a court can identify those jurors whose prior knowledge of the case would render them from rendering an impartial verdict." *Press-Enterprise v. Superior Court*, 478 U.S. 1, at p.15(1986).

In short, for the reasons outlined here and in the electronic media's brief, cameras should be allowed. At the very least, an unobtrusive "pool" still camera should be allowed. The sealing and closure requests should be denied.

What media just called a 'speculative possibility', seems to be answered in the 'affirmative conclusion', just two sentences prior in their brief, with 'an important step' in moving the trial.

January 30, 2004 **Non-Party Media Appendix** of Non-California Authorities in Support of Newspapers' Brief Re: Witness Lists, Jury Selection Procedures, and Cameras in the Courtroom

This appendix has three cases attached, as Exhibit(s) A, B, and C, *Richmond Newspapers*, *Press-Enterprise*, (1984), and *Press-Enterprise*, (1986); However, they are copies of the cases as done by Lexis. Therefore, the page numbers on these copies don't match the page numbers of the particular citations in media's brief, and are noted by Lexis in the text of the opinion with an asterisk and brackets; [*].

Exhibit A is 25 pages, the *Richmond Newspapers* case, minus a cover page and an introduction to the case by Lexis, with the Court's opinion beginning on page 4.

"The narrow question presented in this case is whether the right of the public and press to attend criminal trials is guaranteed under the United States Constitution."

In March 1976, one Stevenson was indicted for murder, tried promptly in July 1976, and convicted of second-degree murder in the Circuit Court of Hanover County, Va. The Virginia Supreme Court reversed the conviction in October 1977, stating that a bloodstained shirt purportedly belonging to Stevenson had been improperly admitted into evidence.

Stevenson was retried in the same court. This second trial ended in a mistrial on May 30, 1978, when a juror asked to be excused after trial had begun and no alternate was available. A newspaper account published the next day reported the mistrial and went on to note that "[a] key piece of evidence in Stevenson's original conviction was a bloodstained shirt obtained from Stevenson's wife soon after the killing. The Virginia Supreme

Court, however, ruled that the shirt was entered into evidence improperly."

A third trial, which began in the same court on June 6, 1978, also ended in a mistrial. It appears that the mistrial may have been declared because a prospective juror had read about Stevenson's previous trials in a newspaper and had told other prospective jurors about the case before the retrial began.

Stevenson was tried in the same court for a fourth time beginning on September 11, 1978. Present in the courtroom when the case was called, were appellants Wheeler and McCarthy, reporters for appellant Richmond Newspapers, Inc. Before the trial began, the counsel for the defendant moved that it be closed to the public: "[There] was this woman that was with the family of the deceased when we were here before. She had sat in the courtroom. I would like to ask that everybody be excluded from the Courtroom because I don't want any information being shuffled back and forth when we have a recess as to what; who testified to what."

The trial judge, who had presided over two of the three previous trials, asked if the prosecution had any objection to clearing the courtroom. The prosecutor stated he had no objection and would leave it to the discretion of the court. Presumably referring to Va. Code § 19.2-266 (Supp. 1980), the trial judge then announced: "[The] statute gives me that power specifically and the defendant had made the motion." He then ordered "that the Courtroom be kept clear of all parties except the witnesses when they testify." The **record does not show that any objections to the closure were made by anyone present at the time**, including appellants Wheeler and McCarthy.

Virginia Code § 19.2-266 (Supp. 1980) provides in part: "In the trial of all criminal cases, whether the same be felony or misdemeanor cases, the court may, in its discretion, exclude from the trial any persons whose presence would impair the conduct of a fair trial, provided that the right of the accused to a public trial shall not be violated."

Later that same day, however, appellants sought a hearing on a motion to vacate the closure order. The trial judge granted the request and scheduled a hearing to follow the close of the day's proceedings. When the hearing began, the court ruled that the hearing was to be treated as part of the trial; accordingly, he again ordered the reporters to leave the courtroom, and they complied.

At the close of the hearing, counsel for appellants [Newspapers] observed that no evidentiary findings had been made by the court prior to the closure order and pointed out that the court had failed to consider any other, less drastic measures within its power to ensure a fair trial. Counsel for appellants argued that constitutional considerations mandated that before ordering closure, the court should first decide that the rights of the defendant could be protected in no other way.

Counsel for defendant Stevenson pointed out that **this was the fourth time he was standing trial.** He also referred to "difficulty with information between the jurors," and stated that he "didn't want information to leak out," be published by the media, perhaps inaccurately, and then be seen by the jurors. Defense counsel argued that these things, plus the fact that "this is a small community," made this a proper case for closure.

Now, you would 'thunk' that at this point, the U.S. Supreme Court would state that the Hanover judge 'did' state specific reasoning, supported by fact, on the record for his decision. Some of the very reasoning as to why this was Stevenson's fourth trial. However, the U.S. Supreme Court ain't had enough to say yet, and totally overlook the facts of *Stevenson's* life. In 1977, the courthouse pride was the 'Ole Hangin' Tree' right outside the front door of the courthouse. It's also the home of the fellow who said, 'Give me liberty, or give me death'. As you can see, these things go hand in hand.

The trial judge noted that counsel for the defendant had made similar statements at the morning hearing. The court also stated: "[One] of the other points that we take onto consideration in the particular Courtroom is layout of the Courtroom. I think that having people in the Courtroom is distracting to the jury. Now, we have to have certain people in here and maybe that's not a very good reason. When we get into our new Court Building, people can sit in the audience so the jury can't be seen. The rule of the Court may be different under those circumstances...."

The prosecutor again declined comment, and the [Hanover] court summed up by saying: "I'm inclined to agree with [defense counsel] that, if I feel that the rights of the defendant [Stevenson] are infringed in any way, [when] he makes the motion to do something and it doesn't override all rights of everyone else, then I'm inclined to go along with the defendant's [Stevenson's] motion."

The court denied [media's] motion to vacate [closure] and ordered the trial to continue the following morning "with the press and public excluded." What transpired when the closed trial resumed the next day was disclosed in the following manner by an order of the court entered September 12, 1978: "In the absence of the jury, the defendant by counsel made a Motion that a mis-trial be declared, which motion was taken under advisement."

"At the conclusion of the Commonwealth's evidence, the attorney for the defendant moved the Court to strike the Commonwealth's evidence on the grounds stated to the record, which Motion was sustained [okay] by the Court. And the jury having been excused, the Court doth [does] find the accused NOT GUILTY of Murder, as charged in the Indictment, and he was allowed to depart [go free]." At oral argument, it was represented to the Court that tapes of the trial were available to the public as soon as the trial terminated.

On September 27, 1978, the trial court granted appellants' [Newspapers] motion to intervene nuno pro tune in the Stevenson case. Appellants then petitioned the Virginia Supreme Court for writs of mandamus and prohibition and filed an appeal from the trial court's closure order. On July 9, 1979, the Virginia Supreme Court dismissed the mandamus and prohibition petitions and, finding no reversible error, denied the petition for appeal.

Appellants [Newspapers] then sought review in this Court [U.S.], invoking both our appellate, 28 U.S.C. § 1257(2), and certiorari jurisdiction, § 1257(3). We postponed further consideration of the question of our jurisdiction to the hearing of the case on the merits. We conclude that jurisdiction by appeal does not lie; however, treating the filed papers as a petition for a writ of certiorari pursuant to 28 U.S.C. § 2103, we grant the petition.

In the view of the U.S. Supreme Court, the validity of the Va. Code was not sufficiently drawn in question by the Newspaper before the Virginia courts to invoke their appellate jurisdiction. The Newspaper never explicitly challenged the statute's validity. "It is essential to our jurisdiction on appeal...that there be an explicit and timely insistence in the state courts that a state statute, as applied, is repugnant to the federal Constitution, treaties or laws."

In both the trial court and the State Supreme Court, Newspapers argued that constitutional rights of the public and the press prevented the court from closing a trial without first giving notice and an opportunity for a hearing to the public and the press and exhausting every alternative means of protecting Stevenson's right to a fair trial.

Given Newspaper's failure explicitly to challenge the statute, we view their arguments as constituting claims of rights under the Constitution, which rights are said to limit the exercise of the discretion conferred by the statute on the trial court. An attack on lawless exercise of authority in a particular case is not an attack upon the constitutionality of a statute conferring the authority. Such claims are properly brought before this Court by way of certiorari, rather than appellate jurisdiction. We shall, however, continue to refer to the parties as appellants and appellee.

The criminal trial which appellants sought to attend has long since ended, and there is some suggestion that the case is moot. This Court has frequently recognized, however, that its jurisdiction is not necessarily defeated by the practical termination of a contest which is short-lived by nature. If the underlying dispute is capable of repetition, yet evading review.

Well, it took the U.S. Supreme Court, three HOWEVER's to find jurisdiction of this issue, which, by the way, was answered in the Hanover Court's decision. The Hanover judge gave his considerations to the varying interests and rights, and gave his reasoning as to why he made the decision, and his decision was based into and upon, facts. The U.S. Supreme Court now wants to imagine as if it's there each and every time a trial begins, and it'll produce a uniform 'policy decision' based on an issue that it wasn't asked to decide.

The Court must have a case or controversy before it can decide to decide to review the records of a trial [certiorari, or certify the records and send them to us]. A case must involve two people, someone to talk to the court on each side of the issue, and someone to answer the court's questions on each side of the issue. At least one of these parties must have presented this specific issue before the court to answer. The court must be able to answer the issue, constitutionally, or it's not within their authority to bother with it.

Here, we have the Newspapers, who did not protest being asked to leave the courtroom, which is a necessity under a system of freedom, since if you wait for the government to say whether it's a freedom or not, then it's gonna be a right, privilege, duty, law, or burden, so it's important to proclaim what it is, when it is. Crying WOLF, once you're inside his rib cage, won't mean much. So, in effect, the Newspapers did not protect their coupling of a free press with Stevenson's right to a public trial in order to preserve their grievance.

On the other side, you'd expect to find Mr. Stevenson, but, lo and behold, it's the Virginia prosecutor, the Attorney General. Guess the white flags were waiving, since that's an elective position in Virginia, and this matter has been floating around for more than four years, elections, publicity, and ability to influence.

Richmond Newspapers has Chief Justice Burger announcing the Court's opinion, with Justice White and Justice Stevens joining in that opinion; until you get to page 581, which is where Justice White wrote a concurring opinion, and when you get to page 582, which is where Justice Stevens wrote a concurring opinion. Justice Brennan wrote an opinion concurring in the judgment, which Justice Marshall joined, but only beyond page 584 of Justice Brennan's opinion. Justice Stewart wrote an opinion concurring in the judgment after page 598, and Justice Blackmun wrote an opinion concurring in the judgment after page 601. Justice Rehnquist wrote an opinion which is in dissent after page 604. Justice Powell decided he wanted no parts in the consideration or decision of the case. The case law book begins this case on page 555, so either the opinion was too long or the justices could only agree with so much. Kinda like cuttin' into an apple and finding part of it has soured.

Justice Rehnquist, now the Chief Justice of the United States, wrote in his dissent of this case, quoting his concurrence in *DePasquale*, I do not believe that either the First or Sixth Amendment, as made applicable to the States by the Fourteenth [Amendment], requires that a State's reasons for denying public access to a trial, where both the prosecuting attorney and the defendant have consented to an order of closure approved by the judge, are subject to any additional constitutional review at our hands. And I most certainly do not believe that the Ninth Amendment confers upon us any such power to review orders of state trial judges closing trials in such situations.

Justice Rehnquist continues with his dissent, The issue is not whether the "right" to freedom of the press conferred by the First Amendment to the Constitution overrides the defendant's "right" to a fair trial conferred by other Amendments to the

Constitution; it is instead whether any provision in the Constitution may fairly be read to prohibit what the trial judge in the Virginia state-court system did in this case. Being unable to find any other Amendment to the United States Constitution, or in the Constitution itself, I dissent.

In *Press-Enterprise Co. v. Superior Court of California, Riverside County*, [Press-Enterprise I, 1984], before voir dire [to speak the truth] examination of prospective jurors began, petitioner, Press-Enterprise, moved that the voir dire be open to the public and the press. Petitioner contended that the public had an absolute right to attend the trial, and asserted that the trial commenced with the voir dire proceedings.

The trial judge agreed and permitted Press Enterprise to attend only the "general voir dire." He stated that counsel would conduct the "individual voir dire with regard to death qualifications and any other special areas that counsel may feel some problem with regard to... in private..." The voir dire consumed six weeks and all but approximately three days was closed to the public. After the jury was empaneled, Press Enterprise moved the trial court to release a complete transcript of the voir dire proceedings.

Mr. Brown's counsel argued that release of the transcript would violate the jurors' right of privacy. The prosecutor agreed, adding that the prospective jurors had answered questions under an "implied promise of confidentiality."

The court denied Press Enterprise's motion, without prejudice [they can bring it up again]. Mr. Brown was tried and convicted of the rape and murder of a teenage girl, and sentenced to death in California Superior Court. After the conviction and sentence, Press Enterprise again applied for the release of the transcript. The judge denied the application.

Press Enterprise then filed a writ of mandate in the California Court of Appeal to compel the Superior Court to release the transcript and vacate the order closing the voir dire proceedings. The petition was denied. The California Supreme Court denied Press Enterprise's request for a hearing. The U.S. Supreme Court granted certiorari, vacated the judgment of the Court of Appeal, and remands the case for proceedings not inconsistent with this opinion. The trial judge should seal only such parts of the transcript as necessary to preserve the anonymity of the individuals sought to be protected.

The Court states that the question of when a trial begins, does not need to be answered here, in this context, since, whether the voir dire process should be open focuses on First, rather than Fifth, Amendment values.

In *Press-Enterprise Co. v. Superior Court of California For The County of Riverside*, [Press-Enterprise II, 1986], Robert Diaz was charged with 12 counts of murder on December 23, 1981, and the state was seeking the death penalty. The preliminary hearing commenced on July 6, 1982, and Diaz moved to exclude the public from the preliminary hearing, under Cal. Penal Code Annodated § 868, which requires such proceedings to be open unless "exclusion of the public is necessary in order to protect the defendant's right to a fair and impartial trial." The Magistrate granted the unopposed motion, finding that closure was necessary because the case had attracted national publicity and "only one side may get reported in the media." Before 1982, the defendant had the unqualified right to close the proceedings. The California Supreme Court rejected an attack on that statute, so the California Legislature amended the statute to include present day requirements.

The preliminary hearing lasted 41 days. Press Enterprise, at the conclusion of the hearing, asked that the transcript of the proceedings be released. The Magistrate refused and sealed the record.

On January 21, 1983, the State moved in Superior Court to have the transcript of the preliminary hearing released to the public; with Press Enterprise later joining in support of the motion. Diaz opposed the motion, contending that release of the transcript would result in prejudicial pretrial publicity. The Superior Court found that the information in the transcript was "as factual as it could be," and that the facts were neither "inflammatory" nor "exciting," but that there was nonetheless, "a reasonable likelihood that release of all or any part of the transcripts might prejudice defendant's right to a fair and impartial trial."

Press Enterprise then filed a peremptory writ of mandate with the Court of Appeal. That court originally denied the writ but, after being ordered by the California Supreme Court, set the matter for a hearing. Meanwhile, Diaz waived his right to a jury trial and the Superior Court released the transcript. After holding that the controversy was moot [over, and doesn't matter], the Court of Appeal denied the writ of mandate.

The California Supreme Court thereafter denied Press Enterprise's peremptory writ of mandate, holding there is no general First Amendment right of access to preliminary hearings. The Court reasoned that the right of access to criminal proceedings recognized in Press Enterprise I, extended only to actual criminal trials. Furthermore, the reasons that had been asserted for closing the proceedings in *Press-Enterprise I* and *Globe*, in that the interests of witnesses and other third parties, were not the same as the right asserted in this case, the defendant's right to a fair and impartial trial by a jury uninfluenced by news accounts. The Court reasoned that if the defendant establishes a "reasonable likelihood of substantial prejudice" the burden shifts to the prosecution or the media to show by a preponderance of the evidence that there is no such reasonable probability of prejudice.

The standard applied by the California Supreme Court failed to consider the First Amendment right of access to criminal proceedings. Accordingly, the judgment of the California Supreme Court is reversed. Through voir dire, cumbersome as it is in some circumstances, a court can identify those jurors whose prior knowledge of the case would disable them from rendering an impartial verdict.

In dissent, Justice Stevens is joined by Justice Rehnquist as to Part II. The constitutional question presented by this case is whether members of the public have a First Amendment right to insist upon access to the transcript of a preliminary hearing during the period before the public trial, even though the accused [person], the prosecutor, and the trial judge have all agreed to the sealing of the transcript in order to assure a fair trial.

The presence of a legitimate reason for closure in this case requires an affirmance. The constitutionally grounded fair trial interests of the accused [person] if he is bound over for trial, and the reputational interests of the accused [person] if he is not, provide a substantial reason for delaying access to the [preliminary hearing] transcript for at least the short time before trial.

By taking its own verbal formulation seriously, the Court reverses; without comment or explanation or any attempt at reconciliation, the holding in *Gannett* that a "reasonable probability of prejudice" is enough to overcome the First Amendment right of access to a preliminary proceeding. It is unfortunate that the Court neglects this opportunity to fit the result in this case into the body of precedent dealing with access rights generally. I fear that today's decision will simply further unsettle the law in this area.

I respectfully dissent.

January 30, 2004 **Non-Party Media Brief** in Support of Rule 980 Applications for Television Coverage of the Trial filed by Courtroom Television Network, Cable News Network LP, LLLP, National Broadcasting Company, Inc., KNTV Television, Inc., and ABC, Inc.

Media, respectfully submit the following memorandum in support of their applications.

Court TV is a national cable television network, dedicated to reporting on the legal and judicial systems of the United States. Since its creation in 1991, Court TV's cornerstone has been to televise civil and criminal trials, and it has televised more than 800 trials and other legal proceedings.

CNN is the world's largest news organization with over a dozen television and radio news networks and websites, as well as several news programming services, produced and distributed domestically and worldwide.

KNTV is the NBC affiliate in San Francisco, and provides news and news programming for the greater San Francisco area.

Two hundred years ago, the court accommodated the public's interest in court proceedings by moving high profile proceedings to a larger building. As the U.S. Supreme Court noted in *Press-Enterprise v. Superior Court*, 478 U.S. 1, at p.10(1986), the probable cause hearing in the Aaron Burr trial "was held in the Hall of the House of Delegates in Virginia, the courtroom being too small to accommodate the crush of interested citizens." Today's technology affords a much easier way to provide access to members of the public who are interested in following this proceeding.

The News Organizations are requesting permission to televise the trial; from the opening statements until the announcement of the verdict; as it occurs in court. Such gavel-to-gavel coverage provides the public with the most accurate and comprehensive understanding of important judicial proceedings, like this murder trial. This Court has a proven track record of conducting fair and orderly proceedings and extensive experience with death penalty cases. There can be no question that there will be media coverage of this proceeding, but only through camera coverage will the public have the most complete and accurate information about the trial.

Finally, as this Court undoubtedly knows, and as the Honorable [Judge] G. experienced in the many hearings he permitted the News Organizations to televise in this case; the cameras are unobtrusive and the News Organizations will fully cooperate with the Court to ensure that all the requirements relating to equipment placement and camera coverage are satisfied. If permitted by this Court, these News Organizations will provide the public with televised access to the proceedings, without interfering with the Court's proceedings in any way.

Although this Brief addresses coverage of the trial, the News Organizations also request the opportunity to brief issues related to access to pre, and post, trial proceedings as those proceedings arise.

California long has recognized the importance of allowing television coverage of trials. As early as 1967, long before technological advances permitted the unobtrusive recording of court proceedings, a California State Assembly committee emphasized that cameras in the courtroom are wholly consistent with our tradition of public trials. The presence of cameras in the courtroom confers numerous benefits on the public. The media, and, in particular, television, play an indispensable role in informing the public about the conduct of judicial proceedings. With the myriad commitments and responsibilities that each person faces on a daily basis, there is simply no time to attend judicial proceedings.

But even if an individual were available to attend trial proceedings, the sheer number of such interested observants in cases like this one guarantees that only a small fraction could be admitted at any given time. The courtroom has limited space. This reality has not been lost on courts and legislatures that have considered the issue. In other words, a courtroom is open only in theory when the general public has no opportunity to view the events transpiring therein.

Furthermore, the duty of the media to keep the public informed about events such as trials falls disproportionately on the television organizations. While newspapers can provide excellent descriptive coverage of court proceedings, they cannot show the public exactly what happens in the courtroom. To enable media to perform its surrogate function most effectively, the maximum amount of information must be available to the public. The most effective means of making accurate, objective information available is through courtroom cameras.

The U.S. Supreme Court has noted that the strong historical tradition in Western jurisprudence in favor of public observation of trials is a practice that predates the Norman Conquest. This tradition assumes even greater importance in our democratic system, where the government and all of its actions ultimately are held accountable by the voters. This observation is particularly true as it applies to high profile cases such as this one. These cases focus public attention on the judicial system, and for better or worse, provide the basis for the public's broader conclusions about the judicial process as a whole.

Moreover, where, as here, the trial has been moved out of a small, closely-knit community that has exhibited an overwhelming concern with the outcome, television coverage is even more important. As Judge G. recognized in changing venue to San Mateo County, this murder has had a significant impact on the citizens of Stanislaus County. Members of that community, and many other communities, responded in force to pleas for help from the Peterson family, and then joined the family in grieving the death of Laci Peterson and her unborn child.

There has been extensive coverage of the murder and Scott Peterson's prosecution because residents of Modesto need to know and understand what happened to the mother-to-be and her child. Modesto's citizens need and desire the catharsis that can only come from public airing of the evidence against Scott Peterson. And regardless of the result, whether Scott Peterson is acquitted or convicted, Modesto's citizens need to understand what the jury considered in reaching that result.

Before continuing with media's **Brief**, it should be noted that what was just written by Media, a non-party, to the criminal court judge presiding over this trial, is that there is a two-pronged offensive towards Scott, the prosecutor, who represents the People in government, and the media, who represent the Public in a criminal trial. Media is arguing to the judge that Laci was murdered, and that Laci's son was unborn. Media also admits that the prosecution of Scott has had extensive coverage by media, even though media forgets that this brief is being written by them, on January 30, 2004, and the Opening Statements of Scott's trial is scheduled for Tuesday, June 1, 2004; which is when the legal prosecution begins.

By permitting gavel-to-gavel camera coverage, this Court can affect the information that the public receives about the trial. The trial will be the subject of intense publicity regardless of how the Court rules on the 980 application in this case. Without cameras in the courtroom, the only information about what happens in the courtroom will come second-hand from accounts by those few members of the public and the media able to fit inside, or from individuals speculating about what has occurred.

Commentators will characterize what witnesses said, rather than being able to show the actual testimony. The media will rely on sound bites from out-of-court interviews, perhaps juxtaposed against out-of-court photographs of participants. Citizens will judge the proceedings with whatever information they possess, however truncated, salacious, or inaccurate. Indeed, Judge G. previously recognized and enunciated the importance of television coverage of courtroom events.

Sounds like media has been watching the TV news corp shows.

Judge G. imposed a protective [gag] order in this case to focus attention on what transpires in the courtroom, which is exactly what will be accomplished by permitting the News Organizations to televise the trial. Indeed, as a practical matter, barring cameras from newsworthy trials merely fuels speculation about the proceedings, and increases the odds of inaccuracies. The antidote for concerns about sensational and speculative media coverage is to provide the public with an accurate and complete view of the actual court proceedings.

This reasoning applies with even greater force to the evidentiary proceedings of the trial. If the Court were to restrict electronic coverage to only certain portions of the trial, such as the opening statement, closing statement, and verdict, those interested in these proceedings would get only a glimpse into the actual machinations of the trial. If the Court has concerns about televising particular parts of the trial, it has the discretion to reduce the coverage as those issues arise.

Such restrictions may contribute to the unfortunate and dangerous popular perception that trials are won and lost based on the attorney's abilities to "wow" the jury, rather than on the actual evidence presented. The jury will bc instructed to base its decision on the evidence presented in between the opening and closing statements. If the public is forced to rely on snippets of the trial, including argumentative summaries of the evidence, rather than the orderly presentation that the jury sees, it cannot hope to completely understand the jury's verdict, leaving the jury and the Court vulnerable to unfair and unfounded criticism.

Allowing televised coverage of the entire trial provides the most complete, most accurate, and most comprehensive information about what has transpired, and the basis for the jury's ultimate decision. The public's interest in being able to follow the entire course of the trial does not conflict with the Court's interest in ensuring the fairness and efficiency of the proceedings. Modern television equipment has evolved to the point where concerns about intrusive cables, microphones, and camerapersons are inapplicable. In fact, it has been nearly four decades since the United States Supreme Court overturned a conviction based on the "considerable disruption" of early-model television equipment.

In fact, any concerns about the adverse impact of full-time camera coverage are belied by the research conducted in various states, including California, which have reached virtually identical conclusions concerning the impact, or lack of impact, on trial participants from the presence of cameras. The results from the state studies were unanimous: the claims of a negative impact from electronic media coverage of courtroom proceedings, whether civil or criminal, are baseless. For example, the state studies revealed that fears about witness distraction, nervousness, distortion, fear of harm, and reluctance or unwillingness to testify were unfounded.

California's report on the effort of electronic coverage of court proceedings is one of the most comprehensive of the state evaluation that have been completed. The California study included observations and comparisons of proceedings that were covered by the electronic media, and proceedings that were not. Not only did California's survey results mirror those of other states, finding that there was no noticeable impact upon witnesses, judges, counsel, or courtroom decorum when cameras were present during judicial proceedings, the "observational" evaluations completed in California further buttressed these results.

For example, after systematically observing proceedings where cameras were and were not present, consultants who conducted California's study concluded that witnesses were equally effective at communicating in both sets of circumstances.

Not surprisingly, the California Study also revealed that there was no, or only minimal, impact upon courtroom decorum from the presence of cameras.

Thus, the extensive empirical evidence that has been collected on the impact of electronic coverage consistently has concluded that such coverage is not detrimental to the parties, to witnesses, to counsel, or to the courtroom decorum. As noted above, Judge G. permitted television access to most of the pre-trial proceedings (excepting only the preliminary hearing), without disruption or prejudice.

The parties here are represented by experienced counsel, whose professionalism and decorum is above reproach, as these proceedings demonstrated. Under these circumstances, there is no cause for concern about the impact of electronic coverage on the Court's proceedings.

As Supreme Court Justice Kennedy told Congress, in discussing whether electronic access of court proceedings should be permitted: You can make the argument that the most rational, the most dispassionate, the most orderly presentation of the issue is in the courtroom, and it is the outside coverage that is really the problem. In a way, it seems perverse to exclude television from the area in which the most orderly presentation of the evidence takes place. *Hearings Before Subcomm. House Comm. on Appropriations*, 104th Congress, 2d Sess. 30 (1966). Justice Kennedy is right. If there is a public benefit to public trials, and there is, then there is also a public benefit to complete access to public trials.

Because "sprawling urbanism has replaced concentrated ruralism," and because "no courtroom in the land could hold even a minute fraction of the people interested in specific cases," the committee recognized that "a trial is not truly public unless news media are free to bring it to the home of the citizens by newspaper, magazine, radio, television or whatever device they have." *Final Report of the Subcommittee on Free Press, Fair Trial, Assembly Interim Committee on Judiciary*, January 5, 1967. In 1981, California adopted California Rule of Court 980, which permitted television coverage of criminal and civil trials.

Fifteen years later, a task force solicited the views of judges, media representatives, victims' rights groups, public defenders, prosecutors, and other representatives of the bar, and analyzed other states' experiences with television coverage of trials. Based on all the evidence that it gathered, the task force found that judges who actually presided over televised trials favored allowing cameras in the courtroom. Ninety-six percent of those judges reported that the presence of a video camera did not affect the outcome of a trial or hearing in any way. In addition, the overwhelming majority of them reported that the camera did not affect their ability to maintain control of the proceedings, nor did it diminish jurors' willingness to serve. *1996 Report of Task Force on Photographing, Recording, and Broadcasting in the Courtroom.*

Based on this resounding support for cameras in the courtroom, the Judicial Council adopted nearly all of the task force's findings, and revised Rule 980. In its current form, the Rule instructs courts to consider eighteen specific factors in deciding whether to permit television access. Of these eighteen factors, none counsels against allowing full camera coverage of the entire trial. Many of them merely raise concerns that are inapposite here.

For example, there are no minors who are expected to testify; no ongoing law enforcement activity; no unresolved identification questions; no threat to subsequent proceedings in this case; nor any threats to witnesses. Furthermore, as set forth in this Memorandum, electronic coverage will not undermine the dignity of this Court, interfere with its operations, or prejudice these proceedings. (See Rule 980 (e)(3)(6); (e)(3)(8); (e)(3)(9); (e)(3)(10); (e)(3)(11); and (e)(3)(7),(12)-(18), respectively.

The parties' objection to camera coverage, while a factor for this Court to consider, is only one factor and should not dictate this Court's decision. Rule 980(e)(3)(iii). Indeed, during the experimental phase of Rule 980, the rule specifically was amended to remove a requirement that the parties consent to allow cameras in the courtroom.

Moreover, the first two factors outlined in Rule 980, which are arguably the most important, weigh strongly in favor of full cameral coverage. Those factors are, first, "the importance of promoting public trust and confidence in the judicial system," and second, "the importance of promoting public access to the judicial system. Rule 980(e)(3)(1)-(2). These concerns are rooted in well established First Amendment principles, and are served by full and complete public access to the entire proceedings. This access can only be accomplished through televised coverage of the complete trial.

In *Richmond Newspapers v. Virginia*, 448 U.S. 555, at p.573(1980), the Court noted that people now chiefly acquire information about trials through the print and electronic media, and that this validates the media claim of functioning as surrogates for the public. Full media access to judicial proceedings is especially important given the pace of modern life and the size of our metropolitan areas.

As noted above, the California legislature recognized the practical difficulties of attending courtroom proceedings in modern cities, in which "sprawling urbanism has replace concentrated ruralism." *Report*, at p.9. Similarly, the Third Circuit acknowledged the practical obstacles that prevent full public attendance at trials, asking rhetorically, "What exists of the right of access if it extends only to those who can squeeze through the [courtroom] door?" *United States v. Antar*, 38 F.3d 1348, at p.1360(3d Cir. 1994).

It is beyond dispute that the First Amendment mandates that criminal trials be open to the press and the public, absent compelling and clearly articulated reasons for closing such proceedings. *Richmond Newspapers*, at p.580, & note 17, press and public have constitutional right to observe criminal trials; and *Globe Newspaper v. Superior Court*, 457 U.S. 596, at p.604(1982), it is "firmly established" that "the press and general public have a constitutional right of access to criminal trials."

This tradition assumes even greater importance in our democratic system, where the government and all of its actions ultimately are held accountable by the voters. The U.S. Supreme Court recognized that "[p]eople in an open society do not demand infallibility from their institutions, but it is difficult for them to accept what they are prohibited from observing." Full public access promotes popular acceptance of "both the process and its results." *Richmond Newspapers*, at p.572, & p.571, respectively.

In *Globe Newspaper*, at p.571, the Court explained that,
The crucial prophylactic aspects of the administration of justice cannot function in the dark; no community catharsis can occur if justice is 'done in a corner [or] in any covert manner'....
It is not enough to say that results alone will satiate the natural community desire for 'satisfaction'. A result considered untoward may undermine public confidence, and where the trial has been concealed from public view an unexpected outcome can cause a reaction that the system at best has failed and at worst has been

corrupted. To work effectively, it is important that society's criminal process 'satisfy the appearance of justice',...and the appearance of justice can best be provided by allowing people to observe it.

Justice Brennan, concurring in the opinion of *Nebraska Press Ass'n v. Stuart*, 427 U.S. 539, at p.587(1976), stated, Secrecy of judicial action can only breed ignorance and distrust of courts and suspicion concerning the competence and impartiality of judges; free and robust reporting, criticism, and debate can contribute to public understanding of the rule of law and to comprehension of the functioning of the entire criminal justice system, as well as improve the quality of that system by subjecting it to the cleansing effects of exposure and public accountability.

As the Florida Supreme Court acutely observed, "newsworthy trials are newsworthy trials, and...they will be extensively covered by the media both within and without the courtroom", whether or not cameras are permitted. *In re Petition of Post-Newsweek Stations, Inc.*, 370 So.2d 768, at p.776(Fla. 1979). Permitting cameras to observe what actually takes place, Judge G. found, "foster(s) accuracy in reporting...." *June 12, 2003, Minute Order*, App. Tab E at 2. Quoting the United States Supreme Court in *Sheppard v. Maxwell*, 384 U.S. 333, at p.359(1966), he explained that it is the disclosure of inaccurate information which "lead[s] to groundless rumors and confusion."

Recognizing these common sense principles, a New York state court granted Court TV's request to televise the trial of four New York policeman charged in the shooting of unarmed African immigrant Amadou Diallo. That court found that televised coverage was warranted because "the denial of access to the vast majority will accomplish nothing but more divisiveness while the broadcast of the trial will further the interests of justice, enhance public understanding of the judicial system and maintain a high level of public confidence in the judiciary." *People v. Boss*, 182 Misc.2d 700, at pp.705, 706(N.Y. Supreme Ct 2000).

Today, June 2004, New York has changed its mind and Court TV had to file suit to see if they could even request to a court to put cameras in a courtroom.

In 1981, a unanimous Supreme Court held that televising a trial, over the objections of two criminal defendants, was not a violation of their due process rights. *Chandler v. Florida*, 449 U.S. 560, at p.576(1981). Chief Justice Burger's opinion emphasized that [a prior, 1965 decision] had not established a rule banning states from experimenting with an "evolving technology, which, in terms or modes of mass communication, was in its relative infancy in 1964..., and is, even now, in a state of continuing change." *Id.* at p.560. The unanimous *Chandler* opinion also observed that "the data thus far assembled was cause for some optimism about the ability of states to minimize the problems that potentially inhere in electronic coverage of trials." *Id.* at p.576 note 11. Therefore, in roughly fifteen years the technological advance that Justice Harlan had anticipated [in his 1965 concurring opinion] made televised coverage of criminal trials acceptable as a matter of Supreme Court precedent.

Now, more than twenty years after *Chandler*, further technological progress has removed any doubt that cameras can be present in the courtroom without any concomitant disruption. It is not surprising, therefore, that several lower courts recently have had little trouble distinguishing the 1965 case, noting that the Court in that case "explicitly recognized that its holding ultimately relied on the then-state of technology[.]" See; *Katzman v. Victoria's Secret Catalogue*, 923 F.Supp. 580, at p.589(S.D.N.Y. 1996), stating that old objections based on potential disruption "should no longer stand as a bar to televised court proceedings"; *People v. Spring*, 153 Cal.App.3d 1199 [no page no.](1984), that presence of television camera during trial did not violate criminal defendant's Sixth Amendment right to a fair trial; *State of New Hampshire v. Smart*, 622 A.2d 1197 [no page no.](N.H. 1993), that televised coverage of high-profile murder trial did not prejudice defendant; and *Stewart v. Commonwealth of Virginia*, 427 S.E.2d 394 [no page no.](Va. 1993), that the presence of video cameras during criminal trial did not violate defendant's due process rights.

More than a dozen states, including Arizona, California, Florida, Hawaii, Kansas, Louisiana, Maine, Massachusetts, Minnesota, Nevada, New Jersey, New York, Ohio, Virginia, and Washington, have studied the potential impact of electronic media coverage on courtroom proceedings, particularly focusing on the effect cameras have upon courtroom decorum and upon witnesses, attorneys and judges. *January 5, 1967 Report*. The positive results of the state court evaluations were further bolstered by the Federal Judicial Center's 1994 study of a three-year pilot program that permitted electronic media coverage in civil proceedings in six federal district courts and two circuit courts. The federal study concluded that no negative impact resulted from having cameras in the courtroom.

These recent court decisions and empirical studies are consistent with the positive experience with televised proceedings that already has existed in this case. Without television coverage of the proceedings, citizens will not be able to exercise their right to observe this trial first-hand. To promote public confidence in and understanding of the judicial system and the outcome of this case, the News Organizations respectfully request that the Court grant the Rule 980 applications of Court TV, CNN, NBC, KNTV, CBS, and ABC.

Oh, what the hell, DNF, too.

January 30, 2004 **Media Request** to Photograph, Record, or Broadcast

By Court TV, of the February 2, 2004 hearing, with a TV camera and recorder.

January 30, 2004 **Media** Request to Photograph, Record, or Broadcast

By Court TV, of the entire trial, beginning with opening statements and continuing through verdict, with a TV camera and recorder.

January 30, 2004 **Media Request** to Photograph, Record, or Broadcast

By Cable News Network LP, LLP, of the entire trial, beginning with opening statements and continuing through verdict, with a TV camera and recorder.

January 30, 2004 **Media Request** to Photograph, Record, or Broadcast

By National Broadcasting Co., Inc., of the entire trial, beginning with opening statements and continuing through verdict, with a TV camera and recorder.

January 30, 2004 **Media Request** to Photograph, Record, or Broadcast

By KNTV Television, Inc., of the entire trial, beginning with opening statements and continuing through verdict, with a TV camera and recorder.

January 30, 2004 **Media Request** to Photograph, Record, or Broadcast

By CBS Broadcasting Inc., of the entire trial, beginning with opening statements and continuing through verdict, with a TV camera and recorder.

January 30, 2004 **Media Request** to Photograph, Record, or Broadcast

By ABC, Inc., of the entire trial, beginning with opening statements and continuing through verdict, with a TV camera and recorder.

Each of the media requests, 980 applications, state that media will be responsible for the increased costs to the court, which are unknown at this time. Not one of the applications had a box to check for the applicant to state if they would help with the increased costs to the prosecutor or to Scott Peterson.

February 5, 2004 **Scott Peterson's Notice of Readiness**

Scott wants to notify the court that his attorney, Mark Geragos, is not currently engaged in trial before any court and is prepared to proceed to trial immediately.

February 9, 2004 **Scott Peterson's Motion** for Separate Guilt and Penalty Phase Juries; Memorandum of Points and Authorities in Support Thereof

Scott motions the court for separate juries; one to hear the evidence and determine not guilty or guilty, and another, if convicted, to hear the arguments on whether to impose the death penalty. Since with just one jury, no one could be on the jury during trial, who did not also know that they could impose the death penalty. Scott would like an evidentiary hearing on the issue of the impact of death-qualified juries on the determination of guilt or innocence. At such a hearing, live testimony and additional, updated documentary evidence could be adduced.

Although the guilt and penalty proceedings in a capital case are bifurcated [separate], a single jury usually hears both. The voir dire [to speak the truth] of a capital jury will therefore cover issues pertaining not only to the determination of guilt or innocence, but also to the ability of jurors to impose death as a punishment. The process of questioning on the death penalty is termed "death-qualifying" the jury, and enables the prosecution to excuse for cause any juror who states that he or she cannot impose the death penalty under any circumstances. This discharge by the prosecution is allowed even if the juror is otherwise qualified to decide Scott's guilt or innocence.

We now have empirical data which chronicles that frightening failure of our judicial system to accurately determine the guilt or innocence of individuals whose lives hinge on that determination. Stated simply, our process sometimes sentences the innocent to death. This awareness should become the new lens through which the judicial system reexamines the constitutional validity of various aspects of our capital justice system. This is not just because, as studies continue to show, it contributes to flaws in the fact-finding process which in turn renders constitutionally invalid any resulting conviction, but also because it is one aspect of the larger problem that is so easy to fix.

Eliminating the factor most easily controlled, the death qualification voir dire, would help even the playing field. This can be readily accomplished by either empanelling two separate juries at the outset, by selecting a penalty jury later should there be a conviction, or, perhaps most efficiently, by selecting a number of death-qualified alternates who will listen to the evidence during the guilt phase and substitute in for the "excludables" should a penalty trial prove necessary. This would greatly help to reduce the likelihood of a conviction-prone jury. Given the inconvenience to the State would be minimal, and given the important interest at stake, the granting of this request would certainly be a reasonable exercise of the Court's discretion.

Alternatively, this Court can find that the California Constitution does not permit death-qualifying the guilt phase jury because the process infringes Scott's right to an impartial jury. By way of this motion, Scott also makes a constitutional challenge to the death qualification process, separate from, but related to, this Penal Code section 190.4, subdivision(c) request. For purposes of this specific request for separate juries under section 190.4, subsection(c), however, this Court need not reach the constitutional issue.

Here, the death qualification process, and its impact on the guilt phase jury, is one of several factors which combine to form a compelling reason to grant separate juries as an exercise of discretion under the statute. The vast adverse publicity, the abnormally high prejudging of guilt, and the strong statistical showings that a death-qualified jury tilts in favor of the prosecution will together have a severe impact on the nature of the jury ultimately selected to decide Scott's guilt or innocence.

Stated differently, this confluence of circumstances make it more likely than not that Scott's guilt or innocence will be judged by a jury that is inclined to favor the prosecution. Although the statute does evidence a legislative presumption in favor of a single jury in death cases, we contend that in this case, any such presumption is rebutted by the overwhelming likelihood that separate juries will help ensure a fair trial. Similarly, any minor economic detriment to the State pales by comparison.

Penal Code Section 190.4, subsection(c), gives the court in a capital case discretion to empanel, for good cause, a second jury for the penalty phase of trial. (See *People v Carpenter*, 15 Cal.4th 312, at p.351(1997), request for separate jury granted. A motion requesting the court to exercise its discretion under the statute may be brought, as here, before the guilt phase begins. *People v. Rowland*, 4 Cal.4th 238, at p.268(1992).

There is no authority affirmatively defining what constitutes "good cause" under this provision, nor how it may be shown. (See, e.g., *People v. Malone*, 47 Cal.3d 1, at pp.27-28(1988); and *People v. Hart*, 20 Cal.4th 546, at pp.640-641(1999), where notion of good cause under subdivision(c) is "elusive". Unlike the situation in most of the cases discussing section 190.4, subdivision(c), the need for a second panel in Scott's case, is to help ensure a fair and impartial jury during the *guilt* phase of the trial. The express language of the statute is susceptible to this reading, particularly in light of the broad overall discretion given the trial court in the jury voir dire arena. Nevertheless, empanelling separate guilt and penalty juries in Scott's case would necessarily be a reasonable exercise of the court's discretion, for several reasons.

Abundant good cause exists in Scott's case. Specifically, it results from a combination of factors unique to this case; the enormous amount of pretrial publicity adverse to Scott combined with the unusually high number of people who have prejudged him guilty combined with the fact that, as discussed, the process of death qualification creates a jury that leans in favor of the prosecution and conviction. In essence, this aggregate of all three factors makes it extremely unlikely that Scott will be able to obtain a guilt phase jury which is not conviction-prone.

First, as was recognized in the change of venue proceedings, the publicity in this case has been unprecedented, not only in its amount and widespread nature, but also in its negativity as to Scott. (See, e.g., *Motion for Change of Venue*, supporting exhibits and declarations, filed 12/15/03). The number of potential jurors who have pre judged Scott and found him guilty based solely upon the press is again huge.

Data submitted previously to the Court showed that in December 2003, *39%* of the people interviewed in Stanislaus County believed Scott guilty of the crimes charged. (See *Motion for Change of Venue*, Exhibit E, ¶6(a)). It is not unreasonable to expect that the adverse prejudgment rate in San Mateo County will be relatively high as well.

The above two factors unique to this case will then interact with an element common to all death penalty cases, the above-mentioned death qualification of the jurors who will hear penalty phase proceedings should they prove necessary. As noted, "death qualification" is "the removal for cause, prior to the guilt phase of a bifurcated capital trial, of prospective jurors whose opposition to the death penalty is so strong that it would prevent or substantially impair the performance of their duties as jurors at the sentencing phase of the trial." *Lockhart v. McCree*, 476 U.S. 162, at p.165(1986).

Empirical studies uniformly indicate a death-qualified jury is more prone to convict a capital defendant than is a non-death-qualified jury. In response, various organizations, including the American Bar Association, have recommended a moratorium on the death penalty. In January, 2000, Illinois Governor George Ryan declared a moratorium on executions in his state and appointed a commission to study its death penalty system. He took this action because 13 people who had been sentenced to death in Illinois were subsequently found to be innocent. As Governor Ryan observed last year, "Our capital system is haunted by the demon of error...." Sanger, *Comparison of the Illinois Commission Report on Capital punishment with the Capital Punishment System in California*, 44 Santa Clara L. Rev., at p.102 & p.11.

Numerous studies over the past 20 years have established that death qualification unfairly skews the jury's fact-finding function, posing a "substantial threat to the ability of a capital defendant to receive a fair trial on the issue of his guilt or innocence." *Lockhart*, at p.185, Justice Marshall dissenting opinion. These studies support the common sense recognition that the built-in consequence of eliminating jurors unwaveringly opposed to the death penalty is a guilt phase jury which tilts in the direction of the prosecution. This result is constitutionally impermissible, and fundamentally unfair.

However, both the United States and California Supreme Courts have found death qualification of the guilt phase jury not unconstitutional. *Lockhart*; *People v. Steele*, 27 Cal.4th 1230, at p.1243; and *Hovey v. Superior Court*, 28 Cal.3d 1 (1980). *Lockhart* was decided 18 years ago. Although expressing serious reservations about the studies the district Court relied upon for its factual findings, *Lockhart*, at pp.168-173, the Court ultimately assumed for the purposes of analysis that those studies did "establish that 'death qualification' in fact produces juries somewhat more 'conviction-prone' than 'non-death-qualified' juries. *Id.*, at p.173. The Court then held, nevertheless, that the Constitution does not bar such result.

During the past decade, our society has become painfully aware of what Justice Marshall observed more than 30 years ago in another dissenting opinion: **the execution of the innocent is an inherent part of the American capital punishment system.** See *Furman v. Georgia*, 408 U.S. 238, at pp.366-369(1972); also at p.290, concurring opinion of Justice Brennan. Because of recent revelations concerning the inadequacies of our capital justice system, basically, innocent people are being convicted and quite probably executed. The constitutional validity of death-qualifying the guilt phase jury needs to be reexamined.

Both the United States and California Constitutions guarantee Scott the right to be tried by an impartial jury selected from a representative cross section of the community. U.S. Const., 6th & 14th Amends.; Cal. Const., Art. I, § 16; *Taylor v. Louisiana*, 419 U.S. 522, at p.530(1975); *Turner v. Louisiana*, 379 U.S. 466, at p.472(1965); *People v. Wheeler*, 22 Cal.3d 258, at pp.265-266(1978); *Rubio v. Superior Court*, 24 Cal.3d 93, at p.97(1990). In the *Lockhart* case, the U.S. Supreme Court considered whether these constitutional guarantees prohibited the removal for cause of "Witherspoon" excludables for the guilt phase of a capital trial.

In *Witherspoon*, excludables were only those individuals excluded from jury service who "made unmistakably clear...that they would automatically vote against the imposition of capital punishment," or would not be able to assess the capital defendant's guilt or innocence impartially.

The District Court in *Lockhart*, based on numerous studies, concluded, "that persons who favor the death penalty are 'uncommonly' predisposed to find for the prosecution and against the defendant, and that death qualification thus "created juries that 'were more prone to convict' capital defendants than were 'non-death-qualified' juries. The Court also found that, for constitutional purposes, the group of excluded jurors is "distinctive and identifiable, since members of this group are currently excluded on the basis of their distinctive and identifiable attitudes toward the death penalty. *Id.*, at p.1323.

The U.S. Supreme Court, in *Lockhart*, stated that the analysis must focus on the entire venire, not the petit jury or individual peremptory or for-cause challenges. *Id.*, at pp.173-174. And, in any event, the Court said, the particular excluded jurors did not constitute a "distinctive" group in the community for the purposes of the "cross section" analysis, essentially because death qualification is not a means to arbitrarily skew the composition of the jury and because Witherspoon excludables are identified for a trial that is within their control. *Id.*, at pp.174-176.

The *Lockhart* court next held that the fact that death qualification produced a jury more prone to side with the prosecution did not render it impartial for constitutional purposes. Constitutional impartiality, the Court stated, could not be defined "by reference to some hypothetical mix of individual viewpoints....[T]he Constitution presupposes that a jury selected from a fair cross section of the community is impartial, regardless of the mix of individual viewpoints actually represented on the jury, so long as the jurors can conscientiously and properly carry out their sworn duty to apply the law to the facts of the particular case." *Id.*, at pp.183-184.

To establish a prima facie violation of the fair cross-section requirement, a defendant must show that: (1)the group allegedly excluded is a "distinctive" group in the community; (2)the group's representation in jury venires is not fair and reasonable in relation to the number of such persons in the community; and (3)the under-representation is due to the systematic exclusion of such persons in the jury selection process. *Duren v. Missouri*, 439 U.S. 357, at p.364(1979).

In *Lockhart*, Justice Marshall was joined by Justices Brennan and Stevens, in a scathing dissent, chastising the Court for its "glib nonchalance" in upholding "a practice that allows the State a special advantage in those prosecutions where the charges are the most serious and the possible punishments, the most severe." Under the majority's decision, the dissent observed, the "State's mere announcement that it intends to seek the death penalty if the defendant is found guilty of a capital offense will... give the prosecution license to empanel a jury especially likely to return that very verdict." *Id.*, at p.185.

Here, we seem to have another case, which the U.S. Supreme Court brought before itself to decide, which requires four of the Justices deciding to review the case record, and yet they disregard the facts of the particular case they are reading, just as they did with the *Richmond Newspapers* case, and siding with the prosecutorial point of view. Since most of the cases deal with defendants who have already been convicted, and then want another jury chosen to decide the sentence, who cares?

Justice Marshall pointed out that "overwhelming evidence" relied upon by the District Court and assumed to be true by the majority for purposes of its analysis, showed that death-qualified juries are more likely to convict than are juries on which "unalterable opponents of capital punishment are permitted to serve." He lamented the majority's "disregard for the clear import of the evidence" and resulting tragic misconstruing of "the settled constitutional principles that guarantee a defendant the right to a fair and an impartial jury whose composition is not biased toward the prosecution." *Id.*, at p.184 & p.192, respectively.

The question in light of the evidence, Justice Marshall emphasized, is whether a defendant is entitled to "have his guilt or innocence determined by a jury like those that sit in noncapital cases, one whose composition has not been titled in favor of the prosecution by the exclusion of a group of prospective jurors uncommonly aware of an accused's constitutional rights but quite capable of determining his culpability [responsibility] without favor or bias." *Id.*, at p.185.

The dissent noted the "essential unanimity" of the evidence produced in the trial court, and the fact that, as the Court of Appeal had found, "all of the documented studies support the district court's findings." *Id.*, at p.190 & pp.187-190. The dissent also observed that the evidence "confirms, and is itself corroborated by, the more intuitive judgments of scholars and of so many of the participants in capital trials; judges, defense attorneys, and prosecutors." *Id.*, at p.188, citing 569 F.Supp., at p.1322.

The actual claim, at issue, was clarified by Justice Marshall, concerning the constitutional analysis of impartiality itself; not whether any particular juror was impartial, but, whether, "by systematically excluding a class of potential jurors less prone than the population at large to vote for conviction, the State gave itself an unconstitutional advantage" at trial. *Id.*, at p.193. In other words, it is the *process* combined with its likely result which is constitutionally infirm, not the result itself. Justice Marshall found precedent for this conclusion in the Court's own prior decision in *Witherspoon*, where, as noted, the Court concluded "'that a State may not entrust the determination of whether a man should live or die to a tribunal organized to return a verdict of death.'" *Id.*, at pp.194, 197; quoting *Witherspoon*, at p.521.

During the past 10 years, the public has become painfully aware of the tragic reality observed by Justice Marshall, innocent people are being convicted and executed. *Lockhart* was written during a time "when capital punishment systems in this nation functioned as if there were no real likelihood that we would execute an innocent person." Rosen, *Innocence and Death*, 82 N.C.L.Rev. 61, at p.62(2003). Times have changed. California has the largest death row population of any state in the nation. Sanger, *Comparison*, at p.105. Given the data gathered in other states, such as Illinois, and the relative numbers involved, it is reasonable to presume that innocent people have likely been sentenced to death in our state as well. *Id.*, at p.114.

This overall change in awareness, which has permeated all segments of society, now warrants a reevaluation of the constitutional validity of death-qualifying the guilt phase jury in a capital case. See, *Atkins v. Virginia*, 536 U.S. 304, at p.320, footnote 25(2002), noting disturbing number of inmates on death row being exonerated; *McFarland v. Scott*, 512 U.S. U.S. 1256, at p.1264(1994), Justice Blackmun stating he now had grave doubt concerning the reliability of capital convictions; and *Callins v. Collins*, 510 U.S. 1141, at p.1145(1994), Justice Blackmun stating, "from this day forward, I no longer shall tinker with the machinery of death." Most important will be a renewed valuing, and updating if necessary, of the data relied upon by the District Court decision in *Lockhart*, which evidence in turn formed the backbone of Justice

Marshall's dissent. As the Justice stated, whether it *proves* the premise is not the point, when we are talking about the right to an impartial jury in a capital trial.

Therefore, in light of all the above, and assuming the Court does not grant Scott's motion for separate juries under section 190.4, subdivision(c), we ask this Court to find that Scott is constitutionally entitled to a non-death-qualified jury to determine his guilt or innocence. Scott simply asks for the chance to have his guilt or innocence determined by a jury like those that sit in noncapital cases. This in turn will ensure that he is convicted or acquitted by an impartial jury which represents a cross section of the community.

We are of course aware of the constraints of stare decisis [prior decisions] and the fact that this Court cannot per se overrule the Supreme Court. Nevertheless, as discussed, the *Lockhart* decision may be distinguished from this case even on constitutional grounds by virtue of the substantial change in the social and judicial topsoil within which the constitutional analysis must take root. Although, admittedly, numerous California Supreme Court decisions have rejected that argument, a closer reading of those opinions, including a historical tracing of the precedent cited, reveals that in fact the seminal California decision of *Hovey v. Superior Court*, did not actually discuss the constitutional issue on its merits but found instead that the evidence submitted was not sufficient to sustain the claim.

Thus California decisions instead rely upon *Lockhart* for the "impartiality" aspect of the analysis. Therefore, given that the data now available establishes that a death-qualified jury is conviction-prone, and given the recent and growing awareness of substantial defects in the adjudication of guilt or innocence in capital cases, this Court can find the California Constitution does not permit death qualification of the guilt phase jury.

In light of the foregoing, Scott respectfully requests that the Court grant him separate juries for the guilt and penalty phases of this trial, as requested.

February 11, 2004 **Prosecutor's Opposition** to Motion for Separate Juries

The prosecutor opposes Scott's motion for separate juries and submits that this court should deny Scott's request for a second jury.

There are many cases that uphold the denial of a second jury. The issue raised by Scott has been raised and rejected before. Scott implies that he has a right to a separate jury in this case, however that is not the law. He argues that some researchers claim that death qualified jurors are guilt prone, but this argument has also been rejected in California.

Scott asks this court to follow the logic of the Federal District Court in *Grigsby v. Mabry*, 569 F.Supp. 1273, at pp.1322-1323(1985), as creating some future constitutional right to a separate non-death qualified jury. However, as Scott points out, and rightly so, that case was reversed by the U.S. Supreme Court in *Lockhart*, which rejected the same kind of claimed constitutional rights made here. "Death qualification," unlike the wholesale exclusion of blacks, women, or Mexican-American from jury service, is carefully designed to serve the State's concededly legitimate interest in obtaining a single jury that can properly and impartially apply the law to the facts of the case at both the guilt and sentencing phases of a capital trial. *Lockhart v. McCree*, 476 U.S. 162, at pp.175-176(1986).

The court in *Carpenter*, did not discuss the issue of a second jury, but merely recited the fact; "At defense request, the court selected separate guilt and penalty juries." *People v. Carpenter*, 15 Cal.4th 312, at p.351(1997).

The California Supreme Court has said: "As we observed in *Gates*, there is no direct authority on the meaning of 'good cause' in this context. There are, however, cases involving the question of good cause for discharge of a juror under sections 1123 and 1089. As to the latter statutes, the facts must 'show an inability to perform the functions of a juror, and that inability must appear in the record as a demonstrable reality.'" *People v. Bradford*, 15 Cal.4th 1229, at p.1354(1997).

The appropriate standard of review when considering a trial court's denial of a separate jury under section 190.4 is the abuse of discretion standard. *People v. Weaver*, 26 Cal.4th 876, at p.947(2001), quoting *People v. Rowland*, 4 Cal.4th 238, at p.268(1992). "Defendant has no right to be tried by separate juries, or to voir dire one way for the guilt phase and another way for the penalty phase." *Id.*

"The Legislature has clearly articulated its preference for a single jury to decide both guilt and penalty, and, provided the chosen procedure satisfies basic principles of fairness, we are aware of no rule requiring the Legislature to select the process psychologically designed to render jurors most favorably disposed toward a defendant." *People v. Kraft*, 23 Cal.4th 978, at p.1070(2000).

February 13, 2004 **Scott Peterson's Reply** to Opposition to Motion for Separate Guilt and Penalty Phase Juries

Scott's motion, does not argue that separate juries are required to facilitate strategic decisions concerning voir dire. Instead, his motion is based upon the *unfair composition* of the *guilt* phase jury he is likely to get if he is not permitted to have separate jury panels.

As it is, given the unique circumstances surrounding this case, the unprecedented adverse media coverage that has permeated all markets and the unusually high numbers of people who have pre judged Scott guilty, Scott will have a difficult time obtaining a fair and impartial jury. When the additional factor of death qualification is added in, that objective will be virtually unattainable, resulting in a jury inclined to favor the prosecution's evidence, reasoning, and viewpoint.

The question under Penal Code section 190.4, subdivision(c), is whether the *specific* factors operating *in this case* constitute "good cause" for separate guilt and penalty phase juries. Although the statute reflects a legislative preference for a single guilt and penalty jury, it also implicitly recognizes that this preference may be overcome. Scott cited *People v. Carpenter*, 15 Cal.4th 312 (1997), as an example that trial courts *do in fact* grant separate juries under the statute notwithstanding a statutory preference for a single jury.

The cases, including those cited by the prosecution, demonstrate that "good cause" under this statute is a fluid concept, completely case-specific. Thus, contrary to what the prosecution suggests, the court in *People v. Bradford*, 15 Cal.4th 1229, at p.1354 (1997, did *not hold* that in all cases, good cause would be defined as "an inability to perform the functions of a juror...." (See prosecutor's Opposition, p.2) Moreover, in *Bradford* the defendant's motion, which targeted the penalty and not the guilt phase jury, focused on difficulties in jury deliberations. We ain't there yet. Hence, the court's discussion of a definition of good cause which had been used in an analogous [different] context was arguably appropriate for that case. *Id.*, at pp.1353-1354. It is not, however, helpful or applicable to this case.

Even if that were the definition of good cause, given the factors set forth in the moving papers, that definition would be met. In *Bradford*, the court also held that mere speculation by counsel that a jury, having found a defendant guilty, could by definition no longer be impartial, did not constitute good cause under section 190.4, subdivision(c). Again, that is not this case.

This Court should therefore exercise its discretion to find good cause under section 190.4, subdivision(c) to eliminate the one factor most easy to control, the death qualification of the jury for the guilt phase. This in turn can be readily accomplished by empanelling separate juries or, as alternatively suggested in the moving papers, selecting sufficient death-qualified alternate jurors.

It is true a court's decision under section 190.4, subdivision(c), is reviewable only for abuse of discretion. But, that principle cuts both ways. The same deferential standard applied in the cases cited by the prosecution where the request was denied would be applied to this Court's decision to *grant* the request. Certainly, under the facts peculiar to this case, it would not be beyond the bounds of reason for the Court to grant this motion.

The decision in *Lockhart v. McCree*, 476 U.S. 162 (1986), has no precedential bearing on the analysis whether in this case, good cause supports the request for separate juries under section 190.4, subdivision(c). The potential constitutional considerations alternatively discussed in Scott's Motion papers, that this, the conviction-proneness of a death-qualified jury and the recent revelations that innocent people are being sentenced to death under our capital justice system, should *inform* the Court's discretion, but, as *factual*, rather than legal factors.

It was within that context that Scott argued that the findings of fact made by the district court in *Grigsby v. Mabry*, 569 F.Supp. 1273, at pp.1322-1323(1985), which were *assumed to be true for the purposes of analysis* in *Lockhart*, should be taken into consideration when evaluating good cause under section 190.4, subdivision(c).

Cases cited by the prosecution, *People v. Rowland*, 4 Cal.4th 238, at pp.267-268(1992), and *People v. Mendoza*, 24 Cal.4th 130, at pp.168-169(2000), both defendants sought separate guilt and penalty juries so that the jury voir dire concerning uncharged crimes evidence, relevant to penalty phase but not to guilt phase proceedings, would not create a bias against the defendant at the guilt phase. In both cases, the Supreme Court held that in itself, counsel's desire to conduct different voir dire for the guilt and penalty phases of a capital trial did not constitute good cause under the statute. Here, Scott seeks to prevent a guilt-prone jury during the guilt phase of the trial.

The prosecution, in citing *People v. Kraft*, 23 Cal.4th 978, at p.1070(2000), argues that California has rejected the contention that death-qualified jurors are guilt prone.(See prosecution's Opposition, p.3). Not so. That's not what the *Kraft* court said, or was even discussing, in the very excerpt quoted by the prosecution.

In *Kraft*, the defendant argued that the jury who had just found him guilty would not be able to give him a fair trial on the question of penalty. That defendant submitted evidence by a psychologist that the guilt phase jury, having unanimously found the defendant guilty on 16 murder counts and 11 special circumstance allegations, would not be likely to give the defendant a fair trial on penalty as would a newly chosen jury. *Id.*, at p.1069. The Supreme Court affirmed that the expert testimony was "general in nature, applicable to a greater or lesser degree in any capital case in which evidence of other crimes is admitted in the penalty phase...." *Ibid.*

It was within that context, that the *Kraft* court stated that "provided the chosen procedure satisfies basic principles of fairness, we are aware of no rule requiring the Legislature to select the process psychologically designed to render jurors most favorably disposed toward a defendant." *Id.*, at p.1070. As quoted, the *Kraft* court established as a predicate requirement, that the "chosen procedure satisfies basic principles of fairness...." *Ibid.* Scott maintains that, under the circumstances of his case and for the reasons set forth in his Motion papers, "basic principles of fairness" will be abandoned if the guilt phase jury is death-qualified.

The *Kraft* court was not speaking to the question of whether a death-qualified jury is more conviction-prone than a jury that is not death-qualified. Furthermore, and this is a crucial distinction, what Scott asks for here is *not* a jury "most favorably disposed toward a defendant", but a jury that is ***not** most favorably disposed towards the prosecution.* It is well within this Court's discretion to endeavor to provide Scott that.

Finally, we note that other than citing the statutory language evidencing a preference for a single jury, the prosecution has not provided a single affirmative reason why this motion should be denied under the facts of this case. Scott therefore can only presume that the very fact an opposition was even filed implicitly reflects the prosecution's recognition that, as was asserted in the Motion papers, the "confluence of circumstances" in this case "makes it more likely than not that Scott's guilt or innocence will be judged by a jury that is inclined to favor the prosecution."

To prevent that result, this Court should grant Scott's request. Scott respectfully requests that the Court grant him separate juries for the guilt and penalty phases of his trial.

It's important to remember here, that the people who say they saw Laci are not people who will fit into the prosecution's theory, so any deviation from due process and procedure would naturally disqualify these people, whether done so, by the prosecutor or by the defense. It appears from the documents that the prosecutor did not want the testimony of Ms. Dempewolf to make it to the stand at trial, already knowing that if what she is saying is true, then she would be a witness in Scott's defense. While the term 'investigation' will be used, there's probably a variety of words that would appropriately fit in front of it.

STANISLAUS COUNTY COURT FILED DOCUMENTS

October 7, 2003 **Scott Peterson's Motion** to Exclude Testimony of Hypnotized Witness Kristen Dempewolf

This motion was filed in the Stanislaus Superior Court.

??? ?, 2003 **Prosecutor's Opposition** to Motion to Exclude Testimony of Hypnotized Witness Kristen Dempewolf

The prosecutor's opposition is not available.

??? ?, 2003 **Prosecutor's Points and Authorities** in Support of Evidence

??? ?, 2003 **Prosecutor's Request** for an Evidence Code, Section 402 Hearing

The request is in connection with the hypnotized testimony.

??? ?, 2003 **Prosecutor's Points and Authorities** in Support of Evidence

SAN MATEO COUNTY FILED DOCUMENTS

February 9, 2004 **Scott Peterson's Reply** to Opposition to Motion to Exclude Testimony of Hypnotized Witness Kristen Dempewolf

The use of hypnosis by law enforcement has been roundly discouraged by the California Supreme Court, the legislature, the Society for Clinical and Experimental Hypnosis, and the International Society of Hypnosis. Indeed, the legislature has found that testimony by individuals who have undergone hypnosis is so suspect that the proponent of the testimony must prove by clear and convincing evidence that the hypnosis "did not so affect the witness as to render the witness' prehypnosis recollection unreliable or to substantially impair the ability to cross-examine the witness concerning the witness' prehypnosis recollection." (See Evidence Code section 795, subdivision(a)(4). The proponent of the testimony must also demonstrate strict compliance with all of the requirements set forth in Section 795.

Given that this is a death penalty case in which there is a "compelling need for ensuring reliability in determining whether death is the appropriate punishment," this Court must exclude Ms. Dempewolf's testimony if there is even a hint of irregularity in the hypnotic procedure. (See *Dustin v. Superior Court*, 99 Cal.App.4th 1311, at pp.1313-1314(5th Dist. 2002), review denied September 25, 2002).

The parties agree that Evidence Code section 795 governs the admissibility of Ms. Dempewolf's testimony. (See prosecutor's Opposition, at 2:10-13). However, the parties strongly disagree on what constitutes compliance with the very strict requirements of Section 795.

For example: Subdivision(a)(2) requires that "the substance of the prehypnotic memory was preserved in written, audiotape, or videotape form prior to the hypnosis." Given that the reliability of hypnotically enhanced testimony is exceptionally suspect, it may be inferred that the record of the prehypnotic memory must itself be reliable. Such is not the case here.

The only so called "record" of Ms. Dempewolf's prehypnotic memory consists of two uncorroborated police reports. Furthermore, the two police reports were made by two different detectives based on two telephone conversations that could have been with any female identifying herself as Kristen Dempewolf. At a minimum, prior to the hypnotic interview, the prosecutor should have either had Ms. Dempewolf read the reports and attest to the accuracy of the police reports, or they should have had her sign a written statement in which she related her full prehypnosis recollection of the events.

Scott would like for the court to take note that the prosecutor contends the prehypnotic "interview" conducted by Dr. Pennington constituted a record of Ms. Dempewolf's prehypnotic memory. In fact, Dr. Pennington's "interview" failed to document Ms. Dempewolf's prehypnotic memory in any meaningful manner.

On the other hand, the "interview" did disclose that prior to undergoing hypnosis, Ms. Dempewolf could not recall the date of the incidents that were purportedly the object of law enforcement's interest. This fact is notable because a review of the hypnotic interview demonstrates that Dr. Pennington questioned Ms. Dempewolf in a manner that required her to answer questions as though she recalled the relevant date, when in fact she did not.

Given the courts', legislature's, and hypnosis community's universal criticism of law enforcement's use of hypnosis, such a flimsy record fails to constitute compliance with subdivision(a)(2); particularly in a death penalty case.

For another example: Subdivision(a)(3) requires that "[a] written record was made prior to hypnosis documenting the subject's description of the event, and information which was provided to the hypnotist concerning the subject matter of the hypnosis." The prosecutor fails to comply with both prongs of the subdivision.

First, as stated above, the two uncorroborated police reports fail to properly document Ms. Dempewolf's prehypnotic memory. Second, the prosecutor claims "Dr. Dale Pennington, the one who hypnotized [Ms. Dempewolf], was briefed on [the two] police reports," and, "Detective Stough's report dated January 19, 2003, indicated that Dr. Pennington was briefed on the reports by Detective Stough (Bates Nos. 2096-2100)." (See prosecutor's Opposition at 3:26-27 and 4:7-9).

In actuality, the Stough report states only that, "I gave Dr. PENNINGTON a brief on the burglary and on the reports of the suspicious van on or about the 24th of December 2002 in front of 516 Covena." (Bates No.2096). The Stough report conspicuously fails to identify which reports, who made the reports, the identity of the witnesses involved in the reports, and any meaningful description of the content of the reports. Simply put, the "written record" provides *no* guidance as to the nature of information provided to Dr. Pennington prior to the hypnotic interview of Ms. Dempewolf. As such, the prosecutor has failed to comply with subdivision(a)(3)(A).

Interestingly, immediately following the language quoted above, the Stough report indicates that "after the briefing Det. BANKS took the Dr. to the scene so he could view that area." (Bates No. 2096). The defense cannot imagine any innocent reason Dr. Pennington would need to personally view the area if the prosecutor's intention was to illicit Ms. Dempewolf true recollection. Indeed, having viewed the scene himself, it is quite plausible that Dr. Pennington could have unwittingly, intentionally, provided cues to Ms. Dempewolf that would have permanently altered her recollection during the prehypnosis interview or the hypnotic interview.

Another example: Subdivision(a)(3)(B) requires that the prehypnotic interview be videotape recorded. As set forth in Scott's Motion papers, it appears that the videotape begins at some point *following* the commencement of the prehypnotic interview, thus failing to comply with this subdivision's requirements.

Another example: Subdivision(a)(3)(D) requires that, "[t]he hypnosis was performed by a license medical doctor, psychologist, licensed clinical social worker, or a licensed marriage and family therapist experienced in the use of hypnosis and independent of and not in the presence of law enforcement, the prosecution, or the defense."

Although Dr. Pennington may arguably have been qualified to conduct the hypnosis, he certainly was not "independent" of law enforcement for the following reasons: (1)the only purported record of Ms. Dempewolf's prehypnotic recollection was in the form of an oral communication by a detective during which the detective "briefed" Dr. Pennington on unidentified "reports" that were drafted by other detectives; thus, Dr. Pennington's sole source of information was law enforcement's own subjective and uncorroborated "reports"; (2)for reasons unknown, Dr. Pennington was taken by a detective to the area in question prior to the hypnotic interview of Ms. Dempewolf: (3)Dr. Pennington's curriculum vitae (See prosecutor's Opposition) reveals that in addition to teaching POST-approved courses, he has served as, *inter alia*, Deputy Sheriff for 3 years, as well as a Reserve Deputy Sheriff for 13 years.

The prosecutor's attempt to style Dr. Pennington as being independent by claiming he is the director/agent of an apparently unregistered business entity should be frowned upon as should Dr. Pennington's submission to the Court of an inaccurate credential. Dr. Pennington's C.V. is noteworthy as well in that (1)it fails to disclose Dr. Pennington's position as Director of Continuing Education for the Behavior Analysis Training Institute; and (2)it lists a 26-year employment tenure as director of "Dale Pennington Associates", an entity that could not be identified via WESTLAW search, which is used by most every legal research person in the United States, of California fictitious business names or via a search of the California Secretary of State's business search portal.

The troubling aspect of the apparent nonexistence of a record of "Dale Pennington Associates" being registered to do business in California is that the prosecutor proclaims Dr. Pennington's independence from law enforcement by stating that "[i]n the instant case, Dr. Pennington conducted the hypnosis sessions as an agent of Dale Pennington Associates."

As to subdivision(a)(4), the prosecutor requests an evidence code section 402 hearing in connection with Ms. Dempewolf. Since the prosecutor has failed to comply with several of the mandatory requirements set forth in Section 795, the request must be denied.

Scott respectfully requests that the Court grant the relief requested in his October 7, 2003 motion.

An Exhibit, attached to Scott's brief, is of 5 members of the staff of the Behavior Analysis Training Institute, Inc., with 91 years of law enforcement experience between 3 of them. Pennington's law enforcement isn't listed, one fellow is a prosecutor, and another teaches interviews and interrogations.

This incident, with the hypnotizing of a defense witness is even more complicated than the one involving the limo driver in the O.J. Simpson case. The police in that case took the limo driver back to O.J.'s house the following day, had the driver stand at the gate and remember what he saw. At trial, when the limo driver was asked to describe what he saw while waiting on O.J., he described what he had seen the following day while with the police, and not what he had seen the night before.

This scenario happens with rape victims having photographs shown to them, robbery victims being shown a 'suspect', and children being told what they did as in committing a crime, and at times, what was done to them in order to convict someone else of a crime. Suggestion, by an authority figure, is very powerful.

What makes this hypnosis incident even more outrageous is that we won't get to find out what the witness saw or knew or thought she saw or knew, before she was hypnotized, nor before police told her things she didn't know or see, nor what was left out of the police report which was taken over the phone from a woman claiming to be Ms. Dempewolf, nor what may have been included in the police report from a phone conversation with Ms. Dempewolf that was never said.

February 9, 2004 **Scott Peterson's** Notice of Motion and Motion in Limine to Exclude Statements Made by Scott Lee Peterson to the Media

Scott would like for the court to issue an order excluding all statements made to media by Scott, or, alternatively, an order requiring that a hearing be held to determine the admissibility of any such evidence the prosecution seeks to introduce. This motion is based on the grounds that the evidence is irrelevant and that the probative value of the evidence is substantially outweighed by the probability that its admission will necessitate undue consumption of time, confuse the issues, mislead the jury, and create a substantial danger of undue prejudice to Scott.

This motion is supported by the attached memorandum of points and authorities, the pleadings and records on file herein, and upon such further argument as may be presented to the Court at the hearing on this matter.

Laci went missing on December 24, 2002. Thereafter, Scott repeatedly went before local and national media in an attempt to facilitate the safe return of his pregnant wife. Regrettably, as time wore on, Scott's media appearances grew to be characterized by questions concerning his relationship with Amber Frey rather than on the search for Laci.

In the prosecutor's own words: "During the investigation the defendant went before the national media with his family to make please for the safe return of his wife and unborn child. Early in the interviews the defendant stirred the media's interest by dodging questions and speaking fondly of his mistress. The defense makes much of the fact that the media has referred to the defendant as an adulterer, but it was the defendant who admitted it on national television." (See January 2, 2004 prosecutor's Opposition to Motion for Change of Venue, at 9:7-15).

Scott does take exception to the prosecutor's characterization of his comments regarding Amber Frey as displaying fondness. In any event, it should be self-evident that Scott was "fond" of some attribute of Amber Frey or else he would not have been involved in an adulterous relationship with her. Hence, there is no dispute that Scott must have been "fond" of Amber Frey.

The defense agrees with the prosecutor's characterization of Scott's media statements in that it sets forth the two sole subjects of Scott's statements: (1)the continuing search for Laci, and (2)Scott's admission of an adulterous relationship with Amber Frey. Since neither of these topics is relevant to the facts alleged in the complaint, the Court must find that all of Scott's statements to the media are inadmissible. Additionally, the prejudicial effect of admitting Scott's media statements would far outweigh any probative value the statements may have.

The statements made to the media by Scott have absolutely no probative value as to the key issue raised in the complaint; namely, did Scott commit capital murder? Comments made by a concerned husband regarding the search for his missing, pregnant wife therefore should be excluded. Additionally, the second category of statements made by Scott, to wit, those concerning his mistress, Amber Frey, are not probative, but are exceptionally prejudicial.

"No evidence is admissible except relevant evidence." (Evidence Code section 350). "'Relevant evidence' means evidence, including evidence relevant to the credibility of a witness or hearsay declarant, having any tendency in reason to prove or disprove any disputed fact that is of consequence to the determination of the action." (Evidence Code section 210). "The trial court has broad discretion in determining the relevance of evidence but lacks discretion to admit irrelevant evidence." *People v. Scheid*, 16 Cal.4th 1, at pp.13-14(1998).

It is also well-settled under California law that "evidence presented on a [n]ondisputed issue is irrelevant and, hence [i]nadmissible, as only relevant evidence is admissible in a trial." *People v. Coleman*, 89 Cal.App.ed 312, at p.321(2nd Dist. 1979), citing Evidence Code sections 210 & 350, and *Krouse v. Graham*, 19 Cal.3d 59 (1977).

The Court must determine the relevance and admissibility of evidence before it can be admitted. (See Evidence Code sections 400 & 402). Given that, as the prosecutor himself has properly noted, Scott's statements to the media were limited to statements concerning the search for Laci, irrelevant to the charges of capital murder, and Scott's admission of an adulterous relationship with Amber Frey, a nondisputed issue, it is clear that all such statements are irrelevant and therefore inadmissible.

Even if the Court should determine that one or more of Scott's statements to the media is admissible, the Court should exclude the statement(s). Evidence section 352 provides: "The court in its discretion may exclude evidence if its probative value is substantially outweighed by the probability that its admission will (a)necessitate undue consumption of time or (b)create substantial danger of undue prejudice, of confusing the issues, or of misleading the jury."

Naturally, the vast majority of potential jurors are likely to be predisposed against a man who admittedly started an affair when his wife was nearly eight months pregnant. Additionally, this evidence would be cumulative in that the prosecutor most certainly will call Amber Frey as a witness and she will undoubtedly testify that she and Scott were having an adulterous relationship. As such, the Court has the discretion to exclude the media statements on the ground that such evidence would be cumulative and necessitate undue consumption of time.

Scott respectfully requests that the Court issue an order excluding all statements made to the media by Scott, or, alternatively, an order requiring that a hearing be held to determine the admissibility of any such evidence the prosecution seeks to introduce.

February 23, 2004 **Prosecutor's Opposition** to the Defendant's Motion Re: Statements to the Media

The prosecutor opposes Scott's motion to suppress statements to the media, since Scott's statements to the various media personnel are highly relevant and extremely probative of the defendant's guilt. Scott's statements concerning Amber Frey support motive for murder. His statements regarding carrying out a large item covered in a blue tarp support how the defendant covered up the murder. His false statements concerning his level of cooperation with the police, and his actions on December 24th show how he tried to turn suspicion away from himself.

Specifically, Scott made statements to Diane Sawyer, Gloria Gomez, Ted Rowlands, and Jodi Hernandez. The people intend to introduce only the defendant's actual statements made to those media personnel. The people do not intend to introduce portions of the aired broadcast that simply involve the newsperson commenting on the interviews.

Here, some parts of the People's case is circumstantial. Therefore, each piece of evidence is important in order for the people to present their case. In his various statements to media personnel, Scott gives statements that conflict with those he told the police, initially lies about his relationship with Amber Frey, lies about his relationship with his wife, lies about information he told Amber Frey, and makes numerous admissions that evidence his guilt.

Scott was interviewed by Diane Sawyer of ABC News on January 24, 2003, where he makes admissions regarding activities on December 24, 2003, [prosecutor meant 2002], and regarding his relationship with Amber Frey and Laci. He lies about what he told the police, lies about when he told Amber that he was married, and lies about his relationship with his wife. His demeanor is also very telling in the interview. He presents himself, quite strongly, as someone who is lying about his involvement in Laci's disappearance.

Scott told Ms. Sawyer that since Laci had been missing he had taken the dog to the park where Laci "walked all those mornings." This was clearly intended to present the impression that Laci was taking a walk in the park on the morning that she disappeared. The prosecutor will present evidence that Laci had stopped walking the dog around the first week in November.

Scott admits that suspicion had turned to him and that it was natural for it to turn to him. He admits having a relationship with Amber, but states that he "doesn't know" why he was having the relationship. He states that Amber was the only woman with whom he had affairs. This was not true. He had had at least one other affair with a woman early in his and Laci's marriage.

Scott states that he had been cooperating fully with the police and that he told the police on December 24, 2002, of his relationship with Amber. This was a lie. In fact, Scott never told the police of his relationship with Amber and denied that relationship to them on December 30, 2002. He repeated this lie to all local media personnel when he was interviewed by them on January 29, 2003.

Scott states that he told Laci about the affair with Amber in "early December [2002]." Numerous witnesses will testify that Laci made no mention of the affair to them, and they did not perceive any evidence of the affair in her and Scott's relationship. Further, Scott told Amber that he told Laci about the affair "after their first date together" in November, 2002.

Scott states that the affair did not cause a rupture in his marriage, and that there wasn't any anger by Laci regarding the affair. He added that Laci was "at peace" with the affair. As incredible as this statement is, Scott obviously made it to throw suspicion off himself. By trying to portray Laci as peaceful about the affair, a statement that no one could possibly believe, he was hoping that investigators would no longer focus attention on him.

Scott calls his marriage "glorious." Again, this was done to throw suspicion off himself. This statement is obviously a lie. If the marriage truly was glorious why would Scott seek an adulterous relationship with Amber?

During the interview Scott refers to Laci and Conner in the past tense, then corrects himself. "She was, is amazing." And in reference to Conner "That was, its so hard." He states that he hasn't been able to go into the room where Conner's nursery was set up. "The door is closed until there is someone to go in there." This statement was obviously designed to convey the impression that he so loved his unborn child that he couldn't even enter the baby's room. This was not true. When the police served a search warrant at his home on February 18, 2003, Scott had turned the nursery into a storage room.

Scott admits that he initially stated that he was going to play golf on December 24, 2002, but decided to go fishing instead. He states that he left home around 9:30 in the morning while Laci was watching Martha Stewart Living. Cell phone records show that Scott left home at 10:08 in the morning on December 24, 2002.

Scott states that he hasn't taken any medication regarding Laci's disappearance because he "needs to experience it" (the disappearance). He admits that the curtains were down in the house on December 24, 2002. He states that this was done to "keep the house warm." He also admits that the temperature that day was approximately 40 degrees. Thus, Scott himself admits that it is extremely unlikely that Laci went walking in the park wearing only a white long sleeve tee shirt as other witnesses have stated.

Scott admits that he loaded large market umbrellas into his truck "that morning." He stated that he was going to put the umbrellas into his shop for the winter, however, when the police got to the house on the evening of the 24th, they were still in the back of his truck. He further admits that his blood would be found in his truck.

Scott states that he told Amber that he was married and Laci was missing "a couple of days after Laci's disappearance." He says that after he told Amber, she went to the police. All of these statements were lies. He spoke to Amber numerous times in the week after Laci was missing and pretended that he was in Europe and that when he returned he and Amber would still be together.

Amber went on her own initiative to the police on December 30, 2002. During that time Scott continued to lie to her about his connection to Laci. He did not admit his connection to Laci until January 6, 2003, when Amber called Scott and confronted him with her knowledge that he was lying to her.

Scott was interviewed by Gloria Gomez, of local KOVR news on January 29, 2003. Scott repeated some of the lies told to Diane Sawyer. He also made additional admissions, and lies, regarding his relationship with Amber.

Scott again stated that he told Amber "a few days after Laci's disappearance" that he was married and Laci had disappeared. This was not true. He also denied continuing to romance Amber after Laci went missing. That was also a lie. As the audio taped phone conversations amply prove, while Scott did not physically see Amber after Laci's disappearance, he did continue to pursue a relationship with her by phone. Even after Amber went to the police Scott continued to contact her, at one point comparing his relationship with her to the movie Love Affair, calling it "a long term caring relationship."

Scott is evasive, and refuses to answer questions that he continued to contact Amber after Laci went missing.

Scott admits cutting his hand on December 24th, "reaching into the toolbox of my truck." He also admits washing his clothes immediately upon coming home from fishing on December 24th.

Scott was interviewed by Jodi Hernandez, of local NBC 11 news on January 29, 2003. He made additional admissions, and gave evasive responses to questions regarding his involvement in Laci's murder. He again states that he left home at 9:30 on December 24th. As shown above that information was not true. He said that he understood peoples' suspicion of him.

Scott was extremely guarded in his responses and wouldn't answer specific questions about the investigation. He stated that he kept a public silence about the case as a "strategy" to keep the media's interest. He stated that the police asked him not to comment about when he informed them about his affair with Amber. That was a lie. The police never told him to keep that information secret. He acknowledges that the police haven't ruled him out as a suspect.

Scott was interviewed by Ted Rowlands of KTVU news on January 29, 2003. He made additional admissions and, again, gave evasive responses to questions about the investigation. Scott repeats his story that he told Laci about the affair in early December. He repeated his story that he put market umbrellas into his truck wrapped in a blue tarp to take to his warehouse for the winter.

Scott repeated his story that he told Laci about the affair and that it didn't put the marriage in jeopardy. He repeated his story that he told Amber about Laci's disappearance "a few days after." He states that after he called Amber she met with the police. Both statements were lies.

Scott stated that the cement found in his warehouse was because of the work he did at his house. The prosecution will present evidence from a petrographer that the cement rings found in his warehouse did not match samples taken from this house. Scott was very "media savvy" in the interview in that whenever he wanted to proclaim his innocence he would speak directly to the camera. This was in contrast to when he was speaking about other subjects when he would either look away, or look directly at the reporter.

This happened enough so that the reporter stated that it was "kind of bizarre" the way he would direct his conversation to the people watching. Scott obviously did this to try and focus public attention away from himself.

A trial court's determination to admit evidence pursuant to Evidence Code section 352 is reviewed for an abuse of discretion. *People v. Brown*, 31 Cal.4th 518, at p.547(2003); and *People v. Gurule*, 28 Cal.4th 557, at pp.654-655 (2002). Here, Scott moves to exclude the statements he made in late January 2003 to various media representatives regarding his actions on December 24, 2002, and his relationship with Laci and Amber.

At the outset it should be noted that Scott has not made a sufficient showing pursuant to Evid. Code Sec. 352 as to why any of his statements should be suppressed. At best, Scott's motion simply provides excuses as to why he made the statements. Such reasoning goes only to the weight of the evidence, not to its admissibility. It is solely a jury question as to what the statements mean, and why they were made.

Further, in order to suppress evidence pursuant to Evid. Code Sec. 352, the probative value of the evidence must be substantially outweighed by its undue prejudice. All relevant evidence admitted by the prosecution is, by definition, prejudicial to the defendant's case. Such is the nature of criminal trials.

Probative evidence is not what Evid. Code Sec. 352 is designed to prevent; "...prejudice for the purposes of 352 means evidence that tends to evoke an emotional bias against the defendant with very little effect on the issues, not evidence that is probative of the defendant's guilt;" *People v. Crews*, 31 Cal.4th 822, at p.842(2003); *People v. Karis*, 46 Cal.3d 612, at p.638(1988).

Challenges to a defendant's statements made under Evid. Code Sec. 352 are rarely, if ever, granted. [See, *People v. Crews*, supra; *People v. Brown*, 31 Cal.4th 518, at p.547 (2003); *People v. Sapp*, 31 Cal.4th 240, at p.276(2003); *People v. Maury*, 30 Cal.4th 342, at pp.409-410(2003); *People v. Kipp*, 26 Cal.4th 1100, at p.1125(2001); *People v. Hayes*, 21 Cal.4th 1211, at pp.1262-1263(1999); *People v. Hines*, 15 Cal.4th 997, at pp.1044-1045(1997); *People v. Gionis*, 9 Cal.4th 1196, at pp.1213-

1214(1995); *People v. Halsey*, 12 Cal.App.4th 885, at pp.891-892(1993).

Further, the evidence is not cumulative in that Scott told different pieces of information to each reporter. The information is not cumulative to the testimony of Amber because Scott told the reporters lies regarding his relationship with Amber, as well as lies about what, and when, he told Amber. As such, Scott's motion pursuant to Evid. Code Sec. 352 should be denied.

February 22, 2004 **Scott Peterson's Reply** to Opposition to Motion Re: Statements to the Media

The prosecutor has provided to the defense in discovery copies of broadcast interviews with Scott with various news outlets and organizations. None of the proffered tapes are uncut, unedited interviews. As such, in addition to the evidentiary problems with admission of such evidence in the prosecution's case-in-chief there is an even more fundamental problem with their admission. Until and unless the unedited uncut version is produced none of these tapes is admissible since there is no foundation for the authenticity of the tapes. Clearly the tapes have been edited, cut and many of the answers by Scott have been spliced and diced in between that of the interviewers.

In *People v. Milner*, 45 Cal.3d 227, at p.240(1988), the court stated that it was not error to exclude an edited version of a videotape of the defendant because of the risk that it might mislead the jury. The Supreme Court affirmed the trial court's exclusion of edited videotapes on the grounds that "the edited version takes things out of context by necessary implication and violates the best evidence rule." *Id.*, at footnote 10.

Any purported statements made by Scott to the media regarding an extramarital affair are not admissible in the prosecution's case in chief. Scott has already stated on the record his position that The Prosecution's filing; Opposition to Motion Re: Statement to the media ("Opposition"), is nothing more than a potpourri of prurient, irrelevant and false allegations designed to titillate.

More importantly, there is no legal basis for the admission of these matters in the prosecution's case in chief. In fact, the statements made by Scott to the media are neither relevant nor material to the prosecutor's case in chief since they are irrelevant to Scott's guilt or innocence. The statements do not amount to admissions or confessions since they relate to collateral matters rather than the crime for which Scott now stands falsely accused.

Furthermore, the statements can not prove some attenuated theory of consciousness of guilt since most if not all relate to Scott's alleged affair with Amber. It is well settled that extrajudicial statements made by a defendant can only come in the prosecution's case in chief if the statement concerns the crime charged.

Even assuming arguendo that the statements made by Scott were not true, they would only go to impeach Scott's credibility as a witness if and when he testifies. Such impeachment, as a matter of law, can only be used in rebuttal rather than in the prosecution's case in chief. As the California Supreme Court has stated in a similar instance of the attempted use of videotaped statements of a defendant: "They were irrelevant to the question of defendant's guilt or innocence. There is a risk, however, that the jury may consider the collateral evidence for the truth of its content, and where that danger exists, the evidence may be excluded." See, e.g., *People v. Coleman*, 38 Cal.3d 69, at p.93(1985), where it was unrealistic to expect jury to disregard truth of assertions contained in letters; and *People v. Milner*, at p.240.

Here, the prosecutor also seeks to introduce statements made by Scott regarding his relationship with Amber. These statements are not material to the issue of his guilt or innocence, and are not probative of the crimes charged. The evidence further creates a substantial danger of undue prejudice to Scott. Obviously the prosecution hopes that a vase majority of potential jurors are likely to be predisposed to guilt against a man who admittedly had an affair when his wife was pregnant and ignore the fact that there is no evidence of Scott's involvement in this crime.

This purported evidence of extramarital affairs is not probative but certainly prejudicial although not on the issue of guilt of any charge crime. Compounding matters the evidence would be cumulative in that the prosecutor and their surrogates have already indicated that they will call Amber as a witness and she will undoubtedly testify that she and Scott had sex.

Amber's testimony that she had sex with Scott will undoubtedly drive up television ratings, however, that bombshell revelation is totally irrelevant to guilt or innocence. As such, the Court should exclude the media statements on the ground that such evidence would be cumulative, necessitate undue consumption of time and create an undue prejudice to Scott.

Lastly, there is no foundation for the admission of any of the so called media statements since all of the items produced to the defense have been edited and not one of the items proffered is an uncut, unedited version of an interview with Scott. As such, there is not foundation for the admission of any of the proffered statements. Until such time as the prosecution has obtained and produced the uncut, unedited versions there is no foundation as to the reliability of the purported interviews.

For the foregoing reasons, Scott respectfully requests that the Court issue an order excluding all statements made to the media by Scott.

February 9, 2004 **Media Request** to Photograph, Record, or Broadcast

The Modesto Bee would like to cover the opening statements, various witnesses, sentencing phase if applicable, and miscellaneous other court proceedings, from February 10th, until TBA [to be announced], with a sketch artist.

February 9, 2004 **Order** of Superior Court of San Mateo Re: Media Request to Permit Coverage

The request by The Modesto Bee is granted, subject to conditions in rule 980, California Rules of Court, and seated as directed by the Bailiff.

February 9, 2004 **Order** of Superior Court of San Mateo Re: Juror Questionnaires

The Court decides that the jurors will be identified by number, and not by name.

February 9, 2004 **Scott Peterson's Notice** of Motion and Motion in Limine to Sequester the Jury

Scott motions the Court to order the sequestration of the jury for the duration of the trial based upon the grounds that sequestration is required due to the extensive and prejudicial media coverage that has plagued this case. This motion is supported by the attached memorandum of points and authorities, the pleadings and records on file therein, and by such other and further argument as may be presented to the Court at the hearing on this matter.

This is a death penalty case. Given that (1)there is no dispute that the media coverage of this matter has been both extensive and prejudicial, and (2)that the coverage has, as the prosecutor aptly put, been "unrelenting[] across the entire state of California", (3)evidence that the volume and hostility of the "media circus" has, if anything, increased as trial in San Mateo County approaches.

See Exhibit D, "New venue, but same media circus" Modesto Bee, February 3, 2004, in which it was reported that this Court had to order removal of a radio station's (KNEW) trailer where a guilt poll was being conducted. In that regard, a check of the KNEW website revealed that (1)the front page features a like labeled "Vote on Scott Peterson Verdict"; and (2) 82.5% of individuals participating in the KNEW guilt poll believe Scott is guilty. (See Exhibit E). Indeed, at first blush the new venue appears to be even more hostile than Modesto.

As such, the only way to avoid "injecting error" into this capital case is to sequester the jury to protect Scott's right to a fair trial and prejudiced jury trial. Certainly if the KNEW death billboard and related poll are harbingers of things to come, the jurors will require exceptionally meticulous handling by the deputies to ensure they are not exposed to such inflammatory and irresponsible press activity. There can be no dispute that the prejudicial media frenzy is likely to reach an even higher pitch once trial begins. As such, the jury must be sequestered.

"In capital cases, appellate courts and legislatures have long recognized the compelling need for ensuring reliability in determining whether death [of a person] is the appropriate punishment. The reason for this disparate treatment is obvious; the death penalty [of a person] is qualitatively different even when compared to a life sentence [of a person]." (See *Dustin v. Superior Court*, 99 Cal.App.4th 1311, at pp.1313-1314(5th Dist.2002), review denied September 25, 2002.)

"We cannot fathom why any prosecutor would want to inject error into a case that carries the potential of death, knowing that if there is a conviction, the error will follow the case for the rest of its appellate life. Now is the time to rectify the prosecutor's error while it is still relatively easy and economical to do so; not wait 20 years down the appellate road." *Dustin*, at p.1314. Although the court was addressing a particular prosecutor's error, the same reasoning naturally applies universally to everyone involved in a capital case.

As the Fifth Appellate District implicitly noted in *Dustin*, a capital defendant (Scott) is entitled to every possible safeguard to ensure that he receives a fair trial. The *Dustin* court also correctly noted that it is desirable to ensure that a capital defendant's (Scott's) substantial rights are protected in the first instance, rather than on appeal.

Sequestration of the jury is a matter left to the sound discretion of the trial court. See *People v. Ruiz*, 44 Cal.3d 589, at p.616(1988); and *People v. Gallego*, 52 Cal.3d 115, at p.169(1991). Although there are no set factors the Court must examine in ruling on a motion to sequester the jury, the Supreme Court has provided some guidance. In disagreeing with Ruiz's argument that sequestration in capital cases should be required, the Supreme Court stated, "First, the defendant (Ruiz) has failed to demonstrate that the publicity in the present case was either extensive or unduly prejudicial to his defense; it is noteworthy that defendant (Ruiz) did not chose to move for a change of venue. Defendant (Ruiz) acknowledges that the California cases appear to require some showing of actual prejudice in order to complain of denial of a motion to sequester the jury." The new venue actually appears to be more hostile than Modesto, so the fact of the venue change should have no bearing on this Court's analysis of the extent and degree of prejudice likely to occur during the trial.

In another instructive ruling the Supreme Court hinted that sequestration may be required upon a showing of "special problems which ma[k]e the sequestration especially appropriate." *People v. Morales*, 48 Cal.3d 527, at p.563(1989). Scott cannot envision a "special problem" requiring sequestration more graphic than "guilt/death" polls conducted in front of the courthouse.

Both the trial court and appellate court have previously determined that the publicity surrounding this case has been extensive and prejudicial. Even the prosecutor has stated, "This case is known worldwide and is indistinguishable from the [Charles] *Manson* case... See attached Exhibit C; *People's January 2, 2004, Opposition to Motion for Change of Venue*, at 19:20-22. "The defendant [Scott] has proven that 'pretrial publicity has been geographically widespread and pervasive' and has failed to prove that jurors in any other country would view this case differently." *Id.*, at 8:3-6, Exhibit C. "As the defendant's [Scott's] own motion [for a change of venue] shows, the case has been covered throughout the world, extensively in the United States and unrelentingly across the entire state of California." *Id.*, at 7:8-10.

As the Fifth Appellate District Court stated, "[T]he potential for prejudice from the release of the [sealed] Materials is enhanced rather than diminished by the arrest of [Scott] and the filing of the complaint against him. The relationship of petitioner to the victims only serves to stimulate the public's appetite for the case, an appetite we would expect the media to satisfy. Release of the Materials would undoubtedly be followed by their widespread dissemination and dissection in every sort of media medium, including daily television with parades of 'experts' endlessly commenting about likely prosecution and defense strategies, opining about strengths, weaknesses and admissibility of the various factual tidbits disclosed by the Materials, and venturing predictions about the probable outcome of the trial against petitioner [Scott]. How fair a trial for both parties; and particularly how an untainted jury could be found anywhere, in the aftermath of such a frenzy escapes us."

Judge G.'s, June 12, 2003 protective [gag] order/decision at page 3, "[I]n the unique facts of this case, there is a clear and present danger [of serious imminent threat to a protected interest] because of the modern media's capability easily to store and recall bits of information in order to relate them at any time including during jury selection. Further compounded in this case is the effect that the publicity is nationwide and cannot be automatically cured by a change of venue or extensive voir dire."

The above quoted ruling, appellate opinion, and prosecution filing illustrate two irrefutable and undisputed facts: (1)the intense unrelenting media frenzy surrounding this case poses a clear and present danger of causing actual prejudice to Scott's, and the prosecution's, right to a fair trial; (2)the volume of media coverage has been virtually uniform throughout the United States, and certainly Redwood City, less than 100 miles from Modesto. To quote the Court of Appeal, "so far as we are aware, the presumption of innocence is still a fundamental constitutional right available to all criminal defendants", including Mr. Peterson. (See attached Exhibit B, at p.6).

In light of the foregoing, Scott respectfully requests that the jury be sequestered for the duration of the trial.

If you wanted a fair cross-section of a community, then an all pro-death jury would not be a fair cross-section of any community, except maybe the one that a fox would encounter when he enters into the chicken pen.

February 11, 2004 **Prosecutor's Opposition** to Motion to Sequester the Jury

Scott has requested that this court sequester the jury in this case. It is clear from the state of the law that sequestering of the jury is not required. It is within this court's discretion to decide to do so or not. The prosecution is opposed to doing so, because of the great toll it would take on the jurors. To keep jurors away from their lives for months on end is not a wise choice.

The law is also clear that all of Scott's concerns can be laid to rest by continuous and strong admonitions to the jury. This way, the jurors are allowed to separate, Scott suffers no harm and both sides are able to have a jury that concentrates on the evidence and not on when they will get to return home.

Penal Code § 1121 allows the court, at its discretion, to decide if jurors should be sequestered. This was affirmed in *People v. Gallego*, 52 Cal.3d 115 (1991). Another court has rejected the same argument being made by Scott here: "Additionally, it is clearly the Legislature's prerogative to enact trial procedures such as are embodied in sections 1121 and 1128, and, once it has done so, neither this nor any court may substitute its judgment for that of the Legislature, in the absence of a constitutional violation." *People v. Dillon*, 34 Cal.3d 441, at p.463(1983); and *Estate of Horman*, 5 Cal.3d 62, at p.77(1971).

"Although defendant [Bunyard] contends that sequestration of the jury in capital cases is a constitutional right, i.e., required by the due process clause of the Fourteenth Amendment, he cites no express authority for that proposition. [Footnote 21] The federal courts which have addressed this issue have refused to recognize any federal constitutional right to have the jury sequestered. See, e.g., *Powell v. Spalding*, 679 F.2d 163, at p.166, footnote 3(9th Cir. 1982); *Young v. State of Alabama*, 443 F.2d 854, at p.856(5th Cir. 1971), certiorari denied, 405 U.S. 976 (1972)." *People v. Bunyard*, 45 Cal.3d 1189, at pp.1219-1220 (1988).

The prosecutor submits that this court should exercise its discretion and deny Scott's request to sequester the jury.

March 5, 2004 **Superior Court of San Mateo**

The Court posts the juror questionnaire on its internet website.

March 23, 2004 **Media Motion** for Access to Jury Questionnaires

The print media coalition in this case, publishers of the San Francisco Chronicle, Contra Costa Times, Modesto Bee, Los Angeles Times, and San Jose Mercury news, along with Associated Press, respectfully requests access to the jury questionnaires in this case.

While this Court has expressed concern about publicity in this case, those concerns are addressed, in this context, by the Court's prior order to the effect that jurors names will remain confidential. For the foregoing reasons, this Motion should be granted.

Jury selection began in this Court on March 4, 2004. This Court previously ruled [decided], on February 9, 2004, that jurors will be identified by number, and not name. The Juror Questionnaire, which this Court posted on its Internet Web Site on Friday, March 5, 2004, explicitly warns prospective jurors, "YOUR WRITTEN RESPONSES ARE NOT CONFIDENTIAL BECAUSE THE QUESTIONNAIRES ARE PUBLIC RECORDS." Thus, the Questionnaires themselves state that they are "PUBLIC RECORDS," and jurors are also warned, "PLEASE RECALL THAT IF YOU REQUEST CONFIDENTIALITY AS TO ANY ANSWER, YOU MUST SO INDICATE."

In short, the Juror Questionnaires, which say in underlined capital letters on their face that they are "PUBLIC RECORDS", should in fact be made available to the public and the press which serves as the public's surrogate.

The U.S. Supreme Court has held that jury voir dire must presumptively be open, "Closed proceedings, although not absolutely precluded, must be rare and only for cause shown that outweighs the value of openness." *Press-Enterprise v. Superior Court*, 464 U.S. 501, at p.509(1984). "The presumption of openness may be overcome only by an overriding interest based on findings that closure is essential to preserve higher values and is narrowly tailored to serve that interest. The interest is to be articulated along with findings specific enough that a reviewing court can determine whether the closure order was properly entered." *Id.*, at p.510.

California's First District Court of Appeal has applied this openness mandate to jury questionnaires. "It follows that the public access mandate of *Press-Enterprise* applies to voir dire itself. The fact that a lawyer does not orally question a juror about a certain answer does not mean that the answer was not considered in accepting or rejecting the juror." *Lesher Communications, Inc. v. Superior Court*, 224 Cal.App.3d 774, at p.778(1990).

The Court in *Lesher*, which like this case was a capital case, the defendant was being tried for a triple-murder, held, "the superior court shall provide access to the questionnaires. The access to the individual juror's questionnaires shall be provided when the individual juror is called to the jury box for oral voir dire."

The Fourth District Court of Appeal reached the same result in *Copley Press v. San Diego Superior Court*, 228 Cal. App.3d 77 (1991), another capital case. The Court first observed, quoting *Press-Enterprise*, '"The value of openness lies in the fact that people not actually attending trials can have confidence that standards of fairness are being observed; the sure knowledge that anyone is free to attend gives assurance that established procedures are being followed and that deviations will become known. Openness thus enhances both the basic fairness of the criminal trial and the appearance of fairness so essential to public confidence in the system."' *Id.*, at p.84.

The Court of Appeal rejected five reasons advance by the respondent superior court for preserving the confidentiality of the jury questionnaires. *Id.*, at p.85. And the Court of Appeal also held that even if some closure or limitation of access is allowed, restrictions on access should be as narrow as possible "so that the salutary nature of openness can be preserved to the largest extent possible." *Id.*, at p.86.

The Court held that "the proper approach is to have the superior court advise the venirepersons that they have the right to request in camera hearings [judge's chambers] on sensitive questions rather than writing their answers in the questionnaire." *Id.*, at p.87. But the Court made clear, "No explicit or implicit promise of confidentiality should be attached to the information contained in the questionnaire; rather the venirepersons shall be expressly informed the questionnaires are public records. Second, the superior court shall provide access to the questionnaires of individual jurors when the individual juror is called to the jury box for oral voir dire." *Ibid.*

The Juror Questionnaires in this case, in keeping with *Copley Press*, do inform venirepersons that they are public records. Since the Questionnaires in this case do inform prospective jurors that they are public records, there is no question that the press and public have a right of access to them. *Copley Press* explicitly mandates when and how the right of access should be fulfilled: "the superior court shall provide access to the questionnaires of individual jurors when the individual juror is called to the jury box for oral voir dire." *Copley Press*, at p.87.

This Court, which has already followed the first part of *Copley Press'* holding by warning venirepersons that "the questionnaires are public records," should also follow the second part of its holding by providing access to the questionnaires of individual jurors when those jurors are called to the jury box for voir dire. That would enable the press to intelligently follow the voir dire of individual jurors, while at the same time not sacrificing their privacy rights, since the questionnaires identify jurors by number and not by name. Moreover, jurors were informed in the questionnaires that they could request confidentiality as to any answer, so jurors have been given a chance to assert privacy claims as to anything they deem particularly sensitive.

The decisions in *Lesher* and *Copley Press* establish that the public has a right of access to jury questionnaires of jurors who are examined during voir dire. The Questionnaires in this case on their face state that they are "PUBLIC RECORDS." The right of access can be safeguarded in this case without sacrificing the defendant's right to a fair trial and without sacrificing legitimate privacy interests of prospective jurors by allowing prospective jurors to discuss truly private matters in an in camera [judge's chambers] hearing.

This motion for access to jury questionnaires should be granted.

February 9, 2004 **Media Request** to Photograph, Record, or Broadcast

KFSN, Channel 30, would like to cover the Motion in Limine, on February 9th.

February 11, 2004 **Order** of Superior Court of San Mateo Re: Media Request to Permit Coverage

The request by KFSN is denied, as no cameras are allowed.

February 10, 2004 **Media Request** to Photograph, Record, or Broadcast

Norman Quebedeau, either a free lance artist, or from the Free Lance Agency, or both, wants to cover all of the proceedings from February 11th to the end of the trial, and make drawings and sketches.

February 10, 2004 **Order** of Superior Court of San Mateo Re: Media Request to Permit Coverage

The request by Norman is granted, subject to the conditions in rule 980, California Rules of Court, and to be seated as directed by the Bailiff.

STANISLAUS COUNTY FILED COURT DOCUMENTS

The subpoena issued to Ted Rowlands, a KTVU reporter, continues for quite a while. Knowing that a subpoena would prevent Ted from talking publicly, as per the court's gag order as a subpoenaed witness, and Ted wouldn't actually testify; which effect was the subpoena directed to, a witness, or to expand the gag order.

June ?, 2003 **Media** Declaration of Service of Notice of Motion (Ted Rowlands)

July 9, 2003 **Minute Order** of Superior Court of Stanislaus County Re: Motion to Quash Subpoena Duces Tecum

July 21, 2003 **Prosecutor's Subpoena of Ted Rowlands**

Ted is not required to appear in person on 8/15/03 at 8:30 in Modesto for a law and motion hearing, if he produces all aired footage of any interview by any KTVU reporter of Scott Peterson; including the interview of Scott Peterson by Ted. Please provide the footage in VHS or DVD format. Ted is reminded, please come to the District Attorney's office at 8:00am on 8/15/03.

July 21, 2003 **Prosecutor** issues Subpoena to KTVU Custodian of Records

The custodian is to deliver to the prosecutor, all aired footage of any interviews by any KTVU reporter of Scott Peterson; this includes the interview of Scott Peterson by Ted Rowland. Please provide the footage in VHS or DVD format, and come by the prosecutor's office at 8:00 am on 8/15/03.

August 11, 2003 **Media Declaration** in Response to Prosecutor's Subpoena

The KTVU custodian of records declares the enclosed video tape is a true copy of original news footage, and related to the case.

December 19, 2003 **Prosecutor's Subpoena of Ted Rowlands**

Ted is required to appear in person, on 1/26/04 at 9:30am in Modesto for Scott's trial as a witness for the prosecution. Ted is reminded, please come to the District Attorney's office at 8:00am on 1/26/04.

SAN MATEO COUNTY FILED DOCUMENTS

January 26, 2004 **Hearing in Superior Court**

January 26, 2004 **Prosecutor Subpoena of KTVU Television**

The subpoena orders Ted Rowlands to appear to testify at trial.

January 28, 2004 **Media** Telephone Call to Prosecutor Re: Subpoena to Ted Rowlands

January 29, 2004 **Media** Telephone Call to Prosecutor Re: Subpoena to Ted Rowlands

January 30, 2004 **Media** Letter to Prosecutor Re: Subpoena for Ted Rowlands

Ted's lawyer is trying to get the prosecutor's attention. The attorney understands that the prosecutor is not seeking Ted's testimony, but if the prosecutor doesn't respond, the quashing process will begin.

February 1, 2004 **Media** Telephone Call to Prosecutor Re: Subpoena to Ted Rowlands

February 3, 2004 **Media** Telephone Call to Prosecutor Re: Subpoena to Ted Rowlands

Ted Rowland's lawyer wants to know what does the prosecutor want to know. Apparently nothing, as the prosecutor does not respond.

February 5, 2004 **Media** Voicemail Message to Prosecutor

Ted's lawyer wants to know what's up, but no response by the prosecutor.

February 9, 2004 **Hearing** Superior Court of San Mateo County

February 11, 2004 **Media Notice** of Motion and Motion of Non-Party Reporter Ted Rowlands to Quash Trial Subpoena; Memorandum of Points and Authorities in Support Thereof

The prosecutor has issued a subpoena for Ted to appear at trial to testify, so Ted is motioning the court to quash the subpoena, on the grounds that the California shield law, Article I, Section 2(b), of the California Constitution together with California Evidence Code § 1070, and the First Amendment of the United States Constitution provide Ted with protection from being compelled to provide testimony. This motion is supported by the attached Memorandum of Points and Authorities, the attached Declaration of Grace K. Won, and on such additional argument as shall be presented at the hearing on this Motion.

In a meet and confer conversation, the prosecutor stated that he's seeking to compel Ted's testimony to testify about conversations he had with Scott, regarding Scott's alleged affair with Amber. Despite repeated requests by Ted's counsel, however, the prosecutor has declined to further specify the scope of the testimony sought or when such conversations may have been broadcast.

The prosecutor's subpoena runs afoul of the California Constitution and Evidence Code which grant journalists a broadly-defined immunity from the compelled disclosure of any "unpublished information" obtained during the course of gathering and disseminating information to the public. Where, as here, the reporter is not a party to the underlying litigation, the shield law erects an absolute bar against compelling the reporter to reveal <u>any</u> unpublished information, including his unpublished eyewitness observations and conversations. The prosecutor's request also contravenes the qualified reporter's privilege enshrined in the First Amendment, which provides an independent source of rights for journalists, separate and apart from those protections accorded by state law.

KTVU Custodian of Records, in response to an earlier subpoena served by the prosecutor, has already provided a sworn declaration authenticating videotape of news footage broadcast on KTVU related to the case.

Here, the State cannot make a sufficient showing to overcome Ted's First Amendment interest in not disclosing the unpublished information that he acquired or generated in the course of newsgathering. This is particularly the case where the prosecutor has provided no explanation for subpoenaing Ted beyond vaguely stating that it relates to a news report concerning Scott's alleged affair with Amber. Ted's testimony is not needed to authenticate the tape of the actual KTVU broadcast.

To the extent that the State is seeking testimony from Ted for the purpose of proving that Scott denied having an affair, such testimony is impeachment material at best, and could easily be obtained instead from non-media witnesses such as Amber or Laci's family or friends, thereby ensuring that important First Amendment protections for reporters are not disturbed.

The California shield law embodied in article I, section 2(b) of the California Constitution and in section 1070 of the California Evidence Code provides reporters like Ted with absolute immunity from being compelled by the State to testify. Article I, section 2(b) states, that a news reporter: "shall not be adjudged in contempt...for refusing to disclose the source of any information procured while so connected or employed [as a news reporter],... or for refusing to disclose any unpublished information obtained or prepared in gathering, receiving or processing of information for communication to the public....

As used in this subdivision, "unpublished information" includes information not disseminated to the public by the person from whom disclosure is sought, whether or not related information has been disseminated and includes, but is not limited to, all notes, outtakes, photographs, tapes, or other data of whatever sort not itself disseminated to the public through a medium of communication, whether or not published information based upon or related to such material has been disseminated." The California Evidence Code § 1070 contains virtually identical language.

Enacted in 1980 by an overwhelming majority of California voters, this constitutional provision provides protection beyond the qualified immunity offered to reporters under the First Amendment. See *Miller v. Superior Court*, 21 Cal.4th 883, at p.899(1999), noting that current version of shield law expanded scope of reporters' protection beyond what the First Amendment provides. The California electorate demonstrated its belief that reporters must be given the maximum possible protection for information obtained in the course of their newsgathering activities.

The shield law immunizes from compelled disclosure any information received, or materials gathered or compiled, during the newsgathering process that have not actually been published. Such unpublished information is protected from disclosure even when closely related information has been published. As noted in *Playboy Enterprises, Inc. v. Superior Court*, 154 Cal. App.3d 14, at pp.23-24(1984), a civil litigant sought audio and videotapes, notes, and other documents relating to an interview conducted by a reporter for Playboy magazine, portions of which had been republished verbatim in an article. The Court noted, "... this material falls squarely within the ambit of article I, section 2 protection whether the published information is an exact transcription of the source material or paraphrases or summarizes it."

Even where information is published, a reporter is shielded from divulging how the news was obtained, from whom it was received, and by whom it was collected, in addition to further unpublished details about the underlying stories. The broadly drafted subpoena issued to Ted exposes him to inquiry that could only serve to elicit this kind of protected information.

Videotapes are self-authenticating under California Evidence Code Section 1553. "A printed representation of images stored on a video or digital medium is presumed to be an accurate representation of the images it purports to represent." Even assuming arguendo that Ted quoted from Scott in a broadcast news report, the fact that Ted quotes from any source does not vitiate the shield law protection. *In re Jack Howard*, 136 Cal.App.2d 816, at pp.818-819(1955), the Court of Appeal held that the publication of a news article containing attributed quotations did not deprive the author of his right to decline to answer whether he ever had a conversation with the purported source.

Indeed, other than identifying his own name, occupation and address, it is hard to imagine what information Ted could provide that would fall outside the ambit of the shield law. Because the practical result of compelling the testimony of Ted would be to extract protected information, the subpoena must be quashed.

In subpoenaing Ted, the State appears to believe his testimony is necessary for its criminal prosecution of Scott. However, the California Supreme Court has held that the State's interest in obtaining evidence for a criminal prosecution is trumped by the constitutional protections afforded to members of the press. "[T]he absoluteness of the immunity embodied in the shield law only yields to a conflicting federal or, perhaps, state constitutional right." *Miller*, at p.901. No such conflicting rights are implicated, much less outweighed, by a prosecutor's need for evidence. *Id.*

In *Miller*, the prosecutor sought to enforce a subpoena against a television station, demanding production of a tape recording of an entire interview conducted by the station with a criminal defendant, including portions of the interview which had not been aired or otherwise published. The trial court found the station in contempt of court, and the appellate court upheld that order, by balancing the people's state constitutional right to due process of law against the shield law. The *Miller* Court found that this balancing of interests was inappropriate, because due process was in no way denied by the shield law.

"[T]here is no need to balance the two rights if they are not in conflict. In *Menendez*, we concluded that whatever the people's right to due process of law in article I, section 29 might mean...it specifically does not mean a right of access to evidence in contravention of previously existing evidentiary privileges and immunities, which include those given to the press." *Id.*, at p.895. Thus, the rule stated in *Miller* demands that the State's desire to investigate and prosecute crimes yield to Ted's immunity as a news reporter from compulsion to testify before a criminal jury.

Such activities, including any conversations with Scott, are protected by the shield law. Ted, therefore, respectfully requests that this Court quash the subpoena ordering him to appear as a witness in the case.

February 11, 2004 **Media Declaration** of Grace K. Won in Support of Motion of Non-party Reporter Ted Rowlands to Quash Trial Subpoena

February 17, 2004 **Media Request** to Substitute Photographer

This request is also an advertisement.

February 18, 2004 **Media Request** to Use Low Powered Binoculars in the Courtroom

Courtroom Artist.com and other artists are sitting in the fifth row and would like to see the faces and exhibits during the trial, with the aid of small low powered binoculars. They are normally used on a regular basis.

February 18, 2004 **Opinion of the Court of Appeal, First Appellate District, Division Two**

The petition for writ of mandate/prohibition is denied. Petitioners are Courtroom Television network LLC, Cable News Network LP, LLLP, National Broadcasting Company, Inc., KNTV Television, Inc., Fox News Network LLC, CBS Broadcasting, Inc., and ABC, Inc., and the Respondent is the Superior Court of San Mateo County, with Scott as a Real Party in Interest. Boy, I'll say.

February 23, 2004 **Judge L.'s Notice** of Motion and Motion to Quash Subpoena; Memorandum of Points and Authorities

Apparently the judge doesn't want to testify at a hearing that Scott subpoenaed him to set for February 23, 2004, and he'd like the court to quash it. The motion doesn't say what the subpoena concerned or when it was served.

March 22, 2004 **Notice of Superior Court of San Mateo Re: Rule 2073.5 of the California Rules of Court**

The court is notifying the parties that the judge is considering a request to provide remote electronic access to all or a portion of the public records in the case, on the grounds that (1) the number of requests for access to documents in the case is extraordinarily high, and (2) responding to those requests would significantly burden the operations of the court.

In making its decision, the court will consider relevant factors, such as: the impact on the privacy of parties, victims, and witnesses; the benefits to and burdens on the parties allowing remote electronic access, including possible impacts on jury selection; and, the benefits to and burdens on the court and court staff.

Five days notice is provided to the parties before the court makes a determination, which will be made on or after March 22, 2004. Any person may file comments with the court for consideration, but no hearing is required or scheduled to take place.

The court does not have the resources to redact driver license numbers; dates of birth; social security numbers; Criminal Identification and Information and National Crime numbers; addresses, and phone numbers of parties, victims, witnesses, and court personnel; medical and psychiatric information; financial information; account numbers; and other personal identifying information. If remote access is provided, the trial judge may make a separate order requiring any party who files a document containing such information to provide the court with both an original unredacted version of the document for filing in the court file and a redacted version of the document for remote electronic access.

No juror names or other juror identifying information will be provided by remote electronic access.

April 6, 2004 **Order** of Superior Court of San Mateo Permitting Remote Electronic Access to Public Court Records

The court has not received any comments from parties or the public in response to its notice. It is ordered that remote electronic access to all documents officially filed with the court in this case be made available on appropriate court-sponsored website, with the exception of any records that are ordered sealed or filed in a Confidential court file.

The court does not have the resources and is not feasible to redact the private information, and as such will not redact the information from documents posted.

March 30, 2004 **Order** of Superior Court of San Mateo Permitting use of Laptop Computer

The court orders that Scott be allowed the use of a laptop computer for purposes of reviewing discovery, including but not limited to, digitally scanned documents in Adobe Acrobat, digital images, digital audio, and digital video, for good cause having been shown.

The court further orders that any laptop made available shall have all necessary software to review the different formats of discovery but the laptop computer shall not have wired or wireless internet access.

Chapter Four

Not So Final Thought

The problem with an incomplete record, is that it is not a record, but, it can have several descriptive possibilities. With some of the 'record' missing, how do you determine what a record would show? Is there some part missing which would shed a different light on the subject?

The prosecutor wants the wiretap recordings released to the public. Scott wants them sealed and not allowed into evidence in court, as being illegally obtained. Media wants the wiretap recordings sealed from everyone but media.

The prosecutor wants some of the warrant material released to the public and some sealed from everyone. Scott wants the warrant materials sealed until trial. Media wants the warrant materials released to media.

The prosecutor wants the autopsy reports released to the public. Scott wants the autopsies to remained sealed and to be protected from public view in court. Media wants the autopsies released to media.

The prosecutor wants a limited gag order, which would leave him free to speak. Scott doesn't want a gag order. Media doesn't want a gag order. Amber wants to gag everyone except Gloria Allred.

The prosecutor [does or doesn't?] want media camera coverage inside the courtroom for the preliminary hearing. Scott wants the courtroom closed during the preliminary hearing, but, if not closed, then he'd like media camera coverage. Media wants cameras everywhere all the time. Amber doesn't want her testimony televised.

What appears is that Scott wants the process closed, so that the actions of those who are responsible for protecting society are viewed in a fair manner in front of the judicial system and therefore the proper actions taken to correct them, and if not closed, then only open access to the proceedings and events of those who put him where he is and of those who intend to keep him there until he's put to death, will expose the truth. In other words, the process, or lack thereof, needs exposure as to how it actually happened and not with or from a point of view that is totally prosecutorial. Either keep it sealed so a fair decision can be reached without public sentiment, or if not, let the public see and judge for themselves.

The prosecutor appears to want the government actions and those materials sealed, but wants the resulting information from those actions to be released to the public, with no one able to publicly respond or counter the prosecutorial information or actions.

On each issue, media has a 'real party' to this criminal case to oppose. Regardless of media's opposition party, the other 'real party' must respond, or reply, or state their position, or all of the above. Fortunately the California Legislature has taken the dilemma of choice of a public trial from the public, fortunate that is unless you're the defendant.

The TV news corps continue to bring up the O.J. trial, saying they keep seeing shades of it, and they appear to be correct. Just as with O.J., it isn't the defense that's creating police corruption, since you can't draw attention to something that which doesn't exist. It's the police and prosecutors who are drawing the attention to the actions and procedures employed toward Scott that are similar to those used with O.J.

The wiretap procedure wasn't followed, police encouraged Amber to lie, deceive, and trick Scott which was designed to produce court evidence; media was fueled in their public inquisition with government leaked false information; police harassed Scott, friends, and family which will produce unusual behavior; police encouraged Laci's family and friends to lie, deceive, trick, and help to snare Scott; government hypnotizes a possible defense eyewitness, knowing their testimony is nullified; and the favorite of alot of prosecutors, keep the evidence away from the defense for as long as possible.

We, the public, have tape recordings that aren't audible to those whose voice are on the recording, a prosecutor who gets caught from the beginning of the trial with the type of rumor and innuendo we've seen on TV for over a year, the needle-nosed pliers that aren't in a police report, a scrunched rug that isn't in the police report, testimony by police officers that Scott was supposed to have said that isn't in the police report, and testimony from officers that is different from the police reports and from their testimony at the preliminary hearing.

Several witnesses have also been caught trying to change their earlier statements. One witness was totally misquoted by a police report, of course, as being against Scott. Innocent actions at the time they occurred, and at earlier hearings, are now actions of a guilty person attempting to cover up a crime and create an alibi.

When asked about the difference in the then and now points of view and statements, the usual response emerges, I don't remember. Well who could ever expect anyone to remember all the Bolshevik these fellows put out there in the past eighteen months.

Did these government servants watch too much TV? Are they counting on the public to back them up no matter what they say?

After such an extensive inquisition, which continues on the TV news corp shows right through the trial, how will anyone ever believe that Scott isn't guilty, let alone, that Scott is innocent. Even if the person who is responsible for Laci's disappearance confesses, and shows up with physical evidence, many in society will still believe Scott is responsible.

If the lies and deceit are converted to public evidence by the TV news corps, and explained away from the trial as irrelevant or not allowed in trial because of a technicality but that doesn't mean it didn't happen or isn't true, then the true public jury decision is but one of secrecy and of a predetermined dominance by information.

If those who write law, execute law, and judge law as written, applied, and executed, can't follow those very same laws, well that doesn't mean that society should say 'to hell with it' and not follow the laws, but, it does present the question; how can we as a government 'expect' we as a society to follow them.

If we could get the legislature to write laws the way they sign them, one ink pen per letter, we'd sure be alot freer, and our laws would be much simpler. Maybe even to the point where government could join the justice system and not have to write excuse laws for their rude, and certainly, unconstitutional behavior.

If we don't demand that the lies, deceit, and trickery be removed from government action, then we must be satisfied with a society whose rules promote its defeat.

Fortunately, at this point in history and within this context, we still have a jury that deliberates in private. These 12 people are the only ones involved in this matter since Laci's disappearance, who do not have an opinion of whether Scott is guilty or innocent. These are the Only 12 people who will begin this matter from that point of view; the Only 12 people to view the Evidence presented in a competent court of law; and the Only 12 people to, therefore, decide the matter.

However, once again we have something more important going on here than whether Scott is innocent in Laci's death, although you won't convince Scott of that, and no one should try. There is something more important going on here than whether Laci was killed by Scott, although you won't convince Laci's family and friends of that, and no one should try.

Because of the extensive, but, prejudicial publicity of Scott and the affair, and the love of Laci as a result of that publicity, the trial was moved to acquire a fair jury. Can a jury be influenced by the TV news corps after a trial begins? If so, in which direction? Will the jurors get a daily update of all the events media says is going on behind the scenes and a re-interruption of the testimony they just heard that day and possibly from witnesses who just left the stand? If so, what rumors and talk will they hear that wasn't allowed in court, and in what direction?

We like to hear about our justice system, its methods, procedures, and actions. The TV news corps are in an excellent position to show us this. If their objectivity must be compromised, in order to gain access to government, and thereby becoming a part of government deception, then we're gonna need some media to report to us on the TV news corp methods, procedures, and actions. If we encourage the TV news corps to perform inquisitions, public prosecutions, and crime investigations, then we must ask the TV news corps to please step in front of the camera.

As one former U.S. President stated, It's a shame, that in America, a person must first prove their innocence. A person is guilty until they prove that.

About the Author

Some of the author's friends say he's a hermit, while other friends say that privacy is his most cherished freedom. Freedom of the press and speech have also been exercised by the author since early childhood. Local, city, and state legislatures, Governors, Presidents, local politicians, the U.S. House of Representatives, and presidential candidates have responded, and benefited from the words written by the author, with a few also feeling their wrath.

Even our country's forefathers knew that one of the hardest things for the average American to accomplish was to be able to address government in a civilized tone, with civilized words. The author tries to prevent the uncivilized practice of public condemnation from returning to government and engulfing society.

Printed in the United States
23173LVS00003B/272